ALLISON CHURCH BROTHERHOOD, LAWRENCE COUNTY (A COUNTRY CHURCH).

History
of the
DISCIPLES OF CHRIST
in
Illinois
1819–1914

Nathaniel S. Haynes, A.M.
Author of "Jesus as a Controversialist"

HERITAGE BOOKS
2011

HERITAGE BOOKS
AN IMPRINT OF HERITAGE BOOKS, INC.

Books, CDs, and more—Worldwide

For our listing of thousands of titles see our website
at
www.HeritageBooks.com

A Facsimile Reprint
Published 2011 by
HERITAGE BOOKS, INC.
Publishing Division
100 Railroad Ave. #104
Westminster, Maryland 21157

Copyright © 1915 Nathaniel S. Haynes

Index Copyright © 2000 Heritage Books, Inc.

— Publisher's Notice —
In reprints such as this, it is often not possible to remove blemishes from the original. We feel the contents of this book warrant its reissue despite these blemishes and hope you will agree and read it with pleasure.

International Standard Book Numbers
Paperbound: 978-0-7884-1458-9
Clothbound: 978-0-7884-8688-3

DEDICATION

To those men and women, few but true, who hold tender and grateful memories of our glorious heroes of the LONG AGO, who are yet forceful factors in the MIGHTY NOW, who are inspired by the splendid vision of the BETTER TIME TO COME—to those elect remnants of the LORD, my faithful and glad fellow-helpers in this labor of love, with sincere appreciation, I dedicate this book.

N. S. HAYNES.

Decatur, Illinois, March 7, 1914.

CONTENTS

	PAGE
FOREWORD	9

CHAPTER I.
THE DISCIPLES OF CHRIST—THEIR PLACE AND PLEA 13

CHAPTER II.
BEGINNINGS IN ILLINOIS 20

CHAPTER III.
CHRISTIAN EDUCATION 33

CHAPTER IV.
THE PERIOD OF CONQUEST—THE ERA OF PUBLIC DISCUSSIONS 68

CHAPTER V.
BENEVOLENCES 88

CHAPTER VI.
LOCAL CHURCHES AND SOME OF THEIR ORGANIZED ACTIVITIES 109

CHAPTER VII.
BIOGRAPHIES 461

CHAPTER VIII.
MISCELLANEA 640

LIST OF ILLUSTRATIONS

	PAGE
J. W. Allen	589
John C. Ashley	564
Atlanta Church	298
Allison Prairie Church Brotherhood	Frontispiece
Mrs. C. C. Babcock	464
Col. E. D. Baker	517
Barney's Prairie Church and Site	415
W. F. Black	633
Bloomington, First Church	281
Bloomington, Centennial Church	281
Bloomington, Second Church	281
Walter P. Bowles	603
E. M. Bowman	106
Clark Braden	633
Mrs. O. A. Burgess	103
J. G. Campbell	517
Carbondale Church	367
Champaign Church	130
Charleston Church	130
Chicago, Englewood Church	150
Chicago, Jacksonville Boulevard Church	150
Chicago, Memorial Church	150
Chicago, Metropolitan Church	150
John J. Cosat	517
Mrs. Persis L. Christian	103
Mrs. S. J. Crawford	103

	PAGE
Danville, First Church	407
Danville, Second Church	407
Danville, Third Church	407
Danville, Fourth Church	407
F. W. Darst	106
Miss Annie E. Davidson	103
Decatur, Central Church	298
Decatur, First Church	298
Decatur, First Courthouse	347
Miss Elmira J. Dickinson	103
Daniel W. Ellege	630
John England	550
Eureka College	33
Eureka Church	415
J H. Gilliland	517
J. R. Golden	461
Thomas Goodman	603
N. S. Haynes	464
Bushrod W. Henry	564
R. E. Henry	461
T. T. Holton	589
Joseph Hostetler	464
D. R. Howe	630
C. J. Hudson	106
Jacksonville Church	298
A. J. Kane	550
W. P. Keeler	106
S. S. Lappin	564
Mrs. Catherine V. Lindsay	103
Long Point Church	347

LIST OF ILLUSTRATIONS

	PAGE
Macomb Church	130
Wm. T. Major	564
Map of Chicago Churches	109
Map of Illinois Churches	109
J. B. McCorkle	570
D. D. Miller	550
G. W. Minier	570
Mt. Pleasant Church	347
M. O. Naramore	106
Normal Church	281
A. D. Northcutt	464
Paris Church	367
Pine Creek Church	347
Pontiac Church	415
Mrs. Lura V. Porter	103
E. J. Radford	589
James Robeson	570
Rockford Church	367
Rock Island Church	367
Wm. B. Ryan	464
Chas. Reign Scoville	633
J. W. Sconce	570
Dr. John Scott	630
C. W. Sherwood	603
E. M. Smith	461
Springfield, First Church	130
O. W. Stewart	589
J. S. Swaford	106
The Sweeney Family	616
R. F. Thrapp	461
John W. Tyler	550
J. G. Waggoner	630
H. L. Willett	633
E. B. Witmer	106
John Yager	603
S. H. Zendt	461

FOREWORD

At the annual meeting of the Illinois Christian Missionary Society in Danville, September, 1911, Min. R. F. Thrapp introduced a resolution directing its State Board to appoint a committee of three to select a competent man to write the history of the Disciples of Christ in Illinois. Mins. R. F. Thrapp, J. R. Golden and R. E. Henry were constituted such committee. In November following they arranged with Min. N. S. Haynes to do this work. Upon the removal of Mr. Thrapp from the State, Min. S. H. Zendt was appointed to fill the vacancy, and upon the removal of Mr. Golden, Min. E. M. Smith was chosen to succeed him.

The task of writing the history has proved to be more protracted and far more laborious than was anticipated. The chief difficulty was in securing the materials. Nearly all of the pioneers were dead. The records of many of the older congregations had nearly disappeared. But the main hindrance was the lack of appreciation by very many of such a volume and their consequent indifference to its preparation. Among a minority of willing and faithful helpers justice requires this grateful recognition of the assistance of Min. T. T. Holton and Prof. B. J. Radford. A decade ago Mr. Holton thought to write the biographies of the pioneer Christian preachers of Illinois. All the material he fortunately secured at that time he graciously turned over to the author. Without his assistance it would have been impossible to make this volume what it is.

A goodly number of the earliest churches of Christ in the State grew out of a reformatory movement that preceded our own. These people were widely known as "New Lights." But, since they now disclaim this name, they are throughout this work referred to as the "Christian Denomination"—their accepted name.

In speaking of those who serve in the high calling of the Christian ministry designations more Scriptural are employed. In this work preachers are not called "elders," but ministers. Some ministers are elders, but all can not be; hence, as a general designation, it is wrong. Besides, there is no perceptible or special affinity between the Disciples of Christ and the Seventh-day Adventists, or the Latter-day Saints, that should lead to the general designation of our ministers as "elders." A true preacher is a servant of Christ, and this relation and its consequent obligations are Scripturally expressed by the word "minister." If an abbreviation is needed, "Min." is easily written and is so used herein. Nor are preachers termed "clergymen," since the Spirit calls the Lord's "flock" his clergy or inheritance. The title "Reverend" and its contraction "Rev." are also avoided. By the mouth of David the Lord says "his name is holy and reverend," and it is not befitting that we so denote ourselves. If this title, which has become in recent years so glibly prevalent among the Disciples of Christ, is to be recognized and used, then why not "Very Reverend" and "Most Reverend," and so on up the scale to the climax of wicked assumption? In this work "Doctor" and its contraction "Dr." are used to indicate a physician only. Its general use as meaning a teacher of religion, or of philosophy, is indefinite, and, if for no other reason, is objectionable.

It is very gratifying that the facts in Chapter II. have been so well authenticated. Many of these, together with the section on slavery in Chapter VIII., were presented in an address delivered by the author before the State Historical Society at Springfield in May, 1913.

The incompleteness of and the inaccuracies in the histories of the local churches are attributable in large measure to the indifference and indisposition of many to furnish the data. Repeated appeals brought no responses. It was with much regret that lack of space compelled the omission of the lists of the names of pastors, where they were furnished, since the growth of congregations has depended so largely upon these faithful servants of God.

The preparation of the biographies has been no less difficult. It is painfully deficient both in the subjects and in their fair proportions of treatment. Without doubt the names of some who are not mentioned should appear, while some of those who do appear should have received less and others larger notice. Many deserving younger men have been crowded out. The names of others may be found in the chapter on education and elsewhere. At best this biographical chapter is an approximation, but it is illustrative of the brave and true men and women to whom the present generation is indebted far more than it is aware. In writing these, the author has brought under contribution the recollections, associations and fellowships of sixty years and such researches as the time permitted.

He has written in the love of the truth and with the best spirit of fairness and justice. It is believed that this volume will be a source of valuable information and joyful inspiration to many multitudes.

THE AUTHOR.

CHAPTER I.

THE DISCIPLES OF CHRIST—THEIR PLACE AND PLEA.

The great apostasy has perplexed all thoughtful people. The mystery of iniquity is an enigma of the later centuries. The church that was founded in the wisdom of God, and redeemed by the blood of his Son, forgot its heavenly origin and divine mission. Its light and power were lost and it became the nesting-place of unclean birds.

That was a sad and sinful age upon which Martin Luther looked out. He beheld everywhere the usurpations of the Papacy. Priests and people were ignorant of the Holy Scriptures. The Pope arrogated to himself the prerogatives of God. The system of indulgences had grown to a scandalous height. John Tetzel, a Dominican friar, preached and peddled licenses to sin in Germany. Darkness covered the earth and gross darkness the people. Then God's great clock struck its spiritual midnight. These appalling conditions awakened and stirred the soul of the earnest German monk. He aroused in Germany a splendid turmoil of thought and precipitated a great battle between divine truth and human traditions. When its smoke had cleared away, these three things stood out clearly: First, the right of private judgment; second, the all-sufficiency of the Scriptures, and, third, justification by faith. Luther was a child of Providence and a mighty man of God. He wrought marvelous results. But even he could not make the journey from spiritual Babylon to spiritual Jerusalem in a day of human life.

Bernhardin Samson, a Franciscan monk, went into Switzerland in 1518 selling indulgences. He was successfully opposed by Zwingli, who appealed to the authority of the word of God. This beginning of the Reformation in Switzerland produced the Reformed Church and the Heidelberg Catechism or Confession, written in 1562.

Meanwhile, John Calvin's great mind was engaged upon the religious problems of the time, and gave to the world the theological system that bears his name, but also the doctrine of the *sovereignty of God*. The Almighty is the supreme Ruler and Arbiter—not the man with the triple crown, whose throne is by the yellow Tiber.

The principles of the Reformation swept across the English Channel. The Anglo-Saxons possess a marvelous power of genius for liberty, and that was fruitful soil. Henry VIII. was on the throne. He had written a treatise denouncing Luther and defending the Pope. Just then his ardor for his lawful wife had cooled and he wished a divorce that he might marry pretty Anne Boleyn. The Pope said "No;" the King said "Yes," had his way and was excommunicated. The Parliament then passed the Act of Supremacy: "That the King, our sovereign lord, his heirs and successors, kings of this realm, shall be taken, accepted and reputed the only supreme head on earth of the Church of England, called the 'Anglicana Ecclesia.' " Thus the chain was broken that tied England to the Papal throne. The Episcopal Church had its beginning, and as the years passed grew gradually away from Papal errors to Protestant principles of Christian faith. And thus came *the denial of the Pope's arrogant claim to the universal headship of the church on earth.*

A joint resolution of the English Parliament, June 12, 1643, convoked a synod to settle the government and liturgy of the Church of England, and to promote a more perfect reformation than had been obtained during the reigns of Edward II. and Elizabeth. What afterward came to be known as the Presbyterian "Confession of Faith" was finally adopted by the Assembly of divines in the month of December, 1646, approved by the Parliament of Scotland in 1647, and by the English Parliament in 1648. Thus arose the Presbyterian Church with its different branches. About 1658 Congregationalism began to grow out of the Puritan movement in England. Out of the religious chaos of the sixteenth century came also the Baptist Church. Their earliest articles of faith were written by Zwingli in 1527. The London "Confession of Faith" was formulated in 1689, and that which held for a century in the United States was cast in Philadelphia in 1742. In their earlier years the Baptists were generally Calvinists. To Roger Williams, Welshman, Baptist, Reformer and founder of the State of Rhode Island, the world is indebted for the principle of the *absolute separation of the ecclesiastical and civil powers.*

On the human side the Methodist Church was the product of the great mind, heart and conscience of John Wesley. His aim at first was to effect a higher type of life in the Church of England, of which he was a member. The first "Articles of Religion" were prepared in 1784. His life and work gave tremendous emphasis to *the doctrine of human responsibility and personal accountability to God.*

Thus for two hundred years the caravans of the Lord moved slowly along the way from spiritual Babylon to spiritual Jerusalem. Wycliffe, Jerome of Prague, Huss, Luther, Erasmus, Zwingli, Melancthon, John Knox, Calvin, Cranmer, John Robinson and John Wesley were the leaders whom the Lord raised up. They aimed and strove to recover the church, the body of Christ, from the ignorance, superstitions, wrongs and oppressions of centuries. With their faces toward the new morning, they searched, struggled and suffered for Christ's sake—a glorious company of God's elect. Severally and successively they led the generations to higher planes of Christian truth and life. The last centuries are debtors to them all. Ours is a splendid heritage from great souls who counted Christ and his truth more precious than their own lives.

But, alas for the frailties of man! The creeds which the reformers thought and hoped to use as fulcrums for the spiritual uplift of the people became barriers to Christian faith. Opinions about doctrines were substituted for personal trust in the Christ. Men were measured not by the word of God in their faith and lives, but by the opinions and creeds of fallible men. Theological warfare ensued. In their pulpits, on the platform and through the press, preachers contended and discussed with one another. The leading questions were of orthodoxy rather than orthopraxy—correct thinking rather than right living. As churches grew in numbers and power, denominational pride dominated. The spirit of Jesus gave place to sectarian rivalries. Men wrangled and raged about their religious opinions. The seamless robe of the Master was rent many times. Bitterness banished brotherly love. Mutual appreciation was murdered by disparagement. Spiritual ostracism supplanted Christian fellowship. Brotherly love was crucified on the cross of sectarian bigotry. The children of God came to hate one another for the love of God —as they supposed. Thus the church of the living God, torn and divided, was shorn of its power. Having lost its divine ideals, it lost its divine aims. The evangelization of the world was forgotten; the salvation of the people was neglected.

Out of this religious travail the Disciples of Christ were born. Assuredly the Christian world needed a new voice. Did they come to the Kingdom for such a time as that? The first thing they said was: "We be brethren. Let us not fight, but let us reason together." After a hundred years, the things they said are now beginning to be heard.

Protestant believers were divided in their teachings and into many religious bodies. However, in the nineteenth century, these divine truths which had been elucidated and emphasized by the great leaders of reformatory movements had come to be the common possessions of all evangelical believers. They all held—and do yet hold—*the right of personal judgment, the all-sufficiency of the sacred Scriptures as the rule of faith and life, the doctrine of justification by faith in Jesus Christ;* all are united in *the denial of the Papal headship of the church;* all affirmed *the supreme sovereignty of*

THEIR PLACE AND PLEA 17

God, individual responsibility and personal accountability to God; all stood for *religious liberty and the absolute separation of civil and ecclesiastical prerogatives and powers.* The Christian peoples who are girdling the earth with this twentieth-century civilization are all united in these things. The Disciples of Christ have pleaded for a return to the word of God and the authority of Jesus Christ, the sole Lord and only Head of the church. The creeds of men may have served their purposes in former times, but they divide God's people, and division is weakness, inefficiency and appalling loss. Bishop Cranston, of the M. E. Church, before the Federal Council of the Churches of Christ in America, said: "The church of Jesus Christ upon earth is constitutionally, intentionally and logically one, and we are staying apart without reason, economy or warrant of Scripture." As a revelation of God, the Bible is all-sufficient and alone-sufficient in the salvation of men and in their preparation for the eternal life. Amid all the clashing confusion of earth and time, only the authoritative voice of Jesus can bring assurance and peace.

The Disciples plead for the reproduction of the Church of Christ, which is his body on earth; for a return to and a restoration of primitive Christianity in all its fundamental elements. What is its basic teaching? What are its divinely appointed ordinances? What its required and essential fruits? What does the New Testament say? To the law and the testimony. "Where the Bible speaks, we speak; where the Bible is silent, we are silent." Assuredly this is a safe and wise rallying-cry.

The Disciples plead for the union of all God's people on the common, catholic grounds of the Bible. Divisions to-day are the crowning sin of Christendom. The Holy Spirit condemned divisions when he spoke through apostles, and Jesus prayed for the unity of all his people "that the world may believe that thou hast sent me." All efforts for Christian union must fail that are based on denominational interpretations of the Bible. Opinions may serve in their places, but they must be subordinated to "thus saith the Lord." Happily, all evangelized believers are now agreed in the catholic elements of the gospel; namely, that Jesus is the Christ to save and the Lord to lead, that the Holy Scriptures can make a man of God perfect and thoroughly furnish him unto all good works, that immersion and the Lord's Supper are the ordinances given by him who has all authority in heaven and on earth, that Christ's people should wear his name, and that they should aim and strive to reproduce his life in their own. Tennyson expressed this goal when he wrote: "Step by step, with voices crying right and left, I have climbed my way back to the primal church, and stand within the porch, and Christ is with me."

It is believed that the Scripturalness and catholicity of the position and plea of the Disciples of Christ are evidenced by the fact that so many ministers—to say nothing of thousands of others—have left the various denominational churches and now stand together on common ground and unitedly serve the one Master. From this multitude the following are noted here as illustrating examples: W. H. Book, from the Baptist Church; M. M. Davis, from the M. E. Church; T. H. Adams, from the Protestant Methodist Church; W. G. Loucks, from the Christian Denomination; J. V. Updike, from the Church of God; James Small, from the Presbyterian Church; A. B. Jett, from the Cumberland Presbyterian Church; C. C. Redgrave, from the Congregational Church; T. P. Bauer, from the Lutheran Church; Claris Yeuell, from the Plymouth Brethren; D. P. Shafer, from the Reformed Church; James Vernon, from the Episcopal Church; C. M. Price, from the Seventh-day Adventists; D. H. Bays, from the Mormon Church, and T. J. O'Connor, from the Roman Catholic Church. Nearly all of these men are living and are, or have been, active ministers of the gospel in the churches of Christ.

Mr. J. Wood Miller, a Presbyterian minister, visited the Englewood, Chicago, Church of Christ on a Wednesday evening in 1912, and read from memory Mark's Gospel to the congregation. Later he sent them the following note:

MY FRIENDS:—Never was I so greatly pleased as in my reception at your church. It is only what could be expected from your most distinctly American of all the churches in the United States that I know of; organized here and having the stamp of the universal church, too, under the head of immersion, the original baptism; Christian, the original name; the whole Word as the only creed, and observing the Supper every Lord's Day, the primitive custom, with every saint a preacher. Having read Mark before perhaps five hundred churches, I recall no larger or more responsive prayer-meeting audience.

CHAPTER II.

BEGINNINGS IN ILLINOIS.

The beginning of the nineteenth century witnessed a widespread revolt against human authority, both Papal and Protestant, in religion. Many men in many places came to see that God alone can be Lord of the conscience. Everywhere these reformers, protesting against the creeds of councils and the dogmas of fallible men, appealed to the Bible alone. Everywhere their aim was the emancipation of the church from the bondage of human traditions and rule. This movement first focalized in the religious body known as the "Christian Denomination." For many years they were called "New Lights," but since they have never recognized this name, it is unfair to so designate them. They were also called the "Christian Connection" and "Christian Church." Throughout this work they are referred to as the "Christian Denomination."

Min. James O'Kelley withdrew from the Methodist Episcopal Church during its first General Conference, held in Baltimore in 1792. In his earlier years he was a classmate of Thomas Jefferson and Patrick Henry. He was a popular preacher and an old presiding elder from Virginia. He urged upon the conference the right of those preachers who thought themselves injured by the appointment of the bishops, to appeal to the general body, then in session. His appeal was in vain. Many individuals and local congregations, either in mass or in part, seceded with him. Appealing for public favor to the public spirit of the time, they for a few years called themselves Republican Methodists.

At the close of the eighteenth century, Dr. Abner Jones resided at Hartland, Vermont. He was a regular Baptist, but he was especially averse to human creeds, which he regarded as walls separating the followers of our Lord. And sectarian names grieved him much. In those years when a man of God got a new thought he was compelled to get a new church to put it in. So Dr. Jones organized a church at Lynden, Vermont, in 1802, with twenty-five members, and another church the same year at Hanover, New Hampshire, and a third at Pierpont, New Hampshire, in 1803.

About that time Elias Smith, then a Baptist minister, was preaching with great success in Portsmouth, New Hampshire. He fell in with Abner Jones, and soon the church under his care was led to adopt the principles and position of the Christians.

Barton W. Stone, a learned and eloquent minister, withdrew from the Presbyterian Church in 1804, and became very actively identified with the Christian Denomination.

Thus there arose simultaneously in the East, South and West congregations that wished to be known simply as Christians. These were remote from one another and without a knowledge of one another's work. They urged the all-sufficiency of the Scriptures as the rule of faith and life, the democracy of the local church, Christian character as the test of fellowship, and the name "Christian" to the exclusion of all denominational names.

Those years were particularly auspicious for the proclamation of such Christian truths. Beginning in the last days of the eighteenth century with the Presbyterians in Tennessee and Kentucky, and continuing to near the close of 1801, there was a most extraordinary revival of religion. Caneridge, Kentucky, was its center; its circumference was almost the outer bounds of the nation. Its slogan was, "The Bible our rule of faith and practice." Many thousands turned to the Lord. Consecrated lives testified to the genuineness of their conversion. Its impressions were deep and its influences abiding.

That revival was the John the Baptist of the movement inaugurated within less than two decades thereafter by the

Disciples of Christ. This also had its beginnings in various localities—East, West and South. It came neither from the Biblical research nor thought of any one man. It was not accidental, but providential. Its members approached the Bible "with all readiness of mind, examining the Scriptures daily."

It is believed by many that Alexander Campbell was the founder of the religious body known as the Disciples of Christ. This is a mistake, and the abundant and incontestible facts of history prove it to be such. It was at least a decade after the beginnings of this movement in various places that Mr. Campbell became the champion and later the most powerful advocate of those principles of Christian truth which differentiate the Disciples from all other religious bodies. This last fact was the occasion that led many uninformed people to call those with whom Mr. Campbell found himself to be in full accord "Campbellites." But this, to the Disciples, has always been an offensive nickname. Now it is no longer in use except in some back precincts where the trees grow tall and the brush thick, and hence the light of intelligence is slow in penetrating.

William Barney came into what is now Wabash County, and settled about eight miles north of the site of Mount Carmel, in 1808. His family then consisted of himself and wife and the following children: George, William, Richard, James, Betsy, Jane, Sarah, Clara and Ann. Shortly afterward, Mr. Barney's three sons-in-law, with their wives and children, also came. It is plain that this was a real Rooseveltian and patriotic family. Other settlers followed. Three forts for protection against the Indians in the locality were built.

Seth Gard came into this settlement in 1813. In 1814 he was a representative in the third Territorial Legislature, and in 1818 was a member of the convention that framed the constitution for the State. Evidently Mr. Gard was one of the leading citizens of that section. He, with Minister James Pool and others, on the 17th of July, 1819, organized the

Barney's Prairie Christian Church. Seth Gard was elected elder and Joseph Wood deacon. His grandson, O. H. Wood, now residing in that locality, has in his keeping the original book containing the record of this transaction. He is now in his sixty-eighth year, has been a member of the congregation for over fifty years, and affirms that from its beginning the Barney's Prairie Church has always stood on apostolic ground. This congregation has had an unbroken and useful life for ninety-six years. Mrs. Eliza Shoaff, Goldengate, Illinois, says that she was born in 1844 two miles north of the Barney's Prairie Church; that her grandparents, Job and Abigail Pixley, came to this locality in 1817, and that not long afterwards they united with the church. Both Mr. O. H. Wood and Mrs. Shoaff unite in affirming the unquestioned statements of their parents and grandparents, that before 1819 there had been a "New Light" church—as they there called themselves—about seven miles from Barney's Prairie, and that it had failed; and further, that when these people met on July 17 they decided to drop the name "New Light" and form a Christian church simply, which they did. Beyond question, in point of time, the Barney's Prairie Church leads all the Christian congregations in Illinois.

The Coffee Creek Church in Wabash County was the second. The original record reads: "At a meeting held at Brother Daniel Keen's on Saturday before the fifth Sabbath in August, 1819, a church of Christ was constituted, consisting of seven members." (See Keensburg.) The testimony of the original records, the history of Wabash County and the memories of the oldest residents of the community unite in affirming that from the first this was simply a church of Christ and has always continued as such.

Stephen England settled near the site of Cantrall, Sangamon County, in 1819. He was a native of Virginia, but grew to manhood in Kentucky. He was a Baptist preacher, but was acquainted with Barton W. Stone before coming to Illinois. Here he was never known as a Baptist minister. Shortly after settling here he invited the people to come to his cabin for public worship. That the people were soul-hungry is indicated by the fact that two women walked two miles to the meeting through prairie grass as high as their heads. On May 15, 1820, he constituted in his own house the first church of Christ in this county. In all there were nine members whose names have come down to us. From that date to this it has always been known as the church of Christ, or Antioch Christian Church. When the village of Cantrall was laid out in the sixties, the place of meeting was moved there and the local designation was changed from Antioch to Cantrall.

In the fall of 1826 the Little Grove Church of Christ, located six miles east of Paris, was constituted by Minister Samuel McGee. Two sisters, Mrs. Mary Morrison and Mrs. Anna Fitzgerald, who had come from Kentucky, were the leaders in the formation of this congregation. From the first it was called "The Little Grove Church of Christ."

MULKEYTOWN.

Mr. T. K. Means was born in Tennessee in April, 1831, and was brought by his parents to Franklin County, Illinois, in 1834. He is still living at Mulkeytown. His mind is vigorous and his thought clear. He says:

The first settlers of this part of the country called themselves Baptists and met at the house of John Kirkpatrick, who settled here in 1818. But these people had been baptized in Kentucky and Tennessee by John Mulkey and his brother Philip, who were Baptist preachers, but went into the Reformation with B. W. Stone early in the last century. It is a fact that John Mulkey was tried for heresy in 1809 in Kentucky. No one now knows when these people left off the name "Baptist" and adopted the name "Christian," for there was no Baptist church and people who held to the usages of that church in this whole settlement.

I have been told that the first man that preached the primitive gospel here was by the name of Underwood. The first preacher I ever heard was Elijah Spiller, who was an old man at that time and had lived here many years. But the man who did most of the preaching was by the name of Silas Reid, who came to the county in 1832. Afterward there came other preachers, of whom I can name Wm.

Bristow, John Hayes, Ulysses Heap, Wm. Chance and then a host of others.

I once heard D. C. Mulkey say that when he came to Illinois in 1832, his elder brothers, John M. and Jonathan H. Mulkey, were then living here and that they were devoted church-members at that time. Then we must infer there was a church organization at that time.

From this testimony of Mr. Means and the lucid preaching of the pure gospel by John Mulkey, Sr., reinforced as he was by the splendid ministry of Barton W. Stone, the writer concludes that the beginning of the Mulkeytown Church of Christ may be fairly placed near the middle of the twenties.

THE SPRING CREEK (MT. ZION) BERLIN CHURCH.

In 1818 Andrew Scott came from Crawford County, Indiana, and located near Richland, in Cartwright Township, Sangamon County. He was a minister whose aim was to teach and preach the true faith and the pure gospel. He at once began to hold meetings in the log cabins of the pioneers. In 1824 he settled near Island Grove—the woods skirting Spring Creek—a mile or two northwest of the site of old Berlin. There he met Theophilus Sweet, a Baptist preacher of the old school. It was not long until Mr. Sweet was in accord with Mr. Scott in his Christian faith and preaching. Their united labors soon developed a Christian Church on Spring Creek that met for worship in the log schoolhouse. It was doubtless organized there. Much as we admire those brave pioneers whose voices rang true to the word of God, still we are reminded that they were fallible. In a time after the beginning of this church, one of its members, named William Grant, accused Preacher Andrew Scott in plain speech of lying. Of his defense the subjoined documents have come down to us:

TAZWELL COUNTY, Illinois, June 30th, 1830.—We whose names are undersigned, having been formerly members of the church at Spring Creek in Sangamon County, by permission of the church in the big grove on Kickapoo, do send to the churches and all whom the presents may concern, that Brother Andrew Scott was and *is* a minister in good standing among us. Signed:

Isaac Carlock,	James R. Scott,
Samuel P. Glenn,	Levina Martin,
Ruth B. Glen,	John P. Glen,
Daniel Vincent,	Nancy Glen.
Ann Vincent,	

I, John Glen, a member of the church of Christ at Big Grove, Kickapoo, do hereby certify that I have known Andrew Scott for forty years, and that I ever did consider him a man of truth and strictly honest.

Given under my hand this 10th day of June, 1830.

Signed: John Glen.

The genuineness of these documents is attested by the following:

I, M. B. Robertson, a Justice of the Peace in and for Sangamon County, Illinois, do hereby certify that the above are accurate copies of letters of commendation received by Andrew Scott, from the above parties.

Given under my hand and seal this 15th day of October, 1913.

M. B. Robertson,

Berlin, Illinois, Oct. 15, 1913.   Justice of the Peace.

From these statements it is clear that there was a church of Christ in Big Grove, on the Kickapoo, in 1830. Nine members of this church had previously been members of the Spring Creek congregation. The latter was formed previous to this time, probably near 1825, the year after Messrs. Scott and Sweet began to work together.

Those who are curious will be interested in the following. On the reverse side of the sheet of paper containing the above testimonials this certificate is written:

This is to sertify that I was at the meten on Spring Creek for the perpes of setlen of Deficelty betwen Brother Scott and Brother Grant he charges Brother Scott ot lying But DiD not prov it it was not setled to the satisfaction of Brother Scott But was left to ware out.

Jesse Wilson.

The church of Christ in Big Grove, on Kickapoo, was short-lived, or soon met in another place under another name.

BEGINNINGS IN ILLINOIS 27

None of the historians mention it, nor is there a tradition of it in the memories of octogenarians. Ebenezer Rhodes was born in Holland in 1780. He came to America, and in 1824 to McLean County, settling in Blooming Grove, five miles south of Bloomington. He was a Baptist preacher and married the first couple in that county. Reuben Carlock was a native of Overton County, Tennessee. He came to Illinois in October, 1827, and settled in Dry Grove, five miles southwest of the site of the present town of Carlock. Minister William Brown, a Christian minister, came to visit his friend, Reuben Carlock, in 1828. In August of that year, Mr. Carlock yoked his ox-team to his wagon, and, accompanied by some members of his family and his guest, Preacher Brown, drove to the cabin of Ebenezer Rhodes for a three-days' meeting. Then and there a little church was constituted. Thereupon the recognized leader, Ebenezer Rhodes, said: "And now, brethren, we must have some articles of faith." Then Reuben Carlock, drawing a small copy of the New Testament from his pocket and holding it up, said: "Brother Rhodes, this book has all the articles of faith we need." Mr. Rhodes at once and in full assurance answered: "That is true." Thereafter he was known as a Christian minister and continued to preach the gospel without the mixture of human traditions until his death in 1842. That little congregation was simply a church of Christ.

In 1815 "Christian Settlement" was founded in Lawrence County, seven miles northwest of Vincennes, Indiana. It was made up of members of the Christian Denomination. For ninety-eight years that country community has been remarkable for its industry, sobriety, thrift and high ideals. In 1828 the church there came fully to apostolic grounds.

The first sermon ever preached in Hittle's Grove, near what became the town site of Armington, was by a Methodist minister named Walker, but he did not form a class. This and other public meetings for worship were held in the log cabin of Michael Hittle. After a time two women

28 HISTORY OF THE DISCIPLES IN ILLINOIS

wished to be baptized, and a Baptist minister, probably Ebenezer Rhodes, was sent for. Finding no church there to vote on the fitness of the candidates, after deliberation it was decided to immerse them on the public confession of their faith in Christ. Thereupon a Baptist church was constituted with seven members. On January 11, 1829, this congregation was reorganized on the following basis: "We, the undersigned, do give ourselves to the Lord and to each other as a church of Jesus Christ, to be governed by his word contained in the Old and New Testaments." This church has had an unbroken life to the present time. This agreement to constitute a church of Christ was signed by seventeen persons.

In 1829 a church was constituted in the southern part of Marion County. It was known as the Mount Moriah Free Will Baptist Church. In 1837 its members dropped the words "Free Will Baptist" and substituted for them "Christian," and since then, to this date, it has been known as "The Mount Moriah Christian Church."

From an old, original record-book the following is taken:

April 30, 1831, the church of Christ on Cedar Fork of Henderson River, Warren County, was constituted upon the belief that the Scriptures of the Old and New Testaments are the Word of God, and the only rule of faith and practice, and are sufficient for the government of the Church.

The location was one and a half miles northwest of the present town of Cameron. This was probably the first church of Christ in the Military Tract. Some of its families became representatives in that part of the State and elsewhere.

The second Sunday in July, 1831, Minister John B. Curl constituted the "Bear Creek" Church in Adams County, and also the "Mill Creek" Church in the same county before the close of the year. Mr. Curl labored diligently through all that section of the State, and three or four other congregations were formed about the same time.

Bushrod W. Henry was a native of Culpeper County, Virginia. He came to Illinois and settled in Shelbyville in 1830. He was then twenty-five years of age. He was a

BEGINNINGS IN ILLINOIS

Baptist preacher and man of superior mental endowments and magnificent personality. In July, 1831, he constituted the "First Baptist Church of Christ in Shelbyville." Within one year he was preaching clearly those Biblical truths commonly held and taught by the Disciples. In 1834 Mr. Henry, with those of like views with him, were summarily expelled from the Baptist Church. Then the congregation in Shelbyville dropped the name "Baptist" and has since then been known as the "Church of Christ." Mr. Henry has two sons living—Judge W. B. Henry, of Vandalia, and Minister J. O. Henry, of Findley. The latter is eighty-six years old. He was a comrade of Richard J. Oglesby in the Fourth Illinois Volunteer Infantry during the Mexican war. Ever afterward they were fast friends until "Uncle Dick" passed over the great divide. Mr. Henry clearly and positively affirms that his father was not assisted by any one except his wife in reaching his conclusions on the teachings of the Scriptures; that together they, husband and wife, reverently and faithfully read themselves out of spiritual Babylon.

By 1832 there began to be some general unity of thought and action among the widely separated Disciples in their efforts to restore the church after the New Testament pattern—in its teachings, its ordinances and its life; so in this year a number of local churches had their beginnings. Most of them still live and have been forceful factors in building society.

The church in Jacksonville had its beginning in that year. Several Christian families came to Morgan County from Kentucky in 1830 and 1831. Fourteen families of Disciples, then called Reformers by many, met together regularly that winter for public worship. In the summer of 1831 Josephus Hiett settled five miles east of Jacksonville. He was the first regular preacher of the Disciples in that section.

James Green and Harrison W. Osborn, of the Christian Denomination, were in that locality at that time. They preached in the courthouse and in schoolhouses as they had opportunity. In 1832 there were good-sized nuclei of Disciples and members of the Christian Denomination in and around Jacksonville. It was in this year that the scholarly and pious Barton W. Stone came from Kentucky into the "Far West," as Illinois was then called. The reputation of this good man had preceded him, for he was an active factor in the Caneridge revival in 1800, whose influences and glory came to be more enduring than the stars. Mr. Stone made a tour through the Prairie State, preaching at Lawrenceville, Carrollton, Rushville, Springfield, Jacksonville and other places. He believed in and labored for the union of all God's people. At Jacksonville he laid his strong but tender hand upon the two separated bodies and left them united in one. This was in October, 1832.

A similar result was effected at Carrollton a few days later.

It may be properly noted here that the Disciples of Christ absorbed the larger part of the Christian Denomination, not only in Illinois, but elsewhere. However, the latter body still lives. The appeal of both parties was to the Bible as, the only recognized authority in religion, and in this way many of the latter concluded that the Disciples were nearer the divine standard than themselves.

The church at Winchester was formed December 1, 1832. The old Union Church, located about ten miles west of Clinton, was constituted October 13 (the second Sunday), 1832. It was formed with seventeen charter members, under the spreading branches of a large white-oak tree, whose decaying stump marks the spot. This and the gravestones in the cemetery that grew around the house of worship, are silent sentinels of faded joys and departed glory. Hughes Bowles was the leader there. He was a product of the Caneridge (Ky.) revival, as were those associated with him in this beginning. His son, Walter P. Bowles, became the best known and most powerful preacher of his time in that section. He and Abraham Lincoln were familiar friends, and long before the immortal emancipator dreamed of place and fame, he said to Mr. Bowles: "Wat, if I could preach like you, I would rather do that than be President." The old Union Church served its community and generation for just fifty years to a day, and then, railroads coming and towns growing, it fell into sleep.

Joseph Hostetler was a great, strong man in his time. In his youth he became a member of the Tunker Church and soon thereafter a preacher. With little help, his own study of the Bible led him to the common basic principles of the gospel. He came from Indiana to Illinois in 1832, and in November of that year organized the West Okaw Church of Christ. It was located about two miles west of the site of Lovington, and became the mother of a number of congregations of like faith in that section. West Okaw still lives and flourishes in the Lovington Church.

In the early thirties a number of families came from Christian County, Kentucky, to Illinois, and settled in Walnut Grove, now known as Eureka. In April, 1832, thirteen Disciples met in the log residence of John Oatman, that stood about one-half mile northeast of the railroad station now there, and organized a church. Since that time it has been known as the Christian Church (or church of Christ) at Eureka, and has been one of the most forceful agencies 'in the entire State for truth and righteousness.

In 1833 churches of Christ were organized at Springfield, Lawrenceville, Decatur, Ursa, Little Mackinaw, ten miles south of Mackinaw town, and elsewhere.

The Mount Pleasant Church, Hancock County, was organized in 1834, and made a remarkable record through eighty years. Mrs. Georgenia Walton has been a member of this congregation for fifty-five years. She is a woman of rare intelligence and spirit. Speaking of the early years, she says: "We were Campbellites in those days. A boy in the M. E. Sunday School was repeating the names of the tribes in Canaan when Joshua led the Israelites into it. This boy said there were Canaanites, Amorites, Jebusites and Campbellites."

This church also produced that great soul, Dr. William

Booz. In the early sixties he sent a communication to the Carthage *Republican* over the pseudonym "Country Jake." The editor was so much impressed with its pungent character that he encouraged him to send weekly contributions. *Thus was born, of these two fertile minds, provincial journalism in Illinois.*

This is less than a bird's-eye view of the beginnings of the Disciples of Christ in Illinois. Across the central and through most of the southern part of the State they continued to grow. Every inch of ground they occupy to-day has been won by battle. They met opposition, often bitter, always determined, from the older religious bodies. Where they are now strong in numbers, intelligent and wealthy and particularly "respectable," they are quickly and cheerfully recognized as "orthodox" and welcomed to the "sisterhood of the churches." Without doubt, with the changing times they have all changed with them, and, by divine grace, for the better.

EUREKA COLLEGE.

CHAPTER III.

CHRISTIAN EDUCATION.

From the first the Disciples of Christ in Illinois have been earnest advocates of mental culture. In the early decades many of the leaders were well-educated men. In the fifties and sixties the question of establishing academies for work supplementing that of the public schools was considered in the annual State meetings. A few such schools were started in addition to the colleges organized. But the Civil War closed all of these, and within five years thereafter the State high schools were begun. But it is a painful and serious fact that the Disciples in Illinois for the last twenty-five years have failed to keep step with the great educational column in the State.

It is a significant fact that the Disciples were the leaders of coeducation in Illinois. Oberlin College, Ohio, was formed in 1833, and from its beginning trained young people of both sexes. So did Antioch College, at Yellow Springs, Ohio, of which Horace Mann was the head. In Illinois, Shurtleff College was founded as Rock Springs Seminary in 1827, and removed to its present location in 1831-32. Young women were first officially admitted to this institution in 1871. Knox College was founded in 1837. It had a female collegiate department from 1849, but it was not "till the early seventies that the same courses were thrown open to women as to men." The school founded at Eureka in 1848 and that at Abingdon in 1853 were both coeducational from their beginnings. So also were the other schools of the Disciples in Illinois.

In 1900 there were 345 colleges and universities in the United States. Of these, 204 are coeducational. It is the prevailing system in the West. Of the twenty-eight colleges in Illinois, twenty-six are open to women. The Disciples have also insisted that education should be affirmatively Christian; hence the Bible has a fixed place in the curriculums of their schools.

EUREKA COLLEGE.

Eureka College was a child of Providence. Its founders were men who walked with God. Central Illinois, into which the first white settlers came, was a land of entrancing beauty. The wide prairies, with grassy billows, reached out until, to the human eye, they touched the horizon. The streams of water were skirted with trees, only a part of which had grown to stately size. Charming wild birds and graceful wild beasts abounded everywhere, untamed and untouched save by the red men. The first immigrants made their homes among the groves. The timber was needed to build their cabins, make their fires and fence their farms. The settlements were known by the names of the groves to which the first pioneers gave names. That one along the west line of McLean County and the east line of Tazewell, which in 1841 became Woodford County, was called Walnut Grove, because those trees, indicating a rich soil, grew there abundantly. Into this place, in the thirties, a number of families came from southern Kentucky. Among them there were Ben Major and William Davenport, who were double brothers-in-law; Elijah Dickinson, Sr.; B. J. Radford, Sr.; William P. Atterberry, R. M. Clark, E. B. Myers, A. M. Myers, Caleb Davidson, M. R. Bullock and Thomas Bullock. Other influential men, as John Darst and A. G. Ewing, came later. The families of the first settlers were generally large and growing.

The schools for the instruction and training of children in that period were of the subscription class, and were often "kept" by impecunious and peripatetic pedagogues. While the pioneers were engaged in subduing their part of the earth, thus helping to lay the foundations of a mighty material empire, they were even more concerned about the mental and

CHRISTIAN EDUCATION 35

moral training of their children. They felt keenly the inadequacy of the ordinary facilities. In the fall of 1847 John T. Jones, an active and well-known minister among the Disciples in Central Illinois, opened at Walnut Grove a select school for the education of girls, on a spot near the present site of Eureka College. In the following winter a malignant type of measles became epidemic in the community and broke up this school.

In the summer of 1848 Mr. A. S. Fisher, a student from Bethany College, came to Walnut Grove. He was engaged by a number of the leading men of the community to conduct a school for a period of ten months. This school opened in a small frame building on September 10. The curriculum included the common English branches, with higher mathematics, natural philosophy, rhetoric, logic, etc. Evidently Mr. Fisher intended to earn his pay. The work of this school was suspended during a "big meeting" that was conducted by Mr. D. P. Henderson, an eminent evangelist of Jacksonville, Illinois. This meeting continued through "many days," and added about one hundred persons to the Walnut Grove Church of Christ. At its close the work of the school was resumed and continued until the following Fourth of July. As the school was successful, Mr. Ben Major and his coadjutors arranged with the young teacher for its continuance. Mr. Fisher submitted the following conditions, which were accepted by the patrons: First, that an addition, properly furnished, be made to the schoolhouse; second, that he be permitted to employ an assistant teacher for the primary pupils; third, that he be allowed the net income from tuition fees for his salary; fourth, that adequate provision be made for boarding all students who came from other localities. At this time a printed announcement of the school was circulated under the name of

WALNUT GROVE SEMINARY.

Miss Sue E. Jones, a daughter of John T. Jones and a graduate, was secured as assistant teacher. The school opened with such an encouraging outlook and growing attendance that the need of a larger building than the one enlarged was obvious. Hence the promoters of the school met in the autumn of 1849 and decided to erect a two-story brick building to cost not less than $2,500. Ben Major led in this enterprise. In December of that year this building was first occupied, and the school was incorporated as

WALNUT GROVE ACADEMY.

Its management was vested in twelve trustees. Of this board, John T. Jones was president and A. S. Fisher secretary. In September, 1850, John Lindsay, a graduate of Bethany College and a young minister, was added to the academy as teacher of Latin and Greek. The first philosophical and chemical apparatus was secured in 1851. In the same year, to the "State Meeting," which assembled with the Walnut Grove Church, the trustees of the academy explained that they were endeavoring to establish an institution of learning where the young people of both sexes might receive the advantages of a liberal education under the care and influence of Christian teachers and free from all sectarian prejudices. They hoped the school would serve the Disciples generally throughout the State.

The year 1852 was a remarkable one in Walnut Grove. The school was abruptly closed one month before the time by a scourge of Asiatic cholera which swept through the community. Its chief victim was Ben Major, the founder of the school. His was a superior combination of head and heart. The best blood of the Huguenots and of Virginians filled his veins. A native of Kentucky and an owner of slaves, from early youth he had serious doubts on the question of human slavery. By the light of divine truth he reached his own purpose and matured his own plans. These were at variance with all his early teachings and antagonistic to all his family traditions and social relations. Having freed his slaves in the fall of 1835, he sent an agent with them to New York and shipped them to Liberia. In 1834, with his family of seven, he moved from Kentucky to Illinois in an ox-wagon. Through a period of eighteen years he served the new settlement at Walnut Grove as counselor, physician, friend and genuine leader. A. S. Fisher justly shares the honor of founding this school. Of him Professor Radford has given this admirable pen-picture:

> He seemed not to us as a man of like passions with the rest. Frivolity was a stranger to him, and that he should make a mistake was out of the question. Grand and peculiar, he might have sat upon his pedagogical throne, a sceptered hermit, but, much to our wonder, he went about the hard drudgery of pioneer school work with a constancy, a punctuality and devotion to duty which was in itself a profitable part of our course of instruction. Professor Neville used to call him 'an arithmetic in breeches,' but this was evidently, to use an arithmetical expression, reducing him to his lowest terms. He was accuracy incarnate. He impressed the ambitious student with the idea that inaccuracy was immoral, and that to make a mistake was unpardonable. With infinite pains and patient repetition, he would lead even the dullest student to understand what had seemed to him hopelessly incomprehensible. The lesson of the hour had the floor, and nothing else was to be recognized but a point of order, and he made a point of order all the time. In the years of his classroom ministry he inculcated upon thousands of youths such lessons of accuracy, industry and attention to the matter in hand as have in no small measure contributed to their success in life.

After thirty-eight years of uninterrupted and self-sacrificing service, he left the college in 1885 and moved to Kansas City, Missouri. There he died in 1903.

The "State Meeting" that convened with the church at Abingdon in 1852 indorsed the movement to build up an institution of learning at Walnut Grove for the education of their sons and daughters and to fit young men for the Christian ministry. There were students then at the school from more than twenty localities in Illinois and also from Indiana and Missouri. The same "State Meeting" also formed a Board of Education consisting of Ministers William Davenport, John Lindsay, George W. Minier, Jonathan Atkinson, A. J. Kane and Prof. A. S. Fisher, the purpose of which board was to consider and report ways and means of establishing academies in various parts of the State under the exclusive management of the Disciples in Illinois.

In 1852 the first post-office was established in Walnut Grove. Before that the nearest office was at Washington, eight miles west. Mr. Fisher was made the first postmaster. Everything was on the general-delivery plan. To add to the burdens of the patient professor, many letters at that time were sent C. O. D., the postage on them being paid by the receivers.

John H. Neville, a graduate of Bethany College, succeeded John Lindsay as teacher in the fall of 1852. One year thereafter the academy began its work with the following teachers: A. S. Fisher, J. H. Neville, Mrs. Sarah Fisher, wife of the principal, and Miss Elmira J. Dickinson.

The Annual Meeting of the Disciples at Jacksonville in September, 1853, received the report from the Board of Education. It was distinctly significant in three particulars: First, coeducational—"that the brethren may endow their sons and daughters with a liberal education;" second, that all education should be Christian—"the Bible should have a conspicuous place in the daily exercises of every school. Having been prepared by the Author of the human mind, it is superior to all human productions in developing morality among any people;" third, an educated ministry—"that only an educated mind is competent to disengage the simple facts of Christianity from the many false dogmas with which they have become entangled through many centuries of false teachings and interpretations. Brethren, shall we have such schools among us and under our control?" These affirmations reflected fully the views of the Disciples in Illinois at that time. However, the Jacksonville meeting did not adopt the report. Other communities than Walnut Grove were ambitious to establish such schools. The assembly decided to confine its activities exclusively to the direct work of evangelizing. Notwithstanding, the meeting voted in favor of raising $10,000 to endow a chair in Bethany College. Of this sum, the people of Walnut Grove raised and paid $2,225.

The academy grew in attendance so that a boarding-hall sufficient for the accommodation of fifty students was completed in the summer of 1854. Its cost was mainly met by citizens of the community. Mr. and Mrs. R. M. Clark, who were admirable Christians, were placed in charge. The hall became a pleasant home for many occupants in the years following.

A music department was introduced with the session beginning in September, 1855. Miss Ellen F. True, of Mt. Vernon, Ohio, was the first teacher. A one-room frame building was erected just across the street from the academy for the use of this department. When not in use by music pupils it was occupied by other classes.

For reasons about which annalists are silent, the people of Walnut Grove desired to change the name of their village and post-office; so a committee of three was appointed near the close of 1854—probably by the trustees of the academy—to choose a new name. Minister John Lindsay, one of the three, reported "Eureka," and the people, believing that *they had found* a favored spot in a goodly land, adopted it.

As the result of an application and some necessary but altogether honorable caucusing, the Legislature of Illinois, by a special act passed in February, 1855, incorporated.

EUREKA COLLEGE.

Under the liberal provisions of this charter the institution has continued uninterruptedly from September of that year to the present time. With the summer of 1855 the academy's work was merged into that of the college. The first Faculty was composed of the following: William M. Brown, president; A. S. Fisher, J. H. Neville, O. A. Burgess, Richard Conover, Mrs. Sarah F. Conover and Miss Ellen F. True. Mr. Burgess remained but one year, preferring the work of the ministry to that of the classroom. He was a man of striking physique and commanding personality. Well developed and finely disciplined, he was self-conscious and self-poised. With the mentality of a master and the tender heart of a woman, he was a regal man whose influence remained with all lives he touched.

The new Board of Trustees turned their attention at once to questions of finance, grounds and a new building. The school had grown steadily in popularity, numbers and efficiency; so enlarged accommodations became imperative. The campus, a tract of about fifteen acres, was the joint gift of Elias B. Myers and James Conover, residents of the community and faithful friends of the school. Its graceful slopes that the bluegrass loves, covered with stately trees of the primeval forest, have always been regarded as an ideal spot for a college. Its charms appeal to the love of the beautiful in nature in all beholders.

President Brown and Minister William Davenport served as solicitors of finance and promoters of the institution in many parts of the State. Within a few months about $60,000 had been secured in interest-bearing notes. One-third of these were to be used in the erection of the new building. Relying upon these notes and college friends, the trustees secured a loan and let the contract for the building in the spring of 1857. It was completed in the summer of 1858, and has been in continuous use since that time. This loan had the personal guarantee of Messrs. John Darst, E. B. Myers and William Davenport, joint-leaders in this enterprise.

The financial panic of 1857 swept the whole country like a cyclone. Banks failed and business was paralyzed. Farmers marketing their products were paid in bank notes, many of which depreciated from 10 to 100 per cent. within from one to sixty days. Printed "Bank Detectors" were circulated and consulted daily and eagerly. These conditions rendered many of the notes held by the trustees valueless, and hindered many patrons from sending their children to the school. The college thus suffered its first reverse. However, the matriculation in this session numbered 276.

Professor Neville left the school in the summer of 1857.

CHRISTIAN EDUCATION 41

The facile pen of Professor Radford has given this picture of him:

> He was singularly handsome, and the contour of his head and the expression of his face suggested the purely intellectual in a greater degree than I have seen in any other person. He loved intellectual exercise for its own sake. The emotional and physical demands must wait upon the mental. He had little patience with mediocrity. Aptness in a student covered a multitude of sins, and dullness would discount a whole catalogue of virtues. His intense intellectuality, which often slid into the minor key of abstractedness, led to many eccentricities, which were copied by us in the sincerest of all flattery—imitation. It was amusing, no doubt—all that awkward and misfit affectation of oddities in gait and manner and abstractedness. But when we call to mind what extravagances are indulged in by the worshipers of Browning, or Balzac, or Kipling; what aping of royal eccentricities, deformities, and even vices, are common in high social life—we shall see that these rustic admirers of the brilliant young teacher were not fools above all that dwell upon the face of the earth.

In January, 1857, Charles Louis Loos came to the college as its president. He was a graduate of Bethany, and had served three years as a teacher in that institution. He was a native of France and had been trained in the Lutheran faith. His acceptance of the position of the Disciples came from a clear conviction of truth and duty. His change of church relation caused much bitterness among his Lutheran relatives. He remained at the head of the college only until the summer of 1858, when he returned to Bethany's Faculty.

He was succeeded in the presidency by Mr. George Callender, who came to Walnut Grove from Liverpool, England, in 1852. He was a Scotchman of fine mind and culture, and was highly esteemed by the students. Three years after his arrival in this locality, on a beautiful summer afternoon, before a large concourse of people assembled on the bank of Walnut Creek, he declared in an impassioned address his joyful acceptance of the common, catholic principles of the New Testament faith, and, with his wife, was then immersed. Mr. Callender did little classroom work, but his frequent lectures were a source of information and inspiration to the students. The session beginning September, 1858, opened with the following Faculty: George Callender, B. W. Johnson, A. S. Fisher, Dr. J. M. Allen, Misses Sue S. Smith, Elmira J. Dickinson and Jane Ewing.

As early as 1849 a society was formed among the students for literary and social culture. It was named "Walnut Grove Literary Institute." Its meetings were held on Friday evening of every week, and were a source of great profit and pleasure to its members. In after years it was incorporated under the name, "Edmund Burke Society." In 1857 the Periclesian and Mathesian Societies were organized, the latter for the help of young men looking toward the Christian ministry. These three societies were composed exclusively of males; so in 1857 the Excelsior Society was formed for the advantage of young women. It continued as a helpful agency until in later years the Edmund Burke and Periclesian Societies declared ladies eligible to their memberships. Through the fifty-six years of the life of the college these societies have continued uninterruptedly. They have been valuable auxiliaries to the direct work of the institution.

In 1860 the college graduated its first class—Mr. E. W. Dickinson. He was then, and has been through most of the years since, a resident of Eureka, and has been one of its most honorable and useful citizens.

To the Faculty of September, 1860, there were added Messrs. R. H. Johnson and J. H. Rowell and Misses Sarah Lamphere and Mary G. Clark, making altogether a teaching force of nine persons. Both the attendance and work of the school were encouraging.

In 1861 came the beginning of the great Civil War. The one thought then uppermost in the minds, and the one passion that then dominated every other in the hearts of all of America's loyal sons and daughters, was the preservation of the integrity of our Federal Union. In response to the first call of President Lincoln for volunteers, five of the seven men who were members of the Senior class—one of whom was a teacher also—entered the military service. It is a fact significant of the loyalty of the Disciples of Illinois to our

CHRISTIAN EDUCATION

flag that, in the awful period of storm and strife, the college graduated only three men. This institution has never been the slavish ally of any political party. Throughout its entire history it has always stood for those immutable principles of civic justice and righteousness that make peoples truly great and assure the life of the republic.

B. W. Johnson succeeded to the presidency in 1862. He had performed the active duties of that office since 1858. He had been a student for three years in the academy, and thereafter by two years' work in Bethany had graduated there. He was probably the best informed man on general history ever connected with the college. During that period many students listened eagerly to his remarkable and charming lectures on this subject.

Mr. H. W. Everest came to the presidency in 1864. Leaving Bethany as a student because of his political convictions, he graduated from Oberlin. He left the presidency of Hiram College to come to Eureka. He was himself an untiring student of broad scholarship, a fine instructor in many lines of knowledge, and of superior executive ability. He was a modest man of fine personality who awakened commendable ambitions in his pupils and impressed them with high ideals. For more than half a century his influence was a potent factor in the lives of many who ever counted his guiding friendship a privilege. During the first three years of his administration the number of students increased from 125 to 225. The close of the Civil War and the resumption of normal conditions contributed to this result. Then he was assisted by some able coadjutors in the school—H. O. Newcomb, a graduate of the University of Michigan, a kindly teacher upon whom "the boys" could always depend in "emergencies," and Dr. J. M. Allen, a lovable and stimulating instructor.

In 1863 the deficit in current expenses became serious. A canvass of the community was made and enough money was secured to tide over for a time. In this and many other emergencies of the college Mr. John Darst was the leading man.

Mr. Darst came from Ohio to Walnut Grove in 1851. Five years thereafter he laid out the town site of Eureka on land that he had previously purchased. He was the embodiment of energy and industry, the soul of honor, "diligent in business, fervent in spirit, serving the Lord." Frequently he subordinated his personal interests to the public good. More than once he mortgaged his land to secure money to help the college. He was officially connected with the school for forty years and was one of its most steadfast and dependable friends. At a meeting held in Bloomington in 1868 to consider the educational interests of the Disciples in Illinois, reference was made to his liberality. Mr. Darst replied: "Indeed, brethren, it has been a sort of selfish thing with me; for I feel a great deal happier than if I did not give." He was the open foe of the saloon, and contributed five sons to the Union Army. He was the helpful friend of young men preparing for the ministry. B. B. Tyler was one to whom he extended practical encouragement. Mr. Tyler said: "I want the world to know what John Darst did for me and for the church of Christ. If I have been worth anything to the world, let the grand good man have the honor that belongs to him."

In 1866 an effort was made to add a few thousand dollars to the endowment, but, inasmuch as the donors were made the preferred borrowers, a large percentage of these notes became worthless through unexpected business failures; so the net result was small. The annual deficit increased in size like a rolled snowball. Overdue debts became an annoyance to the trustees and a very disagreeable inconvenience to the teachers. In this emergency individual claims were surrendered by numerous friends, a loan of $12,000 was secured, and thus temporary relief was attained. Meanwhile solicitors were afield. Among them were Dr. J. M. Allen and Ministers W. T. Maupin and W. G. Anderson.

By 1867 the college had quite outgrown the capacity of the one building used for nine years. Its chapel was too small, the library and museum were overcrowded, and the literary societies needed more room. Hence the chapel building was planned, partly financed and finished in 1868. At the close of eight years' service Mr. Everest resigned in 1872. He was succeeded the following year by A. M. Weston, who had come to the college two years before. He was a graduate of Antioch College under Horace Mann, had served as city editor on a Cincinnati (O.) daily paper, had given three years of his life in the Union Army, rising from a private to a second lieutenancy, and thereafter had given five years to educational work. During the three years of his presidency at Eureka the number of students steadily increased each year.

B. J. Radford, the second, was born in Walnut Grove and has passed most of the seventy-five years of his busy and fruitful life in that community. After more than three years of military service in the Federal Army, he graduated at Eureka in the class of 1866. Beginning at Niantic, Illinois, in 1868 and closing in Denver, Colorado, in 1892, he spent sixteen years in ministerial work, interspersed with teaching. His ministerial work was from 1871 to 1881 at Eureka, and with intervals at Des Moines, Iowa, and Cincinnati, Ohio. Beginning in 1870, he was a college teacher, serving thirty full years, including one year as president of Drake University; the other twenty-nine years were given to Eureka College. He succeeded Mr. Weston in the presidency, continuing two years in that position. His administration of all the interests of the institution was wise. Throughout his life Mr. Radford has been an omnivorous reader, an earnest student, a great thinker, an inspiring teacher and an interesting public speaker. Further, he is a clear and forceful writer, his productions including some genuine poetry. He has an apparently inexhaustible fund of humor and anecdote and is thoroughly democratic in his instincts. His life has been filled with earnest toil and uncomplaining self-sacrifice. During his long career as a teacher he came into personal touch and the range of mental influence with thousands of young people who have passed through his classrooms. Hundreds of these were preparing for the Christian ministry; so he has gripped the lives of a larger number of youth by his potent personality than any other man ever connected with the institution. He has made an immeasurable contribution to the promotion of the Kingdom of God. Since 1886 he has been an associate editor of the *Christian Standard*. With Miss Jessie Brown he was coeditor of *The Disciple* for two years. For a period of ten years he was a popular lecturer on the Chautauqua platforms in Illinois, Indiana, Kansas and Tennessee, and for a much longer time in temperance and social-reform service. He is not without honor in his home community, for he has there united more couples in wedlock than any other man, while he has conducted probably one-half of all the funerals of those who now rest in Olio's silent city. "The Professor" is still strong, active and helpful, and is fairly entitled to be known as the honorable and honored "Sage of Eureka."

H. W. Everest returned to the presidency of the college in 1877. For three years more he led the school with his fine energy and scholarship. During this time a boarding-house for young men, with a capacity for forty-eight, was built. But this hall and that one erected in 1854, having served well their purposes, have gone the way of all earth. Each in its time was full of the romances of youth—its joyous laughter and midnight oil—but now there remain of them only a few fading memories.

In 1881, Dr. J. M. Allen was elected to the presidency. Giving up the practice of medicine, he began his thirty years' service in the college in 1857. He gave the college faithful and efficient work as teacher, solicitor and president. His life was filled with good deeds and self-sacrifice. With a keen sense of humor, apt incident and fitting anecdote, he was always popular. His manifest sincerity and loyalty to truth and right awakened noble ideals in his pupils. His fine character left an imperishable impress upon thousands of young men and women. The college prospered during the four years of his administration.

CHRISTIAN EDUCATION

The teachers here have always received small salaries. Tuition fees are quite insufficient to meet the current expenses of any average school. Another effort was made to increase the endowment, but with limited results. Hence an Aid Fund was begun, and by this method a goodly number of friends gave direct help for thirty years. During that period Minister W. F. Black gave valuable assistance. For the most the teachers have been men and women who were self-sacrificing, esteeming the Christian training and culture of young people greater gain than material riches. And since teachers and taught have been in almost daily personal contact, the influence of this consecration has imperceptibly transformed ideals of life in the students as the vernal sun changes the face of the earth.

The curriculum was broadened with the passing years, and, considering its limited material resources, the college kept pace with educational progress in a marked degree.

In 1884 a commodious audience-room, designed by Professor Radford, was erected on the college campus, called "The Tabernacle." It is 80 by 100 feet in dimensions, seating twelve hundred people. Its cost was $4,000, which was paid by citizens of the community. It stands on gently sloping ground that forms a natural amphitheater. For a period of twelve years the State Missionary Convention assembled there. It has served the college on Commencement and other occasions, and the community for various purposes, including in the later years Chautauqua programs.

In this year the union of Eureka and Abingdon Colleges was effected. The latter had been crippled years before by internal strife, and its popularity and usefulness much impaired thereby. The public schools were growing steadily in efficiency and consequent appreciation. Removed from three to five decades from the period of pioneer school work, many Disciples did not understand the value and functions of colleges owned and directed by themselves. The material and mental steadily overgrew the spiritual in public esteem. Both of these colleges were receiving feeble financial support, and that came mostly from the two localities in which they were situated. In the early eighties it became apparent that both of them could not live. Pres. F. M. Bruner made herculean efforts to save the Abingdon school. He knew its value to the churches of Christ in that part of the State and at large. But it was not so written in the records of destiny. After correspondence and personal consultations, it was decided to unite the college interests of the Disciples in Illinois at Eureka. By this arrangement F. M. Bruner; his son, H. L. Bruner; his daughter, Miss Lettie Bruner, and Mr. W. S. Errett became members of the Faculty of the united school. Up to that date Abingdon had graduated 164 and Eureka 133 young men and women, a total of 297. This number probably did not amount to one-tenth of those who had come under their helpful influences.

Carl Johann became president in 1887. He had served in this capacity during the preceding year while Dr. J. M. Allen was afield for finance. Mr. Johann was a native of Switzerland, near the boundary-line of France. From his sixth year he attended school eleven months in the year, and at the age of fifteen graduated from the high school of his native city—Chaux-de-Fonds. During this period he acquired a knowledge of both the German and French languages, as both were in common use by the people of his native city. He was next sent by his parents to the College of Lausanne, where he completed its course of study in three years. Thereafter he was a student in the Universities of Aaran and Zurich for two years. At the age of twenty he went to Paris, France, to study, but within the year decided to come to America. Here he readily acquired a knowledge of our language. After various experiences as farm-helper, tutor, surveyor and public-school teacher, he came to Eureka in the fall of 1876 as Professor of Modern Languages. He was connected with the college twenty years—eleven years as a teacher and nine as president.

The attendance of students was steadily increasing, so that the boarding-halls were quite inadequate. At this juncture

Mr. and Mrs. W. J. Ford, then residents of Eureka and sincere friends of the school, tendered to the trustees as a gift their beautiful residence, with four and a half acres of ground adjoining the campus, to be made into a boarding-hall for young lady students. The conditions were that it should be suitably enlarged and be known as "Lida's Wood" —in memory of their only daughter. At a cost of $10,000 the building was enlarged, completed and opened for students in the fall of 1888. After being used for five and a half years, this structure was burned to the ground January 11, 1894. It was soon thereafter rebuilt on a larger and better plan. The yard of "The Wood" is covered with native, stately trees and is a charming place. The property has always been a valuable and pleasing adjunct to the educational and social work of the institution.

By 1890 the attendance of students had so increased that the classroom facilities were quite inadequate. The effort for a new building resulted in the completion of Burgess Memorial Hall in 1892, at a cost of $21,000. Of this sum, $10,000 was the gift of Mrs. O. A. Burgess. The building was named by the Board of Trustees that it should stand as a memorial of her deceased husband, who, in its early years, had served as a teacher there and was a distinguished representative of the Disciples. In the session of 1892-93 there were 386 students enrolled, while the teachers numbered nineteen.

In 1890 the trustees bought a five-acre tract near the campus for an athletic park. At the same time they converted a part of the old college building into a gymnasium.

In these years of encouraging progress and helpfulness there were silent and potent forces at work that were soon to challenge the very life of the institution. The first and smaller of the two chief influences was the financial panic of the early nineties. The depreciation of values, the stagnation of business, the tramp of millions of industrious men and women in search of honorable work, and the utter ruin of countless commendable enterprises, were appalling. This depression reached many nations. Naturally, attendance decreased at such educational institutions, while their friends were generally less able to furnish the money they needed.

But the greatest and continuing force with which all such colleges in Illinois must take account is the public-school system of the State. Founded in 1825, it has grown steadily in efficiency and popularity. This enlargement was particularly apparent in the two closing decades of the nineteenth century. In 1870 there were only two public high schools in Illinois; now (1912) there are 365 such schools in towns and cities, with fifty-seven township high schools having a four years' course—a total of 422. Many of them are accredited to the State University. The curriculum of these schools has grown until now it is fully equal to that of the church schools forty years ago. While these colleges enlarged their courses of study and became more efficient in their work, they did not keep up with the State's high schools in popularity. The latter came to be regarded as the "People's College." Since about 1890, courses in these high schools have been elective, while at the present time there is a marked tendency toward vocational training. During this period of high-school growth the commonwealth had added to the two already in operation three additional Normal Schools—one in the eastern, one in the western and one in the northern part of the State. Access is thus made comparatively easy and inexpensive to most of the young people who desire to attend them. Meanwhile, the University of Illinois has continued to grow in every way. The expenses incurred in the establishing, equipment and conduct of this superior system of mental development and culture are largely met by general taxation, while the ever-increasing attendance develops enthusiasm in the student body. These things have had a marked influence toward decreasing the growth of church schools in attendance.

By 1896 an indebtedness of $30,000 confronted the trustees. Minister J. H. Hardin had shown his ability as a solicitor in several fields; so, upon the invitation of the board,

CHRISTIAN EDUCATION

he accepted the presidency. It was understood that, for a time at least, his attention would be given to finance. Under his leadership the debt was paid and 200 acres of land in the corn belt of Illinois was given to the college by Mr. T. A. Bondurant, of De Land, Illinois. Mr. Hardin was a graduate of Kentucky and Missouri Universities, had served as president of Christian University at Canton, Missouri; as corresponding secretary of the American Christian Missionary Society, and in other responsible positions, before coming to Eureka. During his administration the academic garb was first introduced and worn at Commencement.

The grade of work done by Eureka College is indicated, in some degree, by the following facts: The college was admitted as a member of the Illinois Intercollegiate Oratorical Association in 1896. This is composed of Knox, Illinois, Monmouth and Eureka Colleges and Wesleyan and Blackburn Universities. For the ten years next ensuing, Eureka's place was this: 1896, second place; 1897, fourth; 1898, first; 1899, first; 1900, first; 1901, second; 1902, first; 1903, second; 1904, first; 1905, first—six firsts and three seconds for Eureka in one decade became painfully monotonous to the other colleges forming the association. Something had to be done; so in 1906 the young men in Eureka preparing for the Christian ministry were, by a vote of the association, debarred from its membership on the alleged ground that "they are professionals"! And, further, the same spirit and good work that fairly won these honors brought victory in other contests also. The only time Eureka had a representative in the Equal Suffrage Contest, the first place was given by every judge. The Peace Contest is open to all the colleges of the State. Eureka has taken fourth place, and in 1912 secured third, fourteen colleges competing. Even better success has been the order in Prohibition work. One third place, two seconds and two firsts make a worthy record. Twice have Eureka's representatives won high honors in the Interstate Prohibition Contest. One year Eureka's representative tied for first place in thought and composition and ranked

third on the final grade, and in 1900 he took first place.
Robert E. Hieronymus became president in 1900. He was born in Logan County, Illinois, in 1862, graduated from the State Normal in 1886, from Eureka in 1889, and thereafter was one year a student in the University of Michigan. He was a successful teacher in the college from 1890 to 1899, except two years in which he was engaged as superintendent of extension work in the University of California. During his presidency the central heating-plant was installed, and the college buildings were renovated, repaired and modernized. In the library $5,000 was invested and about twenty-five hundred volumes were added thereto.

There were three problems that confronted the administration of Mr. Hieronymus, all of which had been accentuated by some preceding years. First, that of financial support was, of course, continuous. Second, the growing efficiency, popularity and geographical convenience of the system of the State schools, as above noted, imposed upon the church schools a very earnest and serious contest for students. Then, the question of holding growing and capable teachers was to be met—and it is yet. The college has developed some of its graduates into very efficient teachers only to lose a number of them at the time of their larger usefulness to other better compensating institutions.

Through the initiative of President Hieronymus, the Young Men's and Young Women's Christian Associations were formed in the college. He encouraged and emphasized the Student Volunteer Movement and foreign mission service. By means of these agencies the Christian activities of the college were brought up to date, and its religious influences, uniting with those of other Protestant church schools in Illinois, made themselves definitely felt in the State schools of higher education.

For sixty-five years Eureka has been a center of missionary education and activity. The college was imbued with the aim long since. The list of missionaries whom the college has helped to train is a notable one. Of these, three died

CHRISTIAN EDUCATION

before leaving their homes—Miss Lois E. A. Pratz, Miss Alice Ropp and Mr. Oliver Moody. The following, by reason of ill health induced by residence in foreign field, or from other considerations, have either returned to America, or are now elsewhere and otherwise engaged: Mr. E. E. Faris, Mr. and Mrs. Roscoe Hill, Mr. and Mrs. C. S. Weaver and Mr. and Mrs. L. C. McPherson. Those now at work in other fields are Mr. and Mrs. Melvin Menges, Mr. and Mrs. F. E. Hagin, Mr. and Mrs. R. D. McCoy, Mr. Leslie Wolf, Mr. R. R. Eldred, Mr. A. E. Cory, Miss Edna Eck, Miss Bertha Lacock, Miss Nellie Daugherty (who became the wife of Dr. Butchart), Emory Ross, Mrs. Lillie Boyer Hedges, Dr. E. B. Pearson, Lewis A. Hurt, Dr. W. H. Freymire and Miss Frances Irene Banta. But the greatest of all was the beautiful young woman, Miss Ella C. Ewing, who, when on the banks of the great Congo River, mid-continent, she lay dying of African fever, said, "Tell them to come and take my place." In all, fifty-seven missionaries have received their training at Eureka; also, fourteen teachers who have served in the Southern Christian Institute at Edwards, Mississippi, and two in the academy at Hazel Green, Kentucky.

The Illinois Christian Educational Association was formed by a few devoted women in Eureka in 1899. Its object is to help secure the co-operation of friends through the State in the maintenance and enlargement of the college. One dollar a year is paid by every member. Since its beginning about five thousand persons have thus co-operated. The present membership is fifteen hundred. During its thirteen years the association has raised and paid to the college $45,000. In this agency Mrs. S. J. Crawford has been the consecrated and honored leader.

A campaign for a better endowment was inaugurated in the State Missionary Convention held at Paris in 1906. In January, 1912, the trustees reported that the college was entirely free from debt and that it had a bona-fide endowment of $170,000. The credit and honor of this achievement belongs chiefly to Mr. H. H. Peters, who led in this campaign for three years. A multitude of discouragements confronted him daily, but he went forward with the courage, the optimism and the resolute purpose that were simply admirable. However, if the Disciples of Illinois think to conduct a creditable institution of learning for less than $1,000,000 in bankable endowment, they quite misread the signs of the times. The years of paltry parsimony in the best educational work have gone by. This school would have died long since had it not been that John Darst, Dr. N. B. Crawford, James P. Darst, and others while living, according to their financial ability, sustained it by thousands and tens of thousands of their own dollars. Fifty to sixty per cent. of *all* the money paid for this institution has been contributed by the community in which it is located. This generosity has enriched the community.

President Hieronymus brought the college to a standing among and recognition by the other educational forces of the State that it had never before had. During the nine years of his administration he put into the school the best of his fine mind and heart. The burdens were more than he could bear. Broken bodily health compelled him to relinquish the onerous responsibilities.

Prof. A. C. Gray, who had taught in the college since 1908, served as acting president for two and a half years, not wishing to accept its leadership. Mr. Charles C. Underwood became president in February, 1912. He was succeeded by Mr. H. O. Pritchard, September 1, 1913.

If schools are to be measured by the men and women they train and contribute to society, then Eureka College is the equal of any educational institution in the State or the nation. Doing severally their duties wisely and well, her sons are met upon the farm and in the marts of trade, in teachers and physicians, at the bar and upon the bench, in editorial rooms and in the councils of state; and her daughters, if filling less conspicuous places, are no less helpful in serving their times.

The following list of Christian ministers who received

CHRISTIAN EDUCATION

their training chiefly at Eureka indicates in some degree the value of the institution to the church and to the world:

GRADUATES.

Those marked thus * are deceased.

Adams, C. J.
Allen, John W.
Alsup, J. T.
Bain, John.
Barnett, H. M.
Barnett, James A.
Bennett, Harry Gordon
Beshers, R. L.
Boyer, E. E.
Boyer, Thomas A.
Breeden, H. O.
Bullock, J. Harry
Burgess, T. M.
Burnham, F. W.
Cannon, Wm. H.
Carpenter, J. W.
Carpenter, W. J.
Chandler, George F.
Chenoweth, Irving S.
Clark, H. D.*
Clemens, J. A.
Cobb, Abner P.
Coleson, Hiram K.
Cory, A. E.
Crank, J. R.
Dabney, C. B.
Dabney, J. D.
Dale, Hiram U.
Davis, L. F.
Deweese, W. D.
Doan, R. B.
Doney, O. K.
Drummet, Wm.
Ennefer, S. A.
Faulders, L. I.
Finger, S. Daisy
Fisher, Eli*
Fisher, Stephen E.
Garrison, W. E.

Genders, Henry*
Ghormley, J. F.
Gilliland, Ernest A.
Gilliland, J. H.*
Green, W. A.
Hagin, Fred E.
Hallam, S. K.
Harrington, L. S.
Harris, J. E.
Hart, E. J.*
Haynes, N. S.
Heckel, C. A.
Hieronymus, R. E.
Horner, J. M.
Hotaling, L. R.
Huff, A. L.
Huff, Lewie G.
Idleman, Finis S.
Jenner, H. H.
Jones, Silas
Jordan, O. F.
Kern, W. H.
Kindred, W. H.
Kirk, James*
Lappin, W. O.
Lehman, L. O.
Lichtenberger, J. P.
Lyon, Clyde L.
McBean, John L.
McCoy, R. D.
McKnight, J. P.
McPherson, Lowell C.
McReynolds, Paul
Marlow, C. W.
Marsh, Clark
Mavity, Thos. W.
Menges, Melvin
Miller, Geo. A.
Mitchell, Cyprus R.

Nay, Roley
Newton, R. H.
Nichols, Fred S.
Ogle, J. T.
Oviatt, O. Q.
Parke, Myrtle B.
Parvin, Ira L.
Peters, Geo. L.
Peters, H. H.
Pickerell, L. B.
Price, Wm.
Quinlan, J. G.
Radford, B. J.
Radford, Chas. T.
Reichel, H. C.
Reynolds, H. J.
Richards, O. A.
Richardson, W. F.
Rogers, Edwin*
Ross, Geo. W.*
Ross, Charles W.
Rowlison, C. C.
Sealock, B. H.
Serena, J. A.
Seyster, D. F.
Shaw, Herbert P.
Shaw, W. F.
Shields, David H.
Sinclair, C. C.
Sinclair, Ellmore
Sinclair, John A.
Skelton, Leroy*
Smith, F. E.
Smith, F. P.
Smith, J. F.
Smith, O. L.
Smith, W. G.
Sniff, W. W.
Spicer, W. E.

Stauffer, C. R.
Stewart, O. W.
Stivers, J. T.
Street, John W.
Streibich, Harry M.
Sutherland, Jos. R.
Sutton, F. W.
Sweeney, Geo. W.
Thackaberry, F. M.
Thomas, J. N.
Thomas, R. E.
Thomas, S. M.*
Thrapp, R. F.
Tucker, Harry E.
Vawter, S. D.
Ventress, K. C.
Vogel, Peter*
Waggoner, H. G.
Waggoner, J. G.
Waggoner, W. H.
Weaver, Clifford S.
Wetzel, D. N.
Williams, Charles
Wilson, Arthur A.*
Wray, Burton L.
Zendt, S. H.

NON-GRADUATE STUDENTS.

Allen, J. Buford*
Allen, James M.*
Agee, Ivan W.
Asbell, J. M.
Beckelhymer, Isaac
Beekman, J. V.*
Berry, Geo. K.
Berry, J. Festus*
Borop, N. A.
Bowen, F. L.
Bradbury, D. C.
Burr, Amos A.
Calvin, F. N.
Camp, J. W.
Campbell, Walter S.*
Cantrell, C. G.
Carpenter, C. C.
Clements, J. S.
Cloe, J. N.
Conner, A. M.
Coombs, J. V.
Cotterell, Henry A.
Cragun, E. D.
Cummings, Clark W.
Dangerfield, Rachel
Davis, F. S.
Denham, W. W.
Deweese, C. C.*
Dunkerson, Thomas*
Earl, Henry S.
Eldred, R. R.
Engle, Ira
Ennefer, W. L.
Evans, Chas. E.
Fannon, Shorland
Finch, C. A.
Finnell, Rufus
Gains, C. R.
German, W. C.
Gilcrest, R. A.
Gish, Ellis P.
Golden, J. R.
Golightly, T. J.
Hale, A. M.
Harker, J. N.
Harward, H. G.
Hayden, W. H.*
Henry, A. W.
Hiett, J. W.
Hill, Lew D.
Holloman, T. J.
Hougham, C. D.
Honn, D. W.
Howe, D. J.
Howell, R. E.*
Humphrey, W. A.*
Husband, David
Jefferson, S. M.*
Jewett, J. E.*
Johnson, B. W.*
Johnson, J. B.
Johnson, R. H.
Keller, E. H.
Kindred, C. G.
Kitchen, W. G.
Lappin, J. C.
Lappin, S. S.
Ledgerwood, H. D.*
Lessig, Ray S.
Lester, J. N.
McConnell, W. T.
McCune, J. L.
McElroy, G. W.*
McPherson, J. H.*
McPherson, R. P.
Madden, D. W.
Madison, W. D.
Maupin, W. T.*
Medbury, C. S.
Miller, John*
Moffett, F. L.
Moomaw, Otho
Monser, J. W.*
Organ, C. L.
Porter, J. W.
Poynter, D. J.
Poynter, W. C.*
Pratt, B. C.
Ragsdale, Alva
Rowe, G. H.
Russell, W. J.
Rust, W. H.
Scott, F. A.
Scrivens, C. A.
Shirley, Arnold
Shurts, John W.
Smith, J. T.*
Smoot, C. E.
Snively, Geo. L.
Sorey, M. Lee
Speck, J. R.
Spicer, A. R.

CHRISTIAN EDUCATION

Spriggs, E. A.	Sutton, F. W.	Willoughby, W. D.
Stauffer, C. Lee	Sweeney, Z. T.	Wisher, C. C.
Stevenson, Marion	Thomas, G. W.	Wolfe, Leslie E.
Stewart, James F.	Thomas, L. R.	Wright, N. J.
Stout, Elijah*	Tyler, B. B.	York, P. F.
Stout, John E.	Weimer, G. M.	Zinck, Gilbert

To the list of those who were trained at Eureka for the service in the Kingdom of God, the following names should be added: Mrs. Caroline Neville Pearre, the mother of the Christian Woman's Board of Missions; Miss Elmira J. Dickinson, her coadjutor in the national work and the mother of the Illinois C. W. B. M.; Mrs. O. A. Burgess, the president of the national society for twelve years and one of its wisest leaders; Mrs. S. J. Crawford and Miss Anna E. Davidson, who have given to the State Society invaluable assistance.

THE DISCIPLES' DIVINITY HOUSE.

This school originated in 1895, with Mr. Herbert L. Willett as acting dean.

Its purpose is to provide, at the University of Chicago, an organization of all students who look toward ministerial and missionary work. The House is an organic part of the university. In addition to the regular courses of the divinity school of the university, the House offers courses of instruction to graduate students in the origin, teaching, history, aims and literature of the Disciples, for which work credit is given in the university. Since its organization about three hundred students—a few more or less—have availed themselves of its advantages, including a number of missionaries. Mr. Willett is the present dean, and Mr. Errett Gates, who is also a member of the university corps of instructors, is associated with him in its work.

The management of the House is vested in a self-perpetuating board of fifteen trustees who handle all property and appoint the instructors. In 1895 a lot 150 x 175 feet at the corner of Fifty-seventh Street and Lexington Avenue, just opposite the "University Quadrangles," was bought for

$13,000. On this the Hyde Park Church of Christ has a temporary chapel. In addition to this lot, the House has an interest-bearing endowment of $30,000. It is the purpose of the trustees to build on this lot a structure, costing about $150,000, which shall serve as the home of the Hyde Park Church of Christ, for the House with its office, library and classrooms, and which may further serve as the common meeting-place of all Disciples who may be in attendance at the university at any time. Mr. Charles M. Sharp is engaged to lead in this material enterprise, and also to serve as an additional instructor in the House. The library was based on the private library of the late Min. J. T. Toof, to which has been added journalistic and other literature of the Disciples; also German and Scottish literature pertaining to religious conditions of society out of which the Restoration movement grew. This is the only school among the Disciples for the higher training of men entering the ministry of the word of God. The Bible chairs are to furnish college students with a knowledge of the Holy Scriptures. The city of Chicago affords endless facilities for practical work. It is a laboratory of human life.

ABINGDON COLLEGE.

On the first Monday in April, 1853, Patrick H. Murphy and John C. Reynolds opened a school in Abingdon, Illinois. They called it Abingdon Academy. It met in the Christian Church, a plain frame building. It grew and prospered. Messrs. Murphy and Reynolds were graduates of Bethany College. They possessed the educational spirit of the great founder of that institution. It was their purpose to build up a first-class college at Abingdon.

Within a period of seventeen months a three-story brick building, 40 x 60 feet in dimensions, had been erected and equipped, the school had been chartered by special act of the State Legislature under the name of Abingdon College, and in September, 1854, the institution opened its doors for business. The first name written on the registration list was Miss

Elvira Whitman, Cameron, Illinois. She was sixteen years of age. In the class of 1858 she graduated, taught four years thereafter, and in 1862 became the wife of Judge Durham. They traveled very happily together past fifty Thanksgiving Days; when that of 1911 had gone, she went away to the Father's house.

President Murphy was a product of the old church at Cameron. He was scholarly, a good teacher and executive, an eloquent preacher and a fine type of Christian gentleman. The college began most auspiciously. Everybody breathed daily the hopefulness and enthusiasm of youth. The country, the school, the building, the teachers and pupils were all young. The joy of living and learning was the keenest. During the six years of Mr. Murphy's presidency 1,087 students were enrolled, of whom 600 were males and 487 females. In the summer of 1860 Mr. Murphy died of tuberculosis.

He was succeeded in the presidency by J. W. Butler, who had been connected with the college from its beginning. Under his administration the school continued to prosper. New buildings were added at a cost of $40,000, and were fully paid for. The Civil War seriously affected the attendance at nearly all schools. However, the enrollment during nine years of Mr. Butler's ten years' administration was 1,604, of whom 983 were males and 721 females. During the later years of his administration a large number of the supporters and friends of the college concluded that the interests of the school would be promoted by a change in the presidency. These persons gave to Mr. Butler honorable recognition for his faithful and efficient service; still, they insisted upon a change. Mr. Butler fully determined that there should be no change in his official relation to the college at that time. This led to factional spirit and continued contentions. The school lost its prestige and its friends fell away. This was the beginning of the end of the institution.

At this juncture J. W. McGarvey, of Lexington, Kentucky, was elected president, but declined the honor. Mr. Butler served till 1874, and was succeeded by Oval Pirkey, who passed through troubled times. Clark Braden was at the head of the school in 1876-77. In the latter year F. M. Bruner came to the presidency. He was a man of fine scholarship, unflagging industry and commendable ambitions. He fully realized the worth of the college as a factor in general education and particularly its value to the churches of Christ in the Military Tract and at large as well. His efforts through a period of seven years, to reanimate and rehabilitate the college, were herculean and self-sacrificing to a degree. But it was not so written in the records of destiny. The evils of vain ambition could not be undone. In 1884 the institution became affiliated with Eureka College and its doors were closed forever.

But Abingdon was worth far more than it ever cost. It gave to the church and society useful men and women whose influences for good have been widely impressed. Among these may be named A. P. Aten, C. C. Button, M. F. Button, G. T. Carpenter, H. H. Coffeen, George Dew, Judge Durham, Lizzie Dodge Carson, J. H. Garrison, J. H. Gilliland, William Griffin, Josephus Hopwood, Marion Ingles, Mrs. Libbie F. Ingles, G. H. Laughlin, J. M. Martin, C. E. Price, J. H. Smart, A. J. Thompson, J. T. Toof and Emma Veatch Lorman. During the life of the college it had graduated 164 people, and about four thousand had come into direct touch with its helpful influences.

Abingdon College had practically no endowment.

BEREAN COLLEGE.

This institution was organized at Jacksonville, under the general incorporation law of the State, April 25, 1854. Sections 2 and 3 of the charter read as follows:

The objects contemplated by this act of incorporation are to build up and maintain, in the town of Jacksonville, an institution of learning of the highest class, for males and females, *to teach and inculcate the Christian faith* and morality of the sacred Scriptures, and for the promotion of the arts and sciences.

The trustees shall have power to erect the necessary buildings, to

CHRISTIAN EDUCATION

appoint a president, professors and teachers, and other agents and officers; to confer degrees in the liberal arts and sciences, *and to do all other things for the encouragement of religion and learning which are lawfully done by the most approved* seminaries and colleges in the United States.

The first Board of Trustees was composed of Hon. Joseph Morton, President; Jesse Galbraith, Secretary; Joseph J. Cassall, Treasurer; Nathan M. Knapp, Andrew J. Kane, William C. Mallory, Jacob Ward, James Simpson, Samuel G. Weagley, Samuel T. Calloway, Nimrod Deweese, Anderson Foreman, Joel Headington, Jonathan Atkinson and William W. Happy, Sr. The Faculty was as follows: Minister Jonathan Atkinson, President, Professor of Latin and Greek, lecturer on sacred history and instructor in French; William W. Happy, Jr., teacher of mathematics and the natural sciences and instructor in German; Miss Melinda Bond, governess and teacher of history, rhetoric and philosophy; William D. Hillis, teacher of vocal music; Mrs. L. E. Hillis, teacher of instrumental music.

The school opened the first Monday in October, 1854. The term was forty weeks of two equal semesters. During the first year ninety-six pupils were enrolled—fifty-nine males and thirty-seven females.

In addition to academic courses, the study of the Bible was required of all students, and the president delivered every year a course of lectures on sacred history.

The school was located a short distance east of the town on a five-acre campus, a quiet and beautiful place. The first term was held in a frame building located on one side of the ground. Meanwhile, an attractive brick building was erected. It was occupied by the school in 1855. This structure now forms the east part of Pasevant Memorial Hospital. In 1857 Minister Walter Scott Russell came to the presidency of the college. He was born in Cincinnati, Ohio, in 1832, and graduated from Bethany College in 1856, and was a man of unquestioned culture and piety. He was at that time the pastor of the Jacksonville Church also. While his sincerity and Christian excellences were admitted, he was a mystic of the Samuel Taylor Coleridge school of thought. The faith of the versatile thinker was kaleidoscopical. Coleridge says of himself that he became so absorbed in abstract speculation that history, facts, and even poetry, became insipid to him. Mr. Russell became so attached to and absorbed in this theory that the Bible as a revelation from God became secondary to the direct spiritual illumination of the soul by the Holy Spirit. Upon this theory he insisted. His teaching, in both the college and the pulpit, was subordinated to this idea. Some of our leading ministers became the open advocates of this doctrine. The school was fairly successful for four years. But the mystical teaching of Mr. Russell produced a division in the Jacksonville Church of Christ. This rupture forced the discontinuance of the college forever.

Mr. Russell went into the service of the Christian Commission. While caring for sick and wounded soldiers he contracted disease at Vicksburg, Mississippi, from which he died there in November, 1863.

Mr. Campbell, speaking to the students of Berean College in 1858, said: "W. S. Russell is admirably qualified for the responsible position he occupies."

MAJOR SEMINARY

Was founded by William T. Major at Bloomington in 1856. The institution had long been in the heart of its founder. It was first designed as a female orphan school. This aim was soon abandoned and the school became a seminary for the general education and culture of young women under the auspices of the Christian Church. A brick building five stories in height, costing about $20,000, was erected by Mr. Major. It was on Seminary Avenue—the street taking its name from the school—and Lee and Oak Streets. For a number of years the seminary was fairly prosperous. A goodly number of young women were helped to finer ideals and better preparation for their life-work. But tuition fees were insufficient to sustain an efficient Faculty. The public schools grew in popularity, and coeducation found a larger following in the colleges of the time. The attendance of pupils at the seminary did not increase, and hence the enterprise was abandoned in the later sixties.

SOUTHERN ILLINOIS COLLEGE.

In 1856 the Presbyterian Church erected a brick building for a college in Carbondale, Illinois. The structure was enclosed and partly plastered. The Civil War killed the enterprise.

In June, 1866, a convention of members of the churches of Christ in that part of the State was held at De Soto. At this meeting a committee was appointed to negotiate for the Presbyterian building and grounds in Carbondale. In a second convention, held in De Soto in August of the same year, the purchase of the property by the committee was ratified, a Board of Trustees was elected, and Clark Braden was chosen as president.

The title to this property was then vested in Messrs. J. M. Campbell and D. H. Brush. They sold it to these trustees for $10,000, the first named donating $1,000 and the last named $500 on the purchase price. Messrs. Lysias Heap, Pleasant Pope, B. F. Pope, Frederick Williams, Stephen Blair, E. C. Ford, John Goodall, F. M. Goodall and S. R. Hog gave severally $500, leaving a debt of $4,000.

In this unfinished, unfurnished and dilapidated building, the first week in October, 1866, President Braden opened the school with eight pupils. At the close of the first year 155 different pupils had been enrolled. The second year, 1867-68, the enrollment went up to 240 pupils. The third year enrollment was 400 different pupils, of whom 360 were in attendance at the spring term. This was the largest enrollment of any school controlled by the churches of Christ up to that time.

In the session of 1869 the Illinois Legislature enacted a law establishing a normal school in that city, in the southern part of the State, which would make the best donation to such school. There was very keen competition for this institution between Olney, Centralia, Duquoin and Carbondale. The last named was handicapped by its location, being only forty-five miles from the southern end of a State that is four hundred miles long. The chief claim of Carbondale was the great normal school in Southern Illinois College. The city of Carbondale proposed to purchase this school and its property and make them a part of their bid for the State Normal. The Faculty and the churches of Christ in that part of the State were urged to unite and work for the location of the State school there.

President Braden and his wife, in addition to their arduous labors in the college, had spent $4,600 in finishing and furnishing the building. For its current expenses the college had cost no one a cent outside of tuitions. The interest on the $4,000 indebtedness had not been paid. At this juncture of affairs, in a meeting of the trustees and other friends of the college, Mr. Braden urged that the debt be paid off, that a wing to the buliding, which was overcrowded, be erected, and that the State Normal go to Olney, that then led the other cities in the bid. A goodly number of Disciples were in accord with these views. Mr. Braden and his faithful colaborers had built up a great school. From its beginning, normal work had been the leading feature. The clock of time was striking the crisis-hour of Southern Illinois College. The money was not forthcoming, and the property was sold to the city of Carbondale. It is clear that to this growing young college and its normal work, the prime factor of which was Clark Braden, the city of Carbondale is indebted for the Southern Illinois Normal University.

THE BASTIAN SEMINARY.

In September, 1868, Mr. and Mrs. N. S. Bastian opened a school at Sullivan. They were well-educated and cultured people and saw clearly the need at that time of facilities that would supplement the limited work of the public schools.

Possibly there was not a high school in the State at that time—certainly not more than one or two. Mr. Bastian had sold about one hundred scholarships. These were to run five years, which was the life-period of the institution. The curriculum included the studies usually found in the small college of that time. In these there were enrolled from fifty to sixty pupils, never more than seventy-five. The lower grades were in charge of Miss R. Latherman, with an average attendance of sixty-five pupils. The school did good work and exerted a fine influence in the town and on the surrounding community. This aim was most commendable.

Mr. Bastian preached for the Sullivan Church during this time. In addition to all these duties, the principal of the school and his wife boarded a number of the students in their own home to help meet their living expenses. They aimed to apply some of the receipts from the school on the purchase price of the property that was occupied. Mrs. Bastian before her marriage was Miss Eunice Jewett, of Dayton, O. Her father's house had been the stopping-place of many of the pioneers in the Restoration movement. She had a superior knowledge of the Scriptures and was a woman of fine mental and social culture. Her home was a charming place. In addition to all of her domestic and school responsibilities, she was noted for her wise counsel, her ministries of sympathy to the forlorn and benevolences to the poor. In her last illness, after the attending physician had assured her that the end was near, the Sunday-school superintendent, not knowing her condition, came into her room for her advice about the children's program. This she gave, spoke of the Lord's promise and bade the superintendent a final good-by. The value of such a woman is beyond human estimate, and her influence never dies.

After five years of usefulness the school closed from lack of support. With rare exceptions is educational work maintained by tuition fees and infrequent donations.

ALMA INDUSTRIAL COLLEGE.

The thought of an industrial school at Alma originated with Mr. W. S. Ross, a graduate of Abingdon College, and pastor of the Alma Christian Church. The proposition was heartily favored by the community. Subscriptions were secured. Four acres of land were bought, and a good two-story, eight-room frame building was erected thereon. The title to this property was vested in a Board of Trustees. The school opened in September, 1896. It was coeducational and aimed to help worthy young people to start well in life. An option on 420 acres of land was secured, and a printing-office was bought and installed in the building. The aim was to have the boys work part of the time on the farm and the girls in the printing-office, and thus pay part of their expenses. In addition to this labor, every pupil paid $120 per annum. This work and cash secured for each and every pupil during the school year board and lodging, instruction and books. Experience proved that the school could not be maintained on this financial basis. Appeals for assistance in localities from which the school was easily accessible met with meager responses. Debt accumulated; hence, in 1900, the school was discontinued. The property was sold, for public uses, for $3,000, which was said to have been one-half of its value. All debts were settled. The average attendance during the four years was about one hundred per year. The men who served as head of the school or president were H. Y. Keller, W. H. Boles, A. A. Hibner, Clark Braden, W. B. Bedell, P. J. Dickerson and Thomas Munnell. Mr. Munnell died just before the final closing of the institution. His body is buried at Alma. This enterprise was most commendable.

CHRISTIAN COLLEGIATE INSTITUTE.

From 1881 to 1887 this school, which was of seminary rank, was conducted at Metropolis. The prime movers in the enterprise were Messrs. J. F. McCartney, Solomon Tanhauser, T. S. Stone, M. N. McCartney, William Wright and J. M. Elliott.

The sessions were held in the old seminary building that stood at the corner of Katherine and Fifth Streets, opposite the Christian Church. The average attendance during the period was sixty pupils. There were from four to six teachers employed, whose financial support was received from tuition fees and personal donations to the institution.

The curriculum included a normal course, English classics, a business course and instruction in the Bible.

The growing aims and efforts of the high schools in a degree took the ground occupied by this institute; hence it was closed and the property sold.

CHAPTER IV.

THE PERIOD OF CONQUEST.

THE ERA OF PUBLIC DISCUSSIONS.

There were two causes that led to many public debates between representatives of the Disciples and those of other religious bodies. The first was the spirit of controversy that was prevalent in most denominations at the beginning of the movement for the restoration of the New Testament church in its teachings, its ordinances and its life. The sermons of that time were full of denials and affirmations. Minister James Leaton, who was a member of the Illinois Conference and a godly man, was pastor of the First Methodist Episcopal Church in Decatur from 1876 to 1878. During that time, speaking of the changed spirit of public discourses, he said to some friends: "Fifty years ago, whatever might be the sermon subject and text of the average Methodist preacher, the discourse generally closed with these words, 'So you see, brethren, that Calvinism can not be true. Let us pray.'" Secondly, the preaching of the Disciples was new and strange. They appealed to the word of God as the sole and final authority; others appealed to their varying human creeds and went to the Bible for texts to prove them. Great confusion of thought and statement was inevitable. Party spirit was dominant, denominational pride uppermost. The deed was subordinated to the creed. Church people disliked or even hated one another for the love of God. The Disciples were sometimes misunderstood, sometimes misrepresented, sometimes condemned, sometimes shamelessly and shockingly slandered, and very generally counted without the circle of orthodoxy. One of these preachers wrote in 1844 as follows: "I have stood here alone for four years, a mark for sectarian malice to vent itself against. A short time since I was pointed out in a congregation by one of the *called* and *sent* as 'a water-washed, white-faced devil, a wolf in sheep's clothing, a preacher of damnable doctrines.'" To those who live in these better years such bigotry and baseness seem hardly credible. The Disciples were compelled to fight. They have always been ready, and are yet where circumstances require, to defend their teachings in the arena of public debate. In preaching the things which they sincerely believe to be the word of God and the requirements of our Lord, their preachers have many times clashed with others and frequently with unbelievers. The challenges for public discussion usually came from those who opposed. Their evangelists went often unheralded into many communities, proclaimed an affirmative gospel of assurance and hope, and urged the people to read the New Testament. In this way thousands were won to the knowledge and obedience of the truth as it is in Jesus. Many came from churches to the common Christian ground. When local shepherds beheld such losses from their flocks they were filled with denominational fervor and indignation. Feeling fully assured of the correctness of their own doctrinal positions and grieved at the losses of their members by what they conceived to be specious errors, they boldly proposed a public comparison of tenets. The aims of the debaters may not always have been single— the elucidation of the truth—nor the spirit with which they were conducted most commendable; but unquestionably they have seriously jarred "the kingdom of the clergy," broken up an incrusted formalism, and stimulated thousands to Bible reading and study. It is illogical and unwise to condemn a custom because its misuse or abuse is sometimes attended with objectionable features.

Robert Owen, denying our Lord and his religion, openly defied the preachers of the United States to meet him in public defense of their teachings. Alexander Campbell was the only one to respond. The eight days' discussion in Cincinnati, Ohio, April, 1829, assured the American people of the certainty of their Christian faith. The same mighty champion of the truth in January, 1837, in Cincinnati, Ohio, met Mr. "Bishop" Purcell, of the Roman Catholic hierarchy, in a seven days' debate. The book reports of these two discussions are still worthy of a place in any library. Henry Clay was the presiding moderator during the discussion between Mr. Campbell and Minister N. L. Rice (Presbyterian), at Lexington, Kentucky, in 1843. After the close of this discussion Mr. Clay said, "Alexander Campbell is the profoundest theologian and the ablest and most eloquent debater of this age."

The public discussion of religious questions has divine warrant. The inspired apostles were frequently so engaged. Jesus himself was the greatest of all controversialists.

If additional reasons need be cited, note this

CLIMAX OF BIGOTED MENDACITY.

An Irishman who signed himself "The Rev. James Shaw, of the Illinois Conference, Methodist Episcopal Church, America," preached twelve years in the United States. At the close of this period he published a book of 440 pages, of which he was the author, entitled "Twelve Years in America." It was sold in London, Dublin and Chicago in 1867. Two quotations are here made from it. They indicate the religious bigotry of that time, the mendacious slanders of Mr. Shaw, and the conditions that were thrust upon the Disciples and which they were compelled to meet. On pages 164-5 he says:

> Swedenborgians, Tunkers, Shakers, Winebrennarians, Christians and Campbellites form the completion of the minor unevangelical sects, most of whom are immersionists in their views of baptism. The largest of these sects is the last mentioned. They are the followers of the late Alexander Campbell, an Irishman by birth, a Presbyterian minister in his younger days, a Baptist after, and, lastly, the founder of a sect who are numerous in the West. Mr. Campbell was a fine scholar, an eloquent controversialist, and a voluminous writer. He died a year ago. His followers first assumed the name of

THE PERIOD OF CONQUEST

Reformers, then Disciples, now Christians, and by others are known as Campbellites. Mr. Campbell and his followers made an earnest attack on the leading doctrines and institutions of the churches and in their stead offered to the people *salvation through immersion.* He ridiculed the necessity of a change of heart, or the profession of the forgiveness of sins in any other way than by baptism. So easy a form of religion soon took hold of the indifferent and the irreligious: the system became popular, and thousands left the Baptist Church, and some the Presbyterian and others to join it, so that the denomination is made up of nearly all kinds of isms—Unitarian, Universalist, and the apostates from other churches—the only bond of unity among them being *baptism for the remission of sins.*

Speaking of his observations at Niantic, Illinois, Mr. Shaw says on page 294:

In and around this town there was a large number of Campbellites, a sect to whom I have referred in Chapter X. on "American Churches." They viewed with jealousy the encroachments of the Methodists. As they were generally fond of controversy, and their preachers flippant proclaimers of the *"Gospel in the Water,"* their sermons are a strange medley of all sorts of stuff about salvation by immersion. Their style —that of an auctioneer, reserving their wit and railing for other churches, and their praises for their own. Bible, missionary societies, Sunday schools, and colleges, received their loudest denunciations. Things the most sacred they ridiculed and institutions the most solemn they reviled. The Sabbath they disregarded; the forgiveness of sins, a change of heart, they laughed at, unless what was connected with immersion. The divinity of Christ they did not generally believe in; the personality and operation of the Holy Spirit they scoffed at. They were literally immersed infidels, having little of the form or power of godliness. Where evangelical churches were cold and lukewarm, these prospered; but when alive and earnest, the Campbellites sank to their coverts by the waters.

Such choice bits of Christian literature are rare and should not be lost.

The debates conducted by the Disciples in Illinois are a part of their history. It has been impossible to secure reports of all, but the following named will indicate in a fair degree their frequency, influence and the trend of thought of the times:

1840.—Maurice R. Trimble and R. U. Newport, of the "Two-seed Baptists," held a debate at Palestine.

In the forties Bushrod W. Henry held a number of discussions of which no written record has been found.

In this decade Walter P. Bowles held a discussion with James Barger, of the M. E. Church, at the Old Union Church in DeWitt County. The debate was reported greatly to Mr. Bowles' credit.

1848.—At Shelbyville, George Campbell met Hiram Buck, of the M. E. Church.

1852.—W. W. Happy held a discussion about this time with C. W. Lewis, of the M. E. Church, at Jersey Prairie, in Morgan County.

1855.—At Franklin, John S. Sweeney debated with Minister W. H. Pellatt, of the M. E. Church, the proposition that we are justified by faith only is a most wholesome doctrine and very full of comfort.

1856.—Probably in this year John Lindsay debated with David Davis the question of Universalism, at Metamora.

1857.—A. D. Fillmore held a discussion at the Franklin Church, Edgar County, with William Shields, a "Hardshell Baptist."

1858.—About this year the following discussions were held:

At Cruger, O. A. Burgess and John B. Luccock, of the M. E. Church, debated the usual questions of the time. Mr. Burgess was then a young man and had never engaged in public discussions. Mr. Luccock was fully matured and had participated in thirty-one debates before that time. He called Mr. Burgess "a stripling of a boy," and boasted that he would "make a halter and put it on the young colt and tie him up." Before the debate was over, competent critics said that the halter and tie-up had been very effectively applied to Mr. Luccock. He took pleasure in contemptuously referring to Mr. Burgess as a "Campbellite."

In Paris, N. S. Bastian debated the question of baptism with J. L. Crane, of the M. E. Church. Mr. Bastian had formerly been a presiding elder in that conference and had given Mr. Crane his license to preach.

At Mt. Pulaski, A. J. Kane and D. P. Bunn debated Universalism.

At Pontiac, Washington Houston held a discussion with an M. E. preacher.

1859.—At Whitehall, J. S. Sweeney debated the baptismal question with J. B. Logan, of the Cumberland Presbyterian Church. Mr. Logan was at that time the editor of the leading denominational paper published in St. Louis. The discussion was published in book form. Its spirit was fair and fine toned. From that time the Disciples began to increase in that section.

At Glasgow, Mr. Sweeney and Minister Whiteside debated Universalism. Shortly thereafter Mr. Whiteside was taken ill and sent for Mr. Sweeney, who, being at the time in Wisconsin, could not respond to the call. Mr. Whiteside recanted his Universalism, ordered all his books and papers bearing on Universalism destroyed, and shortly thereafter died.

At Lexington, Benjamin Franklin met J. B. Luccock, who was then considered the champion of his denomination in such affairs. He sent his challenge to J. G. Campbell, who was then serving the Christian Church there as its minister. Mr. Franklin was chosen as their representative. People came from near and far. The interest was intense. Mr. Franklin, a plain and homely man, won the sympathy of the unchurched men of the community, a considerable number of whom arranged a private purse among themselves for him. A goodly number of these became Christians in the meetings that immediately followed the discussion.

Probably in the same year the following debates were held:

At Fairbury, O. A. Burgess met B. F. Underwood in a discussion upon materialism and Christianity.

At Lincoln, John Lindsay met J. B. Luccock.

At the White Oak Grove Church in McLean County, James Mitchell debated Universalism with Minister Davis, of Galesburg.

1860.—Robert Foster debated with Daniel Waggle, of the "Dunkard" or Brethren Church, at Chapman's Point, in Macoupin County. Prior to this discussion the Brethren had held the sway in that community. After it they held nothing.

Benjamin Franklin debated with D. P. Bunn the question of Universalism in Decatur. Mrs. Carrie Hostetter, who heard this debate, says that Mr. Bunn based his argument mainly on 1 Cor. 15:22: "For as in Adam all die, even so in Christ shall all be made alive." When Mr. Franklin had clearly and fully replied to his opponent's arguments, he would say, "And now, since my time is not out, I will preach you a sermon." This he would then do. Judge A. J. Gallagher, a man of superior judicial temperament and ability, was the presiding moderator. After the smoke of the battle had cleared, he said to a number of his friends, "The Scriptures being true, hell is a certainty." Judge W. E. Nelson says, "The results of the discussion were very satisfactory to us." From that time the Universalist Church in Decatur began to decline, and has long since disappeared from the map.

At Waukegan, A. R. Knox discussed the same subject. The debate grew out of the visits of a Universalist minister to Gurnee, where Mr. Knox was then preaching. After the discussion there was no Universalist society formed or church built at either Gurnee or Waukegan.

It is a significant fact that Universalist churches flourished in most of the cities of central and northern Illinois fifty years ago, but these are very nearly all now extinct.

1862. About this time William Grissom held a debate with a Mormon elder in Washington Schoolhouse near Ipava. A Methodist minister of that section had said to the elder, "You do not preach the gospel;" but he was not able to cope with the elder. Then Mr. Grissom, a pioneer Christian minister, was sent for. His work with the man from Salt Lake City was so thorough that he was glad to soon move on. A little time thereafter a congregation of Christians was formed there which in later years was merged into the Ipava Church.

1864.—At the Big Creek Church, in Edgar County, Har-

THE PERIOD OF CONQUEST 75

mon Gregg and Marion Brown, a Calvinist Baptist, held a debate. Among other things, Mr. Brown affirmed that the law of Moses is as binding now as it was in any age of the world or on any people. After this discussion Mr. Brown lost the use of his reason for a time. Upon becoming normal he united with the Christian Church and continued in the ministry to the close of his life. The presiding moderator, Mr. Otis Eldredge, also said that this discussion had led him to his Christian conclusions.

At Tuscola, David Walk held a public discussion with a lawyer who was a member of the M. E. Church. Mr. Walk had held a meeting there in 1863 and organized a little church. He was opposed by the three churches that were there at that time. Returning next year, he was compelled to defend his teaching in a public debate. The Presbyterian preacher was slow of speech and the Methodist minister was thought not to be strong enough for the contest; so a well-educated and glib-tongued attorney was chosen for the task. He affirmed that sprinkling is Scriptural baptism, and Mr. Walk that baptism preceded by faith and repentance is for the remission of sins. Mr. Walk, before uniting with the Disciples, had been actively engaged in the Methodist ministry. This fact put ginger into the meeting.

1865.—Probably in this year David Walk and Minister Davies, of the M. E. Church, held a discussion at Berlin.

1866.—At Richview, Clark Braden and J. P. Den, of the M. E. Church, debated the question of baptism.

At the same place Mr. Braden and Prof. H. V. Spencer, of McKendree College, held a discussion on Bible revision.

At De Soto, Mr. Braden met Jacob Ditzler, of the M. E. Church. These men were two of the greatest debaters of that time. It was mutually arranged to consider the questions of baptism, the work of the Holy Spirit and total hereditary depravity; but Mr. Ditzler, for reasons best known to himself, declined to debate the last two when they were reached.

Dudley Downs and Minister Summerbell, of the old

Christian Denomination, held a spirited discussion at Clinton.

John C. Reynolds discussed the question of Universalism with John Hughes at Table Grove. It was about this time that W. K. Pendleton wrote: "The Universalists are full of debate. If all may be saved anyhow, why bother us Christians in our concern to make certain those who have misgivings on the subject? Our faith can not cause us to be lost; and it at least satisfies our anxiety in this life to follow our own convictions of duty."

At Bridgeport, J. K. Speer and George W. Hughey, a presiding elder, met in the arena of discussion. Mr. Hughey was a man of commanding personality and a good voice. In this debate he took the position that the covenant of circumcision (Gen. 17) was the covenant of *grace,* and did not rest infant baptism on the ground that baptism came in the room of circumcision—his discovery. During this debate a preacher of the M. E. Church expressed regret that the Saviour had used the word "baptism" in connection with his religion.

W. B. F. Treat and Minister Abbott debated Universalism at Olney. In this discussion Mr. Abbott declared that the apostles knew no more of grammar than a ten-year-old boy.

1867.—In a schoolhouse near Rural Retreat, in the northern part of Coles County, Harmon Gregg accepted a challenge from James Shaw, of the M. E. Church, and an eight days' discussion followed.

1868.—The most significant discussion of this year was that held at Atlanta between O. A. Burgess and Dr. Chas. H. Burrows, a noted infidel.

The Atlanta Christian Church was feeble at that time and held in contempt by the other churches of the place. Two of its members, Andrew Wright and Jefferson Houser, went to the "union" prayer-meeting that was held the first week in January, and were met at the door of the M. E. Church and requested to leave, as no "Campbellites" were wanted in the meeting, they having been unanimously voted out as arch-heretics.

THE PERIOD OF CONQUEST 77

There was a "Freethinkers" club at Atlanta which included a number of the representative men of the place. Mr. Burrows was their leader and champion. For more than a decade he had traveled and lectured on Free Thought, Phrenology, Spiritualism and Mesmerism. He boldly assailed the doctrines of denominationalism and held out a standing challenge to those who would defend them.

He first met in a public discussion, in Atlanta, Owen Davis, a farmer and pioneer Baptist preacher, January 16-18, 1868, in the Christian Church. The results were not satisfactory to the Christian people of the community. Mr. Davis was an inferior debater.

Shortly after he met Minister Orvis, of the Congregational Church, in a debate. Mr. Orvis was a man of good education and well informed on the questions involved, but not much of a debater.

After this, Mr. Burrows, like Goliath of Gath, defied the hosts of Israel. The Freethinkers were exultant, the friends of truth and righteousness discouraged.

Andrew Wright, father of J. H. Wright, was making wagons in those days. He was a mild-mannered, gentle-speaking man, but counted it a part of his business to earnestly contend for the faith which was once delivered to the saints. This was his opportunity, and in the month of May he had his David, in the person of O. A. Burgess, on the ground.

Mr. Burrows affirmed that "the Book called the Bible is of human origin and fallible in its teachings, and that Jesus was nothing more than a man, born of woman, as other people are." The crowds attending were immense, men coming from other States. The interest was intense, the occasion crucial. Some parts of the discussion were thrilling and climacteric. In speaking of the virgin birth of Jesus, Mr. Burrows said, "It is impossible for any father to swear to his own child," to which Mr. Burgess replied, "This is a high compliment to Dr. Burrows' mother," which so angered Dr. Burrows and his followers that Mr. Burgess was threatened with some of the "hell fire" which he was in the habit of preaching tc his people.

In answer Mr. Burgess said: "I suppose you saw me going out through that window. I have stood where bullets flew thick and can not be intimidated by words. Dr. Burrows well knows that when one party generalizes, his opponent has permit to particularize."

John S. Sweeney passed Mr. Burgess a note which read, "Give it to him; we are all here."

The threat of violence was dismissed, and this incident closed, by Mr. Burgess, as he spoke in his lion-like manner: "Bah! a threat. The last refuge of a lost cause."

In speaking of special Divine Providence, Dr. Burrows said: "I am an old infidel. Why does not God afflict me?" His defiance of the Almighty was blasphemous. While trimming hedge that season a thorn punctured his hand, causing blood poison, which necessitated several amputations, and he was left with one arm and one leg.

Two of his grandchildren were baptized into Christ at Atlanta in 1893, and several since that time, one now working in the Christian ministry.

Mr. Burgess, at the close of the discussion, was presented with a floral bouquet, by Mrs. J. M. Brooks, for the Christian women of Atlanta, as a public expression of their appreciation of his impassioned defense of womanly virtue.

Infidelity lost much of its arrogance in Atlanta, after this.

March 28, 1875, at the age of fifty-one years and six months, Dr Burrows died as he had lived, without God and without hope.

In Duquoin, Clark Braden and R. C. Dennis debated infidelity.

At the White House, or Pleasant Hill Church, in Lawrence County, D. D. Miller and James McMillan on one side debated with John Mack, a Presbyterian minister, the question of baptism and the operation of the Holy Spirit. No reason is given why two preachers should have been pitted against one.

THE PERIOD OF CONQUEST

In the college chapel at Abingdon, Pres. J. W. Butler conducted a discussion with Minister Smith, of the M. E. Church.

At Westfield, Harmon Gregg and Hiram Ashmore, a Cumberland Presbyterian minister, met. Mr. Ashmore affirmed that Jesus Christ is the eternal Son of God.

At Timewell, A. P. Stewart and Minister Yates, of the Baptist Church, held a discussion, which was admirable for its fraternal spirit.

1869.—At Timewell, D. R. Lucas and Minister Thompson, of the Baptist Church, debated on foreordination, election and free-will.

It was probably this year that Clark Braden and G. W. Hughey, of the M. E. Church, debated at Vienna on baptism, the work of the Holy Spirit, the M. E. Discipline and human creeds.

1870.—At Farmer City, R. B. Roberts and Minister Manford, of Chicago, debated Universalism.

Clark Braden and B. F. Underwood held a discussion at Duquoin on Christianity and materialism.

Mr. Braden this year met Samuel Binns at Casey, in discussing the questions of baptism. Mr. Binns was a minister of the Cumberland Presbyterian Church and much enjoyed the sobriquet of "Campbellite-killer." But those whom he "slew" one day were always up and ready for the battle the next morning.

Theodore Brooks and R. N. Davies, of the M. E. Church, conducted a public discussion at Mechanicsburg about this time. Both were men of fine mental development. Great throngs of people attended. Those who heard the debate still refer to it as "a stem-winder."

1871.—S. K. Hallam conducted a discussion at Farmer City with C. C. Marston, on Seventh-day Adventism.

This year Clark Braden met B. F. Underwood twice in discussing Christianity and materialism—first at Time and later at Bushnell.

In the spring of this year G. M. Goode held a discussion

on the questions of baptism at Scottsville, with Ramsey Smithson, a presiding elder of the M. E. Church South. In those days Mr. Goode was called "the Macoupin boy." At the close of the debate Prof. M. G. Lain, the presiding moderator and a member of the Baptist Church, voluntarily gave Mr. Goode a note assuring him that his work was successful and satisfactory in every way. The report of this, going into the regions round about, much disquieted Mr. Smithson's friends, so they demanded that the discussion be repeated, that they might see how "the boy" had so successfully contended with a trained debater. Hence a second discussion of the same questions was held at Girard in the following July. Mr. Goode's friends were well pleased with the discussion and its results. His speeches were logical and always in fine spirit.

1872.—Clark Braden and B. F. Underwood debated Christianity and materialism at Washington.

Mr. Braden also met John Hughes at La Fayette in considering Universalism.

At Dudleyville, in May, Frank Talmage held a debate with T. C. Sharp on baptism and the work of the Holy Spirit. This discussion followed a meeting conducted by Mr. Talmage at that place in which about sixty persons turned to the Lord. Mr. Sharp gave the challenge. His home at that time was in Mt. Vernon, Illinois, where he was the pastor of the M. E. Church. He was accompanied to the debate by one of his leading members, Mr. R. M. Hawley, who, having listened to the discussion with candor, was then baptized by Mr. Talmage.

In September of the same year Mr. Talmage debated at Greenville with Henry Sharp this proposition: "Christianity Is an Enemy to the Best Interests of Mankind." There were only about three Disciples at Greenville at that time. The closing night of the discussion Mr. Talmage extended the gospel invitation. Mr. and Mrs. Frank Smith, who resided seven miles away, accepted Jesus, making the good confession. Inasmuch as they wished to be baptized the same hour of the night, like the Philippian jailer, the minister accompanied them home and baptized them.

1873.—Clark Braden debated infidelity at Bloomington with C. R. Sanborn, who referred to himself as a "Free Congregationalist."

1874.—In a Baptist church six miles east of Dongola, W. H. Boles debated Universalism with Matthew Stokes. Mr. Stokes gave up the battle at noon on the second day. Mr. Boles at once conducted a series of meetings in the near-by village of Moscow, which resulted in fifty accessions, the formation of a church and the purchase of a meeting-house. But the church was short-lived.

At Lovington, C. H. Bliss pitched his tent and began preaching Seventh-day Adventism. A Christian minister, who was not well posted in the sinuosities of this error, in a trial with Mr. Bliss proved unsatisfactory. Whereupon Clark Braden was sent for. He walked direct from the railway station to the tent and said: "Good morning. Here are seven propositions; you can take your choice." It was agreed to debate three of them and then decide about the other propositions. The first round proved quite enough for Mr. Bliss. During the discussion Mr. Bliss' moderator rose up and said, "Mr. Chairman, I rise to a 'pint' of order." Whereupon a Dr. Collet, who had a fine sense of the ludicrous, instantly spoke out so that all the audience heard, "Why not make it a quart?"

In this year an attempted discussion took place at St. Augustine between Minister W. R. Jewell and a Roman Catholic priest whose name is not recalled. O. A. Burgess summoned Mr. Jewell to the town by telegraph. Arrangements were soon made for a three evenings' debate, each disputant speaking one hour each evening. The priest affirmed that "the Holy Roman Catholic Church is the only true church." In his first reply Mr. Jewell used history, to which the priest objected. The moderators sustained Mr. Jewell's contention. The priest then became angry, left the hall and did not return. Mr. Jewell continued for a few days in a course of addresses on the question under discussion.

1875.—W. H. Boles and W. P. Throgmorton, Baptist, held a discussion at Marion. They considered "The Direct Impact of the Spirit, the Final Perseverance of the Saints and the Churches of Which They Were Members." These gentlemen were lifelong neighbors and friends. The debate was conducted in an admirable spirit. Mr. Boles followed it with a successful meeting.

1876.—In the summer of this year Clark Braden debated Christianity and materialism with B. F. Underwood in the city of Jacksonville. Brethren residing there proposed to Mr. Underwood to have this discussion repeated and published. They offered to pay him for his time and copyright. He replied, "Mr. Henderson, I am not ready to publish a debate with Braden."

In the summer of 1875 Col. J. W. Judy, of Tallula, financed a tent meeting conducted by D. R. Lucas in Petersburg. Before that the Disciples had been a feeble folk there, but at the close of this effort the church of Christ numbered 190 members. Before the close of the meeting Mr. Lucas had received several challenges for a public discussion. He accepted that one made by the Presbyterians. They chose Minister D. R. Miller, of the Cumberland Presbyterian Church, to represent them. In the preliminary arrangements he contended for three sessions a day of two hours each. Mr. Lucas was compelled to accept this condition or have no debate. At the end of the fourth day Mr. Miller was worn out and prostrated. This compelled an adjournment of the debate for six months. Then it was resumed and finished. During the discussion Mr. Lucas kept close to the Book and often repeated the maxim, "Where the Bible speaks, we speak; where the Bible is silent, we are silent." In affirming that immersion is the action in baptism, he quoted Acts 8:38: "And they went down both into the water, both Philip and the eunuch; and he baptized him." Mr. Miller replied: "The Bible says baptized, not immersed. Now, what becomes of your oft-repeated maxim, 'Where the Bible speaks, we speak.'" He rang the changes on this quite to Mr. Lucas' confusion. Finally it was agreed to leave to the German Lutheran minister to decide the meaning of the Greek word *baptidzo*. He reported that its primary meaning is "dip" or "immerse." Thus Mr. Lucas recovered his grip upon the audience.

W. D. Owen served as Mr. Lucas' moderator, a Mr. Crozier was Mr. Miller's, while Judge Pillsbury presided. A question of order arose relative to the admission of a definition of *baptidzo* in an old edition of Liddell & Scott's lexicon which the world's scholarship had compelled those editors to omit from all the subsequent editions of their dictionary. The debaters each made his statement, followed by each one's moderator. Then Judge Pillsbury decided in favor of Mr. Lucas. At once a Presbyterian gentleman, who had sandy hair and beard, not satisfied with the decision, arose to say a word. Quick as lightning G. M. Goode, who sat near him, arose and spoke out: "Hold on, my friend. Bro. Lucas will take care of Bro. Miller, Bro. Owen will take care of Bro. Crozier, but, my sorrel-topped friend, if you want anything, I am your man." The hilarity was so general and continued that the moderator declared an adjournment for dinner.

The spirit of the whole community was changed for good by the debate. On its last day Mr. Lucas was invited by and took dinner with a Presbyterian elder who would not even condescend to speak to him during the progress of the tent meeting. Many courtesies were shown by others.

1877.—Mr. Braden debated Universalism with John Hughes at Lewistown.

1878.—Mr. Braden and W. F. Jamison held a discussion at Salem on Christianity and materialism.

Messrs. Jamison, Underwood and men of that class were public lecturers who sometimes published infidel papers and traveled over the country sowing seeds of error, falsehood and unbelief. The only Christian thing to do was to meet them in the arena of public discussion, expose their specious twisters and present the irrefutable evidences of divine truth.

1879.—J. M. Radcliffe and C. H. Caldwell, Baptist, held a discussion at Samoth, which was repeated at the Sevenmile Baptist Church in Massac County.

1881.—William Grissom and J. F. Leake, a Baptist, debated the question of baptism for the remission of sins, at Meredosia. Mr. Leake had previously been affiliated with the Disciples. During the discussion he expressed his regret several times that a stronger man had not been chosen to meet him. Mr. Grissom replied that his brethren thought it unnecessary "to load a cannon to shoot a mosquito." A son of Mr. Leake is now the pastor of the church of Christ at Newton, Iowa.

1883.—At Blandinsville, George F. Adams and William McNutt, Baptist, debated the two following propositions: "The Scriptures teach that the only proper subjects of baptism in water are believers in Christ whose sins are remitted," and "The church of which I, G. F. Adams, am a member is identical in faith and practice with the church founded by Christ and his apostles." Great crowds of people heard this discussion.

At Cuba, G. F. Adams and D. D. Swindle, Baptist, debated this proposition: "The church organization of which I, D. D. Swindle, stand identified, possesses the Bible characteristics which entitle it to be regarded as the visible Church or Kingdom of Christ." Mr. Adams affirmed a similar proposition of the church of his fellowship. This discussion was an intellectual and fraternal treat to those who heard it. Without a single exception, the disputants bore themselves as Christian gentlemen from beginning to end. As often as Mr. Swindle insisted that his church was the church of Christ, that often did Mr. Adams reply, "Then, why do you refuse to call it that?"

In the New Hope Baptist Church, near Samoth, John Mecoy held a debate with Green W. Smith, a Baptist.

1884.—T. L. Stipp and I. B. Grandy discussed Universalism at Hoopeston. Universalists sent the challenge. Mr. Stipp was chosen by the city ministerial association. He was

THE PERIOD OF CONQUEST

its youngest member except one. A series of successful meetings followed the debate.

1886.—U. M. Browder and F. Smith, of the M. E. Church, discussed at Smithfield the following propositions: "The Scriptures teach that the sinner or ungodly is justified in the sense of pardoned, or remission of sins, by faith only," and, "Baptism as commanded in the commission is in order to the remission of past sins." This discussion was full of smartness and sarcasm.

1887.—At Samoth, D. L. Kincaid and Green W. Smith, a Baptist, held a debate.

1888.—In the New Hope Baptist Church, in Massac County, J. M. Radcliffe and G. W. Smith, Baptist, held a discussion.

1889.—A discussion was held at Creal Springs led by J. F. Hight and Robert Huggins, a Christadelphian.

T. L. Stipp and J. T. Pender, of the M. E. Church, debated the questions of baptism and faith alone, at Fisher.

At Bellair, Clark Braden and E. S. Kelley discussed Mormonism.

1890.—In April this year, at McVey, A. C. Layman and Elder Hilliard debated Mormonism. These elders are aggressive and self-assertive. Their entrance into a community is with the avowed purpose of making converts to their faith. The most direct method of defeating their aims is by a public discussion. This debate was held in a large tent and put an end to their advocacy in that community.

At Barry, H. C. Littleton and L. T. Nichols, a Christadelphian, held a discussion. At its close, defeat was confessed, and long since Christadelphian theories and following disappeared from that community.

1894.—In the Oakley Avenue Church, in Chicago, Clark Braden and John Williams held a debate on Adventism. Mr. Williams was the editor of the First-day Adventist organ. His defeat was thorough.

1896.—At Birds, S. C. Hill and Minister Filroe, of the M. E. Church, held a discussion.

In the Azotus Baptist Church, in Pope County, J. F. Hight and G. W. Smith, Baptist, conducted a debate.

1897.—At Joppa, J. F. Hight and R. H. Pique, of the M. E. Church, debated.

And so did J. B. Briney and W. P. Throgmorton, Baptist, at Dixon Springs.

In the West Panther Creek Schoolhouse, in Calhoun County, J. M. Bovee and J. W. Miller discussed instrumental music in public worship.

1898.—J. F. Hight and C. M. Weaver, Primitive Baptist, met in a debate at New Burnside.

In Astoria, H. C. Littleton and M. J. McClure, German Baptist, discussed trine immersion and feet-washing as church ordinances. At its close the German Baptist sentiment expressed itself in the words, "If we had known this man, we would have had a man from Pennsylvania to lead in the debate." The discussion helped the people in the community to a better knowledge of Scripture teaching on these subjects.

At Orchardville, Clark Braden and I. N. White debated Mormonism. Mr. White was one of the twelve apostles of the Josephite party.

1899.—Mr. Braden led in the two debates of this year; first, at Alma, with I. N. White on Mormonism; second, at St. Elmo, with C. H. Bliss on Seventh-dayism.

1901.—Mr. Braden met Minister Hicks at Nebo in a comparison of the church of Christ and the Baptist Church.

1902.—Mr. Braden met J. R. Roberts at Belmont on the subject of "Anti ism."

1903.—And also A. P. Roberts at Olney on the same subject.

At Wayne City, Mr. Braden discussed the questions of baptism with D. B. Turney, of the Protestant Methodist Church. Mr. Turney was a very small man.

1908.—In February, at Colfax, J. Fred Jones affirmed in a public discussion that "the immersion of a proper subject in water is Christian baptism." This was denied by U. Y. Gilmer, of the M. E. Church.

1909.—At Dahlgren, W. H. Boles and J. R. Daley, of the Primitive Baptists, each affirmed in a public debate that the church of which he is a member is the church of Christ. Through the four days there were great crowds and good nature throughout.

J. F. Wright and F. M. Lawley, of the "Reorganized Church of Latter-day Saints," held a debate at Tunnel Hill. "The Saints" furnished the Disciples a boarding-place in their "temple" near Tunnel Hill, and accorded them great respect and hospitality.

In the same year these two men held another discussion at Goreville.

1910.—W. H. Boles met Henry Sparling, one of "the Saints," at Springerton in a six days' debate of two four-hour sessions. The Mormons had a large church there.

1911.—In the Mt. Pleasant Church, in Massac County, D. N. Barnett held a debate with J. R. McLain, a Latter-day Saint.

This led to another discussion at the same place between J. F. Hight and Mr. McLain.

These one hundred specific mentions of public discussions were probably not one-half of the number in Illinois in which the ministers of the churches of Christ have participated. It is apparent that these preachers have fought *all along the line of battle,* from gross materialism to instrumental music in public worship, and generally at such times and places as the advocates of error led in open attacks and aggressive assaults upon the truth. They have successfully met the manifold vagaries of religious and irreligious thought, many-phased infidelity, Universalism, the dogmas of human creeds and Mormonism. Every essential position for which they have contended through the past seventy-five years is now admitted, if not practically accepted, by intelligent evangelical believers. The Disciples are orthodox. Public debates have mostly ceased, not because they were a failure, but because they were a success.

CHAPTER V.

BENEVOLENCES.

Section 1.—State Missionary Activities.

Most of the pioneer preachers were missionaries sent of God and self-supporting. But at a very early day they saw clearly the need of united efforts. At the close of a protracted meeting in Jacksonville, in October, 1834, it was decided to foster a co-operation among the churches. In that meeting B. W. Stone, John Rigdon, Alexander Reynolds, Josephus Hewett, H. W. Osborn, Abner Peeler, Edward D. Baker and others participated. John Rigdon was sent out as the evangelist for six months. This appeal was made to all the congregations in the State to unite in a voluntary association for the spread of the gospel.

In March, 1836, John T. Jones and Guerdon Gates issued the *final* call for a proposed State Meeting in Jacksonville that fall.

In 1839 a State Meeting was held in Pittsfield.

In 1840 a call for "Our Annual Meeting" to assemble in Springfield on Friday before the fourth Lord's Day in September was signed by B. W. Stone, John T. Jones, Peter Hedenberg, D. P. Henderson, Henry D. Palmer, William Davenport, John Rigdon, D. B. Hill and Theophilus Sweet. One object of the meeting was to put "as many evangelists in the field as possible."

In 1842 the Annual Meeting was held in Springfield.

May 18, 1843, a call was sent out from Bloomington for a "State Meeting" to convene there on Friday before the fourth Lord's Day in August following, signed by W. T. Major and H. H. Painter, elders, and R. O. Warrener, evangelist. As stated in the call, the objects of the meeting were "to cultivate acquaintance with each other, to hear of the success of the labors of our teaching brethren, to promote brotherly love, advance the cause of union among the followers of Jesus, and, by teaching the truths of the Bible, edify and instruct each other and all who may attend." This meeting was well attended by brethren from different parts of the State. Co-operation was considered and discussed. At its close J. A. Lindsay and H. D. Palmer became the evangelists in McLean and adjoining counties.

In 1845 the State Meeting went to Pittsfield, and in 1848 to Walnut Grove (Eureka). Whether other such meetings were held in the interims, the extant records do not disclose. During that period of twenty years the facilities for traveling were limited to stage-coaches and private conveyances; hence the distances were, relatively, far greater than now. But the pioneers made the journeys with eagerness, for the "State Meetings" were occasions of mutual assurance, the sweetest fellowship and great joy. They were a source of mutual strength, led to a clearer understanding of Scriptural teaching and did much active missionary work.

In 1839 John Rigdon was engaged as an evangelist in the counties of Adams, Brown and Pike.

The same year "Tobias Grider was appointed to ride as an evangelist in Shelby County, where there were few churches."

November 20, 1842, a co-operation meeting was held at Marion composed of the representatives of eleven churches located in the counties of Franklin, Gallatin, Hardin, Perry, Pope and Wabash. Except two, those eleven churches are extinct. Minister J. M. Mulkey was chairman.

In 1850 there was a co-operation of the churches in Morgan, Scott and Cass Counties, with Ministers Happy and Pyatt as evangelists. In April, 1851, Benjamin N. Humphrey, the corresponding secretary of this co-operation, reported 208 additions by the labors of Evangelists Happy and A. McCollum.

In 1848, A. D. Northcut, who had come from Kentucky,

was employed by the co-operation of the churches in Shelby County as its evangelist. In the first year of this service he added more than three hundred people to the Lord. The co-operation in the same county in 1880 planted congregations at Oak Grove and Mode.

In 1851 the churches in Shelby, Moultrie and Macon Counties were engaged in co-operative missionary work. The following is an exact transcript from the minutes of the meeting:

Proceedings of the cooperative meeting held at church called Bethel meeting house in Shelby County, State of Illinois. In complyance with arrangements made at a meeting held on Sand Creek in the County of Shelby: the brethren from the different named congregations as here follows were in attendance. To make arrangements for evangelizing in the year of our Lord one thousand eight hundred and fifty one. The (brethren) delegates from six congregations were there.

Bushrod W. Henry was made chairman and Henry Y. Kellar, secretary.

The names of the different congregations that were there represented were called for.
1st. West Okaw. Two delegates—James H. Kellar, John Wood.
2nd. Sullivan. Two delegates—William Kellar, N. F. Higginbotham.
3rd. Bethel. Two delegates—J. W. Sconce, B. W. Henry.
4th. Decatur. One delegate—S. Shepherd.
5th. Mud Creek. Two delegates—E. Waggoner, L. McMorris.
6th. Shelbyville. One delegate—John Page.

It was suggested that the meeting adjourn till evening, hoping for the arrival of other delegates. This was voted down on the ground that "it would be giving sanction to a bad precedent—that was, one time to do business and doing it at another." The co-operation then decided to do its work "in the weak congregations and their immediate vicinity." Subscriptions were made as follows: West Okaw, $60; Sullivan, $60; Bethel, $30; Mud Creek, $30; Decatur, $50; Shelbyville, $30; total, $260. At the night session the president suggested two evangelists—one an aged man and the other a young man—"which was unanimously concurred in." Henry Y. Kellar was chosen as "the young preacher," and "B. W. Henry was selected as the senior evangelist." The co-operation decided to "pay the evangelists $26 a month."

In 1854 the second meeting of the Southern Illinois Christian Co-operation was held at Salem. This co-operation included the ten counties at the southern end of the State. The same year, June 14, a district co-operative meeting was held at Batavia. In the sixties there were county co-operations in Tazewell-Mason, Fulton and Iroquois. In 1869, Mason County dropped out of the union with Tazewell and the latter established the church in Pekin. The same year the co-operation of the Northern District met at Batavia, November 12 and 13. In 1881 there were co-operations in the counties of Adams, Christian, Champaign, Douglas, Logan, McLean, Marshall, Pike, Shelby, Tazewell, Woodford and White. Within a year five of these had died a natural or violent death. These few facts indicate the convictions held and efforts made to care for weak congregations and plant churches in new fields by the co-operation of counties singly or unitedly. This work reached through about forty years. Hancock formed a co-operation of its churches in 1892 and continues to hold an annual meeting in the fall.

The American Christian Missionary Society was formed at Cincinnati, Ohio, in 1849. It became the mother of all the wider missionary activities among the Disciples of Christ.

Friday, September 20, 1850, the "State Convention of the Christian Church in Illinois began and held at Shelbyville." Those present were J. Atkinson, Theophilus Sweet, H. W. Osborn, Jas. A. Lindsay, W. F. M. Arny, A. Kellar, Morris R. Chew, Bushrod W. Henry, Wm. Davenport, J. T. Jones, H. D. Palmer, Wm. T. Major, G. W. Minier, John M. Hodge, Elijah Vawter, Alpheus Brown, James D. McPherson, P. H. Murphy and A. A. Glenn.

These men were delegates who represented local churches, counties and co-operations. Other congregations were represented by letters. The number of Christian Churches then in the State was 104, with an aggregate membership of 6,359. During the year then closing, 1,123 persons had been added to the churches.

The first business transacted by this meeting was the organization of "The Bible Society of the State of Illinois, auxiliary to the American Christian Bible Society." Next, "The Illinois State Missionary Society" was organized by the adoption of a constitution and the election of the following officers: President, Henry D. Palmer; Vice-Presidents, Wm. T. Major, Harrison W. Osborn, Bushrod W. Henry; Managers, Jas. A. Lindsay, Morris R. Chew, Wm. Davenport, J. Atkinson, John H. Hodge, John E. Murphy, John Houston, E. W. Bakewell; Recording Secretary, A. J. Kane; Treasurer, William Lavely. Mr. Palmer presided at this meeting, and Mr. Vawter served as secretary the first day and was succeeded by Mr. Minier. Some sessions of the convention were held in the M. E. Chapel, and their pulpit was filled on Sunday, September 22.

At nine o'clock that morning a business-meeting session was held. At ten o'clock, three o'clock and evening public worship was conducted in both chapels. In part of these meetings there were two sermons. On Monday morning the convention heard the "valedictory address by J. Atkinson, and adjourned to meet the next year at Walnut Grove."

In 1852, Mr. Baily D. Dawson was chosen recording secretary and served eight years in this capacity. He is still living in Chicago and has furnished the writer valuable information.

In 1856, Dr. W. A. Mallory became State evangelist and served in this capacity till 1860.

In 1856 the State was divided into fourteen missionary districts, which in 1861 were changed to four and these again to nine in 1864. During this period there was a written constitution, which was frequently changed, and life memberships. Attention and financial aid were directed chiefly to the congregations in Peoria and Quincy. S. T. Calloway was corresponding secretary in 1858. In the Annual Meeting of

BENEVOLENCES

1861 the question of a Students' Aid Fund was proposed, but it was defeated by a majority as not germane to the work of the society.

W. J. Houston served as corresponding secretary and evangelist from 1860-63. In his first report, submitted in 1861, he said that during the year he had traveled 2,500 miles, preached 620 discourses "with numerous exhortations," and "added 374 to the army of the faithful, principally by confession and baptism." For this superior service the society paid him $800. This sum included "one coat received at Paris valued at $12." In 1862 he reported seven hundred discourses and "many exhortations" and over eight hundred additions. "Many new co-operations were organized during the year." That year three other evangelists were associated with Mr. Houston and their accessions totaled 1,349. A balance of $90 due on his first year's work was paid him then.

During this period the society held a few semi-annual meetings, but they were soon found to be impracticable.

John S. Sweeney served as corresponding secretary and State evangelist from 1863-65, and his father, G. E. Sweeney, by special vote of the society, also evangelized under its authority and auspices. One year J. S. Sweeney had sixteen evangelists at work. Mr. Henry C. Latham served as corresponding secretary in 1865-66, but with only office duties. Minister A. H. Rice held the same title, doing active work in the field.

Dudley Down succeeded as corresponding secretary and evangelist, but his devoted toil sapped his energies and sent him, within two years, into rapid decline and premature death.

In 1870 work was begun under the "Louisville Plan," which was adopted at Louisville, Kentucky, in October, 1869. The State was divided into six missionary districts. This was the second period of missionary activity. J. C. Reynolds became corresponding secretary and State evangelist. His first task was to organize the districts and develop a sentiment that would sustain an evangelist in the several divisions.

He was followed in this work, severally, by J. W. Allen, John Lindsay, W. T. Maupin and J. H. Wright. Each did good service, aiming and striving to advance the Kingdom of God by all proper co-operative efforts. Mr. Wright organized the Mt. Morris Church during his seven months' service. There was only a little money that came to support the work and it was a time of transition. During this period E. J. Lampton served as State evangelist and dedicated a mission chapel at Denver that had been built by the Mt. Pleasant country church, all in Hancock County. Before the close of the decade it was clear that the "Louisville Plan" would not be worked in Illinois.

N. S. Haynes was chosen corresponding secretary and State evangelist in 1880 and entered actively upon the work the 1st of the following January. He served in this dual capacity till August, 1885, when he resigned because one member of the Board of Managers thought that too few persons were being added to the churches through the society's work. The next year W. J. Ford served as corresponding secretary. But the convention of 1886 returned Mr. Haynes to this office, and he continued as active manager of the work till August, 1891—a period of nine years and eight months. The chief aim of his administration was a campaign of education for world-wide missions. This was one of the chief needs of the Disciples in Illinois at that time. The Foreign Society had been organized only about five years and its management was feeble. In 1881 he received $44.80 for Foreign Missions, of which $7.35 came from one of the leading churches of the State! Hence he laid hold of printers' ink, church papers and all available preachers for missionary education. In the spring of 1883 he mailed copies of a printed circular appeal, with fifteen thousand envelopes for Children's Day, to 260 of the best Bible schools in the State. Some of the aims and results of his work were the following: He disseminated continually missionary intelligence in every way possible; prepared and published a list of ministers in the State in 1882, and of churches in 1883, both by counties; reported the aggregate value of church property; helped pastorless congregations and ministers without churches, and introduced and urged the co-operation of weak and near-together congregations in sustaining pastors; located the churches of the State and had a map made of the same; later redistricted the State, which arrangement remains unchanged; introduced the desirability of parsonages to public attention, there being only about three in 1880—in 1913 there were 131; urged continually the moral and financial support of our colleges; raised a few hundred dollars to assist in building the first creditable house of worship in Washington, D. C.; led in the formation of two ministerial institutes—the Central, which continues to render helpful service, and one in the Military Tract, which was permitted to die years ago; organized the State Encampment in 1887, which continued twelve years; helped actively in founding and building the Students' Aid Fund; increased the permanent funds from $455 to above $20,000; and in 1890, at the request of Dr. H. K. Carroll, special agent of the United States to secure data of religious bodies for the eleventh census, prepared and transmitted to him a complete list of the churches of Christ in Illinois, on schedules furnished by the Government. July 15, 1890, Dr. Carroll wrote him, saying: "I have received from you Schedules 687 A, B, C, D, E and F. I am very much pleased, indeed, with the work you have done so faithfully and promptly." The maximum for his traveling expenses in any one year was $152.68. Comparing 1880 with 1889, the remittances from Illinois were as follows: To the Foreign Society, $1,007 and $3,815; to the General Home Society, $230 and $3,534; to the State Society, $1,690 and $5,847, and to the State Sunday-school Association, $600 and $2,834. During the nine years and eight months' period, among the congregations organized by the State Society were Champaign, Mason City, Newton, Onarga, Roodhouse and Streator, and among those fostered were Carbondale, three in Chicago (Englewood, Northside and Westside), Galesburg, Keithsburg, Mt. Pulaski, Paxton, Pekin, Princeton, Pontiac, Rockford, Sterling and Taylorville. The associated evangelists during this period were Isaac Beckelhymer, W. H. and Marion Boles, T. A. Boyer, A. Campbell, H. C. Cassell, W. H. Cannon, J. W. Carpenter, J. S. Clements, Jas. Connoran, J. E. Deihl, J. F. Ghormley, E. A. Gilliland, G. M. Goode, J. J. Harris, G. M. Hoffman, D. W. Honn, D. E. Hughes, W. A. Ingram, E. J. Lampton, L. M. Linn, Daniel Logan, L. B. Myers, C. B. Newnan, J. L. Parsons, G. W. Pearl, J. W. Robbins, J. R. Speck, J. Z. Taylor, H. R. Trickett, J. M. Tenneson and R. D. Van Buskirk. Some of these ministers served in the continued meeting only, and others of them in several periods or years.

Min. G. W. Pearl began his service as corresponding secretary and State evangelist Aug. 1, 1891, and closed his term Dec. 31, 1896. No change was made in any way in the conduct of the affairs of the society. Its work prospered and grew steadily in all lines. His management was wise. The evangelists during this period were J. S. Clements, O. W. Stewart, W. A. Ingram, S. S. Jones, Miss Sarah C. McCoy, C. E. Evans, T. A. Boyer, E. A. Gilliland, S. H. Creighton, T. F. Weaver, W. V. Boltz, R. H. Kline, G. W. Griffith, E. J. Ellis, F. L. Moffitt, J. F. Jones, J. P. McKnight.

J. Fred Jones became State evangelist and corresponding secretary Jan. 1, 1896. In 1902 he became "Field Secretary." The period covered by this survey closes with June, 1913, or seventeen and a half years. He states "the ideals during this period" as follows:

1. The organization and support of new churches in fruitful fields.
2. The aiding of weak churches, mainly by evangelistic meetings—about three hundred have been so helped.
3. The support of an evangelist in each district.
4. The needs of village and rural churches have been emphasized and the permanent co-operation of contiguous churches in supporting pastors has been urged.

In 1896 the secretaries of the several missionary districts were made *ex-officio* members of the State Board and are so continued.

BENEVOLENCES

The chief evangelists who were engaged in the State and district work, not including Chicago, were the following: J. T. Alsup, W. B. Bedall, Isaac Beckelhymer, C. H. Berry, R. Leland Brown, J. H. Beard, D. R. Beboit, R. L. Cartwright, W. R. Courter, J. D. and C. B. Dabney, F. L. Dairs, C. E. Evans, O. M. Eaton, W. A. Green, J. J. Harris, L. D. Hill, W. H. Harding, E. M. Harlis, George Hoagland, W. A. Ingram, Gilbert Jones, W. H. Kindred, S. S. Lappin, D. A. Lytle, H. E. Monser, M. W. Nethercutt, E. M. Norton, J. E. Parker, C. W. Ross, F. G. Roberts, T. J. Shuey, C. M. Smithson, E. O. Sharp, Andrew Scott, F. M. Stambaugh, J. E. Stout, H. L. Veach, K. C. Ventress, J. O. Walton and J. D. Williams. Some of these served for longer and others for shorter terms.

The more substantial churches formed were these: Alexis, Beecher City, Bunker Hill, Carlinville, Cowden, Fandon, Freeport, Findley, Havana, Indianola, Joliet, Johnson City, Kewanee, Kinmundy, Moline, Monticello, Ridge Farm, Rock Falls, Savana, St. Elmo, Tamaroa, Tampico, Villa Grove and West Frankfort.

Following the plan of the Foreign Missionary Society, the State Board decided in 1904 to introduce the living-link feature; hence the following churches have paid $200 or more per year for State mission work. Generally the congregations have chosen the mission points or weak churches they have assisted, and quite a number of these have been in their own cities or counties. This list is: Arcola, Adams County churches, Armington, Bloomington First and Second, Champaign, Concord (Tazewell County), Camp Point, Carthage, Decatur Central, De Land, Englewood (Chicago), Gibson City, Jacksonville, Long Point, Mackinaw, Minier, Morgan County Bible schools, a Niantic brother, Normal, Peoria Central, Pittsfield, Paris, Pleasantview (Adams County), Quincy First, Springfield First, and Tazewell County churches.

A goodly number of mission points and weak congregations have been fostered by "Link" offerings or appropriations from the treasury of the society. This list follows: Anna,

98 HISTORY OF THE DISCIPLES IN ILLINOIS

$25; Alexis, $75; Ashland, $100; Bloomington Centennial, $200; Beardstown, $800; Bushnell, $200; Carlinville, $135; Chicago Heights, $25; Chicago Northside, $50; Cooksville, $100; Delavan, $60; Dixon, $225; Decatur, Leaftand Avenue, $272; Elgin, $200; Freeport, $800; Fulton, $825; Findley, $100; Galesburg, $25; Granite City, $300; Griggsville, $230; Havana, $510; Harvey, $250; Hillsboro, $900; Jacksonville (negro), $10; Joliet First, $162; Kankakee, $400; Kewanee, $2,600; McLean, $400; Minonk, $319; Mossville, $158; Moline, $1,600; Mt. Vernon, $250; Paris Mission, $200; Pontiac, $400; Polo, $813; Peoria, Howett Street, $810; Princeton, $50; Quincy Mission, $317; Rock Falls, $230; Rockford, $1,400; Rockford (negro), $50; Redmon, $600; Savana, $271; Springfield, Stewart Avenue, $900; South Chicago, $150; Streator, $2,265; Tampico, $145; Time, $250, and Villa Grove, $388.

THE OFFICE.

Up to 1902 all of the corresponding secretaries had provided offices for the society's work at their personal expense. In that year an office was rented and, through the generosity of friends, suitably equipped with needed furniture. Min. W. D. Deweese was chosen office secretary and did much of the necessary printing up to August, 1913. For several years he has served as treasurer also.

CHRISTIAN COADJUTORS.

The convention of 1910 decided to employ two Christian students in the State University at Urbana to work among their fellow-students—a young man among the men and a young woman among the women. During the three school years following, these coadjutors were paid $25 per month— an aggregate for the period of $1,023. Mr. Stephen E. Fisher, for ten years the pastor of the University Place Christian Church, says:

> The organization of the men and women from Christian Church homes in Illinois who attend the university has proven, under the leader-

ship of these special helpers, very effective. Committees on Bible-school work, church attendance, social life, etc., are constantly active. Many who would not otherwise do so have been led to affiliate with the local church actively during college residence, and about twenty girls in the three years and fifteen young men in the two years have been led to Christ through confession and baptism. When we recall that these are the men and women who will hold the high places of power to-morrow in our nation, the value of this work is beyond estimate.

In 1896 the reported number of churches was 730, with an aggregate membership of 95,257, while in 1913 the numbers given were 692 congregations, with a total membership of 110,736. The value of the houses of worship and parsonages was $4,299,710. The seating capacity of the buildings was 215,990. Mr. Jones gave eighteen of the best years of his life to this work.

In addition to Peter Whitmer, Min. D. R. Van Buskirk and Dr. George D. Sitherwood, all of Bloomington, as members of the State Board gave most valuable assistance; so, also, has J. P. Darst, of Peoria, for twenty-five years.

SECTION 2.—INDEPENDENT AND INDIVIDUAL MISSION WORK.

THE YOTSUYA MISSION, Tokyo, Japan (W. D. Cunningham, Director).—In 1906, J. P. Hieronymus, a banker of Atlanta, received a copy of the *Tokyo Christian*, which, he says, produced a "spontaneous combustion" in him. "I believe in *both organized and individual missions*," he says. He opened an account in his bank for Mr. Cunningham, and since then has received and remitted all sums sent him for this individual mission. In 1912 the amount was $266.81, which came from forty givers. He is pleased to continue as forwarding secretary. This mission has two hundred ropeholders in Illinois, including several organizations, each counted as one.

W. H. WAGGONER was born in Princeton, Ill., March 15, 1868—Sunday morning, just in time for the foreign missionary offering. Educated in the public schools, Eureka College and Yale University. Mr. Waggoner has given his life to lecturing on world-wide missions. He uses maps, charts and pictures with stereopticon. He is a great sower of good seed. His work receives the highest commendation.

BURKEY-SWORD.—Daniel Burkey was reared with the Mennonites and united with the church of Christ at New Bedford, Ill. He said to Mr. Sword in 1908: "I have done little for the Master's Kingdom. I can not preach, but you can. Go into the field, receive what is paid you, and I will pay you the balance." The contract called for $1,500 per year and expenses. This arrangement continued four years. Mr. Sword proved to be a very sane and successful evangelist and Mr. Burkey found great joy in his support. In the period Mr. Burkey paid $776 and Mr. Sword received about twelve hundred people into the churches.

SECTION 3.—PERMANENT FUNDS.

The first suggestion of a permanent fund for missionary work in Illinois came from Mr. E. W. Bakewell, of Normal. At the State Meeting at Jacksonville in 1857 he publicly pledged himself "to be one of eight to give $100, or one of fifty to give $1,000, within a year, toward establishing a permanent missionary fund." Nothing immediately came from this proposition. In 1876 the subject was revived with the view of securing $10,000, the annual interest from which would support the State evangelist. The nation's centennial was thought to be a fitting time to begin the building of a living memorial. The proposition was presented in and indorsed by the State Convention and advertised through church papers and otherwise. Mins. J. J. Moss, A. H. Trowbridge and a few others gave a little time to this work. The two men who started it with $100 each in cash were A. R. Knox and John Doyle. In the early eighties they were followed in like sums by J. O. Bolin, W. R. Carle, John V. Dee, Col. J. W. Judy and S. H. Anderson. In 1880, upon the earnest suggestion of Peter Whitmer, the sum to be raised was placed at $13,000. He was a banker of Bloomington, and for twenty-six consecutive years the faithful and efficient treasurer of this fund. His annual reports were his joy.

The largest gift from any one person came from the estate of Mrs. Sarah A. Starr, of Bloomington, in 1886—$10,000. The Permanent Funds now aggregate $37,504. Of this sum, $5,400 is in annuity bonds. In 1902 the Board arranged to issue such bonds. Mrs. Emily Booth Turner, of Quincy, born in Kentucky in 1825 and a lifelong, earnest Christian, gave to this fund $2,000 on the annuity bond plan. This fund will be increased within two years by $60,000 from the estate of Thomas E. Bondurant. From the estate of Dr. J. H. Breeden nearly $4,000 has been received recently. This income from the regular permanent fund should pay the cost of administration.

STUDENTS' AID FUND.

With the view of assisting young men of limited means in their preparation for the work of the Christian ministry, this fund was started in 1886. The moneys were to be loaned to approved applicants on their notes of hand for varying periods. A committee of three persons chosen by the convention has very efficiently handled this business throughout the twenty-seven years. Later the privileges of the fund were extended equally to young women preparing for special Christian service. August, 1913, this sum totaled $8,219. From September, 1886, to July, 1913, 799 loans were made to 255 students, eleven of whom were women. These loans aggregated $22,264. The results of this stimulating benevolence have been far-reaching. An application came to the committee years ago from Frank L. Bowen. He was well indorsed by the church at Rock Island, but the indorsers said frankly that, in their opinion, it was questionable whether the elements of a successful preacher were in him. The conscientious and judicial consideration of the application placed the committee "on the fence." Finally, J. G. Waggoner said: "Brethren, let's take the risk and give the boy a chance." Then it was so voted. The many years of Mr. Bowen's fine ministry justify the committee's guess, and he will know before whom to lift his hat.

HISTORY OF THE DISCIPLES IN ILLINOIS

SECTION 4.—STATE CONVENTIONS AND PRESIDENTS.

DATES.	PLACES.	PRESIDENTS.
1850	Shelbyville,	H. D. Palmer.
1851	Walnut Grove,	H. D. Palmer.
1852	Abingdon,	W. W. Happy.
1853	Jacksonville,	W. W. Happy.
1854	Decatur,	W. W. Happy.
1855	Charleston,	W. W. Happy.
1856	Mechanicsburg,	W. W. Happy.
1857	Jacksonville,	W. W. Happy.
1858	Bloomington,	W. W. Happy.
1859	Lincoln,	W. W. Happy.
1860	Carrollton,	W. W. Happy.
1861	Eureka,	John T. Jones.
1862	Abingdon,	John T. Jones.
1863	Bloomington,	John T. Jones.
1864	Lincoln,	John T. Jones.
1865	Springfield,	John T. Jones.
1866	Eureka,	John T. Jones.
1867	Jacksonville,	Enos Campbell.
1868	Winchester,	Enos Campbell.
1869	Macomb,	Enos Campbell.
1870	Chicago,	Enos Campbell.
1871	Bloomington,	Enos Campbell.
1872	Bloomington,	Enos Campbell.
1873	Jacksonville,	A. A. Glenn.
1874	Eureka,	J. H. McCullough.
1875	Bloomington,	A. I. Hobbs.
1876	Eureka,	S. M. Connor.
1877	Springfield,	A. I. Hobbs.
1878	Eureka,	A. I. Hobbs.
1879	Princeton,	J. W. Allen.
1880	Bloomington,	A. I. Hobbs.
1881	Jacksonville,	N. S. Haynes.
1882	Macomb,	A. J. Thompson.
1883	Springfield,	G. M. Goode.
1884	Eureka,	S. M. Connor.
1885	Eureka,	S. M. Connor.
1886	Sullivan,	J. G. Waggoner.
1887	Decatur,	J. A. Roberts.
1888	Eureka,	Hiram Woods.
1889	Eureka,	A. N. Gilbert.
1890	Eureka,	J. H. Gilliland.
1891	Eureka,	F. N. Calvin.
1892	Eureka,	A. P. Cobb.
1893	Eureka,	W. A. Maloan.
1894	Eureka,	W. A. Humphrey.
1895	Eureka,	T. T. Holton.
1896	Eureka,	L. B. Pickerill.
1897	Eureka,	N. S. Haynes.
1898	Eureka,	J. H. Hardin.
1899	Eureka,	J. H. Smart.
1900	Bloomington,	N. S. Haynes.
1901	Springfield,	R. F. Thrapp.
1902	Jacksonville,	W. W. Weedon.
1903	Eureka,	J. E. Lynn.
1904	Champaign,	W. H. Cannon.
1905	Decatur,	Geo. A. Campbell.
1906	Paris,	F. W. Burnham.
1907	Jacksonville,	O. W. Lawrence.
1908	Chicago,	H. L. Willett.
1909	Eureka,	J. H. Gilliland.
1910	Springfield,	J. W. Kilborn.
1911	Danville,	J. R. Golden.
1912	Centralia,	Silas Jones.
1913	Jacksonville,	W. W. Weedon.

SECTION 5.—THE CHRISTIAN WOMAN'S BOARD OF MISSIONS.

The first effective call to the women of the churches of Christ in the United States to organize for missionary work was issued in May, 1874, by Mrs. Caroline Neville Pearre, then a resident of Mason City, Iowa. In God's providence

MRS. O. A. BURGESS. MRS. V. T. LINDSAY.
MRS. S. J. CRAWFORD. MRS. ANNIE E. DAVIDSON.
MISS. E. J. DICKINSON.
MRS. L. V. PORTER. MRS. P. L. CHRISTIAN.

this call proved to be bread cast upon the wide waters. On July 26, 1874, Miss Elmira J. Dickinson organized a local woman's missionary society at Eureka—the first in the State. About the same time Pastor J. H. McCullough and wife, of Bloomington; Isaac Errett, then preaching in Chicago, and Pastor J. W. Allen, of Jacksonville, formed similar societies in the churches of these several cities.

The Illinois Christian Woman's Board of Missions was organized by Miss Dickinson at Eureka, Aug. 28, 1874, at the close of the annual meeting of the State Missionary Society. There were present about fifty women, who were encouraged in their action by Mr. John Darst, of Eureka, and Pastor Ira J. Chase, of Peoria. This was the first State organization of the Christian women. It was their expressed intention to become auxiliary to a national society which it was proposed to form at Cincinnati, Ohio, the next October. At this national meeting seventy-five women were present from nine States, ten of whom were from Illinois. Such was the beginning of a Christian activity that has been of incalculable value to the women themselves and the church at large. It has given to their fine minds and true hearts worthy ideals and aims, and has conserved the spiritual life of the churches and brought thousands to the knowledge of the truth and to the service of the Master. On the first Sunday afternoon following the meeting in Cincinnati, Elder Tyra Montgomery formed a woman's auxiliary in the church at Mattoon, of which Mrs. Caroline Montgomery was the first president.

Miss Dickinson was chosen the first president at the formation of the Illinois Society, and for a decade thereafter did the difficult and heroic pioneer work that was needed to lay the foundation of a splendid superstructure. Those who followed in the presidency were Mrs. James Kirk, Mrs. Emma Campbell Ewing, Mrs. O. A. Burgess, Mrs. Persis L. Christian, Miss Anna May Hale, Miss Annie E. Davidson, Mrs. Carrie F. Zeller and now Mrs. Lura Thompson Porter.

The corresponding secretaries have been Mrs. Ella Myers Huffman, Mrs. Happy, Mrs. M. M. Lindsay, Mrs. J. G. Waggoner, Miss Lura V. Thompson (two terms), Miss Rachael Crouch, Miss Gussie Courson and Miss Anna M. Hale.

The treasurers in their order of service were Mrs. John Darst, Mrs. H. W. Everest, Mrs. Cassell, Mrs. M. B. Hawk, Mrs. S. J. Crawford, Miss Clara L. Davidson and now Miss Henrietta Clark.

The superintendents of the Young People's Department were Miss Frank Haynes, Miss Annie E. Davidson, Miss Gussie Courson, Miss Minnie Dennis, Miss Lola V. Hale, Miss Irene Ridgely, Miss Clara B. Griffin, Miss Dora Gutherie and now Miss Effie L. Gaddis.

Miss Dickinson gave the society, in various official capacities, about thirty years of service; Mrs. S. J. Crawford was treasurer twenty-two years; Miss Annie E. Davidson in a dual capacity fourteen years, and Mrs. Porter fifteen years—to September, 1913. Twelve of the women above named have been "field workers;" that is, they have gone through the State as educators and organizers. It may be truthfully said that all of these women in every official position have done their best; hence the work has grown steadily from its beginning. The pioneers in this movement overcame, by their Christlike devotion, uninformed indifference and outspoken prejudice and opposition, and they merit the greater honor. At the first meeting in 1874 there was "a collection taken of $5.41 for the State development;" the total offerings for the year closing with June, 1913, were $24,392. Starting with nothing save prayer, purpose and promise, the auxiliaries and circles reported at the same time were 266, with a membership of 6.277.

In January, 1901, a State paper was started to help in this work. It was called *The Illinois Quarterly*, but became *Mission Leaves* in 1906. It was first issued from Athens, with Miss Anna M. Hale as editor; in 1904 from Eureka, with Miss Annie E. Davidson as editor, and in 1909, first from Cuba, then from Petersburg, with Mrs. Carrie F. Zeller as editor—to August, 1913. There were eighteen hundred of these *Leaves* then in circulation.

The headquarters of the society have been Eureka for two periods, Jacksonville and Springfield. The office is now in the First Christian Church there, and *Mission Leaves* will be issued from that city. Miss Jennie Call is the editor and is also the corresponding secretary.

This movement owes much to Illinois. Its mother, Mrs. Pearre, was trained in this State. So also was Mrs. Burgess, whose superior administrative ability kept her in the presidency of the national society ten years. Mrs. Christian, who was known as a "queen of the platform," and who traveled ten years through the nation in the advocacy of this work, was a product of Illinois. Miss Dickinson, who was first in self-sacrifice, suggested the thought of a missionary training-school. And this was actualized through the munificence of Mrs. Maude Detterding Ferris, a fair daughter of the Prairie State.

The total receipts of the National C. W. B. M. for the year ending September, 1913, were $358,944. This society has in its employ 518 men and women, who are at work in the United States, western Canada, Mexico, Jamaica, Porto Rico, South America, New Zealand, India, China and Africa.

SECTION 6.—CHRISTIAN HOME FOR THE AGED.

This Home is located at 873 Grove Street in Jacksonville. It is a two-story brick, modern building, with forty rooms, that stands on a beautiful lot of two and a half acres. It is the property of the National Benevolent Association and was bought in 1900 at a cost of $6,500. This money was furnished by Mr. John Loar, Mrs. Nancy Henderson and Mrs. Lou Deweese Kaiser—all members of the Jacksonville Church. The two women have passed to the life eternal. Since then a large addition was built to it. There are thirty rooms for the inmates, who are mostly women. Since its opening there have been seventy-eight of these. It has always been full, with a number on the waiting list. The annual current expenses amount to $6,000, which is paid from the offerings made at large to the National Benevolent Association. Admission is limited to members of the Christian Church. The Home is a credit to the Disciples of Christ and most worthy of their support. Mrs. Mary B. Thornberry is the present esteemed and capable matron.

SECTION 7.—CHICAGO MISSIONARY SOCIETY.

Atty. Milton O. Naramore furnishes the following concise data: The Missionary Society was organized in the parlor of old Farwell Hall in 1887. The Christian Churches in the city at that time were the West Side (now Jackson Blvd.), Indiana Avenue, Englewood and the North Side (now Sheffield Ave.) and a few missions. Those present at the meeting were Dr. W. A. Belding, Geo. F. Childs, W. G. Morris, W. P. Keeler and some of the following, who earnestly promoted the co-operation from the first; namely, Mins. J. W. Allen and Blackwell; A. A. Devore, who served as president for several years; A. Larabee, C. C. Chapman, J. G. Hester and H. H. Hubard. Of all these, W. P. Keeler was actively identified with the society from the beginning, has given more years of faithful service than any other, and is still zealous for its usefulness. He was a native of Danbury, Connecticut. About 1855 the family home was where the Great Northern Hotel now stands. Chicago has been his place of residence ever since. In 1899 the society was reorganized and incorporated under the name of the "Chicago Christian Missionary Society." Under the constitution then adopted the society became a representative body consisting of delegates elected annually by the several churches of Christ in Chicago and Cook County. The first officers were: J. H. O. Smith, President; E. A. Orr, Vice-President; E. M. Bowman, Recording Secretary; J. C. Lindsay, Corresponding Secretary; Carl Bushnell, Treasurer; E. W. Darst, Superintendent of Missions, and A. Larabee, Assistant Superintendent. Besides these, an executive board of seven is

W. P. KEELER.
J. S. SWAFORD.   E. W. DARST.   M. O. NARAMORE.
C. J. HUDSON.   E. M. BOWMAN.
                                       E. B. WITWER.

elected annually, to which is committed the entire business of the society. The first board was composed of Milton O. Naramore, Chairman; E. M. Bowman, Secretary; W. P. Keeler, E. B. Witwer, Carl Bushnell, Charles J. Hudson and J. W. Swaford.

One of the most effective means of arousing the churches to the needs of city missions was the plan inaugurated by this board of holding quarterly rallies of all the congregations, at some central place on Sunday afternoons. The first of these was held at Kimball Hall, on Wabash Avenue, near Jackson, in February, 1900. This plan is still continued.

Under the leadership of E. W. Darst, a tireless and devoted teacher of the gospel, city-mission work in Chicago moved forward with new life. In the few years he gave to this service, and during which he laid his own life on this altar, he fully proved the efficiency of this method. Most of the new churches of recent years stand as monuments to his wisdom and consecration. No great enterprise goes forward without a competent leader. Mr. Darst retired only when his failing health compelled. His life closed in a few years.

He was succeeded by W. B. Taylor, who was also an indefatigable servant of Christ. During his term of service the plan of aggressive work in building up new missions through a superintendent was changed. Upon his retirement Asst. Supt. A. Larabee was given charge of this work, and continued therein till the close of his life. His life and work are held in tender and grateful remembrance.

In addition to the contributions of the Chicago churches, the work of this society has been financially helped by the American Christian Missionary Society, the Illinois Missionary Society and the National and State C. W. B. M.

O. F. Jordan has been the faithful and efficient secretary of this society for five years. He has aimed to secure and present annually a tabulated report of the churches of Christ in Cook County, thus giving a bird's-eye view of the growth of the Disciples therein.

SECTION 8.—THE CHICAGO UNION OF AUXILIARIES TO C. W. B. M.

This society was organized in 1894. Its object was to promote the special work of missions as represented by the C. W. B. M. The union has grown from seven auxiliaries with about fifty members to twenty-two auxiliaries and circles with a membership of 547. The quarterly meetings of this union for twenty years have been very helpful to the individual women, to the local auxiliaries and to the congregations with which they are connected. The Chicago Union has always responded loyally to all calls of the National C. W. B. M., and it has co-operated actively with the General Home Society and the City Mission Board in organizing and sustaining missions in Chicago, thus helping to unitize this great work. In 1913 the Chicago auxiliaries raised and paid for their special work, $2,261.

For a number of years the National C. W. B. M. has paid $1,200 for mission work in Chicago.

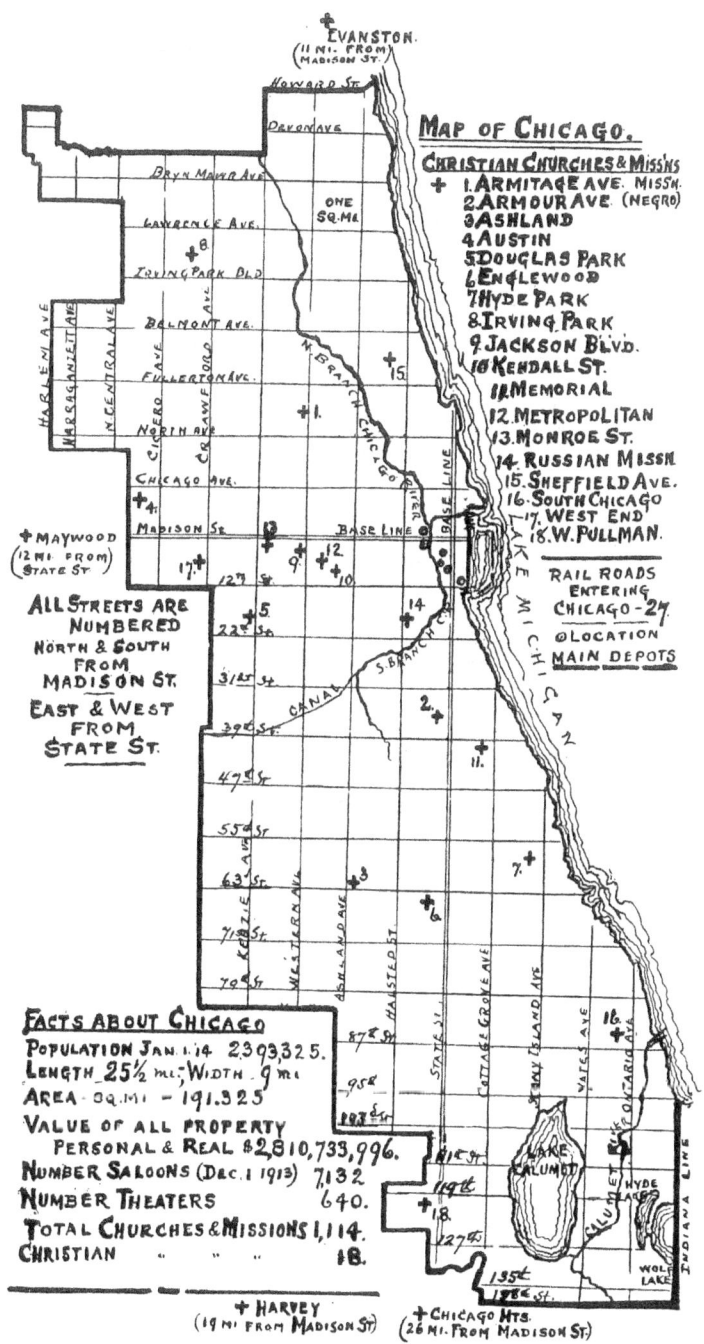

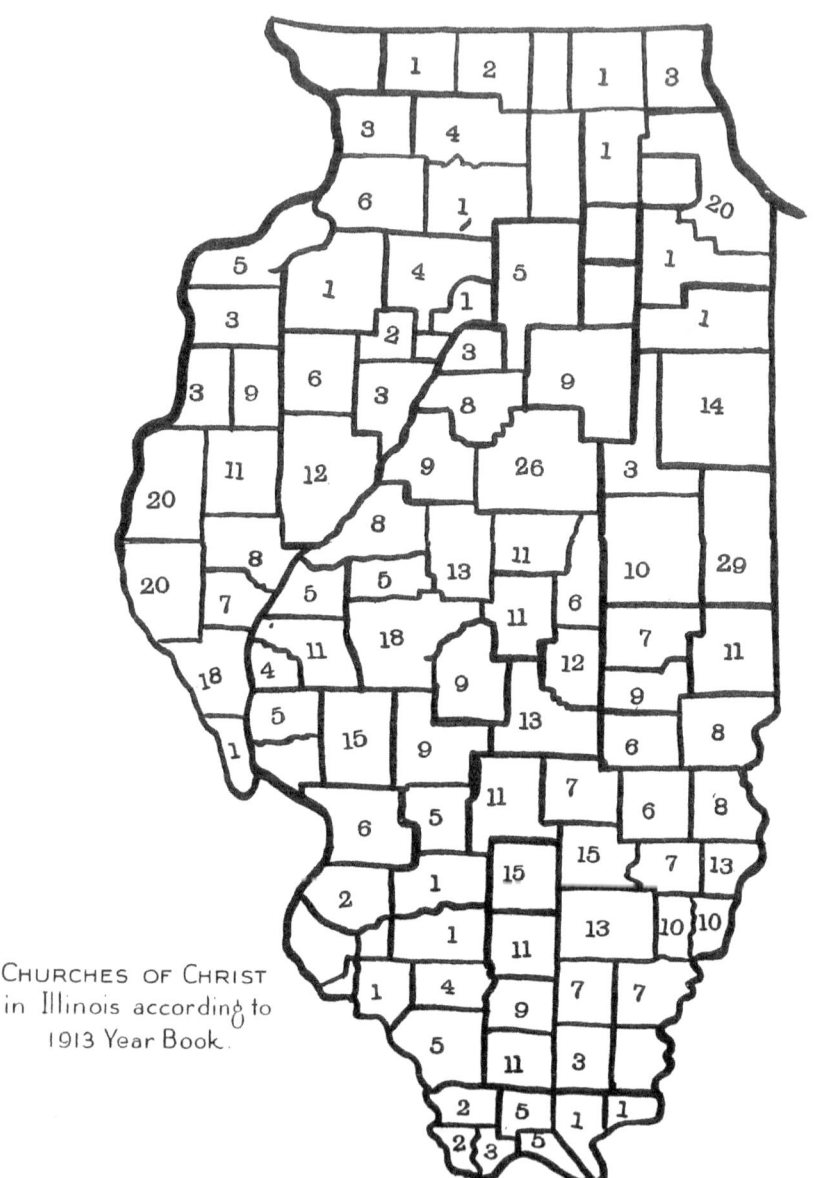

CHAPTER VI.

LOCAL CHURCHES AND SOME OF THEIR ORGANIZED ACTIVITIES.

SECTION 1.

The Churches.

ALEXANDER COUNTY.

The confluence of great rivers seems to impress people with a migratory disposition. The inclination is to move on. In addition to this, the southern extremity of the State has been subjected to the dangers and vicissitudes of great floods. Besides, those who laid out and lotted the town were actuated mainly by a selfish, mercenary spirit. The influences have combined to keep most of its denizens in a state of continual flux. So Disciples have come to Cairo and gone away through the decades.

Cairo First.

Organized 1866, by G. G. Mullins; present membership, 157; value of property, $20,000; Bible school began 1866; present enrollment, 93.

Mr. Mullins was a chaplain in the Federal Army. The Disciples in Cairo had occasional meetings before the Civil War. At the date of organization, so far as can be learned, the following were the charter members: Mr. and Mrs. S. R. Hay, Mr. and Mrs. A. B. Fenton, Mr. and Mrs. Prussia Morrison, Mr. and Mrs. McCauly, Mr. and Mrs. Trambo, J. C. Talbot, Robert Condiff, Mrs. Mary E. Clark, Mrs. White, Mrs. Brown, Mrs. Gilkey, Mrs. Henderson, Mrs. Seely, Mr. and Mrs. Layton, Miss Gilkey, Miss Smith and Mrs. Wilson. S. R. Hay and A. B. Fenton were chosen as elders and J. C. Talbot and Robert Condiff, deacons.

Meetings for public worship were held in the courthouse

until the county clerk turned them out. The erection of a building on Eighteenth Street, between Washington and Walnut, was then begun. Lack of funds delayed its completion for two years, but occasional meetings were held meanwhile therein, seated with planks held on boxes and blocks. In 1867 a successful union Sunday school was held in the courthouse until the county clerk turned it into the street. This houseless school hastened the finishing of the chapel on Eighteenth Street. It was completed in 1868. In 1894 this chapel was moved to the corner of Sixteenth and Poplar Streets. These lots were filled up by the ladies' aid society. The building was repaired in 1901. During its entire life the school has had struggles, occasional successes with frequent failures and not a few discouragements. Always there has been "a remnant according to the election of grace." S. R. Hay, A. B. Fenton, G. M. Alden and J. C. Talbot deserve to be held in grateful remembrance for their sacrifices and faithfulness.

More than forty ministers have served the church. Some of the earlier were Peter Vogel, T. W. Caskey, B. F. Manire, J. C. Mason, David Walk, Alfred Flower and Clark Braden, whose term was particularly helpful. The present building was erected during the pastorate of Frank Thompson. Alden R. Wallace is now the pastor.

Cairo Second.

Organized 1908; present membership, 51; value of property, $300; Bible-school enrollment, 82.

In June, 1908, forty-four members of the First Church signed a paper in which they expressed the belief that the time had come to establish a church of Christ north of Twenty-eighth Street, and thereby agreed to unite in this aim. Officers were elected. The meetings for public worship have been held in a public hall and a store building. The preaching has been done mainly by transient preachers. Floods from the great rivers have very seriously handicapped the work of the churches here.

CHURCHES

ADAMS COUNTY.

Antioch (Golden).

Organized 1843; present membership, 36; value of property, $1,000; Bible school began 1877; present enrollment, 76.

This congregation was formed as the Big Neck Church of Christ, April 16. There were six charter members; namely, H. A. Cyrus, A. R. Hagerty, Joseph, Nancy and Margaret Craig and Mary Ann Thompson. A reorganization was made in 1870 by Min. William Grissom, from which time it has been called Antioch. The first church house was built in 1877, which served till 1913, when a more suitable structure was occupied. It is five miles south and one west of Bowen.

Camp Point.

Organized 1865, by Joseph Lowe; present membership, 458; value of property, including parsonage, $19,000; Bible school began 1866; present enrollment, 337.

Organized in a near-by schoolhouse. Built first house in 1866; the second is a modern structure and was finished in 1912, during the pastorate of W. J. Reynolds, who served this church ten years.

There were thirty-five charter members, among them Joseph Lowe, R. H. Routh, J. W. Miller and Dr. S. G. Moore, who were the elders, and T. G. Odell and G. M. Hess, deacons.

The men given to the ministry were Walter Kline, Ivan Omer and Frank S. Booth.

Clayton.

Present membership, 187; value of property, $6,000; Bible-school enrollment, 102.

Coatsburg.

Present membership, 35; value of property, $2,000; Bible-school enrollment, 50.

Columbus.

Organized 1844; present membership, 151; value of property, $2,500; Bible school began 1881; present membership, 150.
There were no records before 1857.
The church has given Fred Meadows and James A. Seaton to the ministry.

Fowler.

Organized 1861, by Dr. William Hatch; present membership, 36; value of property, including parsonage, $2,900; Bible school began 1896; present enrollment, 33.
The church does good work.

Kellerville.

Present membership, 54; value of property, $1,000.

Liberty.

Organized 1852, by Ziby Brown; present membership, 177; value of property, $3,000; Bible school began 1862; present enrollment, 72.
This congregation grew out of a series of meetings conducted by Min. Ziby Brown, in which he very successfully met the opposition of Romanists and other sectarians. The charter members were Jacob and Anna Connor, E. B., Solomon and Jane M. Rhodes, George Pond, George Benfield, James R. and Elizabeth Howerton, Phœbe A. Vanderlip, Levi and Phœbe Traver, Lovena C. Grubb, Rosena and Elizabeth Vanderlip, Lydia and Rebecca Benfield, Hannah Meacham, James and Margaret J. Dunlap, Nancy A. Malone, Jason and Mrs. Barnard; Ira, Susanah, Samuel, Rebecca and Elizabeth Kimmons; Elizabeth Hunsaker, Susanah and Mary E. Titus, Eliza Malone, and Erastus and Euphrazina Rice. The organization was made in the brick schoolhouse. Min. Elijah L. Craig presided.

CHURCHES

Immediately following the formation of the church, Mr. Bond, an M. E. minister, challenged Mr. Brown for a public discussion. He was accommodated. Later the M. E. Church disappeared from that village. More than twenty ministers have served the congregation. The first house of worship was built in 1853 and the second was occupied in 1907.

Lima.

Organized 1830, by John B. Curl; present membership, 110; value of property, $1,200; Bible school began 1898; present enrollment, 51.

Loraine.

Organized 1892, by S. S. Jones; present membership, 310; value of property, $12,000; Bible school began 1892; present enrollment, 191.

There were 120 charter members. Fifteen pastors have served the church. The first building was erected in 1892. This gave place to a modern structure in 1908.

Marcellene.

Organized 1879; present membership, 50; value of property, $3,000; Bible school began 1879; present enrollment, 72.

Mill Creek (Mendon).

Present membership, 25; value of property, $1,000; Bible-school enrollment, 20.

Mound Prairie (Beverly).

Present membership, 90; value of property, $1,500; Bible-school enrollment, 30.

Mount Hebron (Mendon).

Present membership, 30; value of property, $2,000; Bible-school enrollment, 20.

Payson.

Organized 1868, by J. H. Hughes; present membership, 125; value of property, including parsonage, $4,600; Bible school began 1866.

The church has given Louis Cupp, O. W. Lamonte and O. W. Lawrence to the ministry.

Pleasant View (Camp Point).

Organized 1835, by David Hobbs; present membership, 83; value of property, $3,000; Bible-school enrollment, 65.

The location is three miles southeast of Camp Point. Some say the church was organized by John Ambrose, but the more probable name is given. Among the charter members there were John Ambrose, Nancy Foster, David, Charlotte, Nicholas and Elizabeth Hobbs, Rodney and Rhoda Burnham, Daniel and Lucy Walker. Meetings were held in the residences and schoolhouse till 1848, when a chapel was built. The first pastor was T. J. Matlock, who served in 1849. The church has done good work through its seventy-eight years. It has given to the ministry Elmer, William and Joseph Lowe and R. A. Omer.

Quincy First.

Present membership, 530; value of property, $25,000; Bible-school enrollment, 400.

Min. Livy Hatchett, of Warren County, visited Quincy in 1840. There and then he met Jacob Creath, of Missouri, who addressed the citizens with great ability. Though none made the good confession, some united with us who were formerly Baptists—the wife of Governor Carlin and a Sister Turner. Evidently the church was formed before 1840. In 1844 Mr. Creath reported that his meetings in Quincy had been much disturbed by military maneuvers connected with the Mormon riots at Nauvoo. Min. Patrick Murphy became the first pastor in 1850, when there were only twenty members. Shortly thereafter the chapel of the M. E. Church

South was bought. It stood on Fourth Street, between Jersey and York Streets. This was used until the present building on Broadway and Ninth Streets was erected. Following Mr. Murphy, the church was served by Mins. Simms, D. R. Howe, J. H. McCollough, H. D. Clark, J. T. Toof, F. N. Calvin and others. Governor Carlin was a member here.

Quincy (East End).

Present membership, 71; value of property, $2,500; Bible-school enrollment, 141.

This mission has been fostered by the State Society.

Richfield (Plainville).

Present membership, 20; value of property, $1,500; Bible-school enrollment, 20.

Ursa.

Organized 1833, by Jesse Bowles; present membership, 152; value of property, $5,000; Bible school began 1840; present enrollment, 159.

This was organized as the Bear Creek Christian Church. The local name was changed in 1840. The charter members were Jesse Bowles and wife; Stephen A. Ruddle, wife and daughter; Sarah Crawford, Miss Stephenson, and the Misses Lyttle and Elizabeth Stone.

The pioneer preachers were Stephen Ruddle, Jesse Bowles, John Clark and Levi Hatchet. Mr. Ruddle was born in Bourbon County, Ky., in 1768. He did missionary work among the Indians. Came from Missouri to Adams County in 1829.

Wolf Ridge (Camp Point).

Organized 1892, by John Parrick; present membership, 40; value of property, $1,000; Bible school began 1892; present enrollment, 50.

Of late years the church has paid a little for missions.

Charles A. Cate was a farmer-preacher of this county who

did faithful service for many years. He was born in New Hampshire and died in Adams County in 1908.

John B. Curl was also an active evangelist in the early thirties. His labors were earnest and reached a wide territory.

BOND COUNTY.

Greenville.

Organized 1878, by J. Carroll Stark; present membership, 300; value of property, $4,500; Bible school began 1878; present enrollment, 250.

Isaac N. Enloe was instrumental in having Mr. Stark hold the series of meetings that resulted in the formation of this church.

Among the leading members there are W. H. Dawdy, Cicero J. Lindly, E. E. Wise, C. E. Davidson, E. W. Miller and H. C. Mable.

The two preachers produced were Jesse E. Stone a Talmage DeFreese.

The church is healthy and prosperous.

Mulberry Grove.

Organized 1864, by John A. Williams; present membership, 200; value of property, $3,200; Bible school began 1864; present enrollment, 144.

The charter members were A. J. Morgan and wife, Andrew Steel and wife, A. J. Leigh and wife, C. T. Smith and wife, Hiram Bixby and wife, and Mrs. Barnes.

The German Baptists and United Baptists owned a chapel jointly here. The trustees bought out one party in the spring of 1865 and the other party a year afterward. By 1900 the house was old and poorly located, so then a better location was purchased and a modern chapel built thereon.

Mr. Williams served the church several years. Twelve or more pastors have followed him. The congregation has half-time preaching. There are seven elders, six deacons and five trustees. Evert Elam is clerk.

Smithboro.

Present membership, 30; value of property, $2,000; Bible-school enrollment, 35.

Tamalco.

Present membership, 99; value of property, $800; Bible-school enrollment, 79.

Woburn.

Organized 1859, by John A. Williams; present membership, 50; value of property, $2,000; Bible-school enrollment, 56.

This was the first church in Bond County that was Christian only. In 1859 Jonathan Skates, with his wife and his wife's sister, Mrs. E. M. Lemert—all members of the church of Christ—came from Ohio and settled in this locality. Mrs. Lemert was a woman of fine intelligence and Christian devotion. These, with other Disciples, arranged for monthly meetings in the schoolhouse. In the fall Mr. Williams held a revival and constituted the church.

A chapel was built soon. In 1906 this gave place to a new and better house.

There was a hard pull to pay for the first chapel because of the determined opposition of denominational neighbors. Not a church that opposed in that time has now either place or name in the community.

The first officers were Henry Allen, elder; Jonathan Skates and D. V. Tabor, deacons.

BROWN COUNTY.

Cooperstown.

Organized 1881, by T. W. Cottingham; present membership, 103; value of property, $1,000; Bible school began 1881; present enrollment, 81.

Before this date Mins. A. P. Stewart, Cottingham, Patterson and Stanley had preached here. Like all village churches, this has lost many by the continual change of people. However, this one is still vigorous.

Hazel Dell (Mt. Sterling).

Organized 1870, by Minister Robison; present membership, 70; value of property, $600; Bible school began 1870; present enrollment, 89.

The location is two miles east of Mt. Sterling, on the Ripley road. The chapel was built the same year. The work has been regularly and faithfully maintained, although subject to constant changes in the community. Among the leaders in the earlier days were George Kendrick, Lemuel Coppage, John Dennis and Lewis C. Perry. Mr. Perry was the efficient superintendent of the Bible school for many years.

Mt. Sterling.

Organized 1838, by John Taylor; present membership, 383; value of property, $10,000; Bible-school enrollment, 300.

The first preachers of the Christian Church came to Brown County as early as 1836, and began their work among the scattered pioneer settlers in the vicinity of Mt. Sterling. They were strong, rugged men, deeply rooted in the gospel, and staunch advocates of the Restoration movement. Among these were John B. Curl, Alexander Reynolds, Thomas Brockman, Barton W. Stone, John Rigdon, Jacob Creath, James Ross, W. P. Bowles, Pardee Butler (of Kansas fame), Robert Foster, with an occasional sermon by Alexander Campbell.

John Price, a well-to-do farmer residing two miles east of Mt. Sterling, was one of the first to identify himself with the new movement. He became the most active servant of the Lord. Meetings for preaching, prayer and communion were held in his home, and others in the village in an old blacksmith and wagon shop and next in the courthouse. The first chapel was built in 1853 and still stands on the original site. The city owns it.

The next preachers were D. P. Henderson, J. S. Sweeney

and John Taylor, the latter of whom for many years was the resident minister of the church. He was a man of modest mien and limited education, but had large native ability both as a preacher and leader of men. His long and faithful service gave permanency to this church and introduced the gospel into other communities. Evangelist W. H. Brown also helped the church much.

The pastorate of J. F. Stewart was especially fruitful in both spiritual and material results. On lots that were given to the congregation by him and George F. Tebo the present building was finished in 1887. This was enlarged and reconstructed during the pastorate of Mr. Lorton.

The church is well organized and carrying on aggressive work under Mr. L. G. Huff's capable leading.

New Salem (Mt. Sterling).

Organized 1875, by J. T. Smith; Bible school began 1875.

Four miles north of Mt. Sterling, at the Bell Schoolhouse, a congregation of about fifty members was formed. Among them were some excellent families. Meetings were held regularly on the Lord's Days. In 1877 a chapel was built nearer town, which is known as above written. The pastors at Mt. Sterling have usually served this congregation.

Ripley.

Organized 1842, by John Taylor; present membership, 72; value of property, $4,000; Bible-school enrollment, 112.

For many years Alpheus Brown, a pioneer preacher, resided here and cared for this congregation. During this period it grew steadily and came to have near three hundred members, who controlled the bulk of the wealth in the village and community. Later the church was divided by the Seventh-day Advents and has never regained its power and influence. Ministers Taylor and Brown were the chief factors in its growth. Associated with them as active servants of God there were P. A. Hows, Marion Stout, Nancy Tebo, W. A. Clark, John Adams, L. D. Stoffer, S. Glen, Mrs. Hawkins and Mrs. Hardin. Some of its later preachers were J. S. Sweeney, Mr. Price, J. T. Smith, C. H. Patterson, A. P. Stewart and Mr. Stanley.

A modern house of worship was built in 1904. J. D. Williams is the present pastor.

Timewell.

Organized 1868, by P. D. Vermillion; present membership, 194; value of property, $12,000; Bible school began 1868; present enrollment, 210.

The former name of this town was Mound Station. Previous to 1868 there were some scattered Disciples of Christ in the community, among them Mr. Laughlin, the Coopers, Webb, Oliver Ausmus and other good men.

A strong congregation was organized and a good house built.

The ministers who served the church were Wm. Gressom, Mr. McPherson, D. R. Lucas, T. W. Cottingham, A. P. Stewart, T. M. Weaver and E. J. Lampton.

Two public discussions were held in this house. In 1878, A. P. Stewart met Minister Yates, of the Missionary Baptists. In 1879, D. R. Lucas met Minister Thompson, of the Regular Baptists.

This is a strong church. Pastor W. A. Taylor led in the erection of the present fine structure.

Versailles.

Organized 1869, by W. S. Henry; value of property, including parsonage, $5,300.

Mr. Henry was one of the first elders and A. G. Lucas the first minister. The growth in numbers was slow. In 1874 the frame of a new church building was swept away by a storm. Renewed determination soon rebuilt it. In its earlier years George F. Adams and A. P. Stewart held successful meetings, when some of the most influential people of the community were included in its membership. This church has done good work.

During Mr. Bassett's pastorate A. P. Cobb led in a great meeting.

A new and modern building was erected in 1907 during the pastorate of R. S. Campbell.

The church is doing aggressive work.

BUREAU COUNTY.

The Ross brothers (John, Joseph and Andrew) came from Tuscarawas County, O., and settled in Ohio Township in 1845. Shortly thereafter they organized a church of Christ and built a chapel in their neighborhood. This did good service till 1872, when the place of meeting was changed to Ohio, a town that grew on the railroad three miles north. There the congregation also did good work. But its members moved away, Romanists and infidels came, so that for years the Christian Church has had no regular meetings. The chapel still stands there.

About 1845, Min. Geo. G. McManis organized a church of Christ at Leepertown, which served the community for forty-three years, then it passed away by emigration. It was the first of its faith in the county.

About 1850, J. F. M. Parker, assisted by John Wherry and G. G. McManis, organized at Boyd's Grove the Milo Church. It served its community well for many years, but it is now feeble. The Southerland family was prominent.

Later the Lone Tree Church was formed seven miles southeast of Boyd's Grove, probably by G. G. McManis. Emigration carried it away.

Cragy Sharp, a Scotch Disciple, settled near Lamoille and gathered together a small band there in the schoolhouse. Two of his sons became preachers.

The work at Malden was begun by Elijah Isaacs and John and Andrew Ross. The congregation met in the Forristal Schoolhouse, three miles north of Dover. The Carpenter brothers were reared in this neighborhood, one of whom became president of Oskaloosa College and chancellor of Drake University, both in Iowa.

Neither of the last two named congregations built a church house.

What the name McManis meant to the southern part of this county, Ross meant to the northern part.

New Bedford.

Organized 1866, by Geo. W. Mapes; present membership, 130; value of property, including parsonage, $4,500; Bible school began 1866; present enrollment, 125.

John and Andrew Ross were the pioneer preachers here. There were twenty-two charter members, among whom were Jacob Sells, J. H. Symonds, Levi Baldwin, Henry Thomas and Mrs. Thomas Gibson. At first the church met bitter opposition from its religious neighbors. It became weak, and the chapel that was built in 1869 was sold. In 1887 the congregation was reorganized by Min. G. W. Black, under the auspices of the Ohio Church. Since then it has done excellent work.

Princeton.

Organized 1840, by John G. Yearnshaw; present membership, 282; value of property, including parsonage, $14,500; Bible-school enrollment, 219.

The charter members were James W. Howe, John, Catherine and Daniel R. Howe, John and Eliza Ireland, Daniel Bryant, Clark and Mary Bennett, Rachel and Juliet Radcliff, Elmura Elston, Sarah Minier, Mary Hays, Margaret McElwain and John G. Yearnshaw. Mr. Yearnshaw was chosen bishop, Mr. Bennett, deacon, and Mary Bennett, deaconess, on March 8. The next October four persons were added by conversion under the preaching of G. P. Young. Meetings were held in an upper room until 1846, when a brick house was completed through much toil and sacrifice. Min. G. G. McManis, who had come there in 1844, and his sons went into the woods and cut the timber that was used in the building. It stood until 1870, when the present house was built.

The church has had a varied history. The names of

Mathew Trimble and his son, Wm. C. and Geo. G. McManis, Dr. G. W. Taylor and D. R. Howe are cherished. J. G. Waggoner was twice its pastor. Its present officers are well qualified. C. C. Carpenter is the minister.

Walnut.

Organized 1882, by R. B. Brown; present membership, 242; value of property, $6,000; Bible school began 1882; present enrollment, 147.

Andrew Ross preached the first sermon in the Red Oak log schoolhouse, about three miles from the site of Walnut. A little later G. W. Mapes preached there and the observance of the Lord's Supper was begun. Mr. Brown was assisted in the organization at Walnut by S. S. Jones. Prominently connected with this prosperous church were, or are, Messrs. Brower, McNitt, Wolf, Culver, Kelly, Martin, Potter, Long, Shirk and Ross.

Yorktown (Tampico).

Organized 1891, by J. E. Pierce; present membership, 20; value of property, $2,500; Bible school began 1894; present enrollment, 48.

Mrs. C. C. Babcock held a series of meetings in Woodman Hall in September. She ordained J. E. Pierce, who formed the church with six members. The chapel was built in 1894. With varying fortune it continued till 1899. In that year it supported an evangelist in forming a congregation at Tampico, in Whiteside County, to which it gave thirty of its members. Since then it has gradually declined by removals. It did good work. F. C. Thackaberry is correspondent.

CALHOUN COUNTY.

Bay (Mozier).

Organized 1897, by J. M. Bovee; present membership, 60; value of property, $800; Bible school began 1900; present enrollment, 75.

This congregation was the result of a meeting conducted by Mr. Bovee in the West Panther Creek Schoolhouse. The use of an organ and the beginning of a Sunday school led to a division of the church. Those withdrawing put up a chapel within a stone's-throw of the other house. Then they challenged Mr. Bovee to publicly debate the "organ question." He complied.

Farmers' Ridge (Nebo).

Organized 1856, by J. W. Greer and James Burbridge; present membership, 123; Bible-school enrollment, 100.

George and Richard Williams are preachers here.

Indian Creek (Hamburg).

Present membership, 60.

A small, ultra-conservative congregation, with little influence for good.

CARROLL COUNTY.

Lanark.

Organized 1843, by Garner Moffett; present membership, 122; value of property, $10,000; Bible-school enrollment, 120.

Cherry Grove was five miles northeast of the site of Lanark. Into this place Garner Moffett, David Tripp, William Renner, Thomas and Abraham Moffett, with their families, came in 1840, and a little later David Miller, Emanuel Stover, William Hawk and the McCoy family. Some of these were from Virginia and others from Ohio. Min. Henry Howe preached in this settlement at that time, as did also J. M. Yearnshaw. After the church was formed, it authorized Garner Moffett and David Tripp to preach. Residences and schoolhouses were used for public worship till 1858, when a chapel was built at Stovertown. When the railway was built in 1861, Lanark was started and the chapel moved there. In 1879 a new house was built. This gave place to the present elegant structure in 1907. From the first the church has had many representative people and has done good service. This congregation has given to the ministry Robert and Frank L. Moffett, Wm. B. Clemner and F. A. Sword.

Savanna.

Organized 1904, by C. C. Carpenter; present membership, 25; value of property, $700; Bible school began 1904; present enrollment, 55.

There were thirty-one charter members. Adverse conditions and removals have handicapped the church from its beginning. It owns a lot, but the meetings are held in a hall. A C. E., L. A. society and teacher-training class are maintained. Mrs. C. Gridley is clerk.

Thomson.

Organized 1852, by John Yeager; present membership, 100; value of property, including parsonage, $4,000; Bible-school enrollment, 105.

In 1852, Min. Garner Moffett, of Cherry Grove, established a mission at the Argo Schoolhouse, then called Hague. Soon after, Minister Yeager organized the Johnson Creek Church, with the following charter members: Henry Atherton and wife, Luke Atherton, Cephas Atherton and wife, Thomas Art and wife, Robert Art and wife, Ebon Balcom, Mrs. James Carroll, Mrs. Robert Carroll, Mrs. Alonzo Fuller, Henry Knigh, Amos Shoemaker and wife, and Mrs. Charles Thomalson. Cephas Atherton was the last of these to pass on. He died in 1910. Robert Art was the first elder, and Amos Shoemaker and Thomas Art the first deacons. After Ministers Yeager and Moffett, C. W. Sherwood served the church one-fourth time as pastor for $100 per year. His sermons averaged one hour and thirty minutes. About 1860 the Baptists built a chapel at Bluffville, which was rented for one-fourth time. The district missionary meeting was held here with 130 delegates present. At that time a chapel became a necessity; work on a railway had commenced, so it was built at

Thomson. The rock was quarried by the members and much of the other labor donated by them. J. N. Smith was then the minister. The women of the congregation paid off the indebtedness before the dedication. By reason of its financial weakness the church in its earlier years took L. B. Myers from a real-estate office, G. W. Pearl from a marble-cutter's shop, and C. C. Blakesley from music-teaching, and made good preachers of them. The Thomson Church is proud of three things: they have never had a quarrel, never had a mortgage on their property, and have always paid their ministers every dollar promised. Mrs. C. C. Babcock rendered the congregation fine services as pastor.

CASS COUNTY.

Ashland.

Organized 1892, by G. W. Pearl; present membership, 100; value of property, $3,000; Bible school began 1892; present enrollment, 126.

A former congregation in this town had failed. This one was organized by State Evangelist Pearl. Its pastors have not all been the most worthy.

Beardstown.

Organized 1910, by Chas. W. Ross; present membership, 137; value of property, $5,000; Bible school began 1910; present enrollment, 250.

In the years long since gone, there was a congregation of Christians only here, but even memory of it has faded away.

The present church came from a six weeks' meeting, led by District Evangelist Ross, assisted for a time by Miss Alice Hornbeck, State Bible-school evangelist. First, Mr. Ross made a canvass of the town, visiting 982 homes personally. He found about one hundred persons who had been Disciples, and a ladies' aid society. The meeting followed. Mr. Ross reported 1,220 calls while on the field, challenges to debate and opportunities to side-track in controversies, but the faithful preaching of the gospel in love resulted in a congregation of ninety-seven members.

At first the old chapel of the German Methodists was leased and then purchased in 1911.

Chandlerville.

Organized 1865, by Dr. D. W. Shurtleff; present membership, 199; value of property, including parsonage, $12,500; Bible school began 1865; present enrollment, 180.

In the early sixties, Dr. D. W. Shurtleff preached in the Buck and Pleasant Ridge Schoolhouses, located a few miles east of the town. In 1864 the place of meeting was changed to the village schoolhouse, and Min. John A. Raines ministered to the people there. The chapel was built in 1867, and the present fine structure was finished in 1913 during the pastorate of B. O. Aylesworth.

The church owes much to Dr. N. H. Boone for his help in its first period. After four years of spiritual gloom, Min. H. C. Littleton began to revive the church in 1904. Since then, led by good men, it has moved forward. Dr. H. B. Boone has been Bible-school superintendent for sixteen years.

Philadelphia.

Organized 1837, by Samuel Brockman; present membership, 20; value of property, $1,500; Bible-school enrollment, 25.

In 1850, Princeton, Cass County, was a village of two hundred inhabitants and a good business. Its location was about midway between Virginia and Petersburg. With the coming of railroads, the town disappeared and its site is now farmed. There was a Christian chapel in that Princeton in 1838. Minister Brockman was the first man who preached the primitive gospel in that community and probably formed the congregation. Alexander Campbell preached there one time. John Sybrant, a resident of Jacksonville, and now ninety years of age, became a member of this congregation in 1845. He says that Minister Patton and D. Pat Henderson, both then residents of Jacksonville, were then preaching there; that the elders then were James Conover, Martin Hoagland and Dr. Andrew Elder, and the deacons were Isaac Redding, John Conover and John C. Dennis; that William Black moved there in that year and was shortly made an elder; that Samuel T. Callaway thereafter preached for the church seven years; that a new house of worship was built in 1849 by Joseph Black; that in June a public discussion was held in this chapel between W. W. Happy and Minister Lewis, an M. E. preacher; that E. G. Rice came to the neighborhood, bought the James Conover farm, was chosen an elder and preached for the church; that Eleazer Griffin was their next preacher, but became a schismatic and was dismissed from the church; that in 1866 this church held a meeting in the Garner neighborhood, J. B. McCorkle preaching; that in November, 1866, Minister McCorkle and Dr. J. M. Allen conducted a series of meetings in a wood-shop in Philadelphia, and that the Princeton Church was reorganized there with Charles Elder and John Sybrant, elders, with Ripley Elder and Joseph Black, deacons. The chapel at Princeton was torn down, transferred to Philadelphia and rebuilt there by Joseph Black. It was dedicated in June, 1867, by Min. A. J. Kane, who was then serving the church.

This church formed congregations at Jordonville and Ashland, and gave to the ministry Charles Dean, Charles Elder and Ripley Elder.

It has lost heavily by removals. Abram Bailey, Henry Shafer, Frank Cosner, Mrs. Ruth Harding and Mrs. W. D. Watkins are among the faithful few who remain. Pastor C. E. French, of Virginia, is serving them as he can.

John Sybrant is a beautiful soul who waits in the vestibule of eternity for his glorification.

Virginia.

Organized 1839, by Wm. H. Brown; present membership, 160; value of property, including parsonage, $17,000; Bible school began 1855; present enrollment, 160.

Among the charter members there were probably the following: Mr. and Mrs. Alexander Naylor, Mr. and Mrs. Charles Brady, Mr. and Mrs. John Mosely and Mr. and Mrs. Thomas Mosely. Mr. Naylor was the elder of the church.

It was not till 1843 that Evangelist Brown conducted a great revival in the old courthouse. He was assisted by A. J. Kane and Samuel Church. At this meeting Henry S. Savage, Sr., and Miss Sarah Frances Ward united with the church. Miss Ward became the wife of Mr. Savage. Thereafter she became widely and well known for many Christian works and noble character. Her father and mother, Jacob and Eliza Ward, came into the church at the same time. It was he who gave the lot upon which the first house of worship was built. This was in 1853. It was at the northwest corner of Beardstown and Pitt Streets and was used till 1879. During this period the preaching was intermittent. Robert Foster, John Taft, George Owens, Harrison Osborn, A. H. Rice, J. A. Rains and Samuel Lowe were there, and others who held "big meetings." About 1875 the Black family moved into the city and ever since have added much to the strength of the church.

J. L. Richardson became the first pastor in 1878. In the fall of that year the second church building was finished. It stood at the southwest corner of Beardstown and Cass Streets on a lot one-half of which was given by Mrs. Sarah F. Savage. This building was struck by lightning and burned in 1897. J. D. Dabney was the pastor. He was succeeded by G. F. Shields, who led in the construction of the new building. During the period of the second building, Jas. McGuire, N. E. Cory, Minister Sewell and J. J. Cathcart were pastors.

In the winter of 1888-89, Evangelist W. F. Black held a seven weeks' meeting here which was an event in the life of the church. After this, B. J. Radford supplied the pulpit and pastors succeeded.

The church is active in Christian service.

CHAMPAIGN COUNTY.

The general history of this county says:

"Cyrus Strong, an early settler on the Salt Fork, was a licentiate of the Disciples of Christ. He was the first minister whose name appears upon the marriage records of the county as officiating at a marriage early in the history of the neighborhood. He exercised his gifts in behalf of a religious life.

"Samuel Mapes, a resident of Hickory Grove, of the same denomination, preached at different places in the county and was instrumental in the organization of a church at the schoolhouse in his neighborhood.

"These were the earliest churches of this denomination and its earliest ministers."

Champaign.

Organized 1883, by N. S. Haynes; present membership, 975; value of property, $70,000; Bible school began 1883; present enrollment, 836.

The official records of the State Missionary Society show that this church was constituted by State Evangelist N. S. Haynes. After about two months of intermittent efforts, he gave place to Min. E. L. Frazier, who formed the Bible school and prayer-meeting. He moved to Champaign, but resigned the care of the mission after a short service on the ground that "permanent results promised to be more tardy than he thought he ought to wait for." The care of the mission then went to Min. A. N. Page. He resided in Champaign for about eight years. In 1884, Mr. Page began to give much time to the mission. He bought a cheap lot on White Street, solicited money in Champaign and other counties and practically built the chapel. Then he preached for the congregation till the close of 1885. Some of the pastors who have served the church were B. N. Anderson, S. S. Jones and E. C. Stark.

For the past ten years S. E. Fisher has been pastor, and

FIRST CHRISTIAN, SPRINGFIELD.
FIRST CHRISTIAN, CHARLESTON.
UNIVERSITY CHURCH OF CHRIST, CHAMPAIGN.
CHRISTIAN, MACOMB.

in this period the church has made gratifying growth. Mr. F. B. Vennum moved to the city in 1899 and shortly thereafter bought and gave to the church a much better site. Mr. F. K. Robeson seconded the work of Mr. Vennum and they interested Mr. T. A. Bondurant, of DeLand. A substantial building grew during the pastorate of Jay W. Knight. This was much enlarged and improved in 1910.

During the past decade, more than two thousand members have been enrolled. The church is located at the seat of the University of Illinois and is alive to its opportunities and responsibilities.

Fisher.

Organized 1885, by H. C. Castle; present membership, 236; value of property, including parsonage, $6,500; Bible school began 1885; present enrollment, 222.

This church was the result of a series of meetings conducted by Evangelist H. C. Castle in the U. B. chapel. The congregation occupied their house of worship in 1886, which was remodeled in 1907. J. F. Hollingsworth is in his fifth year as pastor.

Gifford.

Organized 1880, by John M. Smith; present membership, 60; value of property, $1,800; Bible school began 1880; present enrollment, 75.

Meetings were held in the schoolhouse. The church building was finished in 1892.

Homer.

Organized 1856, by Dr. T. M. Hess; present membership, 107; value of property, $3,000; Bible school began 1856; present enrollment, 62.

There were eleven charter members. There was a union chapel in Old Homer, but when it was moved to the new site the legal title passed to the M. E. Church. Dr. Hess built a hall in the new town which was used for public worship. The present house was built about 1875.

132 HISTORY OF THE DISCIPLES IN ILLINOIS

L. R. Conkrite has been given to the ministry and a number of the sisters have married preachers.

Longview.

A feeble congregation with an intermittent life.

Ludlow.

Organized 1869, by R. M. Martin; present membership, 183; value of property, $5,000; Bible school began 1869; present enrollment, 91.

The first records of this church are yet available. The charter members were: J. D. Ludlow, William A. Haley, J. W. Dillon and wife, S. S. Proctor and wife, W. M. Cloyd and wife, W. S. Collier and wife, John Crawford, T. J. Johnson, G. W. Crose and wife, R. G. Braden and wife, Eliza J. Gregg, Belle Neville, Clista W. Dillon, Liddie Braden, Mary A. Dillon, Cassie R. Gregg, A. P. Cloyd and wife, Davis Dillon, J. H. Crawford, C. H. Beach, W. L. Braden, Viola Culbertson, Emily White, and three others whose names are not legible.

The first house of worship, costing $3,000, was completed in 1871 during the pastorate of R. B. Roberts. While J. H. Hollingworth was pastor the building was fully modernized and made beautiful in 1907.

Ira J. Walker served the church through fifteen consecutive years as janitor and organist, free of charge.

Ogden.

Organized 1871; present membership, 60; value of property, $1,000; Bible school began 1871; present enrollment, 50.

Dr. T. M. Hess held the first meetings here about 1860 in an old schoolhouse. In 1872 a church-house was completed. Before the organization of this church the Disciples residing here held membership in the church at Homer. By reason of internal strife, the church disbanded in the early eighties. Through the leading of Mr. B. F. Firebaugh, assisted by Min. L. C. Warren, a reorganization was effected in April, 1886. The old records were lost.

The church has given Walter Martin to the ministry. By the help of Min. S. E. Fisher, a Y. P. S. C. E. was formed in 1908, which is now supporting a native missionary on the Congo.

Rantoul.

Organized 1892, by S. S. Jones and J. S. Clements; present membership, 278; value of property, including parsonage, $12,200; Bible school began 1893; present enrollment, 102.

Meetings were held in public halls till November, 1893, when the chapel was occupied. This received an addition and improvements in 1907.

Before the beginning of this church there was a congregation near the site of Rantoul called Bethany. It served its time and place. Many of its members moved to the town. The building was torn down and the available material used in the construction of the Rantoul chapel.

Sidney.

Organized 1856, by W. P. Shockey; present membership, 68; value of property, $3,500; Bible school began 1870; present enrollment, 80.

The church first met in a building which the Baptists had converted from a dwelling into a chapel. The next year a church was built. All the lumber used in it, except the sills, was hauled on wagons from Indiana. In 1901 a new frame building of modern architecture and construction was erected.

The old records of the church were destroyed.

Some of the other preachers who have served the church were Dr. T. M. Hess, J. W. Monser, Rolla and John Martin and Noah Walker.

St. Joseph.

Organized 1845, by Samuel Mapes; present membership, 237; value of property, including parsonage, $14,500; Bible school began 1845; present enrollment, 84.

As early as 1845 Samuel Mapes came and located in Hickory Grove, five miles northeast of St. Joseph, and began preaching in that and adjoining settlements. This congregation prospered for many years under the ministry of Mr. Mapes, Rolla M. Martin, Mr. McKinney, W. F. Yates and Dr. T. M. Hess.

When the railway was built, the new town of St. Joseph was started. Here meetings were first held in the schoolhouse. Dr. Hess preached for five years and the congregation increased in numbers. Then the M. E. people built a house of worship which the Disciples rented for part time and used for a year. Then they built a chapel of their own in 1880. In this work Mr. Van B. Swearinger, who had come to the community at an early day, was the leading spirit.

During the four years' ministry of J. W. Perkins the church grew. After him came Harmon Gregg, S. S. Jones, E E. Cowperthwaite, J. H. Hosteller, J. Lytle, D. H. Shanklin, M. Metzler, D. H. Palmer and J. T. Davis. Following the pastorate of Mr. Jones, a schism in the church occurred. This was encouraged and led by a former minister, J. W. Perkins. A suit at law followed, which resulted in according the property to those opposed to Mr. Perkins. Two years after this an organ was placed in the church and used.

There are others whose memory should be kept in the church.

In the early years Benny and Alex. Argo were most faithful. Two sisters in the flesh and in the Lord did much to help teach people of their Christian duties. They were familiarly known as Aunt Kit Patterson and Aunt Pop Peters. Aunt Kit was a cripple for many years. She was always at church. When it was dark or rainy she carried a lantern. She was well endowed in mind, had good speaking ability and was prompted by a strong desire to teach people Christ's gospel. She could quote much of the Scripture from memory. Aunt Pop read the Bible through thirty-two times.

During the five years' pastorate of Mr. Davis a new and

modern church building, costing $12,000, was erected. It was first used June, 1909.

There is also a congregation of conservatives here.

CHRISTIAN COUNTY.

Assumption.

Organized 1874, by J. M. Morgan; present membership, 120; value of property, $1,500; Bible school began 1874; present enrollment, 45.

In 1870, Minister Morgan conducted a series of meetings in the Baptist chapel. Several people turned to the Lord. Four years later the organization was effected with twenty-five charter members. The building was erected in 1875.

Berea (Mt. Auburn).

Organized 1868, by John W. Tyler; present membership, 100; value of property, $2,500; Bible school began 1869; present enrollment, 60.

Mr. Tyler held a very successful meeting in the Sanders Schoolhouse, winning sixty-eight persons for the Lord, and organized the church with one hundred members. The first officers were James Sanders and Benjamin Cross, elders, with Wm. Pierson, John M. Abel and Oliver White, deacons. A good frame chapel was built in 1869. The location is beautiful—a high bluff on the south side of the Sangamon River. A cemetery has grown in the rear of the chapel. Mr. Tyler and Dr. L. A. Engle served the congregation for about twenty-five years.

"Uncle Jim Sanders" was a unique character in the community in the early years.

Edinburg.

Organized 1856, by A. D. Northcutt; present membership, 299; value of property, including parsonage, $5,500; Bible-school enrollment, 150.

Meetings were held in the schoolhouse till 1872, when a

frame building costing about $1,800 was erected. This was struck by a cyclone in 1875, which picked up the structure down to the floor and carried it about ten rods. At the time the children were in the house, assembled about the organ and organist, practicing for a religious program. They were all uninjured. The house was immediately rebuilt. It was remodeled in 1901 and is still in use.

A. O. Hargis and Homer Turner have been given to the ministry.

In place of a Christian Endeavor there is a Kulture Klub of thirty young people for Bible study. Active C. W. B. M.

Morganville (Blue Mound).

Organized 1891, by J. O. Southerland; present membership, 100; value of property, $2,000; Bible school began 1891; present enrollment, 56.

In this year there were living five and a half miles northwest of Blue Mound the following named seven Disciples: D. O. Daniels and wife, C. C. Hollier and wife, John Scott, Mrs. Maggie McKinnie and John Hall. Through their effort Min. J. O. Southerland held a series of meetings in the Sycamore Schoolhouse. He baptized forty-two people and organized the Christian Church at Morganville, Christian Co., Ill., with forty-seven members. In August, 1892, a good frame chapel was finished and occupied. At present the elders are T. D. Scott and Elmer Ellis; the deacons, Moses Morgan, Henry Gimnura, David Abel and Bert Wilcox.

Mt. Auburn.

Organized 1840, by A. D. Northcutt; present membership, 200; value of property, including parsonage, $3,500; Bible-school enrollment, 107.

In December, 1836, A. D. Northcutt bought a farm near the site of the village of Osbornville, where Charles L. Osborne now resides. Mr. Northcutt was then a member of the Baptist Church, which was then very Calvinistic. He first disagreed with his Baptist minister because he debarred other church people from a communion service. The date was probably about 1840. The noted Walter P. Bowles was at that meeting, which was held in a Presbyterian chapel about a mile east of Osbornville site. At the close of this meeting, Messrs. Northcutt and Bowles laid hold of such puncheons as they could carry, left the church and went to a near-by grove. The people went along.

Mr. Bowles mounted a stump and preached to them. Thereafter Mr. Northcutt said to his Baptist minister: "I am now done with the Baptist Church." It was not long until Mr. Northcutt and his wife, William Hunter and wife, James Hunter and wife, and James Sanders, formed themselves into a church of Christ. This was the beginning of the Mt. Auburn congregation. These people began at once to meet regularly on the first day of the week for public worship. It fell to Mr. Northcutt to lead and preside at the Lord's table. He had no thought whatever of becoming a minister. However, he soon showed his reverence for the Scripture and his aptness to teach.

The little church grew and he was formally set apart to the ministry. The meetings were held in the Brush Schoolhouse. Mins. John W. Tyler, John Wilson and Mattie Brown preached here. Mr. Tyler once preached once a month for a year. His money pay was $60. When no other preacher was present, Mr. Northcutt officiated. Next the congregation changed its place of meeting to the Hunter Schoolhouse, some three miles northeast of Mt. Auburn, and in 1866 moved into the village. A chapel was built the same year. Later it was improved, and is yet in use.

The work went on till 1875. Then the congregation fell to pieces. For a period of twelve years the house was opened only for funerals—a solemn reminder of deplorable spiritual death. In 1889, Min. M. L. Anthony held a series of meetings and revived the congregation. Since then it has moved forward in a faithful effort to redeem the past.

During the years of depression, Charles T. Cole was always faithful and hopeful. With his the name of Ira Ellis deserves to be remembered. In late years there is a goodly number of earnest men and women, among them John W. Auger.

Pana.

Organized 1905; present membership, 60; value of property, $2,300; Bible-school enrollment, 21.

A small congregation lived here in the seventies and eighties, but failed from a lack of leadership.

Pleasant Hill (Pawnee).

Present membership, 138; value of property, $2,000; Bible-school enrollment, 25.

Taylorville.

Organized 1853, by A. D. Northcutt; present membership, 410; value of property, including parsonage, $30,000; Bible school began 1879; present enrollment, 250.

There were thirty-five charter members. Wm. Singer, B. F. Maupin and J. W. Thompson were chosen elders, with A. J. Sparks and Griffin Evans, deacons.

The Cumberland Presbyterian Church was used for about a year, when a frame chapel was built. It cost $2,500, and at that time was the best in the county. The membership then was about 150. Later an internal strife disorganized the congregation and scattered its members every whither. In 1879, after a year of hard work, Min. S. R. Wilson succeeded in effecting a reorganization with thirty-three members. Wm. Frampton, R. P. Langley and W. N. Long were elected elders, with A. S. Thomas, Morgan Milligan and Joseph Torrence, deacons. Later, L. R. Hedrick was added to the eldership, where he served to the close of his life in 1894. To him the church was and is yet indebted.

The present edifice, "The Davis Memorial Christian Church," was the gift of Mr. and Mrs. Henry Davis, they furnishing most of the money for its construction. It was built during the pastorate of W. W. Weedon.

Among the ministers of the first period of the church, besides Mr. Northcutt, there were Alex. McCollum, Wm. M. Brown, Wm. Vanhooser, John L. Wilson, Thomas Cully, J. W. Tyler and W. T. Maupin.

Mrs. Cordelia Davis Hoover and Mrs. Sarah Davis Deterding were daughters of Mr. and Mrs. Henry Davis. These women were both faithful to the Lord and his work when the church was weak and when it was stronger. Their names are held in tender and loving remembrance. Mrs. Deterding's daughter, Mrs. Maude Deterding Ferris, was the founder of the Missionary Training School at Indianapolis, Ind., giving $25,000 toward this enterprise. At first it bore her mother's name. Mrs. Ferris now supports a missionary in India, Dr. Rosa Lee Oxer, and helps many good causes.

The two auxiliary societies of this church unite in the support of a teacher in the school at Hazel Green, Ky., paying $450 a year.

The New Liberty Church, located three miles southwest of Moweaqua, was organized by A. D. Northcutt in 1853. There were ten charter members. From 1859 to 1875 the congregation reached a membership of four hundred and was a power in the community. Decline marked the years until the formation of the church in Moweaqua, when it absorbed many of its members. In 1902 an ineffective attempt was made for its revival.

CLARK COUNTY.

This is the only county in the State in which no one could be induced to supply the writer with the necessary facts. The primitive gospel was first preached here about 1833 by Daniel W. Elledge. About 1836 he organized the first church. It was located three miles west of Dalson Prairie, and was named the Blue Grass Christian Church. Later he helped build a chapel there. The Darwin Church was organized in this county in 1840 by Min. John Bailey. It was located in the south part of Union Township. There were fifty charter members. A Bible school was begun there in 1873, with John Miller as superintendent. In 1913, there were eight congregations reported in the county, with a total membership of 615. Most of the leaders have been men of very circumscribed vision.

CLAY COUNTY.

Bethel (Louisville).

Organized 1882; present membership, 224; value of property, $1,000; Bible-school enrollment, 103.

This is six miles west from Louisville and was largely made up from Old Union, five miles west.

Bethlehem (Flora).

Present membership, 24; value of property, $1,100; Bible-school enrollment, 95.

Bible Grove.

Present membership, 139; value of property, $800; Bible-school enrollment, 57.

Clay City.

Organized 1871, by Geo. P. Slade; present membership, 88; value of property, including parsonage, $6,200; Bible school began 1872; present enrollment, 100.

About one year after Greenburg Owens settled in Clay City, he secured Evangelist Slade to conduct a meeting there, when, in the small M. E. chapel South, he formed a church of Christ with the following members: William, O. D. and Philadelphia Schooley, Greenburg and Martha Owens, Geo. W. Bailey, Josephine Driskell, Catherine Livings and Sarah A. Bassett. By meetings led by Ministers Slade and John A. Williams, the number was increased to 105 at the close of the first year. The first officers were Greenburg Owens, J. G. Alcorn and J. T. Evans, elders, with O. D. Schooley, A. G. Livings and J. D. Trains, deacons.

A brick chapel was completed in 1872 and first used for a prayer-meeting by the congregation. A parsonage was secured in 1880.

This is a congregation of fine people. While not rich in material property, they have never resorted to anything of doubtful propriety to raise money. They have respected and loved their pastors, paid all their bills promptly, commanded the respect of the community, and have always observed all the missionary days, even though they had no pastor.

The membership has been busy in doing the Lord's work, united and happy. Very few have ever had a tale of woe to tell the pastor. This admirable spirit is credited to Mr. Owens and their other good leaders. Sixty of the first 105 have passed on to the higher life. Mr. Owens was the first to go. Dr. J. T. Evans has long been a pillar of this church.

Flora.

Organized 1855, by William Schooley; present membership, 328; value of property, including parsonage, $16,000; Bible-school enrollment, 218.

This church was organized in an old log schoolhouse that stood a mile west of the hamlet of Flora. The following were the nine charter members: Walter Kinnaman, Henry Kinnaman and wife, Samuel Kinnaman and wife, Felin Poe and wife and James Moore and wife. All of these have finished their work in this life.

When a schoolhouse was built in the village, the congregation transferred its meeting-place there. The first chapel was completed in 1860. It cost $2,000, and served as the meeting-place for forty-three years. The present beautiful and modern building was first occupied in August, 1903, during the pastorate of A. B. Cunningham. During the same period the parsonage was built.

C. W. Marlow is the present pastor.

This congregation has had not a few royal men and women, great children of the King. Among the earlier and continuous residents the names of Wm. Kinnaman, Henry

Kinnaman and wife, Joseph Luse and wife, Alvin Kenner and wife, Jere. Billings and wife, R. B. Henry and wife, S. D. Rosenburger and wife and Albert Green and wife are held in loving and grateful remembrance. From its gates have gone hundreds of faithful people to help and bless the world.

Ingraham.

Organized 1839, by William Read; value of property, $5,000; Bible school began 1864.

In 1840 the place now known as Ingraham was called the "Forks of Muddy." Muddy was on the west and Laws Creek on the east, and between the two was Ingraham Prairie. Marysville was the little hamlet there. When the post-office was established the name was changed to Ingraham, the word "Prairie" being dropped.

William Ingraham was born in New York State in 1801. He came with his parents to Barney's Prairie, Wabash County, in 1807, and to the Clay County settlement in 1838. The same year William Read settled there. In May, 1839, he, with Mr. Ingraham, went to the home of John Rogers to talk about religious matters. They were agriculturists and had taken no part in public worship other than to pray. However, they decided that the gospel must be preached and a church organized; so it was agreed that Mr. Read should serve as evangelist, Mr. Rogers as elder and Mr. Ingraham as deacon. Then they adjourned to meet the next September. Later Mr. Rogers and Mr. Ingraham cordially exchanged their official positions as their experiences had proved their fitness. At the September meeting, Mr. Read read the following:

> That we do here and now constitute ourselves into a church of Jesus Christ, to be known as "The Church of Christ in the Forks of Muddy," and that we will meet together, worship God, and build the cause of Christ in this section, and that our creed shall be the Bible and nothing but the Bible. And now all who agree to this proposition will signify the same by giving me and to each other the hand as a token of said determination.

The three men struck hands, and thus, under a pear-tree, this church was started.

Soon afterward Philo Ingraham and Eli Read moved from Wabash County, who, with their wives and the wives of the first three, made a membership of ten. They entered zealously into the Lord's work, and within a few years had organized congregations of like faith in the present-day limits of Clay, Jasper and Effingham Counties.

Within two years some Methodist brethren moved into the settlement. Soon the theological battle was on, and for a long time was both brave and bitter.

This church developed a sturdy stock of men and women, such as make the abiding world and build the Kingdom of God.

The Ingrahams, Reads, Lollars and Pixleys blessed their generation. The preachers produced were remarkable men. William Ingraham was the true overseer of this church for forty years. Dorman, Daniel and Williard F. Ingraham, William Read the evangelist, Jesse B. Shaddle (who gave over four years to his country's service), G. M. and F. M. Lollar, Gideon Bryan, Albert Meacham and Thomas Wood make up an honorable company.

From a very early date the church observed its annual meetings, which were occasions of great interest and rejoicing. The Bible school was organized by David Hedrick, a Moravian. Later, in the State of Washington, he united with the church of Christ.

The community was intensely loyal during the Civil War.

It is a significant fact that this congregation did not come to the weekly observance of the Lord's Supper till 1874.

There have been three chapels. The first was built of logs in 1848; the second of brick in 1853. Major Waller, of the M. E. Church, preached in this house once every month for a year. The third—a frame—was built in 1872. The Methodist brethren had the free use of this house also. Few congregations have a record that surpassed that of the Ingraham Church.

Liberty Chapel (Flora).

Organized 1911, by C. W. Marlow; present membership, 22.

This church is located five miles southwest of Flora. It grew out of the desire of a few members of the Oak Mound congregation for a more convenient place to worship. They joined with the United Brethren people in the community in building a chapel, which was deeded to them, but used jointly. A union Bible school was maintained. The Disciples increased in the community and the U. B. people decreased, so a legal transfer of the property was made in 1911, Min. C. W. Marlow leading.

The Bible school is up to date and a training-class doing good work.

Louisville.

Present membership, 82; value of property, $1,800; Bible-school enrollment, 45.

McKinney (Sailor Springs).

Organized 1871; present membership, 96; Bible-school enrollment, 85.

This church is located on Levitt Prairie, and was first known by that name. A debate was held in the neighborhood schoolhouse in 1869 which awakened the community. There were twenty-five charter members, some of whom came from the Cooper congregation a few miles west, and others from the Slab chapel a few miles east. The chapel was built in 1871. The first elders were Daniel Reed and Joel Wammack. The church has given to the ministry W. E. Harlow and William Crackel. It is a country church that persists in living by working.

New Bethlehem.

This is five miles northeast of Flora.

CHURCHES

North Harter (Flora).

Organized 1905, by E. S. Thompson; present membership, 140; value of property, $1,350; Bible school began 1905; present enrollment, 100.

This church is located five miles northeast of Flora. It started with eighty-four members, some coming from surrounding congregations. Mr. Thompson was the efficient minister for five years. R. L. Brown followed, and A. R. Tucker is the present preacher. Walter Cox led to graduation fifteen persons in Moninger's "Training for Service." Jas. L. McDaniels is the efficient church clerk.

Oak Mound (Xenia).

Present membership, 98; value of property, $700; Bible-school enrollment, 57.

This is four miles north of Xenia. It was recruited from Old Union. Here most of the young people are church-members.

Old Union (Xenia).

Present membership, 60; Bible-school enrollment, 50.
This is eleven miles west of Louisville.

Red Brush (Louisville).

Present membership, 31; value of property, $1,500; Bible-school enrollment, 80.

Sailor Springs.

Present membership, 80; value of property, $1,800; Bible-school enrollment, 65.

Union Chapel (Louisville).

Present membership, 71; value of property, $1,200; Bible-school enrollment, 47.

Xenia.

Organized 1865, by John D. Williams; present membership, 45; value of property, $1,500; Bible-school enrollment, 58.

The first officers were Gillum Henson and John Dunn, elders; Hiram Gibson and Jackson Barker, deacons. The congregation prospered and did good service in its earlier years. Then a period of wars, led by ultra-conservatives, set in and crippled its usefulness for a long time. At present there are some signs of better days.

CLINTON COUNTY.

Keyesport.

Present membership, 100; value of property, $2,500; Bible-school enrollment, 50.

COLES COUNTY.

Brick (Westfield).

Present membership, 90; value of property, $2,000; Bible-school enrollment, 180.

This church is located about twelve miles southeast of Charleston. It is under the direction of the ultra-conservatives and has monthly preaching.

Bushton.

Organized 1873, by W. F. Black; present membership, 200; value of property, $8,000; Bible school began 1873; present enrollment, 87.

This church grew out of a meeting by Evangelist Black. The town grew after the building of the railroad. The first house of worship was built in 1874, which gave place in 1911 to a modern structure during the pastorate of A. P. Cobb. This church is made up chiefly of substantial farmers who are growing in spiritual interests.

Charleston.

Organized 1840, by Samuel Pepper and Thomas Goodman; present membership, 1,150; value of property, including parsonage, $23,500; Bible school began 1854; present enrollment, 471.

Messrs. Pepper and Goodman were Christian ministers. The former had come from Kentucky and the latter was then residing in Indiana. They came to Charleston, where they united in preaching the primitive gospel and organizing the church of Christ. There were twelve charter members. Of these, the names of James Wiley and wife, Stephen Wiley and wife and Susan Dunbar are now known.

"The town branch" was the place used for baptizing in those years.

They met regularly on the Lord's Days for worship. The first meetings were held in a storeroom where Bushrod W. Henry, with other pioneers, preached. From 1842-46 they met in the courthouse. Then a small red-brick chapel was built on Madison Street, between Ninth and Tenth. This was sold to the Romanists in 1860, when a second brick building was constructed at the corner of Sixth and Van Buren Streets. This was sold to the Episcopalians. The present modern stone edifice was erected in 1905 during the pastorate of J. M. Vawter.

A second and successful attempt was made to organize a Sunday school by Susan Dunbar and Leroy Wiley in 1854.

In 1856, Alexander Campbell spent a Lord's Day with the church.

In the years agone the Wrights, Mintons, Dr. Spears and Dr. Van Meter were prominent and useful families; later, Geo. M. Sefton. All have passed on.

The church has had a line of excellent pastors.

Miss Edna Eck has gone out as a missionary and is serving at Bolenge, Africa.

Charleston is the location of one of the State Normal Schools and the church is awake to its opportunities.

Etna.

Present membership, 65; value of property, $1,000; Bible-school enrollment, 57.

Humbolt.

Organized 1858, by Thomas Goodman; present membership, 161; value of property, $1,500; Bible school began 1897; present enrollment, 92.

The organization was made with seven members in a schoolhouse east of town. Later a frame chapel was built, but not completed. During the sixties and seventies, J. W. Connor, Sr., with his family, resided in the community. He, with his sons—James, Samuel and Americus—preached at times for the church. With their removal the congregation declined. It was revived by Evangelist J. S. Clements in 1897 and began work with thirty-eight members. Mr. and Mrs. E. M. Mullikin were the prime movers in this revival of the church and are yet its leading force.

The church has had, in later years, ten ministers.

Mattoon.

Organized 1859, by J. C. Mathes; present membership, 903; value of property, $18,000; Bible school began 1862; present enrollment, 530.

In its early years, N. S. Bastian, J. R. Lucas, E. L. Frazier, J. M. Streator, G. F. Adams and R. B. Roberts served as pastors.

Oakland.

Present membership, 70; value of property, $2,000; Bible-school enrollment, 79.

Prairie Union (Kansas).

Organized 1868, by John Callcord; present membership, 26; value of property, $1,500; Bible school began 1868; present enrollment, 47.

This congregation is located about five miles northwest

of Kansas. It was formed in the neighborhood schoolhouse, but a frame chapel was soon built, which is still in use. Its beginning was the wish of farmers and landowners of the neighborhood to have a more convenient place for their public worship. They held membership in the church at Kansas; so, without conference or formal dismission, but in perfectly good feeling, they withdrew and began to keep house nearer their homes. Such was the spirit of ultra-independence in those years. The congregation maintains preaching one-half time and a small Bible school.

It has given Daniel K. Honn to the ministry.

Rural Retreat (Hindsboro).

Organized 1857, by W. F. Black; present membership, 86; value of property, $1,000; Bible school began 1857; present enrollment, 100.

This congregation was formed in the Wells', later known as the Wyeth, Schoolhouse, located one and a half miles south of the church site. The chapel was built in 1867 and is located four miles southwest of Hindsboro. It had the services of about twenty-five ministers. Although depleted by many removals and death, it has kept up its public worship regularly. From it the churches at Bushton and Hindsboro have drawn goodly numbers.

Its most prominent, capable and noted member was Miss Helen E. Turner, who became Mrs. Helen E. Moses, who was baptized here.

Walnut Grove (Humboldt).

Organized 1887, by James Steele and David Cotman; present membership, 12; value of property, $1,000; Bible school began 1889.

This congregation is located about eight miles east and north of Humboldt. It was formed in the Honn Schoolhouse. The charter members were John D. Honn and wife, Joseph Honn and wife, A. A. Honn and wife, Isaac Honn and wife, George Toland and wife, A. C. Honn and wife, Robert

McAlister, Mrs. Rachel Caffer, William Newman, J. C. Toland and wife, Mrs. Mace Jones, her son H. B. and daughter Belle, Isaac W. Mace and wife, Mrs. Jessie Moler and her daughter Martha. The first elders were Robert McAlister, A. A. Honn, George Toland and Isaac W. Moler.

A chapel was built the same year.

Next, by changes in the community, the work failed for several years, but was revived in 1910.

Hitesville was a village three miles southwest of the site of Kansas in the early years. The location was beautiful. The church that grew and prospered there had many fine people. It became extinct in 1905.

Stringtown Church was about six miles south of Charleston. For many years it was active and useful, but finally yielded to the law of change. Frank Spitler was its last officer. He kept it going for years by his own efforts. He was a faithful member who went home in 1912.

COOK COUNTY.

Beginnings.

The Disciples of Christ in the United States have always been largely a rural people. It took them fifty years to learn how to do church work in the cities. But during this period they were learning many other things. Chief among these was the meaning and application of the basic principles of Christian truth that gave them birth and being.

In April, 1837, David Cory wrote from Athens, which was about thirty miles from Chicago, saying that he had found only about ten Disciples in the county, and he appealed for a preacher to come to them.

In 1843 some work was done in Chicago looking to the formation of a church wearing only the name "Christian" and appealing only to the word of God as the all-sufficient rule of faith and practice. A Minister Saunders, from Ohio, organized this mission. These people held the materialistic views of John Thomas. In September, 1846, M. H. Baldwin

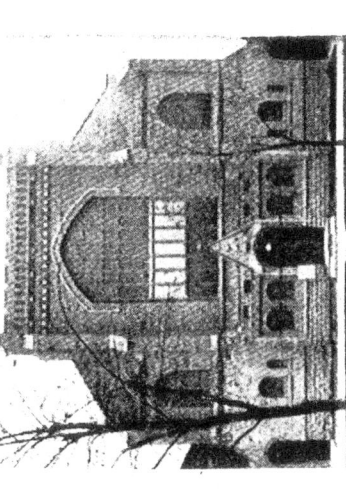

METROPOLITAN.
JACKSON BOULEVARD.

(CHICAGO CHURCHES.)

ENGLEWOOD.
MEMORIAL.

and wife, of Cleveland, O., united with this mission. Next year J. Reese and Miss Laura Balch, of Detroit, Mich., joined. In 1848, Platt Saunders and wife, from Marshall, Mich., and Dr. L. S. Major and wife, from Bloomington, Ill., united with the mission church. In 1849 materialism led to harmful discussions in the public worship; so Mr. L. C. P. Freer proposed separation from the more recently received members, who were called "Campbellites."

Early in 1850 the first church of the Restoration movement was formed in Chicago. The charter members were Dr. L. S. Major, Platt Saunders and wife, M. H. Baldwin and wife, J. Reese and Miss Laura Balch, who afterward became Mrs. Dickey. Lathrop Cooley, of Ohio, was the preacher. Mr. Baldwin was chosen elder, and Mr. Saunders, deacon. From that day to this the divinely appointed worship has been maintained by the Disciples there on every Lord's Day.

At that time the population was twenty-five thousand, and there was not a church building of any denomination better than a one-story, flat-roofed, square-front frame.

The first meetings were held in the residence of Mr. Baldwin, then in an upper room at the corner of Lake and Clark Streets, and next in the old city hall, and then in a schoolhouse in the center of the city. In the latter, M. N. Lord began his ministry.

The first addition to the church was a man named White. He had been converted while serving in the English Army and was a guard over Napoleon. In 1850, James Brenner and Dr. J. H. Millinger and wife united with the church. The first to make the good confession and be baptized were Mrs. D. M. Clark and Mrs. Ann Harris.

In 1852 the church raised $300, and Lathrop Cooley, of Cleveland, Ohio, served as pastor for a year or more. He was succeeded by M. N. Lord. In 1854, Love H. Jameson, of Indianapolis, Indiana, conducted a three weeks' meeting in the city hall, with no additions. This much disappointed and discouraged the church.

In 1857 a frame chapel was started on West Monroe, near Rucker Street, which was finished and dedicated by D. P. Henderson, July 4, 1858. This property was never fully paid for. But in the meantime a considerable number withdrew from the church on mere differences of opinion, and the meetings were held in the old federal courtroom.

In the new chapel, Min. W. H. Hopson held a four weeks' meeting which brought, among others, to the church Mrs. M. D. Raggio, for many years one of the most devoted Christians in the city.

In 1861, Mr. Lord again resigned, after a pastorate of eight years. He, with others, had served earnestly and well, but the lack of spiritual vision had been such during the decade that the church numbered only 120 members. During the Civil War the church was served by N. S. Bastian, W. F. Black and J. S. Sweeney. During the occupancy of this chapel, among its members there were A. M. Atkinson, Ben Davenport, Mr. and Mrs. Henry Honore, Mrs. Abigail Keeler, Dr. and Mrs. Lichtenberger, Mrs. E. B. Stevens, Dr. and Mrs. Warriner and their daughter Belle.

For a short time the congregation met in a room of the old Crosby Opera-house and then transferred to the North Side. The old St. James Episcopal Church at Cass and Illinois Streets was rented. Dr. W. A. Belding, Benj. H. Smith and D. P. Henderson preached here. It was during that time that Ira J. Chase and W. B. Hendryx were ordained to the ministry, and W. B. Craig was baptized there. In 1868, through the influence of Dr. Belding, Mr. H. H. Honore and Dr. L. S. Major paid $5,000 each to a church-building fund. The chapel and lot on the South Side, at Sixteenth Street and Wabash Avenue, were bought and paid for. The congregation moved into it. D. P. Henderson, Isaac Errett and J. S. Sweeney were the ministers, Mr. Sweeney continuing till 1871. In 1869 the church divided. The forty who withdrew, led by D. P. Henderson, formed a congregation and met first in the chapel of the Orphan Asylum on Michigan Avenue, south of Twenty-second

Street. Mr. E. B. Stevens gave this congregation the lot at the corner of Indiana Avenue and Twenty-fifth Street. On this a two-story frame building was erected and used. It was never fully paid for, and twenty years later was lost under mortgage. O. A. Burgess succeeded Mr. Henderson. The great fire, Oct. 9, 1871, reunited the two congregations, and the worship was at the Twenty-fifth Street place. It was known as the First Christian Church. The congregation was served by Knowles Shaw, T. J. Toof, W. J. Howe, S. M. Connor and Isaac Errett. For a few years Potter Palmer and wife were members here. The Disciples in Chicago during those years were prolific in differences and dissensions; so, about 1878, this congregation again divided. At the Sunday morning meeting when the question of separation was discussed and decided, Timothy Coop, a highly esteemed English brother, was present and expressed his surprise and distress of mind. The fifty members who withdrew rented of the Congregationalists their chapel at South Park Avenue and Thirty-third Street. W. D. Owen was pastor there. About twenty-five years afterward he was expatriated. In a year the congregation moved to the old Memorial Baptist chapel on Oakwood Boulevard near Cottage Grove Avenue. Irving A. Searles, J. L. Parsons and Barton W. Johnson preached there. Late in 1880 the congregation moved to Thirtieth Street and Prairie Avenue, renting the brick chapel that stood there. In October, J. W. Allen began a two years' pastorate. In September, 1882, the two churches united. They had increased numerically little, if any, during the period of separation. Meanwhile the First Church was served by Geo. W. Sweeney and O. A. Burgess. The reunited church was known as the Central Church of Christ, and the place of worship was the Prairie Avenue chapel. In December, 1885, Henry Schell Lobingier came to the pastorate, and the next year the church returned to the building at Twenty-fifth Street. Following Mr. Lobingier's resignation, Z. T. Sweeney and G. B. Berry supplied the pulpit, and then Calvin S. Blackwell was pastor for two and one-half years. In 1887 the Central Church began to erect a new house on Indiana Avenue near Thirty-seventh Street. It was used for some eighteen years, when it passel by the mortgage route. W. F. Black left the evangelistic field in 1890 and became pastor of this congregation. For some years it prospered. C. S. Medbury entered the Christian ministry from this church. When they no longer had a home, some of the members, with Mr. Black, met for worship in the Masonic Home, until increasing bodily disabilities ended his work and his life. Other members of the Central formed the First Church in 1899, which was united with the Memorial Baptist.

In all this migratory and painful pilgrimage of more than half a century not a few were found faithful and have gone to the heavenly rest; others deserted the Captain's flag in the days of battle.

Armitage Avenue Church.

This is a small congregation in the northwest part of the city.

Armour Avenue Christian Church (negro; 3621 Armour Avenue).

Organized 1888, by Wm. G. F. Reed; present membership, 150; value of property, $5,000; Bible-school enrollment, 40.

Minister Reed, with eight members, was the beginning. Through feebleness and lack of help, the effort failed and the property used for meetings at 2919 Dearborn Street was sold by the Chicago Missionary Society in 1893, and the proceeds used in buying another church home. Then for ten years the little band led a wandering and forlorn life. In 1903 Min. M. T. Brown came to the pastorate. The present property was then purchased and the congregation took on new life. F. C. Cothran served three years, when G. Calvin Campbell came in 1911. Under his leading the church prospers. The property is fully paid for, and there is a C. W. B. M. and a Y. P. S. C. E. Richard Mathews has been faithful through all these years.

There are about sixty thousand negroes in Chicago, and the thought of their redemption is distressing except to Christian faith.

Ashland Christian Church (Sixty-second and Laflin Streets).

Organized 1899, by J. F. Findley; present membership, 298; value of property, $6,000; Bible school began 1897; present enrollment, 220.

This church had its beginning in the heart's desire of a good Christian man. In May, 1897, W. K. McGregor formed an undenominational school and mission called "The Workingmen's Mission." It united Bible teaching with social features, providing a place where men tempted by saloon influences could meet for mutual helpfulness. This effort grew steadily through two years. Then came Min. J. F. Findley in an evangelistic meeting. There were about fifty charter members. Being compelled to move to Sixty-third Street, near Center Avenue, the life of the little church was thereby imperiled, but God led them into their own modest chapel in September, 1902.

Other than Mr. Findley, the church has been served by Guy Hoover, C. M. Sharp, Guy Hargot, W. R. Moffett and J. F. Futcher, who is now in his sixth year. In its earlier years it was fostered by the Chicago City Missionary Board. "Every phase of church work is active and growing. Over and over again have we proved in our individual lives that God's grace and tender love always have met our every human need."

Austin.

About 1893, Min. A. Larabee interested a few members of the Monroe Street Church in starting a mission in this growing and inviting suburb. Assisted by Pastor Strickland, of the Douglas Park Church, meetings were held on Sunday afternoons in vacant halls or empty storerooms. The work grew encouragingly. George A. Campbell became pastor, and moved to Austin in 1898. The chapel vacated by the Baptists was purchased in 1902. With a fixed home, the congregation prospered. In 1908 this building was destroyed by fire, and then the members were nomads. But a commanding lot was bought and a good building completed in 1910.

Among those who have given fine service here were Mr. and Mrs. L. S. Major, who were pioneers in the church in Chicago; Mr. and Mrs. W. O. Cline, Mr. and Mrs. H. A. Vandercook and family and Mrs. O. A. Kearney and sons.

Chicago Heights.

Present membership, 300; value of property, $30,000; Bible-school enrollment, 300.

The Englewood Church fostered this mission and helped it to self-support.

Douglas Park Church of Christ (Nineteenth Street and Spaulding Avenue).

Organized 1895, by E. W. Darst; present membership, 150; value of property, $12,000; Bible school began 1895; present enrollment, 200.

In the spring of 1894, Messrs. H. F. Layton and A. Larabee, with others, started a Sunday school on Ogden, near Kedzie Avenue. It was successful from its beginning. In May and June, City Evangelist E. W. Darst held a series of meetings. Members of the Jackson Boulevard Church assisted, and Christian ministers of the city. There were thirty charter members. G. W. Doolittle and E. W. Reynolds were elected deacons. Mr. Reynolds served also as the very efficient superintendent of the Sunday school. Trustees were also chosen. The pastors were C. B. Edson, Geo. A. Campbell, Mr. Infield, H. J. Underwood, John Williams and C. L. Wait, who served six years.

In the fall of 1899 the meetings went to a hall at 1812 W. Twenty-second Street, the next spring to a storeroom at

Ogden and St. Louis Avenues. During Mr. Campbell's pastorate lots were purchased on Turner Avenue, near Sixteenth Street, and on these a tabernacle was built, largely by the volunteer labor of the members, in October, 1901. In 1911 this property was sold to the Board of Education. Meanwhile, F. C. Aldinger, S. M. Schoonover, Mr. McBean, Harry F. Burns and Vaughn Dabney served as pastors. In October, 1911, the Douglas Park Congregational Church invited the church to meet with them for public worship in their church home. These union services were maintained until the following March, when this property was bought by the Douglas Park Church of Christ.

Englewood Church of Christ (Stewart Avenue and Sixty-sixth Place).

Organized 1885, by Henry Cogswell; present membership, 600; value of property, $55,000; Bible school began 1885; present enrollment, 600.

In a room on Sixty-third Street and Yale Avenue, September 20, ten adults from the Calkins, Palm and Caldwell families, led by Rollo Calkins, met and covenanted together and so formed this church. Soon after, Dr. Jonathan Pettit attached his name. Mr. Cogswell and Edward O. Sharp served as pastors till the close of 1886. During the next year, Dr. W. A. Belding served. He was a tireless servant of God and a fine leader. A lot was bought on the east side of Dickey Street, now Eggleston Avenue, south of Sixty-fourth Street, and a septagon chapel, costing $3,000, built thereon. By an addition made thereto in 1893, costing $3,500, the seating capacity was more than doubled. Its ugliness repelled all those whose carnal pride was stronger than their Christian faith. B. H. Hayden began a four years' fruitful ministry in January, 1888. During a part of this period the church was helped by appropriations from the State missionary treasury. N. S. Haynes followed in a six and two-thirds years' pastorate, during which the church made substantial progress. Then came E. A. Cantrell in a short ministry. C. G. Kindred became pastor in December, 1899, and continues to the present time. He is a man of great faith in Providence, and with him the church has gone forward to splendid achievements. In 1901 it paid its mortgage debt. In 1902 it became a living link in the Foreign Missionary Society, supporting one of its own daughters, Mrs. Lillian Chalman Shaw, in China. In 1904 it became a link in the Home Society, taking Chicago Heights as its mission point. By about this time the church had gathered $8,000 into a new-building fund. In 1905 it sold its property on Eggleston Avenue and moved into its new home on Stewart Avenue that it had bought from the Cumberland Presbyterians. It is a stone structure and cost, with the contiguous lot and residence on its north side, $21,500. In 1911 the church negotiated a loan of $6,000, mortgaging its own property, to assist the Chicago Heights congregation in the erection of its own fine edifice. An annex to the Englewood building for the use of the Bible school was finished in 1913. It is of brick, cost $18,000 and has twelve classrooms. The church and all of its departments are well officered and organized, and all do efficient service. The budget for 1911 showed $8,752 in disbursements, of which $2,419 went to general benevolences. And by Chicago standards there are no rich people in this church.

It has given to the ministry C. W. Dean, Clark W. Cummings and Charles J. Adams, with William Madison preparing for medical missionary. To write a few names here of the men and women who have under God made this record would be an injustice to many others. Not a few of them are the incarnation of cultured Christian conscience. The presence here of Joseph Badenoch, Sr., and his wife for a term of years was a benediction and of fragrant memories.

In prayerfulness and missionary zeal, in wise perspective and indomitable adherence to high aims, in liberality, hospitality and spiritual democracy, in forbearance and fraternity and all good works, the Englewood Church of Christ holds the first place among the Disciples of Christ in Illinois.

CHURCHES

Evanston Christian Church (Maple Avenue and Greenleaf Street).

Organized 1896, by W. B. Taylor and E. W. Darst; present membership, 135; value of property, $15,000; Bible school began 1896; present enrollment, 150.

The first meetings were conducted in the residence of Mr. M. O. Naramore on Sunday afternoons, beginning Nov. 2, 1895, by W. B. Taylor, then pastor of the North Side Church, Chicago. Jan. 5, 1896, City Evangelist E. W. Darst began an eleven weeks' series of meetings held in Union Hall.

Forty-two people turned to the Lord and thirty-four were received by letters and on statements, so there were seventy-six charter members. Among these were E. E. Starkey and wife, Dr. R. C. Knox and wife, J. W. Work and wife, and M. O. Naramore and wife.

Other ministers who have served this church were E. S. Ames, A. L. Chapman, W. C. Payne, E. V. Zollars, W. D. Ward, and now O. F. Jordan.

Harvey Christian Church (Turlington Avenue, between 153d and 154th Streets).

Organized 1892, by C. H. Knapp; present membership, 209; value of property, $15,000; Bible school began 1892; present enrollment, 234.

The charter members were Mr. and Mrs. G. R. and Miss Mary E. Kenyon, Mr. and Mrs. J. H. Joslyn, Mrs. Maggie Nichols, Mr. and Mrs. F. M. Masher, Mr. and Mrs. John Scoan, Mrs. Jessie Marr, Mrs. C. R. Palmer and Mrs. W. W. Wood.

Meetings were held in various places until 1905, when the present location was secured. The building was completed in 1906.

The pastors who served the church were J. M. McKay, J. S. Clements, W. W. Denham, F. D. Ferrall, T. A. Lindenmeyer, W. E. Orr, Robert Wilson, J. J. Higgs, S. G. Buckner, W. D. Enders, and for two years Asa McDaniel has been the faithful minister. The work grows and the outlook is encouraging.

Hyde Park Church of Disciples of Christ (Fifty-seventh Street and Lexington Avenue).

Organized 1894, by H. L. Willett; present membership, 200; value of property, $7,000; Bible school began 1894; present enrollment, 100.

Prof. W. D. MacClintock was also active in the formation of this church. Meetings were first held in the Masonic Hall on Fifty-seventh Street, east of Washington Avenue, and later in Rosalie Hall. Mr. Errett Gates succeeded Mr. Willett in the pastorate, and during this period the present chapel was built on the lots owned by the Disciples' Divinity House. E. S. Ames has served as pastor since 1900.

In this congregation "one of the most important features has been the adoption of a plan by which Christian union could be practically and effectively realized. This plan does not assume to change the terms of church membership as taught and practiced by the great body of Disciples. It simply recognizes 'members of the congregation' as well as of the church in the technical sense. This plan has been employed since 1903 with the happiest results. It has not caused the slightest friction here."

The church includes forceful people, and is active in many philanthropic and charitable agencies of the city. For a time it supported Mr. and Mrs. Guy Sarvis as missionaries in China. The congregation continues its $600 yearly to the Foreign Society.

Irving Park Church (North Forty-third Street and West Cullom Avenue).

Organized 1898, by E. W. Darst and A. Larabee; present membership, 240; value of property, $10,000; Bible school began 1898; present enrollment, 250.

In May, 1898, the City Missionary Society decided to

establish a church in this place, which is one of Chicago's most beautiful residence sections. Three fine lots were rented and a temporary structure built thereon. City Evangelist E. W. Darst, assisted by A. Larabee, conducted a six weeks' series of meetings. The formation of the church followed. George A. Ragan became the pastor in October following. The south wing of the permanent building was occupied the next month, which is now the Bible-school room. Marion Stevenson came to this pastorate in April, 1901. The main part of the building was occupied in October, 1903. Then came J. R. Ewers, W. F. Rothenberger, A. W. Taylor and C. C. Buckner, who is in the fourth year of his pastorate. During Mr. Taylor's term the Bible-school room was enlarged and fitted into a gymnasium. The building proper was finished and paid for after Mr. Buckner came. It is a frame without architectural beauty, but meets the present needs of the congregation.

The church is well organized and is aggressive. Its most valuable asset is a group of men and women who are growing in all Christian graces.

The Men's Club of this church was largely instrumental in forming the Federated Men's Club of Irving Park, the object of which is to promote and secure political and civic reforms.

Jackson Boulevard Church.

Organized 1873, by George G. Mullins; present membership, 800; value of property, $54,000; Bible school began 1873; present enrollment, 650.

This church was first known as the West Side Christian Church. There were about thirty-five original members. The meetings were first held for a few months in the Jefferson Park Presbyterian Church. Then it had a wandering life till 1878, when it rented fifty feet of ground on Western Avenue, near Congress Street, and placed thereon a frame chapel, which was purchased of the Church of God. Later the rented lots were bought and about $5,000 used in repairs on the building,

After Mr. Mullins, the pulpit was supplied by Knowles Shaw; A. J. White, pastor two years; A. J. Laughlin, one year; J. H. Wright, one year; F. M. Kirkham, and B. W. Johnson.

In 1877, through dissensions, the congregation divided. Those who went out formed the Oakley Avenue Church and built a brick chapel in 1878. They continued till 1895, when they united with the Garfield Park congregation.

J. W. Allen, in 1882, began a very successful pastorate of thirteen years. In 1891 the lots on Jackson Boulevard were bought and the basement of the present building constructed. This was used until 1901, when the edifice was finished during the second period of J. W. Allen's pastorate. Since then the congregation has worn its present local name. In 1895, J. H. O. Smith, and in 1898, Bruce Brown, each began pastorates of two to three years; Lloyd Darsie next served three years, and was followed by the brave and beloved Parker Stockdale, who fell on the front line of battle.

In September, 1901, this church and the "Union Christian Church," worshiping at the People's Institute, united, Roland A. Nichols becoming the pastor. Austin Hunter became pastor in 1910. The church is well officered and organized, and is active, harmonious and prosperous.

In 1911 property adjoining the church lots on the east was bought, and is used for social and other activities. It is known as "The Annex."

Of the charter members, three remain—Mrs. D. M. Clark, Mrs. Maggie Viete and Edwin Stewart, who has long been a faithful servant and officer.

Kendall Street Church (Kendall Street, near Polk Street).

Organized in 1865.

James Bremner, Joseph Badenoch and other worthy Scotchmen formed this congregation. They came from the old First Church while it met on the West Side. They have been ministered to only by their elders, but have given to the kingdom many worthy servants.

CHURCHES

Memorial Church of Christ (Oakwood Boulevard, near Cottage Grove Avenue).

Organized 1908; present membership, 600; value of property, $90,000; Bible-school enrollment, 270.

The Memorial Baptist Church was organized Oct. 19, 1881. It grew out of the University Place Baptist, which was formed Dec. 6, 1868. The young men who have gone out from this membership to preach the gospel are J. C. Chapin, C. A. Lemon, C. J. Price, W. P. Behan, Ph.D., C. A. Callup, Fred Merrifield and Mr. Ernest A. Clement, who made a name for himself in Japan.

The First Christian Church was organized in April, 1899. The Presbyterian Church at Wabash Avenue and Thirtieth Street was secured as a meeting-place. The pastors who served here were Frank G. Terrell, J. W. Allen, Guy Hoover and H. L. Willett, with R. L. Hondley and William C. Hull as assistants.

The Memorial Church of Christ (Baptist and Disciples) came into being June 17, 1908. The Memorial Baptist Church changed its name as above, and on June 19, 308 members of the First Church of Christ united with the Memorial Church of Christ (Baptist and Disciples). Mr. Willett served as pastor till January, 1913, and was succeeded by E. Le Roy Dakin.

All offerings for general benevolences are divided equally between the two bodies.

Metropolitan Church of Christ (Van Buren and Leavitt Streets).

Organized 1897, by J. H. O. Smith; present membership, 500; value of property, $100,000; Bible school began 1897; present enrollment, 300.

The great building known as the People's Institute was erected by a stock company as a center for civic righteousness. Finally the building was sold. The Union Christian Church was organized there July 15, 1897, at the request of the Chicago Christian Ministerial Association. There were 218 charter members. For four years Mr. Smith led this work successfully. Upon his withdrawal, Evangelist C. R. Scoville came to it. He, with W. B. Taylor, city missionary, and part of the membership, decided that it was better to reorganize the church and to change the name to the present one. This was done in January, 1902, with 107 members. Other members went to other congregations. In May, 1903, the Institute was rendered unfit for use by a fire, so the congregation passed that summer in a large tent. In August the church bought property, 116 x 125 feet, two blocks west, at Oakley and Van Buren Streets, for $30,000, which it still owns. A temporary building was erected on the inside lot, the other being covered with storerooms and flats. Meanwhile, the owner of the Institute property died and it was sold at sheriff's sale. The Metropolitan Church, led by Mr. Scoville, bought it for $35,000 cash. On both properties there is a total indebtedness of $40,000. This property, with repairs and an addition, had cost about $110,000. The great building has an auditorium, music-hall, storerooms on the ground floor, two lodge halls, music studios, nine doctors' offices, church library and reading-room, two clubrooms for boys, a gymnasium 45 x 80 feet (which at present is leased for the school work to the Board of Education), a ladies' exchange-room, kitchen, etc. The formal occupancy of this fine building took place in February, 1913, amid much rejoicing.

In all this work the resident pastor, John D. Hull, has been the capable and consecrated helper and leader.

The Metropolitan is well located, and its possibilities of great Christian service are limitless.

Monroe Street Church (corner Monroe and Francisco Streets).

Organized 1891; present membership, 140; value of property, $21,375; Bible school began 1887; present enrollment, 73.

A mission Sunday school was formed and fostered by the Western Avenue Church, and out of this school this congregation grew. C. F. Saunders, J. H. Trunkey, C. M. Mershon, J. H. Norton and Virgil Fry were prominent in this work. J. W. Ingram was the first pastor. The first house of worship, costing $3,500, built on a lot costing $8,000, was built in 1892. In 1895 a union of this congregation with the First Christian Church, then meeting on Oakley Avenue, near Adams Street, was effected. This brought to the church Mr. and Mrs. A. Larabee and Mrs. M. D. Raggio, who were very useful servants of the Lord. At that time the present name of the congregation was adopted. Before this time it was known as Garfield Park Church.

The pastors following Mr. Ingram were Charles B. Edson, C. A. Young, C. C. Morrison, E. A. Ott, A. T. Campbell (two terms) and I. R. Lines. During Mr. Morrison's pastorate the new house of worship was built and first occupied in November, 1901.

The Russian Christian Mission (rented store at 1709 S. Halsted Street).

Organized 1909, by Basil Keusseff; present membership, 40; Bible-school enrollment, 75.

About 1909 the City Missionary Society—E. M. Bowman, president—was anxious to start gospel work among the foreign-born people of the city. Providentially, C. G. Kindred met then Daniel Protoff, who seemed to be qualified to work among the 250,000 Russians of the city; so it was begun. Mr. Protoff's health soon failed, and Basil S. Keusseff was called by the City Board from Pittsburgh. He was doing missionary work there under the auspices of the Baptists. In the heart of the world's steel industry he labored with Russians, Bulgarians, Servians, Croatians, Macedonians and Turks. Mr. Keusseff was born in Bulgaria, converted by the Baptists in Roumania, educated in the American Missionary College in Samokov and in two colleges in England.

Then he was examined by the Military College in Sofia and became an officer in the Bulgarian Army. However, he preferred philology and religion; hence, he became an expert linguist in ten different languages and a minister of the gospel. He organized a Baptist church in Lom, Bulgaria; built a chapel, and edited two newspapers in Sofia. Near Pittsburgh he met Robert Bamber, pastor of the Turtle Creek Christian Church, and soon came to apostolic ground. His work in Chicago is unique and successful. The field is most difficult. All Russians belong to the Greek Catholic Church, and are full of superstition and strongly attached to the church of the Czar; its priests are active in their opposition, as are also the Russian Socialists, Tolstoists, Nihilists and Anarchists. Such opposers challenge the courage of a true soldier of the cross.

The work is carried on in a rented storeroom, but the Chicago Society, with the General Home Society and the State C. W. B. M., hopes to house this mission. For lack of room, all of the Bible school are adults.

Sheffield Avenue Church (Sheffield Avenue and George Street).

Organized 1890, by W. F. Black; present membership, 200; value of property, $15,000; Bible school began 1890; present enrollment, 225.

This was organized as the North Side Church. Prof. W. F. Black, then pastor of the Central Christian Church, began preaching Sunday afternoons in Cook's Hall. The charter members were Mr. and Mrs. Cicero Wallace, Mrs. H. J. Russell, Mr. and Mrs. R. F. and L. R. Priest, Mrs. K. P. Kennedy, Miss Addie V. H. Barr, Mrs. W. H. Bauford and Mr. and Mrs. W. T. Pursell.

Lots were bought at Montana and Sheffield Streets and a frame chapel built thereon. This property was lost under a mortgage. Meetings were then held in Belmont Hall until the present property was secured in 1905. W. B. Taylor was pastor here about six years, and J. Lathrop, Geo. F. Hall,

Thad Tinsley, O. P. Spiegel and Bruce Brown for shorter periods. Will F. Shaw came to the pastorate in September, 1905. He is a sincere and devoted minister and preaches very clearly the pure gospel of Christ. During this time the church has prospered in all excellent service, but has lost many by removals and death. In its membership there have been not a few superior Christian men and women, among them Cicero Wallace, Prof. H. N. Herrick, L. R. Priest, Elias A. Long, W. S. Shearer, John Thrash, L. G. Fertig and Misses Addie Barr and Elsie Fudge—all of them leaders in the public's service.

South Chicago Christian Church.

Organized 1906, by A. Larabee; present membership, 50; Bible school began 1896; present enrollment, 50.

City Evangelist Larabee started this work. The congregation owns no property, but is accumulating a building fund. The meetings are held in Sherman Hall, 9138 Commercial Avenue. The progress is slow because the community is largely composed of foreign-born peoples of other tongues and religions. The church is brave and persistent in the face of overwhelming odds.

West End.

Present membership, 76; value of property, $3,500; Bible-school enrollment, 96.

West Pullman.

Present membership, 64; value of property, $5,000; Bible-school enrollment, 100.

In years past there were churches at Barrington and Palatine. From the former, Ira J. Chase entered the ministry.

A church at Maywood was formed in 1905 and continued for several years, but recently disbanded.

A church at Ravenswood had a similar record.

Chicago is one of the world's greatest mission fields and challenges our courage and consecration.

CRAWFORD COUNTY.

East Union (Palestine).

Organized 1848, by John Bailey; present membership, 150; value of property, $1,200; Bible-school enrollment, 25.

Minister Bailey held a meeting in a log schoolhouse and formed a congregation with fifty members. There was a reorganization in 1858 by Dr. Alfred C. Malone with eleven members, mostly from the Palestine Church. Of these, Samuel Searcy is the sole survivor, aged eighty-four. The chapel was built three and a half miles southeast of Palestine in 1863.

This church has given to the ministry George Hurst, Ralph Harding, J. S. Clements and O. J. Page.

It is active in good works under the ministry of Wright Sparlin.

Hardinville.

Organized 1850; present membership, 103; value of property, $1,000; Bible-school enrollment, 50.

The chapel was built in 1858.

Hutsonville.

Organized 1841, by Alfred P. Law; present membership, 121; value of property, $3,000; Bible school began 1860; present enrollment, 140.

The Disciples met for worship in their homes before the church was organized, which was made in a log house. About 1852 a brick chapel was erected by contributions from the general public, but the legal title soon passed to the M. E. Church. In 1858 the congregation built a house of their own. This was used until 1886, when the ladies' aid society bought a better located lot, on which a better building was erected. In 1911 this house was entirely remodeled and modernized.

In the early days the visits of Uncle Joe Wilson and Uncle Joe Wolf, of Indiana, were looked forward to with great pleasure.

Here are the names of some men and women whose lives have meant much to the church: Ben and Lizzie Frakes, Charles Fiddlar, Curtis Bradberry, Hugh and Sarah Hamilton, R. J. Owens, John T. Shore and wife, Joel Musgrove and wife, Sarah Stark (who taught a Sunday-school class for twenty-five years and was eighty years old when she resigned), Nancy O. Hurst, Sarah McNutt, Charity and Deborah Canady.

There is also a conservative church here with a Bible school.

Landes.

Present membership, 48; value of property, $550; Bible-school enrollment, 41.

Oblong.

Present membership, 144; value of property, including parsonage, $3,600; Bible-school enrollment, 218.

A modern, prosperous church in the oil region.

Palestine.

Organized 1863; present membership, 250; value of property, including parsonage, $5,000; Bible-school enrollment, 150.

Since the waters have swept the site of Kaskaskia away, Palestine claims to be the oldest town in the State. There was a church of Christ here probably in the thirties. In 1840, in this place, Maurice R. Trimble conducted a public debate with a "Two-seed Baptist" preacher. The records have all perished. A reorganization was made by Evangelist D. D. Miller, working in the Fourth District. There were seventy-nine charter members, of whom Press Carver only remains.

The frame chapel on North Main Street was burned in 1855. The present brick house was built in 1874. In 1893 a number of the members who were opposed to the use of instrumental music in the public worship withdrew and put up a frame chapel two blocks south. This is now unused and stands as a monument to mistaken zeal.

The church is prosperous. One Bible-school class is educating an orphan in Porto Rico. E. W. Sears is pastor.

Portersville.

Organized 1875, by Minister Wood; present membership, 65; value of property, $1,500; Bible-school enrollment, 85. There were twelve charter members.

Robinson.

Organized 1867, by A. D. Dailey; present membership, 300; value of property, $12,000; Bible school began 1867; present enrollment, 162.

The original members were N. S. Brown and wife, M. C. Sheppard, Mrs. Mary Callahan, Hickman Henderson and Jas. M. Gardner and wife. The church was a result of a series of meetings held by Minister Dailey. The first house was built in 1882.

West Harmony (Bell Air).

Present membership, 103; value of property, $800; Bible-school enrollment, 65.

Inactive. Chapel built in 1871.

Wirt Chapel (Oblong).

Organized 1862, by G. W. Ingersoll; value of property, $900.

Met in Wirt Schoolhouse until 1875, when chapel was built on land given by Mrs. Deborah Ogden.

CUMBERLAND COUNTY.

Antioch (Greenup).

Organized 1891, by H. C. Kuykendall; present membership, 90; value of property, $700.

This church is eight miles northeast of Greenup. Conservatives are in control.

Brush Creek (Roslin).

Organized 1890; present membership, 25; value of property, $800; has a Bible school.

This is two miles northwest of Roslin. The congregation is fifty to sixty years old, and for a period met in Fairview Schoolhouse.

Corinth (Toledo).

Organized 1876; present membership, 45; value of property, $900.

Two miles southwest of Toledo.

Greenup.

Organized 1887, by Wm. H. Williams; present membership, 43; value of property, $500; Bible-school enrollment, 75.

The organization was effected in the Universalist house of worship. J. D. Borden and John Decker were elected elders, and Messrs. Elstun and Garrett, deacons. The church has been an intermittent one. It gave to the ministry J. D. Borden and John W. Kellum. For several years Charles F. Walden was the efficient clerk.

Hazel Dell.

Present membership, 80; value of property, $1,000; Bible-school enrollment, 50.

I. S. McCash bought a farm two miles northwest of Hazel Dell, and in 1860 moved his family there from Indiana. While he cultivated his farm in summer and worked at the carpenter's trade in winter, he preached regularly within a radius of twenty-five miles. He found a small congregation at the Copland Schoolhouse, which transferred membership to Hazel Dell when the chapel was built there. Mr. McCash was assisted in his pioneer work by an aged brother, Benjamin Duvee, and Daniel Corener, whose home was in the north edge of Jasper County. They went by twos; one would preach and the other would exhort.

Janesville.

Present membership, 70; value of property, $1,000; Bible-school enrollment, 48.
D. T. Gordon is clerk.

Jewett.

Organized 1893, by James R. Parker; present membership, 40; value of property, $600; Bible school began 1893; present enrollment, 80.

The charter members were William, H. O., Harry and Tiney Goldsmith; Rachel Clark, Emma Lamasters, Phoche Prather; C. O., Mattie and Robert Ray; Albert and Maggie Skidmore; Alfred, Jane, William and Emma Williams.

The first chapel burned in 1900 and the second was built. The church was reorganized in 1911 by Evangelist J. E. Stout with forty members, and is now led by better ideals.

There was a division in this congregation in 1909, and the conservatives formed a church that has now fifteen members and a Bible school, but no chapel.

Johnstown (Toledo).

Present membership, 58; value of property, $3,000; no Bible school.
Seven miles north. J. D. Hill is clerk.

Neoga.

Organized 1896, by S. R. Lewis; present membership, 35; value of property, $1,000; Bible school began 1896; present enrollment, 34.

Years ago there was a congregation four miles east called Copperas Creek; also at Neoga, but both passed away. The present church was organized in a hall with twenty-six charter members. The chapel was built in 1898. The congregation is active. Mrs. Maude Frazzel is clerk.

Churches in this part of the State have been led to their serious hurt by non-scriptural ideals.

CHURCHES

Plum Grove (Hidalgo).

Organized 1900; present membership, 80; value of property, $1,800; Bible-school enrollment, 100.

Three miles north of Hidalgo.

Plum Grove (Greenup).

Organized 1900; value of property, $900; has a Bible school.

Six miles northeast of Greenup. A congregation was organized two miles south of this place, in a schoolhouse, by Min. Benjamin Duvee in 1854. This was the first church in the county that was Christian only. Thomas Goodman preached there. When the place of meeting and the name were changed and the chapel built, is not learned.

Toledo.

Organized 1875; present membership, 200; value of property, $3,500; Bible-school enrollment, 167.

The present chapel was built in 1902. The church has grown toward better ideals. Scott Calbert is pastor.

Webster (Janesville).

This is two and a half miles northeast of Janesville.

Min. I. S. McCash constituted a church in 1864 near Hazel Dell, at the Washington Schoolhouse. At that place four of his sons were led to Christ and all of them entered the ministry; namely, Andrew, Levi, Albert and I. N. McCash. Andrew has remained there over forty years. Levi has preached in California and Albert in Washington for nearly as long. I. N. has been more prominent, and, hence, more widely known. This congregation is now divided. About 1865, I. S. McCash also formed a church in the Painter Creek Schoolhouse.

Miss Nellie Morgan, of Jewett, furnished many of the facts in this county.

DEWITT COUNTY.

Clinton.

Organized 1852, by W. G. Springer; present membership, 560; value of property, including parsonage, $18,000; Bible school began 1852; present enrollment, 335.

In the spring of 1857, Walter P. Bowles and Wm. G. Springer held a series of meetings about four miles south of Clinton, in the residence of Hiram Dodson, not far from the location of Texas chapel. During this meeting Mr. Springer proposed that a church-house be built in Clinton, which was approved. W. G. Springer, with Messrs. Wm. Bolin and Samuel Brown, were appointed the committee for this task. Judge David Davis gave the lot, and an old-time brick chapel was finished and occupied in the summer of 1852. In that fall, W. G. Springer, assisted by Wm. Shockey, an able evangelist from Indiana, held a meeting. At its close a church of Christ was organized, with Wm. Bolin and W. G. Springer as elders, and Abram Crum and Milton Parkinson, deacons. There was some preaching by Messrs. Bolin, Springer, Bowles, Wm. Morrow and others, but little growth. Wm. H. Brown, the great evangelist, held a meeting in 1856, and W. P. Shockey in 1858. He also led a public debate on Universalism with Minister Davis. In 1860, J. Q. A. Houston, with Dudley Downs as singer, held a meeting. During this revival the floor of the chapel, filled with a great audience, broke down, causing a panic. Order was restored by the quick singing of the preachers. Mr. Downs then preached for the congregation part of the time for several years. David Walk, Benjamin Franklin, C. F. Short and Leroy Skelton preached in continued meetings and otherwise. In 1865, J. J. Miles settled in Clinton and preached some. Then there followed R. B. Roberts, George Owen, D. D. Miller, J. C. Tulley, Charles Rowe, James Mitchell, James Robinson, John Wilson, Peter Schick, Dr. John Zimmerman, H. G. Van Dervoort, W. H. Crow, Elijah Stout, N. S. Haynes, H. F. Tandy, Geo. F. Adams, Samuel

Lowe and T. T. Holton in various kinds of ministerial service. In the winter of 1866, A. D. Fillmore taught a class in vocal music and preached for the church. In 1871, John Adkinson, who was the main financial support, died. Again the door of the chapel was closed.

In 1881, Miss Mary Welsh, with Mr. and Mrs. Edward Allen, opened and cleaned up the building, replacing the fifty broken panes of glass, and began again the public worship with seven of the members. Since that time the church has grown steadily in numbers and efficiency. The new building was erected during the pastorate of Mr. Young in 1888; also he was the first minister giving full time to a congregation. The pastorate of Mr. E. A. Gilliland was fruitful of great good.

Fairview (Heyworth).

Organized 1887, by J. S. Stagner; value of property, $1,200; Bible school began 1877.

The location is eight miles southwest of Heyworth. The situation is commanding—a bluff on the bank of Kickapoo Creek. There is a well-kept cemetery there.

The chapel was built in 1878. The congregation is now weak. A summer Sunday school is about the only appearance of life.

Farmer City.

Organized 1864, by Dudley Downs; present membership, 147; value of property, $6,500; Bible school began 1868; present enrollment, 160.

This congregation was formed in the old schoolhouse of the town. The chapel was built the next year on Main Street, which served till 1866. Then, during the pastorate of John I. Gunn, the building was moved two blocks east and reconstructed at a cost of $3,500. Other improvements thereon were made during the pastorate of Henry Genders, who died there.

The living charter members are Milan Moore, Mehitabel

Watson, Chas. H. Watson, Catherine Wetzell, James H. Bean, Cynthia Webb, Emma Sangster and Nancy Watson.

The church has never been numerically strong. It has given to the ministry David Wetzell, Joseph G. Slick and Frank L. Moore.

Hallsville (formerly Old Union).

Organized 1832, by Hughes Bowles; present membership, 211; value of property, $1,200; Bible-school enrollment, 82.

The Old Union Church was located about ten miles west of Clinton. Hughes Bowles, with his family, came from Kentucky in 1831 and settled on a farm in that locality. Under the spreading branches of a large white-oak tree, he constituted this congregation on October 13—the second Sunday of the month—with seventeen charter members. It was composed mainly of the Bowles and Hall families. A part, and probably all, of these first members were turned to the Lord at Caneridge, Kentucky. The first elders of this church of Christ were Mahlon Hall, Joseph Hall and Hiram Dotson. Besides these, Darius and Ambrose Hall, with Anderson and W. P. Bowles, were leading members. The first meetings were held in the log-cabin homes of the people and in groves. Among the first preachers there were Hughes Bowles, James Scott, William Ryan, W. P. Bowles, Mr. Painter, Abner Peeler, Isaac Martin, Alfred Lindsay, Sr., John G. Campbell, William Morrow and John England. John Rogers and John Irwin were Kentucky ministers who visited the congregation. Later there were A. J. Kane, J. Q. A. Houston, Dudley Downs, Samuel Knight, L. M. Robinson and T. T. Holton.

The first chapel was built of logs in 1838. It was used jointly by the Disciples, Baptists and Methodists. This fact gave the word "Union" to this place of public worship. As the years passed, "Old" was added. In 1864 a frame building, with a seating capacity of six hundred and costing $3,000, was erected. This was owned and used by the church of Christ only.

These pioneer preachers laid deep and firm foundations. This congregation grew to a membership of four hundred. From first to last near thirteen hundred were baptized here upon the public confession of the Christ.

It gave to the ministry Wm. P. Ryan, W. P. Bowles, Alonzo Henry, Simpson Ely, Harry Barnett, J. A. Barnett, Harry Piatt and John H. Piatt.

Railways came, towns sprang up and Old Union became the mother of congregations. She contributed to "Texas," Maroa, Kenney and Midland, which received the old house; but Hallsville is her direct offspring. On Oct. 13, 1882, the old church disbanded. A decaying stump marks the spot of her birth. This, with the gravestones in the cemetery that grew around the houses of worship, are the silent sentinels of faded joys and departed glory. Here sleeps the sacred dust of brave men and true women awaiting the resurrection of the just.

Kenney.

Organized 1883, by David Wetzell; present membership, 140; value of property, $1,000; Bible school began 1902; present enrollment, 114.

This church was constituted by members who came from the Old Union congregation and those gained in a meeting conducted by Mr. Wetzell in a public hall in 1883. The chapel was finished and occupied in 1884. The next year Robert Orr, W. W. Johnson and F. M. Hubbell were ordained as elders. Messrs. Orr and Johnson continue to serve the congregation as its elders. It grows and does good work.

Lane.

Organized 1850, by Dr. Zimmerman; present membership, 55; value of property, $400; Bible school began 1884; present enrollment, 70.

The meetings of this congregation for a period of thirty-five years were held in the residences of its members and schoolhouses about seven miles east of Clinton. It was first known as Creek Nation and later as Harmony Church. With the coming of a railway, the village of Lane sprang up. It was named for Timps Lane, a representative man of the community and a leading member of the church. Then the chapel and place of meeting were moved there in 1884. It is probable that the Harmony congregation was formed by Min. George Owens in 1867. Mr. Lane died in 1911. The church in the village is not strong.

Long Point (Wapella).

Organized 1851, by William Morrow; present membership, 51; value of property, $800; Bible school began 1858; present enrollment, 41.

This church, located four miles north of Wapella, was formed in a grove near Liberty Schoolhouse. In 1858 the present house of worship was built, costing $2,000. The pioneer preachers who worked here were Wm. Ryan, W. P. Bowles, John Wilson, Dudley Downs and George Owens.

The present elders are Abram Summers, C. W. Short and John B. Turner, who is also correspondent.

At one time Benjamin Franklin debated with John Luccock (M. E. Church) here.

Rock Creek (Waynesville).

Organized 1837, by Hughes Bowles; present membership, 80; value of property, $1,500; Bible school began 1876; present enrollment, 45.

The meetings for public worship alternated between the residences of Peter Crum, at Long Point, and Samuel P. Glenn, at Rock Creek, till 1845, when the first house was built. This served till 1876, when the present house was constructed one-quarter mile south of the first site—four miles east of Waynesville.

This country church has maintained the primitive order of public worship during the seventy-five years of its life.

CHURCHES

Its pioneer preachers were Peter Crum, W. P. Bowles, S. P. Glenn and James Robeson.

Texas (Clinton).

Organized 1850, by W. G. Springer; present membership, 77; value of property, $1,000; Bible school began 1876; present enrollment, 111.

This church is located four miles southwest of Clinton. Its first house was built in 1850 and its second in 1876. The church was reorganized in 1860. Like many country churches, it has lost many members by removal, but maintains its public worship and work. Its elders are B. T. Williams, G. W. Wright and James Justis, with H. White and J. G. Jenkins, deacons.

Wapella.

Organized 1868, by George Owens; present membership, 123; value of property, $2,000; Bible school began 1868; present enrollment, 100.

The meetings were held in the schoolhouse till 1869, when the present house of worship was built. Joshua Carl, Peter Crum and Stephen Riggs were associated with Geo. Owen in forming the congregation.

Mrs. Margaret Carl was one of the charter members. She was baptized by Thomas Campbell in 1826, and at the age of ninety-five years passed to her reward.

O. C. Ives and Richard Short are the elders, with H. Conover and P. O. Scogens, deacons.

Waynesville.

Organized 1894, by R. Leland Brown; present membership, 225; value of property, including parsonage, $6,000; Bible school began 1894; present enrollment, 263.

This church grew out of a meeting conducted by Min. R. Leland Brown. There were eight Disciples at its beginning and eighty at the close. The house of worship, costing $1,800, with a seating capacity of four hundred, was built at once. When the house was dedicated, practical expressions of goodwill came from the representatives of the community, both the churched and the unchurched.

DOUGLAS COUNTY.

Arcola.

Organized 1858, by Dr. W. T. Sylvester; present membership, 270; value of property, including parsonage, $21,000; Bible-school enrollment, 327.

The charter members were John Lanaiger, Dr. Sylvester, Tipton Ward, David Evans and J. M. Harden. Dr. Sylvester was the leading member of this church for about fifteen years. He was an efficient elder and a good preacher until he became a railroad builder.

The congregation was held back for years by hurtful opinions, but has fully recovered itself. It is active in all good works, with W. S. Rounds as pastor.

Camargo.

Present membership, 106; value of property, $10,000; Bible-school enrollment, 125.

There was in the seventies and later a Christian congregation at Hugo, a few miles south of Camargo. The changing tides of human life carried it away, some of its members coming to Camargo.

Hindsboro.

Organized 1863, by Harmon Gregg; present membership, 150; value of property, $6,500; Bible school began 1878; present enrollment, 130.

The Deer Creek Christian Church, located four miles north of the site of Hindsboro, was formed as stated. Besides Mr. Gregg, Thomas Goodman preached much for the congregation. Hindsboro grew by the coming of the railroad, and to this village the membership of the Deer Creek congregation was transferred in 1878. The first chapel was built there the next year, and the present house was erected in 1910 during the ministry of J. S. Rose.

Murdock.

Organized 1902, by R. Leland Brown; present membership, 50; value of property, $1,500; Bible school began 1902; present enrollment, 80.

Newman.

Organized 1869, by N. S. Haynes; present membership, 450; value of property, $23,000; Bible school began 1869; present enrollment, 225.

A series of meetings was begun by Mr. Haynes in the M. E. chapel. When people began to turn to the Lord, the trustees turned him out. The meeting was continued and the church formed in the public schoolhouse. A frame chapel was built about 1874, which gave place to a modern building in 1905. W. G. Pounds and Mr. and Mrs. Bennett were active helpers in the early years.

The church has given L. H. Hooe to the ministry.

Tuscola.

Organized 1863, by David Walk; present membership, 285; value of property, $15,000; Bible-school enrollment, 144.

In 1863, W. B. Wharton and D. K. Walker, two Disciples, were residing in Tuscola. This had then been a county-seat for six years. These two men and their families wished the town should hear the gospel as they understood it, and also a church home for themselves; so they sent for Min. David Walk. He held a series of meetings in the old courthouse and organized a church of Christ with eighteen members. The congregation met in the schoolhouse for public worship. Later, when Mr. Walk returned to Tuscola, he was compelled to defend his distinctive teaching in a public discussion. At its conclusion, members of the Baptist, Presbyterian and M. E. Churches united and prevailed upon the public-school officers to shut the Disciples out of the schoolhouse. This led to the construction of a two-story frame church building. It was used until 1892, when the present brick edifice was completed. The chief cost of the first building was met by John Chandler. Of the charter members, only Mrs. Julia Sloan remains.

The church has always maintained its public worship.
It has given to the ministry Wm. Walling and E. E. Hartley.

Villa Grove.

Organized 1906, by Harold E. Monser; present membership, 110; value of property, $7,000; Bible school began 1906; present enrollment, 142.

Mr. Monser was sent here by the mission board of the Sixth District, and conducted a four weeks' meeting in a tent. During the half-time service of R. L. Cartwright the house was built by the help of the Church Extension Society. The town depends for its life chiefly on railroad work, and the church has been pastorless part of the time, hence has not flourished. Dr. G. L. Kennedy is the clerk.

EDGAR COUNTY.

Some Extinct Congregations.

The second church in the county was known through many years as Big Creek. There is a dim tradition that it was first called "Pickup," but not for a long time. It was organized in the thirties. Its first house of worship was made of hewed logs, with an open fireplace at one end. It was built about 1838 and stood within half a mile of what is now known as the Union Schoolhouse. The elders were Abner Leitchman and Isaac Elledge. The latter was a very good preacher. Harmon Gregg, Sr., and Robert Bloomfield were the deacons. About 1850 the log house gave place to a frame chapel placed within a half-mile northeast. The names associated with this house are Barnett Thomas, Jacob Zimmerly and Ottis Eldridge. In 1882 a new but very inferior chapel was built one and a half miles due south. This was used till 1904, when a part of the congregation went west to Bell Ridge and a part east to Oliver. The old church gave Harmon Gregg and Dudley Downs to the ministry.

In 1840 a church was organized about three miles east of Grandview known as Central. It did good work for about twenty-five years.

The Elbridge congregation was formed in the fifties and flourished for years. The members, "split up by the Civil War," moved away, and the house was sold about 1875 to the public-school district.

Maple Grove was a country church three miles east of Edgar. The property has gone back to the original owners of the land.

Liberty Chapel was six miles east and one mile north of Paris. It, too, has probably gone back to the landowners.

W. F. Black found a "union church" north of Hume and held a characteristic meeting in the fall of 1884. Then most of the people became Christians only. After some years, many changed membership to Sidell and elsewhere. The chapel was sold to be used as a barn, and the proceeds turned into the chapel at Metcalf.

There was never a congregation at Grandview, but "Uncle Tom Goodman," who resided there, was anxious to tell the Methodist and Presbyterian brethren "where they stood." Refusing him the use of their houses, the chapel was built and, in later years, sold to the township.

Asher (Paris).

Organized 1907, by L. Hadaway; present membership, 139; value of property, $4,900; Bible school began 1907; present enrollment, 90.

The location is about five miles southwestward from Paris. The congregation grew out of a Bible school held in the Asher Schoolhouse, re-enforced by members from the old Big Creek Church. There were thirty-eight charter members. The Home Department has 125 members. Like many such, the abler members move to town.

Bell Ridge (Paris).

Organized 1904, by H. M. Brooks; present membership, 319; value of property, $6,000; Bible school began 1904; present enrollment, 162.

This congregation grew out of the old Big Creek Church. It is located ten miles southwest of Paris. There were sixty-seven charter members. The chapel is a creditable one. There have been six regular preachers. Mrs. W. S. O'Hair has served as the very faithful and efficient Bible-school superintendent. The Home Department has 258 members.

Brocton.

Organized 1873, by C. C. Boyer and H. M. Brooks; present membership, 50; value of property, $3,000; Bible school began 1893; present enrollment, 51.

Before the chapel was built in 1893, meetings were held and a congregation organized in the White Elm Schoolhouse, in just what year is not known. Min. C. C. Boyer resided on his farm near here and was the leading man in the movement. Thomas Goodman, J. J. Vanhoutin, James Connor and Harmon Gregg preached here. After the chapel was built, the congregation was reorganized by H. M. Brooks.

The church has given to the ministry two brothers—T. A. and E. E. Boyer.

Chrisman.

Organized 1890, by G. W. Pearl; present membership, 12; value of property, $1,500.

Dr. J. M. Welch, now deceased, led this work in its earlier years. A church building that was owned by the Universalists was bought and used.

The church is very feeble. There were about forty charter members.

Conlogue.

Organized 1872, by Z. T. Sweeney; value of property, $400; never had a Bible school.

The house was built in 1873. Preaching now only periodically.

Dudley.

Organized 1868; value of property, $1,000.

This church is about extinct. Landlordism and ultra-conservatism have proved its undoing.

Hume.

Organized 1875, by C. C. Boyer; present membership, 167; value of property, including parsonage, $2,700; Bible school began 1881; present enrollment, 139.

J. W. Perkins was the first minister. For about six years the congregation worshiped in the old schoolhouse. Squire Hume gave the ground and the chapel was finished in 1881. Miss Maggie Roberts was the first person baptized in the new building. The congregation is now looking toward another house of worship.

To the ministry the church has given T. T. Roberts.

Kansas.

Organized 1856, by A. D. Fillmore; present membership, 350; value of property, $25,000; Bible school began 1856; present enrollment, 250.

This town was laid in 1853 on a flat prairie, where deer, wolves, wild ducks and geese, prairie chickens and snakes made their homes. In 1854 a union chapel was built, the title to which was in the Methodist Protestant Church. The building stood on the present site of the National Bank. Three denominations were interested in the property. In this building the church of Christ was organized with sixteen charter members, as follows: John K. Boyer and wife, W. F. Boyer and wife, Mrs. Katherine Brown, Mrs. Harriett Cornell, Mrs. Evaline Curd, Presley Martin and wife, Mrs. Margaret Atkins, James Wright and wife, Angeline Wilhoit, Sarah Wilhoit, Pendleton Wilhoit and Sarah Arterburn. It was some time afterward that the officers were elected, for the first elders were: Edward Pinnell, J. K. Boyer and N. S. Wiley, with W. F. Boyer, J. G. Wilhoit, W. L. Boyer and A. J. Pinnell for deacons.

The "union church" did not work well; so in 1857 the Disciples put up a chapel of their own. The lot was given by Mr. William Brown, who was an Englishman by birth and "a brother-in-law of the congregation." This building was much improved in 1884. It gave place in 1910 to a beautiful modern edifice erected during the pastorate of B. F. Thomas.

To the ministry the church has given N. S. Haynes, Z. T. Sweeney, Gilbert Zink, Ellis Purlee and Fred Jacobs.

The following incident illustrates the viewpoint and experiences of many Disciples in the fifties and sixties. The services in union chapel were by rotation, the preachers taking their days. A young man from New England came to the village. Having a good voice, he was pleased to assist in the singing at church. He used a tuning-fork to help pitch the tunes. He sang the tenor. Here were two unheard-of things in the community—a tuning-fork and a tenor. This at once brought to his feet one of the aged rulers of the assembly. He informed the young man that he "must drop that pinching-bug and dry up that mule-braying." His indignation spread so that not until the young man was arrested, tried and fined $5 for disturbing public worship, was the wrath of the righteous man appeased.

Little Grove (Vermilion).

Organized 1826, by Samuel McGee; present membership, 40; value of property, $500. Never had a Bible school.

The first organization of the Little Grove Church, six miles east of Paris, was in the fall of 1826, in the home of Samuel McGee. The church was formed through the efforts chiefly of Mrs. Mary Morrison and her sister, Mrs. Anna Fitzgerald. These women, with others in this settlement, had come to Edgar County from Kentucky, where they had come to some knowledge of the Restoration movement. The Little

Grove congregation was always a church of Christ; it was never in any way connected with the Christian Denomination. Meetings for worship were first held in residences, next in the McGee Schoolhouse, and about 1829 in the Prior Schoolhouse. By 1832 the members had increased to near one hundred. People would go sometimes a day's travel to be at the Saturday night and Sunday meetings. It was not uncommon for several of the early settlers to take their families together in an ox-wagon to go to church. In 1835 the congregation began to build a meeting-house, which was finished in 1837 with the seats. This served until 1875, when the present house was built. In its earlier years this church was visited by Alexander Campbell, John O'Kane, Daniel W. Elledge, Love H. Jameson, the brothers Job and Michel Combs, and others. The leading resident preacher up to 1865 was William Hartley, who was assisted by Elijah Ward and other members. The congregation has never been without its active officers and has never had any serious trouble. Hundreds have been members here. Many have come and more have gone. Now only a few remain, mostly women, who meet for worship every Lord's Day. Its wide influences no man may measure. No regular preaching now.

John J. Vanhouten, a grandson of Mrs. Mary Morrison, came to the ministry here.

Metcalf.

Present membership, 125; value of property, $1,500; Bible school enrollment, 70.

Nevins.

Organized 1858, by William Hurtly and A. D. Fillmore; present membership, 19; value of property, $600; never had a Bible school.

This congregation was organized in the country with forty charter members and known as the Franklin Church. The building was moved to the near-by railway station,

Nevins, in 1881, and the church has since been known by that name.

It has given William T. Simms and William H. Simms to the ministry. Both are dead.

Some of those who preached here were Nathan Wright, Thomas Goodman, Wm. Holt, A. J. Frank, W. H. Simms, J. W. Perkins, John N. Mulkey, Hezekiah Williams, Isaac Lamb and H. W. Cuppy.

Oliver.

Organized 1896, by I. J. Lamb; present membership, 100; value of property, $1,200; Bible reading.

A conservative congregation that was re-enforced from the Big Creek Church.

Paris.

Organized 1855, by John C. New; present membership, 1,714; value of property, $65,000; Bible school began 1860; present enrollment, 435.

There were thirty-one charter members. The first house for worship was purchased of the Presbyterians. The second was a two-story brick erected in 1866. The present stone edifice was finished in 1897 during the pastorate of A. E. Dubber. The church has had nineteen pastors and a host of fine men and women. Among those who have contributed not a little to its development were Geo. W. Redmon, LeRoy Wiley, A. J. Hunter, and Fred, Larz and Henry Augustus. Mr. George Brown, for twelve years county superintendent of schools, is the Bible-school superintendent. His is a fine union of head and heart.

From the estate of Mr. Larz A. Augustus the congregation received $25,300. Of this amount, $5,000 may be spent as two-thirds of the membership may vote; the balance is to be held in trust and the interest only "used in the best manner known to said church for the extension of the cause of Christ."

For the past eight years the church has supported Fred E. Hagin as a missionary in Japan.

D. N. Wetzell and W. B. Zimmerman have been given to the ministry.

The church owns a chapel in the south side of the city and conducts a mission there. H. H. Peters is the pastor.

Pleasant Hill (Kansas).

Organized 1870, by Harmon Gregg; present membership, 207; value of property, $3,000; Bible school began 1870; present enrollment, 118.

Is located five miles southeast of Kansas. There were forty-six charter members. A. Boyer and J. N. Shoptaugh were chosen and set apart as elders, and R. Ratts, Ezra Nay and H. Hines as deacons.

A good brick church, contiguous to a cemetery, was built soon after the formation of the congregation and is still used.

This country church has been fruitful in the production of preachers. They were D. W. Nay, S. I. Stark, J. A. Shoptaugh, S. W. Nay, E. F. Kerans, Ross Kerans, Roley Nay and Bruce Nay.

Redmon.

Organized 1907, by L. Hadaway; present membership, 80; value of property, $6,000; Bible school began 1807; present enrollment, 118.

State Line (Paris).

Organized 1862; present membership, 30; value of property, $700; Bible school began 1880; present enrollment, 50.

A number of people entered into an organization calling themselves the Clay's Prairie Church of Christ from the schoolhouse of that name. They met there until 1869, when the house of worship was built. Since then the congregation has been known as State Line because the chapel is near the Indiana line. The first elders were John Hunter (the father of A. J. Hunter), James Watson and Richard Hobbs.

Among its ministers there were Nathan Wright, Abner

Daily, Thomas Goodman, William Holt, G. L. Rude, J. B. Mayfield, Geo. E. and Z. T. Sweeney (father and son), Wm. Simms and W. W. Jacobs.

William Holt, a fine preacher, was the product of this church.

Success (Vermilion).

Organized 1895, by H. Williams; present membership, 75; value of property, $600; Bible school began 1895; present enrollment, 50. F. C. Volker is the clerk.

EDWARDS COUNTY.

Albion.

Organized 1841, by Elijah Goodwin; present membership, 331; value of property, $1,800; Bible school enrollment, 221.

The formation of this church, August 4, was just after the old brick Christian chapel was finished. Daniel Orange, a fine type of Englishman, led in this movement. He was a descendant of the French Huguenots and settled here in 1818. He had heard the Campbell-Purcell debate in Cincinnati in 1836 and was fully persuaded that the doctrinal position of the Disciples was right. The charter members were Daniel, Elizabeth, Elizabeth S. and John B. Orange—a fruitful beginning indeed. Four weeks later Alfred Flower, who married Elizabeth S. Orange—with Charles and Sarah Burns—was added to the number. The first elder was Daniel Orange, and the first deacons were Alvin Kenner and George Goodwin. Elijah Goodwin was employed one-fourth of the time at $50 the year. Like most churches, this one met reverses, but it has grown to wide service and usefulness. The present chapel was built in 1868 and a new building is in process of construction.

Bone Gap.

Organized 1886, by J. S. Rose; present membership, 154; value of property, $1,000; Bible school began 1886; present enrollment, 175.

Mr. Rose was chiefly instrumental in establishing this church, serving it four years. Under his ministry the house was built in 1887. W. D. Walker is correspondent.

Browns.

Organized 1894, by Zacharia Harris; present membership, 144; value of property, $2,500; Bible school began 1894; present enrollment, 134.

The Bonpas Church, located on the eastern border of the county, was organized by Amos Miller in 1838. It served its generation and the remnant finally united with Browns.

Ellery.

Organized 1890, by J. C. T. Hall; present membership, 150; value of property, $3,500; Bible school began 1888; present enrollment, 85.

This congregation had its beginning in a Bible school that was started at the Woods Schoolhouse in 1888 and continued two years. The people of the community were led by Min. J. C. T. Hall in the erection of a frame church which was finished in 1890.

Shiloh (West Salem).

Organized 1862, by J. C. T. Hall; present membership, 125; value of property, $1,500; Bible school enrollment, 109.

The location is eight miles south of Albion. A large per cent. of the people of this community originally came from Kentucky, so it was sometimes called "Little Kentucky." It is noted for its hospitality. The church was organized in the barn of James McKinsey.

West Salem.

Organized 1858, by J. C. T. Hall; present membership, 175; value of property, including parsonage, $13,000; Bible-school enrollment, 235.

This church was formed by uniting the "Long Point" congregation with one that was meeting at the residence of

Jas. F. Barney. James Kinner and Blashel Foster led in this work. The twenty-nine charter members signed the following agreement: "We whose names are hereunto annexed, being immersed believers in the Lord Jesus Christ, do mutually and voluntarily associate ourselves together in a congregational capacity to be known as the Congregation of the Lord at West Salem, taking the Christian Scriptures as our only rule of faith and practice, taking no name as a church name but such as they authorize."

West Village (Albion).

Organized 1858; present membership, 293; value of property, $2,000; Bible school enrollment, 250.

This church is four miles north of Albion. It was a scion of the Little Prairie Church. It was first known as Village Church, but as there was another not far distant by that name, this one was changed to West Village. The first meeting was held in an old log building one and a half miles from the present site. A Bible school was conducted there for a number of years, with occasional preaching. A frame building was erected in 1858, which was used till the present house was built in 1896.

The Curtisville Church was organized by J. C. T. Hall in 1854. A few years later it united with the West Village congregation. But in 1878 it was reorganized and built a chapel. In later years it disorganized.

The charter members were J. T., Nancy J. and Mary Hunt; W. W., Nancy and Edward Willis; Laurie Stroup; W. A. and Sarah T. Inskipp; John T., Ann C. and Eliza Woods; Joe J. Mitchell, Malinda Mann, Harriett McKibben, Harriett Winters, Thomas and Mary Niles, William and Narcissa Scott, and Jane I. Lines.

Little Prairie (Ellery).

Organized 1823, by Elder Alan Emmerson; present membership, 100; value of property, $2,000; Bible-school enrollment, 125.

This church, located about four miles northwest of Albion, was for sixteen years a part of the Christian Denomination. It was organized in the house of Alan Emmerson, near the site of the present church building. The first elder was Alan Emmerson, and the first deacons were Joseph Applegath, Thomas Gill and William Hall. Amos Willis was the first preacher of the Christian Denomination in the county and the first minister of this church. He died in 1840.

The first house of worship of this congregation was a frame—covered, ceiled and weather-boarded with clapboards and plastered with post-oak clay. It had a brick chimney and fireplace. With the passing years, that bear all things away, this superior temple of its time gave place to another frame building that is still in use.

In 1837 the congregation came into the Restoration movement through the leading of Amos Willis, a minister of the older congregation. Later J. M. Mathes, John O'Kane, Moses Goodwin and others served the church.

Marion (West Salem).

Organized 1843, by Elijah Goodwin; present membership, 150; value of property, $1,200; Bible-school enrollment, 82.

This church is in the northwest corner of the county and is on the bank of Sugar Creek. Its first elders were William Foster and N. A. Shelby; its first deacons, Quinton Nicks and B. F. Stark. It was formed in the residence of Quinton Nicks. Meetings were held in the home of N. A. Shelby and others till the chapel was built. Besides Elijah and Moses Goodwin, J. Standish and Cornelius Aids preached there in the earlier years.

It gave George Morrall to the ministry.

New Hope (Browns).

Present membership, 52; value of property, $800; Bible-school enrollment, 44.

Only occasional meetings are held here now.

EFFINGHAM COUNTY.

The East Village Church, after years of work, also disorganized.

Min. Claiborne Wright began the work of the Disciples in this county in 1862. He had settled on a farm east of Mason in 1861. He held meetings in the Craver Schoolhouse, and organized a church of Christ there with the following members: Margaret A. Stephens; Paschal C., Louisa, Celestus, David and Talitha Leonard; Jefferson, Catherine, Claiborne, Charlotte, Catherine M., Wm. T., Ellen Jane and Susan Wright; Michael and Katherine Redinbaugh, Ezra and Phebe Morphew, Margaret Turner, Mary A. Craver, and Wm. D. and Robert D. Porter. Additions to these were made steadily. A large shed used for sheltering sheep in winter was turned into a tabernacle and in this the congregation met for worship. In 1866 the place of meeting was changed to the new schoolhouse three miles east of Mason. After a time debates and divisions occurred, some of the members going to the Universalists and others uniting with the U. B. Church. Min. A. J. Harrell revived the work in 1879, which led to the formation of the church in Mason in 1880.

Beecher City.

Organized 1902, by B. S. Taylor; present membership, 161; value of property, $1,600; Bible school began 1907; present enrollment, 136.

The church was organized in the schoolhouse and met for worship in a canning factory until the chapel was erected in 1907. B. S. Taylor, J. L. Huffcult and M. E. Steele were the three men who were ably assisted by twenty-two women in the church during its first years. Evangelist J. E. Story added 168 people in one meeting and thus helped the congregation to a stronger position.

Dieterich.

Present membership, 65; value of property, $1,000; Bible-school enrollment, 52.

CHURCHES

Edgewood.

Organized 1890, by W. T. Gordon; present membership, 110; value of property, $1,000; Bible school began 1890; present enrollment, 70.

Minister Gordon preached Monday evening, May 19, 1890, in the M. E. Church. A further use of the house was refused him. Then he accepted an invitation from the trustees to occupy the public-school house. When he returned the following July he found the doors closed against him. The managers of the Opera Hall tendered him the use of their auditorium. Following this opening, a church of thirty-seven members was organized the following September. A house of worship was built in 1891.

Dr. Joseph Hall has been the chief leader and supporter of this congregation. There are other faithful servants.

Effingham.

Organized 1890, by W. T. Gordon; value of property, $10,000; Bible school began 1890.

The first work of the Disciples in Effingham began near 1867. There was a partial organization at that date. Occasional meetings were held in the courthouse. A lot was donated in the west part of town and a small frame building was erected thereon. This was burned a few years thereafter. Then, by reason of a lack of good leadership, the congregation went to pieces.

When the beloved H. Y. Kellar moved to Effingham in 1888, he gathered together the remnants and preached to them in the temple until the church building was erected in 1893. The citizens of the city helped liberally in this enterprise.

Elliottstown (Dieterich).

Present membership, 54; value of property, $650; no Bible school.

This place was the residence of Barlow Higgins, who did good work through many years.

Mason.

Organized 1880, by W. T. Gordon; present membership, 125; value of property, $1,700; Bible-school enrollment, 112.

This church received its first impulse from a country congregation east of the town. Meetings were held in the Baptist chapel and the Masonic Hall. The church is much indebted to Minister Gordon. It is doing good service.

Watson.

Present membership, 30; value of property, $500; Bible-school enrollment, 32.

Mins. Wiiford Field, Barlow Higgins, W. S. Mesnard and Frank Shane have done faithful work in this country.

FAYETTE COUNTY.

Arne Prairie (Brownstown).

Organized 1907, by R. Leland Brown; present membership, 17; value of property, $200; summer Bible school.

This is five miles midway between Brownstown and Loogootee.

Bethany (Brownstown).

Present membership, 61; value of property, $1,000; Bible-school enrollment, 65.

This church is about eight miles northwest of Brownstown. It is a new organization and was made up largely of members who previously belonged to the New Hope Church, a near-by country congregation whose chapel burned in 1867.

Bethany congregation gave W. B. Hopper to the ministry.

Bingham.

Organized 1911, by D. R. Bebout; present membership, 15; value of property, $1,000; Bible school began 1911.

A little congregation was formed in 1892 by Min. John Meeks, but it was short-lived. Through the insistence of

Mrs. W. B. Shelton, Mrs. Sarah Hurst and Mrs. Ellen Harper, a meeting was held by Min. C. M. Smithson in 1910 which led to the organization of the church, the next year, of thirteen members.

The meetings were held in the W. C. T. U. temple. Inasmuch as this building was running down, the society proposed to transfer to the people of the town as a union church. When the time for action came, the denominational representatives withdrew; hence the property was deeded to the Christian Church. It was thoroughly repaired and put in a good condition.

Brownstown.

Organized 1871, by Charles Smith; present membership, 206; value of property, $17,500; Bible school began 1871; present enrollment, 190.

An active church of not a few good people. Four Mile, New Hope and Liberty congregations all supplied members to Brownstown.

S. D. Morton and Wm. Rode are true helpers.

Four-mile Prairie (Brownstown).

Organized 1843, by Wm. Chaplin and Wm. Schooly; present membership, 20; value of property, $1,200; Bible-school enrollment, 38.

The first members were Moses D. and John F. Morey, Jacob Tinker and wife, Abner Griffith and wife, Mrs. Campbell, Mrs. Smith and M. W. Hickerson, who was a good preacher. This congregation died and after some years revived. The chapel was built in 1912. This is the home of Min. Geo. T. Bridges.

Liberty (Brownstown).

Organized by Wm. Schooley; present membership, 75; Bible-school enrollment, 70.

This is one of the oldest churches in the county.

It was organized in the residence of Mr. Van Workman.

Later they built a chapel, which was burned down in 1913. Some of the leading members were Mr. Van Workman, Joshua Arnold, Samuel Dayhoof, John and William Sefton, William Buchanan, Joseph Reynolds and William Dively.

Macedonia (Loogootee).

Organized 1868, by Charles Smith; present membership, 75; value of property, $1,000; Bible school began 1869; present enrollment, 75.

Worshiped in the Rush and Eldorado Schoolhouses till 1901, when the chapel was built midway between the two.

Gave C. M. Smithson to the ministry. James Idleman, the grandfather of Finis Idleman, helped form this congregation. The present elders are H. H. Smithson, Elihu Fulton, Samuel Odell, George Underwood, Wyatt Bledsoe and Charles Mills.

Pittsburg (Vandalia).

Present membership, 34; value of property, $1,000.

Ten miles southwest of Vandalia. It was probably formed in the early seventies. The elders now are William Rodecker, John Hopkins and Samuel Jeffs. Mrs. Sarah Collier and Mrs. Horatio Evans are also active members.

Ramsey.

Organized 1851, by Wesley Smith; present membership, 123; value of property, $1,000; Bible-school enrollment, 36.

Among the first members there were Elijah, Elisha and Bazil Prather; Alex. Williams, George Bartlett, William McCary and Jacob Miller. The congregation was formed at Chandler's Schoolhouse. Meetings were held there and in the houses of the members till 1866, when a brick chapel was erected in Ramsey.

St. Elmo.

Organized by W. H. Drummett; present membership, 167; value of property, $9,000; Bible-school enrollment, 189.

Union (Ramsey).

Present membership, 35; value of property, $1,000; Bible-school enrollment, 30.

The chapel was built in 1872 on the farm of John H. Welch, now in Carson Township. It is doing fairly well.

Extinct Congregations.

An old congregation called Antioch, in Bowling Green Township, lived in the seventies. Conservatives paralyzed its activities and, later, their own. Some of the members went to Herrick.

There was a small congregation near the present town of Holliday which died. The original members were Wash. Riley and wife, Wm. Fulk and wife, Griffin Tipsword, Thomas Holman and wife, John and Charles Dunaway.

A congregation at Loudon has ceased to exist.

For years there was a congregation in Vandalia. It perished from a lack of leadership.

There was a congregation in the seventies near Laclede. It was composed mostly of renters and so died.

Ministers.

J. O. Henry was a great force in the churches of this county from 1862 to 1884.

Jacob Miller was a man of strong character, but limited education. At ninety years of age he still resides on his farm near Ramsey.

George T. Bridges grew up near Ramsey. He has always been active, energetic and enthusiastic. His home is south of Brownstown.

John Meeks, Charles Smith and Michael Hickerson were all former preachers, and did unselfish work in their day. All have gone hence.

R. Leland Brown is a native of this county and has been in the ministry since 1869. He has been very active and useful there and elsewhere.

FORD COUNTY.

Gibson.

Organized 1872, by G. W. Campbell; present membership, 430; value of property, including parsonage, $27,500; Bible-school enrollment, 448.

There was occasional preaching for three years in neighboring schoolhouses and the town previous to the organization of the church.

There were nineteen charter members. H. N. Karr and A. E. Pirkey were the first elders, with Andrew Jordan, John Dillingham, A. Canterbury and J. B. Lott, the first deacons. For six years the meetings were held in Union Hall and the church was served by Mins. Clark Braden, W. S. Campbell, F. Collins, J. F. Smith and Samuel Lowe.

By reason of the death of Mr. Lott and financial reverses of Mr. Jordon, the principal financial supports, the congregation ceased to meet. This was in 1880. For ten years following, the local C. W. B. M. kept going. So in 1890 the State Board of Missions sent Min. J. E. Jewett to revive the church. This he did. Mrs. O. H. Damon (*nee* Mrs. J. H. Lott) gave the lot and Mr. Jordon donated the brick. The building was erected and the congregation began work again with about twenty-five members.

The pastors who followed were M. P. Hayden, C. C. Rowlison, R. F. Thrapp, W. W. Sniff, S. E. Fisher, John R. Golden, and L. O. Lehman, who is the present minister.

The building has been much enlarged and modernized. The church has in its membership a superior class of Christian men and women.

Mt. Olivet (Paxton).

Organized 1857, by Marston Dudley; present membership, 84; value of property, $1,500; Bible-school began 1860; present enrollment, 52.

This is the oldest church in Ford County and has contributed of its members to many other congregations. Jacob

Straxer and wife, Marston Dudley and wife, and J. P. Botton and wife began this work. Besides Mr. Dudley, Rolla M. Martin and J. L. Canada ministered to the congregation in its early years. Mr. Botton was the Bible-school superintendent fifty years ago and one of the most useful members.

Elmer Higdon and Ernest Higdon were given to the ministry.

Paxton.

Present membership, 150; value of property, including parsonage, $7,000; Bible-school enrollment, 160.

This church was formed in the seventies. It has given Glen Mills and Jay Bonham to the ministry.

FRANKLIN COUNTY.

Benton.

Organized 1889, by W. H. Ingram; present membership, 200; value of property, including parsonage, $9,000; Bible school began 1889; present enrollment, 100.

This church was organized in the courthouse under the auspices of the State Missionary Society. But it is lacking in spiritual vision.

Christopher.

Present membership, 385; value of property, $6,000; Bible-school enrollment, 240.

This was among the early congregations of the county. It was at first a country church, but the coal interests grew the village into a city. It has kept pace and is active and growing.

Long Prairie (Benton).

Present membership, 50; value of property, $800; no Bible school.

An old country church seven miles northeast of Benton. Irregular preaching.

Miner (Mulkeytown).

Present membership, 108; value of property, $350; Bible-school enrollment, 45.

This is twelve miles southwest of Benton and is one of the oldest churches in the county. It has monthly preaching. Mrs. Adelene Browning is clerk.

Mulkeytown.

Organized 1830, by Minister Underwood; present membership, 380; value of property, $2,000; Bible-school enrollment, 212.

This was first known as the Little Muddy Church because this was the name of the community post-office. Then it came to be known as the "Four-mile Church" because the meeting-place was in the prairie of that name. After the Civil War it took the name of the town from John M. Mulkey, who built the first house on the town site. (See Chap. II.)

Six-mile (Elkville).

Organized 1848; present membership, 88; value of property, $800; Bible-school enrollment, 107.

This congregation was probably reorganized in later years by W. A. Ingram.

Sesser.

Organized 1905; present membership, 48; value of property, $1,875; Bible-school enrollment, 130.

West Frankfort.

Organized 1902, by J. J. Harris; present membership, 132; value of property, $3,500; Bible school began 1902; present enrollment, 120.

Minister Harris conducted a series of meetings in the Congregational chapel which resulted in this organization. The church house is a monument to the devotion and liberality of W. L. Crim, an able preacher.

CHURCHES

White (Plumfield).

Organized 1866, by Matthew Wilson; present membership, 40; value of property, $800; no Bible school.

FULTON COUNTY.

Astoria.

Organized 1863, by J. B. Royal; present membership, 175; value of property, $4,000; Bible school began 1862; present enrollment, 136.

Mr. Royal held the first meetings in the old schoolhouse. The first prayer-meeting was also held there. Dr. B. C. Toler and John Gilliland were the only persons present. The charter members were Thomas, A. S., Uriah, M. J. and Unity Smith; Isaac, Joseph, Ellen, Eliza, Catherine, A. J. and Susan M. Engle; Alexander M. Bride, C. and Eliza Douglas, J. A. Gilliland, I. and Elizabeth Darrow, Philip Wonderlick, B. Munson, Catherine Lane and Dr. B. C. Toler. These twenty-two people signed the following agreement: "We, the undersigned, do agree, and hereby have agreed, to worship together as a church of Christ, to take the Holy Bible as the only rule of our faith and practice, and to call ourselves Christian after the name of Christ our Lord."

The present building was erected in 1885. Dr. Toler was a devoted and efficient leader. W. M. Horton is the pastor.

Bryant.

Organized 1852, by William Howard; present membership, 48; value of property, $1,000; Bible-school enrollment, 50.

This was known first as the New Antioch Christian Church, located in the northwest corner of Liverpool Township. It was organized in the home of T. N. Hasson, with fifteen charter members. John W. Hopkins and Wm. G. Kirkpatric were chosen elders, and T. N. Hasson, deacon. Little progress was made until 1858, when Evangelist Wm.

Grissom awakened the community by the gospel. The chapel was built that year. The meetings were held there until 1870, when the house was moved to the village of Bryant. The church prospered. Removals in the following years contributed not a few valuable members to Lewistown, Cuba and Canton, leaving Bryant a feeble congregation.

H. C. Littleton was given to the ministry. James Wilcoxen was a valuable member here and afterward at Lewistown.

Canton.

Organized 1890, by N. S. Haynes; present membership, 500; value of property, $20,000; Bible school began 1891; present enrollment, 423.

An effort was made in 1878 and another in 1888 to establish a church of Christ in Canton, but neither proved permanent. In 1890 two devoted sisters, Mrs. Nellie Lawrence and Mrs. H. A. Whitnah, visited from house to house all known Disciples of Christ in the town. This led to the organization of the church on August 31, with forty-one charter members, in "Temperance Hall." S. E. Hogue and J. B. Romine were elected elders, with C. L. Whitnah, T. L. Frazier and J. C. Peterson, deacons. The young congregation was nurtured by the prayers and faithful services of some most devoted people.

The well-located lot and first brick chapel cost $12,500. In 1895 a brick auditorium was added. Marion Stevenson was the first pastor. During his term 325 additions were gained in a meeting led by Evangelist T. A. Boyer. Other ministers who have served the church were J. C. and S. S. Lappin, J. P. Lichtenberger, S. H. Zendt, J. G. Waggoner, and now W. W. Denham.

The church has given to the ministry W. H. Betts and August F. Larson.

From the first the congregation has had and has grown very useful Christian men and women. The Whitnah, Lawrence and Frazier families helped much. Their names

CHURCHES

are remembered tenderly and gratefully. The congregation is active in all good works.

Cuba.

Organized 1832, by John Secrist; present membership, 226; value of property, $10,600; Bible-school enrollment, 275.

Ephraim Brown, a farmer, laid out a town about the center of Fulton County in 1834 and named it Middleton. Joel Solomon founded another town in 1836 and called it Centerville. The two were separated by a twelve-foot alley only. Later these two towns were united and named Cuba. Joel Solomon wanted a church; so he put up a chapel and sold it to the Christian congregation in 1837.

Min. John Secrist, of Ohio, held a meeting in the settlement, and in February, 1832, baptized eighteen persons and organized a church with Charles Rigdon and Morgan Hartford as officers. This church is one of the oldest in the Military Tract. The congregation failed to pay for the purchased chapel, and so lost the use of it. Thereafter their meetings were held in residences, schoolhouses, shops, halls and groves until 1863. During the larger part of this period the preaching was done by transients like most pioneer churches had. Among these were John W. Hopkins, Wm. A. Howard, John Rigdon, John Miller, Dr. John Scott and C. P. Hollis. In 1854, Josiah Crawford settled in the community and preached there. In 1857, Wm. Grissom went into Fulton County, held meetings, baptized hundreds and organized country congregations. His ministry at Cuba continued up to 1865. The second church house was built in 1895. The congregation took a pride in loyally supporting and patronizing Abingdon College while it lived, and since its discontinuance it has been equally loyal to Eureka. It is a church with a world-wide vision.

It has given to the ministry H. R. Trickett, D. E. Hughes, J. W. Carpenter, George Snively, L. F. Davis and Charles Day.

The long and excellent service that C. C. Riley gave the congregation is worthy of note. He was born within six miles of Cuba in 1845 and has lived in the town since 1868. He died in 1913.

Ellisville.

Organized 1887, by D. E. Hughes; present membership, 25; value of property, $4,000; Bible school began 1899; present enrollment, 35.

In 1887, Mr. Amzi Byrum, a citizen of Ellisville, invited Min. D. E. Hughes to preach there. There were eight present at the first meeting. The three weeks' revival closed with a membership of eighty-six and the formation of a church. The old chapel of the Presbyterians was used. The new chapel was built the same year. For twelve years a union Bible school was maintained; after that the church held its own school. The village is inland and populations tend away from it.

Ipava.

Organized 1842, by William Howard; present membership, 225; value of property, including parsonage, $10,000; Bible school began 1858; present enrollment, 136.

As early as 1840 there was quite an emigration from Ohio and Kentucky into the southern part of Fulton County. Most of these were members or friends of the church of Christ. Prominent among them was Wm. P. Howard, then a young man. At first meetings were held from house to house. A schoolhouse of round logs, chinked and daubed with mud and straw, clapboard roof, with puncheon seats and floor, was built. In this meetings were held and the congregation formed. This was four and one-half miles southeast of the site of Ipava. This house was soon too small to accommodate the worshipers, hence a church house was built. It was 30 x 40 feet, with eight feet to the ceiling, logs and poles, and roof of lap shingles, riven and shaved. The siding and all finishings were of walnut. This came to be known as the Howard Church. To this congregation

Mr. Howard ministered for sixteen years without financial remuneration, supporting his family by his farm labor.

All the conditions were primitive. The women then did all the spinning and knitting, sewing and weaving—all this in addition to other household cares. In this community, when they would attend the business meeting of the church on Saturday afternoons, they would take their knitting along with them and knit going to and coming from the church. Those living within a radius of two miles of the meeting-house generally walked. These women would travel barefoot, carrying their shoes and stockings. When near the church they would put on these articles of dress. The time and the circumstances required economy. Those who rode went horseback, or in the big farm-wagons. Sometimes they were drawn by oxen. "Old Sam" and "Brin" were useful in those days. The seat-board was an oak plank, cushioned with a sheepskin. Everybody went to church, including the babies.

In addition to Mr. Howard, Hughey Stoops and J. W. Hopkins were two ministers of this community who went, at their own charges, preaching the Word—all self-sacrificing and faithful servants of God and men. After Mr. Howard's removal to Texas, in 1857, Wm. Grissom served the congregation, as did also Wm. Lorance.

By 1867 the building was dilapidated and the congregation disbanded. Part of the members went to Summum and part to the Washington Schoolhouse, where Dr. J. H. Breeden had built up a congregation. In 1869 they purchased the old M. E. chapel in Ipava and repaired it. Thereafter this town was the place of meeting. In addition to Dr. Breeden, P. D. Vermilion, M. T. Cooper and L. M. Robinson served the church. This chapel was not well located; so it was sold and in 1895 a modern structure erected.

Kerton Valley (Havana).

Organized 1889; present membership, 30; value of property, $800; Bible school began 1889; present enrollment, 50.

The deed to the ground was made to the Christian Church, but the various religious people of the community united in building the chapel and in maintaining a union Bible school. The organization of the congregation was perfected by Isaac Beckelhymer in 1912. The clerk is R. L. Cole, R. R. 3, Havana.

Lewistown.

Organized 1874, by A. C. Smither; present membership, 175; value of property, including parsonage, $10,000; Bible school began 1874; present enrollment, 175.

Of the twenty charter members, only three survive. Two of these—Henry C. Hasson and his sister, Miss Celinda Hasson—are residents of Lewistown and active supporters of the one faith. The chapel, still in use, was completed and dedicated by O. A. Burgess. In its construction and in maintaining the current expenses of the congregation, Mr. J. C. Wilcoxen, a royal Christian man, paid one-third of the expenses until his life closed on earth.

Mr. Hasson was superintendent of the Bible school for thirty-four years. Mr. M. M. Beeman succeeded in 1908. He is also the head of the city's schools. The congregation has had its good fortune and ill, but has steadily gained ground and is now a power in its community for good.

It has given to the ministry Marion Stevenson.

London Mills.

Organized 1887, by L. B. Meyers; present membership, 111; value of property, $2,000; Bible school began 1887; present enrollment, 71.

The church at Hermon, Knox County, sent its pastor to London Mills and planted this congregation.

Mr. W. W. Voce has been a strong factor in this church. Miss Mina Fox is the clerk.

The church gave Clarence Brown and Mr. Anderson to the ministry.

CHURCHES

Summum.

Organized 1859, by Dr. J. H. Breeden; present membership, 200; value of property, $2,500; Bible school began 1868; present enrollment, 117.

As soon as Dr. Breeden settled in this village in 1858, he began to work for the formation of a church of Christ there. He soon associated with himself Min. Wm. Grissom, who was a fine evangelist. Among the charter members were Dr. J. H. Breeden and wife, Margaret Horton, Mrs. Clara Weese, Sarah E. Clary, Julia Dary, Elizabeth Dabson and John Thompson.

For possibly forty years the care of the congregation devolved largely upon Dr. Breeden. Among others who served it were A. J. Kane, Wm. Brown, J. B. Royal, Alexander Johnston, J. B. McCorkle, A. G. Lucas, David Sharpless and G. A. Burnett.

The chapel was built in 1865 and is still in use. The church has given to the Christian ministry M. T. Cooper, H. O. Breeden (a son of Dr. Breeden), Guy Shields and Singer De Loss Smith.

The current of young life flows outward as from most inland villages.

Table Grove.

Organized 1851, by Dr. J. H. Hughes; present membership, 112; value of property, $10,000; Bible school began 1851; present enrollment, 163.

Some pioneer preachers of the churches of Christ began to visit this country in 1840. Among them were Wm. Howard, Wm. Muckley, Wm. Rigdon, J. W. Hopkins, Enos Monahan, John Harris, Robert Foster, Wm. Grissom, Wm. Griffin and blind Billy Brown. From their ministry about one hundred persons became identified with the cause of primitive Christianity. The church was organized in the schoolhouse. The officers elected were John Hendrickson and Asa Harlan as elders, with George Harlan and Ewing

McCartney, deacons. The two resident members still living are Mrs. Anna M. Wilson and Addison Abernathy.

After years of meetings in residences, barns, schoolhouses and groves, the chapel was completed in 1868 and dedicated by John S. Sweeney. Later this was replaced by a modern building.

Steven Davis was given to the ministry. This church has never used questionable methods of raising money for its current expenses. The apportionment plan is followed and deficits are unknown.

There was, in 1856, the Hickory Grove Church, three miles southeast.

Vermont.

Organized 1847, by Dr. J. H. Hughes; present membership, 376; value of property, $9,000; Bible-school enrollment, 305.

The second church building was erected in 1891 during the pastorate of Geo. W. Ross. The congregation has given to the ministry J. H. and E. A. Gilliland, Charles W. Ross and Mrs. Nellie Daugherty-Butchart—a missionary in China.

Antioch Mission.

This congregation sustains a mission point. It is located two and one-half miles north of Vermont, has a frame chapel, a Bible school of thirty people and bimonthly preaching.

GREEN COUNTY.

Athensville.

Present membership, 75; Bible-school enrollment, 60.

Carrollton.

Organized 1832, by Barton W. Stone; present membership, 90; value of property, including parsonage, $4,500; Bible-school enrollment, 70.

The church grew for several years, coming to number

120 members. Then it waned through deaths and removals. In 1841 a second start was made with twenty-eight members. Its life has moved like the tides. All of the early pioneer preachers of that section served here more or less. Col. E. D. Baker became a Christian here. Many fine people have had their homes in this church.

Kane.

Present membership, 100 (conservative).

Roodhouse.

Organized 1890, by H. G. Van Dervoort; present membership, 138; value of property, $7,400; Bible school began 1890; present enrollment, 100.

Among the charter members there were Mrs. R. A. Young, Samuel and Sarah Long, Mrs. M. E. Briggs and Mrs. Wm. Heaton. The house was built in 1894.

Union (Greenfield).

Organized 1854, by John S. Sweeney; present membership, 40; value of property, $1,500, no Bible school.

This is in the northeast part of the county. Among the charter members there were E. T. Venderveer, John Barnett, Benjamin Scott, Sr. and Jr., and Edward Prather and wife. J. S. Sweeney held a series of meetings here in 1857, adding one hundred. In 1868, Min. E. P. Bellche debated John Hughes, Universalist, in this chapel. Leroy Pippin is the correspondent.

White Hall.

Organized 1883, by W. S. Jermane and J. J. W. Miller; present membership, 230; value of property, $6,500; Bible school began 1884; present enrollment, 170.

There were twenty-two charter members. A small chapel was bought of the Free Methodists and used till 1903, when the present brick edifice was finished. The present elders are Francis Fowler, W. H. Teter and G. J. Harris.

HAMILTON COUNTY.

Broughton.

Organized 1872, by Minister Truex; present membership, 43; value of property, $1,250; Bible school began 1912; present enrollment, 40.

W. T. Owen and his wife were baptized by Min. J. N. Mulkey, near Mulkeytown, in 1868. The next year they moved to the southern part of Hamilton County. They were the first and only Disciples there. They were solicited to take membership in the Cumberland Presbyterian Church, but declined. On his earnest invitation, Minister Truex came from Roland, held a meeting in the schoolhouse just south of Broughton, and organized a church of thirteen members. This continued till 1880, when a union church house was built in the village which the Disciples used the fourth Sunday in the month. This continued till 1898. For eighteen years, Mr. Owen, though living two miles in the country, served as janitor, superintendent of the union Sunday school and general utility man for the society. The old house went to wreck. Mr. Owen moved away. The congregation scattered. In 1910, Min. Marion Boles held a series of meetings. The next year it was decided to build a church house two miles west of Broughton, which was finished in 1912. Elijah Austin led in this movement. He and G. B. Simmons are the elders.

Dahlgren.

Organized 1906, by Lew D. Hill; present membership, 42; value of property, $1,500; Bible school began 1905; present enrollment, 47.

This church grew out of the Bible school. Meetings were held in homes and the town hall till the church was finished in 1910.

Dale.

Present membership, 35; value of property, $200; no Bible school.

CHURCHES

Liberty (Thompsonville).

Organized 1857; present membership, 55; value of property, $1,000; Bible-school enrollment, 75.

The Lamkin family came to this locality in 1850. There was preaching there through the fifties by John A. and Samuel Williams, and a congregation was formed. The Civil War scattered its members. Thereafter an organization was formed with the following charter members: Joshua Pemberton, James H. Lamkin and John Odle, elders; R. C. Flannigan, Jesse and W. C. Pemberton, deacons; Joel Jacobs, Jas. W. Flannigan, Wm. and Elizabeth Simmons, Sally Lamkin; Charlotte, Mary C. and Millie Pemberton; Sitzma Organ, Martha A. Jacobs, Charlotte Odle, Sallie Ann and Alice Smith. The chapel was built in 1868. The church meets every week to worship. It is six miles south of Thompsonville. W. C. Lamkin, a son of J. H. Lamkin, furnished most of these facts.

McLeansboro.

Organized 1876, by James T. Baker; present membership, 194; value of property, $3,000; Bible school began 1876; present enrollment, 85.

The courthouse was used as the place of public worship till 1880, when the church was finished and occupied. The church has made progress steadily in every way.

Mt. Pleasant (McLeansboro).

Organized 1851, by Moses Goodwin; present membership, 69; value of property, $1,500; no Bible school.

This church was organized in the barn of David Upton, August 22. It met there for worship until 1855, when a log house was built on land donated by Jefferson Garrison. After being used twenty years, this house was torn down and a frame chapel was erected which is still in good condition.

The charter members were Alfred and Nancy Drew, James E. Lee and wife, Jefferson Garrison and wife, Sarah

Smithfeeters, Jane Reynolds and Alice Vaughn. The first elders were James E. Lee and Alfred Drew. From a daughter of Mr. Lee these facts are learned.

The location is six miles north of McLeansboro.

Those who went forth from this congregation as ministers were Thomas Mason, Alfred Drew, William Richards and Steven Hale.

New White Oak (Springerton).

Organized 1885; present membership, 75; value of property, $600; Bible school began 1885; present enrollment, 100.

Mr. J. K. P. White gave one acre of land for the use of the congregation. It is located in Beaver Creek Township.

HANCOCK COUNTY.

Adrian.

Present membership, 98; value of property, $1,500; Bible-school enrollment, 102.

Augusta.

Organized 1850, by James Stark; present membership, 251; value of property, $10,000; Bible-school enrollment, 250.

Mr. Stark was ordained at Jacksonville in 1837 and moved to Augusta in 1842. He was willing at all times to preach the gospel as opportunity offered. Meetings were held in the homes of Benjamin Gould and Wm. Dron. The first chapel was built in 1850. Elders Stark, Dron, Gould, Young and others led the Lord's Day meetings till 1868. Then E. J. Lampton conducted a series of meetings and served as pastor for six years. Since then fourteen other men have served the church in this relation, and about the same number have conducted revivals. Besides these, not a few able and well-known ministers have preached here.

From the first, 1,025 names have been on the roll of this membership, and numbers of these have been representative citizens.

CHURCHES

The church has given to the ministry James McClure, Robert E. Henry and Mrs. Mary Pickens-Buckner.

D. P. Coffman is now one of the beloved members.

Bowen.

Organized 1890; present membership, 250; value of property, including parsonage, $23,000; Bible-school enrollment, 243.

The congregation met for worship in the town hall until 1892, when the present building was erected. In 1907 a new and modern house was occupied. A parsonage followed in 1912.

Among the leading members in the earlier years there were R. T. Lee and wife, Hyram Schulze and wife, W. T. Hough and family and Mrs. Laslie.

The congregation has many members young in the faith and life, full of zeal and ambition for the Lord's work.

Breckenridge (Sutter).

Present membership, 56; value of property, $1,500; Bible-school enrollment, 83.

Burnside.

Organized 1875, by J. H. Garrison; present membership, 68; value of property, $2,000; Bible school began 1875; present enrollment, 81.

The first members were Mr. and Mrs. Alford Pettit, Mr. and Mrs. Wm. Bray (ages eighty-seven and eighty-four—1913), Mr. and Mrs. Wm. Pettit, Mr. and Mrs. Hatch, Mr. Joshua Shreeves (age ninety-two), Mrs. Sarah Decker, D. C. Tyner, with the following four who are still living: Mrs. D. C. Tyner, Mr. and Mrs. E. Glaze and Mrs. O. C. Ing.

Carthage.

Organized 1864, by John Errett; present membership, 360; value of property, including parsonage, $16,000; Bible school began 1864; present enrollment, 236.

Following a series of meetings, this church was organized with the following fourteen charter members: Allen McQuary, H. and Alice Crawford, Elizabeth Scofield, Margaret Crawford, William and Elizabeth Hughes, James M. and Mrs. Mayfield, William and Mrs. Patterson, Virginia Wilson, Mary A. and J. C. Williams.

By the courtesy of the board of supervisors, the meetings were first held in the courthouse. In 1866 a small church building was erected, which gave place, in 1884, to the present structure.

E. J. Lampton was the first pastor. Judge C. J. Scofield served as pastor for several years during the weakness of the church.

These data were furnished by the patriarch of the congregation, "Uncle Jesse C. Williams," who is bright and up to date, although he now (1912) is ninety-four years of age. The church is active in every department, contributing to all missionary and benevolent enterprises.

Dallas City.

Present membership, 334; value of property, including parsonage, $11,500; Bible-school enrollment, 266.

Denver.

Organized 1875, by J. C. Reynolds; present membership, 181; value of property, $3,000; Bible school began 1875; present enrollment, 202.

Thirty-four of the Mt. Pleasant Church in this county, with permission, constituted the church in Denver; thereafter they were formally dismissed by letters. The first officers were: James Black, M. K. Kirk and Geo. M. Browning, elders, with Joseph Dorsey and J. S. McClure, deacons. All of them are dead.

While M. K. Kirk remained there he preached to the church every second Lord's Day. D. C. Barber has been a faithful and useful member for many years.

The congregation has always been active in all good works. It is well officered and organized.

East Durham (Colusa).

Present membership, 40; value of property, $2,500.

Ferris.

Present membership, 60; value of property, $2,500; Bible-school enrollment, 60.

Golden Point (Hamilton).

Present membership, 75; value of property, $4,500; Bible-school enrollment, 91.

Hamilton.

Organized 1893, by Samuel McGee; present membership, 225; value of property, $7,000; Bible school began 1893; present enrollment, 108.

This church was the immediate result of a six weeks' meeting conducted by Minister McGee. For a year the church worshiped in the city hall. During the pastorate of C. G. Blakeslee a church building was completed in 1894. The congregation struggled on for ten years with a half-time ministry by students from Canton (Mo.) University.

There is being built at Hamilton one of the largest water-power dams in the world, and the city has promise of becoming a great manufacturing center. The church there is alert to its opening opportunities.

La Crosse.

Present membership, 90; value of property, $2,000; Bible-school enrollment, 90.

La Harpe.

Organized 1877, by H. P. Tandy; present membership, 522; value of property, $8,000; Bible school began 1877; present enrollment, 225.

A congregation was formed here about 1850, but its life was brief. In March, 1877, Evangelist G. W. Mapes held a successful meeting and the church was organized the following month. Meetings were held in a hall till 1884, when the church was finished.

Mt. Pleasant (Plymouth).

Organized 1833, by Gilmore Callison; present membership, 70; value of property, $2,200; Bible-school enrollment, 60.

Mrs. Hattie McClure-Smith, Muskegon, Mich., and Mrs. Georgenia Daw Walton, Plymouth, Ill., have furnished the data for this history. Mrs. Walton has been a member of this congregation fifty-four years and is its eldest resident member.

Mt. Pleasant Church is located midway between Carthage and Plymouth, ten miles from each, and four and a half miles east of Bentley. Into this locality, in 1833, there came, from near Columbia, Adair County, Ky., Gilmore Callison and his wife Elizabeth, her brother James McClure (who had been baptized in 1830 in Green River, Kentucky, by the pioneer Christian preacher, John D. Steele, and who was the father of Mrs. Smith), Mrs. Betsy Massie (who was a sister of Mr. Steele), Green Browning and others. These five persons met, on the first Lord's Day after their arrival, at the home of Mr. Callison, to "break bread," and then formed a church of Christ. This was the first Christian Church in Hancock County and became the mother of congregations. Plymouth, Carthage, Augusta, Oak Grove, Denver and Bentley are her spiritual children.

The settlers soon gave to the place its name, "Mt. Pleasant." In 1839, Josiah Callison was ordained as an elder and William Smith as a deacon. The two Callisons served this and other communities as preachers. People came from five to twenty-five miles to the public worship. They came on horseback, by wagons drawn by horses or oxen, and were entertained by those living near the grove. Young people walked two to five miles to church.

Robert, John, James, George and Elizabeth Stark united

with the church some years after its formation. The Starks, Pattens, Drawns and others were firm friends of Alexander Campbell in Scotland. Margaret Patten was one of his friends who ministered to him in prison. He called her and her girl companion his "ministering angels." Robert Stark, when he first came from Scotland, and probably James Stark also, made their residence at Mr. Campbell's home in Virginia. Elizabeth Stark married Simeon B. Walton and settled near the church. He united with the congregation in 1843. James and Mary A. Black came from Elkton, Ky., in 1852. He was ordained an elder, and when there was no regular minister preached for the congregation till 1875. William and Lucy Lyon Bridgewater united with the church in 1852.

Mrs. Alzada Groves, an octogenarian, says that when she first knew Mt. Pleasant the women wore homespun, as did the men also—all made by the home folk. The women were proud of a calico dress and sunbonnet. The men wore skin caps and straw hats that were braided and sewed by the women. After her marriage she often walked two miles to church and carried her baby. At church they had "mighty good times."

Mrs. Sarah Huey Daw, another octogenarian, says: "I tell you we had good meetings." After the teaching elders moved to the young towns, some of them would return to preach on Sundays. "I made a good long piece of jeans and gave old brother Grandpa Black a suit of clothes he was pretty proud of."

In August, 1858, or 1859, a district meeting was held at Mt. Pleasant which lasted two weeks. Many preachers were present, among them Thomas Munnell and one of the Erretts. People came from afar.

In the early days it was common to hear wolves howl at night; but their proximity and blood-curdling howls did not keep any one away from church. A mother and her son were driving through the timber one night, when a wolf followed them. The boy drove the horses while the mother sat at the end of the wagon and kept it off with a pitchfork.

At one time Robert Foster settled in the community and preached for the congregations. The members built a house for him on a farm about three miles from the chapel. Before that time, Mr. McClure met a man on the road near Tuckertown who asked him where he lived. Upon his reply the man said: "Why, that is over in the Campbellite settlement. Are they not dangerous? and do they not have humps on their backs, and horns?" Mr. McClure answered: "I am one of them. They are not dangerous, and they look like most people, I guess. Come over to our meetings."

In 1875 the Mt. Pleasant Church built a mission chapel in Denver, Hancock County, and began to establish a Christian congregation there.

As the years passed, many of the members moved to the towns that had grown with the coming of the railways, and the frame chapel that had been built in the forties was becoming old. Some then proposed to disband the congregation. Then a sister urged in a public meeting that all could not go to the towns to church, and the children of the neighborhood were to be cared for. Thus it was decided to go on with the work. A new chapel was built. A tent was secured, and a series of meetings held in a near-by neighborhood which re-enforced the congregation. This meeting was in 1909. The house was remodeled in 1897.

Long time ago ground was given by Simeon B. and Elizabeth Stark Walton for the church house and "graveyard."

J. B. Royal preached for the church when he was a young man, E. J. Lampton, J. C. Reynolds and many other faithful ministers.

This has been an apostolic church and has done a world of good. It has had a host of faithful and truly great men and women. In the winter of 1912-13 a father and his daughter walked four miles by reason of the snow blockading the roads, rather than miss public worship.

This church gave Henry Black, J. O. Walton, Mrs.

Sadie McCoy Crank and Miss Ava S. Walton to the ministry.

Bentley is a mission of the Mt. Pleasant Church. It was formed in the end of the year 1890, and the chapel built later.

Oak Grove (Carthage).

Present membership, 70; value of property, $1,000.

This is about ten miles east of Carthage and was the home church of Dr. Wm. Booz. For many years he made it a practice to preach a sermon here on New Year's Day.

Plymouth.

Organized 1855, by J. R. Ross; present membership, 73; value of property, $9,000; present enrollment, 62.

The series of meetings out of which this congregation grew were held in the M. E. Church. The charter members were David and Susan Palmer, John and Zerilda Ritchey, Jonas and Margaret Myers, J. W. Bell, A. B. Moore, John and Rebecca Madison, John Hendrickson, David and Nancy Wade, Edward Wade, Ann Hooton, Wm. H. Hooton, Isapena Buyher, Thomas and Malinda Burdett, John and Elizabeth Ades, Phebe Ades, John Stark, Uphema Myers, Nancy Browning, Sarah Moore, Francis and Mary Ritchey.

Some of the ministers who succeeded Mr. Ross were H. Young, E. Browning, E. J. Lampton, George Brewster, James Stark and J. Carroll Stark.

Stillwell.

Present membership, 110; value of property, $3,000; Bible-school enrollment, 97.

West Point.

Organized 1864, by David Hobbs; present membership, 160; value of property, $6,000; Bible school enrollment, 145.

Minister Hobbs conducted two meetings here, and at the close of the second formed the church. Among the charter members there were Henry Hindle and wife, Elijah Rhodes and wife, David and Almira Wiggle, Mrs. Joseph McMillan, Mrs. Samuel Barber, Mrs. John S. Kelly and Miss Mary Louis.

The meetings for public worship were held in the little schoolhouse, then in the new schoolroom, then in a hall, next in the Lutheran chapel, and in 1876 in their own building.

The young church was fostered by Mins. John Stark and Joseph Tanner.

Wythe (Sutter).

Organized 1865, by E. J. Lampton; present membership, 30; value of property, $1,500.

Germans have bought the farms, and the life of the church is feeble. H. O. Knox and J. C. McMahan are the only charter members left.

HARDIN COUNTY.

Cave in Rock.

Present membership, 66; value of property, $1,000.

Rosiclare.

Present membership, 146; value of property, $1,500; Bible-school enrollment, 115.

Stone Church (Elizabethtown).

Present membership, 132; value of property, $1,000; Bible-school enrollment, 65.

HENDERSON COUNTY.

Lomax.

Present membership, 150; value of property, $6,000; Bible-school enrollment, 81.

The church maintains preaching and serves the community well.

CHURCHES

Raritan.

Present membership, 20; value of property, $3,000. Inactive.

Stronghurst.

Present membership, 71; value of property, $2,500; Bible-school enrollment, 140.

A varied history.

HENRY COUNTY.

During the sixties and part of the seventies there was a congregation of Christians in Kewanee. It failed by deaths and removals. After twenty-five years the work there was revived.

A part of the members of the first congregation in Kewanee, when it suspended, formed a church northwest of the city, in Burns Township. Its meetings were held in a schoolhouse during a part of the seventies and eighties. Then removals ended its meetings.

For a few years there was a church at Cambridge. Then it was thought advisable to go into a sort of federation. The result was that the M. E. people got the property and the Baptists most of the members. At one time there was in this chapel the "altar" of the Methodists and the baptistery of the Disciples.

There was a small congregation of Christians only at one time in Galva.

At Woodhull there was formerly an active church of Christ which gave Oliver W. Stewart to the Christian ministry. While not extinct, it has shown no desire to be revived in late years.

Kewanee.

Organized 1901, by A. C. Roach; present membership, 366; value of property, $3,000; Bible school began 1901; present enrollment, 225.

The charter members were A. C. Roach, S. J. Batchel,

Geo. W. Bean and wife, Mrs. Ida Deckerhoff, Mrs. Shorba A. Ewing, Thomas Grubbs, Mrs. M. J. Mooney, Eugene Rowe, Mrs. Martha Rodgers, D. S. and Mrs. F. A. Trout, C. G. and Mrs. C. G. Whittaker. Of these, four have died. This membership is made up almost entirely of working people who were deeply depressed by the panic of 1907.

Meetings were held in a hall till 1903, when the old Presbyterian chapel was bought, moved to its present location on East First Street between Elm and Walnut, and repaired.

Lewis Hurt is preparing for the mission field in Africa and Leslie Crown has been given to the ministry. Charles Williams is pastor.

This church was organized and fostered to self-support by the State Mission Board.

IROQUOIS COUNTY.

Cissna Park.

Organized 1906; present membership, 57; value of property, $1,500; Bible school began 1906; present enrollment, 143.

This is a union church. The agreement was as follows:

The undersigned charter members, while retaining their several denominational names, faith and membership, enter into a common fellowship known as the Union Church, and pledge themselves to support this organization in every way consistent with their several views of Christian conduct and duty.

Those signing this compact were Mr. and Mrs. J. C. Sailor, Mr. and Mrs. H. J. Kahney, Mr. and Mrs. R. F. Zehr, Mr. and Mrs. A. C. Ainsler, Mr. and Mrs. L. Stanbus, Mrs. E. G. Dryden, Mrs. Ida Stachell, Mrs. J. Herman, Mrs. W. Landes, Mrs. L. Lesch, Miss Lattie Lesch, Mr. and Mrs. Joseph Burt, Miss Flora Burt, Miss Lillie Thornton, Miss Martha Dryden, Mr. and Mrs. John Lucas, Miss Katie Miller, Miss Lillie Herman, John Dryden, Miss R. Lena Herman, Mr. and Mrs. E. L. Lawson, Miss Nina Crain, Mrs. Carrie Penner and Wm. W. Dryden.

CHURCHES

Darrow.

Organized 1911, by Leslie Crown; present membership, 62; value of property, $4,500; Bible school began 1910; present enrollment, 74.

Darrow is a village on a new railroad. In 1909, Leslie Crown, a student of Eureka College, began to preach in a schoolhouse near there. The church building, modern and up to date, was completed in 1912. Nearly every member of this church is a renter. The land-owners, with few exceptions, gave but little help. Mr. Crown led in this work throughout. He and the resident Disciples deserve much praise, as do also members of other religious bodies who have co-operated in the enterprise.

Donovan.

Organized 1856, by Silas Johnson and Nathan Coughenberry; present membership, 140; value of property, including parsonage, $9,000; Bible-school enrollment, 75.

This organization was made in the Green Schoolhouse west of the Donovan site. There were thirty charter members. For many years the members worshiped in the Bean or Gay Schoolhouses. In 1876, during the ministry of C. W. Poole, who, like his Master, was both carpenter and preacher, a house of worship was built. This building was enlarged and modernized in 1908 during the ministry of J. Newton Cloe.

Fairview (Wellington).

Organized 1892, by Will F. Shaw; present membership, 42; value of property, $2,000; Bible school began 1892; present enrollment, 66.

This country church is about five miles east of Wellington. There were twenty-one charter members.

The ladies' aid society is an active and very helpful force in the congregation. This is one of many instances where the faith of women is greater than that of men.

Iroquois.

Organized by J. F. Ghormley; present membership, 10; value of property, $3,500; Bible-school enrollment, 24.

Martinton.

Organized 1893, by A. R. Crank; present membership, 92; value of property $2,500; Bible school began 1893; present enrollment, 63.

Mr. Crank was serving the congregations at Donovan and Iroquois regularly when he conducted a series of meetings and organized the Martinton Church. The schoolhouse was first used. When the crowds overflowed this, a large tent was pitched. There were about eighty charter members. Of these, only the following names are learned: Mr. and Mrs. Henry Barnball, Mr. and Mrs. Smith Hickman, Mrs. Alma McSaly, Miss Allen Wingard and Mary A. Hathaway.

Milford.

Organized 1877, by C. B. Austin; present membership, 160; value of property, $12,500; Bible school began 1877; present enrollment, 130.

Mr. Austin began his work here in the old Methodist chapel. As soon as results were reached, the doors were locked against him. In an old storeroom the church was organized. Among the charter members were James McConnell, Matilda Endsley, Abijah Perkins and wife, Emma Harmon, Mary Jones and Mrs. Finley Hopkins, four of whom are still living. The first chapel was built in 1879 and the present edifice in 1910, during the pastorate of H. R. Lookabill. James Holton and T. L. Stipp gave good service here and J. M. McDermont was the first pastor.

Onarga.

Organized 1877, by R. D. Cotton; present membership, 75; value of property, including parsonage, $8,000; Bible school began 1877, present enrollment, 77.

The controlling religious force in this community through the seventies was the M. E. Church. To two brothers, James and John W. Cunningham, belongs the honor of establishing a congregation there that should be simply Christian. They were Irishmen who had been led to the knowledge of the truth as it is in Jesus by the preaching of William Poynter. They both resided on their own farms five miles east of Onarga. But not distance, not hard manual labor, not muddy roads nor dark nights could dampen their ardor nor check their Christian courage. Their zeal for Jesus and his truth burned year after year with a quenchless devotion. They were plain farmers.

The charter members were James, John W. and Rachel E. Cunningham, John and Jane Mason, Frank and Martha Dunkins, Lucie M. Parker, Hannah Smith, Robert and Margaret D. Teeter, and Thomas B. and Ellen Weakley.

About fifteen pastors have served the church well.

Pittwood.

Organized 1894, by W. W. Sniff; present membership, 80; value of property, $1,600; Bible school began 1894; present enrollment, 85.

There is a good C. E. society. About ten ministers have served the church.

Prairie Green (Wellington).

Organized 1872, by Jacob B. Blount; present membership, 60; value of property, $1,000; Bible school began, 1872; present enrollment, 42.

This church is located in the southeast corner of the county. It was organized in a little schoolhouse just across the State line in Indiana, but was soon afterward moved to the little old Round Top Schoolhouse in Prairie Green Township. Here the meetings were held till 1875, when the present chapel was built. A reorganization was then made.

Of the charter members the following are still living: J. J. Cowan, who was one of the first elders; Mrs. Elizabeth

Totheroh, Mrs. Nancy Parker, Mrs. Clara Allen, Thomas Guest and John F. Cowan, who helped build the church house. His address is Ambia, Ind. There is a good C. E. society.

Sheldon.

Organized 1890, by W. H. Hayden; present membership, 150; value of property, $6,000; Bible school began 1890; present enrollment, 110.

This church grew out of a series of meetings conducted in a public hall by Minister Hayden, who was supported by the State Missionary Society. There were sixty-five charter members.

The church was erected in 1891.

Watseka.

Organized 1881, by C. E. Elmore; present membership, 350; value of property, including parsonage, $25,000; Bible-school enrollment, 250.

Minister Elmore held a meeting in the spring under the auspices of a county co-operation. There were eighteen charter members, among whom were Capt. John Franklin, E. F. Harris, Prof. L. F. Watson and Cyrus Leatherman.

The meetings were held in a hall for a year, when the old Baptist chapel was bought and remodeled. The next winter Evangelist W. F. Black conducted a successful meeting, in which many of the most substantial people of the community were brought into the church.

The church has given its intelligent and loyal support to its twelve good pastors. The present edifice was erected and the parsonage secured during the seven years' pastorate of B. F. Ferrell.

The church has been actively missionary from the beginning, and planted congregations at Woodland, Sheldon and Pittwood. For twenty-five years Mr. L. F. Watson was a very forceful and helpful member here in many ways. He was eight years clerk of the State Senate.

Mr. S. F. Swinford also did fine work here. Norman H. Robertson is the pastor.

Woodland.

Organized 1887; present membership, 34; value of property, $1,000; Bible-school enrollment, 58.

The chapel was built in 1891. Ten ministers have served the church. Mrs. Sadie Cross is the correspondent.

A church was formed at Buckley in 1892 of twenty earnest Christian men and women, and did good work for seventeen years. Lutherans gradually bought all the farms in the community that were offered for sale, and thus the congregation disappeared. The property was sold by Min. Osceola McNemar at public auction for $1,200, and the proceeds turned to the custody of the State Missionary Society.

The Prairie Dell congregation, in the vicinity of Watseka, has ceased to meet.

JACKSON COUNTY.

Carbondale.

Organized 1862, by Dr. Isaac Mulkey; present membership, 450; value of property, including parsonage, $25,000; Bible school began 1862; present enrollment, 320.

Dr. Mulkey organized this church in the old Presbyterian chapel with the following charter members: Himself, wife and daughter; George Yost, wife and daughter; Daniel Gilbert and wife; Stephen Blair, wife and daughter. Messrs. Mulkey and Blair were the first elders, and Messrs. Yost and Gilbert the first deacons. Dr. Mulkey continued to preach to the congregation, though irregularly, till 1868. The meetings were held in an unsightly old grain-house that stood opposite the Illinois Central Railway station.

Clark Braden organized Southern Illinois College in 1866, and the prosperity of the school contributed to the growth of the church and, indeed, to many congregations in that part of the State. He also preached frequently for the church here.

The basement of the brick chapel was first occupied in 1870. In this a great revival was conducted by Evangelist John Friend. In 1874 this building was finished and dedicated free from debt. It cost $6,000, and was the best in the city. The property was sold in 1901 for a town hall, and the present fine structure finished in 1902.

Elkville.

Organized 1887, by W. H. Boles; present membership, 145; value of property, including parsonage, $2,100; Bible school began 1887; present enrollment, 154.

This church was the result of a tent meeting. The chapel was finished in 1889. The congregation is well organized and active. In the absence of a preacher the worship is conducted by an officer according to the Scriptures. J. J. Thompson is correspondent.

Murphysboro.

Organized 1899, by W. A. Ingram; present membership, 225; value of property, $10,000; Bible school began 1899; present enrollment, 130.

In the courthouse Evangelist Ingram held the meeting under the direction of the State Board that led to the formation of this church. The chapel was built in 1900. The congregation is well organized and active.

Oak Grove (Carbondale).

Present membership, 25; value of property, $500; Bible-school enrollment, 30.

Three and a half miles northeast of Carbondale. School kept up with occasional preaching.

Pleasant Hill (Ava).

Organized 1878, by David Husband; present membership, 100; value of property, $3,000; Bible-school enrollment, 42.

This is ten miles northwest of Murphysboro. About fifty years ago a Baptist church was formed in that section. In their chapel Mr. Husband held a meeting and formed the remnant of Baptists and others into a church of Christ. Among the charter members were the Graffs, Thompsons, Redmons and Lavans. The present chapel was built in 1895. D. A. Thompson is correspondent.

Six Mile (Elkville).

Organized 1848; present membership, 88; value of property, $800; Bible-school enrollment, 107.

Dr. C. F. Mulkey settled in Six Mile Prairie in 1842. His influence doubtless led to the formation of the church there. Mrs. Rosa Kirkpatrick is correspondent.

JASPER COUNTY.

Bogota.

Organized 1851, by Wm. Read and Wm. Ingraham; present membership, 150; value of property, $2,000; Bible-school enrollment, 39.

Wm. Read and Wm. Ingraham began to preach in this neighborhood about 1848. In summer, meetings were held in groves; in winter, in schoolhouses. This church is an outgrowth of the Ingraham congregation. In its earlier years it was known as the Wolf Creek and Honey Church. The charter members were James Bogard and wife, Dixon Woods and wife, Stephen Hams and wife, J. W. Honey, Sr., and wife, David White and wife, Andrew Fisher and wife, Patrick Woods and wife, and Garrison Grove and wife. Of these, Mary Woods is the only one now living.

The meeting-house was built in 1867, repaired in 1890 and modernized in 1912.

Regularly and transiently fifty-six preachers have served the congregation.

It has given to the ministry Geo. W. Tate, J. W. Honey and Benjamin W. Tate.

Christian Chapel (Winterrowd).

Organized 1888, by F. M. Lollar; present membership, 162; value of property, $1,600; Bible school began 1901; present enrollment, 42.

This congregation is located in the southwest part of the county. There were twenty-one charter members, most of whom were from the church at Ingraham. Eleven of these are living. The first officers were John Chestnut and Thomas Blink, elders, with David Morgan and David Sparling, deacons.

The congregation met for worship in a union house until 1901, when the present chapel was occupied. The name was then changed from "Church of Christ at Union Chapel" to "Christian Church, Headyville, Ill." Jas. B. Galloway is clerk.

Latona.

Organized 1855, by Wm. Coble; present membership, 150; value of property, $500; Bible school began 1875; present enrollment, 70.

The congregation was the result of a meeting held by Minister Coble in the Mitchell Schoolhouse. The elders were Joshua Dobbins and Thomas Foster. Meetings for worship were continued in this schoolhouse for years, with Benjamin Duvee, Francis Marion, Jacob Sutherland, Joseph Powell and others as preachers.

Min. Thomas Wall held a meeting in 1871 in the Matlock Schoolhouse and reorganized the church. Then it was called Latona Church.

The church in 1910 gave Miss Myra Harris McLeoud to the foreign mission field, who is at Mahoba, India.

Lis.

Organized 1905, by C. W. Freeman; present membership, 30; value of property, $600; Bible school began 1905; present enrollment, 48.

James Frakes secured the services of ministers at various times, who held meetings in schoolhouses in the neighborhood. The bitter feeling and opposition of "religious neighbors" hindered the formation of a church that would be Christian only. There were nine charter members. Min. G. W. Morrel served the congregation one year. Benjamin W. Tate worked there three years, during which period the numbers were increased and the chapel built. Frank Daugherty is Bible-school superintendent.

Newton.

Organized 1881, by N. S. Haynes; present membership, 140; value of property, including parsonage, $4,700; Bible school began 1888; present enrollment, 117.

About 1858, A. D. Fillmore and S. W. Leonard formed a congregation, but, having no shepherd, the little flock soon scattered. In 1864, A. D. Taylor organized a congregation, but he proved to be unworthy and the church disbanded. Since 1881 the church has maintained its life and work. Meetings for worship were held in the homes of the members and in a hall till the church building was erected in 1891. The impulse to this building was a result of a meeting conducted by Evangelist W. A. Ingram.

A series of meetings was held at the time of the organization in the chapel of the Presbyterians. Their minister was a non-resident who came to their church stately. He and Mr. Haynes exchanged courtesies in beginning the worship on Saturday evening and Sunday morning, his regular date. Immediately at the close of the prayer, in which Mr. Haynes besought the divine blessing on all the services of the hour, the Presbyterian minister stepped to the front of the platform and nodded. A fine-looking young couple came to the front bearing on their arms a very energetic baby boy, which the preacher proceeded at once to "baptize," although he protested by cries and kicks.

Hon. Hale Johnson and Mr. J. W. Honey were valuable servants of the church in its earlier years. Among its pastors, G. W. Lollar and I. G. Tomlinson are well remembered.

The church has ordained to the ministry C. L. Doty and H. G. Kellogg. W. A. Roberts was received from the Christian Denomination, and a Baptist minister also was received. All these additions to the ministry were made during the pastorate of Benj. W. Tate.

Wheeler.

Organized 1883, by J. G. T. Brandenburg; present membership, 65; value of property, $1,500; Bible school began 1883; present enrollment, 60.

There were thirty-one charter members.

Extinct Congregations.

Liberty Church was formed in the forties. It is located a few miles northwest of Hidalgo. The chapel built in 1858 burned down, and the second was built in 1868. The preachers who served there before the Civil War were Daniel Connor, Benj. Duvee, James Duncan and H. J. Sutherland. It did not move to town after the railroad was built, and has gone down.

St. Marie Church, ten miles southeast of Newton, was formed in 1903 by R. Leland Brown. He led the Baptist congregation there to apostolic ground, but the debt on the property was not paid, and after four years all was lost.

The Hunt Church, located one-half mile south of Falmouth, served the community well for many years, but has disappeared.

JEFFERSON COUNTY.

These facts are furnished, after a year's effort, by Mrs. Martha E. Plummer, of Mt. Vernon. Meanwhile, she was separated by death from her husband, Dr. Hiram S. Plummer, with whom she had traveled three and fifty years. She is the daughter of Harvey T. Pace.

Boyd.

Present membership, 70; value of property, $1,000; Bible-school enrollment, 60.

Ebenezer (Mt. Vernon).

Organized 1899, by Marion Boles; present membership, 22; value of property, $900; Bible-school enrollment, 64.

The charter members were Elder J. Newton Brown and wife, Daniel Lewis and wife, W. C. Baker and wife, Grandma Cron, Sophia and George Correll and sister. This little country church has Christian grace and grit. They keep their chapel in a fine condition and pay their preachers promptly. It is six miles north.

Elk Prairie (Ina).

Organized 1852, by J. C. McBrian; present membership, 150; value of property, $1,000; Bible-school enrollment, 40.

The congregation was prosperous until the Civil War, when it was destroyed by internal conflicts. In the seventies it was reorganized by Ministers Heape and Mulkey. Jas. B. Bean is Sunday-school superintendent. It is four miles west.

Fouts (Cravat).

Value of property, $1,000.
Two miles northwest.

Hickory Hill (Mt. Vernon).

Organized 1880, by Wm. Henderson; present membership, 50; union Bible-school enrollment, 50.

This was first known as the Wolf Prairie Church. The charter members were Solomon Ford and wife, Peter Ollomon and wife, John Hodge and wife, Jas. C. Parsley and wife, George Bodine and wife, Edward Carter, Emaline Bradley and daughter, Belle C. Gray, and William Theims and wife.

It has had eighty members and has given to the ministry Elijah Collins, Edward Carter and George Bodine. Mr. Collins is now serving the church. It is seven miles south.

Ina.

Organized 1911, by G. W. Foley; present membership, 25; value of property, $1,000; Bible school began 1911; present enrollment, 35.

The chapel was built in 1910. There were thirteen charter members. Mrs. Nellie F. Hodge is clerk.

Little Grove (Walnut Hill).

Organized 1841; present membership, 100; value of property, $2,000; Bible-school enrollment, 50.

This is a country church in the north edge of the county, but most of its members reside in Marion County. It has constantly and consistently maintained the cause of the Master through seventy-one years. James Kell is clerk.

Mt. Catherine (Woodlawn).

Present membership, 95; value of property, $500; Bible-school enrollment, 54.

Two miles northwest. Mrs. Frank Gaskin is correspondent.

Mt. Vernon.

Organized 1853; present membership, 300; value of property, $3,000; Bible-school enrollment, 210.

At the first formation of this church of twenty-one members, Mins. J. C. Ashley, John E. McBrain, Horace Watrons and John A. Williams were present. Harvey T. Pace and wife were the leaders in this work. In 1854 he bought the old M. E. chapel, remodeled and refurnished it, and gave its use to the congregation. The church grew. After the death of Mr. Pace, this property was lost to the congregation. Others died and moved away, so that there was no organization from 1874 to 1886. Then J. W. Robbins, under

CHURCHES

the auspices of the State Board, reorganized with fourteen members, which was increased to thirty-seven by the close of the meeting. Meetings were held regularly in courthouse and halls till 1889, when a chapel was occupied. A needed addition was made in later years. The church has passed through many trying experiences, but has always had the faithful few.

It has given to the ministry Earl Israel and Charles Starr. Carl Green is the faithful pastor.

Union (Woodlawn).

Organized 1842, by David Chance; present membership, 50; value of property, $1,000.

The charter members were Thomas Howell and wife, Burden Nichols and wife, Elijah Smith and wife, Paul McMillen and wife, and Robin Moore and wife. The present elders are Huston Johnson, A. L. Severs and O. L. Smith. The minister is Otto Timmons. W. J. Bledsoe is correspondent. It is two miles northwest.

On the western edge of the county, three miles east of Ashley, there stood in 1866, in the woods, an old brick chapel which had no floor but dirt. It was called "Old Union," and the congregation that met there is thought to have been the oldest in the county, having been organized in the thirties.

The Antioch congregation, two miles east of Dix, and that at Belle Rive, both having chapels, have both ceased to meet.

This Antioch Church gave Orville Hawkins to the ministry.

In 1913 a congregation of forty members was formed at Waltonville.

JOHNSON COUNTY.

Belknap.

Organized 1896, by G. L. Wolfe; present membership, 44; value of property, $1,800; Bible school began 1896; present enrollment, 54.

This church was the result of a meeting held by Minister Wolfe.

Berea (Vienna).

This is a country church located about five miles from Vienna. It was organized a few years after the Bethlehem Church, and its history is similar in nearly every respect. It has been served by the same preachers. The families of Pickens, Starke, Gage and Albriton have been prominent in the work here. Beverly Albriton was a local preacher who came from the South and settled here. He and his son, George Albriton, have served the church as elders almost continuously.

Bethlehem (Vienna).

Organized 1847, by Minister Wooten; present membership, 30; value of property, $600; no Bible school.

This is thought to be the oldest church of Christ in the county.

Many of the people of the neighborhood came from Middle Tennessee, as did Minister Wooten also. The first meetings were held in a brush arbor. Then a log house was built. In later years this gave way to a comfortable frame building. Norman Mozley, Sr., was the leading spirit. Associated with him were faithful men and women. The church has had the services of able preachers. It has given J. F. Hight to the ministry.

Grantsburg.

Organized 1902, by J. N. Cowan; present membership, 24; value of property, $1,000; Bible school began 1902; present enrollment, 14.

The formation of this church was largely due to the Christian activity of J. N. Cowan and W. B. Bivins, who have served it as elders since its organization.

New Burnside.

Organized 1875; present membership, 50; Bible-school enrollment, 27.

CHURCHES

Vienna.

Organized 1866, by John Lemon; present membership, 56; value of property, $2,500; Bible school began 1866; present enrollment, 57.

During the Civil War, John Lemon and his son Josephus came as refugees from the South to Johnson County. They at once formed a church of Christ at Gum Spring, in 1863, four miles west of Vienna. Its members were also mostly refugees. The house used at Gum Spring was a union chapel. A Baptist church had been first organized there. After the close of the war, many returned to their homes in the South; thus the congregation ceased to be. However, this was the impulse that started the church in Vienna. The first meetings were held in the Cumberland Presbyterian Church. It was not long until the Disciples were denounced as "heretics" and the church door was locked against them. An intelligent lady who witnessed this expulsion said: "Surely these are the Lord's people; for this is the way they treated the Saviour and his apostles." She cast in her lot with them. After Minister Lemon there came Matthew Wilson, John Lindsay and others. R. R. McCall and I. A. J. Parker were helpful in building up the church. A brick house was erected in 1871.

There was a small congregation at Elvira thirty-five years ago that met in a schoolhouse. When Minister Shelt moved away, the members were scattered.

There was a small band formed at Union Hill about 1900, but it did not continue.

PERSONALS.—In the seventies J. W. Bradley, of Clay County, preached in this county; so also did Stanton Field, of Grand Chain. Mr. Field was a farmer, but a great preacher too. He combined the logical faculty with a vivid imagination and a sympathetic heart.

J. M. Radcliff did good service in this and other counties. He was a large man of lion-like appearance, and a fine revivalist.

John F. Mecoy came from Marshall County, Ky. He grew to manhood under adverse circumstances, so that after his marriage his wife taught him to read. He spent his life on his farm, but he became a great teacher of the Bible, a brilliant preacher and a successful evangelist. In Kentucky he led many young men to the ministry. He stood first against slavery and for the Union. He was a born gentleman.

James H. Carter served in the Legislature. S. M. Glasford was a member of the State Senate, and served the Vienna Church as an elder to the close of his life.

Dr. R. M. McCall was assistant superintendent of the State Hospital for the Insane at Anna.

Other Disciples filled various county offices. J. F. Hight has earnestly contended for the faith, and held a public discussion on every occasion for a period of twenty-five years. Now he is serving as county judge. Evidently he is a diplomatist. But he continues to preach to those who are poor and neglected.

KANE COUNTY.

Batavia.

Organized 1852, by M. N. Lord; present membership, 72; value of property, $4,000; Bible-school enrollment, 108.

There were twelve charter members. The public meetings were first held in a room over a store on Wilson Street, a few doors west of South River Street, then from house to house till the completion of a chapel in 1868. This is yet used. Among the earlier ministers who served the congregation there were L. Cooley, Dr. W. H. Hopson, Mr. Phinney, Moses E. Lard, B. F. Hall, J. D. Benedick, J. J. Moss and others. For a long time the congregation has been served by students from the Disciples' Divinity House. Deaths and removals have decimated the membership, and accessions have not kept pace. The church much needs the preaching of the gospel.

John Gunzenhauser resides there and still serves the church well, as he has for many years.

A church was organized in 1841 at Dundee with eighteen members, but never grew to self-support.

Repeated and persistent efforts to establish a church of Christ in Elgin have all failed.

KNOX COUNTY.

One of the first churches in this county was constituted in the village of Henderson about 1838. In the forties J. E. Murphy, Smith Wallace and J. E. Martin preached there. Morran Baker was the leader. In 1850 a brick chapel was built. About 1853 Min. Ziba Brown held a revival which added to the church many prominent families of the community. Then James Gaston ministered to the church nine years. Thereafter the congregation dwindled to its end.

In the early times there was a flourishing church at French Grove, in the eastern part of the county.

At Walnut Grove, also, near Altona, there was a strong church before the railroads came.

In 1850 the Union chapel was built five miles east and one north of Galesburg, and a congregation formed there. This church gave E. B. Reynolds to the ministry. John Spooner was the leader here. Among the preachers were Milton Dodge, Jordan Dodge, Robert Wallace, Patrick H. Murphy, Henry Murphy and James W. Butler.

There was a congregation of Christians in Maquon before and after 1870.

Abingdon.

Organized 1850, by John E. Murphy and Milton Dodge; present membership, 450; value of property, including parsonage, $5,000; Bible-school enrollment, 208.

The pages of the history of the Abingdon Church are covered with smiles and tears, joys and sorrows. Its periods were measured by success and failure. It was a small village in 1849.

Then, some who loved the gospel in its simplicity met

for worship in Indian Point Schoolhouse, an old log building, located about one mile west of the present school site; others met in the home of John Dawdy, south of town; others at Israel Marshall's home northwest, and some in the St. Augustine Schoolhouse. Those Disciples thought it no hardship to ride or walk through mud or snow to worship God according to his word.

In 1850, John E. Murphy and Milton Dodge held a series of meetings in the Indian Point Schoolhouse. The interest became intense. People came from Meridian, Cold Brook, St. Augustine—from far and near—in wagons, on horseback and on foot. Many were obedient to the faith. At the close of the meeting the Abingdon Church was organized.

The charter members were Jane Dowdy (Boydstrum), the sole resident survivor; Thomas and Isabel Roberson, John Boydstrum, Alford and Cassie Dowdy, Elijah Meadows; Jane, Sarah and Julia Meek; Cynthia Brunson, Willis Riggs, Taylor Lomax, Jonathan Bobbitt and wife, John Latimer and wife, John Vertreece and wife, Nathan Bradbury, B. Edmonson and wife, Mrs. John Killam, Israel Maxwell, Eliza and Phœbe Latimore, Lemuel Meadows and wife, William Meadows and wife, Mr. Williams and wife, and Nancy Williams. First elders, William Maxwell and Jonathan Price; deacons, William and Lemuel Meadows.

Besides the two named, the preachers of the early days were John Miller, Livy Hatchett, P. J. Murphy, Isaac Murphy and others.

When the congregation outgrew the first house erected in 1857, they worshiped in the chapel of the Abingdon College building. Since then several houses have been built and used. The last was enlarged and otherwise improved at a cost of $7,000 during the pastorate of F. L. Moore.

During the college period the church was served by Mins. J. C. Reynolds, P. H. Murphy, J. W. Butler, A. J. Thompson, A. P. Aten and B. O. Aylesworth.

The death of the college wrought a division in the church that continued ten years.

From first to last, fifty-two preachers have served the congregation. It is now a fine church, faithful in attendance, missionary to the core and living in the spirit of unity.

In its early years there was neither organ nor choir. They were thought to be sinful. Judge Durham led the songs for many years. The women were taught to keep silent. Mrs. Emma Aten was the first to read a chapter to the edification of the assembly.

Many hundreds have begun the Christian life here, and many have gone in Christ's service into many lands.

East Galesburg.

Organized 1902, by J. M. Morris; present membership, 75; value of property, $600; Bible-school enrollment, 60.

Galesburg.

Organized 1871, by Dr. J. B. Vivion; present membership, 878; value of property, including parsonage, $13,500; Bible-school enrollment, 714.

Meetings were held here in the sixties, and possibly earlier, by a few Disciples in residences, halls and the office of Dr. J. B. Vivion, who was an intelligent and earnest Christian. The church was constituted in his office.

The Swedish M. E. chapel was purchased and Evangelist Knowles Shaw conducted a series of meetings, adding some strength to the congregation. In 1878 the chapel was moved to West Thompson Street, between Broad and Cedar Streets. In 1892 the present building on North West Street was finished and occupied during the pastorate of G. J. Ellis. In late years the church has made rapid and substantial progress.

Henry M. Bruner and John B. Scheitlan were true supporters and leaders in the earlier years.

Hermon.

Present membership, 116; value of property, $2,500; Bible-school enrollment, 106.

Knoxville.

Organized 1869, by J. H. Garrison; present membership, 255; value of property, including parsonage, $17,000; Bible school began 1869; present enrollment, 160.

A church of Christ was formed here as early as 1838. There were twelve members. Among them were Min. Jacob Grum, Dr. Hansford and wife, John Karns, a tailor and clothier, and John Eads, an active Christian. As the years passed, so also did this congregation. It was reorganized in a meeting led by Mr. Garrison in 1869, and has steadily advanced into active usefulness. At that time it was increased by a remnant of members from the Union congregation, that had lived northwest of the town for nineteen years.

This church gave H. J. Reynolds to the ministry.

Meridian Church (Abingdon).

Organized 1839, by John E. Murphy; present membership, 80; value of property, $2,000; Bible-school enrollment, 90.

Five miles west of Abingdon is an imposing structure that for many years has been known far and near as the Meridian Christian Church. Its records are still in a good state of preservation, from which the following excerpts are made:

MAY 4TH, 1839.

We the undersigned, having met at Bro. Meadows' agreeably by appointment for the purpose of forming a Christian congregation upon the word of God to men, and that the New Testament contains the only rule of faith by which Christians should be governed, we do agree to unite as a congregation to attend to the ordinances of the house of God and the means of edification afforded in his word.

After a discourse was delivered by Bro. J. Murphy, the names in the following list agree to become united as a body of Christians upon the word of God: M. Jameson, Sarah Jameson, Lydriam Dawson, J. B. Reynolds, Phebe Reynolds, Charles Reynolds, John Dodge, Theodocia Dodge, Thomas Dodge, Jordan Dodge, John M. Dodge, Margarete Dodge, Rachel Reynolds, Henry Meadows, Polly Meadows, Nancy Meadows, Melinda Meadows, Ephraim Smith, Hannah Smith, Francis Godard, Seth C. Murphy, Irene Murphy, Elizabeth Murphy, Nancy

Murphy, William Murphy, John Fisher, Elizabeth Fisher, Thompson Brock, Jacob Boydstun, Israel M. Marshall, Stephen Howard, John Dandy, James Holland, Martha Howard, Mother Meadows.

After the names of the Disciples were ascertained, it was thought best to have the officers chosen. J. B. Reynolds and Seth C. Murphy were chosen bishops of the congregation. W. Meadows and T. E. Smith were chosen deacons, and John M. Dodge, recorder.

The people met in schoolhouses, in homes, and often, during the summer season, in the shade of the maple-trees—breaking the loaf and heeding the message from some honest pioneer preacher.

The following from the old records are both instructive and suggestive. The first doubtless came from Vincennes, Ind.:

"VINCENNES, January 14, 1842.
"*To All to Whom This May Come,* Greeting:

"That our beloved Bro. Edward Perdue and Sister Jane Perdue, his companion, were members in full fellowship in the Church of Christ at Vincennes and we take great pleasure in recommending them to the care of the Brethren in the Lord wherever they may wish to enroll themselves. Done by order of the church at Vincennes."

"The church of God in Cold Brook, Warren Co., Illinois, recommends to the faithful in Christ Jesus wherever she may choose to attach herself, our worthy and much beloved Sister Sarah Johnson, who has so conducted herself a Christian as to authorize us to commend her to the confidence and watchful care of all God's people.

"Done by order of the church July 8th, A. D. 1842.
"JOSIAH WHITMAN,
"JNO. G. HALEY,
"Elders."

"December 26, 1847, John M. Lodge, who was employed as evangelist, closed his labors with fifty-three additions by baptism.

"February, 1848, brethren were sent as delegates and agreement was entered into that John M. Dodge should be sustained for seven months and to receive eighteen and one-half dollars a month for his services, to proclaim the word of life wherever it was thought best to labor."

Letters received were not simply placed on file, but were made a part of the church record.

During those years many from Kentucky, and other Southern States, found their way into this county. Perhaps as many as fifty letters from the Southern Baptists were placed in the Meridian Church during a period of twenty years.

The roster of the congregation has been revised seven or eight times. Many were received into membership and many have gone out into almost every part of the Union.

They supported liberally evangelists who labored in other fields. This record tells of numerous collections that were taken up for the poor and needy. It tells of the social hour when smiles and tears mingled with joy and gladness. Those who may now read it will learn of the heroic faith and undying devotion of those Disciples to the cause of Christ. It is to-day one of the best communities to be found in the county.

The first church house was built in 1841; the second and present one, in 1880.

St. Augustine.

Present membership, 110; value of property, $3,000; Bible-school enrollment, 62.

LAKE COUNTY.

In the thirties, Darius Gage and two of his brothers, with Benedict Stevens and Emmons Shepard, came from near Cleveland, O., and settled on lands in the northern part of Lake County. A village, located about three miles northeast of Fox Lake and one mile south of the Wisconsin line, was laid out, to which the name of Gageville was given. Some years afterward the name was changed to Antioch, by which it is still known. In this community a church after the primitive order was constituted Aug. 7, 1841, with twenty members, by Min. William Davenport, then of Walnut Grove. It was the first church of Christ in the northern tier of counties in the State. It lived and thrived until about 1910, when the chapel was rented to the German Lutherans.

The Fort Hill Church, three miles south of Long Lake, was organized in 1850 by Min. L. J. Correll. It served its community well for fifty years and then disappeared. While A. R. Knox was preaching for this congregation he baptized in 1856 four heads of families who were Roman Catholics. Of one of these families there are two grandsons who are preaching the primitive gospel.

In the sixties a church was formed at Millburn which did well for some years.

In the seventies the congregations in Lake and McHenry Counties united in employing an evangelist. He was a fluent speaker, but, as soon after learned, of bad reputation. His conduct scandalized the cause he pretended to represent. When the iniquitous embroilment had passed, the cause was prostrate. Some of the churches did not recover, and others only after pain and loss.

In 1849 the custom of yearly meetings was begun. These were continued for forty years. Their chief object was to reach by the gospel those who would not attend the meetings of the congregations. They also cultivated the spirit of loving fraternity among the Disciples, who were mostly fine people in this county.

Min. L. J. Correll came into this county in the early forties and did a yeoman's service. He died in Nebraska about 1908.

Mins. G. B. Willis and A. J. Smith were also efficient preachers.

Gurnee.

Organized 1860, by A. R. Knox and Andrew J. Smith; present membership, 75; value of property, including parsonage, $6,000; Bible-school enrollment, 115.

In the summer of 1859, A. R. Knox began to preach in a schoolhouse four miles west of Waukegan, on the Oplain River. The community was much infected with Universalism and Spiritism. A month's meeting was held the following winter, in which Pastor A. J. Smith, of Antioch, did the preaching. A goodly number were baptized and a church was organized. The meetings were held in the schoolhouse till 1879, when the church building was erected. Before that time, in addition to those already named, John Aylesworth, Wesley Marsh, W. L. Hayden, L. J. Correll and L. A. Dowling served the church.

Waukegan—First.

Organized 1888, by A. R. Knox and E. A. Ott; present membership, 90; value of property, $8,000; Bible-school enrollment, 48.

The first congregation here was wrecked by the evil influence of the unworthy evangelist above referred to. After a lapse of ten years a new start was made. The charter members then were C. M. Cyrus and wife, Phila Winter, Lucretia Emmons, Sarah Calkins, Adelaide Connors; A. R., Jane, Newton, Mary, Emma and Lottie Knox.

This church gave Dewitt Bradbury to the ministry.

Waukegan—West Side.

Organized 1905, by E. N. Tucker; present membership, 89; value of property, $6,100; Bible school began 1905; present enrollment, 117.

LA SALLE COUNTY.

About 1865 there was a Christian congregation in Lostant of near thirty members. It was gathered together by J. G. Waggoner, who was then teaching the public school there. It included in its membership Dr. King and family and Dr. Vandervoort, all of Tonica. Meetings were held in the Baptist and M. E. chapels. When Mr. Waggoner returned to college the meetings soon ceased, deaths and removals occurring. The Baptist chapel there is now waiting for the use of others.

James A. Garfield was interested in building the railroad leading southwest of Streator. A few years after the close of the Civil War he made a trip over the right-of-way with Colonel Plumb. They took dinner with a Mr. Allen and family. It was decided to establish a station near this place.

The people of the neighborhood were so much pleased with Mr. Garfield that they cheerfully approved of the proposition of Colonel Plumb to name the town Garfield.

A few families of the Streator Church who reside in the community have kept a union Sunday school going for some time, but the Papal influences have hindered the building of a church. Meetings are held in a hall owned by Mr. Strosnider, an aged and intelligent Disciple. His daughter, Mrs. Maud Stewart, is the Bible-school superintendent.

Dana.

Organized 1865, by J. Q. A. Houston; present membership, 57; value of property, $8,000; Bible school began 1861; present enrollment, 194.

The Christian people living near Diamond Creek, in the early sixties, in the panhandle of La Salle County, met for public worship in schoolhouses and their own homes. A chapel was completed in the village of Dana in 1868. This house gave place in 1909 to a new and modern structure built of cement blocks.

Four of the first members are living: Mrs. Elizabeth Martin, Dana; Mrs. E. Jones and Mrs. P. Martin, of Minonk, and R. S. Manning, of Nebraska State. Of the earlier preachers, Messrs. Watson, Trowbridge, Lindsey, Crogan, Brokaw, Prophater and Boggs served the congregation.

The Bible school is front rank and the church has grown in power and influence in the community.

W. O. Lappin is the pastor.

Ottawa.

Organized 1913, by J. Fred Jones; present membership, 20; value of property, $2,000; Bible school began 1913; present enrollment, 40.

The Fourth Missionary District led in the formation of the church of Christ in this county-seat. The building and lot formerly used by the St. Paul's Evangelical Church were sold at auction and bought by the District Board. Mr.

George Armstrong, of Ancona, and John Vissering, of Dana, had promised financial help.

C. M. Smithson, the pastor at Streator, and H. H. Jenner, pastor at Long Point, have given valuable assistance.

The Long Point Church gave $200 on the purchase of the property.

Rutland.

Organized 1868, by W. H. Watson; present membership, 180; value of property, $4,300; Bible school began 1868; present enrollment, 100.

Minister Watson held a series of meetings, and at the close, assisted by Min. A. H. Trowbridge, organized a church with thirty-eight members, as follows: John Roe, Abram Mullin, David Mullin, George Boyd, John Ware, G. T. Crumrine, James Rowland and their wives severally; Mrs. Sarah, Mrs. Martha and Miss Maria Crumrine; Jonathan Wilson, James Cox, Mrs. Jane and Miss Elizabeth Wilson, Josiah Richmond, Jesse W. Evans, Samuel Ware, Mrs. Clara Rickey, Mrs. Catherine Ansborn and Thomas Bane; the other names were not secured. Only six of these now reside in Rutland.

A. H. Trowbridge served the congregation eleven years. The Roe, Mullin, Boyd, Richmond and Sutton families have been active forces in the congregation. Wm. Drummet was given to the ministry.

T. Wilson Milteer is clerk.

Streator.

Organized 1870, by J. C. Tully; present membership, 385; value of property, $22,500; Bible-school enrollment, 270.

J. W. Barnhart, a devout and devoted man, was the leader in establishing this church. In 1870 there was a chapel there that members of all religious bodies had paid for, but the legal title was held by the Cumberland Presbyterian Church. In this building Mr. Tully began a meeting in June of that year. After he had preached a few sermons the doors were closed against him. The following Sunday morning the few Disciples met for worship in the front yard of Wm. Ley, on South Monroe Street. Then and there the church was organized. Mr. Ley was chosen deacon and has given the church commendable service in this capacity to the present time. Thereafter meetings were held in a small hall. Charles Rowe became the first pastor, and a small frame chapel was built and occupied the next year. Dr. Streator, for whom the town was named and a leading Disciple of Cleveland, O., held large financial interests there, so he readily gave a location and helped in the building. This chapel was used until 1906, when, during the pastorate of C. D. Hougham, the present modern edifice was completed. Its location is more central.

Following Mr. Rowe came students from Eureka, by whom the pulpit was supplied.

In addition to J. W. Barnhart, whose memory is revered, and Wm. Ley, whose long fidelity is honored, the church also highly esteems Mrs. Mary Anderson. It was here that she left a large and popular church to become a Christian only. When the spiritual life of the church ran low because competent leadership was lacking, she, with a few others, met regularly and maintained the order of the Lord's house.

The church is steadily growing in power and influence in the community and the outlook is bright. C. M. Smithson is the pastor.

Tonica.

Organized 1912, by Chas. P. Murphy; present membership, 19; Bible school began 1913; present enrollment, 100.

Mrs. Chas. I. Haughey and her husband, assisted by Min. C. M. Smithson, of Streator, led in the formation of this congregation. The meeting conducted by Evangelist Murphy was held in the vacant Baptist chapel, which is offered to the Disciples for a small fraction of its value.

There were nine charter members. Min. E. E. Hartley and wife held a meeting early in 1913 which added others, organized a Bible school and a ladies' aid with twenty members.

LAWRENCE COUNTY.

Allison (Vincennes, Ind.).

Organized 1815-28; present membership, 170; value of property, $5,500; Bible school began 1874; present enrollment, 102.

This society was first formed by members of the Christian Denomination. A reorganization took place in 1828, at which time it is probable that the membership came nearer the position of the Disciples. A purely country church, located on a wide, rich prairie, in continuous Christian activities for ninety-seven years is a singular and magnificent record. Its location is seven miles northeast of Lawrenceville. Its first meetings for public worship were held in the homes of the people; then in Center Schoolhouse until the forties, when a neat frame chapel was built. This served for more than fifty years. About 1896 a new, modern and up-to-date building was erected. The church is abreast of the times in a remarkable degree for a country membership. It shows what can be done when the people have a mind to work.

It has given to the ministry C. L. Organ and Mrs. Rochester Irwin.

This community was known from its beginning as "The Christian Settlement." The fine formative influences of those sturdy pioneers have come down through all the intervening years.

Bethany (Lawrenceville).

Organized 1879, by Cyrus Clemments; present membership, 35; value of property, $1,200; Bible school began 1879; present enrollment, 33.

This church is located ten miles north of Lawrenceville. The first Christians only in the neighborhood were Mr. and Mrs. Romelia Norris. Through their efforts Minister Corter first preached in what is known as the "Cornbread Schoolhouse." Later Min. Cyrus Clemments preached there several weeks without visible results. Finally, Miss Frances Judy, a young lady of nineteen, accepted Christ. This led others to obedience, and a congregation was formed. Among the first members there were the following named men and their wives; Romelia Norris, Richard Judy, Jonathan Smith, Amelia Lester, William Kimmell, Henry Bennier, Berry Carter; also these persons with their families: Jackson Grey, James D. Updyke and Mrs. Sarah Groves.

Bridgeport.

Organized 1866, by James McMillen; present membership, 252; value of property, including parsonage, $22,000; Bible school began 1863; present enrollment, 225.

In 1861 members of the Pleasant Hill Church who were residing in the village of Bridgeport built a house of worship there. The lot was given by David Lanterman. Occasional meetings were held therein until 1866, when these brethren obtained formal but willing permission from the mother church to organize in the village. Ministers McMillen and W. B. F. Treat were present and so advised and directed. There were sixty-three charter members. The church has had a checkered history, but the regular meetings conducted by the elders have been held every Lord's Day. Revival meetings were held by representative evangelists. The congregation, having outgrown its old building during the pastorate of George W. Schroeder, a modern brick building, costing $16,000, was erected. Dr. H. V. Lewis gave the parsonage lot. T. H. Lindenmeyer is the present pastor.

Andrew Baird was given to the ministry.

Chauncey.

Organized 1890, by John A. Williams; present membership, 35; value of property, $1,000; Bible school began 1890; present enrollment, 30.

Eleven persons from several congregations, including Baptists, formed this church. Daniel Patton and wife donated the lot. The old M. E. Church was bought, moved onto the lot and remodeled. The church made but little progress, so in 1909 it was reorganized by J. F. Rosboro.

Lawrenceville.

Organized 1833, by M. R. Trimble; present membership, 450; value of property, including parsonage, $25,500; Bible-school enrollment, 350.

This church was the outgrowth of preaching in various sections of the county. An organization had been effected at the Old Center Schoolhouse as early as 1817.

M. R. Trimble had preached at Springhill, and a house had been built there as early as 1820. West of Lawrenceville meetings had been held in Lewis' Schoolhouse and LaMott's barn. Mr. Trimble had preached and conducted communion services in the courthouse yard, and also in the "Old Yellow Courthouse" in Lawrenceville. James Y. Beard, of the Christian Denomination, had also preached there occasionally. This church started with forty-one members. The first officers were C. M. Eaton, Joseph LaMott and Mr. Travis. Soon thereafter Mr. Eaton gave the land in the village for a church building, and paid $1,100 of the money used in its erection, quite a princely gift for those days. The ground was spacious and ample. The house served the congregation till 1895, when a commodious and up-to-date building was erected. This was remodeled in 1908, a good parsonage added and the former parsonage turned into the janitor's residence. This church is a living link in the Foreign Society, supporting Mrs. Fred E. Hagin in Japan. The church has held in its membership many representative citizens who were thoroughly good men. J. W. McCleave was one of these. Thomas A. Hall is the present pastor.

Mt. Erie (Sumner).

Present membership, 25; value of property, $500; Bible-school enrollment, 30.

This is five miles about south of Sumner.

Mt. Zion (Sumner).

Organized 1815, by William Kinkade; present membership, 40; value of property, $1,200; Bible-school enrollment, 40.

Mr. P. W. Sutherland, of Sumner, Ill., has the old church record-book that tells of this beginning. The book is discolored by age, but the writing is very legible. On the first page are the words, "Sold to Ean Miller for 12½, Church Book for Springhill Church." No date is given. On the second page a list of 110 names is started which fills six pages. William Kinkade's is the first, and he was the official elder. Many of these names have utterly faded from the community. It can not be determined from this list who were the charter members. A revision of it is begun on page 7, where it is said to be "a list of the members of the Church of Christ at Springhill." A second revision is begun on page 9, and this entry is added: "Saturday before the first Sunday in November, 1825, the church at Springhill entered a resolution to appoint a clerk to keep a record of all their acts and particular business, and appointed Thomas Spencer." The records of the next ten years follow. Mr. Sutherland says that Mr. Kinkade was a Greek and Latin scholar, the author of a book on the Holy Spirit, a member of the Legislature, the first preacher in the community, and that he organized the Springhill congregation as "the Church of Christ" there. He died before 1833.

There is a lapse in the records from 1835 to 1842, when the following appears:

In the name of Jesus Christ, Amen. The church of God which is in Christ Jesus at Springhill in Lawrence County, Illinois, reorganized October 2nd, A. D. 1842. All names, Creeds, Confessions of Faith, Disciplines, rules and formulas of human invention and contrivance are totally discarded. The Scriptures of the Old and New Testaments alone are the only and all-sufficient standard and rule of faith and practice, of morals and of discipline. No name or names are acknowledged but those contained and used in the Scriptures and therein given to the people of God.

This was signed by M. R. Trimble, William Clark, Robert Johnson and thirty-four names follow. Within five days Ephraim D. Turner and John Fish were appointed deacons, and M. J. Hancock, clerk. The next Lord's Day Alexander Turner and Milan Z. Hancock were chosen elders.

It is admitted that this church was associated with the Christian Denomination till 1835, but whether it then came into the Restoration movement or not till 1842 is not clear. Following the latter date there was much preaching in the Springhill meeting-house by Sylvanus Ades and Wm. Courter and many turned to the Lord.

About 1854 the congregation was reorganized as the Mt. Zion Church, but the former name was much used for the next fifteen years. A frame chapel was built in 1862 through the leading and sacrifice of Henry Vandament. About 1854 Marshall Stivers became an elder, and in this office served the church for fifty years with great good to the people.

Two swarms have gone out from this old hive—Bridgeport and Mt. Erie.

It has given to the ministry Geo. P. Smith, F. M. Shick, B. T. Stivers, J. R. Sutherland and four or five others.

Over 530 people have been members here. Mrs. Melissa Day has been a member since 1854.

Evangelist Harvey Mullins held a great meeting here in 1871.

Pleasant Hill (Bridgeport).

Organized 1843, by M. R. Trimble; present membership, 110; Bible school began 1860.

This church is known as White House or Pleasant Hill. It is located four miles northwest of Bridgeport. In 1842 a company of twenty-six Christians—some from Cornbread Schoolhouse, some from Lawrenceville and some from a congregation of the older Christian Church, including Min. Asa W. Baird—got together under the lead of Maurice R. Trimble. The following January they were organized, accepting no name but the Bible names.

A piece of land was bought for $50 of Daniel Barns. A small but comfortable house was built thereon. This was replaced in 1872 by the larger and more modern building.

Some of the preachers who have served them were M. R. Trimble, Asa M. Baird, D. D. Miller, James McMillan, Harvey Mullins and George Morrell.

Pleasant Ridge (Lawrenceville).

Organized 1834, by M. R. Trimble; present membership, 60; value of property, $1,200; Bible school began 1869; present enrollment, 50.

This chapel is seven miles north of Lawrenceville. Its first local name was McNiece. Its first chapel was burned about 1870. Meetings were then held in Roberts Schoolhouse till 1880, when the present chapel was built. The name was then changed to Pleasant Ridge.

Gilbert Jones was given to the ministry, while George and Thomas Reed are preparing therefor.

Rising Sun (Russellville).

Organized 1877, by J. L. Griffin; present membership, 40; value of property, $1,000; Bible-school enrollment, 22.

This location is about eight miles northeast of Lawrenceville. There were seventeen charter members and the organization was made in the Rising Sun Schoolhouse. The chapel was finished in 1880. This is a good country church and has a fine missionary spirit. A C. E. society.

It has given Frank Powers and Leslie Wolfe to the ministry. The latter is a missionary in the Philippine Islands.

Russellville.

Organized 1840, by M. R. Trimble; present membership, 50; value of property, $1,200; Bible-school enrollment, 75.

For more than seventy years this little church has lived in this little village. In it good people have served God, but to the great world unknown. A house was built in the forties, rebuilt in the seventies and yet serves as the place for public worship. The following preachers have served there: M. R. Trimble, John Howard, Panner Howard, Jacob and Josiah Wolf and Hiram Boyles.

St. Francisville.

Organized 1894, by W. R. Couch; present membership, 121; value of property, $1,500; Bible school began 1894; present enrollment, 83.

Twenty-five Disciples, wishing to hold to Christ as their only creed and the Bible as their only rule of faith and practice, constituted this church. For two years their meetings were held in various places, when the house of worship was erected in 1896. Old Father Gee, at the age of eighty-one, helped to fell the first tree that went into the building. The church has been faithful in the face of opposition, is well organized and is awake to the duty of world-wide missions.

Sumner.

Organized 1850, by Cornelius Ades; present membership, 124; value of property, $12,000; Bible school began 1868; present enrollment, 111.

This church was the result of a series of meetings conducted by Mr. Ades. Meetings were held in the homes of the members till about 1868, when a chapel was built. In recent years this gave place to a modern structure.

The Willow Branch Church was formed northwest of Sumner by Min. H. Y. Keller in 1890. It continued for fifteen to twenty years.

LEE COUNTY.

Dixon.

Organized 1894, by J. B. Wright and T. A. Boyer; present membership, 260; value of property, $5,000; Bible school began 1894; present enrollment, 200.

A tent meeting was conducted here by Ministers Wright and Boyer, resulting in the formation of a church of Christ with 170 members. This was the first preaching by the Disciples in Lee County.

In the early years of the congregation storms broke and perils threatened from within as well as without, but better counsels prevailed, and within a brief period this church has become united, prosperous and useful. S. E. Fisher is the pastor.

LIVINGSTON COUNTY.

Ancona.

Organized 1859; present membership, 191; value of property, $3,200; Bible school began 1894; present enrollment, 82.

Members of the Methodist Protestant and Christian Churches united in building a chapel in 1860. This place proved to be a good recruiting-place for the Disciples. Among the first members were Samuel E. Maxwell, Phineas Green, Alfred Grim, John Showman, Silas Coe, Caleb Mathis, R. W. Hick, Margaret Beckworth and Jessie Carpenter. Others of recent years were Dr. Foredyce, G. W. Mathis, Frank Clark, Geo. Armstrong, John Carrithers, and John, Cephas and Joseph Coe.

In various ways the congregation has been served by Benjamin Franklin, J. B. McCleary, J. W. Monser, Rochester Irwin; Mr. Thompson, a Scotchman; Mr. Nevins, Isaac Slick, Mr. Sabin, W. B. F. Treat; John, Jefferson and Washington Houston, who were great evangelists and singers; Mr. Watson, Mr. Taylor, Perry Hoge, Mr. Spencer and N. J. Wright, whose great meeting led to the erection of the present building in 1894.

The church has given to the ministry C. C. Carpenter and Robert Witchen.

Antioch (Long Point).

Organized 1912, by B. L. Wray; present membership, 24; value of property, $1,500; Bible school began 1909; present enrollment, 45.

This church is about five miles from Long Point, Flanagan and Dana. A Bible school was started in the community about 1887. In 1909, two miles west of the former meetingplace, Mrs. H. P. Thompson formed a Sunday school in a schoolhouse near the site of the present chapel. Min. Rochester Irwin held a tent meeting there in 1909. Out of this grew the building of the chapel. The meeting by Mr. Wray was three years later. The church has half-time afternoon preaching by H. H. Jenner. The credit of this work is largely due to David London, David Carlton and H. P. Thompson.

Fairbury.

Organized 1868, by J. B. McCorkle; present membership, 163; value of property, $8,000; Bible school began 1868; present enrollment, 80.

Minister McCorkle introduced the apostolic faith in Fairbury. There were nine charter members, only one of whom survives. They were Mr. and Mrs. C. B. Thompson, Mr. and Mrs. John Adkins, Mr. and Mrs. Hotchkiss, Mrs. McCurdy, Mrs. Lizzie Spence and Mrs. De Ford.

The first place of meeting was a room over a wagonshop. Later a chapel was purchased of the Presbyterians. In 1894, during the pastorate of J. W. Porter, a more commodious house was built.

The life of the congregation has ebbed and flowed. After various removals, vicissitudes and discouragements, there was a reorganization in 1880 by A. B. Markle. W. C. Chapman is now the pastor.

Mr. M. Hotaling stood by this work for many years and very faithfully. His son, Lewis R. Hotaling, was given to the ministry.

Flanagan.

Organized 1862, by Houston brothers; present membership, 195; value of property, including parsonage, $3,500; Bible-school enrollment, 177.

A few families of the neighborhood met for worship sometimes in their own homes, sometimes in Mt. Zion

Schoolhouse, three miles northeast of Flanagan, and sometimes in the old Berean Schoolhouse, three miles to the southwest. Min. A. H. Trowbridge occasionally rode horseback thirty miles across the country to preach to them. There were few roads then through the prairies. A great impulse was given to the work here and elsewhere by the coming, about this time, of the three brothers—Washington, Jefferson and John Houston—from Kentucky. They settled on farms near Cornell. They were all preachers and fine singers. Among the faithful families of that time there were the Hoovers, Pearsons, Martins, Hopwoods, Wilcoxes and Mouldseas.

J. F. Ghormley, then a student in Eureka College, by a fine effort led in building a chapel in the village in 1881. Thereafter the congregation grew steadily under his ministration and that of J. T. Ogle, E. A. Gilliland, K. C. Ventres and J. T. Alsup, also Eureka students.

The church has never been large. At times so many moved away that it could hardly stand. Those left, by prayer and diligence, rebuilt the numbers. Those who left became active members of congregations in several States.

The church has always been strong in missionary activities in the home and foreign fields. In 1912 it was a living link to Eureka College.

It has given to the ministry R. J. Bamber and J. P. Rollison. Earnest Pearson is preparing for the work of medical missionary.

Forrest.

Organized 1868, by J. B. McCorkle; present membership, 18; value of property, $5,000; Bible school died.

Since its organization this church has never been numerically strong enough to maintain itself according to prevailing standards. Many of its efficient members have moved to other places and others have died. Among the latter, Mr. and Mrs. S. A. Hoyt, John Rudd and John Elmore are held in affectionate remembrance.

Indian Grove (Fairbury).

Organized 1861, by John Miller; present membership, 35; value of property, $1,000.

This location is six miles south of Fairbury. A union chapel was built in 1861 and Evangelist John Miller held a meeting at once. There were about fifty charter members.

In its early period the congregation was served by Ministers Sharples, Spence, Loar, Holloway, Houston, Robenson, Carrithers, Ledgerwood, Poynter and Markle. W. C. Chapman, of Fairbury, now preaches for them Sunday afternoons. A union Bible school is maintained. The church of Christ only keeps up its public worship.

Long Point.

Organized 1889, by I. R. Spencer; present membership, 151; value of property, $9,150; Bible school began 1889; present enrollment, 91.

Minister Spencer led in a series of meetings in the Methodist Protestant chapel and the organization of a church of Christ immediately followed. There were sixty charter members. Ministers of the two congregations alternated in the use of the chapel until 1903. Then the Disciples, led by Min. M. L. Pontius, erected a good building of their own. In addition to a parsonage, built during the pastorate of Rochester Irwin, the church also owns a cottage for its janitor and nine lots for gardening. Mr. Irwin and wife gave fine service here.

The church counts itself fortunate in having had for its ministers, in addition to those above named, F. W. Burnham, S. H. Zendt, H. G. Bennett, L. O. Lehman, F. W. Sutton, J. W. Camp, and now H. H. Jenner.

Pontiac.

Organized 1859, by D. D. Miller; present membership, 377; value of property, $18,100; Bible school began 1859; present enrollment, 275.

This church was the result of a series of evangelistic meetings conducted by Min. Washington Houston. The first meetings were held in the old schoolhouse on the bank of the Vermilion River. The church prospered under the ministry of the Houston brothers, so that the place of meeting was changed to the courthouse to accommodate the crowds of people. The first elders were John Powell, Henry Hill and James W. Perry. Mrs. D. J. Lyon is the sole surviving charter member.

Mr. Newell was a schoolteacher and at the same time a minister in charge of the church. During his pastorate an agreement was made between the Disciples and the Christian Denomination to erect a union house of worship. It was a brick building without any claims to architectural beauty. However, it was honored by the presence of Abraham Lincoln, who delivered an address therein. After five years the legal title was passed to the church of Christ exclusively, and later to Mr. Powell. "The organ question" came up; the congregation became financially involved and disbanded.

Quite a few drifted into other fellowships. But during all the years of spiritual ruin, eight or ten constituted a faithful band and met when and where they could to pray and remember the Lord in his appointments.

In 1873, Min. J. G. Waggoner reorganized the church, since which it has gone steadily forward in usefulness. Charles Rowe became the first pastor. He was followed by students from Eureka. Meanwhile the women of the church bought the church property from the estate of Mr. Powell. The State Board fostered the reviving congregation. During the pastorate of G. W. McColley a new lot was bought and a modern church structure was erected in 1904.

During the days of tribulation, Washington Houston conducted a public discussion in the old M. E. chapel with a representative of that denomination.

The church is now vigorous and prosperous—aggressive in all good works. It is a living link in the Eureka College. B. W. Tate is its efficient pastor.

It has given to the ministry Charles Scrivens, L. F. Starbuck, Frank Cummings and M. L. Bodine.

Saunemin.

Organized 1874, by W. P. Carrithers; present membership, 139; value of property, including parsonage, $5,000; Bible school began 1874; present enrollment, 42.

The organization was formed in the Bethel Schoolhouse. Then it met for worship in a hall in the village. The first chapel was built in 1887 at a cost of $2,000. This was burned in 1904. The same year a much better house was built, and also a parsonage.

The congregation has passed many vicissitudes. Deaths and removals have greatly reduced the membership in late years.

W. P. Carrithers has long been the mainstay in the church. The other two elders are George Moulds and S. D. Vawter. The deacons are Robert Williams, John Farr, W. S. Rustin, C. L. Farner and Mona Fieldcamp.

H. C. Reichel preaches half-time.

LOGAN COUNTY.

It is a source of regret that no written records have been left of the first work of the preachers of the Disciples of Christ in Logan County. Without doubt there was preaching at a number of places in the thirties and forties by W. P. Bowles and his father (Hughes Bowles), by John England, Wm. Ryan, A. J. Kane and others.

The first church of Christ, so far as discovered, was formed about 1848. It was located seven miles west of Mt. Pulaski, on the Springfield road. It was known as the Bridge Church because it stood near the bridge that spanned the stream called Lake Fork. It was probably organized by Father Morrow. At least, he preached there for years. Residing on his farm, it was his custom to come from his home to the meeting-house, riding a mule, with a sheepskin saddle and saddlebags. This congregation continued until about 1860. Then those members who lived on the west of the lake formed a congregation known as the Turley Church and built a small chapel four miles north of the site of Cornland. Those residing east of the lake formed a congregation known as the Buckles Church and built a meeting-house two miles east of the old church and five miles west of Mt. Pulaski. This congregation continued to be an active Christian force until 1905. Then some of its members went to Mt. Pulaski and some to the Lake Fork congregation. The chapel was moved to the Carlisle Cemetery, where it still stands.

In the forties there was some preaching by Christian ministers and some conversions at French's ford, on Salt Creek, south of Lincoln, but whether a congregation was formed, could not be learned.

In late years a congregation was formed at Lawndale, but it has become extinct.

Armington.

Organized 1828, by William Miller; present membership, 222; value of property, including parsonage, $17,000; Bible-school enrollment, 300.

Hittle's Grove and the prairies round about it were as pleasing as any upon which human eyes ever rested. Into that locality, eighty-five years ago, the following named families began to settle: the Hittles and Judys from Ohio; the Albrights from Tennessee; the Burts, Quisenberrys, Hainlines, Dills and Millers from Kentucky, and the Hieronymuses from Virginia.

The first sermon ever preached in Hittle's Grove was by a Methodist minister named Walker, in a log cabin 16 x 16, owned by Michael Hittle.

After a time two women of the settlement wished to be baptized and a Baptist minister was sent for. Finding no church there to vote on the fitness of the candidates, after deliberation it was decided to immerse them on the simple confession of their faith in Christ. Thereupon, a Baptist church was organized with the following charter members: William Miller and wife, Isaac Miller and wife, Walker Miller and wife, and Sarah Miller.

On Jan. 11, 1829, this church became Christian only. The agreement signed with the seventeen names follows:

> We, the undersigned, do give ourselves to the Lord and to each other as a church of Jesus Christ to be governed by His word contained in the Old and New Testaments. William Miller and wife, Jacob Albright and wife Esther, Strother Hittle and wife, Robert Musick and wife, William Darnell and wife Sally, William Burt and wife China, Joseph Lancaster and wife Hannah, John Judy and wife Christena, Jacob Judy unmarried.

These people met for public worship for a short time in their log-cabin homes, then used the log schoolhouse; later a church was built three miles west of the site of Armington. This served till 1865, when a more commodious house was built, one and a fourth miles west of Armington. In 1886, during the pastorate of John T. Owens, lots were bought in the village of Armington and the building moved to them. From this time the congregation was called by the name of the town. The last Lord's Day in August, 1906, the people bade a tender farewell to the old house; on the next Sunday they moved into their new and modern brick structure. J. C. Lappin was their pastor.

Hittle Grove Church was a familiar name to all the old-time Disciples in central Illinois for a period of sixty-five years. Most of the pioneers preached there. In the thirties there were James Mitchell and Abner Peeler; in the forties, W. P. Bowles and G. W. Minier; then later Samuel Knight, James A. and John Lindsey, William Davenport, Leroy Skelton, Baily Chaplain, Samuel and Joseph Lowe, L. M. Robinson, and Isaac and Elijah Stout. In recent years the pastors have been Mr. Edwards, Albert Nichols, J. E. Diehl, Mr. Jennette, E. J. Stanley, C. A. Heckel, J. E. Parker, W. D. Deweese, L. E. Chase, J. C. Lappin, and now R. B. Doan.

In 1857 the church made the following report to the State meeting: "Members, 136; meet twice a month; we break the loaf once a month and have preaching once a month. We pay teaching brethren $2 a day."

The Britt, Burt, Albright, Judy, Darnell, Hieronymus and Mason families have done much for the church.

Atlanta.

Organized 1855, by George W. Minier; present membership, 300; value of property, including parsonage, $14,000; Bible school began 1856; present enrollment, 302.

This church was organized in the Baptist chapel, where meetings were held Lord's Day afternoons the first year. The first elders were C. F. Ewing and Andrew Wright; the first deacons, Jacob Judy and Jefferson Howser; James Shores, clerk. The additional twenty-five charter members were the following: J. P. Hawes and wife, Jefferson Britt and wife, T. H. Dills and wife, Ambrose Hall and wife, John Miller and wife, Calvin Riley and wife, George Dyer and wife, Dr. Arterburn and wife, Mrs. Dr. J. B. Tenney, Mrs. Sallie Strong, Mr. Gill and Mrs. Christenson.

At Atlanta the Disciples were publicly depreciated in the early years by the self-styled orthodox people, as they were in most places. It was a town where infidelity ran riotously. But after the Burgess-Burrows debate in 1868, many phases of religion changed.

The first pastor of the church was W. M. Guilford, who was at the same time principal of the public schools. Those who succeeded him were John Lindsay, W. P. Bowles, R. B. Chaplin, J. W. Monser, Leroy Skelton, Samuel and Joseph Lowe, J. A. Seaton, T. V. Berry, T. T. Holton, R. D. Cotton, R. W. Callaway, Dr. S. H. Bundy, L. M. Robinson, B. O. Aylesworth, L. G. Thompson, J. P. Davis, Mr. Miller, C. E. Selby, R. F. Thrapp, T. B. Stanley, L. W. Morgan, S. S. Lappin, W. R. Jinnett, Ivan W. Magee, and now R. H. Newton.

The first church building was erected in 1856. A modern building was occupied in 1913.

This church has given to the ministry J. H. Wright, Walter Rhodes, Roy A. Miller and Merritt Hoblit, a missionary in Mexico.

Bethel (Emden).

Organized 1853, by William B. Ryan; present membership, 105; value of property, $5,000; Bible school began 1853; present enrollment, 75.

This congregation, located four and one-half miles east of Emden, grew out of the old Sugar Creek Church. A few members, desiring a more convenient place for their public worship, selected the site, which was given by one of the number, Norman Sumner. There were nineteen charter members, as follows: William B. and Elizabeth Ryan, William R. and Elizabeth Shirley, Samuel and Jemima Waters, Jeremiah and Sarah A. Miller, Norman and Margaret Sumner, George G. and Melville Ryan, Jesse P. and Marial Bowles, David and Elizabeth Bowles, James W. and Henry Shirley, and Nancy Bevans, who married John Lumbeck. Of these, only three survive—Sarah A. Miller, and James W. and Henry Shirley. The names of the other sixteen are read on the marble slabs in the four cemeteries located in two States.

The first officers were: Elders, David Bowles and William R. Shirley; deacons, George G. Ryan and Jeremiah Miller; clerk, Norman Sumner, with two trustees. The Christian faith of the Bowles and Shirley families has been so excellent that some of their members have filled the office of elder during the sixty years of the church's life.

The first house was built in 1853. The men went to the forest, felled the trees, cut and hauled the logs together, and, with broadax, foot-adz and such other tools as they had, fashioned and built this first temple for the Lord. For a period of twenty years this house was the happy home of its builders and their children. In 1873 it gave place to the structure that is still in use.

In addition to Mr. Ryan's, the old house heard the voices of Benjamin Franklin, G. W. Minier, W. P. Bowles, Dudley Downs, R. B. Chaplin, Leroy Skelton, Isaac Stout, Peter

Hawes, James Mitchell, Charles Short, Peter Sheik, J. A. Seaton, R. D. Cotton, J. V. Beekman, Samuel Knight, Henry Smithers, S. C. Pruitt and many others. In addition to many of those who also ministered to the congregation in the new house, the following have served there: L. M. Robinson, T. T. Holton, G. W. Warner, H. S. Mavity, J. C. Hall, J. W. Porter, J. E. Jewett, J. A. Barnett, I. L. Parvin, H. B. Easterling, F. B. Jones and R. E. Stevenson.

This church has always been noted for the good common sense of its members. The spirit of brotherliness has always predominated. The people delighted to make others happy. In the period of the old house, families came to church in farm-wagons, seated with chairs which were carried into the house and used on occasion. The blankets and comforters which were used as wraps to protect from cold or rain were brought in at night and made into beds on seats or in a corner on the floor, and there the little ones slept during the worship. This church is proud of the fact that it is a country church. Its watchwords through sixty years have been, "Move Forward." Many of its members have gone out to help in the Lord's work in the world. R. E. Hieronymus began his Christian service here, and W. H. Kindred and Frank Sumner are in the ministry.

The old songs were an inspiration, as they are yet a tender memory with many.

C. R. Bowles has served as superintendent of the Sunday school for thirty years. In the earlier time children were encouraged to commit the Scriptures to memory and repeat them on Sundays. Many now past life's meridian can repeat whole chapters learned in childhood there.

Through sixty years the table of the Lord has been spread on every first day of the week. Preaching is maintained for half-time. The church is alive to all missionary activities. It has no other thought than to live by doing the will of God. The glorious memories of the past unite with the duties of the present in filling these people with high purposes.

Broadwell.

Organized 1863, by C. J. Berry; present membership, 99; value of property, $1,600; Bible school began 1863; present enrollment, 56.

This church was formed in the public-school house with the following charter members: Samuel Buckley, Spencer Grogan, Jacob Eisminger, P. Eisminger, Elizabeth Eisminger, Mary Eisminger, Eliza Lloyd, Nancy Kline, Ellen Kline, May Critchfield, M. Wiley, L. Wiley and M. Wright. These persons organized as "The Church of Christ at Broadwell," upon the Bible as their creed and the New Testament as their only discipline. They "vowed before the Lord, angels and men to walk in obedience to the requirements of the gospel in all things."

The church was built in 1864.

Copeland (Mt. Pulaski).

Organized 1866, by John England; present membership, 100; value of property, $4,000; Bible school began 1868; present enrollment, 125.

This church is located seven miles southwest of Mt. Pulaski. It was organized at the Copeland Schoolhouse. The charter members were Mr. and Mrs. Samuel Harbert, Mr. and Mrs. David Birks, Mr. and Mrs. John Birks, Mr. and Mrs. William Copeland, Mr. and Mrs. Roland Birks, Mr. and Mrs. Abner Copeland, Polly Peters, George W. Whitesides and Maria Copeland.

The church house was built in 1867. An addition and repairs were made in 1906 at a cost of $400. It was modernized in 1911 at a cost of $2,500.

The congregation has been a leading force for good in the neighborhood there many years.

The present officers are: Elders, Elmer Turley, Charles Bowers, Calvin Payne and J. H. Clendenen; deacons, George Bowers, Fred Bellatti, Stephen Edwards, R. Drabing and W. E. Simpson.

Cornland.

Organized 1874, by D. D. Miller; present membership, 120; value of property, $1,350; Bible school began 1875; present enrollment, 72.

A few years prior to the formation of the Cornland Church a congregation had been formed, and a small house erected four miles north of the town site, called the Turley Church.

A series of meetings was held in the Day Schoolhouse in the village by D. D. Miller in 1874, which resulted in the formation of the church there. Of this the congregation four miles north became a part, and that building was moved into town. The congregation was much strengthened by a series of meetings conducted by Min. J. E. Cain in 1875. Many removals have reduced their numbers.

Emden.

Organized 1888, by W. H. Boles; present membership, 94; value of property, $2,500; Bible school began 1873; present enrollment, 70.

A union Sunday school was formed in the public-school house in 1873 with E. L. Carnahan as superintendent. Three years thereafter gospel temperance meetings began to be held there on Sunday evening. Next came some sermons at the same time and place by G. W. Minier and R. B. Chaplin. A three weeks' meeting conducted by Evangelist Boles resulted in the organization of the church with fifty-three members.

The house of worship was completed in 1889 and the organization perfected. Later an addition was built.

The honored names in the congregation include Mr. J. L. Searle, Mrs. Lizzie Bennett and Mrs. Betsy Sumner.

Eminence (Atlanta).

Organized 1838, by its own members; present membership, 180; value of property, $5,000; Bible school began 1845; present enrollment, 62.

This is a country church, located five miles northwest of Atlanta. It has been known by three or four local names. The first building was at Pekin Ford, near Morgan's Mill; hence it was first known as Morgan's Church. Later moved to the present site, where it was known as Smith Ewing or Sugar Creek Church; the latter name, however, held through the larger part of the seventy-five years of its life. In recent years it has been known by the name of the township in which it is located.

The first record reads as follows:

On Lord's Day, June 17, 1838, the Brothers and Sisters whose respective names are hereafter annexed, do agree to live together in Gospel order, as a Church of Jesus Christ, to take the Word of God as the rule of faith and man of our council. The following are the names of the members who joined themselves together on the day above named: Robert Musick, Charles F. Ewing, Mary Ewing, Elizabeth Simmonds, Sarah Miller, Sarah Stroud, James Hieronymus, Barbary Johnson, Melinda Johnson, Catherine Thompson, Esther A. Hawes, Sarah Hawes.

This was a spontaneous organization, originating among and completed by the members themselves. Lord's Day, Aug. 25, 1839, the elders elected were Charles F. Ewing and David G. Thompson, who were ordained on Lord's Day, the 15th of the following month. The records give the names of those who have served the congregation as elders from that day to the present time.

Until 1845 the congregation met for worship where they could. In that year the first house was built, costing $1,000. This served eleven years and was then torn down. In 1856 the second house, costing $1,600, was erected. After being used for thirty-five years it was sold. In 1891 the third building, costing $3,600, was occupied. This was burned in 1901. The same year the present building, costing $6,000, was erected. It has a bell, a baptistery and gasoline lights.

Among the preachers of the earlier years there were Abner Peeler, Hughes and W. P. Bowles, William Davenport, James A. Lindsey, John England, G. W. Minier, William Ryan, Baily Chaplain, L. M. Robinson, John Lindsey, Isaac Stout, Leroy Skelton, Samuel and Joseph Lowe, J. V. Beekman and T. T. Holton. Alexander Campbell visited the church in 1844.

The records show that the church has ordained the following men to the ministry: William Ryan, George Hatfield and George Carlock.

The church now has a resident minister for all the time and is flourishing. Sarah A. Miller, the only living charter member, resides in Atlanta. Elizabeth Howser, who united with the church the next day after its formation, also survives at the age of ninety-four.

In the early days, when harness for horses came into use, with lines to drive with, a member of this congregation bought a set. Not knowing how to attach the lines properly, he hitched his team to the wagon one Sunday morning, placed his wife and children in the wagon, then mounted one of the horses and thus took his family to church and home again. His "style" attracted no particular attention and called out no comments.

One of the laymen produced by this church is responsible for the following:

> Business in Religion and Religion in Business.
> Before national banks were organized we had private or State banks issuing currency, or paper money, as in the fifties. I saw names of private parties placed on the backs of such bills with the dates; so if they failed to pass they could be returned to those from whom they were received as "no good." Now we have currency good in any and all States. If that currency is best that is good in all the States, then that baptism is best that is good in all the churches, and we all know that immersion is good in all the churches.

The following incident deserves to be rescued from oblivion. This picture is from the pleasing pen of Min. T. T. Holton. He says:

> In 1889 G. W. Minier called me to assist him in a meeting at the Sugar Creek Church. He was then in his seventy-sixth year. He said to me, "Bro. Holton, you do the preaching and I'll do the baptizing." This was a very successful meeting. There were forty-three added to the church—thirty-eight by confession and baptism. When

we went to select a place for baptism we found Sugar Creek too scant of water. We crossed the creek and found a beautiful little lake. The venerable Peter Bruner, who had been an elder in the church for a long time, was with us. He had done the baptizing for the church for many years, but had become too frail for the task. While the good elder and I were looking for a pole to test the depth of the water, we heard a splash and, turning suddenly, we saw Bro. Minier swimming around in the lake. It was late in October and there had been two cold spells that froze ice. Bro. Minier was not afraid of water. It was his custom to bathe every morning, sometimes of necessity at great inconvenience. He thoroughly explored the lake and marked a good place for the baptism. He had secreted a towel in his pocket, and, having thoroughly dried and reclothed himself, said, "Brethren, now for the 'Wolf's Den.'" This took us up quite a steep high hill, Bro. Minier in the lead. From the "Wolf's Den" we viewed the landscape. Then Bro. Minier set about gathering some botanical specimens. As we returned to the Bruner home, at his suggestion we visited the Eminence school. Of course Bro. Minier was asked to address the school. The plants he held in his hand he made his text. He gave their common names, also their botanical names, and descanted on the leaves, the bark, the roots, the sap, fruit, etc., to the delight of the whole school. When the day of the baptism came, an urgent matrimonial engagement called him, so I had to do the baptizing. It was the most beautiful scene I ever saw. The lake was surrounded by sugar maples and the leaves were like gold. It was a beautiful afternoon and the great crowd of people gathered there was quiet and reverent. The sloping ground gave all an opportunity to see and hear. I gave an invitation at the water's edge. A young lady came forward. Her mother approached and whispered to me, "My daughter is deaf and dumb. She is educated and I think she understands the step she desires to take." This was the first experience I had ever had in introducing a deaf mute into the kingdom. I took a blank book and pencil from my side pocket and wrote, "Do you believe with all your heart that Jesus is the Christ, the Son of God?" In response she took the pencil and wrote, "I do." And I baptized her.

Hartsburg.

Organized 1870; present membership, 29; value of property, $600; Bible school began 1870; present enrollment, 48.

The early records of the church were lost. A few Disciples living in the country near the village began meetings for public worship. Later a building was erected on the farm of Henry Musick. Within four or five years nearly all of the original members moved away, some to other

States. In 1875, under the lead of Fielding Musick, the chapel was moved to Hartsburg, where it is yet used.

Lake Fork.

Organized 1905, by J. D. Williams; present membership, 100; value of property, including parsonage, $3,200; Bible school began 1905; present enrollment, 100.

This congregation is the product and continuance of the Buckles Church. The village grew up after the railroad was built.

The chapel was built in 1903.

Besides Minister Williams, the congregation has been served by M. M. Snow, D. H. Carrick and M. M. Hughes.

The officers are Henry Horn and W. L. Follis, elders, with C. M. Shinn, Wm. Tebus, Galveston Thuer, E. R. Jones and Obid Gaffney, deacons.

Latham.

Organized 1891, by J. O. Sutherland; present membership, 250; value of property, $15,000; Bible school began 1891; present enrollment, 113.

The church was the first result of a series of meetings conducted by Minister Sutherland. He also served the congregation two terms as its pastor. Those who succeeded him were G. W. Hughes, Mr. Weatherford, Z. M. Brubeck, C. S. Weaver, D. A. Lindsey, and now Ira A. Engle.

The first chapel was built during the ministry of Mr. Sutherland and occupied early in 1892. The present excellent modern structure was erected during the pastorate of Mr. Weaver. It cost $13,325, and was finished in 1910.

This church is largely rural. Its auxiliaries are large and active. In 1912 it paid $325 for general benevolences.

Lincoln.

Organized 1856, by W. H. Brown; present membership, 695; value of property, including parsonage, $29,000; Bible school began 1856; present enrollment, 370.

John England and Walter P. Bowles preached the primitive gospel in various parts of Logan County in the forties and early fifties. One place they visited was French's Ford, on Salt Creek, about four miles south of Lincoln. Among those who became Christians was Miss Sarah Wade, who married Fred Wolf. When the town of Lincoln was started, Mr. Wolf, with others, moved there. He has furnished these facts. He was born in 1831. Thomas H. Denny had bought a farm near Lincoln and settled on it. Being a Disciple, he sent for Evangelist "Billy Brown," who held a series of meetings and constituted a church. There were about thirty charter members, Mrs. Wolf being one of these. The first officers were T. H. Denny and Hopkins C. Judy, elders, and Charles H. Miller and John M. Edwards, deacons.

Meetings for public worship were held in Boren's Hall, in a warehouse and other places. In 1854 they set to build a chapel that was finished the next year. After its enclosure it required a struggle of years to pay for it. The Circuit Court was held in this building in 1856, as the courthouse had burned just before that time. The present modern edifice was erected in 1903-04, during the pastorate of W. H. Cannon.

Other ministers include Dr. J. M. Allen, J. S. Sweeney, Alexander Johnson, Allen H. Rice, Charles L. Berry, George Owen, B. W. and N. H. Johnson, T. V. Berry, H. D. Clark, G. W. Minier, S. C. Humphrey, R. A. Gilcrist, Jesse Gresham, Dr. S. H. Bundy, T. T. Holton, W. H. Cannon, J. E. Jewett, T. F. Weaver, Albert Nichols, E. A. Gilliland and G. W. Wise.

Among those who did much for the church were John A. Simpson, R. C. Maxwell, H. O. Merry and L. P. Hanger; they merit remembrance. Three charter members are still living—Mrs. B. F. Warfield, Mrs. Wielan Ryan and Mrs. Ellen Chowning.

Not many years since the church "had a revival" that is said to have been a distinct injury.

Mt. Pulaski.

Organized 1868, by D. D. Miller; present membership, 361; value of property, $9,000; Bible school began 1868; present enrollment, 271.

Min. D. D. Miller conducted a series of meetings in a public hall on the west side of the public square in the fall of 1868. This resulted in the organization of the church, in the following spring, of thirty members. Of these only two are left living—Mrs. Caroline Snyder and Mrs. Amanda Prompelly, who have continued faithfully. The first elders were Alfred Samms and Samuel Turley.

Through the efforts of Mrs. Pomelia Fisher and others, a lot was bought and a building, costing $2,000, was erected in 1870. In 1906, during the pastorate of David A. Lindsay, the old building was removed and its materials used in the construction of a modern house, costing $10,000.

For a number of years the church was without preaching and the congregation dwindled, but in 1887 a new start was made, since which time the church has gone steadily forward.

The pastorate of Gilbert Jones was especially fruitful.

The Bible school is front rank, while the missionary and benevolent offerings continue to grow.

M'DONOUGH COUNTY.

In 1832 the first Christian Church was organized in McDonough County at a point about one and a half miles north of Blandinsville, known as the Liberty Christian Church. Here the people of two pioneer settlements met to worship, the one known as the Jobe settlement a few miles to the south, and the other a few miles to the north, composed of a number of families, among whom were the Brightwells, Bradshaws, Cyruses and Hustons. In 1842 the town of Blandinsville was laid out and platted. In 1849 Liberty was abandoned as a meeting-place and the church of Blandinsville was organized by the members of the Jobe settlement. And about the same time the members of the north settlement organized the Bedford Church.

Blandinsville.

Organized 1849; present membership, 384; value of property, $25,000; Bible school began 1861; present enrollment, 164.

The history of the church at Blandinsville is not materially different from others of like environments. The following have served as preachers or pastors: James K. Knox, Uriah Long, A. J. Kane, James D. Eads, John Rigdon, Milton Dodge, James R. Ross, Cornelius Ades, Patrick Murphy, Bedford Murphy, J. M. Martin, Robert Lieurance, J. H. Coffee, S. K. Hallam, H. R. Trickett, J. F. Leek, T. H. Goodnight, G. F. Adams, M. P. Hayden, J. Carroll Stark, George W. Ross, William Sumpter, J. S. Clements, W. A. Malone, Clarence Townley, Edward Richey, A. M. Hale, M. C. R. Wolford and D. J. Elsla.

The third house of worship was finished in 1911. It is a modern and beautiful structure with a seating capacity of eight hundred. The congregation has held many admirable people in its membership. It has given Allen Hitch and Wm. Enders to the ministry.

Bushnell.

Present membership, 20; value of property, $2,500; Bible-school enrollment, 23.

Many efforts have been made to establish a good church here, but without success.

Central (Blandinsville).

Present membership, 50; value of property, $3,000; Bible-school enrollment, 60.

Colchester.

Organized 1867, by Cornelius Ades; present membership, 190; value of property, $8,000; Bible school began 1867; present enrollment, 140.

The church was formed in the public-school house. The chapel was built in 1870, repaired in 1901 and burned in 1908. A new brick structure was finished in 1908.

Colmar.

Organized 1906, by Edward Stebbins; present membership, 140; value of property, $1,000; Bible school began 1906; present enrollment, 55.

Fandon.

Organized 1898, by F. M. Branic; present membership, 80; value of property, $1,500; Bible school began 1898; present enrollment, 108.

The church was constituted in Woodman Hall with forty-three charter members. The chapel was first occupied in 1903.

Macomb.

Organized 1845, by A. J. Kane; present membership, 500; value of property, including parsonage, $29,500; Bible school began 1848; present enrollment, 427.

Mr. Kane at that time was a young evangelist; held a meeting of days, at the close of which Dr. Young came and assisted in perfecting the organization. The courthouse was the first place of meeting. A small frame chapel was soon built, which served till 1877. Then a second frame building costing $4,400. The present modern edifice was erected in 1909. Some pastors who served the church were Levi Hatchett, W. W. Hopkins, W. P. Shockley, W. O. Miller, Samuel Lowe, J. C. Reynolds, J. H. Garrison, P. K. Dibble, J. H. Smart and G. W. Mapes two periods.

Those given to the ministry were J. S. Gash, D. H. Shields, Samuel G. Buckner, Champ Clark, G. W. Buckner, Geo. L. Purdy, Clarence I. Timmons and Abram E. Cory, a missionary in China. The membership has always held a number of people who were representative in the community and the kingdom.

Alexander Campbell visited the church in his later years. Mrs. Margaret Martin is now (1913) the only living member who united in the Kane meeting.

New Philadelphia.

Present membership, 86; value of property, $2,000; Bible-school enrollment, 78.

New Salem (Adair).

Organized 1859, by J. B. Royal; value of property, $2,000; Bible school began 1859.

The church was formed in the Wetsel Schoolhouse with sixteen charter members, all of whom have gone to their reward. W. A. Griffin and Daniel Wilson were the first elders, with Josiah Herlocker and Caleb Hipsley, deacons.

The chapel was built in 1867.

M. W. Crim is the correspondent.

Old Bedford (Stronghurst).

Organized 1849; present membership, 125; value of property, including parsonage, $3,250; Bible-school enrollment, 60.

This place is six miles north of Blandinsville. It is a country church that has lived long and done well for its members and the community.

Sciota.

Present membership, 62; value of property, $1,000; Bible-school enrollment, 57.

M'HENRY COUNTY.

North Crystal Lake.

Present membership, 30; value of property, including parsonage, $2,100; Bible-school enrollment, 35.

In the sixties a few congregations were formed in this

SECOND CHRISTIAN CHURCH, BLOOMINGTON.
FIRST CHRISTIAN CHURCH, NORMAL.
FIRST CHRISTIAN CHURCH, BLOOMINGTON.
CENTENNIAL CHRISTIAN CHURCH, BLOOMINGTON.

county by ministers from Lake County. They lived only a few years.

M'LEAN COUNTY.

Ebenezer Rhodes was born in Holland in 1780. Coming to America, he first settled in Maryland, thereafter moved to Ohio, and in 1824 came to Illinois and settled in Keg's Grove, so called because a keg with some whisky in it was found there. Within a few years the name was changed to Blooming Grove, which it still retains. It is five miles south of Bloomington. Mr. Rhodes was a Baptist preacher. He preached whenever and wherever he could get two or three families together. In those early years he preached at Hittle's Grove, Cheney's Grove, Sugar Grove, Long Point, Big Grove, Twin Grove, Dry Grove, Blooming Grove, at the head of the Mackinaw and elsewhere. He was the first preacher in McLean County, and is said to have married the first couple in the county; namely, Thomas Orendorff and Miss Malinda Walker. Mr. Rhodes organized the first church in the county. This was in 1824, in his own house in Blooming Grove. There, so it is said by some, were seven charter members; namely, Ebenezer Rhodes and wife, and his sons (John H. S. and Samuel Rhodes) and their wives, and the other, it is believed, was Jeremiah Rhodes.

Reuben Carlock was a native of Overton County, Tenn. He came to Illinois in 1827, and on October 10 settled in Dry Grove, five miles southwest of the present site of Carlock. Mr. Carlock's family was the fifth to settle in Dry Grove. That was then a part of Tazewell County. In that year the county-seat was located at Mackinaw town. There were then five families in Twin Grove, seven families in Stout's Grove, three families in Brown's Grove, thirteen families in Keg's or Blooming Grove, two families in Funk's Grove and one family in Three Miles Grove. All of the first settlers made their homes along the timber. Indians were then many in this section. Old Town was one of their camps. It was a strip of timber some two miles wide, thirteen miles east of Bloomington. The country was full of deer, wild turkeys, prairie chickens and pigeons. These settlers traded at Springfield and Pekin.

William Brown was a Christian preacher who came from Tennessee to Dry Grove, Ill., in 1828. He was a friend of Reuben Carlock. In August of that year, Mr. Carlock hitched up his ox team, and, accompanied by some members of his own family and his guest, Preacher Brown, drove to the cabin of Ebenezer Rhodes, in Blooming Grove, for a three days' meeting. It was during this meeting that the Rhodes and Carlock families were united in one church. Whether the organization above referred to did not take place till this year, or whether it was reorganized upon receiving the Carlocks, is not clear. But when these families were united in that little church in August, 1828, Ebenezer Rhodes, the recognized leader, said: "And now, brethren, we must have some articles of faith."

Whereupon Reuben Carlock, drawing a small copy of the New Testament from his pocket and holding it up, said: "Bro. Rhodes, this Book has all the articles of faith we need."

Mr. Rhodes at once in full assurance answered: "That is true."

Then and there a primitive and apostolic church of Christ was born. From that time Mr. Rhodes was known as a Christian minister. He continued to preach the gospel, without the admixture of human traditions, till his death in 1842. Later the members went to other local churches. Preacher Brown returned to Tennessee.

Grassy Ridge was another fruitful little vine that served its generation well and then went the way of all flesh. It was located five miles south of Bloomington, on Morris Avenue, and was organized by Min. J. G. Campbell in the White Schoolhouse in 1853 with thirteen charter members. In 1854 a chapel was built on a piece of ground donated by Mr. Campbell. The congregation grew and prospered and did much good. It was pervaded by the admirable spirit of its leader, Mr. Campbell. He saw to it that many of the fine ministers of the Restoration movement preached there. In 1886, by a formal action, the church disbanded, the members uniting with near-by congregations—Lytleville, Heyworth, Shirley, Blooming Grove and Bloomington. Trustees for the cemetery were incorporated under the civil statute.

The Blooming Grove Church was organized again in 1872 by State Evangelist John Lindsay and County Evangelist W. G. Anderson. In 1862 a Sunday school was formed at the Walker Schoolhouse. Mrs. W. J. Rhodes was superintendent, and Mrs. Amos Cox, the wife of a Presbyterian minister, and Miss Sallie Walker were the teachers. A decade later the church was constituted with twenty-six charter members.

The well-to-do farmers moved away, so after a period of thirty-eight years the church was closed in November, 1910. Most of the members have united with the Bloomington Church or with the church at Heyworth.

Anchor.

Organized 1884, by Dr. A. W. Green; present membership, 17; value of property, $1,000; Bible school began 1884; none at present.

Worship was first held in the schoolhouse. The old Antioch Church building was moved to Anchor when its membership was transferred to Colfax. There were thirty-seven charter members, but the church has been weakened by removals.

Arrowsmith.

Organized 1879, by H. G. Van Dervoort; present membership, 142; value of property, including parsonage, $14,250; Bible school began 1879; present enrolment, 134.

This church was the immediate result of a series of meetings conducted by Min. H. G. Van Dervoort in the old United Brethren chapel. However, previous organizations in this vicinity were also contributing factors. Min. Moses H. Knight, one of the earlier evangelists of this county, and

J. G. Campbell began preaching to the people south of Ellsworth in 1858. Later the congregation removed to the West log schoolhouse and an organization of eighteen members was formed under the leadership of Russell Watson. They grew in numbers and strength so that in 1868 a frame building was erected three and one-half miles southwest of Arrowsmith, which was known as the Pleasant Ridge Church. This house was dedicated by Uncle Jimmie Robeson. Later this building was torn down and the material worked into the Arrowsmith Church.

In 1865 a revival was held in the Center Schoolhouse, one-half mile south of the site of Arrowsmith. A small organization was formed which in 1868 united with the Pleasant Ridge Church.

In 1873, Evangelist George F. Adams held a series of meetings in the Martin Valley United Brethren Church. These brethren were very kind to the Disciples until, under the preaching of Mr. Adams, people began to turn to the Lord; then the Brethren turned him and those working with him out of their house. The Martin Valley Church of Christ was formed with sixty-one members. J. G. Campbell helped in this work. These several local congregations came into the Arrowsmith Church at the time of its organization.

This church has a commendable pride in all the Lord's work.

It has given C. D. Hougham to the ministry.

Bellflower.

Organized 1891, by J. S. Clements; present membership, 196; value of property, including parsonage, $12,000; Bible-school enrollment, 139.

Pioneer John England preached the primitive gospel in Osman, a village in the southeast corner of McLean County, in 1875-76. At that time a Sunday school was held there in the public-school house. In 1877 a church of twelve members was formed, probably by John W. Snyder. In 1885 a union church was built to be used one-half time each by the church of Christ and the Protestant Methodist congregation. In 1886, J. H. Gilliland held a successful revival there. But so many of the members moved away that the church disbanded in 1892. Most of those who were left united with the church at Bellflower.

Mr. and Mrs. William McDaniel led the work that produced this church. Min. J. S. Clements held a tent meeting there in the summer of 1891. That fall a house costing $3,500 was built and the church was weak. The present modern edifice was completed in 1913.

Bloomington First.

Organized 1837, by Mr. William T. Major; present membership, 1,666; value of property, $47,500; Bible-school enrollment, 601.

This church was organized in the home of Mr. Major, which was then on the southwest corner of Front and East Streets. There were thirteen charter members; namely, Mr. and Mrs. W. T. Major and their two daughters (Mrs. Elizabeth Hawks and Mrs. Judith H. Bradner) and one son (John —now living at Davenport, Ia.), Mr. and Mrs. Martin Scott, "Father" Maxwell and two daughters, and three others whose names are not known. This little company met regularly for worship in the home of Mr. Major, who was the leading spirit.

About 1840 a small frame church was built on East Street, between Front and Grove Streets. In those years the church was helped by the able ministry of James A. Lindsay, James Robeson, W. P. Bowles, William Davenport and W. H. Brown. Dr. W. O. Warriner was a leading elder and preacher during that period.

In 1856 the lot at the corner of West Jefferson and North West (now Roosevelt) Streets was purchased for $1,500 in gold and a two-story brick building erected thereon at a cost of $8,000. The house was occupied in January, 1857, Charles Louis Loos preaching the first sermon. Some of the leaders in this enterprise were E. H. Didlake, Thomas P.

Brown, Edwin Boston, Dr. E. K. Crothers, F. W. Emerson, Robert Moore, E. W. Bakewell and R. E. Williams, all of whom have passed to the higher life.

The pastors who served the church were Leroy Skelton, T. V. Berry, D. R. Van Buskirk (two terms), Henry S. Earl, J. H. McCullough, A. I. Hobbs, H. D. Clark and B. J. Radford, who filled interregnums. The pastorate of J. W. Lamphear was uniting and healing.

J. H. Gilliland came to the pastorate in February, 1888. He says: "I entered upon the work with fear and trembling." A few years proved him to be a masterful leader. In 1890 the old building gave place to a new and modern structure. In this church Mr. Gilliland's ministry was richly blessed. In 1894, without any outside help, 480 additions were made to the church. There were influential men of fine character who gave him good support, among whom were Dr. G. D. Sitherwood, M. Swan, Henry Kiser, Peter Whitmer, J. T. Lillard, H. J. Higgins and Jacob Bergman, the faithful and much loved doorkeeper in the house of the Lord. Mr. Gilliland came to the church with about four hundred members and left, after a ministry of fourteen and a half years, with a membership of 1,550.

Those succeeding him were Arthur Wilson, W. R. Lloyd and Edgar D. Jones, the present pastor.

Those who have gone to minister to the world's needs through the gospel were Knox P. Taylor, S. M. Jefferson, W. W. Denham, Otto C. Moomaw, D. W. Madden and Mrs. Kate Lawrence-Brown, a missionary in India. N. W. Evans is preparing for the work of the ministry.

The church maintained a mission Sunday school on Moulton Street for forty years. It was closed the last Lord's Day in 1912 because of a lack of teachers.

The church has a fine record for Christian hospitality. From 1853 to 1900 it entertained the State Missionary Convention seven times free. Other assemblies have enjoyed the generosity of its people.

Leroy Skelton, while pastor, fell sick and died July 4,

1870. Alonzo A. Wilson, another pastor, was stricken by the great Destroyer March 4, 1903. J. H. Gilliland, while not pastor of the First Church at the time, yet enshrined in the hearts of its people, fell before the great Reaper Apr. 29, 1912. Few churches have such a heritage of tender and glorious memories of mighty men.

Bloomington Second.

Organized 1902, by J. H. Gilliland; present membership, 565; value of property, $30,000; Bible school began 1902; present enrollment, 276.

This church is a child of the mind and heart of J. H. Gilliland. The First Church approved the movement upon two conditions: first, that one hundred persons enter into covenant to become charter members, and, second, that $10,000 be pledged for the new property. The building is located at the corner of North Evans and East Mulberry Streets and was finished and occupied in November. The entire indebtedness was provided for before the dedication, which was conducted by Mr. Gilliland. He continued as pastor until July, 1909, when he was succeeded by S. H. Zendt, the present minister.

The church has sent into the ministry Alva Ragsdale, W. B. Phillips and Prof. O. L. Lyon, who came from the M. E. Church and is a teacher in Texas Christian University.

Bloomington Third.

Organized 1901, by E. M. Harlis; present membership, 40; value of property, including parsonage, $4,000; Bible school began 1901; present enrollment, 18.

This is a church of negroes. There were thirteen charter members. They now own a beautiful pebble-dash church.

Bloomington Centennial.

Organized 1910, by J. H. Gilliland; present membership, 241; value of property, $25,000; Bible school began 1908; present enrollment, 257.

In February, 1908, a lot at the corner of East Grove Street and Willard Avenue was purchased by Mrs. Aaron Rhodes, Dr. O. M. Rhodes and J. H. Gilliland, with the hope that, in due time, there might be a new church built upon it.

In March following, the officers and members of the Second Christian Church formally resolved to establish a church east of the Illinois Central Railroad, and seventy members signed an agreement to constitute themselves into a church when the enterprise could be placed on a satisfactory financial basis and a suitable building, erected on the above designated lot, should be ready for occupancy.

Action was taken in October following, and the building was completed, furnished and first occupied May 1, 1910. Mr. Gilliland preached the dedicatory sermon. September 1 following, he turned the pastorate of the church over to Milo Atkinson. Previously the incorporated name adopted was "Centennial Christian Church of Bloomington, Ill." It enjoys a strategic location and promises large usefulness.

Buck Creek (Lexington).

Organized 1850, by P. M. Connors and Dr. Young; present membership, 30; value of property, $1,000.

There were thirteen charter members, among them Mr. and Mrs. John Franklin, Sr.; John Franklin, Jr.; Thomas Pirtle, Samuel Scott, Uriah Hanson, William Hanson and Mrs. Andrew Pirtle. The first meetings were held in the groves, residences, schoolhouses, and the barn of John Franklin. In 1869 the first house was built, but several miles west of the first site. It is still in good condition and in use.

The earlier preachers were James Robeson, J. G. Campbell. J. S. Stagner, H. D. Ledgerwood, M. H. Knight and P. W. Schick.

Carlock.

Organized 1836, by Henry D. Palmer; present membership, 250; value of property, including parsonage, $4,300; Bible-school enrollment, 139.

On Aug. 13, 1836, Henry D. Palmer, William Davenport and James Robeson united in a meeting for public worship at White Oak Grove in the wild, open woods. Those mighty men of God, pioneers in a new country and of a better faith, have long since gone to their rewards. On that August day they were young, agile and masterful in their faith. Then and there the White Oak Grove Church was born. For half a century this church held faithfully on its way and ministered to the needs of the community. Most of the pioneer preachers of central Illinois proclaimed the gospel there at various times. Among these was Abner Peeler, who, some now say, organized the church. The meetings were held in the homes of the people, in schoolhouses and groves until 1854, when a house was built. Evidently it was a good house, since it served the church for thirty-five years and was then sold and moved to Congerville for a union church.

The building of a railway grew the town of Carlock. A church building was erected there and on Aug. 13, 1889, the place of meeting was transferred. Thus, after fifty-three years, to a day, of life and service, the White Oak Grove Church "fell on sleep." Among those who contributed to its strength and usefulness there were Jonas Benson, John Benson, Sr. and Jr.; William Benson, Reuben and Abram Carlock and Reuben Brown.

The ministers who have served the Carlock Church were G. A. Miller, C. C. Rowlison, S. T. Spitler, C. S. Medbury, S. H. Zendt, R. L. Beshers, J. S. Smith, J. N. Thomas, E. E. Boyer, and now Miss Myrtle B. Parke.

Colfax.

Organized 1867, by James Robeson; present membership, 308; value of property, $18,500; Bible school began 1867; present enrollment, 300.

The first organization of the Christian Church on upper Mackinaw was in 1859 at the Wiley Schoolhouse, one-half mile west of the present site of Colfax. There the work was carried on four years by Mins. W. G. Anderson, A. W. Green and Speed Stagner. This congregation disbanded in 1863 because the members were so widely separated. They affiliated with more convenient churches of Christ.

In 1867, James Robeson held a meeting in a schoolhouse two and a half miles southeast of the site of Colfax, and instituted a church with sixteen members. This congregation used several schoolhouses until in the early seventies, when a chapel, that was called Antioch, was built two and a half miles north on a piece of ground given by Min. M. H. Knight. The railway came in 1880 and the town of Colfax was born. Meetings for public worship began there in 1881. The membership of Antioch was gradually merged into Colfax. A house was built in 1883. This served the congregation until 1907, when the present modern house was erected during the pastorate of N. H. Robertson.

William Poynter gave the Antioch Church good service. At Colfax there were W. G. Anderson, Dr. A. W. Green, Speed Stagner, M. H. Knight, H. W. Everest, J. F. Ghormley, W. G. Campbell, Jasper Hieronymus, Dr. Sabin, A. L. Sabin, A. W. Dean, J. S. Clements, John Lemmon, John Giddens, J. D. Dabney, J. H. Smart, C. D. Purlee, P. Baker, C. W. Dean, N. H. Robertson and G. R. Southgate.

The church has given to the ministry James W. Knight and Lawrence B. Anderson.

Cooksville.

Organized 1902, by John R. Golden; present membership, 144; value of property, $4,000; Bible school began 1902; present enrollment, 86.

The Blue Mound Church was organized by John S. Stagner in 1862. It was an influential church in the country for nearly forty years—until the railways came through on both sides of it and towns grew up on these lines. It gave four men to the ministry—John S. Stagner and his son, John S. Stagner, Jr.; H. G. Van Dervoort and John R. Golden.

In 1894 members from Blue Mound organized a church

CHURCHES

at Cooksville. A restricting clause was written in the deed to the church lot which led many members to hold themselves aloof. A C. W. B. M. auxiliary was formed in 1902. Through the lead of these women, Minister Golden conducted a revival there in the fall of that year and started the church on its useful way. The old Blue Mound building was torn down and the material used in the construction of that at Cooksville.

Ellsworth.

Organized 1867, by John Houston; present membership, 100; value of property, $2,000; Bible school began 1867; present enrollment, 90.

James Mitchell, James Robeson and G. W. Minier were the earlier ministers; later they were A. A. Burr, Louis Goos, Roby Orahood and A. F. Larson.

Previous to this date there was a church at "Old Town" that contributed to the life of the church at Ellsworth. The Old Town Church was the product of pioneer laborers.

Gridley.

Organized by Upton Coombs; present membership, 50; value of property, $2,000; Bible-school enrollment, 40.

Mr. Gridley, for whom this place was named, gave the church its lot because it was the first congregation to begin work there. John Lambert and William Wilson, who was a Presbyterian, hauled blocks from the timber for the foundation of the building. Among the first members were John and Nancy Lambert, James and Ursley Locke, Silas Greenman and wife, Thomas and Elizabeth Tarmen, and Joseph Huston and wife. Min. James Robeson reorganized the church in 1878. H. D. Ledgerwood preached there eleven years. He was a sincere and consecrated preacher, but the adverse conditions in the community were many. R. L. Beshers, J. E. Prophater, Osceola McNemar and C. H. Scrivens followed.

Reduced by removals, the church has had a precarious life.

Heyworth.

Organized 1872, by J. S. Stagner; present membership, 261; value of property, $10,000; Bible school began 1882; present enrollment, 207.

While serving as county evangelist, Mr. Stagner held a seven weeks' meeting here in the winter of 1871-72. The public hall on the second floor was used. The singing was led by Mr. M. W. Powell without the aid of any instrument. His home was four miles out in the country, yet he missed only one service during the entire meeting. The religious peace of the village was greatly disturbed by Mr. Stagner's plain, earnest and Scriptural preaching. The town was vibrant with arguments on Biblical questions. However, some "who came to scoff remained to pray." There were twelve charter members. To these, many were added during this revival. The baptizing was done in the Kickapoo one mile north of town. The ice was cut away at the place used.

A year later a church building was erected. This served till 1906, when a modern building was erected and occupied during the pastorate of J. P. Givens.

Mr. Stagner became pastor of the church in 1872 and died during the year—a good, brave soldier, who fell on the firing-line.

The earlier years of the church were disturbed by "the organ question," but its vision cleared and it has come to be a strong and useful body of believers. As farmers became well-to-do and moved to town, the churches at Grassy Ridge, Lytleville, Long Point and Fairview contributed to the growth and strength of Heyworth.

It has given to the ministry Frank Davis and Roy O. Ball.

Holder.

Organized 1867, by Robert Moore; present membership, 35; value of property, $1,000; no Bible school.

This church was organized as "The Evergreen Congregation of Disciples." Three years later the name was

CHURCHES

changed to "The Benjamanville Christian Church." This was about the time of the dedication of the building at Benjamanville, at which time the Christian Church of Mt. Prospect united with them. In 1877 the house was moved to Holder and the name changed accordingly. It has never been strong. The ministers who did the pioneer work in the community were Robert Moore, N. O. Lacock, James Robeson and J. G. Campbell.

Hudson.

Organized 1877, by Speed Stagner; present membership, 89; value of property, $3,000; Bible school began 1910; present enrollment, 81.

The East White Oak Church was organized about 1857 in Franklin Schoolhouse by James Robeson. In 1859 a frame house was built. This house stood just over the line in Woodford County, at the center of Section 14 of the White Oak Township. The chief men were J. D. Franklin, Jehu Hinshaw, Zachariah Brown, Cyrus Leatherman, Jesse Chism, Dr. Sabin and his son. It is credited with Jehu Hinshaw and M. H. Knight in the ministry.

After twelve years' service, the congregation, by death and removals, went down. Of the remaining, some went to Carlock and others to Oneida Schoolhouse. In this house, in January, 1877, John Hinshaw, a layman, held Bible-study meetings for two weeks. As considerable interest was shown, Minister Stagner came, conducted a short meeting and organized a congregation of thirteen persons, which took the name of Oneida. Weekly meetings were held there regularly for thirty-two years, when the place of meeting was changed to Hudson. W. D. Deweese is now pastor.

Leroy.

Organized 1888, by T. T. Holton; present membership, 240; value of property, including parsonage, $22,400; Bible school began 1888; present enrollment, 240.

Under the auspices of the State Board of Missions, Mr.

Holton began this work. He secured the use of the Cumberland Presbyterian Church. About forty Disciples were discovered in the community, among them Mrs. Dr. McKensie, Mrs. Devinney and Mr. L. S. Kilborn, superintendent of the public schools. A church of twenty-nine charter members was organized. They covenanted to meet every Lord's Day and proved to be a faithful little band. A series of meetings later by Evangelist J. S. Clements added many.

In 1891 the congregation occupied a chapel of their own. In 1907 they entered a stately and beautiful edifice that was erected during the pastorate of L. E. Chase.

The church has lived and grown through sunshine and shadows. From its beginning there have always been faithful men and women with hope and courage.

Lexington.

Organized 1860, by B. H. Smith; present membership, 285; value of property, including parsonage, $19,300; Bible school began 1887; present enrollment, 189.

J. G. Campbell and James Robeson were the two pioneer preachers of the church of Christ who visited Lexington previous to 1859. In November of that year, Benjamin Franklin held a public debate there with John Luccock, of the M. E. Church. The organization of this church was one of the results of this discussion. The charter members were Mr. and Mrs. C. N. Long, Mr. and Mrs. John Franklin, and Mr. and Mrs. G. T. Dement. A frame building was erected the following year.

The first pastor was Theodore Brooks, who was followed by Joseph Lowe, Samuel Lowe, J. F. Ghormley, M. F. Ingraham and W. D. Pollard, who entered the ministry from this church. In the early seventies the church lost its spiritual life and the house was closed for seventeen years. Some good women opened it again in 1887, starting a Sunday school. Meetings were held by Evangelists T. A. Boyer and O. W. Stewart, which brought to it new life and large numbers. The pastors who followed were J. H. Reece, W. H.

Cannon (during whose ministry a brick building costing $8,000 was erected), E. A. Gilliland, A. A. Wilson, O. L. Smith, George H. Brown, B. H. Sealock and J. P. Givens.

In August, 1912, there were eleven octogenarians who were members of this church.

McLean.

Organized 1903, by Harold E. Monser; present membership, 50; value of property, $5,000; Bible school began 1903; present enrollment, 60.

Some of the pastors have been J. A. Serena, J. E. Jewett, L. B. Appleton, G. E. Duffy and F. L. Starbuck.

Normal First.

Organized 1873, by S. M. Connor; present membership, 420; value of property, $40,000; Bible school began 1872; present enrollment, 192.

There were thirty-three charter members. S. M. Shurtleff and H. G. Fisher were the first elders, and John Gregory and William and Isaiah Dillon the first deacons. The old Baptist Church was first rented for a Sunday school, and here the first meetings were held and the church organized. A frame house, with a brick basement, costing $7,000, was finished and occupied at the close of 1873. This building was remodeled in 1887. It gave place to a new and modern structure in 1912. This was the last work of the lamented J. H. Gilliland.

The pastors who have served the church were S. M. Connor (two terms), H. W. Everest, John Ensell, A. P. Cobb (two terms), G. M. Goode, G. A. Miller, J. H. Wright, E. B. Barnes, J. P. Givens, Andrew Scott, R. H. Newton, W. C. McColley, J. H. and E. A. Gilliland, the present minister.

Normal Second.

Organized 1884, by Preston Taylor; present membership, 28; value of property, $1,700; Bible school began 1884; present enrollment, 38.

This church is located at the corner of Cherry and Linden Streets. It is made up of "colored" people. There were sixteen charter members. It is incorporated under the civil statute and owns its own property.

It has given George Hoagland to the ministry.

Saybrook.

Organized 1868, by James Robeson; present membership, 292; value of property, $10,000; Bible-school enrollment, 202.

In 1860, Min. Jesse Richards formed a small church in a schoolhouse just west of the town, but it soon disbanded.

In 1867, Min. J. M. Stagner began holding some meetings in the Thompson Schoolhouse, one mile east of the town. Conversions were made and scattered members gathered together. In the early winter of 1868 another meeting was held at the same place by Mins. James Robeson and James Mitchell, when others were gained and the church organized. In 1869, G. W. Cline became the pastor. The place of meeting was changed from Thompson Schoolhouse to Harrison Hall, in Saybrook. Several series of meetings were held in this hall. A good church house, costing $3,400, was finished and occupied in the fall of 1871 under the ministry of G. W. Cline. All the materials for this building were hauled from Bloomington. The congregation was unable to pay for this property; so Joseph Newcomb, Sr., one of the members, mortgaged his farm for $1,000 and relieved the situation. It is not known whether the church ever reimbursed him. During the pastorate of H. L. Maltman the building was worked over and made practically new throughout. C. C. Wisher is pastor. The church has also had the assistance of able evangelists and Bible instructors.

Shirley.

Organized 1869, by Jonathan Park; present membership, 168; value of property, including parsonage, $5,000; Bible school began 1870; present enrollment, 60.

This is considered one of the very best country churches in central Illinois.

A new building was erected in 1912. The following ministers have served here: Samuel Lowe, Jonathan Park, Dr. J. M. Allen, G. F. Adams, J. A. Seaton, John Lindsay, G. M. Wood, J. E. Jewett, Miles J. Hodson, G. W. Minier, G. W. Warner, Mr. Doty, Samuel Reynolds, K. P. Taylor, and at present F. L. Starbuck.

Stanford.

Organized 1870, by James Robeson; present membership, 323; value of property, including parsonage, $22,000; Bible school began 1879; present enrollment, 195.

In 1869, "Uncle Jimmie" Robeson held a brief meeting in an upper room with a few believers who desired to be known as Christians only. The next year a frame building was erected and a church of Christ organized. There were ten charter members. A new and commodious brick building was finished in 1900 during the pastorates of Fred Hagin and J. M. Porter. This church paid $30 for missions the first year of its life.

Cassius Garst and Howard Kaufman have been given to the ministry, and Miss Elsie Roth and Miss Vera Morris are efficient singing evangelists.

After James Robeson, the following ministers came: George Cline, John Owen, Isaac Stout, Samuel Lowe, G. W. Minier, W. P. Berry, John Lindsay, H. G. Van Dervoort, C. B. Dabney, J. Fred Jones, Melvin Menges, Fred Hagin, J. W. Porter, S. S. Lappin, C. W. Marlow and N. H. Robertson. Two of these are now successful missionaries on foreign fields.

Twin Grove (Bloomington).

Organized 1841, by James Robeson; present membership, 40; value of property, $3,000; Bible-school enrollment, 50.

This church was organized at the house of Samuel Barker with twenty-five charter members. The families represented in its membership were the Webbs, Barkers, Johnsons, Beelers, Hinshaws, Dickens and Harbord. Of these, Mrs. Martha Hinshaw is the sole survivor. This church has exerted a wide and lasting influence in the community west of Bloomington.

The first house of worship was built in 1848. It gave place in 1868 to a larger building. This was burned down in 1911. A new and better concrete-stone building has grown on the spot where the other two stood.

More than one hundred preachers have ministered to this church. Among them there were James Robeson, William Ryan, W. P. Bowles, Amos Watkins, Dr. Young, Dr. Warriner, William Davenport, G. W. Minier, James Mitchell, J. G. Campbell, Albert Peeler, Jonathan Park, David Lindsay, Sr., William Brownell, Dr. J. M. Allen, O. A. Burgess, John Lindsay, Washington and Jefferson Houston, P. W. Schick, J. W. Owen and J. J. Stagner.

G. R. Southgate and Bert Ross have gone from this church into the ministry.

NOTE.—To Mr. Geo. W. Nance, of Bloomington, is the credit of the good record for this county.

MACON COUNTY.

Antioch (Decatur).

Organized 1850, by John W. Tyler; present membership, 70; value of property, $6,000; Bible school began 1859; present enrollment, 68.

This church was formed in the Salem Schoolhouse, one-half mile west of the present site. In 1864, Mr. Tyler gave the congregation one acre of ground on the south edge of his farm. There, in the same year, a very strong frame building was erected. This was used until 1909, when the present attractive building was begun and finished in 1910, during the ministry of N. S. Haynes. Its cost was about $5,000.

This little country church, located five miles east of

CHRISTIAN CHURCH, ATLANTA.
CENTRAL CHURCH OF CHRIST, JACKSONVILLE.
CENTRAL CHURCH OF CHRIST, DECATUR.
FIRST CHRISTIAN CHURCH, DECATUR.

Decatur, on the C., H. & D. Railway, has given to the ministry B. B. and J. Z. Tyler (sons of J. W. Tyler), W. S. Harmon, C. A. Heckel and J. P. Lichtenberger.

The chief honor for establishing this church belongs to "Uncle John Tyler." Of late years Mrs. Emma Heckel has been its most faithful and useful member.

Argenta.

Organized 1848, by Dr. J. B. Millison; present membership, 65; value of property, $1,500; Bible school began 1883; present enrollment, 26.

This church was formed in a schoolhouse in Newberg, a country village one mile east of Argenta. In 1872 the place of meeting was transferred to the railway village of Argenta. The Clifton and Hill families were prominent in the work of the church in its earlier years.

William Brennan gave the church helpful service in its early life.

Blue Mound.

Organized 1861, by A. D. Northcutt; present membership, 224; value of property, including parsonage, $16,500; Bible school began 1867; present enrollment, 132.

This church was formed in the farm residence of Marshall Randall, two and one-half miles northwest of Blue Mound. The charter members were Marshall Randall and wife, J. C. Rose and wife, Daniel Daniels and wife, William Overman and wife, Denman H. Clements and wife, C. C. Hollier and wife, and Horace Stivers. All of these have gone to their reward. The meetings for public worship were held in the residence of Mr. Randall and in the schoolhouse till 1873. The building of the railway started Blue Mound and turned the village of Randallville back into farm fields. In this, transference of membership was made. Under the leadership of A. D. Northcutt, a U. B. chapel was bought, moved to the town, repaired and used until the present fine brick edifice was completed in 1906. Mrs. Nancy Lewis was one of the leaders in this enterprise. In 1880, at the suggestion of Mr. Northcutt, she was chosen to serve as a deaconness and gave the church faithful and efficient service.

Center Ridge (Maroa).

Organized 1867, by Dr. L. A. Engle; present membership, 60; value of property, $2,000; Bible school began 1875; present enrollment, 35.

This church was organized in the Center Ridge Schoolhouse, where it met for worship for twenty years. In 1887 a neat frame building was erected at a crossroads two and one-fourth miles due west of Emery. It is kept in good condition.

The charter members are the following: James D. Ross and wife and their children Albert F., James M. and Nancy E. Ross; Jordan Simpson and wife, Peter W. Wycoff and wife and son J. W.; D. Jones and wife, Thomas Shockey and wife, W. W. and Edward Shockey, and E. Blackerly. Of these, James D. Ross was the leading spirit. This little church has gone steadily on, serving the community well for forty-five years.

It gave George W. Ross to the ministry.

Mrs. J. D. Lyman is the clerk.

Harristown.

Organized 1861, by Dr. W. A. Mallory; present membership, 180; value of church property, including parsonage, $4,500; Bible school began 1861; present enrollment, 118.

Of the twenty charter members, all except three have passed away. James M. Eyman, Aliff C. Willard and Mrs. Ella J. Averitt are the survivors.

This church has always had fine conceptions of Christian privileges and responsibilities. Probably the one entitled to more honor for this divine outlook was that superior man, J. H. Pickerell. The church has other choice spirits.

A modest, well-kept building has met its needs. The church gave George Hamilton to the ministry. He died in early manhood. But three of its daughters are wives of ministers—Mrs. C. S. Medbury, Mrs. I. N. McCash, and Mrs. R. A. Gilcrist, who recently died.

Oreana.

Organized 1864, by Dr. J. W. Thayer; present membership, 125; value of property, $3,500; Bible school began 1864; present enrollment, 112.

For about ten years the public meetings were held in Zion Schoolhouse. In 1874 a frame building, costing $1,365, was erected. This gave place to the modernized building in 1895.

The earlier ministers of the church were William Brennan, E. C. Weekly, J. B. Millison and John Wilson.

It is in the records that the church paid $50 to missionary work in 1874.

The church has always served the community well. Among the honored families of the church in its early years there were Noble, Boyer, Spooner, Moothart and others.

Maroa.

Organized 1862, by A. N. Page; value of property, including parsonage, $23,700; Bible school began 1869; present enrollment, 210.

This church was organized in the residence of Dr. J. W. Thayer, who was an ordained minister, but whose life was chiefly given to the practice of medicine. There were twenty-four charter members, most of whom came from the Texas congregation in De Witt County. J. S. Clough and M. M. Thomas were the first elders; D. J. Harlan and Samuel Potter, deacons, and Dr. Thayer, clerk.

For several years the meetings for public worship were held regularly in the schoolhouse. The first building was finished in 1869. More than one thousand persons turned to the Lord in that sanctuary. It gave place in 1911 to a new, large and modern structure, during the pastorate of W. H. Harding.

John W. Tyler was the church's first preacher. Dr. Thayer followed for several years. While the church was struggling in its earlier years, it was helped by the ministry of Dudley Downs, Leroy Skelton, John Craycroft, John Wilson and Charles Rowe. During the pastorate of J. V. Beckman the church had a large numerical growth.

Niantic.

Organized 1868; present membership, 364; value of property, including parsonage, $10,500; Bible-school enrollment, 170.

Niantic grew after the railway was built. The first members came from the Long Point Church. Meetings were first held in the town hall. The subscription for building the chapel specifically stated that none of the fund should be used for a steeple or tower. A special fund was raised for this purpose. Among the leading men in the early years of the church were T. A. and J. W. Prichett, George Wree, and Griffin and Peter Chamberlain. B. J. Radford was the first pastor.

From the first the church had a healthy growth. It has always had a part in every good work. Its officers have been efficient. It is strong in material property and apostolic in outlook. Nearly $1,000 is paid annually for general benevolences.

Long Point (Niantic).

Organized 1850, by John Powell; value of property, $1,200.

This location is about two miles south of Niantic. In the late forties several families came from Morgan County and settled there. There were fourteen charter members. The first officers were Nathan G. Averitt, elder, with James Dingman and James Sanders as deacons. Of the original members, Mrs. Elizabeth Chamberlain and Mrs. Rebecca Ford, both daughters of N. G. Averitt, are still living. Mins. A. J. Kane, Dr. John Hughes, John England, A. D. Northcutt and others served the congregation in its earlier years.

Above the entrance door of the chapel is a marble slab, on which are carved the following words: "This building was erected by the Long Point Church of Christ and is dedicated to the worship of almighty God so long as instrumental music is not used therein."

James Dingman and James Sanders were the two strong and unique characters of the community who, in their later years, gave to the congregation its ultra-conservative cast. But the memory of each is rightfully held in high regard. The congregation as such paid $5 to the State Missionary Society in 1865.

It now has preaching one-fourth of the time.

Decatur.

The town site of Decatur was laid out late in 1829. Within a year or two a log courthouse was built near the present spot of the Transfer Station. This house still stands—now in Fairview Park. If its logs could echo all the voices they have heard, the souls of the living would be strangely stirred. In that primitive temple of justice Joseph Hostetler first preached in 1833. The next year there he organized a church upon the Bible as the only rule of faith and practice. In 1835 he gave the infant church a piece of hazel-brush-covered ground at what is now the corner of Wood and Water Streets. On this plot a log church, about twenty feet square, was soon built. Among the charter members of the church there were James and Polly Carter, Landy and Elizabeth Harrold, Joseph Hostetler and wife, Mrs. Martha Williams, Mrs. Rebecca Hanks, Mrs. Elizabeth Cantrall and Mrs. Pratt. Soon there were added Warren G. Strickland and wife, and Mrs. Charlotte Turpin. John W. Tyler, with his family, came from Kentucky in 1836 and shortly thereafter united with the church. Among those who began the Christian life in the log church were Mrs. J. W. Tyler, John and Elizabeth Rucker, and Mrs. Judith Oglesby, a sister-in-law of Richard J. Oglesby.

Carroll Edds came in 1851 and, with Dr. A. L. Keller, formed the first prayer-meeting.

This building served as the place of public worship for twenty years. In 1855 it gave place to the plain brick house that stood at the corner of North Main and North Streets. In this year Ebenezer McNabb came to the town and the church organized the first Sunday school. In the fifties the church grew by conversions and by those of like faith who came from Tennessee, Kentucky and Ohio. For about twenty-five years the church had as its preachers Joseph Hostetler, J. W. Tyler, Bushrod W. Henry, Robert Foster, J. P. Lancaster, James Fanning, G. W. Patterson, Walter P. Bowles, William Morrow, H. Bowles, Tobias Grider, W. W. Happy, Dr. A. L. Keller and A. J. Kane. They were self-sacrificing pioneers, mighty in the Scriptures, heroic in their devotion. The pastors who followed were William Ebert, Alford Paden, Dr. John Hughes, A. J. Taft, W. C. Dawson, P. D. Vermilion, Ira Mitchell, Lucius Ames, A. D. Northcutt, N. S. Haynes, T. W. Pinkerton, E. B. Cake, Simon Rorher and George F. Hall. Interims were occupied by Dr. L. A. Engle, C. E. Weekley and J. W. Tyler. During the pastorate of Mr. Haynes the "little brick church" gave place to a frame building in 1875. It was more attractive, commodious and modern. This church gave to the ministry A. P. Cobb and W. A. Humphrey. In 1893 the lot at Main and North Streets was sold and the building moved to the rear of the newly purchased lot at Edward and William Streets. During the pastorate of Mr. Hall, lots were bought and the Tabernacle erected in 1894 to accommodate his audiences. In 1896 the church was divided and a part returned to the old house at Edwards and William Streets. This is known as the

Central Church of Christ.

Present membership, 800; value of property, including parsonage, $40,000.

During the pastorate of F. W. Burnham, the present

house was built. After its occupancy the old frame building was moved to the corner of Leafland Avenue and Warren Street, where a mission Sunday school was maintained for twenty years. Later the mission was abandoned and the property sold.

The people who remained with Mr. Hall at the Tabernacle organized as

The First Christian Church.

Present membership, 879; value of property, $35,000; Bible-school enrollment, 380.

The building was improved and renamed the "Temple" during the pastorate of F. B. Jones. It was torn down in 1913 to give place to a modern structure during the pastorate of E. M. Smith.

Seventy-two people withdrew from the First Church in 1908 under the lead of the retiring pastor, O. P. Wright, and were organized as

The East Side Christian Church.

Present membership, 75; value of property, $14,000; Bible-school enrollment, 125.

It has made small growth and is heavily in debt. The field is wide and deserving. (The church is dead.)

MACOUPIN COUNTY.

Atwater.

Present membership, 143; value of property, including parsonage, $4,000; Bible-school enrollment, 59.

Blooming Grove (Nilwood).

Organized 1873, by Aslver Solomon and George McElroy; present membership, 64; value of property, $2,000; Bible school began 1874; present enrollment, 58.

This congregation is located six miles east of Palmyra. The charter members were Elizabeth A., Thomas and Sarah Mahan; Mary A. Cleery; James B. and Nancy A. Burleson;

James A. Williams, Rosetta A. Lair, William and Elizabeth Crum, Ellin Slagle, Amiel and Mary Hunt, John A. and Emily Hart. First elders were James M. Lair and Thomas Mahan; first deacons, Amiel Hunt and Richard Cramp.

Berean (Modesto).

Organized 1830, by Jack Nifing; present membership, 25; value of property, $800; no Bible school.

This congregation is located three miles northeast of Modesto. It is "the church of Christ and not the Christian Church." It has Bible classes, but no Bible school. It is opposed to "the pastor," but has preaching one Lord's Day in the month; also is opposed to "so much preach for so much money" and to instrumental music in the public worship. The correspondent is J. C. Roady, Fidelity, Ill.

Boston Chapel (Girard).

Present membership, 60; value of property, $1,800; Bible-school enrollment, 38.

This is four miles east of Girard.

Carlinville.

Organized 1896, by R. A. Omer; present membership, 132; value of property, including parsonage, $14,000; Bible school began 1896; present enrollment, 88.

The charter members were as follows: Rhoda Macknet; H. T., Cleopatra G., Georgia and Harry B. Richardson; John and Lucinda E. Wilson; Emma, Willie and Lelia Giberson; E. A. Utt, Annie E. Glover, Jennie Hayes, Florence and Mary Cunningham, John Taylor, Selma Egnew, Franklin and Susan Smith, Lodusky Miller, William and Jane Clark, Darius Swain, Luther Crowdy, Mary Deeds, Elizabeth Frickers, Jesse H. and Margaret T. Smith: total, twenty-nine. Of these, thirteen are dead and five have removed. M. T. Richardson is the clerk. The church has half-time preaching.

W. A. Green has been given to the ministry.

Gillespie.

Organized 1859; present membership, 84; value of property, $4,000; Bible-school enrollment, 50.

The first congregation grew to number about sixty, but was left without competent leaders and failed. In 1898 the church was revived. Mrs. J. P. Gross is clerk.

Girard.

Organized 1860, by Alexander Johnston; present membership, 177; value of property, including parsonage, $8,000; Bible school began 1860; present enrollment, 166.

C. H. Metcalf says: "The following names are those of the charter members: Sisters Thurman, Moore, Grandma and Miss Kate Eastman, Miss Fannie Eastman, Mrs. Belle Woods, and John Ewing and wife." The church was formed by Evangelist Johnston under the auspices of the State Mission Board. The meetings were held in residences and the Universalist chapel till the completion of the first house in 1865. The present building was finished in 1900. The first elders were John Ewing and James Duncan; later Jacob Deck, J. D. Metcalf, L. J. Thompson, Isaac Moore and Dr. Clark. These were Scriptural elders to whom the church owes very much.

Good revival meetings were held by able evangelists and wise pastors have served the church. It is well organized and has a very honorable record. Leonard G. Thompson was given to the ministry.

Modesto.

Organized 1890, by J. W. McGuffin; present membership, 61; value of property, $2,500; Bible school began 1890; present enrollment, 49.

The charter members were R. T. and E. E. Allyn; P. R. Cox; J. M., Flora and S. E. Allyn; Sarah and Rose Davidson; J. J. Sims, Walter and Fannie Allyn, A. S. Chapman and N. A. Jones.

Oak Grove (Rhorer).

Present membership, 36; value of property, $1,400. Mrs. J. F. Haynes, Modesto, is correspondent.

Palmyra.

Organized 1867; present membership, 392; value of property, including parsonage, $4,500; Bible school began 1867; present enrollment, 300.

There is no record of the earlier years of this congregation. It has given to the ministry of the gospel Messrs. Albert Cherry, Lowell, Perry and John McPherson, three brothers in the flesh and in the Lord, and Miss Inez Humphrey, a schoolteacher in the Southern Christian Institute at Edwards, Miss. L. E. Chase is the efficient pastor, and P. G. Mahon, clerk.

Round Prairie (Bunker Hill).

Organized 1845; present membership, 20; value of property, $500; no Bible school.

The location is six miles southeast of Bunker Hill. Its record of late years is the pathetic and oft-repeated one—deaths and removals, and the occupation of the farms by foreign-born people.

L. S. Mize, Scottville, is the clerk.

Scottville.

Present membership, 160; value of property, $3,000; Bible-school enrollment, 67.

Shaw's Point (Barnett).

Organized 1882; present membership, 64; value of property, $850; Bible-school enrollment, 59.

This is about three miles northwest of Barnett. It was formed after the older church of this name moved to Barnett, and was hence called by the name of the new town.

CHURCHES

Staunton.

Present membership, 50; value of property, $1,200; Bible-school enrollment, 78.

Weak. Paul N. Stone is correspondent.

West Prairie (Dorchester).

Present membership, 12; value of property, $500; no Bible school.

Virden.

Organized 1882, by W. F. Black; present membership, 240; value of property, including parsonage, $3,500; Bible school began 1883; present enrollment, 175.

The charter members were Samuel and Mrs. Mary E. Williams, L. N. Roland, Jacob and Mrs. Cardace Groves, Dempsey and Mrs. Lucy Solomon, James A. and Mrs. Amelia M. Bronaugh, John Aldmon, Henry M. and Mrs. Flora Gates, Mrs. Lizzie Rice, Mrs. D. W. Williams, Mrs. D. M. and Mrs. Maxie Z. Henderson, Mrs. Nancy J. McNight, Mrs. Newton Allen, Mrs. Susan and Mrs. Lottie Plowman, Mrs. Eva Strong, Mrs. Laura Piper, Mrs. Anna Kable, Mrs. Louise Spaulding and Mrs. M. J. Wigginton.

The church has been prosperous from its beginning. The present edifice was built in 1812. S. M. Connor was the first pastor, and A. M. Hale the present one.

Mr. J. P. Henderson has been actively connected with the church from its beginning. His grandmother was Anna Provine, and his grandfather, John Henderson. Both were associated with Barton W. Stone in Kentucky. John Henderson was ordained to the ministry at Bloomington. Ind., in 1821.

Extinct Congregations.

The Sulphur Springs chapel stands four miles west of Waggoner. It was built as a union house in 1852. It is now used only for funerals, a cemetery holding the sacred dust of several thousand people having grown there during the sixty years. At this place a church of Christ was organized in 1857. It prospered, and as the years passed away gave its members to Atwater, Boston Chapel, McVey, Shaw's Point and Waggoner congregations. It disbanded in 1888.

The churches at McVey and Dorchester have died, the latter after a life of thirty-five years. This is the home of J. E. Masters, the oldest Christian minister in the county.

Chapman's Point, so called from John Chapman, who settled there in an early day, was nine miles west of Virden, from whence came the Goode brothers—M. M. and G. M.

MADISON COUNTY.

Edwardsville.

Organized 1889, by J. H. Garrison; present membership, 37; value of property, $4,000; Bible school began 1889; present enrollment, 36.

Mr. E. J. Jeffries and Dr. William Olive led in the work of forming this church. They were heartily assisted by Mr. A. O. French, a prominent member of the M. E. Church. Capable ministers have served here, but the city is so largely made up of foreign-born people that the congregation grows slowly. It has given G. H. Rowe to the ministry. Messrs. Jeffries and Olive are elders, and H. M. Groves is clerk.

Granite City.

Present membership, 260; value of property, $9,000; Bible-school enrollment, 185.

Marine.

Present membership, 60; value of property, $2,000; Bible-school enrollment, 97.

New Douglas.

Present membership, 90; value of property, including parsonage, $2,500; Bible-school enrollment, 72.

CHURCHES

Ridgely (Dorsey).

Organized 1850, by Mrs. Matilda Dorsey O'Bannon; present membership, 10; value of property, $800.

The chapel was built the same year. It is three miles east of Dorsey. The church is in good condition, with monthly preaching by W. H. Groner. G. R. Sutton, Moro, is the correspondent.

Worden.

Organized 1892, by W. Wilbur; present membership, 112; value of property, $2,000; Bible school began 1892; present enrollment, 108.

There were fourteen charter members.

The chapel was built in 1895. Mrs. J. R. Piper is the clerk.

MARION COUNTY.

Alma.

Organized 1867, by John Ross; present membership, 50; value of property, $2,500; Bible school began 1867; present enrollment, 83.

There were fifteen charter members. The church grew steadily for a time. It, like many others, came under the reactionary spirit of the early seventies, by which the numerical growth and spirituality were crippled for years.

Cartter.

Organized 1866, by W. C. Hill; present membership, 35; value of property, $2,400; Bible school began 1866; present enrollment, 36.

The Cartter Church is the outgrowth of the Harvey's Point congregation. In 1808, Captain Harvey and his companion overtook two horse-thieves on the road leading from Salem to Old Foxville, and captured them. In order to get some water, Captain Harvey left his companion in charge of the outlaws. But he left his gun, and when he returned one of the thieves fired upon the captain and killed him. So in his honor the place was named Harvey's Point. This church, in the early years of its life, built a large frame house on the spot where Harvey died. Mins. William C. Hill, J. M. Mulkey and James Snow did much for the church in its earlier years.

G. W. Stevenson came from this congregation to the ministry.

The church grew feeble by removals, so in September, 1911, it was reorganized by Min. J. F. Rosboro in Cartter, the near-by railway town.

Centralia.

Organized 1856, by John A. Williams; present membership, 675; value of property, $35,000; Bible-school enrollment, 835.

This church was formed at Central City. It soon became apparent that the center of business would be moved to Centralia, and hence the church was transferred to that place. The eight charter members were the following: Jacob, Harriet and Simpson Frazier; Daniel Meyers, James and Jane McCarthy, Margeret Whitton and Louisa Hawkins. A lot was bought and a commodious frame building erected thereon. In 1866 this building was burned. Thereafter, for several years, the meetings were held in rented halls. As a consequence, the church continued to become weaker and weaker. In 1872 another frame chapel, costing $2,400, was erected. This gave place in 1909 to a new, modern and beautiful edifice, costing $32,000. This was during the pastorate of J. F. Rosboro.

During the Civil War and for years following, the church sustained serious injury from the bitter political feeling that then existed. The church is alive to all good works.

Donohue Prairie (Kell).

Organized 1898, by C. A. Burton; present membership, 100; value of property, $1,000; Bible school began 1898; present enrollment, 100.

About 1850 a congregation was formed and met for worship in the residence of John Hill, Sr. As the years passed and churches were organized in that section, many of these members united with them. Through the work of W. C. Hill and others, the remnant of the old church was gathered up and a new start was made. The chapel was finished in 1899. The Church Extension Board loaned this country congregation $250, which has been paid. There were sixteen charter members. S. S. Turley, S. C. and Isaac Hill are elders, and the last named is clerk also.

Gaston Grove (Cartter).

Organized 1884, by J. H. G. Brinkerhoff; present membership, 89; value of property, $900; Bible school began 1887; present enrollment, 46.

A meeting was held in the Huff Schoolhouse in 1886 by Minister Brinkerhoff and was followed up by a year's work. There were forty-two charter members, most of whom came from the Mt. Moriah and Harvey's Point Churches. The site was selected and the Gaston Grove chapel was built. Like most country churches, there have been many losses by removals, but the work is maintained.

This church has given A. Leroy Huff to the ministry. Bessie Huff is clerk.

Kell.

Organized 1896, by J. F. Rosboro; present membership, 15; value of property, $1,200; Bible school began 1895; present membership, 30.

The preachers having served the church were C. A. Burton, Clark Braden, W. J. Simer, R. M. Philips, F. O. Fannon and George Foley.

Kinmundy.

Organized 1899, by J. H. Smart; present membership, 110; value of property, $5,000; Bible school began 1899; present enrollment, 134.

E. C. Bargh and his family, with a few other Disciples, had held meeting irregularly for thirteen years. Min. J. H. Smart, then the pastor of the church in Centralia, was engaged by the mission board of the district to hold a series of meetings and organize a church. This was done in the summer of 1899. These meetings were held in the M. E. Church South, and in a public hall. There were fifty charter members. A lot was bought and a good building finished the next year. The church has continued to grow in members and influence.

Lovel Grove (Iuka).

Present membership, 60; value of property, $1,050; Bible-school enrollment, 34.

This church is about one mile south of the village of Omega. In the early fifties this congregation met in a log house about two miles south of the present chapel. It was known as Bee Branch Church. A nice, up-to-date country chapel was built in 1880. In the earlier years, H. A. Vandusen, John A. Williams, John Tinkler, Rolla B. Henry, William T. Williams, H. A. Harrell and William Chaffin ministered to the people. All these have gone to their reward. W. J. Simer has served the church for the past thirty years. What better proof could be given of a genuine preacher and a fine people?

From this church there came to the ministry H. A. Vandusen, F. M. Philips, John Tinkler, W. J. Simer and A. A. Millican.

Mt. Moriah (Mt. Vernon).

Organized 1829; present membership, 135; value of property, $500; Bible-school enrollment, 134.

This is the oldest church in Marion County. It was organized as a Free Will Baptist church and held this name until 1837. In that year it renounced this name for "Church of Christ" and came into full accord with the principles of the Restoration movement. Among the consecrated leaders in the early years there were William Chaffin, David R. Chance, Samuel Shook and Charles Drennen. They were pioneer preachers who underwent hardships and dangers uncomplainingly for the truth's sake.

The first meeting-house was of logs. After its decay three successive frame buildings have been occupied. The second of these was partly wrecked by a windstorm, but was repaired and used till 1904, when the present neat chapel was built. It is located about eight miles southwest of Salem. John A. Williams was the gift of this church to the ministry—a magnificent contribution.

Odin.

Organized 1878, by James M. Hawley; present membership, 188; value of property, $2,000; Bible school began 1878; present enrollment, 113.

There were sixteen charter members. A neat frame church, costing $2,000, was built and occupied early in 1880. Before that the meetings were held in a public hall.

This church gave to the ministry R. Leland Brown. He had served as a deacon and an elder before he was set apart to the ministry of the Word. He has served a number of strong churches, as well as the evangelist of the Seventh and Eighth Districts.

Patoka.

Organized 1875, by Samuel Hawley; present membership, 125; value of property, $2,000; Bible school began 1882; present enrollment, 129.

This church made but little progress for five years. In 1880 it was reorganized by Min. J. D. Morgan. There were then twenty-nine males and eleven females composing the membership. The church then began to grow. A church building was erected in 1882, and in 1905 an addition was built, making it a very neat structure. A large portion of the membership reside in the country south of town. They have erected a chapel and maintain a Bible school there as well as in town. C. M. Ashton is clerk.

Salem.

Organized 1866, by John A. Williams; present membership, 265; value of property, $25,000; Bible school began 1867; present enrollment, 310.

This church was formed in the house of John A. Williams. The members were few in number, but they at once bought a frame building that had been used by the Cumberland Presbyterians. They repaired and used it until 1879. The next year a brick chapel was occupied. This gave way in 1906 to a new and modern building, costing about $22,000. This was during the ministry of F. O. Fannon.

Mr. Williams preached for this church a long time. In its earlier years it was also served by John W. Monehan, John Bradley, J. O. Henry, J. H. G. Brinkerhoff and others.

Sandoval.

Organized 1889, by A. Martin; present membership, 320; value of church property, including parsonage, $6,000; Bible school began 1889; present enrollment, 144.

The meetings of the congregation were held the first year in the Congregational Church. In 1890 the building now in use was erected during the ministry of J. H. G. Brinkerhoff.

Smith's Grove (Kinmundy).

Organized 1882, by Joseph D. Morgan; present membership, 25; value of property, $400; Bible school began 1882; present enrollment, 67.

This church is about seven miles east of Omega. About eighty years ago a log church stood two miles east of Smith's Grove. It was known as the Bluff Church because it stood on a high bank of Skillet Fork, by a rock-bottomed pool that has been used in baptizing through all these years. When the old log house burned down, some of the members formed the Old Union Church in Clay County. In the early eighties, .J D. Morgan gathered together members from the Old Union Church, and others living in Krutchfield Prairie, and formed the Smith's Grove Church. The organization was in a schoolhouse, but a chapel was soon built which the congregation has outgrown. W. J. Simer has preached for this church for twenty-five years. Of it he says: "This place can show more little folks out to Sunday school and church to the square foot than any place that I have ever been. Nearly all of the young folks are members of the church."

Turkey Creek (Odin).

Organized 1867, by A. Martin.

This is a country church that has not grown much in work or membership. It is also called Deadman, and is three miles south of Odin.

Young's Chapel (Salem).

Organized 1883, by John A. Williams; present membership, 82; value of property, $500; Bible school began 1883; present enrollment, 46.

A country church. Preaching services had been held in a schoolhouse in the community for forty years, but no organization was made till 1883. There were about twenty charter members. J. H. G. Brinkerhoff and F. M. Morgan have served the church.

Little Grove Church was two miles southeast of Centralia, and formed in the thirties or early forties. It dissolved about 1870.

Ministers.

J. W. Monnahan was a farmer, teacher and county superintendent of schools in the sixties and seventies. A good preacher and able debater; an energetic and useful man.

Samuel Shook resided on his farm three miles southeast of Centralia. His work was mainly in Marion County in the thirties. He traveled on horseback, followed by his dog "Trip," that lay under the pulpit while his master preached.

William Chaffin also resided on his farm in this county, where he preached in the thirties and also in Clay and Jefferson Counties. He had a habit of placing his hand upon his cheek while preaching, and often said: "I would work my finger-nails off before I would make a price for my preaching." He died before the Civil War.

David R. Chance lived on his farm five miles from Iuka. He was a forceful and useful man, going all over that region. At the table he would sometimes say: "You can tell a preacher by the cups of coffee he drinks—one, two or three; I take three."

Richard Huelin's home was near Walnut Hill in 1840. He was a plain man who knew the Bible and traveled and preached much.

James Snow resided in the same community. He was a good man with a gentle disposition and his preaching contrasted with most of that of his brother ministers. He resided on his farm and traveled widely.

H. A. Vandusen lived on his farm near Omega. He was told that he had hurt a congregation by serving it for nothing. He replied: "I don't know but what that is true." He was a conservative, but earnestly opposed any thought of division on questions of opinion.

It was in this county that an aged M. E. preacher said: "A man can be a good Christian in any denomination except the Campbellite or Mormon."

MARSHALL COUNTY.

The Crow Creek congregation, afterward known as the Salem Christian Church, was located about seven miles south and a little east of Lacon. It was constituted probably in the home of Nathan Owen, just down the hill from the old Salem Cemetery, June 12, 1836. The agreement signed was the following:

> The believers in Christ on Crow Creek mutually agree to constitute themselves in a congregational capacity on the Bible alone, and to take the Scriptures of the Old and New Testaments for their rule of faith, practice and discipline. And to have their names registered together and to live in subjection to each other according to the above-named rule.

This is signed by Nathan and Elizabeth Owen, William B. and Stephen James, Milly Ann Davis, Isaac and Elizabeth Black, I. F. and Mary Ann Miller, Betsy Martin, Susanah Bird, Elder H. D. and Patsey Palmer, Isaac and Eliza Polk, William and Alethee Maxwell. Meetings were held in the homes of the members and in groves when weather permitted. About 1845 a house was built which served the people except during protracted meetings or on County Co-operation days, when they adjourned to the groves. This chapel stood two miles east of old Salem Cemetery. Its walls were of brick made near by, but the lumber was hauled by ox teams from Chicago, a distance of 125 miles as the crow flies. Some of the sons of the men who helped in this work are yet living. In later years it was used for a schoolhouse and was finally torn down.

Henry D. Palmer was doubtless the great spiritual leader in this work through many years and its influences were far-reaching. It was here that Mr. Palmer taught O. A. Burgess the right way of the Lord, saving him from unbelief and starting him on his great career. Nathan Owen was chosen deacon in 1836 and the next year Mr. Palmer was chosen elder. Both of them were resident preachers and farmers, as also John L. McCune. The church grew at one time to a membership of 193 and was visited by all the pioneer ministers in that section of the State. The last remnant of the membership went to Washburn about 1896.

Belle Plain (La Rose).

Organized 1845; present membership, 115; value of property, including parsonage, $4,500; Bible-school enrollment, 92.

Mr. A. F. Hatten, the clerk, says:

The church of Christ at Belle Plain was organized at the headwaters of Crow Creek in a schoolhouse, May 10, 1845, by the following: William, Robert, Rebecca, Olive and James Bennington; Isaac M. and Eliza M. Polke, Elijah and Sarah Vandervoort, Geo. W. and Margaret J. Taylor, James and Mary Martin, Jane Hester and Mary Hatten. The meetings for worship were irregular for several years.

In 1854, at a meeting in James Martin's barn, an unsuccessful effort was made to build a chapel. But in 1856 Pattonsburg, the former name of the town, was selected as the place and the house was built there. It was then called the Liberty Church of Christ. This local name was dropped when the name of the place was changed.

Among the early preachers there were James Robeson, John T. Jones, Amos Watkins, James A. and John Lindsay, and Carrol Ghent. Since then twenty-two others have served the church.

Henry.

Organized 1889, by T. A. Boyer; present membership, 54; value of property, $3,500; Bible school began 1889; present enrollment, 30.

This congregation was the immediate result of a five weeks' meeting conducted by Evangelist Boyer. Many of its members have moved away, so that it has never grown to be strong. Miss Clara B. Waughop is the correspondent.

Toluca.

Organized 1858, by J. Q. A. Houston; value of property, including parsonage, $9,000; Bible-school enrollment, 170.

For about thirty-four years this was known as the Antioch Church and was located one mile west of Toluca town site. Among the first families there were Skelton, Ball, Fetters, Bennington, Stratton and Trowbridge. It was a country church fruitful of great good. Leroy Skelton was given to the ministry. Toluca grew up when the railway was built and the chapel was moved there in 1892. A new building was erected in 1895.

S. S. Lappin began his ministry in this church.

MASON COUNTY.

The following is furnished by Min. R. E. Henry, pastor of the Havana Church:

The first church of the Christians dates its beginning from the coming into the county of Uncle Jimmie Ross, from Morgan County, in 1840. He had been for more than forty years a class-leader in the M. E. Church, but before coming into this county he had been won by the plea of the Restoration. Upon his settlement on Quiver Prairie, six miles northeast of Havana, he began to preach from house to house, and in the spring of 1841, in an unfinished barn, with the assistance of Elder Josiah Crawford of the Old Salem Church, held a revival of several weeks and organized a church. Elder Crawford continued to preach here for many years once or twice a month. A building was later built and, while the work is not kept up at present, occasional services are held in it. Among the early preachers were William Davenport, W. A. Poynter, Andrew Page, John Lindsay and J. I. Judy. Of the charter members Grandma Kroell, formerly Mrs. Atwater, remains in vigorous health and mind at the advanced age of ninety years.

The next church organized in the county some years after the one at Quiver was at Bath, which is still in fair condition.

Some thirty-five years ago the church at Mason City was organized and is one of the strong religious forces in the eastern part of the county for righteousness. They have only recently built a fine house of worship.

The work in Havana was organized about fifteen years ago by the State Missionary Society under the leadership of J. Fred Jones. Before the church was organized, G. M. Goode and J. B. Dabney held a meeting, finding twenty-six who had fellowship with the church elsewhere and ready to organize. Twelve years ago a building was purchased from the Dutch Reformed Church and rededicated by J. H. Gilliland. The first few years the church was supplied by students from Eureka among whom for three years was Joseph Serena. During the pastorate of Louis O. Lehman the work was organized at Topeka and Kilbourne. The work at the former place has been discontinued, while at the latter place a good half-time work is maintained with a Bible school.

There is also an organization of Disciples at Pleasant Plains and a work is maintained as a union church with the Baptists.

In later years Min. J. M. Haughey gave this county excellent service, often walking to his appointments.

MASSAC COUNTY.

Bethel (Grand Chain).

Organized 1885, by George Barrows; present membership, 60; value of property, $1,500; Bible school began 1885; present enrollment, 78.

This church is near Hillerman.

Brookport.

Organized 1885, by Dr. D. M. Breaker; present membership, 60; value of property, including parsonage, $2,600; Bible school began 1885; present enrollment, 79.

This church lived ten years without a building. It has grown and done good service all the time.

Joppa.

Organized 1881, by C. H. Waddell; present membership, 40; value of property, including parsonage, $1,800; Bible school began 1881; present enrollment, 50.

There were seventy-three charter members. The church made no progress for five years. Under the ministry of R. P. Warren new life came to it; but he was killed in 1890 by a runaway horse. Another period of depression followed. Under the ministry of O. J. Page the church took on new life. In 1895 a new building was erected.

Liberty Ridge (Metropolis).

Organized 1867, by Dr. Joseph Brown; present membership, 40; value of property, $1,200; no Bible school.

A country church located six miles northwest of Metropolis. It was organized in a log schoolhouse. Soon thereafter a cheap building was erected which in later years was modernized and rebuilt. In its early years Stanton Fields preached for the congregation.

Little Rock (Unionville).

Organized 1875, by W. W. Dugger; present membership, 80; value of property, $2,000; Bible school began 1875; present enrollment, 75.

This church is made up of negroes. It is located in the east end of the county. They meet regularly every Lord's Day for worship, with half-time preaching. They are doing good work.

Metropolis.

Organized 1864, by Joseph Brown; present membership, 300; value of property, including parsonage, $3,100; Bible school began 1867; present enrollment, 160.

The church was at first made up largely of refugees who had come from Kentucky and Tennessee during the Civil War. After its close many of them moved away. The organization was made in the courthouse. The first church house was built in 1867. It was wrecked by a cyclone and rebuilt.

This church has baptized more than one thousand people. It has given to the ministry J. P. Alsup, B. L. Beshers and T. J. Golightly. J. F. McCartney was one of its most forceful and useful men.

The first pastor was B. C. Deweese; the last, J. S. Clements.

Mt. Pleasant (Brookport).

Present membership, 24; value of property, $800. Conservative.

Samouth.

Present membership, 40; Bible-school enrollment, 50. This is a union church.

Unionville.

Organized 1865, by W. W. Dugger; present membership, 100; value of property, $2,000; Bible school began 1902; present enrollment, 100.

This place is ten miles southeast of Metropolis. Mr. Dugger was invited to preach in the M. E. Church, which he did. The invitation was soon withdrawn. Min. G. W. Hughey, of the M. E. Church, denounced Mr. Dugger as a "Baptist infidel," and of his brethren in faith he said: "They are not Christians, but Campbellites, and Campbellites they shall be called." However, a church was organized that aimed to be Christian only. A small church building was erected which was the first owned by the Disciples in the county. Another and better house has since been built.

MENARD COUNTY.

Athens.

Organized 1838, by John A. Powell; present membership, 201; value of property, $5,500; Bible-school enrollment, 146.

A wagon-maker named Brockman went from Jacksonville to Athens about 1836. He was quite an exhorter and moved those who heard him to tears. About that time a large, well-formed man, with a powerful voice and dressed in homespun, began to preach there; he spoke just as the Disciples preached on Pentecost and afterward. That was John A. Powell, of Sugar Grove. Shortly he secured Evangelist Robert Foster to help in a meeting. There a little congregation was formed. But by reason of a lack of competent leadership, in a few years the congregation went down. Peter Akers, M. E. Church, did what he could in three-hour sermons toward pounding the life out of this little church.

About 1850, Adam Grove, a tailor, located in Athens and began to agitate the question of a church of Christ there. He was soon joined by James Mott, a cabinet-maker, who, with others, began to build a small brick chapel about 1851. The lot cost $10 and is yet owned by the congregation. The trustees at that time were C. R. Pierce, John Jordan, William Price, James Hall, William Primm, Robert Edwards, and A. H. Foster, clerk. The congregation was served by the central Illinois pioneer preachers of those years. During the earlier years of the Civil War the congregation again went to pieces. But it was renewed again in 1864 by the return and faithful ministry of Clayborne Hall. Since then the work has gone steadily on. In 1858 a new building was erected.

Mr. Hall was a faithful man and to him this church is

much indebted. Twenty-one years of his life were passed in Iowa.

Greenview.

Organized 1869, by D. D. Miller; present membership, 215; value of property, including parsonage, $2,700; Bible-school enrollment, 140.

"The church of Christ, meeting for worship at Greenview, Ill.," grew out of the efforts of the church at Sweet Water. Previous to the organizing there was regular preaching for eight months in a hall by Mins. T. W. Raney and D. T. Hughes. All of the charter members except one came from Sweet Water. They were: Wm. N. and Silas Alkine, C. R. Rice, M. M. Ingle; G. W., Elijah C., Nancy and Manda A. Pierce; S. H. Blane, William C. and Elizabeth S. Yowell, D. T. and Martha Hughes, Paulina and Jane Killion, Mary A. Propst, Mary Samson, James Meadows, Lewis and Eliza Yuens, J. H. Applegate, Annie Cogal and Alvina Roberts. These members mutually pledged themselves to faithful Christian service to the close of their lives. The congregation grew in numbers. In 1870, C. R. Pierce and James Yowell were chosen as elders, with Alonzo Matts and Mr. Ingle as deacons. In 1879 the place of meeting was changed from a hall to the Baptist chapel and the two Sunday schools united. Then, being without a pastor, the congregation waned for a few years. Then Joel Shoemaker served as pastor. The church house was not built until 1890. Then there was a reconsecration of the members, led by Min. David Husband. There were about forty persons. Chas. Smoot, J. P. Lichtenberger, C. A. Heckel, W. T. McConnell, Mr. Allen, Lewis Goos, J. W. Flynn and R. D. Cartwright have served the congregation. C. W. Freeman is now pastor.

E. A. Propst has served as superintendent of the Bible school since its beginning. S. H. Blane and family have been most helpful members.

It has given to the ministry Ralph Callaway.

Petersburg.

Organized 1863, by Alexander Johnston; present membership, 620; value of property, $30,000; Bible school began 1863; present enrollment, 275.

In the forties, Aaron B. White, a Christian minister residing in Petersburg, and his sons cleared out the underbrush and built a stand for an open-air meeting just across the street east from his residence. This is the spot on which the present church now stands. Evangelist W. H. Brown preached on that outdoor stand in 1846; with what results it is not known.

About 1860 the Davis, Arnold, Lamar, Capps and Cheaney families were residents of that community and began to meet on the Lord's Days for public worship according to the word of God. The L. A. and Jackson Whipp families came, too, a little later. The most zealous and devoted of all these was Mrs. James W. Cheaney, whose presence in the house of the Lord is to this day an inspiration. The first elders were Dr. K. B. Davis and Robert Arnold. A few years after the organization L. A. Whipp was made an elder, and continues to this time to fill the place with zeal and earnestness. In 1875 a forward movement, led by Mrs. Cheaney, was determined upon. Mr. and Mrs. J. W. Judy, of Tallula, promised their help. When the big tent in which the meeting was to be held was hauled from the depot to the location, Colonel Judy rode astride of it. Some of his friends along the street twitted him. Within two months, they learned that he who laughs last laughs best. The meeting conducted by Evangelist D. R. Lucas resulted in about 260 additions and placed the church firmly upon its feet.

The first house was built in 1876 and the present modern structure in 1909, during the pastorates of W. M. Groves and B. H. Sealock. J. W. Judy and W. G. Green, of Tallula, and L. A. Whipp and A. G. Nance have given the church valuable financial support. The pastorate of M. M.

Goode is remembered to have been of great service to the congregation.

Two public debates were held here—the Lucas-Miller and J. S. Sweeney with Min. "Universalist" Marvin.

The church has had eleven pastors. Dr. D. T. Hughes, Harrison Osborne, John Owen and Dr. L. A. Engle were among the early preachers.

Sweet Water.

Organized 1825; present membership, 115; value of property, $4,000; Bible-school enrollment, 100.

Menard County was a part of Sangamon until the meeting of the General Assembly in 1838-39. The first name of this locality was Sugar Grove, which was applied to it because of the large grove of these trees that grew there. The congregation was first organized as a Baptist church; next it affiliated with the "New Lights," or Christian Denomination; later it became a part of the Restoration movement.

The earliest extant records bear date of 1851. The members of the congregation at that time were the following: William, Elizabeth, Catherine, John N., James, Alvira and John D. Alkine; Thompson, H. D., Tomsey, Margaret and Elizabeth Hughes; Joseph N. Peeler; Amanda and Melissa Whipp; J. N., Franklin, Jemima, Stephen and Ervilla Powell; Lucinda Propst; George, Madeline, Edward and Marea Blane; Arminda, O. P., Nancy, George W. and Louisa Bracken; Charles, Cleva and Susan Montgomery; Jane and Mary Ann Swank; Louisa Gibbs, Malinda Taylor, Angline Shure, William and Thrissa McFadden; William, Elizabeth and Catherine Engle; Elizabeth, Jane and Abner Peccla; Putnam Brown, Cloe Creviston, F. P. Cowan, Hermann and Sarah Sykes. At that date, William Alkine was an elder and William Engle was chosen to that office. Thompson Hughes and Joseph N. Peeler were the deacons. J. N. Powell was an evangelist. Mrs. Elizabeth Propst and her husband were killed on their way to Oregon by Indians.

Wm. Ribea, a minister of the Christian Denomination,

preached in this community after the congregation had left that fellowship. He affirmed that they had departed from the ground they once occupied. He hence instituted a new church, to which some of the members attached themselves.

About 1866 another disturbance arose relative to employing J. K. Speer as their minister. It was held that he taught "soul sleeping" and kindred theories. The questions were threshed out in a public debate in January, 1867. Mr. Speer affirmed that "death extinguishes man's conscious existence." Min. L. M. Linn opposed. The church then numbered about 230 members. About twenty-three persons followed Mr. Speer, including one elder and one deacon. They built a chapel, but discussions among themselves soon ended the society. The Presbyterians bought the house. A few returned to the church.

In the earlier years, Dr. W. A. Mallory, Peter Vogel, T. W. Rainey and E. G. Rice preached for the congregation. For many years C. E. Smoot gave them most helpful service. About thirty others have preached here.

The present large brick church was built in 1861. The old chapel is now used as a dwelling.

The church ordained to the ministry D. I. Hughes, Dr. L. A. Engle and C. E. Smoot.

Tallula.

Organized 1834, by Theophilus Sweet; present membership, 200; value of property, $5,000; Bible-school enrollment, 200.

In October, 1834, "the church of Christ in Clary's Grove" was formed of the six following persons: John Willson, William G. White, Jane White, Jesse L. Trailor, Obedience Trailor and Miss Lydia Ann Caldwell. James W. Simpson and wife came from Kentucky the following year and at once united with the church. Their meetings were held in their residences and the old-time schoolhouse until the chapel was built in 1844. After serving them twenty years, it was sold.

CHURCHES

Besides Mr. Sweet, this church was ministered to by Robert Foster, B. W. Stone, Maurice R. Trimble, W. W. Happy, W. H. Brown and others of the heroes of the faith. But the congregation always met for the divinely appointed worship upon the Lord's Days.

The coming of a railway built Tallula, and the place of meeting and local name were accordingly changed. The Tallula chapel was dedicated by John O'Kane in January, 1865. From first to last, this church has been served by about fifty preachers.

This church has held in its fellowship an unusual number of brainy, forceful and helpful men and women. Colonel Judy and his wife, Dr. J. F. Willson and wife, W. G. Green, and not a few others, were of this class.

MERCER COUNTY.

Keithsburg.

Organized 1864, by Elias Shortridge; present membership, 142; value of property, $5,200; Bible school began 1866; present enrollment, 128.

The organization of the church was made in the old brick schoolhouse three miles east of town. Prayer-meetings were held there every Sunday when no preacher was present. Ministers Shortridge, Speer, Warren, Fiske and Lucas preached there and in the courthouse in the town, which was the meeting-place within a year or two. Levi Ender gave the ground and the first chapel was occupied in 1866. This was enlarged and reconstructed in 1909.

There were about fifty members when the first chapel was built, all of whom have gone hence except Josephus Ogle and wife, of Waterville, Wash., who wait in the dawn of the endless day. They were consecrated members and most helpful to the church.

Among the ministers who have served the church there were J. B. Royal, Mr. Kincaid, M. Jones, L. M. Linn, James Connoran, F. M. Branic, Wm. G. Smith, J. E. Parker, E.

Ward, G. E. Sheerer, A. A. Burr, J. Quinlan, W. E. Meloan, John Larimore and L. F. DePoisters.

S. M. Booie was an efficient and faithful elder in the congregation for fifteen years—till his death in 1893.

The church has given to the ministry F. W. and F. A. Emmerson.

New Boston.

Organized 1902, by G. E. Sheerer; present membership, 152; value of property, $1,000; Bible-school enrollment, 64.

Ohio Grove (Aledo).

Present membership, 40; value of property, $1,000; Bible-school enrollment, 75.

This church is six miles southeast of Aledo. It is an old congregation.

In the sixties there was a congregation at the village of Sunbeam that was probably the progenitor of Ohio Grove.

MONTGOMERY COUNTY.

Barnett.

Organized 1878, by J. S. Sweeney; present membership, 40; value of property, $1,500; Bible-school enrollment, 40.

This was first known as the Shaw's Point Church and moved after the town grew on the new railroad. While in the country, it had a large and influential membership.

Harvel.

Organized 1888, by Isaac Beckelhymer; present membership, 89; value of property, including parsonage, $2,300; Bible school began 1888; present enrollment, 80.

Daniel Adams led in the formation of this congregation. Evangelist Beckelhymer led in a three weeks' meeting and organized with twenty-three members. These meetings were held in the M. E. chapel, for which the community had paid with the understanding that it should be for all Christian people. In another meeting the next year the doors were closed against Mr. Beckelhymer. A chapel was soon finished.

The church was once temporarily crippled by an unworthy pastor from Arkansas. Mr. Beckelhymer is held in high regard by this church. They have had many protracted meetings and have always maintained the order of the Lord's house on the Lord's Day. H. M. Carey is clerk.

Hillsboro.

Organized 1905, by E. O. Sharpe; present membership, 60; value of property, $2,200; Bible school began 1905; present enrollment, 64.

Mr. Sharpe, as evangelist of the Fifth District, first preached in the courthouse in 1904. A series of meetings, continuing fifty-one days, was led by Evangelists Lawrence and Edward Wright. There were seventy-one charter members. Mr. Sharpe became the first pastor. A good lot was bought and the chapel finished in 1909. J. W. Wilkes is clerk.

Irving.

Organized 1853; present membership, 100; value of property, $2,000; Bible school began 1890; present enrollment, 75.

There were eighteen charter members, some of whom were: J. M. Taulbee; James, Nancy and Maria Markham; Elijah, Mary, William and Eliza Osborn; James Osborn and wife and son; Henry Lowery and wife and two daughters. Maria Markham is the sole survivor. They held their meetings in the schoolhouse when it was available and in groves in the summer-time. Ministers Ward and Taulbee preached when a place could be secured. In 1876, Minister Gilbert reorganized the congregation with twenty-one members. In 1878 a chapel was built and L. M. Linn served the church one-half time. W. H. Boles held a great meeting in 1885. Then J. H. Garrison preached for the church. Finis Idleman held the congregation a good meeting. The resident pastor is C. W. Garst. W. M. Berry has led the Bible school faithfully and efficiently as superintendent since its beginning. B. B. Tyler held a meeting here, as district evangelist, in 1863, which he then thought a failure, but it gave J. C. Mason, now of Texas, to the church and to the Christian ministry.

Litchfield.

Organized 1856, by J. C. Reynolds; present membership, 742; value of property, $11,000; Bible school began 1856; present enrollment, 743.

Minister Reynolds was evangelizing under the direction of the State Board when the church was constituted. Among the first who preached there were Ministers Sims, W. H. Brown, J. W. Kellar, J. S. Sweeney and B. B. Tyler.

First a small frame chapel was built. Later a one-room brick building. During the pastorate of Mr. Purlee the present edifice was erected at the corner of Union Avenue and Harrison Street.

Among those who did faithful service in establishing the church there were W. C. Henderson, H. A. Jones, Thomas Harlow, M. C. Hoagland, Mrs. Matilda O'Bannon and Mrs. Adeline Elliott.

Charles W. Ross closed a very successful pastorate of several years in 1913. I. W. Agee is the present pastor.

Pleasant Hill (Barnett).

Present membership, 71; value of property, $1,000; Bible-school enrollment, 58.

Raymond.

Organized 1871, by Minister Ewing; present membership, 156; value of property, $3,000; Bible school began 1871; present enrollment, 151.

Meetings were held in a storeroom for a year when the chapel, which is still used for public worship, was built. Min. J. W. Ballinger reorganized the church in 1875 with forty-three members and served as pastor for two to three years. The officers at that time were J. R. Wylder, Orman White, J. W. Potts, D. J. Parrott and Isaac Dodson, elders; J. H. Nevins, T. J. Scott, W. A. Parrott and S. W. McElroy, deacons. Then there was occasional preaching by sundry ministers till 1890. Isaac Beckelhymer then served as pastor and was followed by others. The congregation has had about thirteen protracted meetings by as many evangelists.

Miss Lou Watson was given to the ministry and served the church efficiently as its pastor.

The congregation is united in its work, has a good C. E. and a well-attended mid-week prayer-meeting. Fred Guthrie is the clerk; C. F. Shaul, pastor.

Waggoner.

Organized 1889, by Isaac Beckelhymer; present membership, 114; value of property, $2,500; Bible school began 1889; present enrollment, 79.

The Sulphur Spring congregation was organized in 1857. Its location was four miles west of Waggoner on the east edge of Macoupin County. Its first elders were W. H. Kent, Wm. Street, Robert Brown and C. F. Richardson. It served the community well during the period of its life and disbanded in 1884. The building is now used for funerals only. A large cemetery has grown around it.

The Waggoner congregation was organized by members from Sulphur Spring. There were about twenty charter members. Jefferson Borton, H. H. Beekman and Willis Plain were the first elders. In 1890 the ladies' aid society bought two lots and the chapel was finished in 1893. Meanwhile the meetings were held in a hall. The same year Mrs. McCoy Crank held a successful revival. The congregation has had eleven pastors. Orin Dilly is in the sixth year of a very helpful pastorate.

Walshville.

Organized 1874, by T. J. Shelton; present membership, 50; value of property, $2,200; Bible-school enrollment, 56.

Min. A. D. Northcutt was prominent in the beginning of this effort. The organization was made in the town hall with ten charter members. With little social influence or means, and overshadowed by three strong denominations, this little band trusted God, went to prayer and work and grew up to an influential position.

The pastors were L. M. Linn, J. H. Garrison, J. H. Smart, H. P. Tandy and L. F. Wood. For several years the Baptist chapel was used. In 1878 a very neat house of worship was built. A number of ministers preached for the congregation through several years. In 1904 their chapel was destroyed by fire. The Bible school secured the privilege of using the M. E. chapel, but was turned out the next year. The second building was finished early in 1908.

J. E. Story, Miss Rachael Dangerfield and Isaac Beckelhymer have served the congregation in recent years. Miss Dangerfield was the pastor when the last house was built.

There is a good C. E., and the congregation is active under the ministry of W. A. Green. T. O. Tiffin is the clerk.

MORGAN COUNTY.

Antioch (Jacksonville).

Organized 1833, by D. P. Henderson; present membership, 40; value of property, including parsonage, $5,000; Bible-school enrollment, 45.

The location is seven miles east of Jacksonville, on the Springfield road. The neighborhood was settled by people from Kentucky, many of whom were Disciples before leaving that State. For a time meetings were held in residences. In 1835 a substantial frame building was erected. This housed the congregation till 1876, when it was sold to Isaac Findall, who moved it to his farm, where it is still used as a shop and carriage-house. In that year the present comfortable house was built during the pastorate of M. M. Goode. He was highly esteemed there for his personal worth and for his work.

A. Campbell and B. W. Stone visited the church in its early period. Mr. Stone died near there and his body rested in its cemetery for a time. Other ministers who served the church were E. G. Rice, M. R. Elder, J. B. Graves, J. W. Strawn and H. P. Shaw. Mr. Shaw and his wife left the congregation to go as missionaries to China.

During the past twenty years many of its members have rented their farms and moved to the city; hence the struggle to exist.

Berea (Prentice).

Organized 1852; present membership, 75; value of property, $550; Bible-school enrollment, 35.

The church was organized August 15, with twenty-five charter members. A part of the agreement was as follows:

> We, the body of Christ, agree to organize ourselves after the primitive practice; to watch over one another and to admonish each other, for our good; to take the Scriptures of the Old and New Testaments for our rule of faith and practice. . . . We agree to continue steadfastly in the apostles' doctrine, in fellowship, in breaking of bread and in prayers . . . to be known as the church of Christ on Indian Creek, meeting at Morgan Schoolhouse No. 2.

Charles Rowe was chosen elder, and Joel Robinson and Wesley Corrington, deacons. Mr. Rowe was a product of this church and served it as elder and preacher for six years. Most of the first members came from the Antioch congregation. It was ministered to at times by most of the preachers of that time and section. Four of its leading members were Joel and Isaac Robinson, Dr. John C. Cobb and Benjamin McIntyre.

Chapin.

Organized 1875, by H. C. Cassell; present membership, 240; value of property, including parsonage, $5,000; Bible school began 1875; present enrollment, 108.

The earliest organization of a church of Christ in this community was the old Mauvaisterre or Jordon congregation, three miles east of the site of Chapin. In March, 1839, nine Disciples of Christ entered into a covenant to observe the ordinances of the Lord as revealed in the New Testament. They were Nathaniel and Martha H. Fisk, Thomas O. and Nancy Taylor, Jane Hill, Mary Boyd, Catherine Gillpatrick, and Nathan J. and Mary Averitt. Mr. Fisk was the first preacher and served the church four and a half years.

Meetings were held in homes and schoolhouses till a chapel was built. It stood in the cemetery that is still used. This congregation grew till its members were scattered through that entire region. For the accommodation of those residing toward the northwest, the Bethel congregation was formed at a point one and a half miles from the site of Chapin. This was a part of the Manvaisterre Church until the time of the Civil War, when Minister McIntire organized a church. The shifting population and the coming of railways long since carried it away.

A colony from the old church moved into Macon County and formed the nuclei of the Long Point and Niantic congregations. It was a fruitful hive, and the influences of the Taylors, Averitts, Boyds, Jones, Tichnors, Bobbitts, Campbells, Strodes, Riggs, Hatfields, Pruitts, Mansfields and many others of their time are yet widely out-reaching. They were heroes of the faith in their day the fragrance of whose memories yet lingers.

In 1877 twenty-four people from the Jordon and Bethel congregations enrolled into the Chapin Church, so this church came of fine spiritual ancestry. The Congregational chapel was bought, which served until the present building was erected in 1902. It has given to the ministry F. W. Burnham and Ivan W. Agee. Since its formation more than five hundred people have been led by it in the way of life.

Concord.

Organized 1868, by William Rice; present membership, 96; value of property, $5,000; Bible school began 1868; present enrollment, 90.

Christian ministers preached about the site of Concord in the early sixties. A chapel was built seven miles to the northwest, which was sold to the Lutherans and then another was built in the town. This house was rebuilt in 1911.

Twenty-four ministers have served the church, which has done good work. S. M. Henderson is an elder and the clerk.

Franklin.

Present membership, 140; value of property, including parsonage, $4,900; Bible-school enrollment, 120.

Jacksonville (Central).

Organized 1832, by B. W. Stone; present membership, 1,200; value of property, $85,000; Bible school began 1860; present enrollment, 900.

This church was organized in October in the old courthouse that stood near the southwest corner of the square. There were seventy-two charter members. Among them were Harrison W. Osborne, Philip Coffman, John T. Jones and Josephus Hewitt—all leading spirits.

The meetings for public worship were continued in the courthouse and residences of the members until a chapel was built on Beardstown Street, which is now North Main Street. This chapel served until the early fifties, when, during the pastorate of A. J. Kane, a two-story brick building was erected on the same street. Joel Hedington taught school in this house. It was in use till 1869, when, during the pastorate of Enos Campbell, a new brick house was built on East State Street. This was enlarged and remodeled in 1888, while A. N. Gilbert was pastor. The present stone structure was finished during the pastorate of R. F. Thrapp in 1906.

Throughout its life this church has always held a goodly number of representative citizens. Its ministers also have generally been men of a high type. Among the pioneers, besides those above named, there were Henry Cyrus, the first pastor; Jerry Lancaster, Jonathan Atkinson, W. W.

Happy and D. P. Henderson. The church was divided during the pastorate of W. S. Russel by his unscriptural teaching. The two parties came to a mutual agreement in 1866, and under the superior ministry of Enos Campbell were welded into one. The teaching of Mr. Russel not only crippled the church for a time, but also affected adversely other congregations in the county and lost to the Disciples Berean College.

W. W. Happy, Sr. and Jr., James Stark and William Gilliam were ordained to the ministry by this congregation.

The pastorate of Mr. Thrapp "was characterized by splendid missionary expansion and progressive civic reform."

This is a great church, abounding in many good works.

Jacksonville (Negro).

Organized 1904, by E. M. Harlis; present membership, 35; value of property, $2,500; Bible school began 1894; present enrollment, 25.

A mission Bible school was begun by Minister Harlis on South Mauvaisterre Street in 1894. This was fostered by the First Christian Church and especially by Mrs. E. C. Ewing. Ten years afterward this mission grew into a church. Mr. Harlis has been faithful in his work. He still ministers to the congregation. The C. E. numbers twenty-five.

Literberry.

Organized 1869, by E. W. Clark; present membership, 160; value of property, $4,500; Bible school began 1869; present enrollment, 176.

E. G. Rice and M. M. Goode were two of the early ministers. The church is now active and zealous.

Lynnville (Jacksonville).

Organized 1833, by Barton W. Stone; present membership, 140; value of property, including parsonage, $4,500; Bible school began 1863; present enrollment, 138.

The church was constituted in the residence of James Leeper. The officers were James B. and William Gordon, elders, with John Banson, James Leeper and A. A. Wilson, deacons. Besides Mr. Stone, among the early ministers there were D. P. Henderson, Dr. Robert Foster, W. W. Happy, Jonathan Atkinson, A. J. Kane, E. L. Craig and E. G. Rice.

The first chapel, built in 1838, was a union house. It was sold for taxes in 1848 and bought by the Disciples. It gave place to the present house in 1882.

This church ordained A. C. Foster and Joseph B. Camp to the ministry.

John B. Gordon was elected to the Legislature, for two or three terms, in the seventies. S. F. Campbell and Geo. W. Camp were leading members of the church and citizens in the community for many years. Mr. Camp was the father of John B., Mark D. and Joseph B. Camp.

In the union chapel Min. Peter Akers, of the M. E. Church, on one Sunday preached four hours in order "to keep the Campbellites from occupying the house the same day."

Oak Ridge (Prentice).

Organized 1876.

The location is twelve miles northeast of Jacksonville. The members of a congregation that had worshiped a period at the old Jordanville Schoolhouse, with some friends, met on March 18, 1876, at the residence of Lewis Hamilton. They decided to build a chapel at the old Stockton Cemetery. This house was finished in 1878.

The charter members were Rosetta Armstrong, Samuel and Catherine Beach, Margaret Coker, Margaret Coulston; Tyre, John, Julia and Anna Brown; Mary Demarest, John Hamilton, J. L. and Mary S. Jordon, Charles Paul, William Robinson, Isaac Smith, and A. B., Elizabeth and Emma Wiswell. The elders elected were John Hamilton, A. B. Wiswell and Tyre Brown.

About seventeen preachers have served the congregation.

Waverly.

Organized 1847, by Austin Sims; present membership, 131; value of property, $5,000; Bible school began 1847; present enrollment, 90.

This is an average church of its class.

Woodson.

Organized 1869, by E. G. Rice and H. W. Osborne; present membership, 151; value of property, including parsonage, $4,500; Bible school began 1868; present enrollment, 93.

This church was the result of a series of meetings conducted by Ministers Osborne and Rice in the schoolhouse in 1868. There were thirty-five charter members, some of whom came from the "Old Concord" congregation. The latter, located about six miles northeast of Woodson, was once a strong and prosperous country church, but the adverse tides carried it away. The Woodson chapel was built in 1869. Ministers Osborne and Rice first preached for the congregation for several years, part time. William Ferguson was for a long time a true and faithful elder, feeding and leading the flock.

Dr. G. W. Miller, a practicing physician of the town, having served the church well as an elder, was ordained to the ministry and has been the pastor for nineteen years.

The church is well organized and active in good works.

MOULTRIE COUNTY.

In 1832, A. H. Kellar, Abram Southern, Rebecca Stevens, and a few other Baptists from Kentucky, with Joseph and Solomon Hostetler and their wives from Indiana, came together in November and organized the West Okaw Church of Christ. Joseph Hostetler was an ordained minister, while his brother Solomon and A. H. Kellar were teaching elders. They were righteous men, full of zeal. The West Okaw Church may properly be called the mother of all the Christian Churches in the county. Its meetings, when the weather compelled, were held in the twenty-feet-square log schoolhouse, with stick-and-mud chimney at the west and with a log left out at the east end for a window. It had what was known as a weight-pole roof. From this point the primitive gospel began and continued to be sounded out. From Cunningham's Grove on the north to Jerry Provolt's at the forks of the Okaw on the south, the seeds of the truth were sown by this pioneer church.

In 1837, Levi Flemming, a zealous preacher, settled on upper Jonathan Creek and laid the foundation of the church there.

Later the Lillys and the Smysers came from Kentucky and settled on Whitley Creek. They were re-enforced by Jackson Storm, a preacher from Tennessee, who, like Apollos, was mighty in the Scriptures; also by Tobias Grider from Indiana.

These Disciples were further helped, as occasion permitted or required, by Bushrod W. Henry, of Shelby County, and John W. Tyler and Geo. A. Patterson, of Macon County. These were all men whose chief learning had been acquired in the school of the great Teacher.

The congregation that could have regular preaching once a month considered itself very fortunate, and if there were no additions at these meetings it was thought something was wrong. There were giants in those days who would successfully grapple with sectarian dogmas and throttle the mightiest champion of human authority as binding on men's consciences.

Levi Flemming and Jackson Storm were two of the pioneer preachers of whom the printed records say little, but their names are in the book of life and long ago they went to their rewards in heaven.

The Wilburn Creek Church, for a long time a flourishing and forceful country congregation, yielding to the law of change, has disbanded.

These men were supremely loyal to the truth and with them the word of the Lord was final.

Allenville.

Organized 1884, by H. Y. Keller; present membership, 200; value of property, $1,000; Bible school began 1895; present enrollment, 113.

The church met for worship in the old Nelson Schoolhouse until the chapel was built.

Arthur.

Organized 1882, by W. F. Black; present membership, 132; value of property, $10,000; Bible school began 1882; present enrollment, 168.

This church grew out of a series of meetings led by Evangelist Black. It was organized in an implement store. A chapel was finished in the fall of 1883. This gave place at the close of 1909 to the present house, costing $8,000. Joel T. Davis was then pastor.

Bethany.

Organized 1881, by S. B. Lindsey; present membership, 180; value of property, $4,500; Bible school began 1881; present enrollment, 89.

There were twenty charter members. The first elders were Charles Ronley, A. S. Younger and G. W. Logan, and the first deacons, W. W. Lennell, William Gough and W. J. Ledbretter.

The house of worship was completed and occupied at the close of 1882.

Cadwell.

Organized 1902, by J. O. Henry; present membership, 86; value of property, $3,500; Bible school began 1902; present enrollment, 68.

Organized in a schoolhouse. Church built the next year. A fine community. Rich soil, with very muddy roads in wet weather. A C. W. B. M.

Dalton City.

Organized 1865, by John W. Sconce; present membership, 75; value of property, $3,000; Bible school began 1865; present enrollment, 51.

About the year 1865, John W. Sconce, assisted by J. W. Tyler, of Decatur, and Jackson Page, of Shelbyville, formed a church of Christ in the New Hope Schoolhouse near Freeland's Point. When Mr. Sconce settled in Dalton City, in 1873, through his earnest effort a church building was put up there and the congregations at New Hope transferred their place of meeting thither.

Gays.

Organized 1869, by Thomas Goodman; present membership, 150; value of property, $1,800; Bible school began 1871; present enrollment, 104.

Met in schoolhouse for two years, when chapel was finished and occupied. The first elders were Edward Rouse and W. S. Colson; the first deacons, W. T. Watson and S. P. Bristow. E. C. Harrison is now the clerk.

Jonathan's Creek (Sullivan).

Organized 1859, by Christie Hostetler; present membership, 70; value of property, $1,500; Bible school began 1862; present enrollment, 80.

Organized in the Lauders Schoolhouse, where it met for three years. In 1862 a church house had been built at the Jonathan's Creek Cemetery, and was occupied. This gave place to a new house in 1891.

David Campbell was given to the ministry.

The church is six miles east of Sullivan.

Lake City.

Organized 1886, by Minister Gates; present membership, 33; value of property, $800; Bible school began 1886; present enrollment, 32.

John T. Howell, John McMullin, and John and Frank Lovings and their families, led in the formation of this church. The chapel was built the same year. There are many Irish Papists in the community. After a few years members of the church began to sell their farms and move. This continued until only a few Disciples are left.

Lovington.

Organized 1832, by Joseph Hostetler; present membership, 408; value of property, $12,000; Bible school began 1865; present enrollment, 324.

On Nov. 17, 1832, a meeting was held at the home of Nathan Stevens, one mile west of the place where Lovington has grown, on the Okaw River, and a church was organized with seventeen members. Joseph Hostetler, who had come from Indiana that year, was the leader in this work. He and his brother Solomon had been preachers in the German Baptist Church, but were now proclaiming the primitive gospel. A. H. Kellar, a farmer and Regular Baptist preacher, associated himself with them. These three were the first elders. The church was known as the Okaw Church of Christ. The meetings for public worship were held in the residences and schoolhouses until 1846. Then a small frame building was erected one mile south of the site of Lovington, on the old Kellar farm—now the Lovington Cemetery. The congregation sustained a steady growth under the leadership of Min. H. Y. Kellar until 1866. In that year a large frame building was erected on the present church site in Lovington. This was used until 1901, when the present church was built. It is a large, modern brick structure, well adapted to the work of the church. F. C. Overbaugh was the pastor at that time. The church now has nine elders and thirteen deacons, the largest Bible school in Moultrie County, with Senior and Junior C. E. societies.

This church has given to the ministry Finis Idleman and Paul E. Million. H. Y. Kellar came from the Okaw Church.

CHURCHES

Smyser (Gays).

Organized 1837, by Tobias Grider; present membership, 180; value of property, $1,000; Bible school began 1858; present enrollment, 63.

This is frequently called the Whitley Creek Church from the near-by stream of water of that name. S. M. Smyser was one of the leading members in the early days; hence it came to be known by his name. Its location is about seven miles northwest of Mattoon. The charter members were John and Synthia Hendricks, S. M. and Rebecca Smyser, Polly A. Hendricks and John Hendricks, Jr. Their names are fragrant remembrances. A church home was built at once. It was used till 1875, when the present house was erected. Tobias Grider, Jack Storms and B. W. Henry preached there in the thirties and forties. S. M. Smyser and A. H. Edwards were efficient elders who served the church for a long time. In the sixties, J. G. Waggoner was "working the roads" in that community. At the time, S. M. Connor was holding a series of meetings there, and became sick. Mr. Smyser said to Mr. Waggoner: "Go home and get ready to preach to-night." Had this church done nothing more in its seventy-five years than produce and give to the world J. G. Waggoner, its work would have been most commendable. J. H. McCormick, E. L. Lilly, J. D. Layton and Henry Boyd are the present elders.

Sullivan.

Organized 1840, by Levi Fleming; present membership, 561; value of property, $15,000; Bible school began 1856; present enrollment, 219.

Before the town of Sullivan was laid out, a little church was formed at Asa's Creek by Min. Levi Fleming, in the home of Levi Patterson. It made little progress until reorganized by B. W. Henry in 1846 with fourteen members. This church worshiped in the schoolhouse in Sullivan, which was also used as a courthouse at that time. The lack of a suitable and permanent place of worship, and internal discord, retarded the growth of the church. Later, A. H. and H. G. Kellar set things in order and a number came in from the Lovington Church. About 1852 a series of meetings, conducted by Mins. John Wilson and B. W. Henry, was held in the M. E. Church. A house of worship was finished and occupied in 1853. In after years revivals were conducted by A. J. Kane, William Mathes, W. M. Brown, Milton Hopkins, W. F. Black, A. I. Hobbs, T. A. Boyer and C. R. Scoville. In the fifties, Mins. J. S. Etheridge, B. W. Henry, H. Y. and Dr. A. L. Kellar moved to Sullivan and contributed much to the growth of the church. Later there came J. R. Lucas, L. P. Phillips, N. S. Bastian and James Hyatt. At the beginning of his second year the church was divided, but was reunited five years thereafter. There followed J. M. Morgan, Dr. A. L. Kellar, Thomas Edwards, L. C. Haulman, E. H. Kellar, J. S. Clements, J. P. Davis, G. E. Platt, B. C. Lamplugh, A. J. DeMiller, J. E. Diehl, J. M. Bovee, Edwards Davis, M. J. Martin, Amzi Atwater, T. F. Weaver, E. W. Brickert, E. E. Curry, H. A. Davis, J. M. McNutt, J. W. Waters, J. W. Kilborn and W. B. Hopper, the present pastor.

In July, 1901, a new and commodious brick building was finished and occupied.

The church has an L. A. society, C. W. B. M. auxiliary and girls' missionary circle.

The church at Sullivan was not singular in its damaging experiences. Not a few of those that are now strong and efficient passed through similar trials. The preachers were not always wise. But their problems were many and the support for their families came largely from their manual toil, and they held to no principles of self-seeking politicians. Oftener disturbances arose from men of partial knowledge and small vision who assumed to be bosses rather than leaders in the congregation. They were generally good men with confused aims. Happily such conditions have largely passed.

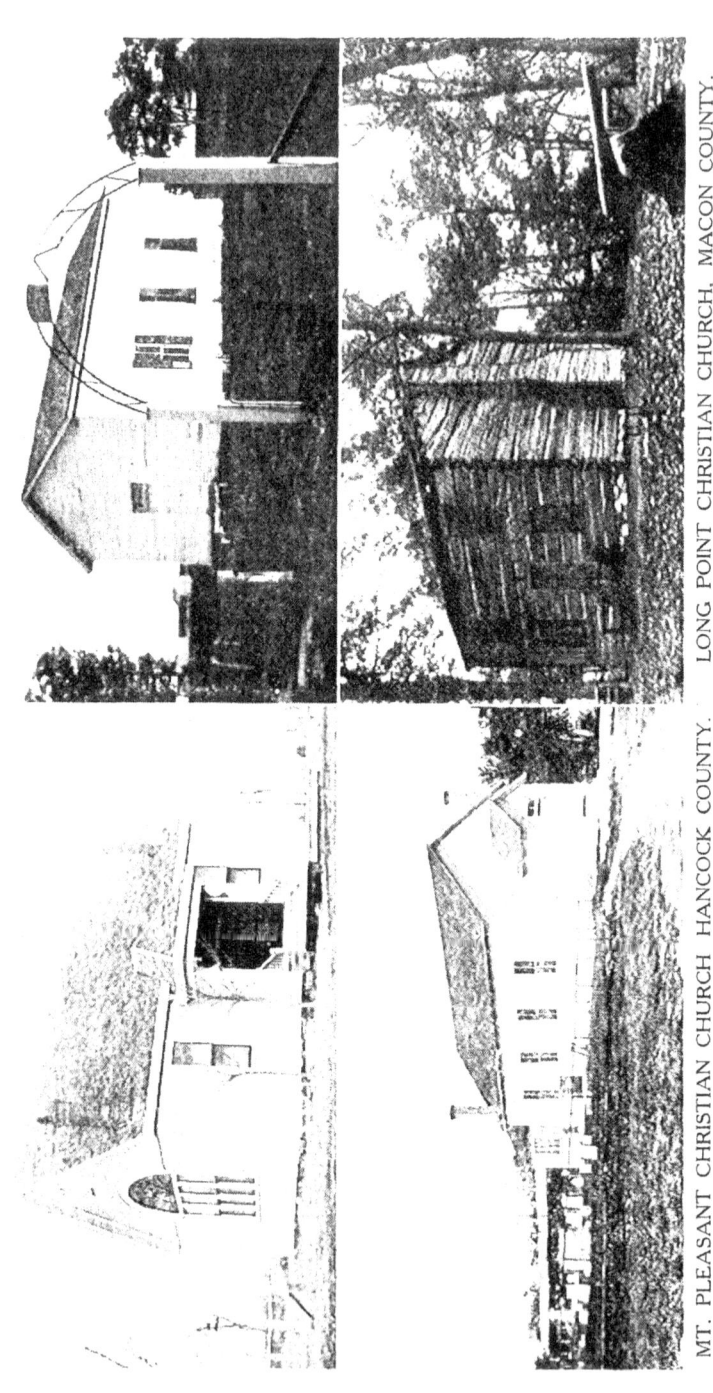

MT. PLEASANT CHRISTIAN CHURCH, HANCOCK COUNTY. LONG POINT CHRISTIAN CHURCH, MACON COUNTY.
PINE CREEK CHRISTIAN CHURCH, OGLE COUNTY. FIRST COURTHOUSE, DECATUR.

Union Prairie (Arthur).

Organized 1870, by Nathan Wright; present membership, 47; value of property, $4,000; Bible school began 1873; present enrollment, 35.

Among the ministers who have served the church, there were David Campbell, Abram Bovie, James Connor, Thomas Goodman, Harmon Gregg, H. Y. Kellar, J. O. Henry, Clinton Hostetler, W. M. Gordon, L. M. Mulligan and John Howell.

The congregation has a good house for worship, located three and one-half miles west of Arthur and one-fourth mile west of the Douglas County line. It was built in 1865. Much of the labor was donated by brethren and friends.

The Haneys and Powels were among the prominent charter members.

OGLE COUNTY.

Grand Detour.

Organized 1894, by J. B. Wright; present membership, 27; value of property, $1,500; Bible school began 1895; present enrollment, 34.

This little church was a child of persecution. Minister Wright began to preach to a few Disciples there in a union chapel. Conversions resulted almost immediately, which called for an organization. This was made with thirty-one charter members. Meanwhile, the legal owners of the property shut the Disciples out of the chapel. The use of the schoolhouse was also denied them. This treatment aroused the interest of others, so that five months thereafter a new church house was ready for use.

A good Bible school and C. E. are maintained.

Mt. Morris.

Organized 1880, by J. H. Wright; present membership, 93; value of property, $3,500; Bible school began 1880; present enrollment, 143.

A few Disciples had held some meetings for worship in

a hall, with an occasional sermon by L. D. Waldo, of Rockford, and D. R. Howe, of Lanark. In March, State Evangelist Wright organized the church with the following twenty-eight charter members: Mrs. Sarah Warner, Mrs. Mary E. Thomas, Mary E. Spielman, Mrs. Anna Long, Mrs. Rose Diehl, Mrs. E. Miller, Geo. S. Kennedy, Wm. S. and Catherine Blake, Charles G. and Sarah Blakslee, Hattie Finnikle, Mrs. Eliza Hammer, Jacob and Susan Keedy, Mrs. Laura Kennedy, Charles and Mrs. Vallee Keedy; Florence V., Fannie and Susan Long; Adam Shaw, Letha Sprecher. Mrs. Susan Thomas, Anna and Mildred F. Thomas, and Mary E. and Clay Wagner. Of these, the seven first named only are living.

A brick building was bought of the Lutherans and remodeled.

The pastors were G. W. Ross, J. H. Carr, T. B. Stanley, J. B. Wright, C. T. Spitler, G. W. Pearl, D. G. Wagner, D. F. Seyster, Mr. De Poister, Mr. Goss, Mr. Hacker, and now H. F. Sayles.

Those given to the ministry are J. H. Shellenberger, Z. O. Doward, D. H. Wagner, J. W. Baker, W. F. Kohl and H. L. Eyrick.

Pine Creek (Polo).

Organized 1860, by Robert Moffett and Charles Sherwood; present membership, 98; value of property, $3,500; Bible school began 1860; present enrollment, 55.

This is one of the truly great churches of Illinois. It is located ten miles southeast of Polo. Into this community there came, about 1857, David I. Funk, Charles Widney, Abram Witmer, David Bovey and other kindred spirits. Mr. Funk was a native of Washington County, Md. For thirty years he had been an elder in the "Dunker" Church, but under the preaching of Mr. Campbell was led to more Scriptural ground. He died in 1876 at the age of eighty-nine years. These men, with their families, began to hold meetings for public worship in the Pennsylvania Corners

Schoolhouse. Here the church was organized. At this meeting Robert Moffett presided and C. W. Sherwood served as secretary. The officers elected were Charles Widney, Abram Witmer, G. T. Johnson, elders, with David I. Funk, Daniel Bovey and John Welty, deacons.

The chapel was built at the same "corners" the same year. In after years a lecture-room was added and other modern improvements made. It still serves the community well.

Of the earlier preachers who served the church, other than Mr. Sherwood and Mr. Moffett, were Geo. F. Johnston, John Ross, Daniel and Henry Howe, L. D. Waldo, Adam Adamson, Mr. Thornberry and Jasper Moss; later came G. L. Applegate, T. B. Stanley, G. W. Ross, J. H. Carr, G. W. Pearl, W. H. McGinnis and J. B. Wright. D. F. Seyster is now in the fifth year of the third period of his pastorate.

The congregation has made very liberal and cheerful contributions of its members to the churches at Mt. Morris, Polo, Grand Detour and Dixon.

Besides, the following men have been given by this fruitful mother to the Christian ministry: Geo. Hamilton, D. F. Seyster, G. A. Miller, L. T. Faulders, C. Roy Stauffer and C. Lee Stauffer. This church has indeed walked well pleasing before the Lord to have had her service crowned with such significant products.

The congregation has been always actively interested in all missionary and benevolent activities. When the question came up in the district missionary convention of trying to establish a church of Christ in the city of Sterling, one of the delegates of the Pine Creek congregation spoke with such confidence and earnestness that the vote was unanimous to begin the effort at once. Henry H. Powell has been Bible-school superintendent for thirteen consecutive years.

Besides the names already written, those of Wilson, Hammer, Drenner, Johnson, Wise, Netz, Pohrer, Wolf, Sheely and Higby will be honored and remembered for fidelity and good works.

Polo.

Organized 1904, by B. H. Sealock; present membership, 94; value of property, $2,000; Bible school began 1904; present enrollment, 112.

There had been occasional preaching in Polo by Christian ministers before the formation of the congregation. The Pine Creek Church gave to it some of its most valued members, but with the kindest spirit.

The Baptist chapel was bought, remodeled and repaired. John M. Grimes is the pastor.

PEORIA COUNTY.

Peoria Central.

Organized 1845; present membership, 635; value of property, $40,000; Bible school began 1855; present enrollment, 792.

There were twelve charter members. The last of these to die was Mrs. Eliza Wadsworth Smith, who passed away in 1904. The first elder was William Tilford, and the first deacon, Sampson Schockley. For a time these Disciples met from house to house to keep the Lord's ordinances, later in the engine-house in the 200 block on North Adams Street, and afterward in the old courthouse. The first church building was erected, costing $3,600, in 1855. It was the first public building in the city with a self-supporting roof. People said it would fall in, but it still stands at the corner of Franklin Street and Seventh Avenue. The present location at the corner of Monroe and Fulton Streets was bought of the "New School Presbyterians" in 1875. It had on it an old-fashioned brick building that was comfortable, but uninviting. Ira J. Chase was pastor at that time. A modern and convenient edifice was erected in 1894 during the pastorate of J. M. Kersey. This building was destroyed by fire early in 1913.

In its earlier years the church had such preaching as it could get. When there was none, Deacon Schockley conducted the worship on the Lord's Day morning. His trade was a brickmason; his business was to serve God. Some of the pastors were John Lindsey, I. N. Carman, D. R. Howe, John Miller, John O'Kane, William Thompson, Ira J. Chase, B. O. Aylesworth, J. B. Mayfield, N. S. Haynes, J. M. Kersey, J. P. McKnight, G. B. Van Arsdale, H. T. Burns, W. F. Turner, and now M. L. Pontius.

The baneful influence of denominationalism is such that the Disciples have found it necessary to come to social as well as ecclesiastical recognition in cities before they have made much growth. This condition has developed a superior type of character. Not a few choice spirits were grown in this church. Among them were Miss Pauline White, a member since 1854, and her sisters. In the last days of the church's weakness, Mr. and Mrs. J. P. Darst were invaluable helpers; the Ford family, particularly "Aunty Ford," a beautiful flower whom God caused to bloom on earth for awhile, that his people might have here an object-lesson of what heaven is to be; the Shockley family; and the schoolmaster who declined a handsome compensation to lead the singing in a near-by congregation, to perform this service in the Central free of charge, C. R. Vandervoort, whose sun set at his high noon. H. C. Reichel and Harry Streibich were given to the ministry.

Peoria—West Bluff Chapel.

This is a mission Bible school. It was the first chapel ever built in one day. The credit of the conception belongs to Mr. A. J. Elliott. The Brotherhoods of the Central and Howett Street Churches, re-enforced by about sixty volunteers of the local carpenters' union, united in building the chapel on May 30, 1910. Min. William Price had laid the foundation.

Peoria—Howett Street.

Organized 1909, by William Price; present membership, 192; value of property, $3,500; Bible school began 1875; present enrollment, 365.

About 1875, Mr. A. B. Tyng, Sr., an active member of the Reformed Episcopal Church, started a mission Sunday school at Cedar and Brotherson Streets. It was called the Tyng Mission. As it was about to be abandoned, the women of the W. C. T. U. assumed the duty of its maintenance. Through the influence of Mrs. F. M. Barrett it passed to the Central Church in 1885. Thereafter a lot was bought at 224 Howett Street, and later a chapel was built thereon. This was during the pastorate of N. S. Haynes at the Central Church. Afterward this building was enlarged. Fostered faithfully by members of the Central, the Howett Street school grew finally into an independent congregation. Among these were J. P. Darst, William Ford and Miss Lorena Simonson, who has given twenty-eight years of service there as a teacher—a rare and beautiful example of efficient devotion. Of late years, Mr. M. W. Rotchford has been Bible-school superintendent and an enthusiastic helper. The neighborhood was as unpromising thirty years ago as a field could well be. The gratifying results are the blessings of the Lord upon prayerful and faithful work.

On June 17, 1841, Dr. P. G. Young reported the organization of a church of Christ, with sixteen members, at Mount Hawley.

In 1842 he reported the organization of a church of forty members at Rome, on the west bank of the Illinois River.

As late as 1888 there was a self-supporting church at Elmore. It sustained a pastor for full time, gave the community helpful service, and contributed to missions.

The changing tides of population carried all these away.

PERRY COUNTY.

Duquoin.

Organized 1857, by Lysias Heape; present membership, 650; value of property, including parsonage, $22,000; Bible-school enrollment, 266.

Previous to 1857 there was monthly preaching in residences by Ministers Pyle, Wells, and Dr. Isaac and J. N. Mulkey. In that year, Messrs. Keyes and Metcalf, the founders of the town, gave the feeble congregation a lot on which the chapel was built. Some of the charter members were Lysias Heape and family, William and Abner Williams, Mrs. McElvain Wells, Mr. Pyle, Isaac Wheatley and family, Daniel and Frederick Williams, John Brown, Robert Parks, Thomas Wiffin and family, and Robert J. Wheatley, who had just moved from Pennsylvania. In after years he was a great man of God and a tower of strength in the church.

In 1857 a financial panic swept the country like a cyclone. Poor crops came the next year, and muttering thunderings of the Civil War were heard. Besides, at that time more papers avowedly infidel were taken and read in Duquoin than those that were Christian. Early in 1861, Mr. Wheatley sent for O. A. Burgess. He preached to an audience of fifty people for days and thought to quit. But, encouraged by Mr. Wheatley, he continued to use his splendid spiritual artillery upon the strong citadel of Satan until seventy persons surrendered to King Jesus. Later W. F. Black, J. Z. Taylor and Ira J. Chase led the church in great revivals.

The eight years' pastorate of J. J. Harris was a rich blessing to the church. In that period the new church was built.

Adam Adcock is now leading the flock in all good ways.

R. A., a son of R. J. Wheatley, has been a faithful member since the Burgess meeting.

Friendship (Tamaroa).

Organized 1867, by P. W. Jones; present membership, 60; value of property, $600; Bible school began 1867; present enrollment, 85.

A country church three miles west of Tamaroa. It was instituted by Mr. Jones, a Baptist minister. In 1869, G. W. Puckett, another Baptist minister, located with the church. On the first Saturday in March, 1870, the declaration of faith, covenant and rules of decorum were repealed and the Bible alone, without any other written creed, was adopted as the rule of faith and practice. Moderator, G. W. Puckett; clerk, S. C. Moore.

The present house of worship was built in 1870. Elders, D. L. Benson, John Miller; deacons, Michael Goos, Abraham Heape.

Besides Mr. Puckett, the following have served the church: Lysias Heape, J. N. and Isaac Mulkey, John A. Williams, Louis Goos, David Husband, and now J. J. Harris one-fourth time.

Two young men were given to the ministry—Louis Goos and C. W. Marlow.

Tamaroa.

Present membership, 50; value of property, $3,000; Bible-school enrollment, 57.

PIATT COUNTY.

Antioch (Atwood).

Organized 1854, by John C. Mathes; present membership, 50; value of property, $1,500; Bible-school enrollment, 50.

The beginning of this church, located about six miles north of Atwood, was unique and significant. Jacob Mosbarger was born in Indiana in 1818 and settled near the site of this church in 1844. He was an infidel. In 1853 a hurt befell him which put him on his back for eleven months. He read everything within his reach and then asked for the Bible. It was to him a book of surprising interest. He read and read until he decided that he should become a Christian; so he sent for Mr. Mathes, in Indiana, to come and baptize him. He came, preached awhile and immersed Jacob Mosbarger and his wife, who was a member of the "New Light" congregation in that community; Gilbert Green and his wife Martha, David Samuels and his wife Ruth, and Gilford Green. These seven were formed into a church of Christ.

They met in the Gregory log schoolhouse. About 1866 a chapel was built which in later years was remodeled. Jacob Mosbarger was elder of this church for forty-five years. During this period he rarely missed one of its meetings. On Thursday afternoons he and his sons always left the field one hour earlier than usual that they might attend the weekly prayer-meetings two and a half miles distant. He was a great and good man of God.

Elijah Goodwin, Joseph Hostetler and J. C. Mathes served the church for twenty-five years. Then James Connor and J. W. Monser did good work here.

Atwood.

Organized 1879, by John C. Mathes; present membership, 112; value of property, $3,000; Bible-school enrollment, 75.

The following is the church covenant:

We, whose names are subscribed, agree with each other, that we will take the Scriptures of the Old and New Testaments, known as the Bible, as the only rule of faith and practice, and that we will take the name "Christian" as the only divinely authorized name and will be known as the Church of Christ at Atwood, Douglas and Piatt Counties.

The county line passed through the center of the town. The charter members were Peter, W. H. and Hannah Mosbarger; Frank and Angelina Browning; Aaron and Anna Shaw; John C., Ruth J. and J. Mathes; Adam Star, Nancy Painter and Nancy Tryon.

The present elders are Wm. White, J. H. Easton and C. M. Flickinger. The chapel was built in 1883, following a good revival by W. F. Black.

Bement.

Organized 1862; present membership, 120; value of property, $4,000; Bible-school enrollment, 125.

There were seventeen charter members, with William Munroe and J. Ruble, elders, and Samuel Hopkins and Thomas Dunn, deacons. Among those who were especially helpful to the church were G. W. Thompson, pastor in 1878-79, who collected the church records; C. H. Bridges, E. H. Graves and C. E. Evans. The church is active and prosperous with good officers.

In 1913, Mrs. Lillie Bowyer Hedges went from this church as a missionary to Central Africa.

Cerro Gordo.

Organized 1883, by H. F. Tandy; present membership, 74; value of property, $2,000; Bible-school enrollment, 67.

This church has had varied experiences that are common to those in small towns. It has lost by removals until it is feeble

De Land.

Organized 1877, by Samuel Lowe; present membership, 199; value of property, including parsonage, $15,500; Bible-school enrollment, 191.

Min. Charles Rowe first preached the plain gospel in this neighborhood in the early seventies. He was followed by Min. S. K. Hallam, who was pastor at Farmer City. Among the charter members there were Mrs. Martha Bondurant, Thomas E. Bondurant, Mr. and Mrs. Joel Churchill, and Mr. and Mrs. H. G. Porter, all of whose services to the congregation were invaluable.

A union chapel was built, the Protestant Methodists sharing it one-half. During the pastorate of J. M. Francis a new building was erected, which was much enlarged and improved during the pastorate of W. T. McConnell. J. H. Stambaugh is now pastor. The church is active in all good works.

Hammond.

The church here was organized about 1875 by the Macon County Missionary Co-operation, Min. Thomas Cully serving as the evangelist. The ultra-conservatives have long since taken it off the map as an active force for truth and righteousness.

Monticello.

Organized 1911, by Andrew Scott; present membership, 39; value of property, $2,500; Bible school began 1911; present enrollment, 131.

In years past a church was organized here, but it failed. The charter members of the present congregation were Mrs. Hattie Eshelman, Gussie and Mrs. L. M. Baker, Mrs. J. L. Hicks, Mrs. J. Hough, Mrs. Cora Johann, W. M. and Mrs. Hannah Holden, R. M. Wilkens and wife, Mrs. Elizabeth Cramer, Mrs. Lillian Henry, Mrs. J. C. Miller, Pansy Dooling, L. E. Bowyer and wife, J. D. Duffy and Mrs. Hanna T. Anderson.

The unused Baptist chapel was bought.

PIKE COUNTY.

Atlas.

Organized 1908, by J. R. Campbell; present membership, 140; value of property, $4,000; Bible school began 1910; present enrollment, 90.

There were two families in this village who called themselves Christians only. The spiritual life of the place had run low, so they decided to organize a church of Christ. Several successful meetings were held. A house of worship was occupied in 1910.

Leonard Angel was ordained to the ministry.

Barry.

Organized 1842; present membership, 275; value of property, including parsonage, $18,000; Bible-school enrollment, 250.

The earlier records of this church were burned. It has served the community well.

Bee Creek (Pearl).

Organized 1911, by G. W. Williams; present membership, 60; value of property, $500; Bible-school enrollment, 40.

This congregation is five miles south of Pearl. It is feeble.

Chambersburg.

Present membership, 326; value of property, including parsonage, $7,500; Bible-school enrollment, 166.

An old church with a good record. Oscar Dennis is correspondent.

Detroit.

Organized 1882; present membership, 133; value of property, including parsonage, $6,000; Bible-school enrollment, 152.

An old church that has served the community well. Glen Fields, Pittsfield, is the correspondent. It is a fine community.

El Dara.

Organized 1873, by W. H. Crow; present membership, 190; value of property, including parsonage, $3,500; Bible school began 1873; present enrollment, 100.

This church was the first result of a meeting held by Mr. Crow. There were twenty-four charter members. Of these there are now (1913) living: Mrs. Martha Coley, Mrs. Cynthia Worsham, Mrs. Charlotte Pursley, Mrs. Ethel Pursley-Brown, Mrs. Jennie Pursley-Reynolds and Mrs. Mary Hewitt.

The church continues to do good work. J. W. Pearson is the pastor.

Green Pond (Pearl).

Present membership, 100; value of property, $1,500; Bible-school enrollment, 60.

This church dates back to the log house with puncheon floor. It is alive under the half-time preaching of S. R. Lewis. Geo. Graham, R. R. 1, is correspondent.

Griggsville.

Organized 1876, by R. H. Moss; present membership, 116; value of property, $4,000; Bible school began 1876; present enrollment, 75.

The churches of Christ in Pike County had long desired to plant a congregation after the New Testament pattern in this thrifty town. Its New Englandism was slow to accept anything that had its beginning west of Boston.

D. R. Lucas held a great tent meeting shortly after the organization. It proved an expansion, but not a growth. Since then the work has been difficult and slow. A large house was planned, but never finished. The present house was built during the pastorate of J. E. Diehl. J. D. Dabney is the pastor.

Independence (Pittsfield).

Organized 1858, by James Burbridge; present membership, 160; value of property, $2,500; Bible school began 1882; present enrollment, 101.

At first the congregation was called the Highland Church of Christ. In 1882 it took the village name. James Burbridge, Robert Nicholson and Andrew Main led in the movement. The present building was completed in 1866. Most prominent in this work were Joseph Troutner and Robert Nicholson.

The church has had the services of thirty-seven ministers.

Martinsburg.

Present membership, 75; value of property, $2,000; no Bible school.

An old church of good but conservative people.

Milton.

Present membership, 250; value of property, $2,000; Bible-school enrollment, 142.

An old church that has done much good work. It has always had many superior people. C. E. Bolin, Jr., is correspondent.

Nebo.

Organized 1885; present membership, 200; value of property, $5,000; Bible school began 1885; present enrollment, 165.

The first elders were G. W. Burbridge and N. B. Grimes, with T. J. Shaw, James Burbridge and G. N. Creech, deacons. There were about fifty original members. J. J. W. Miller served as pastor for a number of years. J. D. Harpole and T. L. Minier are among the active members.

New Canton.

Present membership, 75; value of property, $2,000; Bible-school enrollment, 67.

A weak church.

New Hartford.

Organized 1851, by Hardin Gooden and David Roberts; present membership, 150; value of property, $3,000; Bible school began 1851; present enrollment, 152.

The first officers were Wm. Shambaugh and W. H. McClintock, elders, and W. R. Mathes, Jonathan Goble and D. K. Harris, deacons. All of them have passed on.

Meetings were held in the schoolhouse till 1856, when a chapel was built, which was used until 1903, when the present building was erected.

From first to last, about six hundred people have held membership here. The church has entirely transformed the life of the community. J. W. Pearson is now pastor.

There is a Y. P. S. C. E. and C. W. B. M. Elmer Attor, Pittsfield, is correspondent.

Old Pearl (Straut).

Present membership, 60.

An old church of conservatives five miles south of Pearl.

Pearl.

Organized 1885, by C. H. Maynard and M. L. Anthony; present membership, 277; value of property, $2,000; Bible-school enrollment, 200.

This congregation was formed in the M. E. chapel. It struggled along till 1894, when its own home was finished.

To this an addition was built in 1906. H. S. Van Dervoort and M. L. Anthony held successful revivals. The church is active in all missionary and benevolent work.

It has given O. C. Bolman to the ministry. Min. W. H. Kerns furnished these facts.

Perry.

Organized 1837, by David Hobbs; present membership, 330; value of property, $4,000.

Near the site of Perry, in the residence of Nicholas Hobbs, this church was organized, with the following among the charter members: Abraham Chenoweth and wife, Gideon Bentley and wife, William Van Pelt and wife, Samuel Van Pelt, Nicholas Hobbs and others. Mr. Hobbs, Mr. Chenoweth and William Van Pelt were the first elders and they taught the people the Word for a few years.

The first house of worship was built in 1839. Four years thereafter, W. H. Brown, the great evangelist, held a series of meetings, and the multitudes attending were so great that one side of the chapel was removed and a shed was added to accommodate the people. This house gave place in 1851 to a more commodious building, and this to the third house in 1880, during the pastorate of John T. Smith.

Two of the early preachers were Wm. Strong and John Curl. The first pastor was David Hobbs.

The helpful families in the church have been the Chenoweths, Dorseys, Brownings and others.

Pittsfield.

Organized 1836, by Mr. Jacob Hodgen; present membership, 600; value of property, $15,000; Bible school began 1855; present enrollment, 37.

The first meetings for public worship that aimed to follow the apostolic pattern were held in the house of Mr. Hodgen. Then they met in various halls in the then village, and next in the courthouse.

In 1841 the organization was completed, with the following charter members: W. H. Strong and wife, Jonas Clark and wife, Jacob Hodgen and wife, Jonathan Piper and wife, John G. Shastid and daughter (later known as Mrs. Cowden), Joseph Sanders and wife, Caroline Barber and Calista Bennet (afterward Mrs. Holmes). The elders were Jacob Hodgen and Jonas Clark; the deacon was Joseph Sanders. Soon after this time many others were added, among whom were the Wyatts, Bennetts, Hendricks, Rubles, Quimbys and Johnsons.

Among the early-day preachers, there were Wm. Gale, W. H. Strong, James Burbridge and Charles Bolin. Mr. Strong became the first regular minister in 1839. In the same year the "State Meeting" was held with this church.

In 1844 a small frame chapel was bought from the Congregationalists. This gave place, in 1853, to a two-story frame building.

The lower story was owned by a stock company and used for school purposes. This house was used for twenty-five years and was filled with many sacred memories.

In 1890, during the pastorate of W. A. Meloan, a modern brick structure was erected. Five years later, two rooms were added during the ministry of Geo. L. Snively.

To the Christian ministry the church has given C. G. Kindred, W. H. Cannon and Clarence Rainwater. The pastorate of H. D. Clark is very tenderly remembered.

The church has many honored names of men who grew large in character and usefulness, among them Hicks, Barber, Hall, Swan, Steers, Binns and Chamberlain.

Pleasant Hill.

Present membership, 231; value of property, $2,500; Bible-school enrollment, 90.

This church is about forty years old and has done good work. W. E. Turnbaugh is correspondent.

Rock Hill (Nebo).

This is six miles west of Pearl.

Rockport.

Organized 1869; present membership, 44; value of property, $3,000; Bible-school enrollment, 69.

F. M. Curver, S. Lomax and J. Ogle formed this church. By removals and deaths it soon failed. It was revived by Min. T. J. Keller and started again with 115 members. Upon the removal of Mr. Keller, another disbanding followed. In 1911 he returned, and through his efforts the congregation again began to work with fourteen members. A modern chapel, with a concrete basement, was built and the outlook is better.

Time (Pittsfield).

Present membership, 15; value of property, $1,000; no Bible school.

This is seven miles southeast of Pittsfield. The community has been seriously handicapped by infidel notions.

POPE COUNTY.

Dixon Springs.

This church is five miles east of Grantsburg, near the road leading from Vienna to Golconda. It is of the ultra-conservative class.

Thirty years ago there was a church at Golconda that aimed to be Christian only, but removals and deaths dissolved it. Within the last decade, Mins. K. A. Williams and R L. Cartwright conducted meetings there. Some turned to the Lord. Again, those who could serve as leaders moved away. Mr. Kimball led the first effort.

Delwood.

Organized 1912, by E. C. Stark; present membership, 12.

Mr. Stark recently located in this community and needed a church home for himself and family. Aided only by the Lord, he went to work to make one. As nearly always in the beginning, the preaching of the primitive gospel raised the ire of sectarians. They demanded a public debate. Mr.

Stark accommodated them. Then they denied him the further use of the public-school house. His teaching was grossly misrepresented, and a boycott was made as effective as could be.

PULASKI COUNTY.

America.

Organized 1889, by I. A. J. Parker; present membership, 55; value of property, $1,500; Bible school began 1889; present enrollment, 30.

Christian Chapel (Pulaski).

Organized 1890, by I. A. J. Parker and S. A. Holt; present membership, 75; value of property, $1,000; Bible school began 1899; present enrollment, 50.

Grand Chain.

Organized 1858; present membership, 73; value of property, $2,500; Bible-school enrollment, 80.

PUTNAM COUNTY.

Putnam.

Organized 1850, by D. R. Howe; present membership, 100; value of property, $2,000; present enrollment, 50.

This place was called Snatchwine until the railroad came. The chapel was built in 1866 and is still in good condition. This little church was fruitful in preachers. First, there was John Wherry, a farmer, a strong, prayerful and true man of God. Next, his son-in-law, J. F. M. Parker, then his two sons J. E. and Lesly Parker, Mr. Malone, Mr. McCurdy, and possibly others. William Drake is correspondent.

RANDOLPH COUNTY.

Mt. Summitt (Leanderville).

Organized 1887, by David Husband; present membership, 40; value of property, $1,000.

In 1844, Herman Husband, with his wife, came from

Somerset, Pa., and settled in the southern part of this county. They were both earnest Christians. The first meeting conducted by a Christian minister was by Wm. Lile in 1855, in the home of Mr. Husband. Next, Lysias Heape preached there. He was a great preacher, and his sermons usually were from two to three hours long. A schoolhouse was built near by during the Civil War and was used for public worship. Dr. Hezekiah Hodges, a country physician, and Wm. Frederick, a miller, preached there. These men, with Mr. Husband, supported themselves and their families by their daily labors while they proclaimed the gospel. In 1886, Min. L. M. Linn and H. D. Banton held a meeting and formed a church at Rockwood. They were followed by Dr. Isaac Mulkey. The church passed away. In 1869, Peter Vogel, of Duquoin, held a meeting and formed a congregation at Mill Creek. J. Buford Allen served as its pastor. It also failed. About 1872, John Friend and John Jones, two young men from the Bible School at Lexington, Ky., held a meeting at Mt. Summit and formed a congregation. It continued only a few years. J. T. Baker gathered a congregation at Baldwin, but it also failed. In 1886, David Husband, a son of Herman Husband, held a seventy-one days' meeting and reorganized the Mt. Summit Church. Then they were turned out of the schoolhouse. The first name on the subscription-list to build a chapel was Albert Conder, a boy five years of age, who pledged a coonskin. The house was built and dedicated free from debt. It still stands and is used in worship.

David Husband and T. J. Holloman were given to the ministry by this county.

RICHLAND COUNTY.

Antioch (Olney).

Present membership, 81; value of property, $590; Bible-school enrollment, 47. Like many others, nothing more could be learned.

Berryville (Parkersburg).

Present membership, 80; value of property, $1,000; Bible-school enrollment, 47.

Calhoun.

Organized 1864, by Erastus Lathrop; present membership, 66; value of property, $700; Bible school began 1864; present enrollment, 58.

The first meetings were held in the schoolhouse and grove till 1867, when the chapel was built.

During this period the preaching was done mainly by Minister Lathrop, an aged and godly man, and Marion Shick. A. J. Brittain and James Hundley were the first elders, with Harry Barney, Henry Dean and Lewis Van Matre, deacons. All these are dead except Mr. Brittain. The church has had high and low tides in its life. It has always maintained worship on the Lord's Day when without a preacher. Has a C. E. society.

John Crawford was given to the ministry.

Noble.

Organized 1884, by H. M. Sanderson, Sr.; present membership, 72; value of property, $2,000; Bible school began 1885; present enrollment, 40.

A good C. E. society. J. W. Whitaker was given to the ministry.

Olney.

Organized 1866, by W. B. F. Treat; present membership, 280; value of property, $3,000; Bible school began 1866; present enrollment, 195.

For ten years there were only a few members, who worshiped in a rented hall. G. W. Morrell, a much-loved resident minister, was the chief servant of the church during this period.

A commodious house of worship was built in 1896, to which additions were made in later years. The church is harmonious and hopeful, with good organized activities.

CHRISTIAN CHURCH, CARBONDALE.
CHRISTIAN CHURCH, ROCKFORD.
MEMORIAL CHRISTIAN CHURCH, ROCK ISLAND.
FIRST CHRISTIAN CHURCH, PARIS.

CHURCHES

Parkersburg.

Present membership, 124; value of property, $1,500; Bible-school enrollment, 150.

A good C. E. society.

Prairie Hall (Claremont).

Present membership, 35; value of property, $1,000.

ROCK ISLAND COUNTY.

Moline.

Organized 1906, by O. W. Lawrence; present membership, 152; value of property, $6,000; Bible school began 1906; present enrollment, 200.

The house of worship was built in 1909. The church was formed and fostered by the State Board of Missions. Mr. W. F. Eastman was the leading spirit.

Rapids City.

Organized 1847; present membership, 10; value of property, $1,000; Bible-school enrollment, 24.

This was once a prosperous coal-mining community, but when the mineral was exhausted the town lost its population. A fine brick building was erected in 1850. Messrs. Steele and Shadle were the first elders. Ministers Lucas and Sherwood were among the first preachers. By removals and death the church went down and the house was closed for many years. The same was true of the M. E. Church. Mrs. C. C. Babcock revived the work in the seventies. Now there is only a small Bible school. Perry Willard is the elder.

Rock Island First.

Organized 1868, by C. W. Sherwood; present membership, 725; value of property, including parsonage, $45,500; Bible-school enrollment, 353.

In March, 1856, a few Disciples met in Rock Island for public worship. These meetings continued for two years, when it was thought best to discontinue them. Through the invitations of P. L. Mitchell and Mrs. Almyria Holt, the State Board of Missions sent Evangelist C. W. Sherwood there in March, 1868. Just twelve years to a day from the last meeting held in 1858 the Disciples again met and the organization was effected. Some of the same wine was used on both occasions, having been faithfully kept by Mrs. Holt, and the same basket, containing a dollar or two in nickels and dimes placed therein ten years before, and cared for by Mrs. Holt, the former treasurer, was used at that time. In April, Minister Sherwood reported to State Sec. Dudley Downs that the mission then numbered thirty persons.

Mr. Mitchell rented the hall over the post-office, which was used as the place of meeting. In 1870 he purchased the old Baptist chapel, remodeled and refitted it, and gave it to the congregation.

During this period 746 people had been received, but there were but 370 when they left the old house, the difference having gone in the usual ways.

In 1895, Mrs. Mary Wadsworth offered to replace the old chapel with a new and commodious structure as a memorial of her beloved father, P. L. Mitchell. The conditions were that the congregation should furnish and care for the building and that its doors should be open to all who would enter, without price. With many tender memories and tearful hearts, the old home was left. The new one was first fully occupied in January, 1896. Since then the church has continually grown in strength and usefulness.

It has given Frank L. Bowen and Fred S. Nichols to the ministry.

Rock Island Second (Thirty-sixth Street and Fifteenth Avenue).

Organized 1913, by J. Fred Jones; present membership, 45; value of property, $2,500; Bible-school enrollment, 110.

For several years a Bible school had been conducted

CHURCHES

under the superintendency of Dr. J. D. Nichols. In the church there were twenty-five charter members.

SALINE COUNTY.

Eldorado.

Organized 1903, by Gilbert Jones; present membership, 100; value of property, $2,000; Bible school began 1903; present enrollment, 75.

Mr. Jones was residing here while serving as evangelist of the Eighth Missionary District. The church grew out of meetings conducted by him in the public-school building. There were thirty-three charter members. The same year a lot was bought and a chapel built thereon. Before leaving it, Mr. Jones placed the church well upon its feet.

J. H. Bramlet, J. A. Davis, Mrs. C. E. Osburn and family, S. S. Karnes, with the Bean and Banks families, contributed much to the progress of this church.

Harrisburg.

Present enrollment, 100; value of property, $2,200; Bible-school enrollment, 108.

Stone Fort.

Organized 1898, by I. A. J. Parker; present membership, 25; no church building; Bible school began 1898; present enrollment, 25.

Miss Flora Parker is clerk.

SANGAMON COUNTY.

Auburn.

Organized 1868; present membership, 70; value of property, $3,000; Bible school began 1868; present enrollment, 40.

One or two efforts to form a church here that should be Christian only had come to naught. But in the spring of 1868 the following named Disciples constituted themselves into such church: A. G. and Mary A. Harvey, John and Laura Piper, George W. and Margaret Hackley, M. G. and

Mary E. Wadsworth, A. M. and Salome T. Black, and Nancy F. Wineman. Meetings for public worship were held on the second floors of store buildings. A good Bible school was held. Preaching for half-time was arranged.

John Piper and G. W. Hackley, two carpenters of limited means, led in the building enterprise. The former gave the lot. On a $600 subscription they began to build a house. When the structure was about ready for the doors and windows, it was wrecked one night by a hurricane. It was the only building in the town that was damaged. The next day the two carpenters began on the work again. After two or three years the building was finished. These facts attest their faith and heroism.

Barclay.

This congregation grew from the Wolf Creek Church, located two miles southeast, which was one of the early churches of the county, and prosperous and influential in its time. As indicating the conceptions of "discipline" then current, the following transcript is made from the original records of the Wolf Creek Church:

Jerry Richerson husband of Alley Richerson.
    The above named person is excommunicated from this congregation for the following disobedience.
    He dissembled from the Brethren, almost altogether. (Forbiden Hebrews 10 & 25). His works were those of the flesh. (Galacians 5 & 22-23.) we are commanded to withdraw ourselves from every person who walks disorderly. Second Thessalonians 3rd & 6, and first Corinthians 5 & 4 says, In the name of our Lord, Jesus Christ, when you are gethered together and my spirit, with the power of our Lord Jesus Christ, to deliver such an one unto Satan for the destruction of the flesh that the Spirit may be saved in the day of the Lord Jesus. This done Feb. 7th, 1841.
                                                            W. M. ELLIS, Clerk.

On the same day and in the same formal manner, Alley Richerson was excommunicated because "she did not meet with Brethern on the first day of the week to commemorate the death and suffering of our Savior, violated even the laws of morality, in her conversation; in short, she refused to live that character and carry out that principle taught in the Christian Religion," etc., etc.

The Wolf Creek Church was organized Sept. 3, 1837, with Adam J. Groves, Rezin H. Constant and Melitus W. Ellis as elders, and Samuel Wilson, James Taylor and William F. Elkin as deacons. Up to Feb. 5, 1849, there had been 282 members.

The old building was burned, so that in 1890 the chapel in Barclay was built and the congregation met there. Removals and the influx of miners decimated the congregation so that only a small Sunday school is kept going.

Berlin.

Organized 1825, by Andrew Scott; present membership, 80; value of property, including parsonage, $1,500; Bible school began 1867; present enrollment, 100.

(See Chap. II.) In its early years the church was served by Andrew Scott, Theophilus Sweet, Judge J. W. Taylor, A. J. Kane and Dr. Mallory. Charles O. Rowe came from Indian Creek and so strengthened the congregation that a frame chapel was built in 1842, one and a half miles northwest of Berlin. Then it was known as the Mt. Zion Christian Church. The elders then were Mr. Scott, William Grant and Henry Ellis. Then Harrison Osborn and Robert Foster served the church for six years. It was here, in 1855, that Mr. Foster, removing his coat in order to immerse thirty converts in Spring Creek before a large assembly, disclosed the fact that he was wearing his "boiled shirt" with the bosom behind. In 1859 a new chapel was built in Berlin, which thereafter became the place of meeting. This town was the boyhood home of War Governor Richard Yates. Early in 1861 he visited the place and made a "war speech" in the Christian chapel that greatly perturbed the congregation. Two of his sisters, Mrs. Martha Scott and Mrs. Elliott, were members here. A four days' public discussion was held in this house during the Civil War. Since then sixteen pastors have served the church.

Buffalo.

Organized 1875, by G. M. Goode and J. B. Allen; present membership, 125; value of property, including parsonage, $4,000; Bible school began 1875.

Two pastors, G. M. Goode, then of Illiopolis, and J. B. Allen, then of Mechanicsburg, conducted a series of meetings in the schoolhouse in the fall of 1874. The work was purely missionary on their part and resulted in eight conversions. The organization of thirty members was made early in the following January. T. J. Underwood, John Jacobs and Samuel Garvey were chosen elders. A church building, costing $2,000, was erected the same year.

Cantrall.

Organized 1820, by Stephen England; present membership, 125; value of property, including parsonage, $3,300; Bible-school enrollment, 29.

(See Chap. II.) In 1819 a band of pioneers made the first settlement north of the Sangamon River, a few miles northwest of Springfield. Stephen England was the leader. He was born in Virginia in 1773. When quite young he was taken to Bath County, Ky. There he married Anna Harper. They became the parents of twelve children. The family moved to Madison County, O., in 1813, and in the fall of 1818 to Madison County, Ill. Mr. England was a Baptist preacher in Kentucky, but was never known as such in Sangamon County. In June, 1819, he first preached to his neighbors who assembled in his home. The next year (May 15) he formed a church with the following members: Stephen and Anna England, Jachoniah and Nancy Langston, Levi and Fanny Cantrall, Mrs. Adelphia Wood, Mrs. Sarah Cantrall and Mrs. Lucy Scott. This was the first church organized in this county. These nine people then signed the following agreement:

We, members of the church of Jesus Christ, being providentially moved from our former place of residence from distant part, and being baptized on the profession of our faith and met at the house of Stephen England, on a branch of Higgins Creek, in order to form a constitution, having first given ourselves to the Lord and then to one another, agree that our constituion shall be on the Holy Scriptures of Old and New Testaments, believing them to be the only rule of faith and practice.

In 1823 a log meeting-house was built one and a half miles southeast of the site of Cantrall, near what is now known as the Britten Cemetery. The cracks were chinked, and greased paper was used for the windows. This primitive temple was built by the volunteer labor of the settlement. In 1846 the second house was built in the village, and the third in 1873. Mr. England continued to serve the church till his death, preaching his last sermon sitting. He solemnized the first marriage in the county in his own home. On one occasion a couple came from Fort Clark, now Peoria, to be married by him.

The congregation was served by about all of the pioneer preachers of central Illinois. It gave John England and R. E. Dunlap to the ministry. Besides these, many great and good men and women have gone forth from this church.

David England served the congregation as an officer over half a century. George T. Sayles as an efficient elder for forty years, and later, John and Robert Grant and John S. Lake have given invaluable service. The names of Carlile, Livi and John T. Canterbury, Hiram Powell, "Uncle Jack" Cline and Carlile Witts are cherished.

The church has always been missionary. It was never affiliated with the Christian Denomination.

Clear Lake (Springfield).

Organized 1865, by A. J. Kane; value of property, $1,500.

The charter members of this church were H. D. Turley and wife, M. D. Whitesides and wife, B. Turley and wife, J. Cartmel and wife, C. Churchill and wife, B. F. Whitesides and wife, Mrs. Black, T. King and Mary F. Turley.

Its house of worship was built the same year. For many

years the church was a strong force in the community for truth and righteousness. Its most active and useful members were H. D. Turley and family. Denominational opposition was active for a long time. It was here that A. J. Kane baptized Dr. W. A. Mallory.

By deaths and removals the church has become feeble. The remnant are dividing between Riverton and Springfield Churches.

Dawson.

Organized 1887; present membership, 30; value of property, $2,500; Bible school began 1887; present enrollment, 30.

The chapel was bought of the Presbyterians. The congregation has lost by removals. The influx of coal miners adds to the difficulties to be met.

Illiopolis.

Organized 1866, by C. P. Short; present membership, 408; value of property, including parsonage, $17,600; Bible school began 1868; present enrollment, 240.

The original members of this church were Mr. and Mrs. A. C. Ford, Mr. and Mrs. W. F. Garvey, Mr. and Mrs. John C. McGuffin, Mr. and Mrs. Thomas Bourland, W. L. Roberts, W. N. Streeter, F. M. Green, Mrs. Mary Ruby, Mrs. Sarah Dake, Archibald Boyd and Mrs. Mary Skeen.

For a long time the meetings were held in the M. E. Church, with only occasional preaching. But this privilege was withdrawn and the meetings were held in the public-school house.

On a cold, misty, windy day in November, 1867, the congregation met in the street in front of a hotel, as the schoolhouse was undergoing repairs. At this meeting there were eight conversions to Christ, and the determination to build was reached. A plain frame house was finished and occupied in August, 1868. This served the church until 1909, when the building was reconstructed, enlarged and modernized during the pastorate of Robert A. Sickles.

The church has always had some admirable men and women. The present pastor is B. H. Sealock.

It has given to the ministry John McGuffin and Charles O. Williams. Possibly H. M. Brooks should be credited here.

Loami.

Organized 1892, by C. S. Medbury; present membership, 150; value of property, $1,500; Bible school began 1892; present enrollment, 75.

The church was organized with sixty-eight charter members. A convenient frame building, costing $3,400, was occupied the following January.

The church has had twelve pastors and has done fine service.

Mechanicsburg.

Organized 1845, by Walter P. Bowles; present membership, 175; value of property, including parsonage, $3,500; Bible-school enrollment, 100.

Mr. Bowles and Dr. Robert Foster preached the apostolic gospel in the early forties in this community. The people met in residences, barns, groves and schoolhouses. There were about thirty charter members. The first officers were Wm. S. Pickrell, John Churchill and John Dawson, elders, with James McRee, Joseph Green and Wileby Churchill, deacons. The house of worship was finished in 1856. Mr. Pickrell gave the lot and made the brick used in the construction. It still stands, having received only modern improvements. The dedication sermon was preached in August, 1856, by A. Campbell. Besides Ministers Bowles and Foster, A. J. Kane, W. H. Brown, W. A. Mallory, A. D. Northcutt, and John Wilson, who was a product of this church, served the congregation in its earlier years.

By 1885 the tide had gone out so that John Garvey, with twenty-four women, constituted the membership. Miss Emma Pickrell, a daughter of Wm. S. Pickrell, during this period superintended the Bible school and administered the Lord's Supper with grace and fidelity.

In 1887, Evangelist W. F. Black conducted a great revival, since which the work has moved forward.

This church is noted for the number of great, noble and helpful people it has produced. The Pickrells, Garveys, Churchills, Elkins and others are enshrined in the hearts of many.

Pleasant Plains.

Organized 1869, by John Wilson; present membership, 102; value of property, including parsonage, $4,000; Bible school began 1870; present enrollment, 78.

W. M. Brown preached the gospel in this community in the early years. There was a congregation of Christians formed four miles east of the town site and worshiped there for several years. The town grew when the railroad was built. The church was formed in a hall. In 1870 the house of worship was built. A period of strife and division ensued, but gradually disappeared.

In the earlier years, A. J. Kane, G. W. Minier, Ministers Osborn, Norton, Burton and John Lemmon served the congregation.

Riverton.

Organized 1876, by Dr. W. A. Mallory; present membership, 90; value of property, $6,000; Bible school began 1876; present enrollment, 50.

Meetings for public worship had been held in school-houses in the neighborhood of Riverton for years. The first name of the town was Howlet. This was the home of Dr. Mallory. He first preached in the village "little brick school-house" in 1874, and then baptized the first converts there— Louise Fox and Georgiana Flagg. In 1876, Evangelist Logan conducted a series of meetings with about fifty converts to Christ. A small building was then rented and regular church work begun. But the M. E. congregation offered more rent and got the use of the room. Then the Christian congregation went to the Good Templars' Hall. Next, the Opera Hall was used. Then Temperance Hall again. Jacob

Bunn, of Springfield, gave the congregation a lot, but they were unable to build a chapel thereon. The death of Dr. Mallory proved a severe loss to the congregation, and they scattered. A few stood true to their convictions of Christian truth and duty; they were Emma King and Mrs. Amanda Steele and her daughter Etta, who is now Mrs. Etta C. White, the church clerk.

During the pastorate of J. B. Briney in Springfield, he preached here occasionally. In 1894, B. F. Flagg and Archie Neal led in an effort to revive the work. Min. J. O. Sutherland conducted a series of meetings and reorganized the church. The next year an effort was made to build a chapel, but it only partially succeeded. But the women held true until the house was finished, furnished, and even modernized and improved. The ashes made by burning the mortgage were turned over to the church clerk to keep.

Riverton is a coal-mining town. Its population is shifting. The congregation is composed of laboring people. The legalized groggeries do their fatal work. It is said that ministers do not wish to reside there.

Rochester.

The first church by this name was formed in Rochester Township, independent of the South Fork congregation, in 1841. A. Richardson and B. Williams were elected elders, with S. West and W. Bashaw, deacons. This congregation was served by Mins. W. M. Brown, A. J. Kane, W. P. Bowles and W. A. Mallory. For years it was strong and a power for good in the community.

Organized 1877, by A. J. Kane; present membership, 90; value of property, including parsonage, $2,500; Bible school began 1877; present enrollment, 50.

With the coming of the railroad, the town grew and the place of meeting was changed. The first elders were W. P. Clark and J. McClure, with W. Windsor and S. Wolford, deacons. The chapel was built in 1877.

A. J. Kane and W. A. Mallory served the church for

several years. There followed a few ministers whose lives did not vindicate their calling, and disturbance ensued. The church, however, has recovered and is doing good work.

Springfield—First.

Organized 1833, by Josephus Hewitt; present membership, 992; value of property, $133,000; Bible school began 1848; present enrollment, 450.

Were this not a great and good church, it would be untrue to its antecedents. Minister Hewitt was a man of superior versatility and eloquence, and passed like a comet through the Springfield sky. In the residence of Mrs. Garner Goodan, located on the lot now occupied by the Chicago & Alton passenger station, the church was constituted in October with the following charter members: Philo and Martha Beers, Joseph and Lucy Bennett, Alfred and Martha Elder, Dr. James R. Gray, Mrs. Garner Goodan, Mrs. Ann McNabb, William Shoup, Reuben Radford and Elisha Tabor. To these were soon added America T. Logan, wife of Judge Stephen T. Logan; Gen. Jas. Adams, Lemuel and Evaline Highy, Mordecai Mobley and wife, George Bennett and wife, Col. E. D. Baker and wife, the Woodworth family and others.

The passing years further brought to and took away from this fellowship Alexander Graham, its second minister; Wm. H. Brown, its third, and great evangelist; William Lavely and Daniel B. Hill; A. J. Kane, whom it added to the Christian ministry; Jonathan R. Saunders; Mary Logan, who became Mrs. Milton Hay; J. W. Taylor, who was an earnest preacher and served four years as county judge; John G., Thomas C. and Wm. F. Elkin; Richard Latham, J. H. Pickrell and his sister, Mrs. H. P. Pasfield, and many others whose names are held in sacred remembrance. In that honorable company, A. J. Kane may easily be counted the leader. The gospel, working through his clear mind and pure heart, gave direction to the thought and character of the church. His wife, Mrs. Caroline Beers Kane, was the last one of the old guard to pass to the church triumphant.

The first house of worship was of brick, completed in 1834, and stood on the north side of Madison Street, between Fourth and Fifth; the second in 1853, at the northeast corner of Sixth and Jefferson; the third in 1882, at the corner of Fifth and Jackson, built during the pastorate of J. Buford Allen; the present splendid edifice was finished in 1912, during the pastorate of F. W. Burnham, and stands on the southeast corner of Sixth and Cook Streets.

This church has now many good people who abound in good works. They supported Mrs. Susie C. Rijnhart in Tibet; paid $2,500 to build a dormitory in Tokyo, Japan, when Miss Rose J. Armbruster went out there, and pays $600 yearly to the Foreign Society. Dr. Paul Wakefield and his wife, who is a daughter of Mrs. Lindsay, went out from this church to China, and E. T. Williams left its pastorate thirty-five years ago for the same field. He is secretary of the American Legation at Peking. The church has entertained the National Missionary Convention twice and the State Convention six times.

The pastors have mostly been noted men. Besides those already named, the list includes the names of D. R. Howe, L. B. Wilkes, T. T. Holton, H. W. Everest, J. M. Atwater, J. Z. Taylor, E. V. Zollars, J. B Briney, A. P. Cobb, J. E. Lynn and F. W. Burnham.

Among the now forceful members are H. C. Latham, Charles P. Kane, B. R. Hieronymus, L. H. Coleman (whose son, C. B. Coleman, entered the ministry and is a teacher in Butler College), Mrs. Catherine Lindsay (for thirty years president of the C. W. B. M. auxiliary), G. A. Hulett, C. E. Brown and Mrs. Mary L. Morrison. Others equally worthy, both among the dead and the living, have their names in God's book of remembrance.

Springfield—Stewart Street.

Organized 1905, by C. C. Morrison; present membership, 550; value of property, $10,000; Bible-school enrollment, 264.

This church was the result of a tent meeting conducted by C. C. Morrison in the southeast part of the city while he was pastor of the First Church.

A good property costing $9,000 was completed and occupied in May, 1906. This congregation was nourished and helped by the other two churches of the city. It does good work. The pastors were R. A. Finnell, H. H. Jenner and Gifford Earnest.

Springfield—West Side.

Organized 1902, by J. E. Lynn; present membership, 674; value of property, $45,000; Bible-school enrollment, 346.

On the 5th of January, 1902, this church was organized, its Bible school formed and its building dedicated. There were ninety-eight charter members and twelve were added that day. The church has grown seven-fold, possesses an admirable spirit and is doing excellent work. In 1910 an addition was made to the building, costing $14,000.

The church has given Chester Gruble to the ministry.

Salisbury.

Organized 1875, by John Lemmon; present membership, 50; value of property, $5,000; Bible school began 1875; present enrollment, 57.

This is an inland village in the northern edge of the county. The subscription paper for building the house had some unique conditions; as, "The house should be used for religious purposes only; that no entertainment that required admission fee at the door should be given there, or any political meeting held there; and when not in use by the owners, the church of Christ, it should be open to all religious proclivities." It has served the community well for a third of a century.

South Fork (Rochester).

Organized 1832, by W. P. Bowles; present membership, 75; value of property, $1,000; Bible-school enrollment, 50.

This congregation is located southwest of Rochester. It

was organized in the residence of Thos. Baker, that stood one and one-half miles west of the town site. The charter members were W. P. Bowles and wife, A. Bowles and wife, Joseph Walter, Elizabeth Bowles, Anna Payne, J. Baker and wife, Thos. Baker and wife, A. Richards and wife, W. Poor and wife, E. Delay, D. Stokes and L. Gooden.

The church now has preaching part of the time.

Williamsville.

Organized 1842; present membership, 200; value of property, including parsonage, $11,800; Bible-school enrollment, 137.

This church was first organized in the home of W. F. Jones. At first it was known as the Fancy Creek Christian Church. There were members scattered from Wolf Creek to Fancy Creek; hence, about thirty of them withdrew from the Wolf Creek congregation and organized at Fancy Creek.

Meetings for public worship were held in the homes of the people until 1856, when the Lake Schoolhouse was secured. In 1858 a house of worship was built in Williamsville, and thus the name of the congregation was changed. In 1852, W. Jones and James Lester were chosen elders, with G. W. Constant and J. Barr as deacons. In 1866, A. J. Kane ordained T. M. Helm and A. W. Elder as elders, and F. A. Merriman, C. Turley and J. Groves as deacons of this congregation.

Minister Kane served the church for several periods as preacher in charge.

J. S. Sweeney held a public discussion here with Minister Davies, of the M. E. Church. By this, many people in the community were helped to a better knowledge of the Scriptures.

This church is composed of excellent people. For many years it has been noted for its liberality and fidelity in all Christian work.

The Richland congregation, twelve miles westward of Springfield, and four miles east of Pleasant Plains, was a country church of the early time. For many years it was the home of John Wycliffe Taylor and his wife, Aunt Sallie.

SCHUYLER COUNTY.

Bader.

Present membership, 90; value of property, $1,000; Bible-school enrollment, 75.

Bethany (Rushville).

Organized 1871, by Alpheus Brown and A. S. Robinson; present membership, 30; value of property, $600; Bible school began 1871; present enrollment, 37.

The church has been served chiefly by the pastors in Rushville.

Browning.

Organized 1894, by L. F. Davis; present membership, 12; value of property, $1,000; Bible school began 1894; present enrollment, 48.

Meetings were held in a hall for a year and a half, when the chapel was built.

Camden.

Organized 1865, by Henry Smithers; present membership, 45; value of property, $1,500; Bible school began 1865; present enrollment, 92.

The church was reorganized in 1871. Besides Mr. Smithers, the following ministers have served the congregation: W. T. Dunkerson, Martin Sharples, Alpheus Brown, Henry Pruett, B. F. Shepard, C. B. Newnan, J. O. Walton, D. E. Hughes, Hervey Scott, C. B. Dabney, Geo. Chandler and W. E. Roberts.

Frederick.

Organized 1890, by D. E. Hughes; present membership, 12; value of property, $1,000; Bible school began 1852; present enrollment, 59.

A Sunday school was begun in 1852. A number of Disciples resided here, for whom J. B. Royal and Orin Dilley preached occasionally. The church was organized at the close of a meeting conducted by Minister Hughes. A chapel was built at once.

As preachers, D. L. Kincaid, W. G. Groves, L. F. Davis, Isaac Beckelhymer, J. W. Knight and Clyde Lyon have served the congregation. Removals and indifference have made the church few and feeble.

Pleasantview.

Value of property, $600; Bible-school enrollment, 60.

Ray.

Organized 1895, by D. E. Hughes; present membership, 75; value of property, $2,000; Bible school began 1890; present enrollment, 84.

Public worship was conducted in the schoolhouse until the chapel was built the next year. Besides Mr. Hughes, H. C. Littleton, G. W. Ford, J. W. Carpenter, G. W. Ross, H. L. Maltman and Evangelist J. D. Williams have served the church.

Rushville.

Organized 1833, by Barton W. Stone; present membership, 225; value of property, $5,000; Bible-school enrollment, 200.

The first preaching in Schuyler County by a Christian minister was about 1829 by James Hughes. He was on his way home from Ohio to Missouri and stopped at the home of Benjamin Chadsey, one of the prominent early settlers. This was two and a half miles northeast of Rushville. The preaching of Mr. Hughes was eagerly welcomed by the scattered Christians in the community.

In 1832, Barton W. Stone came up from Jacksonville and held a series of meetings in the old log courthouse in Rushville. His preaching awakened great interest in the community. In 1833, James W. Davis and James Urbank came from Kentucky to continue the work. The organization of the church was perfected December 29.

The first house of worship was built in 1834 and the present one in 1874. The congregation has passed through high tides and low tides of prosperity and spiritual life.

SCOTT COUNTY.

Exeter.

Organized by David Hobbs; present membership, 88; value of property, $1,500; Bible-school enrollment, 78.

Glasgow.

Present membership, 45; value of property, $1,000; Bible-school enrollment, 40.

Manchester.

Organized 1864; present membership, 68; value of property, $1,500; Bible-school enrollment, 45.

Two of the charter members were James F. Curtis, who was baptized by Mr. Campbell in 1832, and Mrs. Eliza Billings, who is the sole survivor. J. R. Belvins is the clerk.

Winchester.

Organized 1832; present membership, 300; value of property, $7,000; Bible-school enrollment, 140.

Early in the thirties a few families of Disciples came to Winchester. They soon found one another. As a result, they instituted regular weekly meetings in their homes for public worship. They "broke bread," read the Scriptures and exhorted one another. Among them there were Levi Harlan and Theophilus Sweet, to whom, doubtless, belongs the honor of this beginning. In 1838 this church had 100 members. In the earlier years a lot was secured in the southeast part of town and a substantial brick house built thereon. This served the congregation until 1855, when it was sold to the Roman Catholics. A more central place was secured and a

CHURCHES 385

two-story brick structure was erected and furnished in 1866, during the pastorate of T. J. Marlow. A modern edifice was completed in 1913.

Among the early preachers here there were William Strong, John T. Jones, D. P. Henderson, W. H. Brown, J. S. Patton, W. W. Happy, John Atkinson; then David Hobbs, N. S. Bastian, E. P. Belsher, J. H. Coats, J. S. Sweeney and others.

The church has the usual auxiliaries and is in a healthy, growing condition.

SHELBY COUNTY.

About 1837, Min. B. W. Henry organized a congregation near his home on the west side of Okaw Township. Two or three years later a log house was built for the double purpose of school and church, and was so occupied for about twenty years. Among the pioneer preachers who worked there were B. W. Henry, Tobias Grider, Fleming, Goodman, Storm, Mulkey and Sconce. In the early fifties it was active in co-operative missionary work. The changing tides of human life later on carried it away.

In 1871, Min. P. P. Warren organized the Bethany congregation in Windsor Township with fifty-three members. From 1860 preaching had been kept up at this point by Ministers Warren and Tobias Grider, under the direction of the Sand Creek Church, and the converts thus made were received by this congregation until the new organization. Minister Warren served Bethany once per month for more than twenty years. The chapel was built in 1871. The congregation gave A. J. Nance to the ministry. It died by conservatism.

The Green Creek congregation was formed in Big Spring Township about 1850 and did good service. In 1855, Evangelist Thomas Goodman organized the Mount Pleasant congregation in Prairie Township, and this absorbed the first named. The meetings were held first in the Baker, and next in the Forrest, Schoolhouse.

13

James Carr preached for this congregation for thirty years, and died there in 1880 in a good old age, loved and respected by all. Others who preached here were Tobias Grider, Wm. Colson, A. A. Lovins, J. I. Seward, J. M. Morgan and Isaac McCash.

In January, 1880, Min. L. M. Linn held a meeting of days in Shelby Township and formed the Oak Grove congregation with thirty-six members. A union chapel, part Unitarian, was built. The spiritual life is feeble.

In 1873, Tobias Grider formed the Union congregation in the Hidden Schoolhouse, on the line of Okaw and Shelby Townships, with fourteen members. It died at the close of thirty years.

Min. B. R. Gilbert organized the Zion congregation on the west side of Todd's Point Township in 1878 with thirty-two members. The same year a chapel costing $1,200 was built. The church met regularly for worship on the Lord's Days and maintained a mid-week prayer-meeting. It died of conservatism.

In April, 1860, Min. John Sconce formed a congregation in a log schoolhouse near the northeast corner of Todd's Point Township with fifty-eight members, which was known as Welborn Creek Church. A chapel costing $1,200 was built in 1871, located three miles north of the site of Findley. The growth of towns on railways reduced its strength, but its dissolution was hastened by a contention of two of its men over a stalk-field. It disbanded about 1900. The house still stands there. Its remnants went to Findley and Bethany Churches.

The Pleak congregation, six miles southeast of Moweaqua, was formed with twenty members by Min. J. D. Morgan in 1880. A substantial chapel was built in a few years, but the title never passed to the congregation. A political quarrel divided the membership and killed the church. F. M. Pleak, the leader of this work, died in 1902.

Many of these were sincere but mistaken efforts to justly apply the great principles of the gospel.

Ash Grove (Windsor).

Organized 1832, by Jackson Storm; present membership, 400; value of property, $4,000; Bible-school enrollment, 80. This location is four miles southeast of Windsor. For many years it was known as the Cochran's Grove Church. It was organized in a log residence. Some time later a log chapel was built, which was used till 1858. Then a large frame building was erected, which in turn gave place to the present building in 1887. The site of these four buildings has changed but little. The lot, with the adjacent cemetery ground, was given to the congregation by Greenup Storm, one of the strong and godly pioneers. The thirteen charter members were: John Storm, Sr., and wife, Wm. Duggar and wife, Wm. Bennett and wife, Daniel Green and wife, John Storm, Jr., and wife, Joseph Dickerson and wife, and Stella Good. The church has had a long, useful and honorable life. It was the mother of Windsor, Gays and Lower Ash Grove, a conservative society. W. B. Bennett served the congregation fifty years as an elder. Most of the pioneers of that section preached there. H. H. Harrell served the church ten years. It is now in sympathy with world-wide missions. It has given to the ministry James Brady, W. R. Storm and Homer Storm.

Brunswick.

Organized 1860, by B. W. Henry; value of property, $2,000; Bible school began 1869; present enrollment, 57.

For many years this was known as the Antioch Church of Christ. The charter members were John, Sr., Sarah S., James and Mary, Andy and Elizabeth Barrickman; Martha Christman, Rebecca Galyer, W. H. Jackson, Leah James; William, Isaac, Sr., Samuel, Nathan, Eleanor, Lydia and Ellen Killam; E. J. and James Miller, Jacob Morehouse, Hiram and Rachel Pogue, Henry and Isabel Prichard, H. C. and Margaret Robertson, John and Eliza Smith, and C. L. Scott.

When the village of Brunswick grew up about the church its name was changed to harmonize therewith. The present chapel was built in 1868. An organ was first used in 1910

Cowden.

Organized 1899, by W. Bedell; present membership, 120; value of property, $2,100; Bible school began 1899; present enrollment, 145.

This church started right and has grown steadily in usefulness. It is well organized. The active members include the McMillen, Mason, Reynolds, Ballenbaugh, Prater and Jewett families.

Findlay.

Organized 1906, by H. E. Monser; present membership, 90; value of property, $6,000; Bible school began 1906; present enrollment, 94.

Mr. and Mrs. A. H. Terry moved from Shelbyville to Findley in 1903. The Christian Church there was so conservative that it was doing little. In 1905, through the influence of Mrs. Terry, an auxiliary to the C. W. B. M. of twelve members was formed. A meeting by Mr. Monser in November, 1906, resulted in the organization of a church of eighty-eight members. It is active and aggressive. A brick building was finished and occupied in January, 1909. Miss Olive was set apart to the ministry by this church. There is also a conservative church here.

Henton.

Organized 1850, by B. W. Henry; present membership, 127; value of property, $4,500; Bible-school enrollment, 100.

Mr. Henry and others preached for several years in this community before 1850. There were twenty-five charter members in the Prairie Bird Church. This beautiful name gave way to Henton when the railroad came and the village started. The first elders were Lindsay McMorris, Chatter

Kelly and Elijah Waggoner, and the first deacons, J. T. and W. M. Smith. The first house was built in 1857.

J. O. Henry was here ordained to the ministry.

Herrick.

Present membership, 25; value of property, $2,000; Bible-school enrollment, 84.

Mode.

Organized 1880, by L. M. Linn; value of property, $500.

Evangelist Linn, working under the auspices of the County Co-operation, held a meeting of weeks in the winter of this year and formed the church with fifty-one members. A union chapel was built shortly thereafter. Now there is only a small Bible school.

Moweaqua.

Organized 1896, by M. Ingles; present membership, 258; value of property, $6,000; Bible school began 1896; present enrollment, 119.

William Richhart led in the formation of this church. On his invitation the first sermons by a Christian preacher were delivered by Minister Doty. There were forty-two charter members.

A good church building was soon put up. A. R. Spicer was the first pastor.

New Liberty (Windsor).

Organized 1871.

About 1840 a log chapel was built in the northeast corner of Windsor Township. It had two chimneys and a dirt floor.

Ministers Grider, Henry, Storm, Fleming and Goodman preached there. The resident members formed part of the Sand Creek Church till 1871, when a separate congregation, called Wolf Creek, was formed. The log house had then disappeared, for meetings were held in the Dodson and Baker Schoolhouses till 1874, when a chapel was built. The name was then changed to New Liberty. It gave Jesse Baugher to the ministry. About 1880, under the lead of P. P. Warren, it became ultra-conservative.

Rocky Branch (Tower Hill).

Organized 1850, by B. W. Henry.

Meetings were held in Rose Township by Ministers Henry, M. R. Chew and Edward Evy about this date in residences, in Black Log Schoolhouse and in a grove. One of these, conducted by Mr. Henry, resulted in fifty conversions. The consequent congregation passed through many experiences, prosperous and adverse. Many times all efforts ceased. A neat chapel was built. Now no meetings of any kind are held.

Sand Creek (Windsor).

Organized 1834, by John Storm; present membership, 25.

This place is three and a half miles northwest of Windsor. The eleven charter members were Benjamin Weeks and wife, Joseph Baker, wife and son, Ashley Baker and wife, Louis Ledbetter and wife, Sarah Bougher and Rachel Wallace. Min. Tobias Grider gave one acre of land for the building-site. The first house was of logs, built in 1834; the second, a frame, built in 1857, and the third, a brick, built in 1874.

For fifty years this congregation was prosperous and useful. It enrolled from twelve hundred to fifteen hundred members, and gave to the ministry Isaac Miller, Nathan Rice, P. P. Warren, A. A. Loomis and L. P. Phillips. In the log chapel in 1850 a missionary co-operation, including Shelby, Moultrie and Macon Counties, was formed. Peace and prosperity continued till 1889, when Min. Daniel Sommer came and began an aggressive opposition to the use of instrumental music in public worship and other "innovations." This church had never used an organ and had no thought of introducing one until the preaching of Mr. Sommer created a desire and a demand for its introduction.

This led to a division in 1904 and to a suit at law for the property. This was decided by the State Supreme Court at the October term, 1905, in favor of the conservatives, they being the majority. It was here that the pigmy and disloyal "Address and Declaration" was issued in 1889 (see Chap. VIII.). By that act this church wrote "Ichabod" in large letters upon its record.

Those members who protested against these puerile proceedings have since then conducted public worship and work in a near-by schoolhouse. They have been faithful and blessed of God.

Shelbyville.

Organized 1831, by Bushrod W. Henry; present membership, 500; value of property, $7,500; Bible school began 1831; present enrollment, 140.

This church was constituted as the "First Baptist Church of Christ in Shelbyville." Mr. Henry's sermons reflected his growing knowledge of the Scriptures and called out the opposition of his conservative Baptist brethren. Their doctrinal differences widened so that Mr. Henry and his friends were excluded from the Baptist fellowship. By 1834 they had discarded the name Baptist, and by 1836 had fully organized "the church of God in Christ in Shelbyville." The first elders were B. W. Henry and J. J. Page. The former giving much of his time to evangelizing, the care of the church devolved chiefly upon Mr. Page. For thirty-five years he was a most faithful elder in every way as set forth in the New Testament. Reuben and Martha Wright, Mrs. Enfield Tacket and Mrs. Polly Smith were also among the first members whose devotion to the church was long known. Mr. Henry continued his ministry with the congregation as he was able. About 1845 the first church house was built. It stood diagonally across the street from the present building. This was used until about 1878, when the brick building still in use was finished. In 1849, A. D. Northcutt served the church, which prospered under his ministry.

About the same time, Min. W. H. Brown held a public debate in the Christian chapel. General Thornton served as presiding moderator. The discussion resulted in greatly strengthening the church of Christ.

Some of the pastors who have served the church were N. S. Bastian, Dr. A. L. Kellar, Theo. Brooks, J. G. Waggoner, and now W. G. McColley. It gave O. P. Wright to the ministry.

J. Fred Miller, Wm. Chew, W. F. Turney and J. W. Loyd are held in grateful remembrance. J. D. Miller and W. C. Kelly have been active and efficient members for the past twenty years.

The church is well organized, with an average aggressiveness.

Stewardson.

Present membership, 320; value of property, $2,000; Bible-school enrollment, 142.

Tower Hill.

Organized by W. H. Boles; present membership, 50; Bible-school enrollment, 46.

Windsor.

Organized 1857; present membership, 273; value of property, including parsonage, $3,500; Bible school began 1860; present enrollment, 110.

It is not known who of the pioneers planted this congregation or the exact year. It was served in its earlier period by those ministers who laid the foundations of the Restoration movement in that section. Later, there were Z. T. Sweeney, Thomas Edwards and J. H. Hite. Many protracted meetings were held by Ellis Zound, Isaac Mulkey, W. F. Black, Wm. Patterson, James Connor and E. J. Hart. A. D. Fillmore, the sweet singer, led the church. The chapel was built in 1859. In the later seventies, Dr. Jesse Yoar left by his will $1,000 to the congregation to be permanently invested for its benefit.

J. H. Price and Thomas Henry were elders and strong men in the community. Mr. Henry served in the House of the General Assembly of Illinois. J. D. Bruce, a deacon, is the sole surviving charter member.

ST. CLAIR COUNTY.

East St. Louis First.

Organized 1890, by J. T. Boone; present membership, 445; value of property, $34,000; Bible school began 1890; present enrollment, 149.

This church had what most people call a feeble beginning. There were eight women, residents here at the time, who had been Disciples at various other places. These united their heads and their hearts to have a church home that should be Christian only. A third-floor hall was secured and Minister Boone, then a resident of St. Louis, Mo., conducted a two weeks' meeting with thirty additions. Then the thirty-eight members organized and moved to another hall. Next, meetings were held in a schoolhouse until the growing congregation moved into their chapel at Seventh Street and St. Clair Avenue. There they met for nineteen years. In 1910 they moved into the beautiful modern edifice at the corner of Washington Place and Belmont Avenue.

The church has had fifteen pastors, the present minister being Meade E. Dutt.

There is a strong Papal following in this city, yet this church of Christ has moved steadily forward. Many things have happened in their Christian service which have caused their hearts to rejoice. Their prospects are bright.

East St. Louis—Lansdowne.

Organized 1905, by C. O. Reynard; present membership, 120; value of property, $4,000; Bible school began 1905; present enrollment, 162.

This was the second church in St. Clair County that aimed to be Christian only. There were thirty-two charter members. The first meetings were held in a portable school building, the use of which was secured for this purpose by Mr. D. Walter Potts, city superintendent of the public schools. A chapel was built in a short time.

Mrs. Agnes Potts, whose father was a minister and who is the oldest member of the congregation, had much to do with its organization. The first elders were J. H., A. A. and D. Walter Potts. There are many "Potts" in this church, but the material is good.

STARK COUNTY.

La Fayette.

Organized 1847, by John E. Murphy; present membership, 62; value of property, including parsonage, $5,000; Bible school began 1848; present enrollment, 46.

The charter members were Charles, Tyrus, Laura, Ezra and Emiline Himes; Lewis H., David T. and Polly M. Fitch; Henry Hardman, Hyram Nance, William and Maria Lake, and Melia Dunbar. The first elders were Charles Himes and John Bryan; the first deacons, Lewis H. Fitch and William Lake.

Fifteen members were added Aug. 21, 1848. There were nearly one hundred on the roll at the end of 1858.

The earlier ministers, besides Mr. Murphy, were M. P. King, F. M. Dodge and Messrs. Woodruff, Sick, Yearnshaw, Davenport, Arne and Adams.

The first money paid for missions was $7.40. It was collected and paid over by the church treasurer, W. Lovely, to the State Missionary Society, meeting at Walnut Grove, Sept. 5, 1851.

These data are taken from the first records of the church by Irvin Ingles.

Toulon.

Organized 1849, by David McCance; present membership, 82; value of property, $5,000; Bible school began 1855; present enrollment, 65.

The organization was made in the old courthouse, with the following charter members: David McCance and wife, Edward Wilson and wife, Elijah McClennahan and wife, Henry Sweet and James Boles. The congregation grew, so that meetings were held next in the schoolhouse, then in Temperance Hall, which was the place of meeting till 1855, when the present church building was erected.

Robert H. Newton and Clyde Lyon have gone from this church into the ministry.

There was a church also at Wyoming, but it was short-lived.

A church with six members was formed at the residence of Ephraim Barth, in the south part of this county, in 1846.

STEPHENSON COUNTY.

Freeport.

Organized 1906, by O. F. Jordon and J. M. Taylor; present membership, 60; value of property, $4,000; Bible school began 1906; present enrollment, 60.

This work has been difficult and slow, but under the pastorate of E. T. Cornelius it has advanced to hopefulness. The meetings have been held in the courthouse, Y. M. C. A. building and, for a considerable time, in the Masonic Temple, but a chapel in the near future is a possibility.

A small congregation was formed in this county in 1840 by Henry Howe.

About 1847, Dr. W. P. Naramore formed a church of Christ about two miles west of Oneca, where he then resided. It was known as the Mt. Pleasant Church and still lives.

TAZEWELL COUNTY.

The first sermon preached in Little Mackinaw Township was in the home of Thomas F. Railsback by Min. John Oatman in 1831. This residence was four miles south and one-quarter mile east of Mackinaw town. In Mr. Railsback's residence the Little Mackinaw Church was organized in

1833, but its local name was applied later. The original members were Thomas F. Railsback and wife Louisa, A. B. Davis, Catherine Allensworth, and Benjamin Herndon and wife Nancy. For many years they met in a log schoolhouse one-half mile south—at the Gaines Cemetery. Here rests the sacred dust of these six godly pioneers.

Min. James A. Lindsey was the first preacher in charge. Others who followed him were Wm. Ryan, Wm. Davenport, H. D. Palmer and G. W. Minier. From 1853-63 their meetings were held one mile north in the Four Corners Schoolhouse. In 1863 a church building was erected two miles eastward. This place is three miles north of Minier. For nearly forty years at this place this church did admirable work. For decades the Little Mackinaw Church was well and widely known. New towns grew as the railways were built. Out of this hive there went swarms of Disciples, to Mackinaw town, to Minier, to Concord and to Lilly congregations. And so the dear mother died, and in 1893 her house was sold. The records are with W. L. Dickson, Minier, Ill.

The Antioch Church was located six miles south of Fremont and one and a half miles east of the village of Dillon. It was organized in the middle thirties and was the first church in that township. Those forming it were Jesse Fisher, Jerome Waltmire, William Dillon, Abner Rulon and others. The first building was erected in 1838 and the present one in 1858 at a cost of $600. It is beautifully located and is yet in good condition. The congregation has disappeared. Its records are with William Bennett, Delavan, Ill.

Tennessee Point Church was about three miles northeast of Fremont. It consisted of only five families; namely, the Front, Speece, I. Stout, Shaw and A. N. Page. Their meetings were held in a schoolhouse. It disappeared with the forming of the Concord congregation.

The Hieronymus Grove Church house, located four miles northeast of Armington, was built, at a cost of $3,000, in 1869 by Enoch Hieronymus, deceased. The congregation organized in October. It did good work for forty years and then disbanded, its members uniting with other near-by churches of Christ. All of its original members have passed except B. R. Hieronymus, of Springfield, and Wm. Darnell, of Stanford.

For a little while there was a small congregation in Fremont, but they never owned a chapel. Wm. Gaither, Stephen Stout and Wm. Johnson and wife were members there. They united with the Antioch congregation.

At the village of Boynton a church grew and served for many years, but finally failed by reason of removals and the formation of congregations in other towns. The Armington people are giving the Boynton community some attention.

An earnest effort was made to establish a church after the primitive order at Delavan. Mr. Jerome Waltmire, a sincere and devoted Disciple, moved there to reside and led in the effort. Through his work a good church house was built and a congregation gathered. Delavan had a large percentage of people of New England blood and traditions and they were mostly satisfied with the denominational phases of faith and life. The effort failed and the property was sold.

Concord (Minier).

Organized 1870, by George Campbell; present membership, 90; value of property, $1,000; Bible school began 1870; present enrollment, 107.

A Sunday school was formed in the Black Jack Schoolhouse about 1863, about eight miles northwest of the site of Minier. Beginning in 1867, Mr. Slater taught the school there for two years and often preached on Sundays. He made a number of converts. Others who preached there in the early days were James Robeson, James and Ira Mitchell, Bailey Chaplin, Caleb Hainline, Eli Fisher, G. W. Minier and Isaac and Elijah Stout. These ministers received little or no remuneration for this work. Those meetings were attended by multitudes and many became Christians. There were forty or more charter members, thirty-one of whom brought letters from the Little Mackinaw Church. It was about this time also that the congregation at Tennessee Point disbanded and some of those members came here.

Under the leadership of Min. Isaac Stout a church house was completed in 1872. Most of the materials, except the heavy timbers and walnut seating, were hauled from Peoria. Samuel Nutty gave one acre and a half of ground for the site. An addition was made to this building in 1894. Mr. Campbell conducted the worship when the house was first occupied and gave to the place and congregation the local designation "Concord," and he prayed that it might never become a discord.

Since then, preaching has been maintained half-time, but rarely has the observance of the Lord's Supper been omitted. A good Bible school and C. W. B. M. are maintained.

Deer Creek.

Organized 1906, by A. L. Huff; present membership, 91; value of property, $1,400; Bible school began 1896; present enrollment, 50.

This church came of the conscious need of divine truth by a number of Disciples. The charter members were Mr. and Mrs. D. C. Slyter, Mr. and Mrs. W. H. Peifer, Mr. and Mrs. J. M. Davis, Mr. and Mrs. W. S. Foster, Mr. and Mrs. Albert Wagner, Mr. and Mrs. H. E. Graham, Dr. C. M. Chapman, Miss Ruth Chapman, Wilford Miller, Isaac Malone, Albert Foster, John P. Hall, William Therolis, Mrs. Nancy S. Bogardus, Mrs. Fanny M. Stumbaugh, Mrs. Seville M. Mooberry, Mrs. Sadie Ammerman, Mrs. Alice Ransburg, Misses Grace and Cora Ransburg, and Miss Adda Ten Eyck.

The meetings were held in a public hall. Then the Presbyterian chapel was bought and improved.

Lilly.

Organized 1837, by James A. Lindsey; present membership, 79; value of property, $1,500; Bible school began 1871; present enrollment, 90.

In 1859 a number of members peaceably withdrew from the Mackinaw Church and formed a congregation at the Mt. Pleasant Schoolhouse, the former meeting-place. It was one mile south of Lilly, which grew after the building of the railway. In 1871 the present chapel was erected there, which has since been the meeting-place. The church has never been strong, but has done good work.

William Lindsay, one of its charter members, devoted his best energies to this church as an elder for more than forty years.

Mackinaw.

Organized 1837, by James A. Lindsey; present membership, 509; value of property, $20,000; Bible-school enrollment, 417.

Min. James A. Lindsey came from Kentucky to Illinois in 1824 and settled in the eastern part of Mackinaw Township, Tazewell County. It is probable that meetings for public worship were held in his residence. A meeting was held in what in later years was known as Mt. Pleasant Schoolhouse, and from the record made at the time the following is copied:

On Saturday, the last day of September, 1837, a meeting was held at a schoolhouse. Elder Jas. A. Lindsey addressed the meeting, urging the propriety of organizing a church in our immediate neighborhood on purely gospel principles. Before adjourning, the Disciples present mutually agreed to procure letters of commendation from the churches where they held membership and at a future meeting effect such an organization. Accordingly, on the following Thursday, the 5th day of October, a meeting was held at the residence of Michael Hittle, and the church was fully organized. The following preamble was presented:

"We whose names are herewith subscribed, all having been immersed on a profession of our faith in Jesus Christ the Son of God, do agree to associate and co-operate as a church of Christ, to be known by the name of the 'Congregation of Disciples of Christ,' and meet for worship in Tazewell County, Ill., Township 24 North, Range 2 West of the 3rd. Principal Meridian; taking the Scriptures of the Old and New Testament for the articles of our faith, and the law of our Lord as exhibited in the New Testament and the precepts taught by our Lord and his Apostles, together with the examples of the churches set in order by them, as the law and rule of discipline. May the Lord help us to know and do his will."

The foregoing was then signed by the following persons: James A. Lindsey, Jane Lindsey, Michael Hittle, Mary Hittle, R. F. Houston, E. I. L. Houston, Nehemiah Hill, Emely Hill, Jas. Lindsey, Mariah Lindsey, Jesse E. Jackson, Catharine Jackson, Elijah Sargent, Elinor R. Miller, Elizabeth Lindsey, Delila Lindsey, Wm. Lindsey, Alfred Lindsey, John Lindsey, David Lindsey, Samuel Flesher, Geo. Hittle, Nancy Hittle: twenty-three.

R. F. Houston was chosen clerk, Geo. Hittle and Samuel Flesher were chosen elders, and Michael Hittle and Nehemiah Hill as deacons. James A. Lindsey, being at that time an efficient preacher with extended acquaintance, was chosen as evangelist and authorized to administer all the ordinances and perform all the duties usually recognized as belonging to a preacher of the gospel. It was unanimously agreed on that occasion to meet on the first day of every week for worship if not providentially prevented, or by general agreement to meet with congregations at near-by neighborhoods. Alexander B. Davis, clerk of Little Mackinaw Christian Church, was clerk of this meeting.

Such was the beginning of this church, at first called Mt. Zion, that has come steadily on its way through seventy-six years. Ordinarily no records were kept of meetings in those early times. The names of those coming into the church were added and cases of discipline were noted. Names and dates of additions to this church indicate a regular growth, mostly by primary obedience.

The following deserved tribute has been paid to the memory of three of those pioneers:

Samuel Flesher, though not a preacher, was well read in the Bible, of unblemished character, fluent in exhortation and delighted in the public service of the church. The church sustained a serious loss when in May, 1841, he was accidentally drowned.

George Hittle, though his German brogue somewhat hindered his speech, by his earnest zeal, his deep piety, his thorough knowledge of the Bible and withal his cheerful, social manner with everybody, had a power not often excelled as a leader. Often as he stood before the little gatherings, telling of the supreme love of the Saviour, his deep-feeling exhortation had a joyous effect on all that heard. He died in 1842.

Michael Hittle was active as a deacon for more than twenty years.

He held steadfastly to the supremacy of the gospel and helped in its furtherance, particularly in charity for the needy. He died in 1888.

In the earlier years the congregation enjoyed the preaching of Ministers Lindsey, Davenport, Palmer, Jones, Peeler, Robeson, Major and Minier. In 1846-47, William Davenport rode horseback from Eureka once a month and preached three sermons each time to the church. He was paid $2.50 per trip.

Up to 1848 the congregation had no settled place for its meetings. In that year they decided to hold the regular meetings in the village of Mackinaw, and soon built a church house there, which was the first in the township. This house was first seated with six-inch boards laid on some kind of supports. On these the people sat the day the house was first used and listened attentively to Henry D. Palmer preach a sermon three hours long. The second house was built in 1875.

This church finds much satisfaction in the fact that it has always been missionary in sentiment and practice. In 1850, James A. Lindsey went as a delegate to Shelbyville when the State Missionary Society was organized. He was made chairman of that meeting and counted it one of the supreme joys of his long and faithful ministry. The church record shows that $10 was contributed to State Missions Aug. 31, 1851.

The church holds in sacred and honored memory the names of not a few men and women; among them are Solomon Puterbaugh, H. J. Puterbaugh and wife, and George Patterson.

About three thousand people have been members of this church.

It has given to the ministry John Lindsey and Roscoe Hill.

Malone (Green Valley).

Organized 1866; present membership, 20; value of property, $1,200; Bible school began 1866; present enrollment, 52.

This church is six miles southwest of Green Valley. The

first records were lost. A reorganization was made in 1879, when the location was changed four miles and a new house built. Like all country churches, the numbers are continually reduced by removals. The Bible school is Evergreen. There have been thirty-seven preachers who have served here.

Minier.

Organized 1874, by charter members; present membership, 222; value of property, $12,000; Bible school began 1874; present enrollment, 150.

The charter members were the following: James E. and Ann P. Railsback, N. P. and Catherine Williams, Louisa Railsback, Mary Elliff, T. L. Minier, Jennie Edmiston, John F. Quigg, Elizabeth and Betsy Johnson, Lou Ireland, Lou McDowell, Carrie Baker, Sophia, Rodney J. and Mary Mitchell. All of these were former members of the church of Christ at Little Mackinaw. The first officers were R. J. Mitchell and J. B. Chaplin, elders, and B. N. Ewing, J. W. Chidister and L. L. Munn, deacons.

The church has had some superior people, one of whom was Rodney J. Mitchell.

Pekin.

Organized 1876, by W. F. Richardson; present membership, 250; value of property, $5,000; Bible school began 1876; present enrollment, 310.

This church was organized by the Tazewell County Christian Co-operation. It was the first result of a month's series of meetings led by Mr. Richardson. There were thirty-two charter members. Of these, Mrs. Emma Inman is the only faithful member remaining here now. The Co-operation rented the Universalist chapel for one year. The management of the congregation was given temporarily to a business committee. Later Joseph Hiett, B. R. Hieronymus and J. E. Jewett were chosen elders, and J. S. Salee, William Hiett, James Newkirk and Jobe Hedges, deacons. During the pastorate of T. T. Holton, a lot was purchased for $500 and a chapel, costing $3,000, was built thereon. Later, it was enlarged and improved.

During the first years the pulpit was supplied by Profs. B. J. Radford, H. W. Everest and others. The first pastor did the church much harm.

The records made commendable mention of Mrs. Frances E. Van Etta for her wise and efficient services.

The church has all helpful auxiliaries.

Washington.

Organized 1834, by Richard B. McCorcle; present membership, 110; value of property, $3,700; Bible-school enrollment, 70.

The following were the charter members: Richard B. McCorcle, Isabel McCorcle, James and Mary McClure, John and Martha Johnson, William Holland, Sr., Peter and Catherine Scott, Dr. and Mrs. Goodwin, Ruful and Catherine North, Eliza McCorcle, Levi and Mrs. Moulton, Josiah and Mrs. Yager.

This church has had its ups and downs. Many of its members have gone West to found homes in the newer country. They are faithful Christians in Iowa, Kansas, Nebraska and other States. At Ulysses, Neb., twenty-six of the charter members were from the Washington Church. It is not now as strong as formerly.

The first building was erected in 1850, a brick which is now used by the German Lutheran congregation. More room being needed, the second house was finished and occupied in 1869. This building was burned the following February. The third house was completed and occupied in August, 1870. This was burned in October, 1876. The fourth and present building was first used in July, 1877.

The church has given to the ministry three brothers—B. W., R. H. and J. B. Johnson, sons of John and Martha Johnson—and James Kirk.

The church still has its face toward the future and is purposeful.

UNION COUNTY.

Anna.

Present membership, 115; value of property, $5,000; Bible-school enrollment, 108.

Toledo (Cobden).

Present membership, 50; value of property, $1,000; Bible-school enrollment, 36.

This is one of the oldest churches in the State. Converts were immersed here as early as 1836. This is the home of. Min. C. S. Towne, now past eighty, an able writer and faithful preacher. Robert Brown, R. R. No. 1, is the correspondent.

VERMILION COUNTY.

July 12, 1836, Dr. W. Walters wrote that he had organized a church of Christ in Danville; also four others in Vermilion County; further, that he had gone twenty-two miles west of Danville and there organized another church. W. S. Shockey and Hughes Bowles were associated with Dr. Walters in these evangelistic labors in those early days.

About 1875 there was a small congregation at Fairmount, but the chapel was sold under the mortgage and the members scattered.

Alvin.

Organized 1897, by T. L. Stipp; present memoership, 85; value of property, $2,300; Bible school began 1887; present enrollment, 60.

This congregation was the first direct result of a series of meetings conducted by Evangelist Stipp, with seventy-five additions. The place was an old building that had been used for a saloon, but became a public hall after the town expelled the traffic. The sittings were chiefly boards placed on the ends of beer-kegs. An old pool-table added to the furnishings.

The chapel was built the next year. Mr. Stipp continued

his ministry half-time for three years. Since then the life of the congregation has been precarious. However, a good school is maintained and the public worship is kept up regularly.

Antioch (Rossville).

Organized 1866, by James Connor, Sr.; present membership, 195; value of property, $12,500; Bible school began 1868; present enrollment, 191.

This location is six miles southeast of Hoopeston. The congregation grew out of a meeting of days conducted by Minister Connor, who served the church several years. The charter members were Mrs. Huldah Brown, Joseph Heaton and wife, Samuel B. Smith and wife, Joseph Youngblood, Frank Youngblood and wife, David Newman and wife, John Norton and wife, John Oliver, Peter Marlatt, Thomas Bietz and wife and Mrs. Mary Kight. All of these have gone to their long home except Joseph Youngblood and Mrs. Thomas Bietz.

In 1868 two acres of ground were secured and a frame chapel built thereon. This was a union chapel, being shared in its uses by Methodist brethren. It was added to in 1890. In 1910 a new structure of brick, fully modern and very convenient and pleasing, was erected.

This is known as the Antioch Church of Christ. It has always had the missionary spirit. Every year the congregation makes its offerings to all the regular benevolences. In 1911 they amounted to $240.

This church has given to the Christian ministry Turlie McConnell, Eldon Norton, Rudolph Heicke and Orren Orahood.

Irving Cromkite, R. R. 2, is the clerk.

Bethany.

Organized 1875, by J. C. Myers; present membership, 20; value of property, $1,500; Bible school began 1875; present enrollment, 40.

The location is five miles northwest of Danville. It is also known as Lone Oak. For years the congregation held large influence for good in a wide community. Preachers who made their opinions of equal authority with the Scripture came and sowed the seeds of dissension. Wrangling supplanted worship, and vilification of men the praise of God. The congregation was divided and feebleness followed.

Bismark.

Organized 1880, by T. L. Stipp; present membership, 100; value of property, $3,000; Bible school began 1880; present enrollment, 60.

Mins. J. J. Cosat and J. C. Myers were associated with Mr. Stipp in forming this church. There were about forty charter members. The first officers were Riley Chandler, Wm. Wilson and Samuel Munnell, elders; with David and Andrew Claypool and Wm. Holland, deacons. The church was rent with division on the question of instrumental music, Sunday school and missions. Finally, those opposing these things withdrew. The congregation then reorganized and turned its thought and effort to do the things that please God. They have semi-monthly preaching, but the public worship every Lord's Day. J. J. Cosat is the pastor.

Catlin.

Present membership, 212; value of property, $5,000; Bible-school enrollment, 161.

Central Park (Danville).

Organized 1909, by E. M. Norton; present membership, 47; value of property, $1,500; Bible school began 1909; present enrollment, 57.

This congregation is also known as Brook's Chapel. It is in a suburb of Danville, with both electric and steam roads, and has a fine class of citizens.

The faithful work of Minister Norton led also in building the chapel. Roy Cronchite is the pastor.

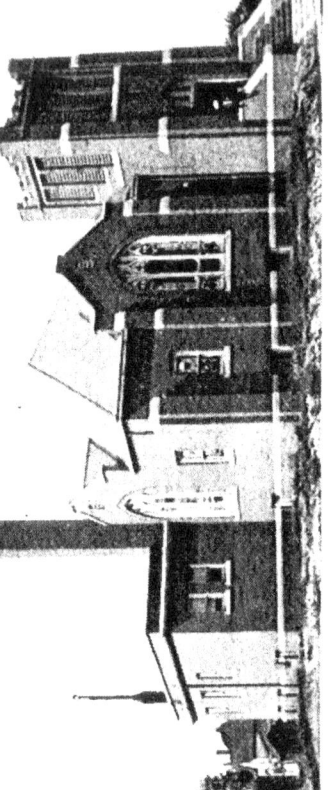

FIRST CHRISTIAN.
SECOND CHRISTIAN.
(DANVILLE CHURCHES.)
THIRD CHRISTIAN.
FOURTH CHRISTIAN.

CHURCHES

Center Point (Fairmount).

Organized 1891, by B. N. Anderson; present membership, 50; value of property, $1,500; Bible school began 1891; present enrollment, 57.

The location is six miles southwest of Fairmount. The congregation contributes to missions and other benevolences. There is a good Bible school, with Adda Smith, superintendent. The elders are E. L. Hawkins and E. F. Hines. Geo. F. Hedges is the clerk. Half-time preaching by Pastor H. H. Williams.

Cheneyville.

Organized 1891, by J. N. Lester; present membership, 109; value of property, $1,500; Bible school began 1891; present enrollment, 77.

The present elders are J. M. Swaner and Frank Dice, with Quince Teagarden and Oscar Young, deacons. B. T. Nicholson is the pastor. This is his first work in Illinois. He is an alert and earnest minister.

Danville First.

Organized 1871, by John F. Rowe; present membership, 407; value of property, including parsonage, $35,000; Bible school began 1871; present enrollment, 261.

Minister Rowe conducted a meeting of days in Lincoln Hall, on West Main Street, near the location of the Plaza Hotel, which resulted in the formation of this church. There were about forty members. H. A. Coffeen, Parley Martin and Geo. Dillon were the first elders. Soon thereafter a small chapel was built on Franklin Street where 415 is now. This was used till 1895, when the present commodious edifice was erected on the corner of Oak and Seminary Streets, during the pastorate of S. S. Jones.

W. R. Jewell first preached for the congregation, meanwhile editing a secular paper.

The church and Bible school are thoroughly organized for efficient service. In 1912, $450 was paid for missions.

In the years of struggle, Mr. and Mrs. Hiram Woods were most valuable members.

Danville Second.

Organized 1899, by S. S. Jones; present membership, 100; value of property, $10,000; Bible school began 1899; present enrollment, 72.

This church was formed in a rented building in Germantown, which is now a part of Danville, with seventy-five charter members. It was later incorporated as "The Second Church of Christ."

Danville Third.

Organized 1902, by S. S. Jones; present membership, 770; value of property, $20,000; Bible school began 1902; present enrollment, 396.

This congregation is the outgrowth of a mission formed by the First Church in the northern part of the city in 1901. Those directly interested "covenanted together to form a church to be known as the Third Church of Christ of Danville, Illinois." The meetings of the congregation were held in a hall, a storeroom and the Garfield School building till the completion of the church building in 1904. It is located on the corner of English and Walnut Streets.

S. S. Jones was the first pastor.

Danville Fourth.

Organized 1904, by E. M. Norton; present membership, 120; value of property, $12,000; Bible school began 1904; present enrollment, 95.

There were about seventy-five charter members. The elders are Jehiel Vance, Jacob Knee, John Hilman, Joseph Boles and Harris Smith, with Dr. Redmon, Dell Peeler and Edward Swisher, deacons. Its location is at the northwest corner of Fourth Street and Cunningham Avenue. The ministry of S. S. Jones in Danville was richly blessed.

CHURCHES

Fithian.

Organized 1884, by B. A. Anderson; present membership, 11; value of property, $1,000; no Bible school.

Formerly this church was a power for good in the community. Death and removals have nearly dissolved it. Fithian is a good little town in a fine agricultural section.

Georgetown.

Organized 1901, by S. S. Jones; present membership, 198; value of property, $7,000; Bible school began 1901; present enrollment, 145.

This congregation started with ninety-two members in January, and before the close of the year had housed itself in a good brick building.

James H. Hewitt has been one of the most valuable factors in the church. F. H. Vernon is the pastor.

Henning.

Organized 1898, by J. W. Street; present membership, 140; value of property, $2,250; Bible-school enrollment, 139.

The church was constituted in a hall. There were seventeen charter members, most of whom have moved away or died. With experiences that are common to village congregations, it prospers and does good.

C. C. Gaumer is the pastor. Miss Edith E. M. Seymore is correspondent.

Hoopeston.

Organized 1873, by Rolla M. Martin; present membership, 535; value of property, including parsonage, $20,000; Bible school began 1873; present enrollment, 270.

This church of Christ had its beginning almost with the city. The few members there first met in storerooms and shops. J. F. Mathers and Rolla M. Martin were the early preachers.

The first house of worship was built in 1873, under Mr.

Martin's ministry. The present brick edifice was erected in 1899, during the pastorate of R. H. Robertson.

Hoopeston is a city of superior intelligence, and the church of Christ is abreast of the times. Andrew Scott is pastor.

Indianola.

Present membership, 68; value of property, $3,500; Bible-school enrollment, 67.

Lowe's Chapel (Danville).

Organized 1876, by J. C. Myers; present membership, 68; value of property, $2,000; Bible school began 1876; present enrollment, 50.

This chapel is eight miles southeast of Danville. Mr. Myers, like his Master, was a carpenter, so after forming the congregation he built their chapel.

James A. Fishback is elder; Oscar Huff and Joseph Fishback, deacons, and J. J. Cosat, minister for one-fourth time. The church has never been strong, and has been further handicapped by ultra-conservative preachers.

No. Eight (Armstrong).

Organized 1888, by Wm. Hamilton; present membership, 23; value of property, $400; Bible school began 1892; present enrollment, 37.

This congregation was formed in No. 8 Schoolhouse, in Champaign County, with about eighty members. When the chapel was built, in 1892, it was located in Vermilion County, five miles southwest of Armstrong.

Among the charter members were O. P. and Allen McGlaughlin and wives, Anthony Long and wife, James Stuckey and wife, John Jeakim, Mary and Carrie Robertson, Viola McGlaughlin, and Jessie and Flora Tattershell. From the first, 157 persons have held membership here. Harley Fetters is clerk.

CHURCHES

No. Ten (Potomac).

Organized 1870, by Rolla M. Martin; present membership, 270; value of property, $1,500; Bible school began 1870; present enrollment, 131.

The charter members were George, George W., Irene, Jr., Margaret, Samuel, Matilda and Irene French; Hosea, Alonzo, Ellen, Warren and Sarah Knight; Caleb and Mary J. Albert; William, Martha, Samuel, John and Rebecca McGee; Jane Sweet, Rebecca Clemm, Louisa Cronkhite and Mary Tillotson. The first officers were Hosea Knight, elder, with George French and Caleb Albert, deacons. To the original twenty-three members, 321 have been added.

The church is wide awake to Home and Foreign Missions.

It is served by four elders and fourteen deacons. E. C. Creighton is the clerk, and E. M. Norton, pastor. It is located six miles southeast of Armstrong.

Oakwood.

Organized 1886, by Minister Pine; present membership, 129; value of property, $5,000; Bible school began 1886; present enrollment, 130.

There were fourteen charter members. In 1892 the congregation was reorganized by S. H. Creighton with 114 members. The house is modern, the Bible school front rank and a mid-week prayer-meeting. Geo. J. Huff is the pastor full time. Contributes to Home and Foreign Missions. W. D. Rogers is the clerk.

Potomac.

Present membership, 125; value of property, $3,500; Bible-school enrollment, 103.

Prairie Chapel (Rossville).

Organized 1865, by Rolla M. Martin; present membership, 74; value of property, $2,000; Bible-school enrollment, 110.

This chapel is five miles west of Rossville. A few scattered neighbors were gathered together by Minister Martin at old Blue Grass. They soon moved their place of meeting to the home of Simon Armentrout, thence to the Bratton Schoolhouse till 1866, when the present building was bought of the United Brethren and moved to the present site. It has been repaired several times and is now a creditable house.

The congregation has grown through trials and struggles to efficiency.

Minister Martin served the church twenty years. C. F. Gaumer has served the church for the past eight years. There is a good board of thirteen officers. Charles Villiars is the clerk.

Ridge Farm.

Organized 1899, by C. E. Evans; present membership, 50; value of property, $3,000; Bible school began 1899; present enrollment, 48.

P. F. York is the pastor of this church. It contributes to missions, and is striving to attain unto the best things in Christian service.

There is a good board of six officers. L. C. Osborne is the clerk.

Rossville.

Organized 1894, by S. R. Creighton; present membership, 264; value of property, including parsonage, $12,000; Bible school began 1894; present enrollment, 154.

Sidell.

Organized 1895, by S. H. Creighton; present membership, 125; value of property, including parsonage, $7,500; Bible school began 1895; present enrollment, 138.

For a few years, meetings were held in the Maple Grove Schoolhouse, a few miles southwest of Sidell. These led to the building of a union chapel in the north end of Edgar County in 1882. In 1884, Evangelist W. F. Black conducted a meeting of days there, when most of the congregation became Christians only. These he then organized into the Antioch Christian Church. In about ten years this congregation was absorbed by others, and the chapel was sold and turned into a barn.

Evangelist Creighton held a meeting in Sidell in the Baptist chapel in 1895 and organized a church of Christ of about one hundred members. Among them were members from Antioch, a goodly number of Baptists and converts to the Lord.

The church has given Clay F. Gaumer to the Christian ministry and Mrs. Marie Jackson McCoy to the mission field in Japan.

Union (Danville).

Organized 1838, by Jacob Swisher; present membership, 60; value of property, $1,000; Bible school began 1850; present enrollment, 50.

The location is seven miles northwest of Danville. This congregation has been served by all the first and second generation of Vermilion County preachers, among them Robert Sears, H. H. Gunn, W. P. Shockey, Wm. Mapes, R. M. and J. L. Martin, J. H. Broom, Abner Hubbard and J. H. Mavity.

It has given the following men to the Christian ministry: Wm. Pilkington, J. H. Martin, J. J. Cosat, T. L. Stipp, O. B. Gravat and P. L. Cunningham.

The church was divided through the preaching of ultraconservatives. These damages have been measurably repaired by the ministry of J. J. Cosat, who is serving the congregation for the twenty-fifth year as its pastor. They maintain a good Bible school and C. E.

Bertha White, R. 2, is the clerk.

Walnut Corners (Danville).

Organized 1843, by H. H. Gunn; present membership, 98; value of property, $2,500; Bible school began 1875; present enrollment, 72.

In the early forties the Stony Creek Church was constituted some ten miles northeast of Danville. It continued in a prosperous condition till 1856, when the new railroad started a town three and a half miles away, called State Line, Ind. Then most of the congregation moved into a new brick building in that town. However, a cemetery had grown near the old church. For the convenience of funeral occasions, the house was remodeled and repaired. After some years a Bible school was formed for the neighborhood, and from this school grew the Walnut Corners Church. The school is front rank and there is a good C. E.

J. C. Myers, J. J. Cosat, W. H. Kerr and others have served the church. John Smith and Irvine Cunningham are the elders.

Westville.

Organized 1866, by R. M. Martin; present membership, 40; value of property, $1,600; Bible school began 1907.

This church was first organized on the site of Westville. It grew to a membership of four hundred and exercised a wide influence for good in the surrounding community. Then a strong ultra-conservative preacher was engaged to serve the congregation. Under his teaching, in six years it sickened and died, and its members were scattered to the four winds.

In 1907, Min. E. M. Norton gathered up and reorganized the surviving remnants. A building formerly used by the Presbyterians was bought. It was much damaged by a stroke of lightning in 1912, and the title is in litigation. So a union school is held in the Congregational chapel. A. C. Ellsworth and C. M. Snooks are the elders.

Willow Springs (Grape Creek).

Organized 1870, by J. H. Martin; present membership, 40; value of property, $1,000; Bible school began 1870; present enrollment, 50.

It is located one mile southeast of Grape Creek. The

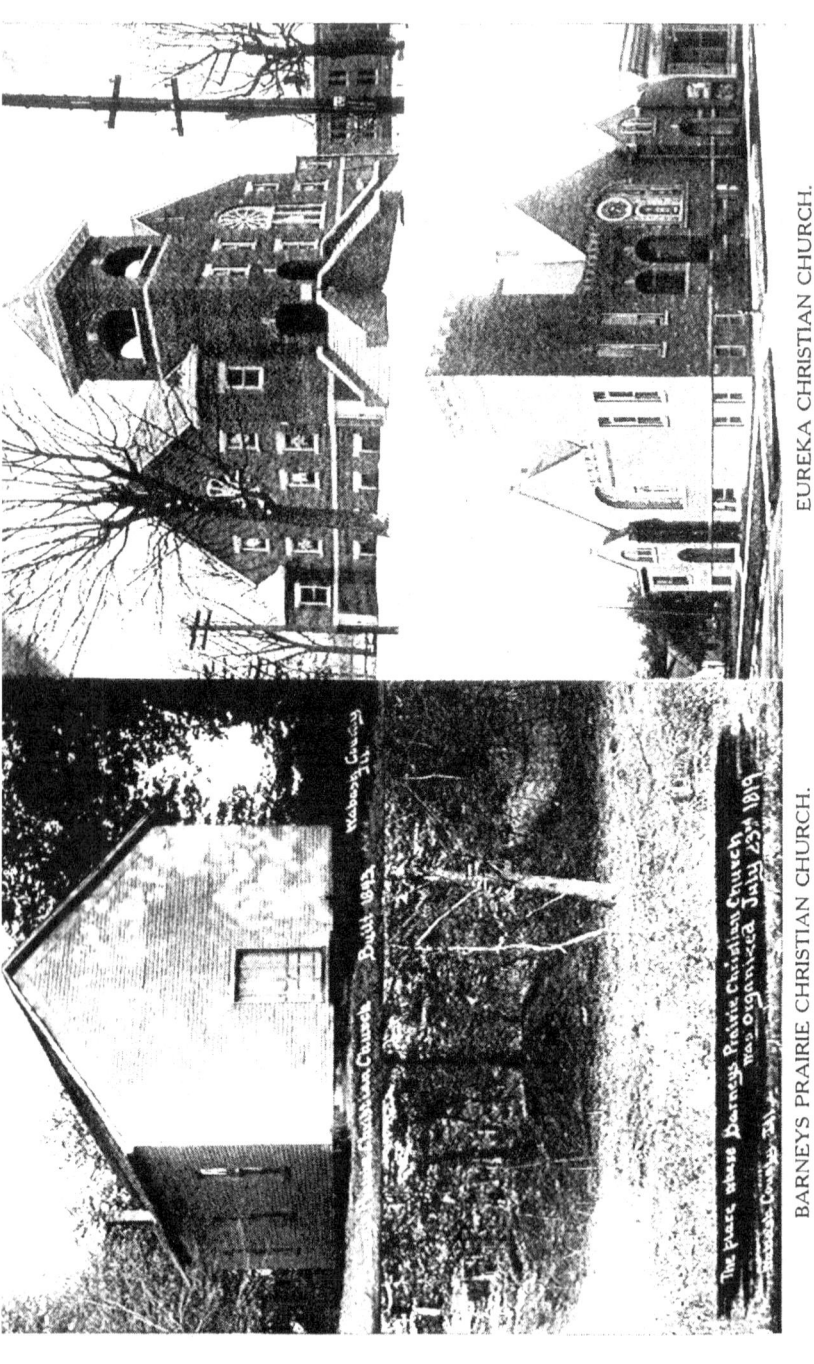

EUREKA CHRISTIAN CHURCH.
PONTIAC CHRISTIAN CHURCH.
BARNEYS PRAIRIE CHRISTIAN CHURCH.
WHERE BARNEYS PRAIRIE CHURCH WAS ORGANIZED.

spiritual life is feeble. Samuel Jumps and John Wilson are the elders.

WABASH COUNTY.

Adam's Corners (Allendale).

Organized 1851, by William Courter; present membership, 75; value of property, $1,000; Bible-school enrollment, 33.

At a meeting the fifth Lord's Day in June, at the residence of Allen R. Jackman, it was decided that, for the convenience of that part of the Barney's Prairie Church living in that neighborhood, a congregation be established at Adam's Corners. Soon afterward a union chapel was built. This was burned. Then the Christian congregation built a house of their own.

Mr. Courter served both as minister and elder. Under his untiring efforts the church grew to be strong and influential. It is still one of the best country congregations in the county. Many of its members are leading citizens. Geo. W. Morrell preached here three years with fine results.

A flourishing Bible school and the regular worship are well attended.

Allendale.

Organized 1891; present membership, 117; value of property, including parsonage, $3,700; Bible school began 1891; present enrollment, 143.

There were forty charter members. The chapel was built the same year.

There is an efficient Y. P. S. C. E. and Bible school, of which F. S. Gray has been superintendent since the church was started, except three years. John Walser is clerk.

Antioch (Keensburg).

Organized 1886, by Logan Gillaspie; present membership, 70; value of property, $1,200; Bible school began 1886; present enrollment, 50.

This congregation is thirteen miles southwest of Mt.

Carmel. There were fifteen charter members. James H. Dinnel and A. B. Denham were chosen elders, and W. B. Stewart, deacon.

The first chapel was built as a union house in 1870, but in 1886 the legal title passed to the Christian congregation.

A. B. Denham, an efficient elder for twenty-six years, was recently lost by removal. James Deputy is clerk.

Barney's Prairie (Allendale).

Organized 1819, by James Pool; present membership, 140; value of property, $1,350; Bible school began 1860; present enrollment, 110.

William Barney, with his family, left the banks of the Genesee River, in New York, in 1808. They came by raft down the Ohio River to the mouth of the Wabash. There the raft was sold and a keel-boat bought. In this they pushed upstream to Ramsey's Rapids, afterward the site of Bedell's Mill. This was eight miles up-river from the site of Mt. Carmel. His family consisted of Mr. Barney, his wife and his twelve children and three sons-in-law. (See Chap. II.) The male members of the family struck out through the forest to find a place on which to build their cabins. They reached a beautiful stretch of land, covered with grass ten feet high, and afterward known as Barney's Prairie. Shortly afterward came Mr. Barney's three sons-in-law. They were Ranson Higgins, Philo Ingram and William Aldridge.

Other settlers were then in that section and still others came afterward. Among these were Seth Gard and Gervaise Hazelton. These two men located Palmyra, two and a half miles north of the site of Mt. Carmel, near the river Wabash, Apr. 22, 1815. But Palmyra was abandoned in 1821 because of its unhealthiness. The Indians had so told the settlers, and it proved true.

This section was then in Edwards County, which was created by an act of the Territorial legislative body in 1814, and which reached north to the Canadian line.

CHURCHES

Joseph Wood came to the settlement about 1815. Ira Keen and others came from Ohio, New York, Virginia and Kentucky—all by the rivers.

Fort Barney was built in 1811. It was northwest of Palmyra. Fort Wood was southwest and Fort Compton northeast of Palmyra. These places were from five to eight miles apart. These forts were built by placing large poles firmly in the ground, reaching up about twelve feet, the top ends hewed off to sharp points. Early settlements were made round about these forts for protection, since the Indians had murdered several families near Fort Compton.

On a woodland spot, midway between the forts, a meeting assembled on July 17, 1819, and then and there organized the Barney's Prairie Christian Church. Seth Gard was elected elder; Joseph Wood, deacon, and Jarvis Fordice, clerk. The number of charter members is not known, but they had mostly come from the East and were the most intelligent and influential people in the settlement. (See James Pool, Seth Gard and Joseph Wood in biographies.) Some of these people had been members of the Christian Denomination, known at that time as "New Lights." But when they formed the Barney's Prairie Church, they renounced the name "New Light" and decided to be known simply as Christians. This is the written record, which is confirmed by the testimony of D. H. Wood—now near seventy years of age—a grandson of Joseph Wood, the first deacon. He has been a member of this church for fifty years, and through all these years had heard that this church started on apostolic ground.

The congregation met later near Fort Barney, in a grove near the prairie. Here a stand was built and surrounded by seats made of split logs, smoothed on the flat sides. They were more substantial than comfortable. Public worship was held here when the weather permitted; otherwise, in dwellings or barns. In 1843 a chapel was built. This has been repaired and refurnished and is still in use.

This was the first church of Christ in Illinois.

Bellmont.

Organized 1896, by Erastus Lathrop; present membership, 110; value of property, $800; Bible school began 1876; present enrollment, 75.

The first members were Dr. N. Briston and wife, Christ Shoenert and wife, John J. Sloan, A. W. French and wife, Wm. H. Davis, A. P. Manley, John G. McClary and wife, Mariah E. Knowles, Eliza J. Rigg, Nancy Jane Carter, Lafayette Read, Alice Bristow, Clara Briston, Lydia E. Kimbel, T. H. Burton, Ellen Imes, Nancy J. Parmenter, Elizabeth Sloan, Thompson Davis and Elizabeth M. McClary. Messrs. Briston, McClary and Baird were chosen elders, and Burton and French, deacons. The organization was made in the office of Dr. E. T. McClane, where the meetings for public worship were held till 1879, when the Silvan M. E. meeting-house, that stood five miles north of the village, was bought. As it was a very strong building, it was torn down, moved to town and rebuilt. This was done mainly by the volunteered labor of the members. Since then it has been much improved.

The church has been fruitful of good. D. M. Durham is the pastor.

Keensburg.

Organized 1819, by its members; present membership, 180; value of property, $5,000; Bible-school enrollment, 100.

The original record reads as follows:

At a meeting held at Brother Daniel Keen's on Saturday before the fifth Sabbath in August, 1819, a church of Christ was constituted consisting of seven members: 1—Thomas Thompson: 2—Nancy Thompson: 3—Daniel Keen: 4—Polly Keen: 5—William Arnold: 6—Ely Reed: 7—Dennis Sayles.

The record shows that John Auldridge was chosen as the first elder, and Daniel Keen, the first deacon; that meetings were held monthly and that additions were made to the church at these meetings, and also that several were dropped from the record for various reasons. In 1825 the church reported twenty-eight members in good standing.

This was the Coffee Creek Church, located one-half mile east of the site of Keensburg. The place of meetings was changed to the village in 1882.

This congregation has from its beginning, in 1819, always been a church of Christ; it was never of the Christian Denomination. Such is the united testimony of the oldest residents of the community, the original records of the congregation and the history of Wabash County. It was, therefore, only six weeks younger than the Barney's Prairie Church.

Lancaster (Mt. Carmel).

Organized 1842, by Maurice R. Trimble; present membership, 95; value of property, $1,000; Bible-school enrollment, 85.

Lancaster was formerly known as Round Prairie. In the life of Elijah Goodwin (pp. 183-4) the following lines appear:

> During this year [1842] a Methodist preacher named Dickens made an appointment on Round Prairie to preach on baptism. There being no meeting-house in the settlement, one of our brethren opened his large barn for the occasion. The preacher came and put in two days preaching on the subject. The brethren sent me word that I must come and give them a two days' meeting and preach on the same subject. This I could not do, but sent them an appointment, promising to give them two days' preaching in one. I went and preached in the same barn five hours without leaving the stand. I spoke on the subject, action and design of baptism. Preached two hours and thirty minutes and gave an intermission of fifteen minutes. Then I resumed the subject and preached two hours and thirty minutes more—all before leaving the stand. The large barn was full of people and a great multitude stood outside before a large door the whole time, giving the most earnest attention.

Elijah and Moses Goodwin, H. A. Hayward, James Pool, Joseph Ballard, and probably others, had preached the apostolic gospel in this community previous to Elijah Goodwin's five-hour sermon. Alfred Flower came later.

This church organized the third Lord's Day in October and had the following charter members: William Ridgeley and Robert Johnson, elders; Horace A. Woodward and John Higgins, deacons, with Wm. Clark, Sophia Woodward, Hiram and Polly Couch, Lydia McMillen, Martha Jones, Sarah Russell, Nancy and Elizabeth Lewis, Maria Courter, Sarah Pryant, Warren and Tamar Winders.

Mr. Woodward, one of the first deacons, was a famous showman in his early life and had built the large barn (where big meetings assembled), in which to keep the animals of his menagerie during the winters. He died in Grayville in 1878. The organization of the church is still celebrated by an annual meeting the third Sunday in October. Public worship, a basket dinner and a home-coming of former residents, make it a delightful occasion. Min. W. R. Couch has written these words: "The most, perhaps all, of the charter members of the Lancaster Church were converted under the preaching of Elijah and Moses Goodwin and Maurice R. Trimble at the old stand on Barney's Prairie." The last of them to go home to God was Elder John Higgins, of blessed memory, who died in 1902.

The church has given to the ministry James McMillen and James E. Moyer.

This is now a weak church. I. G. Williams is the minister in charge.

Lick Prairie (Mt. Carmel).

Organized 1830, by Joseph Wasson; present membership, 125; value of property, $600; Bible-school enrollment, 45.

This church is located twelve miles west of Mt. Carmel. Among the charter members there were Adam, Samuel, John and Andrew Baird; Eli Moore, Thomas and William Hill, John Steward, Samuel and Eban Putnam, and all their wives severally. This was organized as a church of the Christian Denomination, but in 1853, when another chapel was built, it became a part of the Restoration movement. Elijah and Moses Goodwin did efficient service at this place.

The first house of worship was of logs, built in 1831. This was used for fourteen years. Then another log house was built one mile south of the present site. By 1853 the congregation had outgrown the building. Then a union chapel was built, the Universalists using it one-fourth of the time. Elements so conflicting were not peaceable. After twenty-eight years of confusion, the old house, being unfit for use, was torn down. In 1881 a neat frame chapel was built and called the Garfield Memorial Church.

Maud (Mt. Carmel).

Organized 1896, by Geo. W. Morrell; present membership, 90; value of property, $1,200; Bible school began 1896.

This church is located about five miles west of Mt. Carmel. It was the first general result of a meeting held in the schoolhouse there by Minister Morrell. The charter members were James, Winifred and Lula Bell; John and Vashti Williams; Henry Obold and wife; J. R., Jr., Virginia, Jane and Flora V. Brines; David P. Wright, Harris Roll and wife, David K. and Rosaline Seiler, David H. and Susan Brown, Hannah Aborn, Anna Fearheiley, Mary Read, Samantha Van Senden, Mary E. Halbig, Irene Bell, Rose Getz and Cassie Shellhorn.

Mrs. H. Aborn and husband gave one acre of land and the chapel was built thereon in 1896.

This church is in a farming community and is sustained wholly by farmers. Since 1901 they have the "Annual May Meeting." Meetings for worship are held forenoon, afternoon and evening, a free basket dinner intervening. In the afternoon the anniversary sermon is preached and the church roll is called. There are two elders and four deacons. D. M. Durham is now pastor.

Mt. Carmel.

Organized 1862, by D. D. Miller; present membership, 760; value of property, $15,000; Bible school began 1862; present enrollment, 335.

This church had thirty-three charter members. Only one of them—Maria L. Filton—is left in the community. The first officers were, elders, John A. Morgan and Charles Redman; the deacons, Amos Walter and Daniel Titus.

The first house of worship was built in 1864, which was enlarged and remodeled in 1893. The first meetings were held in the courthouse and were violently opposed by religious bodies then established in the city. But it has grown to be strong and representative. All departments of Christian growth and service are aggressive.

Besides Mr. Miller, who worked under the auspices of the State Missionary Society, the following evangelists held meetings here: Franklin, Black, Clements, Ingram, Coombs, Courter, Pearl, Updike, Martin, Scoville, Thompson and Wilhite.

W. W. Weedon is the pastor.

WARREN COUNTY.

Alexis.

Organized 1897, by J. C. Alsup; present membership, 60; value of property, $3,000.

Berwick.

Organized 1902, by D. E. Hughes; present membership, 58.

Cameron.

Organized 1831; present membership, 290; value of property, including parsonage, $6,500; Bible-school enrollment, 144.

This church, with its antecedents, is one of the oldest and most interesting in the State. Its first name was Coldbrook, because a cold spring there formed a cold brook. The location was one and a half miles northwest of the site of Cameron. It was on the old trail leading from Peoria to Oquaka and about midway between the sites of Galesburg and Monmouth. A little town grew up around the Coldbrook Church that was called Savana. With the building of the railroad in 1854-55 the place and name of the church were changed and the village faded away.

The original record-book is still in the possession of the Cameron Church, and from it the following facts are gleaned:

"On the 30th day of April, 1831, this church was constituted upon the belief that the Scriptures of the Old and New Testaments are the only rule of faith and practice and sufficient for the government of the church." The names of the seventeen persons who signed this covenant were these: William M., Elizabeth, Elijah, Sr., Margaret, Sr., Elijah, Jr., Margaret, Jr., Davidson; Henry E., Elizabeth and John G. Haley; John E. and Frances Murphy; Richard and Nancy Ragland, and William, Sarah, Josiah and Julia Whitman. Three of these men were preachers—William Whitman, John E. Murphy and Elijah Davidson—and as many as eight of them were good public speakers. Squire Whitman, a nephew of William and Josiah Whitman, with his wife and sixteen other members of this church, went to Oregon in 1850 by the old caravan route, and there helped to found the town of Monmouth and to plant the college there.

The Coldbrook congregation called itself "the Church of Christ on Cedar Fork of Henderson River," Warren County. The record-book says: "Second Saturday in Feb., 1832. Agreed to send four dollars by Elijah Davidson, Jr., to St. Lewis to purchase a record-book for the church and one gallon of wine."

"Second Saturday, Aug., 1833. Agreed to meet on every Sabbath for worship."

For two years the record-book was made to do duty for other than church business. For example, on the first page there is a "Receipt for Felon," apparently from the pen of Henry Haley. It reads: "Bathe the part affected in ashes and water, take the yolk of an egg, six drops of the spirits of turpentine and a few beet leaves cut fine, a small quantity of hard soap, and one teaspoonful of snuff or fine tobacco, then add one teaspoonful of burnt salt and one of Indian meal and apply to the part affected." The records of personal business transactions also appear. But in June, 1834, "the church appointed four brethren to transcribe the church book, leaving out all that the church now believes unnecessarily committed to record."

The second Saturday in June, 1832, the church debated the question, "What encouragement should be granted young gifts by the church?" It was decided that it was the duty of every individual member to teach the Scriptures to the best of his ability, and those having the ability to teach publicly should be given letters of recommendation by the church.

In December, 1834, some parties wished to be married, so a few members of the church met on the 11th of that month and "appointed Alex. Reynolds to solemnize the *right*." But the following month the church took time by the forelock for the matrimonial business and authorized Joseph and Isaac Murphy, in addition to Elijah Davidson and William Whitman, who had been previously appointed, "to solemnize the *right* of matrimony." In December, 1838, the church granted one, J. R. Melton, this right, but the following March they examined his case, found him to be an impostor and excluded him from the church.

In May, 1834, the congregation received by immersion "Bro." Richard, a colored man; in 1838, Sister Polly, a colored woman, and in 1843 by commendation Sister Susan Richardson, a colored woman.

This church grew and prospered. It had the word, the spirit and the blessings of the Lord. In its earlier years it was served by Mins. Alexander Davidson, Levy Hatchett, Patrick H. Murphy, J. W. Butler, J. C. Reynolds, L. S. Wallace, George W. Lucy, S. T. Shelton and Alexander Johnson, who were all farmers.

Two deacons were chosen in 1833, but not till 1850 was an elder elected in the person of Samuel Shelton. In 1839 three swarms went out from the fruitful hive. The second Sunday in February the church granted permission to organize a congregation "across the creek." This became the Talbot Creek Church. The last Lord's Day in March, twenty-two persons received letters who became the nucleus of the Monmouth Church. June 26 there were twenty-six persons who received letters and formed the Meredian Church.

These Christians aimed to be strictly apostolic, but only with the passing years did they come to see some minor matters clearly. In the late thirties Elijah Goodwin, of Indiana, visited the congregation and preached one Lord's Day morning. Then a leading brother, presiding at the table, proceeded to break the loaf into small pieces convenient for each to take one. Whereupon, Mr. Goodwin spoke aloud: "Don't, brother. Let the disciples break the bread." The effect was like a thunderbolt from a clear sky. Silence brooded for a minute. Then the people saw, and from that time the custom was changed. On one Sunday morning the congregation met for worship, but the preacher failed to come, so a social meeting was held. During the singing of the closing hymn, a stranger, who was passing through to another State, went forward to accept Jesus as his Saviour. The leaders were puzzled; so they sent the stranger back to his seat in the chapel, extended the customary invitation and announced the invitation hymn. Then the earnest traveler was received according to their custom and went on his way rejoicing. The brethren had to be "regular."

When Mr. Campbell preached in the State before railways were built, he was often conveyed from place to place by friends. One of these called his attention to the great fertility of the soil and the wealth that would be produced from it. He replied: "Yes, but how hard it will be for the people to live as Christians." Naturally, there was a widespread wish to see him and hear him preach. A crowd of people waited to welcome him. In it was a man of bucolic habits who, as the great preacher approached, said to his wife: "Arise, Peggy, and behold him with your natural eyes."

In 1860 the old chapel was moved from Coldbrook to Cameron. In 1890 a new house was built. Since then Clark H. Marsh was given to the ministry.

Coldbrook No. 2 (Cameron).

Organized 1839; present membership, 200; value of property, including parsonage, $4,200; Bible-school enrollment, 114.

The Talbot Creek Church was formed in the northeast corner of Monmouth Township at the home of William Hopper, March 3, of forty-three members, most of whom were of the mother congregation and five miles northeast of it. Some of the ministers who resided near the Talbot Creek congregation and were members of it were S. L. and Thomas Wallace, John E. and Joseph E. Murphy and F. M. Bruner. In 1845 the congregation built a small frame chapel. In 1860 a more commodious house was built two miles east and one mile south of the former place, which is four miles north of Cameron. Here a modern frame building was erected in 1895. The name Talbot Creek gave place to Coldbrook. This is three miles nearly north of the first place of this name. It is a living and flourishing country congregation.

Gerlaw.

Organized 1859; present membership, 100; value of property, including parsonage, $8,000; Bible-school enrollment, 109.

In 1859 a number of members from the Talbot Creek Church organized at Mauch's Grove, a few miles north. When the railway was built and the town started, the meeting-place was changed to Gerlaw. At a critical time in this congregation, Min. J. W. Kelsey rendered very helpful service.

Monmouth.

Organized 1839; present membership, 930; value of property, $30,000; Bible-school enrollment, 247.

This congregation was a child of the Coldbrook Church. In March of this year twenty-two persons received letters and these became the charter members of the Monmouth

Church. This city is the center of United Presbyterianism in Illinois. The Christian Church has grown slowly but steadily to influence. Pastor D. E. Hughes has served it well for more than a decade.

Roseville.

Present membership, 160; value of property, including parsonage, $5,000; Bible-school enrollment, 73.

Youngstown.

Present membership, 230; value of property, $2,500; Bible-school enrollment, 80.

WASHINGTON COUNTY.

Ashley.

Organized 1871, by John A. Williams; present membership, 90; value of property, $800; no Bible school.

Mr. Williams conducted a series of meetings in the Baptist chapel, but formed the Christian congregation in the residence of Robert Coffey. The charter members were G. W. Cammack and wife, Thomas Graves, Byron Marrow and wife, Wallace Coffey and wife, Drew Foster and wife, Mollie Hammond and I. J. Reeder and wife. For years the church did good service, but is now feeble in every way.

It gave F. M. Morgan and one other to the ministry.

This was the early Christian home of J. F. Winters, who has been for many years one of the most helpful members of the First Church in Lincoln, Neb.

WAYNE COUNTY.

Baily.

Organized 1867, by Jas. A. Chowning; present membership, 65; value of property, $1,000.

For eighteen years this congregation met for worship in residences, groves and schoolhouses. In 1885 a chapel was built on the farm of Daniel Logan.

To the ministry this little congregation has given Daniel Logan, Samuel and Charles L. Wood. The latter is reported as a strong and effective preacher and a member now (1913) of the State Legislature.

Beech Bluff (Fairfield).

Organized 1912, by Wylie H. Keen; present membership, 26; no church property; Bible-school enrollment, 70.

This congregation, located about six miles southeast of Fairfield, is one of its children.

Black Oak (Fairfield).

Organized 1909; no church building.

This is a mission point of the Fairfield Church. It is six miles east and north of there. It was organized with forty-five members and did well for several years. Then a traveling preacher of the ultra-conservatives came in and measurably crippled its usefulness.

Boyleston.

Organized 1890; value of property, $800.

This is a child of the Fairfield Church, six miles west. In this small village five denominations sought to control. The house was completed in 1892 and the little church promised good until an ultra-conservative preacher came in and divided them.

Buckeye (Jeffersonville).

Organized 1840; present membership, 85; value of property, $500; Bible school began 1869; present enrollment, 73.

In 1839 a number of families emigrated from Columbiana, Carroll and Stark Counties, O., and settled in Lamard Prairie. All of these were Disciples. Among them there were Jesse Milner, Isaac and Edward Whitaker, Jonas and Fentore Lumm, John Morlan, Martin Emmons, Noah Towns, James McNeeley, John Skelton, James A. Maslan and Townsend Richards. About the same time a few families came from Tennessee and settled in the same neighborhood. Among them were the Butcher and Candle families, Edward Puckett and others, who were also members of the Christian Church. At that time Lamard Prairie was very sparsely settled, there being only a few squatters there. There was neither church nor school near this settlement. The first work of these settlers was to locate their homes, build their houses and clear up a little land for cultivation. Their next work was to build a house that would answer the double purpose of school and church. They called this house "Buckeye," and it still stands as a memorial of those royal pioneers. It is not now known all who went into this church, but among them were a number of preachers who did good work in establishing the primitive gospel in this and adjoining counties. Buckeye was indeed a glorious and fruitful mother. About thirty ministers have served here.

The chapel was built in 1871.

In 1850-52 another large immigration came from central Ohio and settled in the western part of Lamard Township. Among them were Isaac and George Brock and John Bunting. The two last named were preachers who helped much in building up the Christian Church.

Cisne.

Organized 1854, by Peter Stine and George Brock; present membership, 150; value of property, $2,500; Bible school began 1878; present enrollment, 140.

This church was organized at the Way Schoolhouse, where it met until 1874, when it moved to Cisne. The house was built the previous year.

George Brock, Peter and Stephen Stine, J. C. Ashley, Michael and John Flick and others came from Monroe County, O., in the forties and early fifties and settled near the site of Cisne. They were all Disciples. They all knew the Bible. Many of them carried a copy of the New Testament in their pockets and were prepared to give a "thus saith the Lord" for all doctrinal questions. They wielded a molding influence in the community and left a rich legacy to their posterity.

Oscar Eaton entered the ministry here.

The congregation has steadfastly discouraged all games of amusement.

Fairfield.

Organized 1853, by J. C. Ashley; present membership, 320; value of property, $5,000; Bible school began 1878; present enrollment, 225.

The beginning of the record is this:

> The names of the members of the Church of God in Fairfield, Wayne County, Illinois. The following named persons met and organized upon the Word of God alone as the only Rule of Faith and Practice, constituted this the 18th day of October, A. D. 1853. Minister present, Elder J. C. Ashley. Names of Disciples: William McNeely appointed Deacon; Sampson Wickersham, George W. Turney, J. M. Kenner, America Kenner, Cyntha Ann Edmonson, Antha Wickersham, Bridget E. McNeely, James T. Organ, James Austin, R. P. King, Parlia Ann Ayles, Virginia Spooner, Edwin A. Spooner, Ermess Organ, Charles Lichtenberger and Jane his wife.

Meetings for worship were held in residences, courthouse, opera-hall and Cumberland Presbyterian Church until 1883, when a building was erected.

Harry Holmes and J. C. Hall were given to the ministry.

This church has been exceptionally wise in establishing three congregations in its adjacent territory. It is still fruitful in all good works.

Frame (Mill Shoals).

Organized 1842; present membership, 65; value of property, $1,000; Bible-school enrollment, 60.

About 1842 a few Disciples from Tennessee settled in and around Turney's Prairie, about six miles south of Fairfield, and formed a congregation in the Walker Schoolhouse. This is now known as Frame. Some of the charter members were William Boye, P. J. and Thomas Puckett, Joseph Odell, John Shruseberry and Anderson Walker. They toiled together and met great opposition in building up primitive Christianity in their community.

Jeffersonville.

Organized 1861, by D. D. Miller; present membership, 83; value of property, $1,600; Bible school began 1871; present enrollment, 98.

The church was organized in the schoolhouse and set in order when the house of worship was occupied in 1871. At this time, Jasper Branch, Jesse Ward and John Morlan were chosen elders and continued for many years true servants of the Lord.

The church has the honorable credit of giving to the ministry the Lappin brothers—S. S., J. C. and W. O. Lappin—also Daniel Logan, Jr.

Keenes.

Organized 1911.

Middleton (Keenes).

Present membership, 85; Bible-school enrollment, 100.

Mount Erie.

Organized 1911, by O. M. Eaton; present membership, 52; value of property, $1,800; Bible school began 1911; present enrollment, 125.

This congregation was the result of a series of meetings held by Evangelist O. M. Eaton. The church building was erected in 1912. I. G. Williams is serving the church as minister.

Oakwood (Goldengate).

Organized 1895; present membership, 130; value of property, $2,000; Bible school began 1908; present enrollment, 250.

A congregation was organized in a barn in the village of Goldengate. The ministers present and participating were Z. A. Harris, H. H. Peters and C. L. Wood. Meetings for public worship were held in the public-school house, which after a time was closed against the Disciples. The congregation, being then without a house in which to meet, disbanded. In 1908, Min. I. G. Williams held a meeting in the Oakwood Schoolhouse, two and a half miles north of the village, and in the same year Min. W. H. Keen organized a congregation there. A good chapel was built.

Pleasant Grove (Jeffersonville).

Organized 1854, by J. C. Ashley; present membership, 200; value of property, $1,000; Bible school began 1870.

This congregation was a swarm from the old Buckeye hive. It is four miles west of Buckeye and was formed for the convenience of the members residing in the community and for the purpose of extending the gospel. Among the charter members there were George and Isaac Brock, Joseph Phillips, Townsend and Sylvester Richards, George Simmons, Robinson Lappin, Henry Henthorn and Jesse Ward.

This church is apostolic in its faith and practice. From the first there have been men in the congregation able to speak to edification. It has turned out a good many preachers, but not of the professional class. It has preaching one Sunday in the month, but the communion service has not been omitted ten times in fifty years, except on unusual occasions. Quietly and without discord, the work has moved steadily on through fifty years. A goodly number of the men and women who received their Christian training in this country church are now scattered from Ohio to the Pacific Coast, but they are in the front ranks of useful service.

A plain frame chapel, built in 1866, is still in use. About fifty preachers have served here.

Pleasant Hill (Cisne).

Organized 1873; present membership, 65; value of property, $1,000; Bible-school enrollment, 60.

This congregation is located four miles northeast of Cisne. There was preaching in the community from 1855 by Ministers Schooley, Jerry Butcher and Barney Robertson. When the chapel was built, the church was organized with about twenty charter members. Meets every Lord's Day for worship with or without a preacher.

Rinard.

Organized 1909, by E. E. Violett and Adam K. Adcock; present membership, 40; value of property, $1,700; Bible school began 1909; present enrollment, 48.

Church building occupied in 1910.

S. E. Fugate has entered the ministry.

Six Mile.

This is one of the oldest churches in the west side of the county. Willard T. Luther, Wm. Hill, H. Swan, Rose Rich and others did the early preaching. But its growth was due to John Wright, the first elder, and Samuel Wood, a young man and one of the first converts. Besides Samuel Wood, the congregation has sent out Charles L. Wood and W. W. Solomon as ministers.

Turney's Prairie.

Organized 1839, by Moses and Elijah Goodwin; value of property, $1,200; Bible school began 1845.

This congregation was formed at the Anderson Walker Schoolhouse. It is not known when the first house of worship was built. The present is a neat frame chapel, where the members meet regularly.

J. T. Purvis has entered the ministry.

Wayne City.

Organized 1887, by J. S. Rose; present membership, 125; value of property, $1,200; Bible school began 1888; present enrollment, 70.

The congregation was organized in the M. E. Church. There were sixty charter members. J. M. Lee, J. C. Ashley and W. W. Reid were chiefly instrumental in the formation of the church, and its first elders.

There is a ladies' aid and Y. P. S. C. E.

Zif (Clay City).

Organized 1878, by J. C. Black and W. W. Weedon; present membership, 42; value of property, $1,000; Bible school began 1878; present enrollment, 31.

Congregation met in residences and schoolhouse till the chapel was built in 1896.

In former years there were churches at Barnhill, from which came W. W. Weedon; Gum, that gave W. M. Garrison and Leander Harrington to the ministry; at Brown's, at Blue Point, at Brush Creek, at Pleasant Hill, at Gethsemane and other points, but by reason of emigration and new congregations springing up in new villages grown by railroads, all these organizations have disappeared.

WHITE COUNTY.

Ashland (Mill Shoals).

Organized 1883, by W. H. Johnson; present membership, 57; value of property, $1,000; Bible school began 1883; present enrollment, 40.

This is a country church in the northwest part of the county. The congregation was formed under the lead of Mr. Johnson as president of the County Co-operation.

George B. Carter gave for a building-place an acre of ground from the corner of his farm, on which there was a fine grove of ash-trees; hence the local name of the church. The house was built in 1884.

Bryant's Valley (Crossville).

Present membership, 100; value of property, $1,000; Bible-school enrollment, 100.

Carmi.

Organized 1851, by P. K. Dibble; present membership, 125; value of property, $20,000; Bible-school enrollment, 130.

The twelve charter members were as follows: Mr. and Mrs. Daniel Hay, Mr. and Mrs. Samuel R. Hay, Mr. and

Mrs. D. G. Hay, Mrs. Mary Robinson, Mrs. Sarah Kearney, Mrs. Robert Gamble, Miss Susan Wood, Miss Mary DeTest and Miss Shoemaker.

At first meetings were held in the courthouse. Many came into the church. The first house was a small brick, built in 1852; the second, a frame, built in 1867, and the third and present modern edifice in 1905, during the pastorate of Frank Thompson. Alfred Flower was the first pastor.

The church is active and ambitious for the highest usefulness.

These members of this church have served the county: Jessè Grissom as treasurer, William Poynton as circuit clerk, Arthur Poynton as deputy, and Otis Downen as deputy county clerk.

Mrs. Mary Robinson was the widow of Gen. John M. Robinson, who served in the United States Senate from Illinois from 1830 to 1841 and was a justice of the State's Supreme Court when he died.

Enfield.

Organized 1868, by W. H. Crow; present membership, 77; value of property, $1,800; Bible school began 1868; present enrollment, 55.

Jonah Marlan and Naomi, his wife, were the leading spirits in this organization. He, Jacob Fleck and J. B. Holmes were the first elders. Mr. Crow resided in Enfield at the time. He was teaching in the public school as well as preaching. Other faithful members were Mr. Stile, Tolvin Rice, G. W. Berry and J. B. Odell. There were faithful sisters too. The chapel was built in 1890.

Grayville.

Organized 1840, by Elijah Goodwin; present membership, 165; value of property, $5,000; Bible-school enrollment, 164.

Minister Goodwin began to preach in Grayville in 1837. The following were the seven charter members: Daniel

Buckley and wife, Jeremiah Ruth and wife, Martha Lumb, Sarah Mills and her sister, later Mrs. B. W. Kenner. Mr. Buckley was the first elder, Mr. Ruth the first deacon.

Besides Mr. Goodwin, among the preachers of the earlier years there were Andrew Beard, D. K. Biddle, Moses Goodwin, J. W. Allen, W. P. Slade, Mr. Goff and W. F. Black.

The first building was erected in 1844 and the present one in 1872, the latter during Mr. Allen's pastorate.

The church has passed through many trials, but is now alert and active. Its roll has many honored names.

Mill Shoals.

Organized 1911, by themselves; present membership, 62; value of property, $1,200; Bible school began 1911; present enrollment, 50.

Disciples residing here had owned a lot for some time. In 1911 they decided to build thereon and a neat frame chapel went right up. Then they organized and began to keep the ordinances of the Lord.

The outlook is bright. The elders are J. B. Johnson, L. D. Harland and Goodwin Pucket.

Seven Mile (Carmi).

Organized 1839, by Moses Goodwin; present membership, 90; value of property, $800; Bible-school enrollment, 70.

This church, located six miles northwest of Carmi, was one of the pioneer churches of White County. The following is a copy of a paper that was written by one of the original members, Dr. Martin Johnson: "The Christian Church at Seven-mile Prairie was organized on the 24th day of February, A. D. 1839, by Elder Moses Goodwin, upon the following constitution; to-wit: 'We take the Scriptures of the Old and New Testaments as the only rule of our faith and practice.'" Those who then signed this agreement were Arthur Johnson, Lucy Johnson, John Johnson, Polly Johnson, A. L. Johnson, Luranah Johnson, Martin Johnson and Comfort Johnson. These eight people—and other baptized believers who later affiliated with them—came from the Old Union Church of the Christian Denomination in Gibson County, Ind. Another entry, on August 21, of records show that there were twenty-eight members, that Moses Goodwin had moved to the Prairie and united with the church, and that he and A. L. Johnson were elders of the congregation, with John and James M. Johnson, deacons. Hon. W. H. Johnson, of Lancaster, Ill., writing of these people and this church, says:

My great-grandfather, Arthur Johnson, and wife, and my grandfather, John Johnson, and his wife, original or charter members of the Seven Mile Prairie Church, had been charter members of the Old Union Church in Indiana, which organized over one hundred years ago. About the time the church in Seven Mile Prairie was organized, Elder Moses Goodwin succeeded in bringing Old Union Church, as a whole, into what was called the Campbell Reformation. Elijah Goodwin, whose mother (then the wife of my Grandfather Johnson), brother Moses and two sisters (Mrs. Luranah Johnson and Mrs. Axie Crabtree) lived in the Prairie, often visited the neighborhood and preached here. Moses Goodwin and Fenton Lumm, both natural orators and splendid preachers, lived in Seven Mile Prairie and their labors took in all the surrounding country. My uncle, Arthur Johnson, one of the first elders, was an able preacher and a strong defender of the faith, but never became an evangelist. He conducted three public discussions successfully. Frank Murdock, S. F. Rogers, Barton W. Kello and Isaac Kello were faithful ministers sent out by Old Seven Mile Prairie Church.

There have been three chapels. The first of logs, with a long shed on the south side, built on the land of John Johnson. The second, a frame, near the east end of the bridge over the creek. The third stands on the Carmi and Mill Shoals Road nearly a mile east of the second house.

This church has contributed much to the production of other congregations. Its members held clearly defined convictions of Christian truth and were filled with the spirit of conquest.

Springerton.

Present membership, 100; value of property, $1,000; Bible-school enrollment, 84.

WHITESIDE COUNTY.

Coleta.

Organized 1847, by Henry Howe and John Yager; present membership, 71; value of property, $2,500; Bible school began 1855; present enrollment, 75.

In 1837 the Yager family came from Ohio and settled in Genesse Grove, about three miles from the site of Coleta. The Stanley, Crum and Nance families, from different places, soon followed. John Yager, then a young farmer and minister, began to preach at the Grove and to the widely separated pioneers more or less regularly. Min. Henry Howe came down from Wisconsin and held a protracted meeting. Then the church was formed with the following members: John Yager and wife, Mrs. Rose Ann Crum-Wick, John Moxley and wife, Mrs. Margaret Ann Crum-Wick, Miss Rose Ann Crum, Clement D. Nance and wife, Mrs. David Nance, Benjamin Tripp, Mrs. Sarah Jane Crum-Stanley and Samuel Landis and wife. The following were converted during Mr. Howe's meeting: Thomas J. Stanley and wife, Pleasant Stanley, Wm. Stanley and wife, David Nance, John T. Crum, John Hill, John Shepherd and wife, Miss Ruth Nance, Nathaniel Landis, Mr. Sperling and wife, and Dr. Hopkins and wife. These thirty were the charter members. This meeting was held in the house of John Moxley. The place of baptizing was Moxley's Ford, and was for many years. To these were soon added Wm. Crum and wife, John Tryer and wife, Dr. Dodd and wife, C. W. Sherwood and wife, Oscar Royer and wife, Fred Strand and wife, Henry Mason and wife, James Mason and wife, C. B. Peugh and wife, and Mrs. Polly Harrison, who came from North Carolina and was well known for her fidelity to the Lord's work.

John Yager and Clement D. Nance were the Scriptural elders for many years. The first deacons were Thompson and William Crum and David Nance.

The first meetings were held in the cabins of the settlers,

next in the schoolhouse till 1864, when a chapel was built, mainly by John Yager. This gave place to a more modern building in Coleta about 1885.

C. W. Sherwood, E. J. and F. B. Stanley were given to the ministry.

This congregation was composed of substantial people and exerted a fine influence in its own community. It was a willing helper in establishing churches of Christ in that part of the State.

Erie.

Organized 1870, by J. N. Smith and Chas. W. Sherwood; present membership, 100; value of property, $4,200; Bible school began 1870; present enrollment, 58.

In the early sixties, Erie was known chiefly for its sand-fleas and Jim Pratt, a local and noted infidel. His aim was to run every preacher out of the town who tried to preach the gospel there. Whereupon, at the solicitation of Mr. Matthews, a loyal and royal Disciple, Pastor J. N. Smith came down from Lanark and ground Mr. Pratt through the mill of a public debate. The next spring, Mr. Smith returned and organized a church with thirteen charter members. Of these, Luther Matthews and Mrs. Carrie Matthews-Greidly are the only survivors.

They first met in the schoolhouse. In 1871 an old chapel was bought and remodeled. Later, a good house was built.

Among those who served the congregation there were John Yager, L. D. Waldo, D. J. Howe, T. B. Stanley and Mrs. Clara C. Babcock. The feeble condition of the church led Mrs. Babcock to take up its care. She served it three terms, aggregating fourteen years.

Fulton.

Organized 1896, by N. S. Haynes and Mrs. C. C. Babcock; present membership, 40; Bible school began 1896; present enrollment, 45.

The church has never secured a firm hold in the community. It has given Frank Bear to the ministry.

Rock Falls.

Organized 1905, by H. E. Monser and W. E. Spicer; present membership, 200; value of property, $2,300; Bible school began 1897; present enrollment, 272.

About 1890, Arthur Babcock, son of Mrs. C. C. Babcock, gathered together in his own home a number of children who were not attending Sunday school. The number grew to near one hundred. An appeal to the general public for means to build a chapel was well answered. Mr. Morrell gave the lot. Mrs. Babcock conducted a meeting of days at the dedication and about twenty were added to the Sterling Church. The organization of the Rock Falls congregation was delayed till 1905.

Elmer Frost and Walter Miner became ministers.

Sterling.

Organized 1875, by Knowles Shaw and J. J. Moss; present membership, 276; value of property, $3,500; Bible school began 1875; present enrollment, 163.

The churches of Christ in northern Illinois, though few in numbers, have always been aggressively missionary.

They led in and financed the effort that produced the Sterling Church. Evangelist Knowles Shaw conducted a tent meeting that continued thirty-three days. There were about seventy-five charter members. For five Lord's Days the Coleta congregation came *en masse,* bringing provisions to feed all the hungry, and for three Sundays the Pine Creek Church did the same.

The first elders were W. F. Eastman, J. S. Detweiler and Geo. W. Nance, and the first deacons, R. B. Colcord and J. D. Nance.

Six great meetings have been held by evangelists since the first one.

The church has given to public service Miss Mary Kingsbury, a missionary in India; Mrs. Clara C. Babcock, G. W. Pearl, S. H. Zendt, L. O. Lehman and Miss Rachel Crouch.

In 1880 the State Board fostered the church by $360 and Peter Whitmer, of Bloomington, by $400, both on condition that the congregation purchase and pay for a chapel, which was done.

Tampico.

Organized 1900, by J. S. Clements; present membership, 95; value of property, $3,500; Bible school began 1900; present enrollment, 60.

This year the State Mission Board sent Knox P. Taylor here to hold a two weeks' Bible-school institute on condition that the Yorktown congregation follow up with a meeting. This was done, but it cost Yorktown thirty of its own members.

WILL COUNTY.

Joliet First.

Organized 1897, by John Williams; present membership, 50; value of property, $8,200; Bible school began 1897; present enrollment, 45.

There were twenty-one charter members. The house of worship was finished and dedicated free from debt in 1905. This was largely due to the liberality of Col. D. H. Darling and his wife, who were devoted members of the church. Slow but steady progress is made now.

In 1905 the Central Church was organized with forty-two members by Sec. J. Fred Jones. It grew out of a factional spirit and after a short period disbanded.

WILLIAMSON COUNTY.

The early churches were organized in residences, groves and schoolhouses. Some of them were short-lived, but served as seed-sowers in planting the primitive gospel. The exact dates can not be given, but they were planted in about the following order and principally by the men named below: About 1840 a church was formed in the Pulley settlement, northeast of Marion; one in the Crain settlement, west of

Marion; one in the Goodall settlement, east of Marion; another north of Spillertown, where a log chapel was built. Then came the Lake Creek Church in the northern part of the county and Bond Church in the northwest corner. These all served their time and have long since become extinct.

Wm. H. Willford, of Tennessee, was one of the first Christian ministers who came to this county. About 1840 he located near Crab Orchard. He owned the first printing-press in the county and issued a small paper called the *Western Monitor*. He also published a few books and preached the gospel.

Arch T. Benson, a Marion merchant, preached the gospel from house to house in a very acceptable and sympathetic manner.

Among others of the early preachers were Dr. Bundy and William Spiller, of Marion; Cyrus Heape, of Tamaroa; Mathew Wilson, of Carterville, and Isaac and Newton Mulkey, of Mulkeytown.

Carterville.

Organized 1885, by J. J. Hudson; present membership, 290; value of property, $10,000; Bible school began 1885; present enrollment, 225.

Met in hall till chapel was built in 1888. The commodious brick structure came recently. Active church, with good C. E.

Creal Springs.

Organized 1895, by J. J. Bobbitt; present membership, 50; value of property, $700; Bible school began 1895; present enrollment, 40.

A product of the Eighth District. Only a Bible school has been maintained for several years.

Fordville (Carterville).

Organized 1868, by Mathew Wilson; present membership, 25; value of property, $500; Bible school began 1870; present enrollment, 74.

Three miles southwest of Carterville. When Mr. Wilson reached the community to preach, it was dark and no one had brought a light. He began by saying: "Seeing that you people are in darkness, I will proceed to give you the light of the gospel." The chapel was built in 1870. Repeated swarms from this Christian hive have reduced its numbers.

Herrin.

Organized 1864, by Samuel Wilson; present membership, 145; value of property, including parsonage, $5,000; Bible school began 1864; present enrollment, 184.

Meetings were held in the schoolhouse till 1867, when a modest chapel was built. It gave way in 1898 to the present building.

The original members were Newton Bradley, Samuel Stotlar, William and Louisa Williams; George, Nathan and Sarah J. Cox; Eliza Spillar, Eliza Stotlar and "Grandma" Lawrence.

Johnson City.

Organized 1904, by Gilbert Jones; present membership, 90; value of property, $2,000; Bible school began 1904; present enrollment, 54.

This congregation was the result of a five weeks' meeting conducted by District Evangelist Jones. There were sixty charter members.

The chapel was built at once. Mr. Jones worked thereon in the daytime and preached at night. This task, including manual and ministerial labor, was the gift of Mr. Jones.

Marion.

Organized 1865, by H. T. Banta and A. T. Benson; present membership, 430; value of property, including parsonage, $18,500; Bible school began 1865; present enrollment, 213.

The house of worship was erected in 1875 and remodeled in 1901. A goodly number of representative people have always belonged to its membership.

Reeves.

Organized 1905, by F. L. Davis; present membership, 125; value of property, $2,000; Bible-school enrollment, 80. Chapel built in 1896. Irregular preaching.

Shiloh (Marion).

Organized 1866, by Mathew Wilson; present membership, 100; value of property, $800; Bible-school enrollment, 48.

Three miles north of Marion. Organized in a grove. Have done good work and do yet.

West Chapel (Carbondale).

Organized 1897, by F. M. Phillips; present membership, 35; value of property, $800; Bible school began 1899; present enrollment, 60.

This is six miles south of Carterville. Organized in schoolhouse. Chapel built in 1894.

A congregation at Grange Hall, and another at Rall's Grove, both having chapels, have ceased to meet.

WINNEBAGO COUNTY.

Rockford.

Organized 1856, by A. P. Jones and Wm. Hayden; present membership, 291; value of property, $25,000; Bible-school enrollment, 369.

There were thirty-five charter members in this organization. The church made feeble progress and disappeared in the early nineties. The property was sold for debt. Other Disciples moved into the city and the Central Christian Church was formed by Min. L. E. Prather in 1898. During the seven years' pastorate of O. F. Jordan, a stone chapel was bought and paid for, but during the next ministry, that of W. B. Ward, this property was sold and the present property, better located, was bought. Wm. B. Clemner, the present well-equipped and efficient pastor, led in the erection of this fine building.

CHURCHES

WOODFORD COUNTY.

The county-seat of Woodford has had three locations. This fact has naturally led to changes in population. The first was Versailles, located four miles southeast of Eureka, the second, Metamora, and the third, Eureka. There was a congregation of Christians at Versailles in the early years, and also a second one when the place had become wholly rural, but both passed away. At Metamora there was formerly a self-supporting church of Christ, but later the community became so Romanized that only a union church has been maintained for two decades.

The Panther Creek congregation was the second church of Christ formed in the county, according to the testimony of Mr. Aaron A. Richardson. It was located about five miles southeast of Eureka and about six miles southwest of Secor. It was organized about 1840, with Amos Watkins and James Robeson, elders, and Warren Watkins one of the deacons. The first meeting was held in the residence of Amos Watkins, says Mr. Richardson. "The first time I ever remember being at church was in this house. John Hibbs preached the sermon. My grandmother united and Elmia and Martha Watkins were baptized that day." This church continued until about 1860. Many of its members had moved away. Of the remainder, some went to Secor, others to Palestine.

Palestine congregation was located about seven miles east and south of Eureka. The meeting-house of the Panther Creek Church was moved there. It carried on its work for about fifty years, but has ceased to be.

A congregation was formed at Cram's Schoolhouse, about two and one-half miles northeast of the site of Secor. This was probably about 1848, as the McCords, Patricks and Billberrys were among its members. This was known as the Panther Grove Church. Sympson Y. Barnard and Wm. Berry were the first elders. Meetings were later held in Willow Tree Schoolhouse and finally moved to the village of Roanoke.

446 HISTORY OF THE DISCIPLES IN ILLINOIS

There was a flourishing church at Bowling Green, a village eight miles southeast of Eureka, in the early fifties. For some years this was the home of Min. James Robeson. This congregation long since passed away.

The Partridge congregation was located west of Metamora, but conservatism finally closed its doors.

Cazenovia.

Organized 1903, by E. O. Sharp; Bible school began 1903.

The church at Washburn planted a mission here. The meetings were held in a storeroom, the use of which was given by its owner, Mr. C. B. Pickerell. Mr. Sharp was the evangelist of the Fourth Missionary District when the organization was effected with twenty-seven members. Thereafter, the preaching was by the pastors of the Washburn congregation and Eureka College students. During the ministry of B. L. Wray, a substantial chapel was built, the church became self-supporting and was fairly prosperous. But removals and death soon weakened it.

Now the congregation is made up of members of various denominations and is ministered to by Fred Carr, of Eureka.

El Paso.

Organized 1864, by John Lindsay; present membership, 250; value of property, $12,000; Bible school began 1864; present enrollment, 125.

For twenty years this church was feeble. The following was the beginning:

We, the undersigned disciples of Christ, do hereby constitute ourselves into a congregation of Christ for the purpose of worshiping God together in El Paso, taking the Bible as our rule of faith and practice, and to be known and styled the Christian Church in El Paso, Illinois.

The forty names which were subscribed were these: J. H., Juliett, Mary L. and L. B. Moore; M. R. Bullock, John and Margaret Canfield, Jane and Alice Dixon, Maggie Himmond, Jackson Luttril, Sarah C. Bayles, Lucenda and Evar-

CHURCHES 447

gatine McLord, Mary Packard, Elizabeth King, M. Potter; F. J., S. J., Martha and Maria Barnard; Mary Ann Stephenson, Mary Brewer, Amanda J. Willis, John and Hannah D. Hibbs, Mary Smith, Elizabeth O'Neal, Esther Reeves, M. W. and Julia Y. Thompson, Hannah Montgomery, D. P. and M. A. Harber, Agnes and Elmira Gibson.

John Hibbs and D. P. Harber were chosen elders, with F. T. Barnard and (afterward) Cyrus Gibson, deacons.

This meeting was held at 10:30 A. M. on July 4, 1864. John Lindsay and James Robeson both preached.

The church was then constituted by the labors of Mr. John Lindsay, working in the service of the Woodford County Co-operation.

J. H. MOORE, Chairman.

A small frame chapel was built in 1865. The pulpit was supplied for fifteen years. But El Paso did not increase in population as rapidly as it was surmised at that time that every railroad crossing would. The church lapsed from the spring of 1881 to December, 1886. Then E. J. Lampton held a meeting of days and reorganized the congregation with thirty-four members. This was the beginning of the permanent growth of the church. J. E. Jewett, J. D. Dabney and C. S. Medbury were then pastors. During the latter's ministry the congregation grew, and the present building was finished in 1895.

Eureka.

Organized 1832, by John Oatman; present membership, 805; value of property, including parsonage, $23,400; Bible school began 1852; present enrollment, 526.

In April, 1832, what was then known as the Walnut Grove Church of Christ was organized in the log-cabin residence of Min. John Oatman, that stood about one-half mile northeast of the railway depot now there. The thirteen charter members were the following: John Oatman and Nancy, his wife, and their children, Eliza, Joseph, Clement, Jesse and Hardin Oatman; Daniel and Rhoda Travis, Joshua and Mary Woosley, and Samuel and Rebecca Arnold.

Meetings were held in the residences of the settlers, in groves and in the barns of Daniel Meek, Caleb Davidson and Ben Major until the summer of 1846, when the "old meeting-house" was built. It stood on the spot now occupied by the Soldiers' Monument in Olio Cemetery. This building was used until 1864, when a two-story brick house was erected on the site of the present structure. At that time the pulpit was filled by H. W. Everest, Dr. J. M. Allen and A. G. Ewing. The present edifice was erected in 1901 during the pastorate of N. S. Haynes.

The Sunday school was organized in 1852 with Ben Major as superintendent. Previous to this a Bible class had been conducted by Min. John T. Jones, which met in the homes of its members. The school was broken up in 1852 by cholera.

Mr. Oatman served the church three years. In 1836, Ben Major and Elijah Dickinson, Sr., were elected elders and continued with active efficiency until relieved by death— the former in 1852 and the latter in 1862. Min. William Davenport was the local minister of the church from 1835 to 1855. When he was away the elders led the public worship. From 1855 to 1868 the pulpit was supplied, in addition to the three above named, by O. A. Burgess, C. L. Loos, William Poynter and B. W. and R. H. Johnson. In 1868, A. S. Hayden became the pastor of the congregation, serving three years. During the next fifteen years the pulpit was filled by B. J. Radford, H. W. Everest and Dr. J. M. Allen, very much the longer part of the period falling to Mr. Radford. The two brief pastorates during this period were those of J. H. Berry and B. J. Pinkerton. The pastors who succeeded were J. G. Waggoner for two terms, W. H. Cannon, N. S. Haynes, A. W. Taylor and D. H. Shields.

Great special meetings were held with the congregation by Evangelists D. P. Henderson, James Robeson, Alexander Proctor, William Davenport, Knowles Shaw and George F. Hall.

This has been, and is yet, one of the great churches of

the State. For eighty years it has been noted for its cheerful hospitality, generous liberality and its manifold good works.

Minonk.

Organized 1865, by John Roberts; present membership, 69; value of property, $3,200; Bible school began 1867; present enrollment, 75.

The first meetings were held in the old East Side Schoolhouse once a month, alternating with the Baptists, Presbyterians and Methodists. The first elders were Craigie Sharp, Sr., Jonathan Macy and Joseph F. Burt. The deacons were Wm. Norris, J. T. Taylor and J. L. Vance.

The building was first occupied in 1867. It was remodeled in 1907.

About 1870 the harmony and usefulness of the congregation were seriously impaired by strife over the use of an organ in the public worship.

The pastors were J. C. Stark, A. H. Trowbridge, J. F. Ghormley, S. D. Vawter, G. A. Miller, Paul H. Castle, F. E. Hagin, D. H. Shields and Byron Piatt. These were at intervals as death and removals depleted the membership. The church house was closed from the fall of 1897 to the close of 1904. Then W. F. Kohl, the pastor at Rutland, revived the remnant and reorganized the congregation with eighteen members.

Since then, J. H. Bullock, C. D. Hougham, H. C. Reichel, Ernest Reed, Silas Jones and F. M. Morgan have served the church. R. L. Beshers is the present pastor. Clara B. Vance is the clerk.

Mt. Zion (Eureka).

Organized 1855, by John T. Jones and William Poynter; present membership, 40; value of property, $1,500; Bible school began 1855; present enrollment, 38.

On April 29, in the schoolhouse which stood near the site of the present chapel, "the church of Christ, meeting for worship at the head of Walnut Grove," was constituted with the following members: Joshua, Sarah V., James, T. C. and Eleanor R. Jones; Jane Todd; William S., Sarah C. and Rhoda J. Magarity; Robert Carr; R. R., Mary A. and John Grady; William T., Senith A., Mary and Elijah Woosley; Margaret and P. Buckner Stitt; Martha, Peter, Susan and Mary Crow; James R., Letitia A. and Adolphus G. Oatman; David and Martha Harber; Mary and Lucy W. Parke; Mary W. and Lorenzo Bateman; James, Nancy O., J. Pleasant and Eliza J. Mitchell; Robert, Harriett, Sarah A. and John Foster; Robert and Mary A. Nance; Solomon, Thomas, Wilson, Sarah A., Nathan and Sarah Tucker; Harriett, Ellis, Caroline and Nancy J. Trunnel; Patsey Parker, Albert U. Barber, Isaac Swearingen, Jacob A. Casart, Alonzo Pratt, William Higgens, George Davier; John O., Sarah, William, Susan and Nancy Mitchell.

Most of these brought letters from "The Church of Christ, Walnut Grove." Joshua Jones, Robert Foster and Wm. S. Magarity were elected elders; William Mitchell, James R. Oatman and Wilson Tucker, deacons; James R. Bateman, clerk, and William Mitchell, treasurer.

This little congregation, located about four miles northwest of Eureka, has always held a large percentage of most excellent Christian people.

About 125 preachers have ministered here. Many of them were college students who have gone forward to the first rank in the ministry.

Roanoke.

Organized 1872, by J. B. McCorkle; present membership, 20; value of property, $2,500; Bible school began 1872; present enrollment, 30.

The first meetings were held in the old Bunch Schoolhouse, then at the Willow Tree Schoolhouse.

While the meetings were held in these places, 1872 to 1874, Min. Rufus Gish, a "Dunkard" preacher, used to debate with Mr. McCorkle.

Mr. D. F. Fanber gave lots for the church building, and the chapel was dedicated by Dr. J. M. Allen in 1874. Ministers McCorkle and W. C. Poynter served the congregation on alternate Sundays for several years, and the latter continued his service after the decease of the former.

Messrs. D. T. Fanber, C. M. Stephens, B. G. Kindig and J. R. Wilson were some of the men who did faithful work in the earlier years.

Secor.

Organized 1862, by James Robeson; present membership, 30; value of property, $1,000; Bible school began 1862; present enrollment, 50.

Minister Robeson, assisted by Min. John Lindsay, held a meeting of days in an old corn-crib, during which over forty people turned to the Lord.

The first elders were James M. Richardson and H. B. Mathews, and the first deacons, Aaron A. Richardson, Henry B. Smith, and Garrett and Rankin Armstrong.

The congregation met for worship in the little old schoolhouse until the chapel was built. As the years passed, an increasing percentage of Germans came into the community. The church finally divided on questions of opinion. In 1898 the conservatives received a deed to a lot that specifically proscribes the use or placing of any musical instrument on the premises, the organizing of any societies of any kind, and the permission to preach in the house by any one who favors these prohibited things. That both congregations have maintained only a feeble life under all the circumstances is apparent.

Washburn.

Organized 1864, by David Sharples; present membership, 250; value of property, including parsonage, $10,500; Bible school began 1864; present enrollment, 297.

Evangelist Sharples was in the service of the Woodford County Co-operation when he held the meeting that resulted in the formation of this church. There were thirty charter members, the larger part of whom came from Vernon Schoolhouse, two miles southeast, and the old Salem Church, seven miles northwest of Washburn.

In 1867 a substantial building, just across the line in Marshall County, was dedicated by Min. Theodore Brooks. In 1890 it was moved to a more suitable location nearer the center of the village, remodeled and enlarged. Additional improvements were made in it during 1912.

The following pastors have served the congregation: John L. McCunne, Charles Rowe, David Sharples (two periods), Hugh B. Rice, John D. Henry, Theodore Brooks, A. P. Cobb, J. A. Brenenstuhl, R. E. Dunlap, William Hayden, W. A. Humphrey, S. S. Lappin, I. H. Fuller, J. W. Kilborn, H. H. Jenner, Rochester Irwin and R. G. Jones.

The church has always held its ministers in high esteem, for they have been very worthy men. From the first, it has grown in numbers and influence. No discord has ever stained its fair name nor hindered its admirable progress. It has always responded promptly to all calls for benevolent work. It is well organized and officered.

It has given to the Christian ministry L. B. Pickerell, Stephen E. Fisher, Charles Richards and Gilbert Gish.

Section 2.

Bible Schools.

The Disciples of Christ in Illinois were slower in the appreciation of the value of Sunday schools than other evangelical bodies. Their first work was to clear away the theological debris of the centuries by teaching and preaching the word of God. Very naturally, this advocacy was addressed to adult rather than to adolescent minds. Only with the passing years was the necessity and duty of child-training recognized. With it came questions about methods and many meetings for conference and fraternal discussions. To the State Meeting that convened in Springfield, Aug. 30, 1865, Eli Fisher, evangelist in the Second District, reported:

"In reference to the Sunday-school enterprise, I have to say that there is little interest taken in it." From the extant information, it is a fair conclusion that only from one-third to one-half of the churches of Christ in Illinois had Sunday schools at that time. All of them were primitive and many suspended during the winter.

An effort was made to convene a State Assembly in the Sunday-school interest at Macomb, Feb. 19 and 20, 1868, but the attendance was more local than general. An institute was held there November 11-13, the same year. The State Missionary Convention met there in 1869 and gave some attention to Sunday-school work; so also did the convention in Chicago in 1870. In the early seventies, Mr. L. H. Dowling served as Sunday-school evangelist for a time. The State Convention held in Jacksonville in 1873 resolved in favor of a State Assembly in the interest of Sunday schools, to convene in the following October. It appears that this meeting did not convene until the spring of 1874, when the State Sunday-school Association was organized. Thereafter, these meetings were held for eleven years in the month of May, with limited and somewhat local attendance. At these meetings, primary questions were considered and interest in the work was stimulated. The State Missionary Convention at Springfield, Aug. 29, 1877, declined to take over the work of the State Sunday-school Association; so it convened for its business on the morning of the 30th. Ira J. Chase was president, and that forenoon addresses were made by B. J. Radford, N. S. Haynes and J. Carroll Stark, the last named speaking on "How to Interest Children in Church Services." The total receipts for that year were $75, and the expenditures were $35. In 1882 the question of a closer relation of the two State Assemblies came up again, but with no definite results.

In the early eighties a meeting of the executive committee of this Association convened at the residence of N. S. Haynes in Decatur. Its chairman, Min. J. W. Allen, said that its object was to inaugurate aggressive work in behalf of the Sunday schools in the State. He proposed very earnestly that Mr. Knox P. Taylor be recalled from Texas and be given this business. This was done, although not a dollar for his support was in sight and offerings for all general Christian activities were then small. For about two years all the meetings of this executive committee were held in the same place where it first met, always including free entertainment. The return of Mr. Taylor to the State was a godsend. No man has ever given a superior service to Illinois. His vocabulary was limited, but his soul was large. His sincerity and piety left imperishable impressions upon all with whom he associated. Frequently his hosts saw him upon his knees in communion with his Father. He taught people by eye-gate and ear-gate, *the Bible first*, then methods of school work. Having come through denominationalism, he had much sympathy for his brethren who were still enmeshed therein. He believed the plain truth, and taught it as though all who heard him accepted it. Mr. Taylor continued in the active service of the Association till 1900, and thereafter as his waning strength permitted.

The Association generally met in May. The following are the places that afforded free entertainment to its members, the years and additional evangelists: Sullivan, 1886, J. Jones; Decatur, 1887; no report for 1888; Jacksonville, 1889. Mr. S. W. Leffingwell then became assistant evangelist, but, finding his need of a better knowledge of the Bible, he turned himself into Eureka College for a year's study under the lead of Prof. F. M. Bruner. Then he continued with the Association till 1894. Charleston, 1890, J. M. Morris and David Husband; Bloomington, 1891, when the four evangelists last named reported sixty-one additions to the churches; Lawrenceville, 1892, Mrs. Sarah C. McCoy and Charles Ballard; Olney, 1893, G. W. Warner; Carthage, 1894; Decatur, 1895, Miss Anna M. Hale; Peoria, 1896, Miss Hale; Danville, 1897, Miss Hale; Decatur, 1898; Eureka, 1899, when the State Sunday-school Association ceased to be and its work was properly committed to the

State Missionary Society. Under its direction, Min. A. C. Roach worked from 1901-03. He organized missions at Bradford, Cambridge, Wyoming and Kewanee, but only the last named of the four infants survived and grew into a church. Min. M. McFarland was Bible-school evangelist in 1905, and Min. Marion Stevenson from Sept. 1, 1905, to Feb. 28, 1907. Mr. Stevenson combined a fine knowledge of the Scriptures with the best modern Bible-school methods; hence his period of service was the beginning of clearly defined and definite aims in Bible schools. A fruitful harvest continues to grow from his wise seed-sowing.

Mr. Clarence L. DePew entered this work Oct. 1, 1907, and continues therein. His aim has been to bring the schools up to the best national ideals, first in grading them, and, second, in making them "Front Rank."

Graded schools have the following classification: First, the family, which includes (1) the Home Department, who are non-attendants, and (2) the Cradle Roll, which includes infants, from birth to three years.

Second, Elementary, including (1) Beginners, four and five years; (2) Primary, six to eight years; (3) Juniors, nine to twelve years.

Third, Secondary: (1) Intermediate, from thirteen to sixteen years, and (2) Seniors, from seventeen to twenty years.

Fourth, Adult, all over twenty years of age.

A Front Rank school aims and tries to conform to the following standard:

1. Workers' conference at least monthly, using a prepared program and library.
2. Teacher-training class.
3. Graded school, using graded lessons.
4. Bibles owned generally and used in the school.
5. Organized classes. All secondary and adult classes holding International certificates.
6. Service, which includes (1) definite instruction on temperance, (2) evangelistic or direct efforts to lead the

members of the school to become Christians, and (3) missionary education and offerings.

In 1911 there were 169 Front Rank schools, of which sixty-five had reached all the requirements and were awarded the seals and pennant. These numbers grew steadily, so that in July, 1913, there were 202 in the Front Rank, of which eighty-two had reached all the requirements.

In 1913 there were in *all* the Bible schools of Illinois forty-three hundred organized adult classes, of which twelve hundred belonged to the Disciples. In the teen age they then had eighty-six organized classes. For several years they have had more than four times as many students and graduates in teacher-training than were enlisted in all other schools in the State combined. For the year closing July, 1913, they had 1,048 out of a total of 1,360 in teacher-training classes in Illinois.

In sixty years the Disciples have come from the foot to the head of the evangelistic class in the appreciation of and efficiency in the Bible school—one of the greatest agencies for the salvation of the world.

In 1907 there were 223 that contributed $1,293 to the National Benevolent Association. To the same cause, 246 schools in 1913 contributed $3,195.

There were 627 schools reported in 1913, with an aggregate membership of 81,576.

Section 3.

Christian Endeavor.

The Endeavor movement was begun in February, 1881. A few years thereafter many young people in the churches of Christ in Illinois organized themselves into these societies. They were classified into Senior, Intermediate and Junior. These grew steadily. The first years were filled with the enthusiasm of youth, and in a measure the movement became interdenominational. Among the Disciples in Illinois the high tide was reached in 1897, when they had, of the three classes, 577 societies, with an aggregate membership of ten thousand or more. During the later period of the Eureka Encampment, which ran from 1885 to 1899, the young people occupied a Saturday with very profitable programs. Up to that time, the sphere of the Christian Endeavor had not been clearly defined; so there was a tendency to make a church within the church. Local church officers, instead of helping and directing, generally held themselves aloof, while missionary secretaries actively encouraged separate and special contributions. The State Endeavor Society had a complement of officers. For the young people all this had an educational value. When the tide of enthusiasm reached its crest it at once began to recede. By 1905 it was decided that so many State officers were not needed; hence they gave place to a superintendent. Min. H. H. Peters gave gratuitous but efficient service in this position for four years, resigning in 1910. Later, State Endeavor was incorporated in the work of the State Missionary Society. In 1913 there were 284 societies reported, with an aggregate membership of 9,571.

The Endeavor work has been helpful to the Disciples of Christ in Illinois. 1. It has taught many young people to take active parts in public worship and continues to train others for service. 2. To many of them it has opened the window of world-wide missions and they have seen something of human needs. Their support of mission places in the State was most commendable. 3. It has cultivated the spirit of fraternity and co-operation among the young people of the various communions and has promoted the idea of Christian union. 4. The failure of some local societies in their virility or their lives has been due not so much to their unwillingness to serve, as a lack of practical encouragement by church officers. Very rarely has an Endeavor society risen above the spiritual level of the church of which it is a part. Its present need is the active and practical encouragement by the spiritual officers of the churches.

Section 4.

The Brotherhood.

The organization of the Brotherhood among the Disciples of Christ was made during the National Missionary Convention at New Orleans, La., in 1908. Mr. R. A. Long, of Kansas City, Mo., was the first president, and through his ability as an organizer and his financial liberality, the movement was given wide publicity and made good progress.

The organization in Illinois was effected at the State Missionary Convention at Eureka in 1909. Toller Swift served the first two years as president, and was followed by Min. J. A. Barnett to the present time.

The Brotherhood aims to promote general church interests. It seeks to train the men of the churches for greater and more effective service. It encourages Bible study and the organization of men into large Bible-study classes. A number of young men have already been led into the Christian ministry through the observance of Men's and Boys' Day by the churches. The men have become more generally interested in missions, benevolences and educational institutions. Many students have been induced to attend the colleges of the Christian Church through this agency. Investigation of these educational institutions and a report on their equipment and needs has been made by the National Brotherhood. A helpful service has been afforded in the large number of conferences conducted upon men's work in the churches. It affords a common platform, program and agency for the co-operation of all benevolent activities. These aims are commendable, but too general to insure the continuance of this Brotherhood in Illinois. When they determine to build up and sustain a representative Christian college, they will have an object worthy of their splendid abilities.

The work of the Brotherhood, local and general, is wisely and well directed by the secretary of the National Society, Mr. E. E. Elliott, Kansas City, Mo. According to his annual report in 1913, there were 933 local Brotherhoods affiliated with the national organization, of which over two hundred were in Illinois.

SECTION 5.

Ministerial Associations.

There had been meetings of ministers of the Christian Church in Illinois previous to 1873, with varying aims. On July 14 of that year fifteen preachers from the central part of the State assembled in Springfield. This meeting was in response to a call signed by H. W. Everest, Thomas Munnell, and J. W. and J. B. Allen. Mr. Everest was then pastor of the Springfield Church. He stated that the object of the meeting was, if thought best, to form a Ministerial Union, the aim and work of which should be to place the State missionary work upon a better footing, and especially to devise some ways by which the weak and languishing churches could be helped.

This Ministerial Association was formed the next day with A. J. Kane, president; H. W. Everest, vice-president, and N. S. Haynes, secretary. Nine of the preachers present pledged $500 to begin the work, which was to be done under the direction of the State Missionary Society. The Ministerial Association of Central Illinois grew in numbers and did very efficient service for a period of six years. Its second meeting was held in Jacksonville, in May, 1875; the third at Peoria, in May, 1876; the fourth at Normal, in May, 1877.

There was a special meeting of this Association at Springfield in August, 1877, when it was decided to make the aims and work of the Association more directly ministerial than they had hitherto been. In 1878 the Association met in August at Eureka, in 1879 at Princeton, and in 1880 at Bloomington, which was the last.

In the spring of 1882 the Central Illinois Ministerial Institute was organized, and has continued to the present time with very helpful annual meetings.

R. E. HENRY.   J. R. GOLDEN.
S. H. ZENDT.   R. F. THRAPP.   E. M. SMITH.
Committee.

CHAPTER VII.
BIOGRAPHIES.

George F. Adams.

Born in Elizaville, Ky. Died in 1884, at Blandinsville, Ill. Educated in the schools of his native village and the Bible College of Kentucky University. He came to Illinois about 1870. Held several pastorates, for which work he was not well fitted, but in the evangelistic field he was an unusually brilliant and successful preacher. Many were well taught and brought into the church through his ministry. His early death came by an accidental gunshot wound.

J. Buford Allen.

Fleming County, Ky., 1847.   1902, Spokane, Wash.

Was the youngest of three brothers who served in the Christian ministry—Dr. J. M. and J. W. Allen being the other two. Was educated in the public schools at Bloomington and at Eureka College. He began the study of law with Judge W. E. Nelson, of Decatur, but soon decided to enter the ministry. Besides other congregations in Illinois, he served the First Church in Springfield for a period of seven years. His health failing, he moved to Hutchinson, Kan., and later to Spokane, Wash.

Mr. Allen was a clear and vigorous thinker, a sincere and frank man and an efficient preacher.

John W. Allen.

Kentucky, 1843.

Mr. Allen was a native of Fleming County, Ky. He was well born and has always been a fine type of a Christian gentleman. After three years' service in the Federal Army, during which time he "did duty" at Donaldson, Shiloh and Vicksburg, he graduated at Eureka in 1867. He ministered to the church at Grayville, Ill.; served as State evangelist for one and one-half years; was pastor at Shelbyville and Jacksonville, and the following sixteen years in Chicago, two years with the South Side Christian Church, two years with the First, now a part of the Memorial, and twelve years with the Westside, now the Jackson Boulevard Church. That was the period in which the Disciples in the commercial metropolis were coming out of religious contention, chaos and confusion into sympathetic activities and orderly co-operation. It was a time of stress and storm, and Mr. Allen put into it virile years of his splendid life. To no one man is our cause in Chicago more indebted for a saner spirit and better vision than to him. His ministry has always been Scriptural, unselfish, forceful, sympathetic and constructive. Since 1895 his work has been in Spokane, Wash.

William G. Anderson.

Jefferson County, Ind., 1818.   1908, Colfax, Ill.

Came to McLean County in 1855. In 1858 he settled on a farm of 350 acres on the upper Mackinaw. When the railroad was built, the town of Colfax was located on part of his land. This, with the underlying coal, placed him in good pecuniary circumstances. Mr. Anderson received a limited education, but he had fine common sense and was devoted to duty. He preached much in the pioneer days, served as field solicitor for Eureka College five years, and was a public-spirited, progressive and aggressive citizen.

John Clinton Ashley.

On Atlantic Ocean, 1800.   1850, Walnut Hill, Ill.

He was one of the pioneer preachers of the Restoration movement and a coworker with A. Campbell. He was on a missionary tour from Ohio into Illinois when he sickened and died. His body was buried at Walnut Hill.

Dr. John Kossuth Ashley.

Portsmouth, O., 1824.   1905, Cisne, Ill.

A son of the former. Having graduated in medicine from the Ohio State University at Athens, he practiced his profession in that State for ten years. He came to Wayne County in 1856, and continued his work there till the close of his life. He was an intelligent, broad-minded and useful Christian man.

The Ashley family was interesting and distinguished. John M. represented Toledo (O.) district in Congress for a long term of years, and was a trusted adviser of President Lincoln in the dark days of war. Later, he was appointed territorial governor of Montana by President Grant. E. M. Ashley was engaged in the department of public surveys for a long period. During this time he entered the land on which the city of Denver, Colo., now stands.

Mrs. Alice Porter, of Albion, is a daughter of Dr. Ashley.

Aaron Prince Aten.

Near Eaton, O., 1839.

Mr. Aten came to Illinois in 1849, where he grew up on a farm. Educated at Rochester Seminary and Abingdon College. Received the A.B. and A.M. degrees, and later the LL.D. degree from another institution. He was ordained to the Christian ministry in 1860 and has preached continuously since. With his ministerial service he has united educational work through many years. He was pastor of the churches at Rochester and La Fayette and Abingdon, meanwhile serving as principal of Rochester Seminary and eight years as professor of belles lettres in Abingdon College. From 1861-65 he was recording secretary of the I. C. M. S. and a member of its board of managers. In 1864 he was the evangelist of the society in the old Tenth District. In 1876, Mr. Aten left Illinois. Since then he has been busy in his twofold service in Texas, Tennessee, Kentucky, Kansas and Oklahoma. In 1913 he was pastor of the Southside

Christian Church in Oklahoma City. Besides, he has done considerable editorial and literary work.

It goes without saying that Mr. Aten has been a very active man, but his good habits have helped to wide and varied usefulness and continued efficiency.

Elias Ayles.

Was born in Washington County, O., 1831. He became a Christian in 1863 and began preaching at once. He was also a railway engineer. Loss of hearing came with advancing years, so that he was compelled to cease work. He is a man of fine character whose life has been filled with good works. He resides at Fairfield.

Mrs. Clara Celestia Hale-Babcock.

Fitchville, O., 1850.

Her father was a Methodist preacher of the most rigid type. The daughter was zealous in her religious life and was quite content with the teachings of her church. She was past her twenty-fifth natal day before she ever heard a sermon from any other class of preachers. Curiosity led her to attend church one evening in Sterling, Ill., when Evangelist Geo. F. Adams was conducting a series of meetings there. As she passed out, Mr. Adams said to her: "I hope you enjoyed the services." She made no reply. He repeated the inquiry. She answered: "I can't say that I did." He asked her what there was in the meeting that she did not approve. Several persons had publicly confessed their faith in Christ. Waving her hand, she said: "Is that all there is in it? Dare you make it so easy to get into Christ?" He answered: "You must be accustomed to the use of the mourners' bench." "Surely I am," she replied. He said: "You are the very woman I have been looking for. If you will bring me a Scriptural authority for it, chapter and verse, I will install it to-morrow night." She said, "I will," and passed on, Mr. Adams remarking, "You know there are no records of conversions outside of the Acts of the Apostles,

A. D. NORTHCUTT. JOSEPH HOSTETLER.
MRS. C. C. BABCOCK.
N. S. HAYNES. WILLIAM B. RYAN.

so it must be there." Mrs. Babcock did not sleep that night till she had read the Book of Acts. Not finding what she read for, in the morning she visited her pastor and asked him where she could find in God's word authority for the altar. He answered: "Where have you been? Have you been listening to that Campbellite exhorter over the river?" She said "Yes." Then he said: "He will lead you to the devil, for they are not orthodox. They don't believe in the Holy Spirit or in prayer." She replied that she had not gone from choice, "but you have not answered my question." After some other such conversation, the pastor said that the altar for those trying to come to Christ was not commanded, but the church teaches it as a good method. Then she asked: "How much does the church teach that is not in the Bible? If you have one human plan, how shall we know the divine plan? It weakens my faith." A few evenings later Mr. Babcock persuaded his wife to hear Mr. Adams again. On that occasion she witnessed Scriptural baptism for the first time, and the sermon was on baptism. Passing out, Mr. Adams asked her about the Scripture for the use of the mourners' bench. She replied frankly: "It is not there and we have no right to use it." He inquired: "Have you been baptized?" "Not according to that form," she answered. "Will you not obey Christ in the Bible way?" he asked. She went home sad and thoughtful. The next morning she went to see her pastor, who prayed with her and scolded her. "Will you immerse me?" she asked. "No, no; you have been baptized according to your father's faith and the church's teaching," he answered. She said: "What does the Bible teach? You must show me where the Scripture commands sprinkling or I shall go down into the water like my Saviour." A week later, Mr. and Mrs. Babcock were baptized by Mr. Adams. With Bible in hand, she went from door to door of her friends, many of whom turned to the Lord. She did not formally unite with the Sterling Church until she first measured its teachings and practices by the word of God. Later, she went out into the service of the W.

C. T. U. in Illinois. Being in Erie on a Sunday, she was induced to speak to the Christian congregation in the forenoon. The presence and approval of God were so manifest that she was led to continue in the service of that congregation. Later, after wise counsel and mature deliberation, she was ordained to the Christian ministry in 1888. Her work proved a great blessing to the church in that part of the State. She proved herself both a good evangelist and pastor. She has conducted twenty-eight fruitful meetings and has made about fourteen hundred converts, one thousand of whom she baptized with her own hand. The little church of Erie she served altogether fifteen years. In that community she preached 172 funeral sermons. She was the first woman in Illinois to enter the Christian ministry. In all this splendid service she had the cordial moral support of her husband. After twenty-five years of this work, she has retired to the quiet of a Canadian farm home.

George E. Bacon.

Madison, Ind., 1851.   1896, Aurora, Ill.

Came with his parents to Kansas, Ill., in 1854. His mischievous disposition in boyhood was irrepressible. Coming to maturity, he entered the ministry, but soon decided that he was unwilling to make the full surrender that its obligations impose. He became a lawyer and State's attorney of Edgar County. In 1886 he was elected to the State Senate and returned in 1890, serving eight years. He was a fluent and brilliant orator. In the formal eulogies pronounced by representatives of the General Assembly upon John A. Logan, Mr. Bacon's far surpassed all others.

Col. Edward D. Baker.

·London, England, 1811.   1861, Ball's Bluff (Va.) Battlefield.

At the age of four years this boy was brought to Philadelphia, and at the age of fifteen he was teaching school. He was admitted to the bar in Carrollton, Ill., in 1830; the next year married Mrs. Mary Ann Lee, and in 1832 participated actively in the Black Hawk War.

It was shortly after his marriage that he was immersed and became a member of the church in Carrollton. It is not probable that he was formally set apart to the Christian ministry, but his ardent disposition, superior ability as a public speaker and his sincere devotion to the pure gospel led him to its public proclamation for near a decade. He also baptized some converts. Min. W. H. Cannon, pastor of the Central Church, Decatur, says that his own grandfather, Hardin Goodin, whom he knew well, was immersed by Mr. Baker in Honey Creek, Pike County. Nor was this an exceptional instance. He was also associated with those Disciples in the early thirties at Jacksonville in their first efforts looking toward co-operative missionary work.

In 1835 he moved to Springfield. There he met and became the sincere and lifelong friend of Abraham Lincoln. Two such magnificent and magnanimous souls could easily understand and love each other. This friendship proved of incalculable value to the Federal Union in the black night of bloody horrors in which both suns went down.

In 1837, Mr. Baker was elected to the House in the Legislature and in 1840 to the Senate. In 1844 he beat Mr. Lincoln for the nomination for Congress on the Whig ticket, and was elected. But Mr. Lincoln's feelings were reflected in the fact that a baby boy who came into his home in 1846 was named Edward Baker Lincoln. While representing the Springfield district in Congress, Mr. Baker raised a regiment of infantry and saw active service as its colonel in the Mexican War. Meanwhile, his official duties calling him to Washington, he addressed the House of Representatives wearing his military uniform. In 1848, Colonel Baker, rather than contest a second time with Mr. Lincoln the nomination for Congress, moved to Galena. There he was nominated on the Whig ticket, and elected. Mr. Lincoln was returned from the Springfield district. In 1851, Colonel Baker was engaged in superintending the construction of the

Panama Railroad. In 1852 he moved to California. In San Francisco he quickly took a leading place at the bar, and for eight years was one of the representative and most influential citizens of the State.

Upon the urgent invitation of friends he was induced to move to Salem, Ore., in February, 1860. Such was his fidelity to principle, his commanding ability, his matchless eloquence and urbanity, that he was elected to the United States Senate at the next meeting of the Oregon Legislature.

In 1912, Mr. E. R. Kennedy published a volume entitled "The Contest for California in 1861," in which he clearly shows that it was chiefly through the statesmanship of Colonel Baker that the Pacific Coast was then saved to the Union. The book is charmingly written and is a distinct contribution to American history.

With the coming of the Civil War, Mr. Baker was busy in the United States Senate. However, he raised a regiment in New York and Philadelphia of sixteen hundred men and was commissioned to command the brigade to which it belonged. It was encamped near the Capital. On August 1, 1861, members of the Senate hastily summoned Colonel and Senator Baker to the chamber to reply to a speech to be delivered there that day by Senator Breckenridge, of Kentucky. He came in, laid his sword upon his desk, and sat down to listen. His reply is classed among the great orations of the world. James G. Blaine says that its delivery was the most extraordinary of any occurrence that ever transpired in the Senate chamber.

October 21, having stood at the head of his brigade for hours against great odds, he was struck by four or five rifle-balls almost simultaneously and fell in death—"as gentle and pure and unselfish and generous and eloquent and valiant a man as ever cheerfully gave his life for a noble cause." Mrs. Judith Bradner, a charter member of the First Church in Bloomington, passed on in 1912 at the age of ninety-eight years. She at one time entertained at dinner in her home Stephen A. Douglas, Abraham Lincoln and Edward D.

Baker. She described Mr. Baker as a most attractive personality, a fine conversationalist and an engaging presence, at once commanding and kindly. A marble statue inscribed "Baker" stands in one of the rooms of the nation's Capitol.

Dr. J. W. Ballinger.

Emmerson, Mo., 1837.   1879, Niantic, Ill.

Most of the life of Mr. Ballinger was passed in the State of his birth. In the five closing years of his life, which were devoted to the Niantic community, he gripped the people as few men can. In the places of his residence he served as elder, teacher, physician and minister. He was careful to remember the poor, but held continuously the good will of all classes. He was one of the truest friends of humanity and the noblest pattern of manhood.

N. S. Bastian.

Was of Holland descent and a native of New York State. He received a liberal education, and throughout his life was esteemed both for his learning and culture.

He became a member of the M. E. Church in early life, and shortly thereafter entered the Christian ministry. In 1843 this church wished to send a missionary to one of the districts of the West African coast. Mr. Bastian was asked to go. After consideration, he answered: "Christ died for me. I will go." His first child was born there. The native chiefs came from far to see a white baby and make it a present. The child lived only a few months. After a time, Mr. Bastian was sent to Europe on business connected with the African mission. He left his wife there and set sail. On his voyage, one evening just after he had retired to bed and before he had closed his eyes, apparently his wife stood before him. Ere he could address her, she vanished. When he landed in Europe he met orders from his Mission Board to return to America. Landing in New York, he was met by a member of the Board, to whom he said, "Have you heard from Africa?" The reply was, "Yes. And Sarah is dead." This was Mr. Bastian's wife. On comparing the day and the hour, he found that his wife had gone to be at home with her Lord at the moment when he saw her appearance to him on shipboard.

Mr. Bastian's studies of the New Testament had unsettled his thoughts on the subject of Christian baptism. Finding himself more in harmony with the Baptist than with the Methodist Church, he peaceably changed his ecclesiastical affiliation. Coming West, he soon fell in with the Disciples. He was at once attracted and charmed by the Scripturalness of their preaching and the simplicity of their plea; hence, he was not long in casting in his lot with the people whose teaching and practice were so fully in accord with his own conclusions. Some of his Methodist brethren said that the fact of his "joining the Campbellites" was proof that "he was rattled;" whereas, his thoughts and aims were only moving in wider orbits.

His sacred dust and that of his second wife—a Christian woman of the highest type—repose in unmarked graves at Sullivan, Ill. Nor is a memorial window there in the house of God for these, his faithful servants.

Archibald T. Benson.

Tennessee, 1818.   1894, Marion, Ill.

Came to Williamson County when a young man, and shortly thereafter became a Christian and a preacher. His ministry reached out to many places in that part of the State. In the years of his active service, he baptized more converts, married more couples and conducted more funerals than any preacher in the county. He served as chaplain of the 128th Illinois Volunteer Infantry during the Civil War. He was noted for his hospitality and many good works.

Charles J. and Thomas V. Berry.

St. Andrews, New Brunswick.   1871, Lincoln, Ill.
St. Andrews, New Brunswick, 1822. 1882, Creston, Ia.

Charles J. came to Boston when in his teens, and for a

period was a member of the Tremont Temple Free Will Baptist Church. His moral convictions were strong, and his opposition to slavery and all secret societies became so radical that, as his pastor, Nathaniel Colver, put it, "Charles compelled the church to disfellowship him." Meanwhile, by the aid of the *Millennial Harbinger,* he came to a knowledge of the Restoration movement. Whereupon, he helped his brother Thomas in the formation of a church of Christ and instituted worship on the Lord's Days after the apostolic example. In 1855 he succeeded James Darsie as pastor of the church at Connersville, Pa. He came to Illinois in 1859, and resided at Princeton, Abingdon and Lincoln, at which places, or in the surrounding sections, he labored assiduously in the gospel till his death, which came by tuberculosis.

Thomas V. also came to Boston in his teens, and there learned the trade of a piano-maker. In 1845 he learned the gospel from a Mr. Dungan, of Baltimore, who had gone to Boston to buy leather goods. To the little church formed there Thomas gave most of his earnings from his manual labor for hall rent, etc. He graduated from Bethany. Coming to Illinois in 1860, he first served the Bloomington Church seven years and later the churches at Princeton, Lincoln and Monmouth.

These brothers were the sons of Methodist parents. The home was one of regular prayer and practical piety. They were men of a high spiritual type and gave their time to genuine service.

Dr. James M. Bell.

Sangamon County, Ill., 1856.

Educated at the University of Michigan. Was elected to the House of the Legislature in 1910-12. Dr. Bell is a member of the church at Rochester.

Prof. W. F. Black.

Moorefield, Ky., 1839.   1908, Chicago, Ill.

Mr. Black's early years were passed in schoolrooms as student and teacher. He graduated at Asbury, now DePauw

University, and spent some time at Hiram while J. A. Garfield was there. He entered the ministry at the age of eighteen, and for many years was a very popular and successful preacher. He served as pastor at Terre Haute, Greencastle and Indianapolis, Ind., and Tuscola and Chicago, Ill., and was president of the Northwest University, now Butler College, in 1872-74. He was best known as a great evangelist. His meetings in cities, towns and country were equally successful—the additions were counted by hundreds and by thousands. Many of these were leading and influential citizens of their communities. He did his work without the aid of professional singers or special helpers. His custom was to teach the people the Scriptures and follow this lesson in the same meeting with a great sermon. Illinois owes much to his self-denying and faithful service, for not a few of her feeble congregations were thereby saved from death to large usefulness, and many from all classes of society were led to know and to walk in the better way. He is held in tender memory by a host of grateful friends.

William Henry Boles.

Perry County, Ill., 1850.

Educated in country schools, Ewing College and Butler College. Entered the Christian ministry in 1870. Served the churches at De Soto, Marion, Carbondale, Duquoin, Pekin and Christopher as pastor. Mr. Boles has been widely and well known for a quarter of a century as a live wire. He has been a successful evangelist and a popular lecturer, speaking to many multitudes on Mormonism, the liquor traffic, evidences of Christianity, Romanism, and other subjects that delude and enslave people in error. He was never known to run away from a public discussion when it was thrust upon him. He is industrious, genial, democratic and enthusiastic in his work. Over eight thousand people have been added to the churches by his ministry. In March, 1888, he conducted a series of meetings in Duquoin. At its beginning he entered into an agreement with Dr. A. J. Fishback, a rationalist of local notoriety. First, the doctor was to hear every sermon preached by Mr. Boles. Second, for two hours a day, four days in the week, they were privately to consider the fundamentals of Christianity. Third, if the doctor was convinced that the Bible came from God and that Jesus is divine, he should quit the "Freethinkers" and preach the gospel henceforward. Fourth, if Mr. Boles should be convinced to the contrary, he should quit the pulpit and take the platform for infidelity. Before the meeting closed, Dr. Fishback became a Christian. To the close of his life, nine years thereafter, he was an able minister of Jesus Christ. Mr. Boles is a brave and unselfish patriot, and bears in his body the marks of the Lord Jesus.

Dr. William Booz.

Woodford County, Ky., 1831. 1901, Carthage, Ill.

Those who were personally acquainted with this gentleman called him a noted physician, preacher, philosopher and friend. His father's family came to Illinois in 1837, and in 1839 into Hancock County. Orphaned of his parents at the age of fourteen, he was one of six children left penniless and alone. He appealed to the judge for the privilege of choosing his own guardian, which was granted. In the home of this friend he became one of the family. The only schoolbook he there had was an English novel, from which he would read aloud to the pleasure of the whole school. By his persistence and pine-knot efforts, at the age of fifteen he secured a subscription school, which he taught in the kitchen of David Mason's cabin. The money thus earned was used to enable him to make some trips to Carthage and to buy and borrow some books. For three years he studied medicine, for his great ambition was to be a physician. Meanwhile, he taught schools as necessary. He became a Christian under the ministry of Gilmore Callison and began to preach at the age of seventeen. His knowledge of the Bible soon became remarkable, and later he was widely recognized as an eloquent preacher. A minister of another church asked Dr. Booz to come to Pontoosuc at one time and meet an opponent in a public discussion. So well was the work done that the opponent failed to appear the second evening.

All his life he was a country doctor. Despite his early disadvantages and later handicaps, he rose to wide recognition. At one time he had the entire practice in 170 square miles around his home, except in twelve families. He had patients all over western Illinois as well as in Iowa, Missouri, Ohio and Kentucky. When he began the practice of medicine at the age of twenty-two, he laid down certain rules, from which he never deviated through the forty-seven years of his professional work. He was always a hard student—a progressive, a discoverer, a leader. During the period of his practice he rode more than one-half-million miles, mostly through the brakes of Crooked Creek. He regarded a call to a bed of pain as a call to duty. Through trackless forests, bridgeless streams and Egyptian darkness, he made countless trips to the homes of suffering, and ofttimes where no compensation could be expected except the love and gratitude that followed him to his dying day. He was the embodiment of cheerfulness, and his peculiar personality inspired his patients with confidence.

Without personal political ambition, he was a leader in politics.

He wrote well. His papers for township literary societies were gems of pathos, wit and homely good sense. In the early sixties he sent a communication to the Carthage *Republican* over the pseudonym, "Country Jake." The editor was so impressed with its pungent character that he encouraged him to send weekly contributions. *Thus was born provincial journalism in Illinois.*

In medicine Dr. Booz was a genius, to the world a Christian, to his contemporaries a philosopher, and to his family and to all people, a gentleman. He was the soul of honor, justice and generosity. There was not a selfish or mean streak in him. The pride of his Kentucky blood was apparent in his exalted character. And a country doctor all his life *because he wanted to be!*

Thomas E. Bondurant.

Near Mechanicsburg, Ill., 1831.   1905, De Land, Ill.

His parents were Kentuckians who came to Illinois in 1828. In 1854, Mr. Bondurant entered 290 acres of land in Piatt County, under the graduation act of Congress, at fifty cents per acre. He moved there in 1856, which was his home to the close of his life. The year before he had attended Eureka College, but, becoming engrossed in his business, did not return.

Mr. Bondurant was never married. In 1861 his mother and a sister, Miss Mary E. Bondurant, went to De Land, and the three constituted the family. Throughout his life he was a farmer and live-stock man. He was a shrewd and far-sighted business man. His advice to men starting in life was, "Buy land." He continued to follow this maxim, and accumulated large property.

He came into the church in 1851, and for fifty-four years was an intelligent and active Christian. He always stood openly for the better things in life and against the saloon and kindred evils. And he was never willing to compromise with wrong. He was generous to many worthy causes while he lived, but did not talk about his benefactions.

At the time of his decease, his estate was valued at about $450,000. By his last will, the larger part of this wealth is to be used, after ten years, for educational and missionary purposes. His end was peace.

Hughes Bowles.

Virginia, 1786.   1846, DeWitt County, Ill.

This man came from Virginia to Caneridge, Ky., and was probably a product of the great revival held there in 1801. His education was limited, but he was a great reader and a good historian. He united with the Baptist Church and was licensed to preach. He soon decided that denominationalism was wrong, and he believed that God had revealed to every man his whole duty in plain and unmistakable terms in the Bible.

He settled on a farm in DeWitt County, near the site of Old Union Church, Turnbridge Township, on the banks of Salt Creek, in the spring of 1830. He had then been married twice and was the father of twelve living children. Members of his family maintained the farm of two hundred acres while the father gave his time to preaching the gospel. His trips were made on horseback and reached from ten to fifty miles. The storms of the winters, the miry sloughs and swollen streams of the springs and early summers frequently challenged the faith and courage of the itinerant preachers. But Mr. Bowles seldom missed an appointment.

He was well versed in the Scriptures and could almost quote the New Testament from beginning to end. Associated with him in his Christian work there were Abner Peeler, powerful in argument and appeal and a true prophet's vision; James Scott, who spoke with the "old Baptist tone," and when the weather was warm would, in the progress of his sermon, lay off his coat, unbutton his collar and sleeves and plead most earnestly with his hearers; and Alfred Lindsey, mild, gentle and with wonderful winning power. Ten dollars was the largest sum Hughes Bowles ever received for holding a meeting, which was at the Lake Fork Church. This money he gave to a Mrs. Frakes, a widowed sister in the Lord, who was thrown from her horse, breaking her hip, while going to his meeting. He was a kind and sympathetic man, but very positive. All his children were in the fold ere their father went away to be with the Good Shepherd.

David Bowles.

Bourbon County, Ky., 1825.   1911, Emden, Ill.

David was the oldest son. He was a farmer, residing on Delavan Prairie, in Logan County. He read much, was decidedly conservative and a good public speaker. He assisted in the organization of several churches within the radius of his Christian service.

March 10, 1903, from his home in Emden, Ill., David Bowles wrote to T. T. Holton. From his communication the following is taken:

I do not know of a meeting-house in this part of the State before 1840. The people met for worship in the summer-time in the groves, in the winter-time in their dwelling-houses. The houses were nearly all log cabins eighteen feet square. Two beds in this room. A big fireplace in one end. No windows. Glass could not be had. So, you see, this left but a small meeting-house. But you would be surprised at the number of people that would get into one of these houses for worship. The young women and some married women would pull off their shoes and get up on the beds, till sometimes there would be from eight to ten on each bed. Some people may say, "This is unreasonable—the beds could not hold them up." They were not such bedsteads as we have now. Usually there was but one post to the bedstead. Holes bored into the logs of the wall with a two-inch auger and a strong rail sharpened to fit was inserted and strong rope cords made at home of hemp made them very strong. Still, once in awhile, one of these cords would break and let them to the floor. Soon everything would be quiet again. With all our glorious meetings we would sometimes have some of the ridiculous. I will only name one or two. One cold winter day we met at old Father Hall's. Bro. Walter Bowles was to preach. The house was just such as I have described, with a loft laid with large clapboards. A ladder going up in the right-hand corner by the fireplace. The door shut. A lamp lighted. Brother Walter stood right by or under the ladder that led to the loft. He was lining his hymn, when a big tomcat raised a racket up in the loft and came tearing down the ladder. Brother Walter rather dodged. But some of the older ones were able to sing the hymn. The house was so crowded that none could kneel. Everybody's face was turned toward the fire. While Brother Walter was offering prayer the cat that had got whipped came and sat down in front of the fire. The cat that had whipped came slipping through the crowd, and, seeing the one he had whipped sitting before the fire, he aimed to give him a big lick. But the other saw him in time to slip out of the way. The boss cat went right under the fore-stick into the fire and came out squalling and carried the fire and coals back through the crowd. Old Mother Hall saw it would set the house on fire. Broke in with a broom on him. Everybody in the house saw it, and Brother Walt brought his prayer to a close very quickly. Soon we were dismissed.

I will give just one more to show the inconveniences we had to labor under. We had prayer-meeting at old Bro. James Ferrice's one night. The old grease-lamp was stuck in the wall of the house just about as high as a man's shoulder. Bro. Ambrose Hall was up talking. Forgot himself and threw his head back, and the blaze was all over his head in an instant. Some of the brethren sprang to him and extinguished the flame. So that brought that meeting to a sudden close. This is enough of the ridiculous.

William F. Bowles.

Kentucky, 1829.

William F. Bowles was brought by his parents to Illinois in 1830. He became a Christian at thirteen and served the Old Union Church as deacon and elder for many years. A great student of the Bible, his judgment was regarded as based upon truth and justice. He always helped in the aggressive work of the church, and his conclusions on church government were rarely questioned. His one son and four grandchildren are all prominent in the work of the church. He is the sole survivor of the family that came to Illinois, and resides with his son in Des Moines, Ia.

Walter P. Bowles.

Kentucky, 1811.   1863, Illinois.

This man was the most forceful and noted of this remarkable family. He was the son of Hughes and Ruth Prather Bowles. During his mature years he was called by nearly all of his acquaintances "Wattie Bowles."

He was physically a man of the finest type. Standing six feet and one inch in his stocking feet, his weight was 190 pounds. Rarely could any man follow him with ax, cradle or scythe. He could stand with both feet in a half-bushel measure and shoulder four bushels of wheat in one sack.

There was an admirable co-ordination between his physical forces and his mental energies. At about the age of twenty-two he was married to Miss Isabel Wallace, a daughter of Col. Andrew Wallace, who served in our army in the war of 1812. At that time Mr. Bowles could not read. His wife proved herself to be a fine teacher—her husband an unusually bright pupil. Five years thereafter he could quote nearly all of the New Testament from memory, and before the close of his life, most of the Old as well. His memory was extraordinary. He knew the map of Palestine better than most people know their own State.

Of course Mr. Bowles was a farmer, owning and cultivating his land. But shortly after his marriage he became a preacher. Those who heard him, testify that he was powerful and eloquent. His superior ability to sing and induce others to sing, added much to his efficiency. He was mighty in prayer as well. Sometimes he would stop in his discourse, drop down upon his knees, and passionately plead for the salvation of sinners. In plowing-time he would work in his fields Saturdays till 11 o'clock A. M., then come to his house. Then he would whet his razor on his boot-leg, hone it on the palm of his left hand, and shave his face clean and smooth without the aid of a mirror; then grease his boots, wash up and redress; after eating his dinner, he would saddle his horse and gallop away ten to thirty miles and preach Saturday night and Sunday in a residence or schoolhouse to fifteen or more people. For this work he received not a dollar. His reward was the sweet consciousness of duty well done and that God was pleased. Thus he traveled through DeWitt, Sangamon, Morgan, Logan and McLean Counties. At one time he held a "big meeting" in the barn of John Campbell, in Tazewell County, at which three hundred additions were received.

Mr. Bowles lived in a farmhouse in Turnbridge Township. He was a pronounced antislavery man and a lifelong friend of Abraham Lincoln, who was entertained a number of times in the hospitable home of Mr. Bowles. In the earlier period of Mr. Lincoln's life, on one of these occasions he said: "Watt, if I could preach like you, I would rather do that than be President."

Mr. Bowles was absolutely fearless. In one of his meetings in a schoolhouse two young men got to playing cards.

He asked them to desist, urging that it was quite out of place. In a few minutes they were at it again. The preacher said they must stop it. When they started their game the third time he walked back to them, grasped each one by his collar with his vise-like hands, led them to the door, bumped their heads together and told them to go. They went.

At one time Mr. Bowles and his cousin, John G. Campbell, of McLean County, were driving together in some kind of a one-horse rig. At high noon they came to the home of a pioneer farmer, located not far from the present site of Waynesville. The farmer and his "hired man" had just come in from the field, when the following conversation took place:

"Hello, neighbor," called out Mr. Bowles; "we wish to go to New Jerusalem and have stopped to ask you about the way."

"To where?" asked the farmer.

"To New Jerusalem."

"Never heard of any such place. This road leads up to Bloomington."

"No," answered Bowles, "we are going to New Jerusalem. But we are hungry. Now, if you will give us our dinner and feed our horse I will tell you the way to New Jerusalem."

"The devil you will," answered the farmer. "I will give you your dinners and feed your horse for fifty cents."

When they had finished dinner, Mr. Bowles pushed back a little from the table and began to preach to them the way of the Lord. When they rose from their places it was to go to a near-by stream, where Mr. Bowles baptized the farmer, his wife and the hired man—the entire family.

His body sleeps in Old Union Cemetery, within six feet of the spot where stood the pulpit in which he had preached hundreds of times.

God always provides the man for the time, and Wattie Bowles was a child of Providence.

Christopher C. Boyer.

Edgar County, Ill., 1839. 1908, Edgar County, Ill.

Mr. Boyer resided on a farm all his life in the county of his birth. However, for a long period he was an active but a conservative and useful minister, chiefly in Edgar, Coles and Clark Counties. His financial compensation for his ministerial labors was always small. He was the father of Min. T. A. Taylor and Prof. E. E. Boyer, of Eureka College.

Clark Braden.

Trumbull County, O., 1831.

Mr. Braden graduated from Farmers College, Cincinnati, O., in 1860. No one aided him by a dollar after he left the country district school. For ten years he labored, taught and attended school as he could. Aiding his younger brothers and sisters, in their struggles for an education, delayed the completion of his own course. His father and mother were pioneer Abolitionists and active teetotaler-temperance advocates from 1835 to 1855. Mr. Braden was himself in line with the enemies of slavery from his youth. He cast his first vote for Freesoil in 1852. He stumped and voted for Fremont in 1856, and for Lincoln in 1860. In this work his life was twice in peril from friends of the saloons and thrice by Mormons. He made war speeches and carried a gun as a soldier in the 127th Illinois Volunteer Infantry.

Many years of his life have been given to educational work. In this field he filled many positions, from the teacher of a "deestrick skule and board round" to the presidency of three colleges.

He has served in the Christian ministry for fifty-seven years and has been pastor of thirty-five churches. He has been a voluminous writer and has edited one political and one religious paper. He has delivered more than six thousand lectures. He has conducted 133 public discussions, on nearly all topics agitating the public mind. Twenty-six of these discussions were in Illinois. He was endorsed for more than one hundred other debates at which his opponents failed to appear, including "Seventh-dayists," infidels and Mormons. For more than twenty years it was a standing formula with these errorists, when they challenged for a debate, to condition, "any one except Braden." Some of his opponents, when hard pressed by Mr. Braden, unceremoniously fled from the halls where the discussions were in progress, amid the jeers and hisses of audiences. His debates and lectures have reached through many States and Provinces of Canada. In April, 1872, Mr. Braden sent a challenge to the great agnostic, Robert G. Ingersoll, to debate in Peoria. When asked by Colonel Wright, "Why do you not accept?" he replied, "I am not such a fool as to debate. He would wear me out." Mr. Braden's last public discussion was successfully conducted in his seventy-eighth year. A prominent minister declared in a church paper that Mr. Braden, by his assaults upon errors and his earnest advocacy of the truth, had saved the Pacific Coast from a tidal wave of infidelity. Mr. Braden was sometimes criticized for his neglect or disregard of the social amenities of life. However, he was always a companionable man, when he had time. A fine physique has enabled him to do the work of two or three men. He has been "a crank all his life and grows no better," for he is now an active advocate of Christian socialism. The storms of eighty years have not cooled the ardor of his love for "the truth as it is in Jesus." For more than sixty years he has studied, investigated, written, taught and debated, and through these six eventful decades his master aim has been, "Accept the Christ's teachings, live the Christ life, realize the Christ character."

Dr. J. H. Breeden.

Sullivan County, Ind., 1834.   1911, Ipava, Ill.

Dr. Breeden was a born leader of people. He came from Pike County, Ill., about 1858, and settled in the village of Summum, in Fulton County, to practice medicine. At that time his material possessions consisted of his wife—a woman of superior mind and heart—one son, a pony, a dog, a little house furniture and his medicine-case. He began life there in a two-roomed house, in which he resided for a long time. His first concern was the formation of a church in his new home, after the primitive order, for he had learned the word of God and how to preach it. He was chiefly instrumental in establishing the church in Summum, and its care devolved mainly upon him for many years. Besides, he was active in preaching the gospel in the communities around and about. Meanwhile, his work as a physician grew and increased and became very extensive. In this he was sincere, prudent, frank and kindly, so that his friends were counted by thousands. He was a genial and companionable man. With the acquisition of property his liberality grew. He was the friend of every good cause and the liberal supporter of every good work. For a term of years he served well as a trustee of Eureka College. During his life and by his last will he contributed thousands of dollars to advance the kingdom of God. He was a brotherly man, skillful in his profession, successful in business and a good preacher as well. H. O. Breeden is his gifted son.

J. H. G. Brinkerhoff.

Hackensack, N. J., 1844.

Came with his father's family to Illinois in 1852. Educated in common schools, Steele's Seminary, Indiana Normal, and graduated in law at McKendrie College. He has taught in high schools twenty years, been frequently engaged in newspaper work and has preached the gospel as well.

H. M. Brooks.

Meigs County, O., 1855.

Was educated in the school of hard manual work and trained in the common and select schools, U. C. College and literary correspondence courses of two universities. He was an ordained minister in the Christian Denomination for four years. In January, 1889, at Illiopolis, Ill., he united with the Christian Church during the pastorate of U. M. Browder. He served the Paris Church with much efficiency; also preached for the Kansas and Bell Ridge Churches in Edgar County, and the church at Tuscola, besides churches in other States. He has organized five congregations and induced fourteen young men to enter the Christian ministry. He conducted the funeral of Dennis Hanks, who taught Abraham Lincoln to read. Mr. Hanks died at the age of ninety-three years from the effects of a runaway.

Theodore Brooks.

Came from Troy, N. Y., to Lexington, Ill., in 1860. The recently formed church there had invited him to become its pastor. He served this congregation and that at Lincoln half-time each. Mr. Brooks was a scholarly man, with a ready command of a fine vocabulary. Of companionable disposition, he was a superior conversationalist. As a preacher he was fervent and interesting. It was his custom when he came to Illinois not to preach "first principles" and to never give, at the close of his sermons, the public invitation for people to accept the Saviour. One Sunday in June, 1861, when preaching in Lexington, he was informed that a lady wished to present her letter and be received into the congregation; so he gave the invitation. While the hymn was being sung, a gentleman passed up one aisle and his sister the other—both to make the good confession. The preacher, learning the facts, cried out, "O God, forgive my lack of faith!" His continued ministry in Illinois was most helpful to both congregations and preachers.

George Matthew Brown.

Kentucky, 1816.   1893, Pike County, Ill.

He was a brother of Wm. H. Brown, and was usually called Matty Brown. He was peculiar to marked eccentricity, but did useful work in Pike County and elsewhere.

William M. Brown.

Kentucky.   1863, Tennessee.

This man was a striking personality. He was six feet and two inches in height and of fine form, weighing two hundred pounds. His head was large, his face strong and clean-shaven, and his dark hair he wore long for a male and decidedly pompadour.

He came to Springfield in 1841 and for a time was pastor of the church there.

He was elected as the first president of Eureka College, but his service was only nominal.

His chief work was that of an evangelist. In this sphere he was probably the most noted among the Disciples during his period of service in Illinois. He was regarded as a powerful preacher. His sermons united argument with impassioned appeal. In dealing with what he considered denominational doctrinal errors he was often as inexorable as logic could be, even to rasping. On one such occasion, a woman auditor, not in sympathy with all his teaching, personally expressed the wish that she "might have his scalp for a scrub-brush." At one of the earlier State Meetings held in Springfield, the mountain-top was reached on the Lord's Day. It was the custom then, at the close of the communion, to shake hands throughout the assembly. Some of the elder brethren would embrace each other and weep tears of joy. On this occasion, Mr. Brown and the gentle Barton W. Stone were quite carried from the usual self-poise by the ecstacy of joy. Then Mr. Stone cried out, "Brother Brown, you speak too harshly of people's errors. Dear brother, when you find a stone across the path of truth, just carefully roll it away, but don't try to spat the man who laid it there." It is said that a sermon that he delivered at Mt. Pulaski, following the Kane-Bunn debate on Universalism, was such a terrific indictment of other Protestant preachers and so filled with ginger and salt. that several days passed before those in the great audience regained sufficient composure to talk about the discourse.

To his aggressiveness he added a brilliant imagination. His pictures of heavenly things were sublime. Great crowds attended his meetings and many were turned to the Lord. After all, a sweet tenderness was in his soul. Conducting a meeting in Bloomington in a cold winter, he was entertained in the inviting home of Dr. R. O. Warriner. After the evening meetings, going home the doctor led his little daughter Belle by the hand. The child, tired and very sleepy, as all normal children should be in such circumstances, cried. Then Mr. Brown would sing to her:

> "Rings on her fingers, bells on her toes,
> She keeps boohooing wherever she goes."

The churches at Springfield, Bloomington, Pittsfield, and at many other places in the State, are yet much indebted to this great preacher. He became chaplain in the Thirty-eighth Illinois Volunteer Infantry, and, contracting a cold at the battle of Chickamauga, died ten days later.

Uriah Marion Browder.

Jamestown, O., 1846.   1907, Dayton, O.

Mr. Browder was a pastor and evangelist and a public debater in Illinois for a period of the seventies and eighties. He was clear in thinking, masterful in logic, and forceful in the presentation of the truth, which he never questioned or compromised. He was the author of several books.

Francis M. Bruner.

Kentucky, 1833.   1899, Iowa.

Mr. Bruner was of German ancestry and rugged pioneer progenitors. His boyhood and youth were passed upon his father's farm in Illinois. He graduated from Knox College in 1857 with the honors of his class. He went to Europe in 1858, where he spent three years at the Universities of Halle in Prussia and 'l Ecloe de Paris in France. Some time was also passed in the great libraries, the museums and art galleries of Berlin and London. He was a diligent student and an indefatigable worker, so that he came to a strength of intellect, breadth of scholarship and greatness of character that made him the peer of the best men of his time. He was captain of Company A of the Seventh United States Colored Infantry one year, during which time he contracted the germs of relentless disease from which he was never thereafter free. In 1866-67 he was a member of the Illinois Legislature, serving with high honor.

In 1870 he became president of Oskaloosa College, Iowa, where he served efficiently as executive, teacher and solicitor for six years. He was induced to accept the presidency of Abingdon College in 1877. Into his efforts to restore the school to its former prosperity and usefulness he threw the indomitable energy of all his splendid faculties; but the seeds of its death had already been sown. With the union of Abingdon and Eureka Colleges he became the head of the Bible Department. The ripest fruit of his whole life was there gathered by the young men who sat in the shade of this great tree. After four years there, failing health compelled his resignation.

Mr. Bruner was a great teacher of the word of God. His much learning did not make him mad in either mind or heart. Intellectual pride and self-righteousness had no place in him. Cast in a heroic mold, he was genuinely humble and loving. In health and sickness, in prosperity and adversity, in appreciation of his worth or its lack, he was a great soul who moved forward unwaveringly to his high aims.

John Buckles.

Illinois, 1822.   1909, Illinois.

In 1822, when John Buckles was three weeks old, his parents left White County, Ill., to find and make a home in that part of central Illinois now known as Logan County. John was the third child, and on this journey was carried in the arms of his mother, who rode on horseback. The distance was about 150 miles as the crow flies. The hardships of such a trip are unknown to most people of this day.

At that time there were only six families living within the present boundaries of Logan County. John's father, Robert Buckles, was a man of iron mold. Without the education of schools, he answered clearly all the questions that pertained to his business and life. At the outbreak of the Black Hawk War he was one of the first to enlist, and bunked with and fought side by side with Abraham Lincoln. John's mother, Mary ("Polly") Birks Buckles, was one of the uncrowned heroines of history. She was the mother of fifteen children. The family residence was a mud-daubed cabin. In this for many years she did all the cooking before an open fireplace, made all the clothing for her family from the raw materials, and when her husband was absent from home at some distant market, or at war, she would fell the trees and cut the wood for use during the cold winters. It was a new land upon which the Buckles babies first looked out. Small growths of trees skirted the streams of water, and the wide prairies, reaching out in every direction to the horizon, were seas of grass and wild flowers. Wolves howled, foxes stole and wildcats screamed. Great herds of agile deer moved gracefully hither and thither, and countless thousands of wild chickens made the prairies vocal with their thrummings in the early mornings of spring. And there were 'coons in those days. Later in his life, John Buckles said: "Well do I remember the winter I captured thirty of these midnight travelers, and the day I received my first money—fifteen dollars in silver—for their hides. It was one of the happiest events of my life." He attended school altogether about one year. The house was made of logs, with the ground for a floor, split logs for seats and the children's knees for desks. In his early manhood he assisted his father in driving hogs to Racine, Wis., and sheep to St. Louis, Mo. In his twenty-second year he helped a neighbor drive a herd of cattle to the New York City market, and again in the following year, 1845. It was he who led the largest ox before the drove. The time required for the round trip was 130 days—one hundred in going and thirty in returning. His pay was twelve dollars per calendar month. Such experiences cultivated his inbred industry and thrift, taught him independence of judgment and self-reliance, and developed his sagacity, courage and force. By commendable methods as farmer and stockman, he accumulated good property and lived a long and useful life. He was an open foe of the organized liquor traffic, a helpful friend of our college and a sincere disciple of our Lord. His life is a heritage to his children and his children's children.

O. A. Burgess.

Thompson, Conn., 1829. 1882, Chicago, Ill.

Mr. Burgess came of Puritan stock. His mother trained him in the straitest thought of Calvinism. Her death came in 1843, which led the son to seek the Lord. He failed to receive the blessing at the "mourners' bench" and turned away from religion, believing himself given over to hardness of heart or predestined to be damned. He attended Norwich Academy, New York, and came to Metamora, Ill., in 1847, where he taught three years. He became a Christian in 1850 under the ministry of Henry D. Palmer. Shortly he went to Bethany College, reaching there with $4.50, but by resourceful labors graduated in 1854. His life thereafter was passed in Illinois and Indiana, where he served as teacher in Eureka and president of Butler College, pastor of churches and as a mighty champion and triumphant defender of the truth of the gospel against all opposers.

Thomas D. Butler.

Shrewsbury, England, 1838.

The chief event of Mr. Butler's childhood was a visit of Alexander Campbell to his native city in 1847. It was then arranged that Thomas should be sent to Bethany College in a few years. But his father dying soon, postponed the visit of the son until he reached his majority. In 1859 he spent sixty days and nights in crossing the Atlantic. Mr.

Butler has done but little ministerial work in Illinois except in a general way. He served for a time the church at Batavia and on the editorial staff of the *Christian Century*. He is widely known as a writer, his contributions having appeared many times in the *Millennial Harbinger,* New York *Independent, Christian Standard* and other papers. He is a man of fine mental and spiritual culture. His literary taste is discriminating and refined. His wife, Marie Radcliffe Butler, was for a long period well known as a charming writer. Mr. Butler firmly believes the gospel as it is written in the Book.

W. F. Burnham.

Chapin, Ill., 1871.

Educated in public schools, Illinois College and graduated at Eureka in 1895. He learned telegraphy and worked at the business in Illinois and Montana for a period of five years. He served as pastor in Carbondale, Charleston, Decatur Central, and is now with the First in Springfield. In Mr. Burnham are combined the qualities of a successful minister. He is the secretary of the National Commission on Christian Unity.

Judge Albert G. Burr.

Western New York, 1829.   1882, Carrollton, Ill.

Was brought by his widowed mother to Illinois in 1830. The first home was near Springfield. He was almost entirely a self-educated man. At the age of twenty he taught a school at Vandalia. In 1850 he went to Winchester and in 1856 was admitted to the bar. He served two terms in the Legislature and was a member of the Constitutional Convention of 1862. In 1868 he moved to Carrollton, where he resided till the close of his life. He was a member of the fortieth and forty-first Congresses. In 1877 he was elected circuit judge, and served in this position till the day of his final victory. As a jurist, Mr. Burr was eminent and had few equals. His analyses of intricate questions were clear and explicit and his decisions satisfactory. As an orator he was well-nigh perfect. In his early years he entered the

Christian Church, and to the close of his life he was not only a member, but a support and an inspiration. When there was no other one present in the Lord's Day meetings to preach, he proclaimed the unsearchable riches. While he filled high positions and was the peer of any man, he was not in the least ostentatious or distant. He had a genuine affection for and was intimately associated with the common people. As man and jurist he made it the rule of his life to do justly and love mercy. He frequently expressed himself in verse. The following was written by him about 1852:

LIFE'S VOYAGE.

Though waves may swell and billows rise,
And threatening clouds hang o'er the skies,
  O'er me and mine—
Though driven on where breakers roar,
And ragged rocks surround the shore,
  I'll not repine.

Though riding on the maddened wave,
To time and circumstance a slave,
  I'll bear my lot;
I'll raise aloft religion's sail,
And strive to ride throughout the gale,
  And falter not.

Though friends upon the sea of life
Are from my bosom torn in strife,
  And by the swell
Of ocean wave, borne from my side,
I'll bid them with a stoic's pride
  A long farewell.

Though all desert me in the gloom
And leave me o'er life's sea to roam
  Without one friend,
Still I will always onward keep,
Triumphant o'er the raging deep,
  Till life shall end.

Alexander Campbell.

Was born Sept. 12, 1788, in the County of Antrim, Ireland. He was descended from Scotch and Huguenot ancestors. Both his physical and mental constitution was vigorous and well balanced. From his earliest years he was trained by his learned and accomplished father in habits of severe application. He was a graduate of the University of Glasgow. Reared in the strictest school of Presbyterianism, he early formed and cultivated habits of piety and a taste for theological studies. From his youth he had a profound reverence for the word of God.

He came to America in 1809 and joined his father, Thomas Campbell, in western Pennsylvania. From that time father and son were one in their aims, spirit and work. Both were deeply impressed with the conviction of the evils and inherent sinfulness of sectarianism. Their first advocacy was the repudiation of human creeds as tests of fellowship, and the union of all our Lord's people upon the catholic truth of the Bible as the only authoritative standard of faith and practice. Taking their stand upon the principles set forth in the "Declaration and Address," neither foresaw the conclusions to which he would be led. They and those associated with them searched the Scriptures as free as possible from party bias. From these investigations they concluded that sprinkling for baptism and infant membership in the church were unauthorized of God. They were therefore accordingly immersed and united with the Regular Baptists. It was stipulated, however, that they should not be required to subscribe to any creed or articles of faith other than the Bible. After a few years in this fellowship they found it prudent to withdraw. There were prejudiced and intolerant men who held a leading influence in the Redstone Association who were unwilling to break from the Baptist name, creed and traditions. They stirred up fierce opposition against those who stood for the catholic truth of the New Testament. Hence the Campbells, and others who held to the principles of the "Declaration and Address," cut loose from their religious connections and entered untrammeled upon the advocacy and the defense of the plea for the return to primitive Christianity.

Alexander Campbell died in 1866.

Thomas Campbell lived a full century in advance of his generation. He was a rare and beautiful soul. In him the vital elements of Christ's gospel united in charming fruition. At the age of ninety-one he passed on.

W. H. Cannon.

Near Pittsfield, Ill., 1862.
Grew up on the farm. Educated in the public schools, Eureka College and Drake University. Has been pastor at Sterling, Illiopolis, Lincoln (two terms), Lexington, Eureka, Chapin, Pittsfield, and now at Central in Decatur. Mr. Cannon is a man of very clear perception and a superior minister.

W. R. Carle.

In 1870, Mr. Carle was elected to the lower house of the twenty-seventh Legislature of Illinois on the Democratic ticket. He was a successful business man and accumulated much property. He was a member of the Wapella Church, which town was his home. In religion he was conservative, but held that Christians should pay one-tenth of their income to the Lord's work. He did something for two of our colleges in his last years. He was never married, and for many years made his home with his uncle and aunt, Joshua and Margaret Carle. They were natives of West Virginia and were immersed by Alexander Campbell.

Joshua Carle claimed that he was the first among the pioneers to "publicly teach the universal priesthood of all believers."

Thomas Carlin.

Near Frankfort, Ky., 1789.   1852, Illinois.

Came to Illinois in 1812, settling near Carrollton. He was twice elected to the State Senate. Commanded a battalion in the Black Hawk War. Was elected Governor of the State in 1848, serving four years. Historians say he was one of the best Governors the State ever had. Mr. Carlin was a member of the church of Christ in Quincy.

W. P. Carrithers.

Sullivan County, Ind., 1829.

Came with his parents to Illinois in 1847. Educated in the public school. Served in the ministry for forty years. His preaching was mainly in Livingston, Marshall, Ford and McLean Counties, but he also worked in Missouri, Iowa and Nebraska. Mr. Carrithers is a gentle, earnest and faithful man whose ministry was distinctly constructive. His home is at Saunemin, where he quietly awaits the day of his coronation.

John Chandler.

Was born near Cynthiana, Ky., March 25, 1822, and is now (1913) a resident of Decatur, Ill. His early education was such as was afforded by the winter country schools of Kentucky and Ohio at that time.

Crawford County, Ill., was organized in 1817. Coles County was cut out of Crawford in 1831, and Douglas County was cut out of Coles in 1857. Mr. Chandler came to what is now Douglas County in 1838. Here he became a schoolteacher and an official. Before the division of Coles County, he served as assessor and treasurer; after the division, he was deputy sheriff, then served as county clerk two and one-half years by appointment, and the next four years by an election in Douglas County. He was in the Mexican War.

Mr. Chandler was the presiding moderator in the debate between David Walk and the M. E. attorney at Tuscola in 1863. Shortly thereafter, he became a Christian. When the little congregation needed a house of worship, he furnished $3,450 of the $3,800 that it cost. He never received any money returned. The building was a two-story frame. Mr. Walk said that his wife would conduct a "day school" on the first floor, but this aim was not realized. The most of Mr. Chandler's many years were passed on his farm. He has lived a long, an honorable and a useful life—a public-spirited and intelligent gentleman.

Thomas Campbell lived a full century in advance of his generation. He was a rare and beautiful soul. In him the vital elements of Christ's gospel united in charming fruition. At the age of ninety-one he passed on.

W. H. Cannon.

Near Pittsfield, Ill., 1862.

Grew up on the farm. Educated in the public schools, Eureka College and Drake University. Has been pastor at Sterling, Illiopolis, Lincoln (two terms), Lexington, Eureka, Chapin, Pittsfield, and now at Central in Decatur. Mr. Cannon is a man of very clear perception and a superior minister.

W. R. Carle.

In 1870, Mr. Carle was elected to the lower house of the twenty-seventh Legislature of Illinois on the Democratic ticket. He was a successful business man and accumulated much property. He was a member of the Wapella Church, which town was his home. In religion he was conservative, but held that Christians should pay one-tenth of their income to the Lord's work. He did something for two of our colleges in his last years. He was never married, and for many years made his home with his uncle and aunt, Joshua and Margaret Carle. They were natives of West Virginia and were immersed by Alexander Campbell.

Joshua Carle claimed that he was the first among the pioneers to "publicly teach the universal priesthood of all believers."

Thomas Carlin.

Near Frankfort, Ky., 1789. 1852, Illinois.

Came to Illinois in 1812, settling near Carrollton. He was twice elected to the State Senate. Commanded a battalion in the Black Hawk War. Was elected Governor of the State in 1848, serving four years. Historians say he was one of the best Governors the State ever had. Mr. Carlin was a member of the church of Christ in Quincy.

W. P. Carrithers.

Sullivan County, Ind., 1829. Came with his parents to Illinois in 1847. Educated in the public school. Served in the ministry for forty years. His preaching was mainly in Livingston, Marshall, Ford and McLean Counties, but he also worked in Missouri, Iowa and Nebraska. Mr. Carrithers is a gentle, earnest and faithful man whose ministry was distinctly constructive. His home is at Saunemin, where he quietly awaits the day of his coronation.

John Chandler.

Was born near Cynthiana, Ky., March 25, 1822, and is now (1913) a resident of Decatur, Ill. His early education was such as was afforded by the winter country schools of Kentucky and Ohio at that time.

Crawford County, Ill., was organized in 1817. Coles County was cut out of Crawford in 1831, and Douglas County was cut out of Coles in 1857. Mr. Chandler came to what is now Douglas County in 1838. Here he became a schoolteacher and an official. Before the division of Coles County, he served as assessor and treasurer; after the division, he was deputy sheriff, then served as county clerk two and one-half years by appointment, and the next four years by an election in Douglas County. He was in the Mexican War.

Mr. Chandler was the presiding moderator in the debate between David Walk and the M. E. attorney at Tuscola in 1863. Shortly thereafter, he became a Christian. When the little congregation needed a house of worship, he furnished $3,450 of the $3,800 that it cost. He never received any money returned. The building was a two-story frame. Mr. Walk said that his wife would conduct a "day school" on the first floor, but this aim was not realized. The most of Mr. Chandler's many years were passed on his farm. He has lived a long, an honorable and a useful life—a public-spirited and intelligent gentleman.

Bernard J. Claggett.

Lexington, Ill., 1861.

Educated at Wesleyan. Farmer and banker. Served as mayor of Lexington and in the House of the Legislature; elected in 1892. Long time a member of the Lexington Church.

J. S. Clements.

Edgar County, Ill., 1856.

His grandmother, Mary Holland, came out of the Presbyterian Church with Barton W. Stone at Caneridge, Ky., and his mother was baptized by Maurice R. Trimble in southern Illinois. He grew up on the farm, attended the public schools and was five years at Eureka. He has been in the ministry thirty-eight years, an energetic pastor and successful evangelist in Illinois, Missouri and Kansas, having added near ten thousand members to the churches. His single purpose has been to preach the pure gospel and follow the Master. "If I had my life to live over again, I would do just what I have done, barring a few mistakes."

L. E. Chase.

Coolville, O., 1876.

Grew up on the farm. Attended the country school, the village high school, Hiram College and the University of Illinois. Taught school at nineteen. The first year of his married life he worked on a farm and preached to weak churches in Ohio. For this service, he received twenty-five cents in money and much valuable experience. Then he went to a small church in Michigan for full time at $300 per year. While there, the advice and encouragement given him by A. P. Frost, the father of Miss Adelaide Frost, were worth as much to him as years of college work. After five years in Michigan, he came to Illinois, where he has served the churches at Armington, Leroy, Carbondale, New Bedford and Palmyra. He was converted in a little country M. E. church. While he never joined the church, his Methodist brethren treated him most fraternally. He has helped in the building of three houses of worship, and has received more than two thousand into the church.

A. P. Cobb.

Wooster, O., 1853.

Mr. Cobb's family came to Decatur in 1867. Here he attended school, and while in his teens learned the machinist trade. He was strong in body and vigorous in mind, and made good progress in both lines of work. In those years he was in the school of adversity as well. Graduating at Eureka in 1878, he entered the ministry. As a pastor he served the church at Normal two periods, at Springfield six years, at Des Moines, Ia., and San Antonio, Tex. For ten years he served as an efficient evangelist in the United States and Canada. He held successful meetings in Boston, New York City, Minneapolis and other great centers. For fourteen years he has been the platform manager at summer Chautauquas. In him industry, large energy and capacity for work, with thirst for knowledge and wide readings, have united in producing a scholar of more than average attainments.

The Connors.

James Connor was born in Tennessee in 1810, was brought to Indiana in 1812, and died there in 1893. His ministry in Illinois reached only from 1859-65. He resided on his farm near Humboldt. That was the time of monthly preaching and protracted meetings. He worked in Coles, Moultrie and Douglas Counties. He was a preacher for more than sixty years.

S. M. Connor was a son of James Connor. He served the Normal Church two terms and the churches at Girard and Virden. His period of work in Illinois was from 1878-88. In laying the foundation of the church at Normal he stood brave and firm against bitter sectarian opposition.

Daniel Connor, a brother of James, resided in Cumberland County for about thirty years, and preached in that part of the State.

John H. Coats.

A preacher for many years and a long-time elder of the church in Winchester. Military service in Company A, Sixty-eighth, and Company K, Fourteenth Illinois Volunteer Infantry. Captured and several months a prisoner in Andersonville. Treasurer of Scott County for several years, member of the Illinois Legislature in 1882, and Presidential elector in 1896.

Nathan E. Cory.

Ohio, 1837.

Mr. Cory attended the Baptist College at Franklin, Ind., and Oskaloosa College, Ia. He was a lay preacher in the Methodist Church before uniting with the Christian Church in 1857. Besides holding a great number of meetings in Illinois, he served the churches at Monmouth, Virginia, Mt. Sterling, Barry, Colchester and Augusta. He has been a faithful preacher of the word of God and his ministry has always been constructive. Between four and five thousand people were added to the church in Illinois by his labors. He is father of A. E. Cory, a missionary in China.

John J. Cosat.

Vermillion County, Ill., 1844.

Grew to manhood on the farm, receiving only such education as the common schools of the time could give him. Returning to civil life in the summer of 1865, he began as a teacher in the public school, in which he continued for about thirty years. He became a Christian in 1866, and four years thereafter was ordained to the ministry by the old Union Church and the venerable Rolla M. Martin. Since then he has preached almost continually on Saturdays and Sundays, much of the time without financial compensation. He has fostered weak congregations, brought into the kingdom about three thousand people, organized churches and endured hardness as a good soldier of Jesus Christ. Mr. Cosat's is a peaceable disposition, but he has always been ready to defend the truth. Being invited there in 1893, he held two public discussions in Labette County, Kan., with Priest Peter Ferrell, of the Roman Catholic Church. The propositions were the following: "The Holy Scriptures alone furnish all the necessary knowledge to obtain pardon and everlasting life," and, "To pray acceptably to God, our prayers should be addressed to the Holy Virgin, saints and angels." In 1895 he debated the question of instrumental music in public worship with Min. William Elmore, at Bismark, and in 1898 the same question with Min. J. W. Perkins, at Georgetown. Mr. Cosat has stood for better things in Christian life, and his ministry has been a very great help to the congregations in Vermilion County.

His military record was one of unusual brilliancy and thrilling to a degree. Being away from home on a visit, at the beginning of the Civil War, he enlisted in the Fifth Wisconsin Infantry. He was under the command of General Sheridan at Harper's Ferry, Martinsburg, Winchester and Cedar Creek; later, under General Meade at Petersburg, Sailor's Creek and on to Appomattox. On the morning of Apr. 6, 1865, Lieutenant-General Ewell had placed his corps in rifle-pits on the brow of a hill south of Sailor's Creek. This Confederate force was savagely and simultaneously assaulted by the Second and Sixth Federal Corps, and with such skill and determination as to virtually destroy it. In this assault, Mr. Cosat and five of his comrades were separated from their regiment, with the Confederate forces between them. The official report of Thomas S. Allen, colonel in command of the regiment, War Records, History of Appomattox Campaign, page 953, gives the names of the six men; to-wit: Sergeant Angus Cameron, Corporals Charles Roughan and August Brocker, and Private John W. Davis, of Company C, and Corporal John J. Cosat and Private Herod W. True, of Company I, all of the Fifth Wisconsin Volunteer Infantry. Sergeant Cameron suggested that they try to capture General Ewell. The six men ran across an open field and took position in a fence row that had grown up in dense brush. The sergeant crawled to the end of this, and reported that General Ewell, his staff and body-guard, probably a hundred in all, were riding directly toward them. The sergeant ordered that, when the Confederates came within hearing distance, they move in single file with cocked guns out of the brush—the sixth man stopping at the edge—and he himself would demand the surrender. General Ewell, thus completely surprised and supposing there were many Federals concealed in the brush, at once ordered his adjutant-general (Beglar) to unfurl the white flag, which he did. Shortly thereafter this immortal six had the honor of presenting to General Meade this famous old, battle-scarred veteran of the Confederacy, his staff and body-guard, as prisoners of war.

Walter R. Couch.

Wabash County, Ill., 1839.

The parents of Walter R. Couch settled in Wabash County in 1816. At the age of sixteen he became a Christian at the historic Barney's Prairie Church under the ministry of William Courter, who was one of the faithful preachers of the early days. When a young man he began to preach. He graduated from Northwestern Christian University, now Butler College, and thereafter gave eleven years to churches in Indiana. He then returned to Illinois. While he managed his farm in Wabash County, his time and talents were mainly given to the service of the churches in that and contiguous counties. For fifty years he has been actively and faithfully identified with the work of the Lord, and his generous and helpful services have been widely influential in promoting every good cause.

William L. Crim.

Washington County, Ind., 1829. 1910, West Frankfort, Ill.

He taught school in his neighborhood and served three years in the Union Army during the Civil War. He came to Franklin County in 1865, but did not enter the ministry till four years later. Thereafter his farm was the center from which he radiated in all directions—conducting meetings, holding public discussions and organizing churches. He was an earnest student of the Bible itself. In preaching a sermon on "Sanctification" he quoted 130 passages by his memory, as shown by a stenographic report. His knowledge of the Scriptures was comprehensive and profound; his sermons clear, forceful and impressive. He lived close to nature and near to God.

Daniel H. Darling.

Painesville, O., 1834.   1909, Joliet, Ill.

Was educated in the schools of his native town. His life-work was teaching and training the young. Before reaching his majority he began his work at Toledo, O. Next, he was principal of the school at Lockport, Ill., for three years, and then superintendent of schools in Joliet up to the beginning of the Civil War. He returned to this position in 1882, and continued therein till 1896, when failing health compelled his retirement. His fine character left imperishable impressions upon the multitudes of children.

He was rejected, because of his size, by the recruiting officer in Chicago in 1861. Then he went to Michigan, where, receiving authority from the Governor, he raised Company C of the Seventh Cavalry. He was engaged in all the campaigns of the Army of the Potomac and participated in many battles. He was wounded at Gettysburg, but would not leave the field till the battle ended. After the close of the Civil War he continued in the military service on the Western plains against the Indians. There he was colonel in command, and helped in opening the Overland Mail Route to California. He retired by reason of broken health.

Mr. Darling entered Christ's service in early life, and was active and earnest therein to its close. In Joliet he worked and worshiped with the Baptist Church until he thought the time had come to form a congregation after the New Testament pattern. He was its leader and support in every way.

William Davenport.

Jessamine County, Ky., 1797. 1869, Nebraska City, Neb.

Mr. Davenport was a man of large physical, mental and spiritual strength. He became a lawyer, and his fine presence and oratorical powers gave promise of a brilliant career. In early life he united with the Baptist Church, but, hearing the advocates of the primitive gospel, he was captivated by the simplicity and Scripturalness of their teaching. He then united with the church of Christ and entered its ministry with characteristic enthusiasm. He came with his family to Walnut Grove (Eureka) in 1835. There he settled on his farm, but his life's work was preaching the gospel, of which he was a powerful advocate. His public ministry reached many places, both near and far, in Illinois and was greatly blessed. He was also one of the leaders in founding the school at Eureka, and, having married a sister of Ben Major, helped to cast that community in a superior mold.

Miss Elmira J. Dickinson.

Hopkinsville, Ky., 1831. 1912, Eureka, Ill.

Few women in Illinois exerted a wider or better influence on her generation than Miss Dickinson. Her father brought her in 1835, with his family, to Walnut Grove, now Eureka. This was her place of residence throughout her life. She was in almost all of her Christian service a true pioneer. Beginning her teaching with the "little ones" in the academy, she continued her work in the classroom through twenty-nine years. She was actively associated with the Woman's Christian Temperance Union, and traveled in its interest during its formative period for five years. It was her desire to serve in some foreign mission field, and, as the Disciples of Christ had not then reached this point in their growth,

Miss Dickinson asked the Baptists to send her out. They could not accept her unless she would become a Baptist, which she could not do. The Woman's Union Missionary Society of New York were financially unable to send her. Thus was she providentially kept at home for a larger service. She became the founder and leader of the Christian Woman's Board of Missions in Illinois, and one of the most efficient co-operants in their national society. Her self-imposed task of laying the foundation of this work in Illinois was a most difficult one. As a missionary advocate and educator she was an unwelcome visitor in many places. Not a few wished that she would pass them by. She was keenly sensitive to all this uninformed indifference and crass opposition, but with a divine vision she bore it all and worked on. The years vindicated her wisdom, and a multitude of Christly women now rejoice in the magnificent results and move forward. Her life was thoroughly devoted, and her moral courage the finest. She was a true handmaid of the Lord, whose work will survive all the mutations of time.

Dudley Downs.

Edgar County, Ill., 1838.   1869, Minnesota.

Mr. Downs' parental inheritance was excellent. He went to school in the country and at Paris. He entered the Christian ministry early in life. After one year in Pennsylvania, he returned to Illinois, where his work was chiefly done. He served at Wapella and Clinton, and was State Evangelist for several years. Also, he helped edit a monthly Christian paper for several years.

Mr. Downs was a man of sweet spirit and gentle disposition, but he was full of moral courage and energy. He was wholly consecrated to his work and wore himself out in it all too soon.

W. F. Eastman.

New York, 1847.   1909, Illinois.

Mr. Eastman received a liberal education in his native State and was for a time a schoolmaster there. He was well read and versatile. He became a Disciple from intelligent conviction, and throughout his life was as true to his ideals as the needle to the pole. In him, gentleness and firmness were united so as to remind one of his Master. His estimable wife was an earnest Congregationalist, so that his church life was lived alone. In a modest but becoming manner he always showed his colors. Every one that knew him knew that he was a member of the church of Christ. He was the prime mover in the formation of the church at Sterling. Thereafter, he went West, and, by a mistake in judgment in business, he lost not only the means he had accumulated, but was left heavily involved. He then came to Moline, Ill., and engaged in the newspaper business. This paper he made one of the most influential in northern Illinois. Again he took his own place in planting a church of Christ in that city as its sustaining force. He was serving as postmaster there in 1909. As the end approached, he took $500 from the bank and paid the last dollar of indebtedness that he had unfortunately incurred more than twenty years before that time. Then he said, "I will never have a home on this earth, but will have to wait for a mansion in heaven."

L. N. Early.

Boone County, Ky., 1848.

Attended public and private schools at Petersburg, Ky. Taught ten years. Next, after seven years' work, graduated with first honors from the classical and Biblical schools of Kentucky University. Later, did work in the University of Missouri, where he received his A.M. degree, and at Harvard. Has served the church at Grayville, Kansas and Danville Second. Is a good teacher and preacher.

Caleb Edwards.

Brighton, England, 1832.   1905, Quincy, Ill.

Was brought to Cincinnati, O., in 1844, and came to Edwards County in 1848. He did not begin to preach till 1864. From that time to the close of his life he gave himself to a most sincere and upbuilding ministry. He was unassuming, gentle and steadfast, and was loved by many people. He dropped dead on a street in Quincy.

Daniel W. Elledge.

Bourbon County, Ky., 1813.   1890, Yoncolla, Ore.

Daniel W. Elledge was one of our true pioneer preachers. In 1816 his parents brought him from Bourbon County, Ky., to Edgar County, Ill. They were high Calvinists, and commonly called, in the vernacular of the time, "Hardshell Baptists." They were ambitious to make a Baptist preacher of this son, and hence gave him unusual attention. The schools of the community were not of a very high grade. Any man who could read, write and teach arithmetic was considered a competent master. But young Elledge hungered for knowledge, was a keen observer and thoughtful. In later years, on one of his preaching-tours, he met a college-bred minister who, after hearing him preach, said, "Bro. Elledge, where did you receive your education?"

"Down in Edgar County, at the Big Creek Schoolhouse."

"You use good language for one with only a common-school education."

Mr. Elledge was a student of the Bible from his boyhood. Shortly after his marriage in 1831, Michael Combs came over from Indiana and held a meeting in the neighborhood. He organized a Christian Church. Mr. Elledge was one of the converts and soon thereafter began to preach. At first his efforts were poor, but he improved rapidly. The earlier years of his ministry were confined mainly to Edgar, Clark and Coles Counties, where he preached in log cabins of the people, in schoolhouses and in groves. He was a logical reasoner and an earnest exhorter. Many were turned to the Lord by his preaching. About the year 1833 he moved to Clark County, and settled on a new tract of land some three miles east of Dalson Prairie. While he improved his farm and from it supported his family, his preaching was steadfastly continued. About 1836 he organized his home church, six miles west of his residence and three miles west of Dalson Prairie. This he named the Blue Grass Christian Church. Later he helped build their house for public worship.

The path of his ministry was marked by converts, congregations formed and their houses built. Not infrequently he was associated with Nathan Wright and Michael Combs, of Indiana, and Thomas Goodman, of Illinois, in what were called "Big Meetings." And they were big in clear-cut teaching of the Bible, big in fellowship and hospitality, big in sincerity and simplicity, big in Christian joy and helpfulness, and big in results, for they were the enduring foundation of our civilization. They were big in everything except the financial compensation of the preachers. There was little money in circulation, and frequently these pioneers were squeamish about "taking pay for preaching." But the pioneer sisters knew that a man needed food and clothing, so every now and then they gave Bro. Elledge a pair of home-made woolen socks, and on one occasion they gave him enough of homespun "Blue Jeans" to make him a pair of trousers. As his physical weight had come to be 230 pounds, it is apparent that this was a liberal donation. Many of the early settlers kept a few sheep and raised flax to make their own clothing.

Game was plentiful in southeastern Illinois. At one time Mr. Elledge had seven deer hung up in the woods. On another occasion, having killed one of these fine animals about a mile from his home, he left it on the ground till he could "get the old mare and sled to haul it home." On his return he found that a panther had dragged the carcass to the side of an old log and had covered it up with leaves.

While Mr. Elledge cleared and cultivated his land, he carried a copy of the New Testament in his pocket. When he sat down to rest he would read it. At one time, he was preaching at the home of Robert Downs, father of Dudley Downs, in the southern part of Edgar County. Because of the crowd of people, the preacher stood just inside the entrance door, and, turning around, he saw one of Mr. Downs' three large hounds standing with his front feet on the threshold, stretching his head upward. Quick as lightning the preacher's big fist smote the hound's jaw, knocking him out into the middle of the yard. "My book tells me to beware of dogs," said Mr. Elledge, and went on with his sermon as though nothing had happened.

In 1853 he sold his farm and moved to Putnam County, Mo. He settled within three miles of the Iowa State line. In that new country he began his work again as a frontier, pioneer farmer and preacher. For a number of years he stood alone in that region as an advocate of the New Testament order. According to the customs of the time, the Methodists took pleasure in calling him "the fighting Campbellite preacher." But in one public discussion they learned to respect him. His ministry in northern Missouri was signally fruitful in people turned to the Lord and churches constituted.

In 1865, Mr. Elledge sold his farm and moved to Oregon, where he continued his earnest ministry through the Grand Ronde Valley, at Eugene, at Portland, at Salem three years, and at various places in the State of Washington.

When the infirmities of his body became such that he could not stand in preaching, he sat and taught the people the word of God. He fought a good fight, he kept the faith, and on his little farm near Yoncolla, Ore., in his seventy-fourth year, he finished his triumphant course and went away to receive his eternal crown.

John Ellis.

The vital data of this good preacher failed to come in answer to earnest requests. It is probable that he was associated with the Christian Denomination, but he preached for a few of the churches of Christ in Madison County, Ill., in the early seventies. Later he served some kindred congregations in western Pennsylvania. He was then an aged and feeble man. In answer to protests against his holding to his ministry under such conditions, he replied that he wished to go on to the close of his earthly life. Let the following poem (his production) be his memorial. It was popular for a long period and is worth preserving.

The writer is indebted to Min. A. J. Carrick, Montezuma, Ia., for these copies:

THE WHITE PILGRIM'S GRAVE.
(Written at Johnsonburg, N. J., 1836.)

I came to the spot where White Pilgrim lay,
   And pensively stood by his tomb;
When, in a low whisper, I heard something say:
   "How sweetly I sleep here alone.

"The tempest may howl and the loud thunders roll,
   And gathering storms may arise;
Yet calm are my feelings, at rest is my soul,
   The tears are all wiped from my eyes.

"The cause of my Master impelled me from home,
   I bade my companion farewell:
I left my sweet children who for me now mourn,
   In far distant regions to dwell.

"I wandered an exile and stranger below,
   To publish salvation abroad;
The trump of the gospel endeavor to blow,
   Inviting poor sinners to God.

"But when among strangers, and far from my home,
   No kindred or relative nigh,
I met the contagion and sank in the tomb,
   My spirit to mansions on high.

"Go tell my companion and children most dear,
   To weep not for Joseph, though gone;
The same hand that led me through scenes dark and drear,
   Has kindly conducted me home."

REPLY TO WHITE PILGRIM.
(Written at Yellow Springs, O., 1843.)

I called at the house of the mourner below,
   I entered the mansion of grief;
The tears of deep sorrow most freely did flow;
   I tried, but could give no relief.

>
> There sat a lone widow, dejected and sad,
> By affliction and sorrow oppressed;
> And there were her children in mourning arrayed,
> And sighs were escaping their breast.
>
> I spoke to the widow concerning her grief,
> I asked her the cause of her woe;
> And if there was nothing to give her relief,
> Or soothe her deep sorrows below.
>
> She looked at her children, then looked upon me
> (That look I shall never forget),
> More eloquent far than a seraph could be;
> It spoke of the trials she met.
>
> "The hand of affliction falls heavily now,
> I'm left with my children to mourn;
> The friend of my youth lies silent and low
> In yonder cold graveyard alone.
>
> "But why should I murmur or feel to complain,
> Or think that my portion is hard?
> Have I met with affliction? 'Tis surely his gain—
> He has entered the joy of his Lord."

M. R. Elder.

Illinois, 1836.   1907, Harristown, Ill.

Mr. Elder was an active and useful preacher in west-central Illinois for forty-five years. His disposition was genial, his heart tender and sympathetic, and loyalty to the Lord supreme.

Ashley J. Elliott.

Evansville, Ind., 1862.   1910, Peoria, Ill.

Mr. Elliott was a "railroad man" of fine mind and habits. His business brought him into contact with many men and its conduct was recognized as exceptionally forceful and efficient. Without obtrusiveness, every one who wished knew where he stood. He was never ashamed of his Master or his church. He hated intemperance of all kinds, including the use of tobacco. He was resourceful and had perspective and initiative. To him belongs the honor of first "building a church in a day."

John England.

Kentucky, 1811.   1884, Illinois.

John England was a son of Stephen England. The family came into Sangamon County in 1819, where Stephen England formed, in the following year, the first church of Christ in central Illinois. It is now known as the Cantrall Christian Church.

John England's education was very limited. He grew up before the schoolhouses were built. What he learned, he knew well. He became a blacksmith, wagon-maker, farmer and preacher. As a minister he was well and widely known and very useful. He moved with his family to Logan County, where he entered forty acres of land, and as the years passed added to it until he owned 140 acres, where he resided the larger part of his life. This was near Mt. Pulaski. He preached at the Antioch Church, now Cantrall; Athens; Wolf Creek, now Barclay; Fancy Creek, now Williamsville; Mt. Pulaski, at different places along Lake Fork, and elsewhere. His memory of the Scriptures was surprising. He always had conscientious scruples about taking money for preaching. This, to some, was a very wholesome doctrine and full of comfort. Indeed, in everything Mr. England was finely conscientious. His son, A. T. England, says that his father was "always, in his deals, afraid he would get the better of the other fellow." Further: "If, in the evening, the topic of conversation would run upon anything of a financial character, in five to ten minutes he would be sleeping; but if there would be anything said pertaining to the Scriptures and the life beyond, he would be standing on his feet in a few minutes talking. He never seemed to be the least tired or skeptical about his hope for the future world. His mind was earnestly set on what good he might do other people. I have known him to ride fifteen miles home after preaching at night before he went to bed. I used to think the people gave him such wonderful troubles about coming to settle difficulties in the churches. One of the sisters sent for him one day, and when he got there she told him that she 'had terribly fell out with her man' and was so troubled that their little boy would necessarily 'have the husband's stock somewhat.' There and then she wanted father to tell her if they couldn't cut one of the boy's blood-veins and let the husband's part of the blood run out of him —then he would be purely of her blood."

"Uncle John" England's hospitality was known afar in that day, when the latch-string always hung outside of the door. Quoting again from his son: "Billy Brown, A. J. Kane, Walter Bowles and the Pickrells from Mechanicsburg would often come to our place. You better believe I had a hustling time taking care of their horses. It didn't make any difference what denomination a preacher was, we always kept him for nothing. Sometimes the old folks would go away, and my older sister and I concluded we would charge the people for staying all night. She did the cooking and I tended to their horses and made out their bills. The first thing I bought with my part of the money was a pair of boots with red on the tops. I was ten years old, and oh, but I stepped high, for this was the first pair of boots I ever had. Father would scold me like everything when he got home."

John England was a true servant of God and his fellow-men—self-forgetful, self-sacrificing and supremely loyal to his Christian convictions. He died in great hope of the life to come.

Robert Seymour Ensign.

Dalton, Mass., 1836.   1912, Long Point, Ill.

Was of Puritan lineage and Revolutionary stock. Both of his grandfathers served with distinction in the Colonial Army. He was a manufacturer of woolen goods and a farmer. He came to Illinois in 1864, settling on a farm near Dana. There he was a schoolmaster and filled such civil offices as he was elected to. While yet a young man, he became a Christian, uniting with the Baptist Church. He united with the church of Christ at Dana on his coming there. Later he moved to the vicinity of Long Point. It was at his suggestion that the work there was started that led to the organization of the church of Christ. He was one of its charter members, and was chosen one of its first elders, in which capacity he served to the close of his life. He was a modest and unassuming man, of ability and genuine worth, and had the moral courage to apply the principles of our Lord's teachings to personal conduct in all of life's practical affairs.

Alfred Flower.

Albion, Ill., 1822.   1907, Worcester, Mass.

Beginning in his early manhood, Mr. Flower gave sixty-five years to the ministry of the gospel. Most of his work was done in Illinois, but he labored also in Indiana, Kentucky, and in the closing period of his life in New England. At this time he spent his winters in Florida, where he preached continually. The church in St. Petersburg was founded and fostered by him. In him, there was a fine correlation of mind and heart. He was a man of superior spiritual fiber, broad culture and genuine sympathies. His expository sermons were interestingly illustrated and most helpful. In his prime, he often arose at three or four o'clock in the morning to reach his appointments, and much of his ministry was without financial compensation. His faith was always serene and his love sincere. His patience never grew weary and his enthusiasm never faltered. He moved toward the land of eternal dawn with the hopefulness of youth. He was a son of God and a friend of men. Mrs. Sarah Flower Adams, author of the hymn, "Nearer, My God, to Thee," was his cousin.

Dr. Robert Foster.

Tennessee, 1814.   1875, Palmyra, Ill.

Mr. Foster was a unique character. Small in body, he was in mind alert and quick to learn and understand. At the age of fifteen he was baptized by Philip Mulkey in Tennessee. His father was a high and stern Calvinist and drove Robert from home when he became a Christian. So he came to Illinois with Tandy Trice, a pioneer preacher. The period of his youth must have been diligently improved, for he became a successful physician and remarkable preacher. The Christian ministry was the absorbing and consuming work of his life. His labors were chiefly in central Illinois, where he was associated with D. P. Henderson, W. P. Bowles, B. W. Henry, A. J. Kane and other mighty men of that time. How much this part of the State is indebted to his zeal, toils and sacrifices, only a few know. After he was well started in the ministry, he made a visit to his childhood's home in Tennessee. While there, he conducted a meeting of days, and baptized his mother, two brothers and a sister. His proud father gave him no countenance, and he came away without even seeing him. In April, 1836, he started horseback on an evangelizing tour, and the next November reported 150 baptisms. In 1837 he was associated with B. W. Stone in a meeting in Lynnville.

In December, 1838, he was married to Miss Mary A. Burnett, near Palmyra. They began housekeeping in a log cabin on Wolf Creek, north of the site of Riverton. One of their sons, W B. Foster, became a brilliant and successful preacher, but died in his young prime. Several other children survive.

At one time, Dr. Foster had a lucrative medical practice in Carlinville, but this could not tie him to that profession. His desire to preach pushed all else aside. His generosity knew no limit. It was that trait in him that led Dr. Bostick, of Scottsville, to say: "Robert Foster is the smartest man I ever knew, but has the least common sense of any man I ever saw." John M. Palmer said that Robert Foster would give away the last dollar he had, then borrow another dollar and give that away.

He is said to have been the ablest and most convincing preacher in the State on the Bible way to become a Christian. Claiborn Hall, long a great man of God at Athens;

Thos. E. Bondurant, first at Mechanicsburg, and M. M. and G. M. Goode, first at Chapman's Point, were turned to the Lord by Mr. Foster. He called the younger Mr. Goode his "son Timothy." Preaching on the conversion of the jailer, and replying to the contention that there were infants in this family, Mr. Foster said: "This jailer had one daughter. She married a shoemaker who was lame in one leg and blind in one eye. How did I learn this? Why, just like the preachers who say there were babies in this family who were baptized. *I inferred it.*" His sermon on Philip and the eunuch was made very striking by modernizing the Scripture to suit the then prevalent conception for conversion.

Some amusing incidents are told of him. In those days it was the custom to have high, boxed-up pulpits. Mr. Foster was too short to see over the big Bible; so he was provided with a box on which to stand. When he began to exhort, he could not stay on the box, so his head would appear and disappear behind the high enclosure. A little girl in the audience witnessed his movements and was much troubled thereby; so she began to cry, saying: "Mother, why don't they let him o-u-t?"

Some of the good sisters somewhere had given him a stiff-bosomed shirt. They were shocked to notice at an out-of-doors baptismal occasion, when Mr. Foster removed his coat, that he had his shirt on front part behind, so occupied was he with his work. He was always himself. He did not "put on" or play a part. His eccentricities were as natural as the color of his eyes or the shape of his face.

At the close of his life, he said to George Sims, an aged comrade in the gospel: "Brother Sims, what a blessed thing it is that a Christian can die and exchange his old, wornout body for a spiritual one with Christ."

Chas. W. Freeman.

Greenup, Ill., 1859.

Grew up on the farm. Attended country school, County Normal and State School at Normal, Ill. He was a teacher for eleven years in the country and town schools. When twelve years of age he made a violin of a cigar-box and learned to play about eighty pieces by ear. Later he studied music. Before his conversion, he made music for dances; since then he has made music more earnestly for the Lord. The first three years of his preaching were connected with his work as a schoolmaster. During that period he received less than three dollars for his ministerial service. His work in Illinois was mostly in southeastern counties. Mr. Freeman has been an earnest and efficient evangelist, having led in eighty revivals. He baptized his own mother on the seventieth anniversary of her birth. His preaching always rings true to the word of God, of course.

Seth Gard.

Came from an Eastern State to Barney's Prairie settlement, in what is now Wabash County, in 1813. He was a man of ability, initiative and perspective, and was probably the leading man in that section. He was a member of the third Territorial Legislature, and was also a member of the convention that framed the State Constitution in 1818. He was the first elder of the Barney's Prairie Church. To him, with Min. James Pool, Joseph Wood and others, is due the honor of starting that church on the apostolic basis. Mr. Gard died in 1845.

James S. Gash.

Kentucky, 1833. 1909, Illinois.

Mr. Gash turned to the Lord at the age of thirty. He began preaching at once. His ministry was confined to the Military Tract. For many years he led the singing in his home church at Macomb. At the time of his death he had united more people in wedlock than any minister in McDonough County. He was a brotherly man of sweet spirit and a consecrated and helpful Christian. His end came by apolexy. The democracy of the gospel was well illustrated in his spirit and life.

J. H. GILLILAND.

COL. E. D. BAKER.

JOHN J. COSAT.

J. G. CAMPBELL.

Clay F. Gaumer.

Knox County, O., 1870.

Grew up on the farm. Taught school and attended school, graduating with honor from the Ohio Northwestern University in 1893. Was principal of the public schools at Sidell, Ill., for nine years, when he resigned to enter the ministry in 1903. Mr. Gaumer has given the churches of that part of Vermilion County helpful service. He was elected to the forty-fourth General Assembly of Illinois on the Prohibition ticket; and again in 1906 by a large majority.

James H. Gilliland.

Illinois, 1855.   1912, Illinois.

Mr. Gilliland was born on his father's farm near Vermont. While a boy he lived and worked there. He graduated from Abingdon College in 1875, and from Eureka in the class of 1880. The following year he received from the latter institution his master's degree.

He served the church at Mechanicsburg four years and at Harristown until he was called to Bloomington in February, 1888. His service in that city has been well called "a monumental ministry." Under his wise leadership and forceful, Scriptural preaching the congregations there grew from one to three, with large, modern, well-equipped buildings paid for, and the number of Disciples increased from four hundred to about twenty-five hundred. The ministry of very few men is crowned with such substantial and abiding results.

As a man and a minister, Mr. Gilliland was unassuming and wholly without ostentation. His master ambition was to be a capable and faithful preacher of the Word. He read widely and wisely, and thought profoundly and clearly upon all the great religious problems of our time. His last work was the preparation of an address on "Twenty-five Years of Christian Work in Bloomington," read by another at the seventy-fifth anniversary of the formation of the Christian Church in that city. In its closing he said: "The ministry of the Word is the transcendent calling. It is a God-revealing,

Christ-uplifting and Bible-interpreting calling. The preacher may well visit the critic's school, but his residence is at the interpreter's house. The ministry is a man-saving, a truth-seeking, a world-redeeming calling. The minister is the champion of the needy, the advocate of the poor, the protector of the helpless, the apostle of every good cause. Honored with the presence of God and his power, clothed with the authority of Jesus and the truth, directed by the principles of faith, love and sacrifice, the ministry is the supreme calling among men."

In his passing, the cause of truth and righteousness sustained a distinct loss. The hearts of thousands were touched with sincere regret and sorrow. "He sets as sets the morning star that goes not down, but melts away into the light of heaven."

Archibald A. Glenn.

Nicholas County, Ky., 1819.   1901, Wichita, Kan.

Mr. Glenn was of Scotch-Irish lineage. His paternal grandfather came from Ireland to America just before the Revolution. His mother was a Kentuckian—a woman of refinement and great strength of character.

His father's family moved to Indiana in 1820, from there to Vermilion County, Ill., in 1823, and afterward to Schuyler County. The father died in 1832, leaving his family but little property. Archibald, then a lad of fourteen, with his mother, kept the family of six younger children together and managed the farm. When his brothers were older and able to work, Archibald went to Rushville, learned the printing business and published a paper in the interests of the Whig party. Next, he went to Mt. Sterling and became a bookkeeper in a store. In 1853 he was elected county clerk. This was the beginning of his political career. He served as superintendent of schools in Brown County one term. He was a delegate to the convention that amended the State's Constitution in 1862. General Lippencott, State Auditor in 1868, regarded Mr. Glenn as one of the most capable members of the State Board of Equalization. He was elected to the State Senate in 1872, and became president of that body and *ex-officio* Lieutenant Governor in 1874. The little school training that Mr. Glenn received was in the country schools. Technically, he was not an educated man, but he came, by reading and absorbing the contents of many good books, into the possession of a prodigious fund of information that he used with commanding ability.

He was a member of the church of Christ at Mt. Sterling and was a staunch and true Disciple. Always and everywhere and in all things he stood four-square for the best things of life.

Galen M. Goode.

Macoupin County, Ill., 1842.

Grew up on farm. Attended public schools. Began preaching about 1863. He has served the churches at Illiopolis, Harristown, Normal, Buffalo, Hartsburg and Lexington, Mo. Besides, much miscellaneous Christian work. He has been a genial man of fine humor and wit and always devoted to the truth. He is the father of Min. W. S. Goode, of Ohio.

M. M. Goode.

Illinois, 1835.

A brother of G. M. Goode. Was a very active and useful preacher in Illinois in the earlier years. Entered the ministry in 1862. Served at Antioch, Berea and Literberry, in Morgan County, and Petersburg. These two brothers had quick wit and fine humor and were most enjoyable companions. But he went to Missouri more than thirty years ago.

In August, 1867, he conducted a public discussion at Palmyra, Ill., with Min. Richard McVey, of the M. E. Church. One of the speeches of Mr. Goode was full of unction, and as he spoke a Mr. Vancamp pressed his way to the front to make the good confession; he was at once followed by two sisters, Misses Lucy and Leona Gardner, Richard Allyn and Taylor McPherson. Then Mr. Short, who was Mr. McVey's moderator and a teacher in the female college at Jacksonville, stepped to the front and exhorted the people to come forward and confess the Saviour. It was a moment of profound spiritual pathos. At the meeting for immersion the following day a number of others turned to the Lord.

Thomas Goodman.

Virginia, 1808.   1888, Charleston, Ill.

In early manhood he was a schoolmaster and a merchant, and accumulated some property. Meanwhile, he was preaching some, and the conviction grew in him that he ought to be wholly consecrated to the work of the Christian ministry; hence, to this work he gave his life and in it spent most of the means he had acquired.

He came to Illinois in the pioneer days. While yet a schoolteacher he would often ride horseback to his appointments, preach Saturday evening and twice on the Lord's Day, then ride most of the night to begin his school work Monday morning. Later his preaching-tours were so extended that two or three days' riding was required, and on these trips as often as necessary he swam his horse through swollen streams.

"Uncle Tom" Goodman was one of the most intense men. His was the material of which heroes and martyrs are made. He was never kept in his bed by sickness a whole day in his life until his last illness, that lasted only three days. He never voted, but when Mr. Lincoln was a candidate for the Presidency in 1860 the conscience of the preacher was sorely tried, such was his admiration for the great man. To have stipulated a term of ministerial service for a named amount of money would have been to Mr. Goodman well-nigh an act of sacrilege. It was said of him that if one would quote from memory or read a passage in the New Testament, he could at once name the chapter and verse. In his preaching he often became so impassioned with the love of the truth and his desire for the salvation of people that he dashed little flecks of foam from his mouth like a mighty warhorse in battle. He conducted the funeral of Thomas Lincoln, the father of Abraham Lincoln, a few miles southeast of Mattoon, where the sacred dust of the paternal progenitor of the great Emancipator lies entombed. Thomas and Nancy Lincoln were members of the Christian Church.

Mr. Goodman, with patient and well-directed aim, humbled himself through his life; so God has highly exalted him.

John R. Golden.

McLean County, Ill., 1876.

Grew up on farm. Learned carpenter's trade. Educated at Eureka College. Was pastor at Moweaqua, Walnut, Gibson and Westside Church in Springfield. Was elected to the House of the Legislature on the Prohibition ticket in 1906.

Elijah Goodwin.

Ohio, 1807.   1889, Ohio.

Elijah Goodwin belonged to Indiana, as that was his home most of his life. But since no man did more to plant the Restoration movement in Edwards, Wabash and White Counties than he, these lines are due here. At the age of fourteen he became a member of the Christian Denomination. Four years later he was licensed by their conference to preach. In a few years his preaching began to distress their older ministers. He soon identified himself with the Disciples. His ministerial labors in the counties above named, as well as southern Indiana and northern Kentucky, were incessant. Besides, he did considerable editorial work. His book of sermons entitled "The Family Companion" was published in 1873. If any one thinks he was only a common backwoods preacher, let him learn his mistake by reading it. At the time of his decease his talented and accomplished wife was the editor of the *Christian Monitor*. The closing words of the last of three poems she wrote on the death of her husband follow:

"His glorious crown of silver hair!
His face like marble, pure and fair;
His folded hands, in holy calm,
Worthy to bear the martyr's palm.
I'll lay white flowers upon his breast,
Emblem of his peaceful rest;
Never more for him shall be
The pain of death's Gethsemane."

Moses Goodwin

Was a younger brother of Elijah Goodwin. He had little of school training, but knew the Bible from end to end. He was strong both physically and mentally, and was a born orator. No one ever went to sleep or became indifferent when he was preaching. Through the teaching and preaching of Maurice R. Trimble, of Knox County, Ind., Moses came fully into the Restoration movement a little before his brother Elijah. While Moses Goodwin was preaching for Union Church in Gibson County, Ind., that congregation came over bodily into "gospel order," as they called it, without change of name, officers or records. The only change apparent afterward was that the mourners' bench was used no more and penitent believers publicly confessed their faith in the Christ and were baptized for the remission of sins.

Moses Goodwin settled in White County, Ill., some time before 1840. Feb. 24, 1839, he organized the Christian Church at Seven-mile Prairie, which became the mother of all the churches of Christ in White County. His labors were constant and successful, but they undermined his health. He died at Grayville about the time he reached his prime.

Harmon Gregg.

Illinois, 1830.

Mr. Gregg was born in a log cabin a short distance west of the site of the city of Charleston. Indians were still living thereabout. In the winter-time he attended school in a log house when the days were not fit to break and scutch flax. In 1849 the California gold fever attacked him. He crossed the plains with the view of gathering gold by the basketful. Like many others, in this he was disappointed, and after two years returned to Illinois. The trip had cost him two years of schooling.

In the southeast part of Douglas County there was a community of intelligent settlers. It came to be known as Rural Retreat and is yet so called. A debating society was formed and its weekly meetings were held in the schoolhouse. In these meetings Mr. Gregg soon became an active participant.

It was not long until the Disciples in the community encouraged him to preach. He was modest and timid, but they insisted. Thus it was that he was led into the ministry. His work was done mainly in Douglas, Coles and Edgar Counties. Associated with him were A. D. Fillmore, Thomas Goodman, Gershom Rude, Joseph Hostetler and W. F. Black.

One day Mr. Gregg was plowing in his field. A neighbor residing five miles away called on business. In the course of the conversation the caller misquoted a passage of Scripture, which Mr. Gregg corrected. Then the neighbor so persistently besought him to come over and preach in their schoolhouse that a promise was given. The results were conversions among the people, the organization of a church of Christ and the building of a substantial church. His ministry was continued there four or five years. A good sister remarked to the preacher one day that honey-bees always did well for a man who lived amicably with his wife; whereupon, she gave him a colony. This was the sole material compensation received from that congregation for those years of service. Frequently Mr. Gregg's preaching was of the militant type. It could hardly have been different. In those years he and his brethren, pleading for the authority of Jesus Christ and the word of God, were often called "water-dogs" by pious denominationalists. Sometimes even women would shake their fists in his face and mutter their dissent. But this preacher was always true to the word of God.

Tobias Grider.

Monroe County, Ky., 1800.   1880, Shelby County, Ill.

At the age of twenty he married and moved to Indiana, where he soon became a Christian and began to preach. He came to Illinois in 1836, and settled on Sand Creek in Shelby County, where he died. As a proclaimer of the gospel, he labored under many disadvantages, but by persevering industry he supported his family from his farm and gained a good knowledge of the Scriptures. His life was filled with self-sacrifices for others' good. He was never called an eloquent preacher, but his sermons were full of Bible truth, logically stated, and he was a powerful exhorter. Many hundreds were won to Christ by his ministry, in which he continued faithful unto death.

W. M. Groves.

Hancock County, Ill., 1865.

Educated in the public schools of his native county and Abingdon College. As pastor, he served the churches at Stillwell, Columbus, Rushville, Carrollton, Girard, Shelbyville and Petersburg. He is a leader among the Odd Fellows of Illinois. He was first elected to the State Legislature in 1909, and is now (1913) serving his third term.

John I. Gunn.

Scotland, 1866.

Educated at Evanston, Ill. Served several years as a minister in the M. E. Church. Mr. Gunn combines the literary and spiritual in fine proportions, and his ministry is pleasing and profitable.

George F. Hall.

Near Clarksville, Ia., 1864.

Mr. Hall began his mundane career in a log cabin and grew up on the farm. He attended the district school and four and a half years in Drake University. He has read widely and written much. In 1904 he received the Ph.D.

degree from what was then known as Ruskin University. The aggregate sale of his books has been about one hundred thousand volumes. He paid his way in school by his own labors. Thereafter he served as pastor five years in Kansas and seven in Illinois. Meanwhile, he was afield as a very forceful and successful evangelist. And he gave not a few lectures on a variety of subjects. For nearly seven years he preached Sunday mornings at Bush Temple of Music, Chicago, to multitudes of people. In this work he was unassisted save by the volunteer offering of the people who attended there. Mr. Hall is vigorous in body and brain. He is not easily abashed or discouraged. His sermons have always rung true to the word of God.

J. C. T. Hall.

Ewel, England, 1818. 1901, Albion, Ill.

Was brought by his parents to America in 1821, and later into Edwards County. At the Little Prairie Church there he became a Christian and a minister. He worked with his hands to support himself and family while he preached, and was successful both in his secular business and his public ministry. He was a lover of good books and had a large library. He was firm in his faith, a man of sweet and gracious spirit, and, with his increasing means, liberal to a fault. For about sixty-one years he continued his public service in southern Illinois, but particularly in Edwards County. A short time before his death he said: "It is the last step that a man makes that takes him into heaven."

Jonathan Hall

Was for many years an efficient elder of the Old Union Church. Beginning in 1873, he served as judge of DeWitt County for four years.

Caleb Hainline

Was baptized by Abner Peeler in August, 1836. He began as a local teacher in the Hittle's Grove Church in 1840, continuing until his death in 1901—over sixty-one years. In 1871 he preached fifty-nine sermons, married three couples, and received a total compensation of $2.10.

J. E. Harris.

Fulton County, Ill., 1854.
Educated at Abingdon College. Is a farmer and grain-dealer. Served three terms as mayor of Bushville, and was elected to the House of the Legislature in 1904-06.

J. J. Harris.

Summit County, O., 1853.
Grew up on the farm and with decidedly infidel notions. Fortunately, marrying a Christian of intelligent convictions, she led him to the knowledge of the truth. Then he attended Bethany College a year. He served as pastor in Ohio and Michigan, and came to Illinois in 1887. His eight years' pastorate at Duquoin was a great blessing to the church in every way. Since then he has resided in Marion and has evangelized and served congregations. He was the evangelist of the Eighth District three years, and has been a public advocate of prohibition. Mr. Harris is one of the common people, a man of fine common sense and a true preacher. His ministry in southern Illinois has been distinctly constructive.

W. W. Happy.

Kentucky, 1806.   1875, Illinois.

At the age of eighteen, Mr. Happy united with the Baptist Church. He came to Jacksonville in 1830, and soon thereafter became a member of the church of Christ there. In the thirties he was twice elected to the lower House of the Illinois Legislature from the Jacksonville district as a Whig. He served his constituents with fidelity and efficiency.

When about thirty years of age, he was urged by his brethren to give his life to the Christian ministry, and shortly thereafter entered upon this work. He traveled through the

State with Mr. Campbell in 1853 in the interest of Bethany College, and frequently preached for the churches they visited. Later, the great reformer said of Mr. Happy that in intellectual endowments he was the equal of any man in the West, and that his grasp of the scheme of redemption was quite superior. He was a great thinker and had the courage of his convictions. His affiliation with the Russell defection grew out of his deep spiritual desires and his longing to be right with God. His return to the church in later years was evidence of his Christlike humility. He was a Christian pioneer of noble character, who gave his life in unselfish devotion to the gospel's advocacy. He died in humble circumstances.

J. M. Haughey.

Jamestown, O., 1833.   1912, Mason City, Ill.

Became a Christian in 1859 at Rothchild's Schoolhouse, west of Lincoln, Ill., under the preaching of Minister Goodsell, of the Baptists. In June, 1861, he took charge of the Baptist Church in Mason City, and the following winter transferred his membership to the church of Christ in that place. Thereafter, his ministry was continuous till failing health compelled his retirement. He never sought to serve a church because of the salary, but supported his family by the newspaper business. In his ministry he walked throughout Mason County and added multitudes to the Lord.

On one occasion he was preaching, in a schoolhouse packed full of people, on "The Four Baptisms." Just in front of him sat an old gentleman with steady eyes on the preacher. He spoke first of the baptism of suffering; second, of water, and, third, of fire. "Now I come to the baptism of the Holy Spirit," said the preacher. Just then the old gentleman extended his arm full length, and, pointing his index finger almost into the speaker's face, said, loud enough for all to hear, "Yes, sir, and it's the only baptism I'd give a snap for, by ginger." He had formed the habit of saying "by ginger" in his youth, and it stuck.

Robert Moffett Allison Hawk.

Indiana, 1839. 1882, Washington, D. C.

Brought with his father's family to Carroll County, Ill., in 1846. Educated in common schools and at Eureka College. First lieutenant of Company C, Ninety-second Regiment Illinois Volunteers, in 1862. Promoted to captaincy early in 1863. Lost his right leg in the battle of Raleigh, N. C., the day of Lee's surrender. Breveted major by President Johnson for meritorious service. Was county clerk of Carroll County from 1865 to 1878. Was elected to forty-sixth and forty-seventh Congresses from the Fifth District. On the night before the assembling of the convention of his district to nominate him for the third time, Major Hawk was stricken by apoplexy and died within a few hours at his rooms in Washington, D. C., at 11 P. M., June 29, 1882. General and Mrs. John A. Logan were with him at the time of his death. Major Hawk was a large man in every way—physically, mentally and morally. He was a commanding personality, and commanded the confidence and respect of all who knew him. He was a faithful Christian man.

Morgan P. Hayden.

Deerfield, O., 1845.

Graduated at Hiram College. He served two periods in Illinois covering twelve years—at Ludlow, Blandinsville, Augusta, Watseka, Rockford, Washington and elsewhere. Mr. Hayden has a fine knowledge of the Bible, out of which he has enriched his generation.

Lysias Heape.

York County, Pa., 1813. 1889, Illinois.

Mr. Heape's family moved to Ohio in 1816. He was baptized there in 1832 by Wm. Dowling. He came to Perry County, Ill., about 1835. Soon he was chosen as an elder of a congregation near Duquoin. In the discharge of his Scriptural duties he was soon led into the work of the ministry. In his experience he had the privations and the joys of a pioneer preacher. From 1847 to 1855 he was employed by a Co-operation of Christian Churches in southern Illinois.

D. P. Henderson.

It is humiliating to the writer that such a fine character and useful life fails of a befitting mention from a lack of the facts. Mr. Henderson was, at different times, actively associated with the churches of Christ in Illinois for fifty years. He was a successful pastor and evangelist and a resourceful leader in co-operative missionary work and Christian education. He was a writer and editor as well. He worked in the thirties in Morgan County and one of his pastorates was in Chicago. T. T. Holton says of him: "He was a model of grace for an old man and very winning and persuasive in his address. I think in his youth he could have courted a princess. He was a man of wonderful energy, though slight of build." When clerk of the court in Jacksonville, he preached in villages and country churches on the Lord's Days. His great meeting in Louisville, Ky., in which five hundred additions were received, called special attention to him. During his pastorate there, the great pillared Temple at the corner of Fourth and Walnut Streets was erected. In its basement the Foreign Christian Missionary Society was organized. In the same place a daily morning prayer-meeting during the Civil War was held, and the unity of the congregation was thus conserved. He was an earnest Union man, and there were influential numbers there who differed with him. Mr. Henderson was thoroughly democratic. He knew nothing of snobbery save as he saw it in others. While a forceful leader, he was admirably conciliatory. He was a fine example of the *suaviter in modo, fortiter in re.*

Bushrod W. Henry.

Culpeper County, Va., 1805.   1879, Shelbyville, Ill.

Became a member of the Baptist Church at the age of nineteen and soon after began to preach. Came from Tennessee to Shelby County, Ill., in the fall of 1830. His ministry among the Baptists there was fruitful, resulting in the formation of several congregations. In 1832 he began to preach clearly three things: "The Bible as an infallible guide, baptism for the remission of sins, no name but Scriptural names for the followers of Christ to wear." In reaching these conclusions, his son, J. O. Henry, testified that his father was helped by no human being except his wife. Sympathizers with the views of Mr. Henry early began to be called "The Henry Party." These questions were debated until in 1834, when Mr. Henry and his friends were summarily excluded from the Baptist Church. This date was recalled because it was associated with the "sickly season" which occurred in that year.

Before this time among the converts of Mr. Henry were Willis Whitfield, Colonel Vaughn and Silas Rhodes, who never left the fellowship of the Baptist Church.

He was a man of prodigious industry. He led the work on his six-hundred-acre farm and traveled and preached in many places—a strong, valiant and intelligent proclaimer of the Word. In the earlier part of his ministry he was county evangelist for two years in Shelby. The first year he received as salary enough blue jeans for a pair of trousers, one pair of home-made woolen socks and $1.25 in money. The next year his salary was five dollars in cash. He was the first Disciple of Christ to take part in Sunday-school work in that county, helped in the organization of the State Missionary Society at Shelbyville in 1850, and was one of the original trustees of Eureka College. He was a mighty spiritual force in his time, all the while exemplifying his preaching by his daily life. In 1868 a venerable and stately man went into the church in Springfield one Lord's Day morning and sat down well forward. He declined an invitation to preach, but presided at the table. He said: "This is an institution of the Lord's own appointment. The command to do this in remembrance of him is so gentle that it sounds like a request of one who loves us and desires to be remembered. That member of the church of Christ who has no providential hindrance and yet refuses to be present and bear a part in this memorial service, deliberately decides, for that time at least, he will not obey his Lord." That man was Bushrod W. Henry.

Mrs. O. W. Stewart and Mrs. Errett Gates are two of his grandchildren.

James O. Henry.

Culpeper County, Va., 1827.   1914, Findley, Ill.

Was the eldest son of Bushrod W. Henry. He was a preacher of the gospel for sixty-five years. Most of his ministerial work was done in Fayette and Shelby Counties. He served in Company E of the Fourth Regiment Illinois Volunteers during the Mexican War. He and Richard J. Oglesby were in adjoining companies, and formed a friendship there that continued through their lives. Ever afterward when they met it was "Jim" and "Dick" until the latter came to honors. When Mr. Oglesby was the last time Governor, Mr. Henry took luncheon with him at the Mansion. Then they slowly walked together to the entrance of the State House grounds. The time of their final separation had come. "Well, Jim," said the Governor, "we have been friends for a long time. In life you took one course and I another. If I had my life to live over again, I would pursue the course you have followed." Then they shook hands for the last time on earth and the eyes of both of the old boys were more than moist.

Rolla B. Henry.

1887, Clay County, Ill.

The earlier years of his ministry were given to Ohio. In Illinois he preached for congregations in Clay County, where he also served as county judge for a number of years. He never allowed his official duties to interfere with his regular ministerial work. He was a fine Christian gentleman who commanded high respect and general esteem.

William C. Hill.

Zemuree, Tenn., 1828.   1908, Illinois.

His parents brought him to Illinois in 1829 on a packhorse. They went to Montgomery County, but afterward settled on Turkey Creek, south of Odin, in Marion County. He had the education imparted in backwoods subscription schools. He became a Christian in 1841 under the ministry of Mr. Schooly, and began to preach in early life. His ministry in southeastern Illinois reached through sixty years, during which he immersed about five thousand people. His work was in the pioneer settlements and for many years in private houses and groves. He encountered intense bigoted sectarianism, generally ignorant and superstitious. He was a valued counselor and rarely equaled as a controversialist in private personal encounters. Many congregations grew from his labors. His sincerity in all he said and did, his earnest, sympathizing nature and his power in exhortation enabled him to win many souls for Christ, while his own life strengthened and confirmed their faith. His many and great sacrifices have had their reward.

Judge Andrew Hinds.

Eden, Vt., 1822.   1887, Lena, Ill.

Was admitted to the bar in 1846, and came to Stephenson County, Ill., in 1849. There he taught school, farmed, served as county treasurer and county judge and as a member of the board of supervisors for twenty years. While a member of the State Legislature, he introduced the Hinds prohibitory liquor bill. It did not pass, but was an important step in the right direction. He was one of the most trusted men in his county, and was an intelligent and faithful Christian.

David Hobbs.

Shelby County, Ky., 1807.   1876, Liberty, Ill.

Mr. Hobbs was trained up in the Baptist Church. His education was such as the common schools at that time afforded. He came to Illinois in September, 1830, and settled near the site of Columbus. There he taught school as he had in his native State. He also owned and tilled a farm. He early became an earnest and devout student of the sacred Scriptures. This led him to reject the custom of "relating an experience" on becoming a Christian, and to the adoption of the Scriptural order. In 1832 he preached in the residence of John Yeargin, who had preceded him from Kentucky. This was the first sermon in Gilmer Township. With ten others, he moved to Concord Township. It is claimed that on Apr. 24, 1835, he organized the church, on the Bible as the all-sufficient creed, known now as the Pleasant View congregation. He served this church as elder and its principal teacher till 1850. While a resident of Adams County, he associated with John B. Curl, T. S. Brockman, James McPherson and Wm. H. Strong in the pioneer work of the gospel. His ministry was extended into the contiguous counties and beyond. In 1850 he sold his farm and moved to Pike County, where he gave himself more exclusively to preaching.

Mr. Hobbs would never accept any civil or military office and held himself wholly aloof from politics. He was six feet and three inches tall, well proportioned and very strong. Having read himself to the apostolic ground, his ministry was fruitful of great good.

Jacob Hodgen

Was born in Hodgenville, Ky., in 1793, and came to Pike County, Ill., in 1832. Mrs. Emma Crow, of Pittsfield, has written of him as follows:

He was in turn a wagon-maker, farmer and merchant. He was one of the grand characters among the pioneers of the county and the church. Of the strictest integrity, sturdiest manhood and unwavering faith, he was a man whose faith and opinions commanded the respect of his fellow-men. His genial and whole-souled nature made him a host of friends, and his enthusiasm in the cause of Christianity made his house the home of the ministry so that it was known as "the preachers' hotel." It was said of him that whatever the need, he stepped into the breach, whether it was to pray, to preach, to plead or to cry.

Such was the character and spirit of the man who helped so much in laying the foundations of a purer gospel in Pike County.

Mrs. Sarah A. Holman

Was a unique personality. She was intelligent, cultured, independent, self-reliant, and had visited many places of interest in the United States and had traveled throughout Europe, Egypt and Palestine. She first visited the Central Christian Church in Peoria during the pastorate of N. S. Haynes. At that time she looked as if she might be fifty years young; her actual age was seventy-two. She was a widow. Her husband had lived and died a member of the Baptist Church—a devout Christian man. Her only living child was a married daughter, who soon after passed away. Mrs. Holman said to the pastor, in a personal interview, that when a young woman she had heard Alexander Campbell preach, and that she could not conscientiously become a member of any church but the Christian; that her home had never been where there had been such a congregation, and so through her life she had stood aloof from all churches. Within a few weeks she was led by the pastor to publicly accept Christ and place her membership in the Central Church. She was not then a resident of Peoria, but was later. When she came to be baptized it was found that the baptistery had sprung a leak and was empty. "There it is again," exclaimed Mrs. Holman; "the Lord intends that I shall never be baptized." The minister assured her that the Lord had nothing to do with the leaky pool, but maybe the devil had. At the conclusion of her baptism three days afterward, she said to the two women that assisted her: "And now, ladies, what do I owe you?" They were shocked and protested. She answered: "It is my custom to pay those who assist me in any way." When further protest would have been rudeness, they each accepted the five dollars that she gave each of them and turned it into the church hymnal fund. Mrs. Holman passed to the life to come, at the age of ninety-three years. During the twenty-one years in which she was a member of the Central Church, she gave to it, to Eureka College and the Church Extension Society the aggregate sum of $22,000.

William Holt.
Illinois, 1837.   1880, Illinois.

Mr. Holt was born in Edgar County. His ministry was mainly there and in the surrounding territory. He was highly esteemed as a man and was an able and brilliant preacher. Familiar with the Scriptures, he presented their teaching in a clear, logical and forceful manner. The results of his ministry were abiding. His sun set at his life's noon.

Thomas Tilghman Holton.
Aberdeen, O., 1839.

Nature cast Mr. Holton in a large mould. His grandfather, William Holton, served through the War of 1812 and was in the battle of Tippecanoe. There he commanded a company in which were four of his brothers. He was also a member of the first legislative body of Virginia, his adopted State. From Fanquier County he migrated to Mason County, Ky., where William Holton, the father of the subject of this sketch, was born. His mother was Sally Price Tilghman, a native of Albemarle County, Va. Both branches of his family were of pre-Revolutionary stock.

He enjoyed superior educational advantages. He went to the country school, to Aberdeen Seminary, to the Southwestern Normal School at Lebanon, O., and graduated from Bethany College July 4, 1862. Before he was seventeen he was a schoolmaster at Genntown, O. On a certificate marked 100 he conducted a school of eighty-five pupils efficiently for nine months. Leaving Bethany after graduation, he served as vice-president of Jefferson College, near Louisville, Ky., of which O. A. Bartholomew was president. Early in 1864, Mr. Holton became the head of Falmouth Academy. Miss

Sally E. Holton, his sister, served as assistant. Under their lead this school did superior work for two and a half years. In 1866 he became pastor of the church at Vincennes, Ind. In 1868 he became pastor of the church at Springfield, Ill. Next he served the Berlin Church, and at the same time was principal of the public schools there for three years. In 1873 he moved to Lincoln and served the church there and at Atlanta half-time each. Thereafter, with Lincoln as the center, he ministered to many churches; as, Broadwell, Mason City, Pekin, Old Union, Hallville, Emden, Bethel, Delavan and Eminence. The Old Union Church he served fourteen and a half years. In the meantime, he moved to Tallula and served the church there four years, and to De Land also, with the same period of pastorate.

During his first years in Lincoln he did considerable secular work, clerking in bank and bookstore. Later, he served eight years as circuit clerk in Logan County. Thereafter, when his political principles had improved and his civic perspective became clarified, he stood for the State Legislature on the Prohibition ticket and received five thousand votes.

His religious experiences have been marked. When a young man at school, he had for his room-mate Ira J. Bloomfield, who won his star in the Civil War. The two attended Sunday school and church together. Being well intentioned, they decided to become members of this church, provided they could be immersed. The minister, however, desired that they should "conform to their religious usage." They were likely lads, so the preacher left with them a booklet entitled "Immersion Not Baptism." This declared that immersion was "unscriptural, inconvenient and indecent." When the dominie returned he found the lads unchanged. "Well, now," he said, "boys, we want you, and will immerse you if that is your choice." Whereupon, they declared that neither he nor his church had any right to do an unscriptural and indecent thing in the name of the Lord. In 1858, Mr. Holton was baptized by Min. Marsena Stone and received into the Baptist Church. He related no visions nor wonderful experiences. The formula that the preacher used was this: "My brother, upon a confession of your faith in the Lord Jesus Christ and by his authority, I baptize you into the name of the Father and of the Son and of the Holy Spirit, for the remission of sins." Up to this time this young man had thought to become a lawyer. Now the good Baptist sisters urged him to prepare to preach the gospel; thus God changed his life purpose. During his four years at Bethany he changed his church affiliation. On one occasion, George W. Minier said to him: "Brother Holton, you are entirely too modest." So he entered into the active work of the ministry only by the urgency of the lamented preacher, J. Z. Taylor.

Mr. Holton's life has been very active and fruitful. He has been much in demand for public addresses, at Commencements, on Memorial Days, at Old Settlers' Reunions, Fourth of July celebrations and Ministerial Institutes. He has united in marriage six hundred couples, has preached one thousand funerals, and led near two thousand persons into the kingdom of God. Such facts indicate his wisdom, his worth and his place in the confidence and affections of the people. He has filled a large place of usefulness, preaching in schoolhouses and doing most all sorts of miscellaneous and unclassified Christian work.

In 1907 he moved to Bloomington. Since then, his helpful ministry has been continued in the regions round about.

Joseph Hostetler.

Kentucky, 1797.   1870, Illinois.

Joseph Hostetler was a remarkable man. He is properly classified with the pioneer preachers of Indiana, but his services in Illinois entitle him to this notice here.

He was of German blood and German Baptist parentage. Though a typically mischievous boy, under the influence of his mother he very early in life learned to love the Scriptures, particularly the biographies of the Old Testament characters. In the great revival of 1811 he wished to enter the church, but his parents thought him too young. But one of his companions, of his own age, was received upon the following experience, which illustrates the prevalent thought of the time on the subject of conversion. When asked to describe the work of grace upon his heart, the lad sobbingly replied: "I don't know as I has any work of grace to tell. I is a poor sinner."

"Do you believe in Christ?" asked the leader.

"Oh, yes, ever since I can recollect."

When further asked if he had dreamed anything remarkable, he related, in substance, as follows: He went to bed *as usual* in great distress; dreamed that he was going he knew not where, when the devil met him and was hurrying him off toward hell; thinking himself lost forever, just then a young man met them and rescued him; and that he then awoke in a transport of joy. Whereupon, a gray-haired deacon arose and said: "Brethern, I have been a Baptist for twenty-five years, and ef I ever heerd a experience of true grace, this boy has given us one. So it is with the poor sinners. They are goin' they know not where 'tel the Lord meets 'em. I can interpret this dream. He's powerfully converted. Glory to God." This incident impressed young Hostetler deeply. As he had no such experience, he read the Bible through and with remarkable persistence searched the New Testament, where he learned that his faith in Christ and repentance toward God should be expressed in his public confession of the Lord Jesus and his baptism "for the remission of sins." In his nineteenth year he was thus received into the German Baptist Church by his uncle, Adam Hostetler.

Shortly thereafter he was married and about the same time authorized by the church to preach. On that solemn occasion his uncle presented him with a small Bible, saying: "Preach and practice only what you find in this Holy Book." Many things were yet confused in the thought of this young preacher, but he made daily use of the Bible and an English dictionary. About 1824 the first volume of the *Christian Baptist* fell into his hands, which he read with eagerness, but not with entire approbation. He was strong, self-reliant, clear-minded, purposeful, and with a tremendous capacity for work, both physical and mental. In mature life he spoke both the English and German languages with equal ease and fluency. He was noted for the accuracy of his speech, both in his private conversation and in his public addresses.

Mr. Hostetler came to Illinois in 1832 and settled on a farm about twenty miles east of the then village of Decatur. There he served as a pioneer farmer and preacher, organizing in that year what was then called the Okaw Church. He entered Decatur the same year to preach. The Methodists and Presbyterians had preceded him, and, according to the custom of those days, bitterly denounced his discourses as Campbellism, Romanism, infidelity, etc. Such men as he are never intimidated, and a number of the people, hearing his message, believed in Jesus Christ and were baptized. The first church in Decatur, that was Christian only, was organized there by him in 1833. He moved there the next year, and during his two years' residence supported his family by the practice of medicine, for which he had fitted himself by his unflagging industry. He returned to Indiana in 1836.

During this period of four years, he met Bushrod W. Henry, a mighty, resolute and deeply religious Baptist preacher. He also met John W. Tyler, also a Baptist minister of fine mind. Both of these men had come from Kentucky to Illinois in the early thirties. Under the guiding influence of Mr. Hostetler, Mr. Tyler discarded his "articles of faith" for the Scriptures solely and dropped his denominational name for Christian only. Mr. Tyler conducted the obsequies of Mr. Hostetler, and in his funeral discourse stated this fact as it related to himself. Mr. Hostetler returned to Lovington, Ill., in 1861, where he passed the remnant of his days. He was a self-reliant and aggressive leader of men.

Daniel Radcliffe Howe.

Ohio, 1819.   1905, Illinois.

James Howe, the father of the subject of this sketch, was a native of Virginia and a Baptist preacher. He was a member of the Mahoning Association and came with its members into the Restoration movement. So spiritually D. R. Howe was both free-born and of the blood royal. In his youth he attended private schools in Ohio. In 1835 he came with his parents to Burean County, Ill. There at Leepertown he went to school six weeks to George W. Minier. A little knowledge of Latin and Greek he got by the help of his brother-in-law, Amos Hays. At twenty-one he taught the first school ever held in Green County, Wis. He became a Christian in his eighteenth year and thereafter preached some for seven years. Then he became a settled minister of the church at Princeton at a salary of $250 a year. He served there through a period of ten years, during the last half of which he received $1,000 per year. He served the churches at Washington two terms, Peoria, Springfield, Minonk, Quincy, Putnam, Henry, Lanark two terms, Monroe, Wisconsin two terms, two terms at Princeton, and Ulysses, Neb. Besides, Mr. Howe was a very successful evangelist and a noted builder of church houses. He was one of the finest men of his time. In him there were combined in an unusual degree the elements of a great gospel preacher. He enlightened the mind by a knowledge of the Scriptures and then appealed to the heart and conscience with great earnestness. Withal, he had fine business ability. During the fifty years of his active ministry he missed the public worship on the Lord's Day only eight times.

In 1860 he was elected to the House of the State Legislature, where he gave the great war Governor of Illinois faithful support.

John Houston.

Near Blandinsville, Ill., 1848.

Educated at Abingdon College. Farmer, live-stockman and banker. Elected to the House of the Legislature in

1908, 1910 and 1912. Mr. Houston has been an elder in the Blandinsville Church for thirty-five years.

The Houston Brothers.

They were Washington J., John Quincy A. and Jefferson P. Houston. All natives of Bourbon County, Ky. Moved to Bloomington, Ind., in 1840, and to Illinois in 1857, settling in La Salle County.

Washington J. Houston.

Kentucky, 1814.   1873, Illinois.

Was a very successful evangelist, baptizing several thousand converts, chiefly in central Illinois. He preached for a time under the auspices of the State Board of Missions, served as financial agent of Eureka College, and met all errorists in public discussions as they desired. His closing years were spent at Marshall, where he died.

John Q. A. Houston.

Kentucky, 1821.   1870, Illinois.

He was employed as an evangelist in Marshall and Livingstone Counties, and also by the State Board. He was a sweet singer, which contributed to his ministerial work. His labors reached south to Centralia. While engaged at Maroa in raising funds to complete the church building, he sickened and died there.

Jefferson P. Houston.

Kentucky, 1816.   1892, Missouri.

His work was confined to Livingstone and near-by counties.

John S. Howard.

Tennessee, 1807.   1890, Ohio.

With his father's family came to Illinois in 1817 and became a part of the Christian Settlement on Allison Prairie. He became one of the earlier preachers in that section. He resided in Russellville, where he proclaimed the gospel and in the regions beyond. A true man and faithful servant of God, he passed on at the age of eighty-three.

William A. Howard

Came from Kentucky and settled in the southern part of Fulton County about 1840. He there cleared and cultivated his farm. His most used tools were his ax and mattock. He was a strong man, both physically and mentally. For years he chopped, grubbed, split rails and worked his land six days in the week, and preached two or three sermons on the Lord's Days. Often he would walk five miles, preach two sermons in a schoolhouse, and return to his home congregation for a discourse in the evening. Like most men of his time and place, he was clad in homespun. He was a devout man, well versed in the Scriptures and gave himself to his Master's work. In a wide territory he was well known and tenderly loved by many people. He moved to Texas in 1857.

Charles E. Hull.

Salem, Ill., 1862.

Mr. Hull has been a merchant, an editor and otherwise usefully and successfully engaged. He was elected to the House of the General Assembly in 1879 and to the Senate in 1896 and 1904. He is an active member of the church at Salem.

Andrew J. Hunter.

Indiana, 1831.   1913, Paris, Ill.

Shortly after his birth, the parents of Mr. Hunter moved from Greencastle, Ind., to Illinois, and settled on a farm in Hunter Township. He graduated from Edgar Academy in 1848 and began his business life as a civil engineer. Then he studied law, was admitted to the bar and in a few years became a prominent attorney. In 1864 he was elected to the State Senate. He was a member of the National House of Representatives in the fifty-third and fifty-fifth Congresses, and rendered efficient service on various committees. During the latter, he voted for the appropriation of fifty million dollars to be put into the hands of President McKinley for carrying on the war with Spain. Mr. Hunter was a lifelong Democrat, but he was always stronger than his party, because he possessed the confidence and respect of the people on account of his character. His heart always beat in sympathy with the sons of toil, for from them he sprang. Hence he championed the interests of the laboring people. He was a large-hearted, generous and broad-minded man, a splendid "mixer." In the days of his prime he was a superior platform orator. For more than fifty years he was a member of the church at Paris. In addition to serving the church as trustee and elder, during all this period he was the chief usher stationed at the main entrance at both Sunday meetings, where he received the people with dignity and cordiality. And thousands found pleasure in going to worship there because of this sincere and hearty welcome.

Harrison T. Ireland.

La Porte County, Ind., 1848.

Came to Marshall County, Ill., in 1855. A farmer. Was elected to the House of the Legislature in 1904-6-8-10. Mr. Ireland has long been a useful member of the Washburn Church.

James E. Jewett.

Belfast, Me., 1844. 1912, Lincoln, Ill.

Came with his parents to Illinois in 1856, who settled on the wild prairie in Livingston County four miles northeast of Gridley. His education was received in the public schools of that time. Mr. Jewett came of fine, patriotic stock. One of his grandfathers, John Cochran, was a member of the "Boston Tea Party," a soldier in the Revolution and an inmate of a British prison for nine months. His paternal grandfather was a soldier in the War of 1812. He himself enlisted Aug. 7, 1862, as a private in Company G, 129th Illinois Infantry, in which he served with superior courage and distinction till the close of the war. He followed the flag through all that high carnival of blood and death that led to Atlanta, to the sea and to the "Grand Review" at Washington, D. C.

Returning home, he went to the farm, next to the schoolroom as teacher, and then to the ministry of the gospel. He also read law and was admitted to the bar, but only little of his time was given to the practice of this profession. He was also prominent in some of the fraternal societies of the State, and filled a number of minor civil offices with recognized ability and credit.

His mind was always alert and his life full of action. His disposition was genial and kindly and his companionship pure and helpful. He sought and saw the best in human life and was serene in adversity.

Hale Johnson.

Indiana, 1847. 1902, Illinois.

Mr. Johnson's father, Dr. John B. Johnson, served as assistant surgeon during the Civil War. His grandfather was a Baptist minister who was a chaplain in the War of 1812. Hale Johnson inherited the fighting blood of his ancestors. At the age of seventeen he enlisted in Company D, 135th Indiana Infantry. He, with his father's family, came to Illinois in 1865.

Mr. Johnson was an attorney. His residence was in Newton. He became a Christian in 1870. To the close of his life he was a praying, active, sincere man. His church came first in his life. His generosity was unfailing. His last contribution, made the day before he died, was to a Christian Orphans' Home. He was open-minded, always willing to investigate and learn what would contribute to the religious, social and civic betterment of society.

At one time he was mayor of the city of Newton. In 1882 he left the Republican party because it refused to submit a prohibition constitutional amendment to a vote of the people. In a public address he gave Min. N. S. Haynes the credit of pulling him loose from his old party moorings. Thereafter, he was one of the most effective, prominent and influential party Prohibitionists in America. He served well on committees, State and national. In 1896 he was nominated for Governor. Later in the same year he was placed on the national ticket for the Vice-Presidency, with Joseph Levering for the office of President. During this campaign he stumped in more than thirty States, speaking day and night. While party Prohibitionists have rarely been successful as such, the fruits of their self-sacrificing and heroic labors are manifest in the growing public sentiment that finds increasing expression in State and national legislation. The Christian conscience of the nation has decreed that the liquor traffic must die. The handwriting is even now on the wall.

Mr. Johnson's death was tragic. He had gone to a country merchant to try to persuade him to settle a debt peaceably. The merchant became enraged and shot him. A few hours later the assassin committed suicide. Mr. Johnson's untimely death was deplored, particularly among Prohibitionists. They placed a beautiful monument over his grave in the cemetery at Newton.

William H. Johnson

Was born near Enfield, Ill., in 1841. The family from which he came has been noted for its intelligence, patriotism and loyalty to Christian convictions for a hundred and fifty years. His grandfather, Arthur Johnson, was a soldier in the Revolution. The subject of this sketch received such education as the time and place of his residence afforded. He became an attorney and a Christian of intelligence and culture. Enlisting in 1861 in Company I, First Regiment Illinois Cavalry, he was made first sergeant, and after four years of service he was mustered out as first lieutenant of Company I, Eighty-seventh Regiment Illinois Volunteer Infantry. In 1880 he was chosen an elector and voted directly for Garfield for President. In 1882 he was elected to the State Legislature. He has served several congregations as preacher in charge. He is a modest, sympathetic and all-round Christian man.

John T. Jones.

Cincinnati, O., 1795.   1877, Eureka, Ill.

Mr. Jones was one of the true leaders of the Restoration movement in Illinois in its beginning. In 1831 he came from Cincinnati to Jacksonville. There he gave the church for fifteen years active and efficient service. He moved to Eureka in 1847. He was a gentleman of fine intelligence and culture. His hospitality was cheerful and his dignity commanding. With the beginning of the college, he was made a trustee, and for twenty-five years never missed a board meeting. His discrimination between things fundamental and incidental was superior. When objections were urged to voluntary meetings of individuals and representatives of congregations for the most effective dissemination of the truth, he was one of the first to answer these clearly and conclusively. He was a minister, a schoolmaster and a writer. His counsel was always wise and his spirit amiable and conciliatory. His influence was distinctly constructive. The memory of the just is his.

S. S. Jones.

Bath County, Ky., 1859.

Educated in country schools, at Ladoga (Ind.) Normal, Owingsville (Ky.) Seminary, North Middletown (Ky.) College, and in classrooms as a teacher. Came to Illinois in 1884, and for a decade he served the churches at Homer, Champaign and St. Joseph. In 1894 he became pastor of the First Church in Danville, which he continued to serve for eight years. Then he went to the Third Church, where he continued for ten years. When Mr. Jones went to Danville the Disciples numbered about 150, with a property worth about $3,000. At the close of his eighteen years he left four churches whose combined membership is near two thousand, all well housed in properties whose aggregate value is about $85,000. He received into the congregations there near two thousand people, fourteen hundred of whom were by primary obedience. That work will be his enduring memorial.

E. A. Jordon.

Rockport, Ind., 1880.

The facts in this sketch were furnished the author by Mr. Jordon in writing.

His parents were both devout members of the Roman Catholic Church. He attended the public schools. In 1888 the father sold his farm, moved to New Boston, Ind., in the same county, and there engaged in the grocery and saloon business—a business not thought to be inconsistent among Roman Catholics. The son was then placed in the parochial school there, which was taught by the sisters. In this school the doctrines of the Roman Church were given prominence and the rudiments of true education were sadly neglected. At ten years of age he was confirmed by Bishop Donahue, of Indianapolis. Shortly thereafter, his mother died, leaving three sons. She had dedicated this son in his early life to the priesthood, and her dying request of her husband was that he would send this son to St. Meinrod Monastery to prepare him, that she might thus fulfill her vow. In that institution, which was in charge of the Benedictines, he remained eight years. He completed the college course and received the A.B. degree. Then two years were passed in the seminary, where he took the minor vows and deacons' orders. He was held to this work by the memory of his mother's vow. It was a custom of the seminary for the students to be sent out on Sundays to near-by hamlets, to conduct "missions" or religious services. He, with others of his fellow-students, went to Eddyville one third Sunday in the month. They found the room they expected to use occupied by a band of people who called themselves "Christians." Min. Ira Scott, an elderly man, preached. He announced that the Catholic students were there to conduct their "mission" and asked the people to remain and hear them. This kindness caused the students to feel rather small, since they had remained outside the building through Mr. Scott's meeting. At the close of the students' "mission," one of them, Loyola Chatron, challenged Mr. Scott to debate the question which of the two churches was right. Chatron was well versed in the traditions and doctrines of Rome, was brilliant, and had recently come from the Jesuit College in Rome. He had a mighty good opinion of himself. Min. W. B. F. Treat represented the church of Christ and Mr. Chatron the Romanists in a week's public debate. Mr. Treat's powerful logic in presenting the word of God and facts of history was irresistible. The first result of the discussion was that five students of the monastery left the Roman Church. Mr. Jordon was one of these. For a year thereafter he was tossed about on a sea of doubt. He regarded all Protestants as alike. Finally, he found the people who took the word of God as the only rule of faith and practice. He was baptized by Min. J. T. Jacobs, of Rockport, Ind., and greatly enjoys his freedom in Jesus Christ. He later baptized his father, who had opposed his son's leaving the Roman Church in every possible way. Mr. Jordon is pastor of the church at La Harpe.

Jacob Judy

Became a Christian in Greene County, O., before he was fifteen years of age and just before a church of Christ was organized in his home. This was early in August, 1828. He applied for and received a letter, of which the following is a copy:

The Baptized Church of Jesus Christ, meeting at Brother Jacob Darst's, Greene County, Ohio, believing the Scriptures of the Old and New Testaments to be the Word of God and the only and all-sufficient rule of faith and practice to any Christian Church, and whereas our Brother Jacob Judy, having requested a letter of dismission in order to join a church where God in his divine providence may cast his lot, This is to certify that he is a member in good standing and in full fellowship with us and his brethren in the Lord, and when received by you he is dismissed from us. And may the God of all grace preserve you and him to his Heavenly Kingdom is the prayer of your brethren in the Gospel bonds.

Done by order of the church when met on Saturday before the third Lord's day in August, 1828.   JACOB DARST, Clerk.
Signed in behalf of the Church.

Mr. Judy's recollection was that this was a Baptist church. He came to Illinois in 1824. He helped to build the first house in Mackinaw, and then assisted Mordecai Mobley, who lived and kept a store in this building. Later, Mr. Judy built him a home in Hittle's Grove, and was one of the active Christian men of the neighborhood. Later his home was in Atlanta, where he died in September, 1903. Had he lived till the following January, he would have been one hundred years old. He always wished to say a word or two at every meeting. The substance of his talks was: "Let us love one another. How great is the goodness of God." These words will always go with his memory.

J. I. Judy.

Mackinaw, Ill., 1832.   1913, Independence, Mo.

Mr. Judy became a Christian in 1848 under the preaching of Walter P. Bowles. He gave about forty years to the ministry. His work was mainly in Tazewell, Logan, Mason and Fulton Counties. For a period of twenty years he received an average of one hundred persons by conversion, and organized twelve congregations. His work also reached out into Iowa, Missouri and Arkansas.

Col. J. W. Judy.

Clark County, Ky., 1822.

During the years of his active life, Mr. Judy was one of the most favorably and widely known men in the State. He was colonel of the 114th Illinois Volunteer Infantry. In the siege of Vicksburg he was on the firing-line for forty-five days. He came to Illinois in 1851, and was a farmer in Menard County. After the war, he served as a member of the State Board of Agriculture, and during a period was its president. He was an expert on thoroughbred cattle, and traveled from ocean to ocean as an auctioneer of such live stock. He is a fine type of Christian gentleman. His wife, Mrs. Kate A. S. Judy, was a daughter of J. W. Simpson, of Clary's Grove Church, and was highly esteemed by many for her Christian activity and usefulness. The home was at Tallula, where Mr. Judy waits in the twilight of life for the eternal morning.

Andrew J. Kane.

Guilford County, N. C., 1817.   1896, Springfield, Ill.

Both of Mr. Kane's parents died in his infancy. He grew to manhood in the home of his eldest brother, Morrison Kane. This was in Indiana. At Indianapolis, in 1836, he became a Christian under the preaching of John O'Kane and Love H. Jameson. At twenty-one he began life for himself. He went to Chicago, thence to Peoria, and on to Sangamon County in 1839. His first work there was to assist in building the first bridge across the Sangamon River. By trade he was a carpenter. Uniting with the church in Springfield, he was led by its members to give his life to the Christian ministry; hence, he began the study of Hebrew, Latin, Greek and English Literature under private tutors. Later, he was ordained by the church. Of Mr. Kane's ministry, T. T. Holton has well written:

> His field of labor was central Illinois, though he at times passed the border of the State. He went on horseback with his saddle-bags behind him—in one side was his Bible; in the other, baggage. He rode through a country sparsely inhabited and when there were but few settled pastors. No man was better known than he—no voice more widely heard in those early days of the settlement and development of central Illinois. Meetings were held, churches organized, infant congregations cared for, and occasionally an encounter was had with some champion of opposition in public debate. Some of his evangelistic meetings were marvelously successful for the time, and his converts ran into the thousands. He regarded not the clouds or the wind. I have seen him ride up to his door with his ears frozen and his beard bristling with icicles, but never for a moment thinking

ANDREW J. KANE.　　DAVID D. MILLER.

JOHN W. TYLER.　　JOHN ENGLAND.

of quitting his work. It was with great reluctance that within a year of his death, at eighty years of age, he found he must relinquish all further efforts to preach.

Mr. Kane was a passionate lover of the Bible. He devoured its great truths. He was jealous of its integrity and its interpretation. Always abreast of the times in religious thought, he vigorously opposed the trend of destructive criticism. Judge W. E. Nelson said of him: "He was a most efficient preacher of the gospel—a man of great power—deeply convinced of the authority and sovereignty of God, of the divinity of the Christ and of the force and authority of the Bible." He was a reasoner rather than an exhorter, but his sermons appealed both to the imagination and the conscience. A careful reader and painstaking student, this master workman was heard by intelligent people, even in his closing years, with delight. A wide-visioned man, he assisted in the organization of the State and General Missionary Societies. One who knew him well said: "When Bro. Kane stands like a giant before the congregation, shuts his lips together, runs his left hand under his chin, and gives an emphatic look upward and all around, you are going to hear something."

> "His life was gentle; and the elements
> So mild in him, that Nature might stand up,
> And say to all the world, This was a man."

Dr. A. L. Kellar.

Oldham County, Ky., 1827.　　　　1908, Covina, Cal.

Was the youngest of eight children. He received, for his time, an exceptionally good education in Bacon College, and graduated from the medical department of the University of Louisville, Ky., in 1851. In the same year he was ordained to the ministry. He came to Decatur, Ill., in 1852 and began his practice there, but most of the years of his active life were passed at Sullivan. There he was one of the most persevering and efficient men the church ever had. His medical practice was very large, but much of it paid him little or no money. His disposition was most charitable. For forty-four years he practiced the healing art for both body and soul. He was rugged in body, vigorous in mind and energetic in action. His faithful services were a distinct contribution to the foundations of society in the counties of Macon, Moultrie and Shelby. He was well known and highly esteemed by many for his integrity of character. Min. E. H. Kellar, of California, is his son.

H. Y. Kellar.

Oldham County, Ky., 1825.   1902, Effingham, Ill.

Mr. Kellar and his brother, Dr. A. L. Kellar, were sons of A. H. Kellar, a Baptist minister who came to Moultrie County in 1832. There meeting Joseph Hostetler, he chose to be simply a Christian and assisted in the formation of the West Okaw Church of Christ. H. Y. Kellar's education was limited to the common schools of that time, but he came to be a well-informed and well-developed man. For a number of years he served as a schoolmaster. In 1847 he was ordained to the ministry by the West Okaw Church. He served congregations in Indiana, Kentucky, Missouri, Iowa and California, but the larger part of his ministry was given to Illinois, both as evangelist and pastor. He assisted in the organization of the State Missionary Society at Shelbyville in 1850, and was a member of its board of managers for many years. He was always the advocate of an educated ministry. He was an earnest preacher, but not a disputant. He was a ready helper in every good work, a wise counselor and a faithful servant of God and his fellow-men.

Nathan M. Knapp.

Member of Winchester Church. Member of the Constitutional Convention of 1847, of State Legislature in 1850, and paymaster in the Federal Army in the sixties. Retired with rank of lieutenant-colonel. Mr. Knapp was a man full of vigor and action and exerted a wide influence.

James Worcester Knight.

Illinois, 1869.   1902, California.

Was a son of Moses H. Knight. Attended school at Eureka. Was engaged in the newspaper business and in the public advocacy of good citizenship. In this later work, Sec. J. Fred Jones met him in 1896 and induced him to enter the ministry. He served the churches at Browning, Youngstown, Frederick, Carlinville and Champaign. When the University Place Church was nearing completion in 1902 under his leadership, ill health compelled him to go to California, where he died the next spring.

Moses H. Knight.

Vermont, 1830.   1878, Illinois.

Mr. Knight's parents were devout old-school Presbyterians, while an uncle, who had much influence over him, was an earnest Congregationalist. He was educated in a Baptist school. These surroundings greatly perplexed him in his religious views. He came to Illinois in 1850, settling in the western part of McLean County. He heard Min. J. G. Campbell present the simple New Testament teaching, and accepted with joy. He was ordained to the ministry in 1858, and continued faithfully therein for a period of twenty years. He served the churches at Lower and Upper White Oak and various communities in the northeast part of the county, where he was associated with Mr. Campbell in evangelistic work. In his preaching trips he traveled horseback or walked. Much of his service was without financial compensation. He was a pure, true and efficient servant of God and men.

A. R. Knox.

New York, 1824.   1914, Waukegan, Ill.

Shortly after his marriage in 1846, Mr. Knox, with his wife, came to Lake County, Ill. Both were active members of the Baptist Church. He was a "licentiate" and she a pioneer and leader in all church work. He heard that a minister had been traveling in Kentucky, Ohio and Indiana, and that his "preaching was tearing Baptist churches all to pieces." On inquiring, he learned that the name of this disrupter was Alexander Campbell. There were at that time a few Disciples scattered through that section who had come from Ohio. Some of them loaned Mr. Knox a copy of the "Christian Baptist." Before they had read the book half through, he and his wife were in full accord with the principles and aims of the Restoration movement. To these their lives were devoted. They were the parents of Mrs. Louise Kelly, so widely and favorably known as a Christian woman of superior ability and usefulness. For more than half a century, Mr. Knox lived and labored in Lake County for the primitive gospel. With a well-informed faith, he was as immovable as a mountain. In his evening-time he waited in the twilight of the eternal day.

E. J. Lampton.

Was born in Kentucky, reared in Missouri, became a Christian in 1852, entered the ministry in 1859, and continues therein. He gave twenty years' work to Illinois, during which time he baptized about three thousand people and added not a few others to the churches. His work, like his character, is of the substantial kind.

S. S. Lappin.

Wayne County, Ill., 1870.

The same year his parents moved to Missouri. Six years thereafter, while the family was returning in a movers' wagon to their former home in Illinois, the father died and was buried on the way. S. S. Lappin grew to his majority on the farm, working there and in stores, and attending and teaching schools. At the age of six years he had read McGuffey's old "Third Reader" through three times, having learned the words by spelling them aloud to his mother, whose eyesight was too dim to make out the letters. At twenty-one he began to preach in schoolhouses and country churches, but was still selling goods in a store in Fairfield.

After one year in Eureka College, he served the churches at Toluca, Washburn, Paxton, Atlanta and Stanford. He entered the editorial office of the *Christian Standard* in 1909, where he continues as its managing editor. Through the school of early adversity, his native endowments, with grace and grit, have led him to a place of great usefulness.

He has two brothers who are twins, and were born after their father's death: John C., a teacher in Phillips University, Enid, Okla., and William O., a teacher in Atlantic Christian College, Wilson, N. C.

Richard and Henry C. Latham—Father and Son.

James Latham, the father of Richard, was the first settler within the bounds of what is now Logan County. He was a Virginian, but came to Illinois from Union County, Ky., where all of his ten children were born.

Richard Latham was born about 1799, and came to Illinois in 1819, soon after locating at Elkhart. There he was married and built the best residence of the early settlers. This home came to be known near and far as one of unusual hospitality even in that period of domestic generosity. He became a Christian during the wide-reaching revival in which Robert Foster was the chief factor. For several years he went to the Lake Fork Church, eight miles east of Elkhart, and rarely missed a meeting there. When not there, the order of the Lord's house was maintained in his own home. This led to the formation of the Elkhart congregation. In 1852 he moved to Springfield. He was soon made an elder of the church there, and filled this place till his passing in 1868. Of him a writer has well said:

> Of the character of Richard Latham we find only good to record. He was a man whose honor was dear to him as his own life and whose word was sacred as his oath. While his career in the main savored little of adventure or striking achievement, it was enriched throughout by kindness and the benefactions which quietly but ceaselessly welled up from the bounty of his nature, endearing him to all with whom he came in contact. For miles around he was known as "Uncle Dick," and the whole community looked to him as arbitrator,

guardian and adviser, rarely questioning the wisdom voiced in his gentle counsels.

He presided at the Lord's table in such a way as to make all present feel thrilled and worshipful. When his sacred dust was borne away to its final resting-place, the number of gray-haired men who followed was a sight to see.

The epitomized character of Henry C. Latham may be written in four words—an ideal Christian gentleman. He is a worthy son of an honored sire. For many years he has been steadfast and reliable in the First Church of Springfield. There is no part of the worship that he has not led and no part of the service that he has not performed, and all has been done well. He has been a lifelong student.

John Lemmon.

Sangamon County, Ill., 1838.

Grew up on the farm and attended the public school. Enlisted in Company D, Thirty-third Illinois Volunteer Infantry. Lost his right leg and index finger on his left hand in the battle of Black River—the last stand the Confederates made outside of Vicksburg.

After the war, attended Bible College at Lexington, Ky., three years. Then taught school. Entered the ministry in 1874. Has served fourteen congregations in central Illinois, that at Buffalo seven years.

Mr. Lemmon is a man of clear and deep convictions—sincere, frank and outspoken. When a ministerial institute had given a half-day to the consideration of an unprofitable subject, he then publicly asked: "How long will it take this kind of talk to convert the world?" He holds that the same wise economy should be used in the management of public trusts as is exercised in one's personal business.

Silas White Leonard.

Louisville, Ky., 1814.   1870, near Centralia, Ill.

His parents dying when he was quite young, he was adopted by a Captain White, a Baptist, who reared and educated him in Ohio. He began to preach the primitive gospel at the age of twenty, but spent much time in teaching vocal music for the next eight years. About 1848 he, with A. D. Fillmore, published "The Christian Psalmist." It was in figure-faced notes and was the first hymnal having the music ever in use among the churches of Christ. It reached a circulation of 560,000 copies. In 1856 he moved from Jeffersonville, Ind., to his farm near Centralia, where he resided to the close of his life. From that point he went out and preached in many places. He was a sweet-spirited, but an aggressive and progressive, preacher.

Five days before his death he rode nine miles horseback and gave a temperance lecture. The cold thus contracted hastened his demise. He had just finished a new "Psalmist" in both kinds of notes, at a cost of $3,000, and had placed the material in the publisher's hand when his call came.

Cicero J. Lindly.

Near St. Jacobs, Ill., 1857.

Graduated in scientific and law departments of McKendree College and admitted to the bar in 1879. He has farmed extensively and has been active in civil life for many years. He has served as county judge in Bond County, was Presidential elector in 1884, and served also as Railroad and Warehouse Commissioner. Was elected to the House of the Legislature in 1902, 1904 and 1906. Mr. Lindly is an active member of the Greenville Church.

James A. Lindsey.

Kentucky, 1792.   1872, Illinois.

Mr. Lindsey came to Illinois in 1824 and settled in Tazewell County. At that time he was a Baptist. In 1827 he associated himself with the Disciples. He was a reverent and faithful student of the Bible, and early in his life became a preacher of the primitive gospel. He resided on his farm. He carried a small copy of the New Testament in his pocket, and as he plowed he read and thought on the Word. This was a custom of most of the pioneers. He was the leading spirit in the formation of the Mackinaw Church in 1837, which at once formally recognized his ability and fitness to preach the gospel and commissioned him thereto. After that, his wife superintended the farm and his sons did most of the work there. One year he evangelized on the condition that his brethren pay the wages of a male helper on his farm. Most of his ministry, reaching through sixty years, brought him little or no money compensation. Much of his work was done in Tazewell County, but he also evangelized and formed congregations in McLean, DeWitt and Marshall Counties, also west of the Illinois River. His style of preaching was exegetical. He read and unfolded a chapter, more or less. His sermons usually continued from one and a half to two hours. He taught people publicly and from house to house. This was the business of his life. Once where he stayed overnight he so taught the host and his wife that they expressed the wish to enter the Christian life. The next morning, before leaving, he immersed them. He patiently bore the derision that was too often thrown at the Disciples in the earlier years. As he rode quietly along the roads he sometimes would hear people say: "There goes a Campbellite. See the hump on his back." He was ardently missionary in his convictions, teaching and life. Three of his sons were preachers. From his home near Lilly, where he had resided for thirty-eight and a half years, he passed to his great reward.

John Lindsey.

Christian County, Ky., 1821.   1887, Eureka, Ill.

Came with his parents to Tazewell County in 1824. Was a son of James A. Lindsey. Graduated at Bethany College in 1848. For some time was a traveling companion in the ministry with Alexander Campbell. Was a teacher in Walnut Grove Academy and a valuable helper at Eureka College in many ways through many years. He served as pastor with many churches, but was more engaged in evangelistic work. About five thousand persons were added to the churches through his efforts. Mr. Lindsey's life was a very useful one to his time. He was always outspoken on the right side of every moral question.

Henry C. Littleton.

Ipava, Ill., 1851.

Received such education as the common schools afforded. After his baptism by Dr. J. H. Brinkerhoff in 1867, he served as a lay preacher. Then he traveled with some of the strong preachers of that time, by whom he was instructed in the things pertaining to the kingdom of God. He served the churches at New Philadelphia, Bryant, Cuba, La Harpe, Barry, Mason City, Pekin and Astoria. He was a single-purposed, guileless and industrious preacher whose service was always constructive. He moved to Iowa in 1900.

F. M. Lollar.

Ingraham, Ill., 1840.

Mr. Lollar grew to manhood on a farm in Clay County and attended the subscription and public schools of his community. He entered the military service in October, 1861, and served four years and three months in Company F, Forty-sixth Illinois Volunteer Infantry. He was discharged with the rank of captain. Upon his return home he attended school and taught schools. He did not begin to preach until 1882. Then he served the Ingraham Church part time for twenty years and the Union Chapel Church for eleven years. He held many successful revivals in Clay and Effingham Counties. He was a good man of fine common sense, whose work the Lord richly blessed. He moved from his farm in 1904 to Olney and from there in 1908 to Wynne, Ark.

Fenton Lumm

Was another of the old-time preachers of White County. He lived in Seven-mile Prairie. His labors were contemporaneous with those of Moses Goodwin. While he always resided on his farm, he was a man of some culture. He was a pleasing and inspiring speaker. A man who had been reared a Methodist heard Mr. Lumm preach one day. At the close of the sermon, with tears streaming down his cheeks, he turned to the man who sat next to him and said: "That is the first Methodist sermon I ever heard in my life."

Jonas Lumm, of Grayville, who was also an old-time preacher, was Fenton's brother.

Alexander McCollum.

Washington County, Pa., 1820.   1895, Taylorville, Ill.

Grew up on a farm in Miami County, O., and received his early education there. Taught school and studied medicine, but did not graduate. First united with the Baptist Church, but, hearing Alexander Campbell in a public debate, he took the Bible alone as the rule of his faith and practice. Was licensed to preach in 1844 as a man of recognized ability. He came to Morgan County about 1850. In that section he was associated with D. P. Henderson, W. W. Happy and others in evangelistic work. He became the pastor of the Taylorville Church in 1856, but in 1858 moved to a farm in Locust Creek Township. There, in a settlement of Ohioans, he formed a Christian congregation that gave P. D. Vermillion to the ministry. This band never built a chapel. In 1863, Mr. McCollum returned to Taylorville, where he resided till the close of his life. He rendered the church there most valuable help. From that place he preached in all the surrounding region for miles and years. He led Mrs. Henry Davis to the Lord—she was the mother of Mrs. Hoover and Mrs. Detterding, both of honored memory. Mrs. Davis and her husband built the present house of worship in Taylorville.

Mr. McCollum lived in a time when liquor was in most homes, but he never knew its taste. In his ministry he was intrepid and aggressive. On one occasion he entered a denominational assembly in the country. The regular minister did not come; so the leaders, after a private consultation, asked the unorthodox McCollum to "make a few remarks." He opened up with such unction that there were tears in many eyes and not a few fervent "Amens." He came to the great commission, and the tears gave place to disappointment and the "Amens" to vexation. Next he stood on Mt. Zion under the throne of the King and amid the fiery tongues of Pentecost. The preacher's words did not affect the people like those of Peter. There were hurried nods and whisperings among the leaders, and a concerted move among them toward the door. The people followed— so did the preacher, proclaiming insistently the word of the Lord. It was an irregular panic, and looked like a flight from fire or an invasion of Indians. Away went the people down the main road with the preacher a close second, still making himself heard and understood. He told them about Philip in Samaria. At another sign from the leaders the people took to the woods in squads and singly. The peerless defender of the faith poured the truth into the squads as he came upon them. An elderly man, out of breath, heard the whole story of the eunuch's conversion; a woman with a babe in arms heard for the first time about the salvation of Lydia. Had it not been for the saplings and pawpaw bushes, the whole history of conversions would have been declared.

John Byram McCorkle.

Lawrenceville, Ill., 1819.　　　　　　1882, Eureka, Ill.

His father, Richard B. McCorkle, with his family, moved to Tazewell County about 1830 and settled a few miles north of Washington. There he built a strong log residence that furnished a home and a safe place for women and children during the raids of Indians upon the early settlers. His eldest daughter married John Johnson, and became the mother of three noted preachers—B. W., R. H. and J. B. Johnson.

During his early manhood, J. B. McCorkle marketed farm products at Ft. Dearborn, now Chicago. He seized every opportunity for his mental discipline and the acquirement of knowledge, including night schools. In his Christian service he was was much helped and encouraged by Sanford Gorin, an older elder of the Washington congregation. He moved to Eureka in 1869. He served the college as financial agent, preaching as he went among the churches. He evangelized under the auspices of the missionary co-operation consisting of Woodford, Tazewell and McLean Counties. During his public ministry, which he continued as long as his bodily health permitted, he baptized over one thousand persons. Most of this work was done at his own charges, supporting his family meanwhile by other means. His hospitality was so generous that his home in Washington was nicknamed "The Campbellite Hotel." In this, many of the pioneers were entertained. Often in his evangelistic meetings he sang a solo just before his sermon. His faith in the word of God was abiding. Daily in his home his family assembled for worship.

W. H. McGinnis.

Missouri, 1838.   1904, Illinois.

Entered the Christian ministry through the action of the church at Louisiana, Mo., in 1860. The same year he came into Illinois, where he continued his work to the close of his life. He wrote a few years before his decease: "As you probably know, my preacher-life has been a very humble and uneventful one. My first regular work was in the counties of Brown and Schuyler in 1862. At that time I was almost the only Christian preacher, outside of Quincy, in all that region between the Illinois and Mississippi Rivers. The Civil War was then on. Hundreds of soldiers were being brought back—sick, wounded, dying and dead. Many nights I rode on horseback, through mud and darkness, to be at the places where soldiers were to be buried, and give consolation through the preaching of the gospel. In the first five years of my ministry, although I baptized many hundreds of people, I did not receive enough money to buy my clothes. The first State convention I attended was in Bloomington in September, 1863. On the first morning of the convention the ground was covered with a heavy frost—a splendid corn crop was in ruins. A sadder-faced audience I never looked into. Robert Foster said: 'Let us brace up. I move that the janitor make a fire, and that Bro. Fillmore lead us in one of his best songs.' Both of these things were done, and through our prayers the Lord's work moved on gloriously."

While Mr. McGinnis was a faithful preacher of the Word, he was pre-eminently a man of peace. Through the gentleness of his spirit and the sweetness of his disposition, the influences of his consecrated life were as wholesome and abiding as the sunshine.

John Henry McGuffin.

Scott County, Ky., 1844. 1891, Illiopolis, Ill.

Came with his parents to Illinois in 1857. Educated in the public schools and the Mechanicsburg Academy. Enlisted in the Tenth Illinois Cavalry in July, 1862, and at the end of three years was mustered out as corporal of Company G. He was engaged in secular business till 1886, when he entered the ministry. He was a man of fine character and did efficient service in the few years of his ministry.

George G. McManus.

Jefferson County, Ky., 1804. 1888, Odessa, Tex.

Began preaching in Ohio in 1824. In 1843 came to Princeton, Ill. Did much pioneer work in Bureau County with a most unselfish and devoted spirit. He served as county judge for several years. Moved to Kansas in 1873, where he lost his wife by a fire. Mr. McManus was one of the Lord's great men.

Jo Major.

Walnut Grove, Ill., 1834. 1913, Eureka, Ill.

A son of Ben Major. For many years a trustee and liberal financial supporter of Eureka College. He was captain of Company A, Eighty-sixth Illinois Volunteer Infantry. A braver man never followed a flag in all the fortunes of war. His patriotism was wholly unselfish and his Christian life modest.

William Trabue Major.

Frankfort, Ky., 1790.   1867, Bloomington, Ill.

For many years this name was as familiar to the people of Bloomington as the name of the city itself. He was educated at Georgetown, Ky., and came to Bloomington in 1835. His removal to Illinois grew out of his aversion to negro slavery. He was a descendant of the Huguenots and was a man of earnest religious convictions.

For six years he was a member of the Baptist Church, but in 1830 he was excluded from the fellowship of that body because he held and advocated religious views which he believed to be more in harmony with the Bible than those preached by the Baptists at that time. It was in this way that he came thus early into the movement looking to the reproduction of the New Testament church. He was the leading spirit in the organization of the Christian Church in Bloomington. He built, almost single-handed, its first house of worship. Through the active years of his life he gave the congregation his thought, prayers, time, energy and means. When no minister was present, he preached, and frequently baptized candidates. He presided well at the Lord's table and exhorted his brethren to fidelity and good works. While the orthodoxy of the Disciples was for years a perennial question with his religious neighbors, Mr. Major knew whom and what and why he believed, and was as immovable as a mountain.

The growth of the city and his foresighted investments brought to him considerable property. He was a public-spirited citizen. The first public hall for general uses was erected by him at the southeast corner of Front and East Streets, in 1852. In this the first Republican State convention was held in May, 1856. In this year he also founded

WILLIAM T. MAJOR.

BUSHROD W. HENRY.

JOHN C. ASHLEY.

S. S. LAPPIN.

Major Seminary, which, next to his church, he loved and prized.

Dr. William A. Mallory.

Kentucky, 1822.   1884, Illinois.

The parents of Mr. Mallory came from Kentucky to Illinois in 1827, and settled in what is now Clear Lake Township, Sangamon County. His mother's brother, John Dawson, came with them. Mr. Mallory became a Christian at Clear Lake in 1844, under the preaching of A. J. Kane. He began teaching school in 1841. At the same time he began the study of medicine with Dr. John Todd, of Springfield. Later, he pursued his medical studies at Laporte, Ind., and then practiced his profession, for a time, at Beloit, Wis. In 1847 he was in the Louisville (Ky.) Medical College, and in 1848 located at Fort Madison, Ia. Near that city he was married to Miss Susan A. Johnston in 1848. They returned to Springfield the next year.

In August, 1852, he began the publication of the *Christian Sentinel*. From this date, his thought and energy were mainly given to the work of the ministry. In March, 1856, he entered the service of the State Missionary Society, in which he continued until the outbreak of the Civil War.

He was commissioned by Governor Yates, in January, 1862, as a recruiting officer. This work resulted in the enlistment and organization of the 114th Illinois Volunteer Infantry, in which Dr. Mallory became captain of Company C. After one year's service at the front, he resigned by reason of ill health.

Thereafter, his time and energies were given chiefly to the work of the gospel. His ministry was confined to central Illinois. He resided at Howlet, now called Riverton. One of the sermons that he preached with great power was based on these words: "For the time is come that judgment must begin at the house of God; and if it first begin at us, what shall the end be of them that obey not the gospel of God? And if the righteous scarcely be saved, where shall the ungodly and the sinner appear?" It was a sermon not soon forgotten. He was a man of fine courage and cultured conscience, of kindly heart and generous helpfulness. His active and useful life was cut short by typhoid fever and blood poisoning.

George Watson Mapes.

Near Auburn, N. Y., 1828.   1898, Des Moines, Ia.

The earlier years of his life were passed in Ohio and Indiana. In 1852 he united with the Baptist Church. In 1853 he brought his family to Bureau County, and the following year united with the church of Christ in Ohio Township. He bought and cultivated a new farm, but was ordained to the ministry in 1856. From 1868 his time was wholly given to the ministry. He planted a congregation in his home neighborhood and others elsewhere in that county, was a successful evangelist, and served as pastor at Putnam and Princeton, leading at the latter place in building the chapel that is still used. At Washington and Macomb, two terms, where a chapel was also built during the time, he also was pastor. Then his ministry was given to Missouri and Iowa. Mr. Mapes was a good business man, but in his life the material was always subordinated to the spiritual. He was gentle and earnest, kindly and strong. Failing health did not abate his zeal. "I must die with the harness on," he said, and so exchanged his cross for his crown.

Geo. W. Martin.

An elder of the Winchester Church. Captain Company H, 129th Illinois Volunteer Infantry. Served one term as sheriff of Scott County and three terms as circuit clerk. Died in 1910, in Harvard, Neb.

Rolla M. Martin.

Monongalia County, Va., 1816.   1878, Danville, Ill.

Came with his parents to Illinois in 1820, who settled near Georgetown, Vermilion County. There were many Indians then in Illinois. Mr. Martin grew to manhood on his father's farm. He attended a few subscription schools for a little time, but most of his mental training was acquired by his personal efforts. His mother was solicitous and ambitious for her son, and so got for him all the books she could. The Bible was the chief one in the collection. The books young Martin studied with earnestness and persistence—ofttimes by the light made by the burning of hickory-tree bark or a grease-lamp. Such was his progress and growth, that at the age of seventeen he became a teacher. His early manhood was spent chiefly in the schoolroom. At twenty-five, he was ordained to the ministry and continued therein until his death.

Mr. Martin was a large man in every way. His weight was 250 pounds, well built, of superior mental powers, of fine personality and noble bearing. He was a prince among men. He was a forceful speaker, with fine reasoning ability. His life falling in the formative period of the Restoration movement, he was frequently led into public discussions. In these, he wielded the sharp sword of the Spirit with unusual power. Religious errors fell before his Biblical logic like grain before the sickle. On one occasion, Mr. Martin, with H. H. Gunn and George Y. Stipp—the father of T. L. Stipp—held a public debate with three Universalists. It was an interesting time. Riding homeward with one of his opponents, he said: "Bro. Martin, see, here is water; what doth hinder me to be baptized?" Mr. Martin responded: "If thou believest with all thine heart, thou mayest." The man replied: "I believe that Jesus Christ is the Son of God." Then and there the man was baptized. About 1856, Mr. Martin held a public discussion at Myersville with an M. E. preacher named Garner. He insisted that Philip and the man of Ethiopia did not go down into the water, but only near to it or only to it, and Philip sprinkled water upon the man. Mr. Martin replied by quoting, in a like way, Matt. 8:32: "The whole herd of swine ran violently down a steep place to or near the sea and perished on dry land." During this debate, Mr. Martin was accosted on the street by a member of the M. E. Church, named Smith, who inquired: "Suppose a man makes the good confession, as you require, and on the road to the water to be baptized a limb from a tree falls on him and kills him, what would you do with him?" Mr. Martin promptly replied: "I would bury him."

Mr. Martin was a soul-winner as well as a defender of the truth. During his ministry he baptized more than three thousand people and formed a goodly number of churches. For many years he was the only Christian minister residing in Vermilion County. His trials for Christ's sake were many. He often rode long distances to his appointments, through all kinds of weather and roads and across swollen streams that endangered his life. Twice he was elected treasurer of Vermilion County, but declined further civil service because it hampered his work as a preacher. He still lives in the lives of multitudes.

J. D. Metcalf.

Hopkinsville, Ky., 1834.   1887, Girard, Ill.

Was brought, when a year old, by his parents to Illinois. They settled in Greenfield. Mr. Metcalf moved to Girard in 1856, and there resided to the close of his great and good life. He was a successful general merchant, lumber dealer and banker. He became one of the leading citizens of that community, and was held in high esteem both for his personal worth and his public spirit. He served the church most efficiently as an elder for twenty-one years, when his life closed. His Christian outlook was world-wide, and in his last will he remembered State, Home and Foreign Missions in $1,000, severally. His head was clear and his heart tender, and his influence for Christ will be felt till time falls asleep on the bosom of God.

David D. Miller.

Zanesville, O., 1815.   1895, Illinois.

Mr. Miller was of German-Scotch blood. His grandfather, John Miller, held the rank of major in the Revolutionary Army. In 1798 he colonized Millersburg, Ky. His father, Adam Miller, was a high Calvinist and an old-school Baptist who farmed and preached. The boy, David, could not believe that God was a respecter of persons; so he ran away from home to attend a Methodist camp-meeting. This did not help him. His father moved his family to a four-hundred-acre farm in Cass County, Mich., in 1854. There he worked on his farm, went to school, learned the trade of carpenter and read the Bible earnestly.

In 1859 he returned to Ohio. Here he became a Christian in 1841 at the Brushy Creek Church, which was twenty miles from his home. Through the influence of Elder Baker, who was the ablest attorney in Licking County and a great bishop of the congregation, Mr. Miller entered the ministry. His first work was that of a missionary, or evangelist, in four counties of central Ohio, under the direction of the Elizabethtown Church. His salary was to be $200 a year, which he was to collect himself. Mr. Miller says: "Then I thought of the dying Irishman, who willed $200 each to his several sons. When the boys inquired where the money was to come from, the father replied: 'You must look after that yourselves.'" He said further: "Much of my best work was done outside of the pulpit. I would sometimes form classes of young people in a neighborhood and explain the Scriptures to them." In his autobiography he gives this incident also: At the Yearly Meeting at Austentown Valley, the birthplace of the Restoration movement in the Western Reserve, fifty ministers were present and eight thousand people assembled. All the churches and schoolhouses for ten miles around were used for overflow meetings. William Hayden preached the anniversary sermon, opening with these words: "A quarter of a century ago to-day we met on this ground as a Baptist Association. We resolved to throw away everything but the gospel, and there was not a man among us that knew what the gospel was; but we have found out what it is, thank God." He paused, wiped the tears from his face, stretched his hands toward the vast throng, and said: "See here; what have we done in twenty-five years? We've set hell afire, made the devil mad and astonished the natives." Then, Isaac Everritt, who sat beside Mr. Miller, whispered in his ear: "That's Billy Hayden; he says what he pleases." In that meeting Mr. Miller was an active participant.

He followed his inclination for evangelistic work, for which he was well fitted. Ohio, Michigan, Indiana, Kentucky, Illinois, Iowa, Missouri and Kansas are all indebted to his self-sacrificing toil. During the forty-one years of his ministry he baptized about four thousand people, engaged in eight public discussions and did an immense amount of hard gospel work. He was a man cast in an iron mould, but with a tender heart and cheerful disposition. For his faith in God he would have as willingly have gone to the stake as he did to breakfast. His temperament was poetic, and patience the woof of his soul. In politics, he was an Abolitionist—by heredity and environment. He lived and died in the fear of the Lord and the love of man.

James J. W. Miller.

Illinois, about 1831.   1907, Illinois.

Began to preach at the age of eighteen years. Educational opportunities were limited, but he grew into the use of pure and forceful language. His field of labor was limited to Pike, Calhoun, Green and Macoupin Counties, but he did considerable work in Missouri. In his revivals he laid the beginning of many churches. He was a man of high ideals, candid and devoted to truth and duty. His industrious habits were well known. When not preaching, he was engaged in manual labor. For fifty-five years he proclaimed the glad tidings to his fellow-men.

George W. Minier.

Ulster, Pa., 1813.   1902, Chicago, Ill.

Mr. Minier was of German and English parentage. Both of his grandfathers were soldiers in the Colonial Army. He was educated at the Athens University, Pennsylvania. At

GEORGE W. MINIER.

JAMES ROBESON.

JOSEPH B. McCORKLE.

JOHN W. SCONCE.

the age of nineteen he became a schoolmaster in New York State. In those early years he also developed his ability to speak in public.

He came to Illinois in 1837 and settled in Bureau County, where he resided for ten years. While there, he surveyed the State road from Peru to Knoxville and taught schools. One of these was at Leepertown.

Jan. 1, 1839, he was married to Miss Sarah Ireland. To this union six sons and six daughters were born. In 1839 he surveyed a part of the Illinois River bottom about Starved Rock.

In the spring of 1841 he was immersed by Dr. P. G. Young in or near Magnolia, Ill.

In 1847 he came to Bloomington and opened a high school for young people. The next year he conducted the same kind of school at Mackinaw.

In 1851 he moved to his farm in Tazewell County, near the Little Mackinaw Church. He got his land from the Government with soldiers' warrants. The land cost him eighty-three cents per acre. Soon after he became a Christian he was induced to enter the ministry. He was with Alexander Campbell on a part of his tour through Illinois in 1853. In the earlier years of his ministry, he preached now and then at Bloomington, Elkhart, Fremont, Mackinaw town, Little Mackinaw, Hittle's Grove, Washington, Waynesville, Le Roy, Springfield, Peoria, Pekin and elsewhere. During those years he was associated with H. D. Palmer, Wm. T. Major, William Davenport, Andrew Ross, William Ryan, O. A. Burgess and other distinguished men. In 1867, in company with Messrs. Blackstone, Boyer and Stroud, he platted the town that bears his name. It is located three and a half miles south of his old home.

In all-round culture and Christian character, there were few, if any, superior to Mr. Minier in the period of his prime. He was rated high in educational lines. Frequently he was called upon for lectures. In schools, sometimes his subject was trees; then again it was birds. He was president of the North American Forestry Association, also of the State Horticultural Society. He was also a member of the National Peace Society and an earnest advocate of its principles; also of all temperance work.

In his young manhood he was very handsome. His elegant appearance and refined manners attracted all classes. He was welcomed by the young as well as the old. Little children would run out to meet him where he was being entertained. With his brethren in the ministry he was always cordial and entirely free from any feeling of jealousy. He never preached a long sermon, and his services were in wide demand for weddings and funerals and other public or semi-public occasions. He never used tobacco in any way, in which he was in striking contrast with some of his contemporaries. He could easily quote from Milton, Young and, especially, from Shakespeare. "He saw sermons in stones, books in brooks and good in everything." In the pulpit he was a teacher. His speaking was on a dignified level. He depended upon the truth of God, presented distinctly and carefully. He never got lower than a high level.

There was in him a fine sense of humor. While he did not encourage unseemly demonstrations, he enjoyed a ripple of appreciation that fit the occasion. At one time, a good, sedate sister called him to account for creating what she called "unholy levity" in the congregation. In all kindness, he responded:

"My dear sister, you would forgive me if you knew how much I keep back."

He had his troubles, as other men have, but he never intruded them on his friends. He never went around looking "blue." At one time one of his friends said to him: "Bro. Minier, how do you seem so cheerful when you have been walking through deep waters?" He replied: "My dear brother, trouble is the last thing in the world to nurse. I must save my strength to do my work. I will not waste time on what can not be remedied. Any trouble that comes to me I will not lay upon the hearts of others."

One of his moral axioms was this: "When we have done what we can to make the world wiser, better and more beautiful, we should be satisfied."

"Only the actions of the just smell sweet and blossom in the dust."

Mordecai Mobley.

Was one of the early settlers of Sangamon County, where, in 1824, he was married. In his youth he was "wild," but in the wave of religious interest that passed over that county by the preaching of Dr. Robert Foster, Mr. Mobley became a Christian. He continued in the Lord's service with great energy. He served as justice of the peace, and was connected with the land office at Springfield. Meanwhile, he was active in the church there. He moved to Dubuque, Ia., in 1850, and at once set about to establish a church there. He was not a preacher, but he taught the people who met for public worship on the Lord's Day and led them in all good works. President Lincoln made him postmaster at Dubuque. He was a man who sought first the kingdom of God. At eighty-five years he died in Washington, D. C.

F. L. Moore.

Illinois, 1857.

Mr. Moore was born three miles west of Clinton, among the blackjack and sassafras trees. He is still considered to be a young man. When he was twenty-eight years of age, his education had neither limit nor boundary line. Then he left the jeweler's bench and spent four months in Eureka College. That he might continue his work there, he asked a loan of a small sum from a rich man, who refused and severely criticized him for having left a good business and wasting his time in college. The most of his ministerial work has been done in Missouri and Kansas, as pastor, evangelist and Bible-school evangelist. His ability as an artist and an engraver has greatly helped in his blackboard and chart work. In late years he has served the Abingdon Church with efficiency. Mr. Moore has never found time to waste with the higher critic and has never overtaxed his mind in trying to find out whether Moses wrote the Pentateuch with a goose-quill pen or not. He has never had any more sense than to believe that the gospel is the power of God unto salvation, and has baptized multitudes. He hopes to preach until he is ninety, and then move out on a little garden-farm.

G. W. Morrell.

Illinois, 1831. 1909, Illinois.

One of the self-sacrificing and devoted preachers of the earlier years. His ministry was chiefly in Richland, Wayne, Wabash, Clay, White and Lawrence Counties. To him, the church in Olney is much indebted. His ministerial labors reached also into Indiana and Ohio.

The Mulkeys.

The Mulkey family came to America from Sweden about 1650 and settled on a part of the territory watered by the Delaware River and Bay. Their history is an interesting one. They were men of earnest Christian convictions and high moral purpose and courage. As far as known, there was only one exception—he was a shocking pervert.

William F. Mulkey.

A successful business man and a faithful Christian. He represented his district in the House of the Twenty-ninth General Assembly. He refused a nomination to the State Senate in 1880.

John M. Mulkey,

For whom Mulkeytown, in Franklin County, received its name, with his brother Jonathan H., came from Tennessee to Illinois in the early thirties. He built the first house on the site of Mulkeytown in 1837. The post-office was called Little Muddy, because it had been previously established at the house of John Kirkpatrick, who lived near Little Muddy Creek. The name was not changed to Mulkeytown till after the Civil War. Another brother, Dr. C. F. Mulkey, came from Tennessee to the same locality in 1832, and was engaged for a time with John M. in the mercantile business.

Philip Mulkey

Came to this locality in 1835 and spent the balance of his life in preaching the gospel and teaching school. His four sons, three of whom are named above, all preached, but were chiefly engaged in other business.

John Newton Mulkey.

Tompkinsville, Ky., 1806.   1882, Glasgow, Ky.

John Mulkey, the father of John Newton, moved from Tennessee to Kentucky about 1801, and settled on Mill Creek, some two miles from Tompkinsville. In 1809, while preaching a sermon at the home of William Simms, from the tenth chapter of John, and making a strong effort to maintain the doctrine of Calvinism, his own arguments convinced himself that this teaching was false. The Stockton Valley Association, to which the Mill Creek Church belonged, called him to account. The upshot of the matter was that John Mulkey left the Baptists and took many of the Mill Creek Church with him. These met together on the third Saturday in November, 1809, and, after prayer, organized a church on the Bible alone, rejecting human creeds, confessions of faith and books of discipline. This congregation came to be known as the "Bible Alone Church." Hence, it is plain that his son, John Newton Mulkey, was as near religiously free-born as any one of his time. He began to preach in East Tennessee in 1831. In the summer of 1832, two miles west of Wolf River, Clay Co., Tenn., in the Liberty meeting-house, he preached a sermon on "The Weekly Meeting of the Church to Break Bread." He came to Illinois in 1857, settling in Perry County. He was reckoned the most powerful preacher of this name, and the equal of the best of his time. He preached the Word clearly and with unusual sympathy for all those whom he addressed.

While supporting his family from his farm for twenty years, he did efficient ministerial work in southern Illinois. The closing years of his life were passed in Kentucky. It is estimated that he preached ten thousand sermons and immersed nearly that number of believers.

Dr. Isaac Mulkey

Came to Illinois in 1846. He united the healing art and the work of the ministry. His preaching was continuous. He resided in Carbondale and died at Ashley.

Besides these named above, other Christian preachers of this family went West—some to Missouri, some to Arkansas and others to Oregon.

Patrick H. Murphy.

Warren County, Ky., 1828.   1860, Abingdon, Ill.

Came to Warren County in 1833. Became a Christian at the old Coldbrook Church at the close of 1840, and was formally ordained to the ministry in 1850. Was educated at Galesburg and Bethany College. Mr. Murphy and J. C. Reynolds opened an academy at Abingdon in 1853. By its efficiency the school quickly grew into popularity. This led to the beginning of Abingdon College in 1854. Mr. Murphy became its first president and filled the position most successfully till his early death. Meanwhile, he served the Abingdon Church as its pastor. He was a fine scholar, a good executive and a high type of Christian gentleman. His demise was an irreparable loss to the cause of Christian education in western Illinois.

Clement Nance, Sr.

Pittsylvania County, Va., 1756.   1828, Floyd County, Ind.

This man was never in Illinois, and he died two years before the dissolution of the Mahoning Association, by which action Alexander Campbell was formally separated from the Baptists. The appearance of this notice of Mr. Nance here would seem to be an anachronism. What, then, is its apology? Probably not more than once in a century have a man's posterity been so impressed by the blood and faith of a great progenitor. Mr. Nance became a Christian in the Methodist Church in 1773. In 1790 he received license to celebrate the rites of marriage as a Baptist, giving bond for the same with a security in the sum of $2,500. He was married to Mary Jones and they became the parents of twelve children. Their descendants, with their families, now number about thirty-five hundred, and are scattered throughout the middle and far West. Mr. Nance came from Virginia into Kentucky in 1803, where he stayed about eighteen months. It is highly probable that during this time he met Barton W. Stone, for thereafter to the close of his life he was a steadfast advocate of the principles of the Restoration movement.

Some of his descendants were the Burtons of Woodford County, of whom Mrs. B. B. Tyler is one; the Richardsons of Adams and Woodford Counties, of whom are A. A. and Min. Frank Richardson; John Oatman, the founder of the church at Eureka, married a daughter; the Mitchell, Long, Harber and Nance families all carry the blood of Clement Nance, Sr., as do many others in a less ratio. "Uncle Jimmy Robeson" was his son in the gospel. Most of his posterity have been Disciples of Christ. In a larger or smaller degree the churches at Eureka, Mount Zion (near by), Secor, Bloomington, Lexington, Sterling, Blandinsville and Quincy have received his marvelous impress. He laid his wand of empire on generations and sends his message of high purpose down the ages

Dr. W. P. Naramore.

New York, 1824. 1910, Illinois.

His parents died when he was young. He grew to manhood on a farm near Chardon, O., in a family named King. They were most earnest Disciples and gave this young man an excellent Christian training. He graduated at Williams Medical College in Ohio at the age of twenty-one. Coming to Stephenson County, Ill., in 1846, he entered upon the practice of medicine. Finding in his new home no church built after the apostolic pattern, he proceeded to establish one. About two miles west of the village of Oneca, his then place of residence, was the Van Meter settlement. There he established the Mt. Pleasant Church of Christ and ministered to it many years. Of that congregation, Judge Andrew Hinds was an active member. Later, Dr. Naramore preached in the Baptist chapel in Lena and elsewhere in the county. Meanwhile, he continued in the practice of his profession assiduously. While he never sought any public office, he was a member of the State Legislature in 1859-60, and also a member of the State Constitutional Convention in 1862. He introduced Judge J. M. Baily and R. R. Hitt into public life. He greatly desired to enter the Federal Army during the Civil War, but the men enlisting in a large section of Stephenson County positively insisted that he stay at home and care for their families while they were away. This he did free of charge to all of them. For twenty-five years he was president of the Old Settlers' Association of that county.

He was always firm in his Christian faith. His intelligent conscience permitted no concessions to error or compromise of gospel truth. His sincerity, wide information, admirable spirit and steadfast devotion to high ideals made him a superior Christian man. His fine character commanded the fullest confidence and highest esteem of all his fellow-citizens.

William E. Nelson.

Sparta, Tenn., 1824.

Mr. Nelson's mother was a devout Presbyterian and his father a member of the same church. When William was about eighteen years of age, he attended a union revival, in which Methodists, Baptists and Presbyterians participated. During this meeting those who "got through" laughed immoderately. But William failed of "the blessing." Then he betook himself to his father's office, who was an attorney, to pray. It was not long till he, too, was laughing; whereupon, the minister assured him that he was accepted by the Lord. He then united with the Presbyterian Church, and he became quite "a respectable member." However, he was disquieted about his baptism. Shortly, a "Campbellite" preacher named Hooker passed that way. But the sheriff locked the courthouse against him. Then the preacher took to the woods. William was inclined to hear him, although he thought this minister had no more religion than a horse. That sermon on "Rightly Dividing the Word" set him to thinking and to reading the Bible. Seven years later, another preacher of the same fellowship passed that way. Nine miles north of Sparta, he preached in a schoolhouse to just four people—a man and his wife who were simply Christians, the negro janitor and young Nelson, who had gone out on horseback to hear the sermon. There he halted the formal closing of the meeting to make the good confession. Shortly thereafter, he was immersed in a creek. His mother cordially encouraged her son in his chosen course.

Mr. Nelson came to Decatur in 1857. During all the years of his virility he was an active and helpful member of the church. His custom was to read one or more books of the Bible through at a sitting and every week; thus his knowledge of the Scriptures came to be comprehensive and profound. He was elected a circuit judge in 1876 under the new law, but failed of a re-election in a district that was overwhelmingly against him politically. In 1886 he was chosen county judge, in which position he served eight years.

Mr. Nelson is probably the most widely known and best loved man in Macon County. In 1912 the city of Decatur named one of its public parks for him. The experiences of eighty-nine years have not frozen the cheerful humor and keen wit out of him. At his eighty-eighth birthday he wrote the following:

Verbal Inspiration of the Bible.

Numerous articles have been written to prove the verbal inspiration of the Bible, all of which make numerous quotations from the Book itself to prove the proposition. For instance: "The word of the

Lord came to Ezekiel, saying." The fault of this method is apparent in that it makes the Book itself the witness; but it must be remembered that a good many persons do not accept the Book as from God.

In the matter of a divine revelation two factors must be considered: First, God, who *knew* the *truth* concerning facts unknown to man, was sovereign, and had power to make promises and keep them; and man, who did not *know* and was to *learn* and *obey*, considering the powers of his *reasoning*, and capability to *understand*.

In considering these factors, the nature of both must be taken into view. God had created man, and, being omniscient, knew that man had *ears* and a *mouth*, and could speak and receive and communicate with ideas in the use of language composed of words.

Knowing this, God made his revelation to man in *words* that the man could understand. If he did not, then His revelation *misleads* instead of *improving*. This we can not believe with our idea of God's omniscience and goodness, and the very purpose he had in view in making the revelation. Hence the words were chosen by Him with the view to man's *information*, and must have been selected by God as suitable and apt to convey to man God's idea.

This is the common-sense view and is the simple argument for verbal inspiration. It is irrefutable in man's reason and proves verbal inspiration without the Book as witness. It appeals alone to man's capability to reason—an argument addressed to man's common sense.

Andrew D. Northcutt.

Montgomery County, Ky., 1813. 1890, Christian County, Ill.

Mr. Northcutt was of Welsh extraction and a self-made man. His grandfather, Jeremiah Northcutt, served seven years as a soldier in the Colonial Army and was present at Yorktown at the surrender of Cornwallis. Mr. Northcutt's school privileges were very limited, but his persistent industry fitted him for the work of teaching. He came to Illinois in the fall of 1836, and for fifty-four years he resided, successively, in Sangamon, Shelby and Christian Counties. He was a successful farmer and stock-raiser and he was a successful preacher as well. He entered the church in 1843 and the work of the ministry shortly thereafter. With his pioneer neighbors he ate and slept, exchanged work in the harvest-fields, joined in the drives to the markets in the genuine spirit of Christian democracy. With them he toiled and sweat six days in the week, and to them he sweat and preached on the seventh.

But he was not an exhorter. His speech ran evenly and calmly always. He was a man of superior natural powers of mind; analytic, logical, clear and argued with a force peculiarly his own. He was energetic and tireless in the organization and upbuilding of churches among the people of central Illinois, at a time when churches were few and far between, and the visit of a minister of any denomination an event in the community. As illustrating the denominational feelings at the middle of the nineteenth century, he related the following incident: The Methodist Sunday schools along the Sangamon River westward from Decatur united in the celebration of the Fourth of July in an assembly that convened in one of the inviting natural groves contiguous to that stream. Among the banners carried in the procession was one representing a big frog in the act of jumping into the stream traced below, and across the form of the ugly amphibian was printed the word "Campbellite"! However, Mr. Northcutt cherished well-defined friendships for his old-time friends.

Harrison W. Osborne.

Kentucky, 1800.   1883, Illinois.

Was baptized by Barton W. Stone in 1817, and two years thereafter was ordained to the ministry. Thus he early became actively associated with Mr. Stone in his reformatory work. Mr. Osborne came to Morgan County about 1830, and was an earnest preacher in the Christian Denomination until the union of the "New Lights" and the "Reformers" into the Jacksonville Church of Christ by Mr. Stone in 1832. Thereafter, to the close of his long and useful life, he was a faithful teacher of the truth as it is in Jesus. He was a small man physically, but with superior mental endowments and spiritual culture. He rode horseback over a wide territory and was very prompt in meeting all his engagements. His manner was modest and his voice gentle, but he emphasized those teachings of the Scriptures with great earnestness that his hearers most needed. Colonel Judy says of him: "He was quite eloquent, hewing close to the line all the way through." His last years were passed at Berlin, Sangamon County. There his beautiful and winsome character so took hold of the community that many of the young people thought they could not be married without "Uncle Harrison," and his services were in wide demand for funerals. When the burden of years became heavy upon him, he said: "I am waiting for my Saviour's welcome on the other shore."

George Carroll Owen.

Poplar Grove, Tenn., 1812.   1890, Columbus, Kan.

His father was a well-known Methodist preacher in his locality in Tennessee. The family came to Macoupin County in 1830. Three years later, George united with the Methodist Church. In a short time he entered the Christian Church and its ministry. He was abundant in labors in that section of the State as a forceful and convincing preacher. His life was passed on the farm, and his ministerial services were mainly without money compensation. Later in life, he preached in Mississippi, Louisiana and Kansas. While on the way to fill an appointment, his last illness smote him and death took him. He had been a preacher about fifty-five years, and had aided in the organization of many churches.

A. N. Page.

Mrs. Mary A. Grove Page was baptized in 1836 in a meeting held at Panther Creek, Woodford Co., Ill., by those great pioneers, William Davenport, James Robeson and Jas. A. Lindsey. Her husband, A. N. Page, was baptized by Henry D. Palmer in 1844. Mrs. Page said that her husband was converted by a personal study of the Word, and when the minister came along he was baptized. Immediately thereafter he began what would now be called cottage prayer-meetings. His neighbors were invited to his home and to the homes of two other families of the community, where they sang, studied the Bible, prayed and observed the Lord's Supper. With this start, Minister Palmer called him to the ministry. In this service he continued fifty years. He did missionary work in Woodford, Mason, Tazewell, Livingston and other counties. He led many people in central Illinois to Christ, and he was there known and loved by many.

Oliver J. Page.

Edwards County, Ill., 1867.

Was a teacher in Eureka College. Served as principal of the Metropolis High School and pastor of the church there. Elected to the House of the Legislature in 1898.

Henry D. Palmer.

Charleston, S. C., 1781.   1861, Illinois.

Mr. Palmer, in his early manhood, was a carpenter. Before his conversion it was his custom to work seven days in the week. He cared nothing for God. The church nearest his home in Tennessee belonged to the Presbyterians. One of its members was a good Christian woman who was a neighbor of the Palmer family. She often invited them to go to meeting with herself and family, but Mr. Palmer always replied: "I am too busy." One Sunday morning she stopped and first asked Mrs. Palmer to go with them. She replied: "I'll go if Henry will; you ask him." So she went out to his shop and said: "Won't you go to church with me to-day?" He replied: "No, I haven't time." Then she said: "Henry, some time you'll have time to die," and left him. That proved the alarm-bell to him. Shortly he went into his residence and said: "Wife, let's go to church." They went, and kept going. They together read the Bible and prayed. In due time they wished to unite with the church. As they objected to being sprinkled, the Presbyterian minister immersed them. Just before he was baptized he took his tobacco from his pocket and threw it far away, saying: "I read in the Bible that we must put away all filthiness of the flesh." As he continued to study the Bible, he found that he could not subscribe to the Westminster Confession of Faith; so in kindness he withdrew and united with the Baptists. He came to Illinois first in 1819, and for a time was associated with the "Christian Settlement" that had been formed the year before in Lawrence County, seven miles northwest of Vincennes, Ind. The locality is now known as Allison Prairie. The settlement was founded and the church there formed by the good people of the Christian Denomination. Mr. Palmer was then formally affiliated with them. He left there and went to Indiana, but returned to Illinois in 1835 and settled on Crow Creek, in Marshall County. There he bought a farm, on which he made his home to the close of his life. Thereafter, his course was that of the brave and self-sacrificing pioneers. He traveled and preached far and near. He was one of the strongest preachers of the period, and most of the infant churches of central Illinois were helped by his able, Scriptural sermons. He was present and helped in the formation of the General Christian Missionary Society at Cincinnati, O., in 1849. In 1850 he was at Shelbyville, and assisted in organizing the State Missionary Society and was chosen its first president.

He taught O. A. Burgess the way of the Lord, baptized him and induced him to become a preacher.

I. A. J. Parker.

Farmington, Tenn., 1840.

When a little child, was taken with his father's family to Tippah County, Miss. There he grew to manhood. His father was a Christian preacher, so the son received a good education for that day. He became a Christian in 1858. At seventeen he became a schoolmaster and continued in this work until the Civil War began. He enlisted in the First Alabama Federal Cavalry and was honorably discharged as first lieutenant. He came to Johnson County, Ill., in 1865. There he has been a farmer, merchant, schoolmaster, singing teacher and preacher. In 1888 he was elected to the House in the General Assembly. Mr. Parker is a man of fine character. He is modest, cultured and sweet-spirited and devoted to the truth as it is in Jesus. His ministry in southern Illinois has been a blessing to many. He has taught 113 singing-classes and in this way won the hearts of the young people, and then won them to Christ. He has evangelized, established congregations and cared for them. One elder said: "Bro. Parker has completely transformed the character of this community during his ministry."

Two of his sons, W. A. and B. E. Parker, are Christian ministers, and also his son-in-law, E. W. Sears.

John F. M. Parker.

Knox County, O., 1838.   1906, Galesburg, Ill.

When a child he came with his father's family to Illinois. Was educated in the public schools and Berean Christian College at Jacksonville. He entered the active ministry at the age of nineteen, in which he continued forty-five years. He organized and built up the church at Putnam, which was his home. His ministry extended over the southern section of the Military Tract. He served as State evangelist of Minnesota for several years, where his heroic work was fruitful of results that remain to this day. His faith was rich and strong, his life gentle and peaceable, his character beautiful and winsome. He gave himself heartily to the Restoration movement, although the active years of his life were passed on his farm, where most of his ten children grew up. Within eleven months he lost a son, a daughter, his farm and his wife. But then he said: "I know whom I have believed, and am persuaded that he is able to keep that which I have committed to him against that day." Mins. J. E. and L. G. Parker are his sons.

Abner Peeler.

No name is met more frequently among the pioneer preachers of central Illinois than Abner Peeler's. He was abundant in labors, preaching the gospel over a wide scope of the new and sparsely settled country. Yet little of him went into the written records of the times. He was a man of varying moods. In the thirties he, with Hughes Bowles, began a meeting of days in a log-cabin residence of one of the brethren. Within a few days the meeting failed to come up to Mr. Peeler's expectations and he became discouraged. He told Mr. Bowles that he was too sick to help that evening, and that he would lie down on the bench and listen to the songs and sermon. Such difficulties challenged the courage of Mr. Bowles, so he then preached with such power that several persons went forward to make the good confession. This at once restored Mr. Peeler to his normal condition of health. He was instantly upon the floor, and, without coat or boots, made such an exhortation that the entire assembly was moved and a number of others turned to the Lord. After that, Mr. Peeler was often referred to as "the preacher who exhorted in his stocking feet." But he was a farther-seeing man and advised his brethren to move out of the woods and settle on the prairies. At one time he resided in White Oak Grove, in Woodford County.

L. B. Pickerill.

Woodford County, Ill., 1853.

Educated at Eureka and at the Bible College, Lexington, Ky. His ministry has been wholly given to the churches of Christ in Illinois, which he has served faithfully and well.

William S. Pickrell.

Montgomery County, Ky., 1807. 1870, Mechanicsburg, Ill.

Accompanied by his brother, Jesse Pickrell, he came to Sangamon County in 1828. Together the two brothers had three horses and $300. He entered land where Mechanicsburg now is and later laid out that village. He was a man of public and patriotic spirit, and came to know personally every man of prominence in the then large county of Sangamon. In the Black Hawk War he messed with his friends,

Abraham Lincoln, John T. Stewart and Elijah Iles. He became a major in the State Militia.

He became a Christian in 1842. At once he took an active and leading part in the church. A man of superior capabilities and spirit, he served the congregation with great efficiency in every position. When no preacher was present, he spoke well to the people. He was always ready for every good work—to instruct the untaught, to encourage the discouraged, to strengthen the weak, comfort the sorrowing, to assist the needy and help bury the dead. His home was noted for its hospitality near and far. Many found a cheerful welcome. At a "State Meeting" held there in 1856, his home entertained sixty-four delegates. As his ten children grew of age to attend public worship, those who, for any reason, were required to stay at home, cried. One of his daughters became the wife of Harvey N. Edwards, another of George Pasfield, and a third of Wm. Bayard Craig. The last, Miss Emma, led the congregation in a period of weakness—superintending the Bible school, presiding at the Lord's table, and doing whatever needed to be done until the tide turned in the congregation's life.

Mr. Pickrell was a tall, large man, with a florid complexion and gracious manner. He was a prince of the Lord's.

J. Henry Pickrell.

Mechanicsburg, Ill., 1834.   1901, Springfield, Ill.

Was a son of W. S. Pickrell, and widely and most favorably known to many still living. He was a most faithful Christian everywhere and in all things. He was always willing to assume the hardest tasks, always cheerful, hopeful, full of faith and forgetful of self. He was heard to say that he had not missed a prayer-meeting in forty years.

W. O. Pinnell.

Oldham County, Ky., 1824.   1899, Paris, Ill.

Was a fine farmer, stockman and banker in Edgar County. He was active in raising the Seventy-ninth Illinois

Volunteer Infantry, in which he served as captain of Company H. He was a member of the Twenty-eighth General Assembly, served as county clerk in Edgar and as mayor and postmaster at Paris. He was a member of the congregations at Kansas and Paris.

James Pool

Came to the Barney's Prairie settlement in what is now Wabash County from Hamilton County, O., in 1815. He was the first minister of the Barney's Prairie Church and continued in that relation until his death in 1854. He was a godly man and very considerate of the feelings of others. On one occasion he entertained a brother overnight. Early next morning he built a rousing fire in the open fireplace in the room where his guest was sleeping. He thought to further please him by playing on his violin. The guest arose and said: "Bro. Pool, you have offended me." Whereupon, Mr. Pool, laying his violin on the fire, said: "I will never offend you again." Such condescension to the Christian weakness and prejudice indicates the spirit of this good minister of Jesus Christ, who, through thirty-three years of pioneer toil, laid deep and strong the foundations of this great church.

William C. Poynter.

Barren County, Ky., 1821.   1899, Albion, Neb.

Came with his father's family to Illinois in 1836, settling at Palestine, Woodford County, which was then a part of McLean. Shortly thereafter, he became a Christian under the preaching of Wm. Davenport, and at once a diligent student of the word of God. He carried his Testament in his pocket and in a few years could quote most of it from his memory. In 1852 he lost one of his arms by an accident. This turned him from farming to preaching. His ministerial work was mostly in Woodford County, but it reached over much of central Illinois. In Iroquois County he was a pioneer, laying the foundation at Watseka, Woodland and Onarga, in the Spring Creek community. In Boone County,

B. J. RADFORD.

OLIVER W. STEWART.

T. T. HOLTON.

JOHN W. ALLEN.

Neb., he did similar effective work. His preaching produced an intelligent faith in men that lasted and held them steadfast to Christian duty. Mr. Poynter filled a number of civil offices. Of his two sons who reached maturity, the elder, W. A. Poynter, held several honorable positions in the State of Nebraska, one of them being Governor, while the younger, D. J., is still a preacher and an editor there.

J. A. Reed.

Ohio County, Ind., 1842.

Is a farmer and resides at Mason. Served through Civil War in the Eighty-third Indiana Infantry. He was elected to the House of the Legislature in 1906.

John C. Reynolds.

Kentucky, 1822.   1906, Illinois.

Mr. Reynolds came to Illinois in 1839. He settled in Warren County, a few miles west of Abingdon. He was licensed to preach in 1850 by the Meridian Church of Christ. He graduated at Bethany and was one of the founders of Abingdon College. In this school he served as teacher for six years. For two years he was president of Christian University at Canton, Mo. The other years of his active life were given to the work of the Christian ministry in Illinois and Missouri. In 1867 he became the proprietor and editor of the *Gospel Echo,* and continued in this work for a period of six years. He grasped and clearly understood the subjects to which he gave his attention. His method was distinctly didactic. He was as humble, sincere and guileless as a little child. His sympathies were as wide as the needs of humanity. His faith was always serene, his work led by high ideals and his life a benediction to his generation.

Elbert G. Rice.

Columbia, Tenn., 1823.   1892, Jacksonville, Ill.

Came with his parents to Illinois in 1832. Their home was made near the present village of Riggston. His training in the public and subscription schools was supplemented by his lifelong readings and study. Thus he came to be a well-informed man, with good ability to think, reason and preach. He knew the Bible well and was sincerely devoted to the Restoration movement. Mr. Rice was a successful farmer throughout his life, in Cass County for fourteen years, but most of the time in Morgan. He served frequently as an evangelist, but was particularly a friend of the weak and needy congregations. These he would help until they could help themselves, and then turn to other like places. In him were united many admirable traits. He was an intelligent, modest, gentle and strong, highly esteemed man and much loved by all. For many years he was a very valuable factor in the Jacksonville Church. His life and ministry were richly blessed of God. Of his eleven children, nine are living.

J. M. Riggs.

His grandfather, Scott Riggs, came to Illinois in 1815 and settled on Allison Prairie, in Lawrence County, which was then a part of Crawford. He was a blacksmith, farmer and preacher. He served as a member of the first Legislature of the State in 1818. He was active in uniting the Christians and Disciples in that part of the State. He moved to Scott County in 1825, and was a member of the church at Exeter at the time of his death.

J. M. Riggs served one term as sheriff of Scott County, was a member of the Twenty-seventh Illinois Legislature, of the Forty-eighth and Forty-ninth United States Congresses, was nineteen years a member of the Winchester Board of Education, and an officer of the board during the entire period. He has long been an active member and efficient officer of the Winchester Church.

James Robeson.

South Carolina, 1797.   1888, Secor, Ill.

The family of James Robeson moved from South Carolina to Kentucky on horseback in 1798, settling at the present site of Hopkinsville. There he grew to manhood on a farm on a part of which the courthouse now stands. He attended such schools as were within reach at that time, and afterward a select school conducted by Barton W. Stone. In 1813 he became a Christian under the ministry of Mr. Stone, and shortly thereafter entered the ministry. About this time, Mr. Stone and Clement Nance, Sr., were starting on a preaching tour from New Albany to Crawfordsville, Ind. Young Robeson accepted an invitation to accompany them. On the return trip they stopped overnight at the home of Mr. Nance, and, according to the custom of the time, had preaching. Young Robeson said to the girls in the Nance family that they should not tell any one that he was a preacher. But they, with true girlish impulse, spread the report quickly and widely. That evening he was impressed to preach his first sermon before a large audience and in the presence of Messrs. Stone and Nance. This was the beginning of a laborious and fruitful ministry that reached through a period of seventy years. He traveled with Mr. Stone not a little, preaching from house to house and holding series of meetings in the fall season. During these earlier years, Mr. Robeson was profoundly impressed by the beautiful spirit and strong life of Mr. Stone. These preaching tours reached into Tennessee and Missouri also.

In 1822, Mr. Robeson was married in Kentucky to Miss Jane A. Earle. They were the parents of eleven children.

In 1835 he sold his lands in Kentucky and freed his twenty slaves, giving the State his bond for $100,000 for their maintenance. Coming to Illinois, he settled in Tazewell County on a piece of land that is now the north edge of Eureka. After a short residence in Washington, he moved to a point eight miles southeast of Eureka and there started a town that he named Bowling Green. Here he was engaged in merchandising. But he held to his preaching constantly and faithfully in all the regions around his places of residence. Much of his preaching was in the hewed-log schoolhouses, so he came to be called the hewed-log preacher. In the earlier years of his ministry he was opposed to a preacher's receiving money for their public services, but later he came to see the Scripture teaching on the subject. Reverses in his secular business probably accentuated this.

In 1841 he was elected to the State Legislature. He declined a second term on the ground that no preacher has time to so use. He was associated with Ben Major and Thomas Bullock in leading the movement that resulted in the organization of Woodford County from slices of McLean and Tazewell Counties in 1841.

In 1857 he sold his farm and moved to Secor. Thereafter, he was engaged in evangelistic work for about eight years under the auspices of the McLean County Co-operation. In the later years of his life he was known as "Uncle Jimmy Robeson." He was one of God's elect. In his sermons the love of God for man predominated. He was a fine exhorter. Many, many great audiences were moved to tears by his persuasive pleadings. Sitting in a chair, he preached his last sermon at the age of ninety-one. He was mighty in prayer, his supplications now melting his hearers into tears, now lifting them to the gates of glory. His courage equaled his pathos. On one occasion, at Money Creek, twelve miles southwest of Lexington, McLean County, he conducted a very successful meeting. Among the number was a wife whose husband swore that he would shoot any man who baptized her. His neighbors said he was a dangerous man and tried to dissuade Mr. Robeson. He replied: "If she comes, I will baptize her, knowing that I will be doing my Master's will." A great concourse of people assembled at the usual place on the banks of the Mackinaw the next Sunday. The husband was there with his gun in hand. Mr. Robeson first offered one of his powerful prayers that touched and subdued all hearts. The wife was baptized without disturbance. A short time thereafter, Mr. Robeson baptized the husband at the same place.

BIOGRAPHIES

Levi Mac Robinson.

Susquehanna County, Pa., 1831.

His early life was spent on the farm. His education began in a log schoolhouse. At eighteen he was converted in the United Brethren Church and began at once in the active service of the Lord. He came to Mt. Pulaski, Ill., in 1860 and served congregations thereabout. Through the loving and faithful ministry of Dr. J. M. Allen, Mr. Robinson united with the Christian Church. Since then, until the heavy hands of the years laid their disabilities upon him, he was an active and faithful preacher in many fields in central Illinois. From his home in Mt. Pulaski he responded to many calls from many people and places. There he is now, a highly respected and revered citizen.

Charles O. Rowe.

Delaware County, N. Y.   1893, Laramie, Wyo.

Mr. Rowe was first a blacksmith, and the action of the smith characterized, in a measure, his public ministry—he hit hard licks. He began to preach at the Berea Church, in Morgan County, in 1852. His last sermon was on Christmas Day, 1892, on "Posting the Books for Fifty Years." He did successful work in Illinois for many years. Mr. T. T. Holton furnishes the following incidents that will portray the man and his manner:

THE SAPSUCKER SERMON.

When pastor of the church at Berlin in the sixties, he was walking to church on Sunday morning when his attention was attracted by a sapsucker at work. He was impressed and said to himself, "That bird never planted the tree, and had it been left to him there would have been no sap there." Instantly the sermon he had prepared for that morning was placed on file and he proceeded to make some shoes that would fit, as was his manner. He spoke of human parasites, hangers-on, deadbeats; legislators who traveled on passes while the masses paid their railroad fares, and members of the board of equalization who did the same; of the leeches and bloodsuckers of society; of loafing big boys who ate the bread of their mothers' toil; of "sanctified" husbands who loafed at stores while their wives made the living; of the fellows who came to help after the fire was out, and, by contrast, of the praise and credit that should be given honest laborers in all necessary industries. The sermon was remembered many years. Another incident was

THE PIOUS DOG.

Mr. Rowe began a protracted meeting in a country church in Illinois. The first night the people came in crowds and with them came many dogs—he guessed the number at sixty. In the main there was no particular disturbance until two of the unfriendly curs came into collision. He met the emergency by saying just before dismission: "Now, brethren, the dogs are all right. They seem to enjoy being here. They like to come to church. They like to be with their folks. A dog would rather be with a man than to be with another dog. I find no fault with the dog or his master. But, brethren, dogs have no souls. The preacher has no mission to dogs, and the attendance of so many dogs with different dispositions, and different views upon the subjects of the day, may cause a clash and seriously interfere with the meeting. Now, will you not all just tie up your dogs to-morrow night at home and see how we will get along without them." The suggestion was fully acted upon. The next night Mr. Rowe was well up on Jacob's ladder in his sermon, when a startling crash was heard; the door flew wide open, and a great dog, with chain about his neck and an attached post upon his shoulders, moved to the front of the platform, stopped and looked with evident satisfaction at the audience. The sermon ended and every one laughed. The post was detached and the dog led out. Mr. Rowe concluded the meeting as follows: "Brethren, there is a great lesson for all of us in what we have seen here to-night. This pious dog has taught us what we should not forget. He wanted to come to meeting to-night because he had been here before. I have just learned that he has been a regular attendant. You can not keep the regulars away. You can not tie them up so they will not break away and come. Brethren, get the habit of being here and you will like it and can't be kept away. Then, this good dog wanted to be with his folks. He chose his society. He was restless away from those who befriended him. So ought those to be who stay away from the house of God. Wake up and come where you will enjoy your best friends. This brave dog tugged at his post that held him and never let up till he was with his folks in the house of the Lord I close with one suggestion, that this pious dog be allowed to be present every night of the meeting if he chooses to come. Let us be dismissed."

Andrew Ross.

In the year 1845, John, Joseph and Andrew Ross, three of the sons of Min. William Ross, a Methodist preacher of

Tuscarawas County, O., came to Illinois and settled in Ohio Township, in the northern part of Bureau County. These sons were following in the religious footsteps of their father. John was an ordained minister, while Joseph and Andrew were class-leaders in the Methodist Protestant Church. Before leaving Ohio, John had become somewhat skeptical about the Scripturalness of some of the teachings of the church of which they were members. In their new home the three brothers began a careful and sincere study of the Scriptures to satisfy themselves on these questions. This investigation led them to leave the Methodist Church, to be immersed and to identify themselves with those who desired to be known as Christians only—rejecting human creeds and accepting the Bible as the sole Scriptural guide. They began preaching these truths from house to house, and soon organized the Ohio Township Church of Christ. About this time, John Ross built a new barn, in which meetings were held for a time. Here George McManis and Minister Parkerson helped them in protracted meetings. Later, the congregation met in the new schoolhouse. Afterward, a chapel was built on the farm of John Ross. These Disciples met with opposition from their religious neighbors. Hence, they were called upon to defend their teaching. This made them thorough Bible students and able exponents of the word of God.

John Ross moved to Pine Creek, in Ogle County, where he served the church. Later, he moved to Alma, Ill., where he resided till his death. Thereafter, the chief responsibility devolved upon Andrew. He continued to look after his large farm through the week, preach for the congregation on Sundays, and usually invited a large number of his hearers to go home with him to dinner. He reared a large family of his own and some adopted children besides. He was diligent in business, generous with his accumulations, fervent in spirit and walked in fear of the Lord and the high favor of men. At ninety his heart rests upon the divine promises and his eye is fixed upon the eternal city. He is of the class that has greatly enriched the world.

George W. Ross.

Macon County, Ill., 1855.   1910, Vermont, Ill.

His early life was passed upon the farm. He attended the public schools, Kentucky University, and graduated from Eureka College in 1881. Nearly all of his ministry was given to Illinois, the closing seventeen years with the Vermont Church as its pastor. Three days before his death, he drove fifteen miles to conduct a funeral. His wish was to "die in harness."

Charles W. Ross, one of the most capable preachers in the State, is his son.

Joseph B. Royal.

1816.   1898, Vermont, Ill.

Became a Christian in Sangamon County. Like his Master, he was a carpenter before he became a preacher. His home was at Vermont for many years. With that town as a center, he preached throughout the Military Tract. He baptized about four thousand persons. The strength of his life was given to his generation. It was a time of sacrifices. Preachers' salaries were small, and ofttimes a part was never paid. But his heart was in his work. He went afoot or on horseback to his appointments. He preached in homes, barns, groves, courthouses and schoolhouses. For more than fifty years he held steadily on in his ministry till the disability of age laid its hand upon him. In his prime he was a power in the pulpit.

John L. Routt.

Eddyville, Ky., 1826.   Denver, Col.

Was brought in his infancy by his parents to Illinois. Served as captain of Company E, Ninety-fourth Illinois Infantry, through the Civil War. Was appointed Governor of the Territory of Colorado by President Grant, and after its admission as a State in 1876, he was twice elected as its chief executive. Mr. Routt was probably the first man among the Disciples to pay $10,000, in one sum, to the work of the church. This he did toward the erection of the First Christian Church in Denver, Col., of which he was a member.

Gershom L. Rude.

New York, 1808.   1890, Illinois.

In early life, Mr. Rude learned the blacksmith's trade. He spent some time in Ohio, where, at Harrison, he became a Christian and at once entered into active service in the church. He became associated with George Campbell and Sidney Rigdon, who afterward became a Mormon. Later, Mr. Rude moved to Indianapolis, Ind., and just outside its limits he had his shop. In this city his devotion to the Lord and his ability as a public teacher of the Word was recognized. He was associated with Mins. John C. New, John O'Kane, Henry R. Pritchard and Love H. Jameson.

Mr. Rude came to Edgar County in 1855 and located a few miles northeast of Paris. Here, upon his farm, he opened a blacksmith shop, united with the Paris Church and began to preach on Sundays. The passing years were more and more given to the work of the ministry. He went where he was invited. His work extended into Coles County, and in Edgar County there were few communities where he did not preach, oftentimes without money and without price. Through life he was an incessant and discriminating reader. His knowledge of the Bible was such that he would locate quickly almost any passage read or quoted to him. He clothed his thought in good language. His style was clear, argumentative and very dogmatic. In his best years his ministry turned many to the Lord. Withal, he was a good singer, and usually started the songs in his meetings. He was generous, benevolent and kindly in heart. He was, during the Civil War, an ardent Unionist and the incarnation of moral courage. Political feeling was unusually warm in the southern part of Edgar County, as well as elsewhere, during that period. Mr. Rude was preaching in those parts then. Before beginning his discourse there on one occasion, he said: "Some people are always crying peace, peace. In the name of God, if you want peace, why don't you have it? You cry peace with a revolver in each pocket and the devil in your heart." People often became so angry with him for his preaching that they furiously declared that they would never hear him again; but these generally did hear him again, and many of them, sooner or later, became Christians only.

William B. Ryan.

Virginia, 1800.   1877, Missouri.

Mr. Ryan's family moved to Logan County, Ky., in 1818, and from there to Logan County, Ill., in 1830. The latter trip was made in an ox-cart and required three weeks' time. The settlement was in Eminence Township. His first home there was a log cabin, in which the family passed the winter of "the deep snow."

In 1839 he and his wife were baptized by Walter P. Bowles. He at once began to preach. He was affectionately called by most people "Uncle Billy." As a pioneer preacher, he was a favorite with the early settlers in Logan, Tazewell and DeWitt Counties. His meetings were held in dwellings, schoolhouses, mills, or anywhere he could assemble an audience. One of his favorite expressions was, "Remember the warning of Mt. Sinai." He was a great admirer of Alexander Campbell, who was once his guest. When traveling north from Springfield in 1853, Mr. Campbell was accompanied by G. W. Minier and others. They stopped at the home of Mr. Ryan for dinner. They found Mr. Ryan busy making ax-handles. These Mr. Campbell examined, making suggestions as to their weight, size, shape, etc. The two hours' visit was much enjoyed by all. As they left, Mr. Campbell expressed himself as being much pleased with Mr. Ryan. His home on the border of the "Big Prairie" was the stopping-place for most travelers passing through that region. His hospitality knew no bounds. His latch-string was always out. Abraham Lincoln was often his guest. A business letter from Mr. Lincoln to him is a much-prized keepsake of his grandsons. He, with eighteen others, organized the Bethel Church in the northern part of Logan County. He was its first pastor, and there he passed many pleasant and profitable years. His was a busy life. He worked on his farm to support his family, served four years as associate judge in his county, and was a soldier in the Black Hawk War. He was twice married. Few men can show more clean pages in the "Book of Life."

Judge Charles J. Scofield.

Carthage, Ill., Dec. 25, 1853.

Grew up to his fifteenth year on a farm. Then began the classical course in Christian University, Canton, Mo. Graduated with A.B. degree in 1871. Then taught three years in Carthage High School. Meanwhile, read law and was admitted to the Illinois bar in June, 1875. Began at once the practice of law. In October following, he was appointed master in chancery of the circuit court of Hancock County, which position he filled for ten years. Meanwhile, he was a busy lawyer. In June, 1885, he was elected one of the judges in the Sixth Judicial Circuit, comprising the counties of Adams, Hancock, McDonough, Fulton, Brown, Schuyler and Pike. Re-elected in 1891, thus serving on the circuit bench twelve years. He declined the third nomination. In 1893, Judge Scofield was appointed by the Supreme Court of the State one of the judges of the Appellate Court for the Fourth District to fill an unexpired term of one year. At its close he was reappointed for three years, thus serving four years on the Appellate bench and until his service as circuit judge terminated. On the death of Judge Scott in 1909, Judge Scofield was urged to become a candidate for the nomination to the Supreme Court, but declined because of his disinclination to enter personally into a political contest. Since his retirement from the bench in 1897, his practice has extended throughout Illinois and into other States. The class of his cases has made him, in considerable measure, a lawyer's lawyer.

Mr. Scofield became a Christian at the age of twelve. Coming to maturity, he found the church at Carthage financially weak; hence, he began to supply its pulpit. This led to his becoming its pastor, which place he filled for about twenty years. Such salary as was paid him was turned to the work of the church.

In every way Mr. Scofield is a man of the highest type. His power of analysis is unusually superior, and his grasp of a subject is masterful. Preachers who hear him in a sermon are delighted.

John W. Sconce.

Nicholas County, Ky., 1824.   1910, Kansas.

Mr. Sconce came with his parents to Vermilion County, Ill., in 1830, and in 1836 to Shelby County. At the age of nine he started to school. The only book he had was a copy of the New Testament, his parents being too poor to buy others for his use. He was baptized by Bushrod W. Henry in 1841. He began to preach at the White log schoolhouse, Todd's Point Township, in 1849. The same year he located on a farm six miles north of Shelbyville. The churches of the county engaged him to preach in destitute places. His ministry was fruitful and many were turned to the Lord in various localities. In 1863 he moved to a farm in Moultrie County, where, for ten years, he continued the same kind of work that he had done in Shelby. His family was supported mainly by his farms. In 1873 he settled in Dalton City. Chiefly through his labors, a church of Christ was established there.

In 1876 he moved to Mt. Ayr, Ia. In that new country he continued successfully his pioneer work as a preacher. Ten years thereafter he moved to Attica, Kan. There he continued in the same sort of work until the infirmities of age compelled him to give it up. Of such as he the Lord will make up his jewels.

In such sacrifices of self have the beginnings of the Kingdom been laid through all the centuries.

BIOGRAPHIES

Andrew Scott.

Melrose, Scotland, 1857.

Came to America in 1863. Educated in the public schools of Canada and at Hiram College. Established the first church of Christ at Portage la Prairie, Man., Can., in 1881. In Illinois he was the very successful evangelist of the Sixth District for three years. He has served as pastor in the churches at Normal, Danville and Hoopeston, where he now is. Mr. Scott's Scotch heart always beats loyal to the truth as it is in Jesus.

Charles L. Scott.

On a farm in Edwards County, Ill., 1876.

Was principal of public schools in Grayville. Elected to the House in the Legislature in 1908, 1910 and 1912.

Dr. John Scott.

Vermont, 1790.   1883, Prairie City, Ill.

Was one of the strong men of his time—physically, mentally, morally and spiritually. He was a farmer, a schoolmaster, a surveyor, a physician and a preacher. When about eighteen years of age, he made the trip, on board "The Clermont," from New York to Albany. He came into Fulton County in 1839. There he, with other pioneers, formed what came to be known as the Scott Settlement. It was about five miles north of the site of Cuba. He later made his home elsewhere in Fulton County, and at these places had for his neighbors and friends the families of McBeth, Bell, Rigdon, Oglesby, Reed, Markle, Dr. Speer, Bangman, Boynton, Wheeler and Levi T. Scott. The wife of Levi Scott was Mary Doyle, whose family came from Kentucky to Peoria County in 1835. For many years the Doyle family were influential as Christians in that county. For about twelve years after coming to Fulton County, Dr. Scott gave much time to preaching in the cabins of the pioneers, in log schoolhouses and elsewhere. On canvas, he made an outline of Solomon's Temple and its furniture, by which to instruct people through eye-gates. During this period he was associated with the Christian Denomination. In 1851, Michael and Job Coombs, brothers and ministers of the churches of Christ in Indiana, came that way. Through their preaching, Dr. Scott and a considerable number of friends were led to accept the more apostolic teaching. They were baptized on a Monday forenoon in the transparent waters of Lost Grove Creek as it ran its way among blooming flowers and singing birds. In 1855 there was a considerable exodus of these people into McDonough County. They located on new farms near the site of Bushnell. Here Dr. Scott again took up his faithful and loving ministry and continued in it until handicapped by the burden of years. He was a strong and true man, whose life was full of good deeds.

These facts were furnished by a step-grandson, I. N. Scott, New Sharon, Ia.

Walter Scott

Was born in Moffat, Dumfrieshire, Scotland, Oct. 31, 1796. His parents were people of fine intelligence and culture. They were all members of the kirk. He was educated in the University of Edinburgh. When a young man, on the invitation of his uncle, George Innes, he came to New York. For a time he taught a classical school on Long Island. Later, he went to Pittsburgh. There he soon made the acquaintance of a fellow-countryman, Mr. George Forrester. In his home he found a welcome. Mr. Forrester was a minister of the Haldanean school. At that time he was conducting a school and also preaching to a small membership whom he had collected together. He invited Mr. Scott to examine the Scriptural claims of pedobaptism, in which he had been trained up. He made a faithful investigation of the subject. His reverence for the authority of God's word led him to the conclusion that it was a defenseless relic of the Papacy and wholly without divine warrant. Hence he was

CHARLES W. SHERWOOD.

JOHN YAGER.

WALTER P. BOWLES.

THOMAS GOODMAN.

immersed by his friend, Mr. Forrester. He at once became an earnest and persistent student of the Holy Scriptures. He opened a classical and English high school, but these duties he did not permit to interfere with his assiduous and systematic study of the Bible. It was not long until, on one of Mr. Campbell's visits to Pittsburgh, he and Mr. Scott became personally acquainted. Both were men of brilliant and admirable qualities. They were further attracted by their mutual conclusions on great Scriptural questions. From that time they were co-operants in the reproclamation of the gospel as it was first preached by inspired men.

David Franklin Seyster.

Pine Creek Township, Ogle Co., Ill., 1858.

Trained in country schools, high school and Eureka College. Preached first sermon in 1888 at La Claire, Ia.; walked across Mississippi River on the ice to reach there. Has served the churches at Coleta, Pine Creek three terms, Kankakee, where he also preached Sunday afternoons for two years in the State Hospital by appointment of its superintendent, Lynnville, Mt. Morris, Lanark and Savanna. Everywhere his work has been fruitful in additions and spiritual results.

Cragy J. Sharp.

A native Scotchman who settled in Bureau County in 1848. A successful farmer and preacher. Associated with the Ross brothers in the church near Ohio. Fine Bible scholar and preached without money compensation from one to three times every Sunday for years. He helped a number of young men in securing their education at Abingdon, among them G. T. Carpenter.

Charles W. Sherwood.

Keepskill, N. Y., 1830.   1877, Rockwell, Ia.

Came to Whiteside County, Ill., in 1842. There he grew up on a farm near Coleta. His parents were Methodists and most excellent people. Charles resided in a community of Disciples of Christ and became a Christian only at the age of twenty-one. At the "social meetings" on the Lord's Day he began to speak, which led into the ministry. Then he farmed in the summer-time, mended shoes during the winter, and preached on Sundays as he could find opportunity. As he sat on his bench a copy of the Bible and Webster's Dictionary lay open before him—so he kept pegging away. As a preacher he was popular with all classes because he preached the truth in love. He was a fine, all-round minister who traveled from place to place with his horse and buggy. His evangelistic labors were chiefly in northern Illinois, where he baptized about six thousand persons. Editor B. W. Johnson once referred to him as "the noble-hearted Sherwood, the Lion of the North."

W. J. Simer.

Marion County, Ill., 1849.

Was educated in the public schools and has applied himself diligently to reading and study at home. Began to work for himself at the age of seventeen and to speak in public at twenty-five. He taught school and has a good library. He resides on his own farm, has always been a public-spirited citizen, and for over thirty years a faithful preacher. He is a man of fine common sense, sweet disposition and kindly impulses, and is popular among all classes and ages of people. His post-office is Kinmundy.

James W. Simpson.

Kentucky, 1804.   1861, Illinois.

After his marriage to Miss Emma Hathaway, near Mt. Sterling, he came to Illinois in 1835 and settled in Clary's Grove, Menard County. There he soon became the leading man in the church, and never for one minute faltered in his devotion to its best interests and in his defense of the primitive gospel to the day of his death. As an elder for years, he conducted the public worship when no preacher was present, teaching and admonishing his brethren and continually abounding in all good works. His house was the minister's home. He was one of the Lord's great men. He was the father of Mrs. J. W. Judy and Mrs. S. B. Callaway.

Jerome H. Smart.

Missouri, 1842.   1913, Clovis, N. M.

Mr. Smart joined the Baptist Church when he was fifteen years of age. He gave the Government over four years of military service in the Twenty-fourth Missouri Volunteer Infantry. At the close of the war he entered Abingdon College, from which he graduated in 1868. During this time he changed his church affiliation. The plain gospel overcame his temperamental Baptist proclivities. After his graduation, he taught in a school two years. Then he entered the ministry. His work was at Macomb, Colfax, Centralia, Winchester, Waukegan and Danville chiefly. Besides this, he was associated with the Christian Publishing Company for twelve years. Mr. Smart's ministry was always safe and constructive.

H. H. Smithson.

Marion County, Ill., 1843.

As soon as he was able to perform manual labor, he worked in a mill until he was of legal age, meanwhile attending the public schools three months every year. In 1865 he moved to Fayette County, where he taught in the public schools and preached for twenty-eight years. Thereafter, for a decade he gave himself wholly to the ministry. His life has been faithful and useful.

C. M. Smithson.

Fayette County, Ill., 1877.

A son of H. H. Smithson. Grew up on a farm. Attended public schools and Austin College in Effingham. Taught six years in public schools. Began his ministry in 1900. Served county and village churches. Pastor at Grayville, Mt. Vernon, Flora and St. Elmo. Is now at Streator. He is ambitious to be helpful beyond the local field of his labors.

George L. Snively.

Mr. Snively was born in the same house and immersed in the same baptistery in Cuba that his father was. He became a Christian under the ministry of H. C. Littleton. Soon thereafter Mr. Littleton said to him: "How would you like to go to school and prepare to preach the gospel?"

"Do you think I could do it?"

"Yes," was Mr. Littleton's assurance.

Mr. Snively attended school at Eureka and the Bible College at Lexington, Ky., but he did not graduate. However, by attendance at university lectures, correspondence courses and personal application, he grew to be a very capable and efficient minister.

For a number of years he was associated with his father in the county clerkship of Fulton County and other lines of business, which gave him a good commercial training. Meanwhile, he was preaching upon the Lord's Days. After several successful pastorates, he became the first general secretary of the National Benevolent Association of the churches of Christ, in 1901. The results of his five years of service in this capacity were exceedingly gratifying. Then he was successfully associated with the Christian Publishing Company, St. Louis, Mo.

Following his earnest desire, in 1907 he became a general evangelist. Here God has used him in turning thousands to the Prince of peace. He has also come to be one of the most efficient men in the "dedication of new churches," in which work he has won hundreds of thousands of dollars to sacred uses.

Mr. Snively has always been too busy and earnest, and the needs of the world have been too insistent in his conscience, to give any time to untaught questions or doubtful disputations. He believes the Book and preaches the truth.

BIOGRAPHIES

Ellis J. Stanley.

Whiteside County, Ill., 1842.

Came to his manhood in his native county. Took a little turn at military service the last year of the war in the 156th Regiment Illinois Volunteers. Attended Bethany College. Most of his ministerial work has been done beyond Illinois, but here he has served the Table Grove and Armington congregations and elsewhere.

Thomas B. Stanley.

Carroll County, Ill., 1851.   1912, Cedar Rapids, Ia.

In early life, Mr. Stanley dedicated his life to Christ. Besides his home and his congregation, he was trained in the public schools and at Eureka College. He was actively engaged in the ministry until failing health interfered. Then his aim was to constantly serve others as he was able. He worked with the congregations at Coleta, Normal, Atlanta and elsewhere. His ideals were high, his life's aim single and his fidelity to God's word unquestioned.

E. C. Stark.

New Harmony, Ind., 1853.

This man is a good preacher, with continuing experiences. He grew to manhood in White County, Ill., with such educational advantages as the public schools of the period afforded, but all the time since he has read and studied. He joined the M. E. Church at sixteen, but two years thereafter united with the church of Christ at West Salem, Ill. He taught school and preached in Edwards County for ten to thirteen years, served four years as evangelist in Virginia, then, for a period of eleven years, with the churches at Fisher, Farmer City, Delavan, Champaign and others in that section. Went to an abandoned farm in southern Illinois to solve the old-age problem. But he is still active and useful as a preacher. Here are a few of his pick-ups: He has found a new church, indigenous to southern Illinois, calling themselves "Social

Brethren." One of their preachers, in explaining to his congregation the words of Jesus, "Suffer little children to come unto me," said: "The Lord allowed little children to suffer that they might come unto him." Another one of these preachers read the words, "prepare you victuals," in Josh. 1:11, "prepare your vehicles," and explained it by saying, "Grease the axles, tighten the nuts, etc." One of the accredited ministers of a strong church in southern Illinois said, "The only Bible in the world was hid in the cornerstone of a temple," but he did not know what temple. Again, the same preacher, in explaining 1 John 1:9, "His seed remaineth in him," said, "Jesus and John the Baptist did not marry; their seed remained in them." In the course of a public discussion between Mr. Stark and Min. John Ralph, Baptist, the latter said: "Mr. Stark seems to think that I am an 'ignoramemus.'" David Morse, a prominent Cumberland Presbyterian preacher, said in a funeral sermon, "Everything that lives shall live again in human form."

Mr. Stark is a fine character.

J. Carroll Stark.

Stow, O., 1830. 1908, McMinnville, Tenn.

He had the advantages of the farmer boys of those days and in that section. To these he added two years in Hiram College. At the age of twelve he was baptized by Alanson Wilcox, and to render this act of submission to his Master's will he walked three miles and returned before changing his clothes. He was in the work of the ministry at twenty. Before coming to Illinois, he served churches in Ohio, New York, Indiana, Missouri, Iowa, Minnesota and South Dakota. In this State he served at Princeton, Ohiotown, Belleplain, Antioch (now Toluca), Augusta, Table Grove, Greenville, Salem, Duquoin, Blandinsville and Hamilton. Besides this, he evangelized in twenty-two States and Provinces. His public ministry reached through fifty-eight years. He held many formal debates on various subjects pertaining to religion. Probably the last of these was in 1903, on "Instrumental Music in the Church of Christ," at Henderson, Tenn., with Joe S. Wallick. His last pastorate was at Tullahoma, Tenn. Later, he moved to a ranch near McMinnsville, and preached almost every Sunday to the mountain people, although he was in his seventy-ninth year.

Mr. Stark was a brave and true soldier of the great Commander. He was passionately devoted to his Leader, and carried his banner triumphantly through the storm and smoke of every battle. Sincere and frank as a child, he could have but little patience with the duplicity of sectarian chiefs. Yet his heart was as tender as it was true.

James Stark.

Auchtermuchty, Scotland, 1815. 1892, Augusta, Ill.

Mr. Stark came to America with his uncle, John Deon, in 1835. Mr. Deon was acquainted with Alexander Campbell in Scotland, and they became his guests upon their arrival at Bethany. While there, Mr. Stark was baptized by Wm. Hayden. Shortly thereafter, he moved to Jacksonville, where he took membership in the church and was associated in its work with John T. Jones, D. P. Henderson, Josephus Hewitt, W. W. Happy, Peter Hedenburg, Philip Coffman and others. He was ordained to the ministry by this church in 1837. Like nearly all of the pioneer preachers, he was compelled to provide for the material needs of himself and his family by secular work; so he engaged in a general merchandising business there, and also in Augusta, whither he moved in 1842. His education was obtained by his own efforts. He was well informed in the affairs of church and state. In the pulpit and on the platform he was a fluent and eloquent speaker. In the church he enjoyed the personal friendship of Mr. Campbell, B. W. Stone, James Challen and O. A. Burgess, and in the State was personally acquainted with Abraham Lincoln, S. A. Douglas and Col. E. D. Baker. He was a member of the House of the General Assembly in 1846, and was a Presidential elector in 1860, casting his official vote for Mr. Lincoln. In his social relations he was affable, and as a public speaker pleasing, so that he was heard with enthusiasm by public audiences. A great man, with clear convictions of truth, right and duty, he fought a good fight and kept the faith.

James F. Stewart.

Peelar Station, Va., 1847.

Was a mail-carrier, farmhand, carpenter and lumber merchant. Attended the public schools and Eureka College. Gave Illinois churches ten years of upbuilding work. He has a son in Johnson's Bible School preparing for the ministry, which he considered "a far better place for such work than Chicago."

Oliver W. Stewart.

Mercer County, Ill., 1867.

Grew up on the farm. Graduated from Woodhull High School and from Eureka College in 1890. Evangelist in Illinois three years and served as pastor of the church at Mackinaw. Was a leader of the Illinois Christian Endeavor Union. In 1896 he became actively identified with the Prohibition party, and since then he has given himself almost exclusively to this work. In 1902 he was elected from the Hyde Park District in Chicago to the State Legislature, where he served with unusual efficiency. Of one of his speeches there, Senator L. Y. Sherman said: "It was the finest and most eloquent speech I ever heard in an Illinois Assembly." Mr. Stewart is the ablest advocate of Prohibition principles who has graced the rostrum in twenty years. He is sane and sensible, wise and witty, persuasive and practical. His frank fairness, irresistible logic of facts, superior vocabulary, fluency of utterance and fine presence unite in making him a most interesting and persuasive orator.

At the national convention of the party at Indianapolis in 1904, a circular on the subject of the candidacy of Gen. Nelson A. Miles was distributed. Among others, the names of James A. Tate and Oliver W. Stewart were signed. Both of these are members of the Christian Church. The *Voice*, which was then controlled by John G. Woolley, called the document a "Campbellite" circular. It was a gratuitous insult. Seven years thereafter, Mr. Woolley ate his own words on Prohibition in a most shameless degree and thereby became "the lost leader." No one has found occasion to question Mr. Stewart's loyalty to the principles of the purest patriotism.

T. L. Stipp.

Illinois, 1848.

Mr. Stipp was the son of a Predestinarian Baptist minister and was born in Vermilion County, where the larger part of his life has been passed. He graduated in the law class of the University of Michigan in 1871, but a change coming into his life-purpose, he was ordained to the work of the ministry in 1875. He has served twenty Illinois churches and four in Indiana. His ministry has been especially helpful to the weaker churches. Through all kinds of adverse and disagreeable conditions he has traveled on horseback to keep his engagements with them and very often at small financial compensation. His good business ability led him to buy Illinois land when the price was low, and to hold it. His seven living children are active members of the church of Christ.

Barton W. Stone.

Near Port Tobacco, Md., 1772. 1844, near Jacksonville, Ill.

Mr. Stone's father died when he was a little child. In 1779 his mother moved with her large family of children and servants to the backwoods of Virginia, in Pittsylvania County. Some of his brothers were soldiers in the Army of the Revolution, and the family was otherwise subjected to the vicissitudes of the war. From childhood, he had a deep hunger for knowledge. He was early sent to school and made unusual progress. After five years in the country school, his teacher pronounced him a finished scholar. He soon decided to qualify himself for a barrister. In 1790 he entered Guilford Academy, in North Carolina, and determined to acquire an education or die in the attempt. There he completed the academic course. While there, in much agony of soul, he turned to the Lord, uniting with the Presbyterians. With it came the desire to preach the gospel. His special preparation for the ministry was attended with great anguish of mind. The Osage Presbytery licensed him to preach in 1796. He was presented with a Bible, not the Confession of Faith. Then he started on a preaching tour over the mountains that brought him, at the close of the year, to Caneridge and Concord, Ky. With these churches his ministry was richly blessed. In the fall of 1798 the Presbytery of Transylvania met to ordain him to the pastorate of the two congregations. He declined to subscribe unqualifiedly to the Confession of Faith, but answered, "I do, as far as I see it consistent with the word of God." His study of the Bible was with an open mind and many prayers; so within two years he was relieved from the perplexity and distress in which the labyrinth of Calvinism had involved him. Henceforth he was a free man. With the turning of the century, he caught the spirit of, and became an active participant in, that great revival that marked the beginning of a new era in Christian teaching and life. Mr. Stone and his coadjutors preached that God loved the whole world and sent his Son to save men; that the gospel is the means of salvation, but it will never be effectual to this end until believed and obeyed by us. "Man-made creeds we threw overboard and took the name 'Christian,' the name given to the disciples by divine appointment first at Antioch." "The sticklers for orthodoxy amongst us writhed under these doctrines," says Mr. Stone. "The sects were roused. The Methodists and Baptists, who had long lived in peace and harmony with the Presbyterians, and with one another, now girded on their armor and marched into the field of controversy. These were times of distress. The spirit of partyism soon expelled the spirit of love and union; peace fled before discord and strife, and religion was stifled and banished in the unhallowed struggle for pre-eminence." This was in 1803. The next year, Mr. Stone formally withdrew from the Presbyterian Church. Thus the ship of the common, catholic gospel, whose compass had been lost for fifteen centuries, was again launched upon the wide sea of human life. Mr. Stone continued an earnest student of the Scriptures; so after a time he was immersed, as were many of those associated with him. "The churches and preachers grew and were multiplied." They came gradually to apprehend the application of their principles to the details of doctrine and duty. Mr. Stone, after his removal to Lexington, Ky., made a trip to Meigs County, O., for the purpose of immersing a Presbyterian minister named William Caldwell. While there he preached, on its invitation, to the Separate Baptist Association then assembled there. He says: "The result was, that they agreed to cast away their formularies and creeds, and take the Bible alone for their rule of faith and practice—to throw away their name 'Baptist' and take the name 'Christian'—and to bury their association, and to become one with us in the great work of Christian union. Then they marched up in a band to the stand where Mr. Stone was preaching, shouting the praises of God, and proclaiming aloud what they had done. We met them, and embraced each other in Christian love, by which the union was cemented." Mr. Stone says of Alexander Campbell when he first came into Kentucky: "I heard him often in public and in private. I was pleased with his manner and matter. I saw no distinctive feature between the doctrine he preached and that which we had preached for many years, except on baptism for remission of sins. Even this I had once received and taught, as before stated, but had strangely let it go from my mind, till Bro. Campbell revived it afresh." When Mr. Stone moved to Georgetown, Ky., he met John T. Johnson, "than whom there is not a better man. We plainly saw that we were on the same foundation, in the same spirit and preached the same gospel. We agreed to unite our energies to effect a union between our different societies. This we easily effected in Kentucky." Mr. Stone came to Morgan County, Ill., in 1832, and resided on his farm four miles from that place. Thereafter, he preached with great earnestness.

He was a finely educated man, speaking the French language, reading the Hebrew and teaching the Greek and Latin. He was a most successful teacher, and often turned to this profession for the support of himself and family.

Mr. Stone is justly entitled to far greater credit and honor for his work in the Restoration movement than has ever been given him. Like truly great men, he was simple and transparent. On one occasion, he entered the home of John T. Jones just as the family was going to dinner. The good wife, as was the custom, began to apologize for her dinner. Whereupon, Mr. Stone replied: "Sister, if we are Christians, it is good enough and we ought to thank God for it; if we are not Christians, it is too good for us." At another time, Charles W. Jones, a son of John T., was conveying Mr. Stone from the town to his farm by a conveyance drawn by one horse. He thought the horse was being driven too hard, and asked Charlie if he had ever heard the horse's prayer to his master. The driver answered he had not. Then Mr. Stone said: "On the hill speed me not, down the hill push me not, on the plain spare me not and in the barn forget me not."

When he joined the innumerable host of just men made perfect his body was buried in a locust grove on his farm. When the farm was sold it was reinterred in the Antioch Church Cemetery near by. Later, it was taken to Caneridge, Ky.

Isaac Stout.

Clinton County, O., 1822.   1900, Pekin, Ill.

Was brought by his parents to Illinois in 1827. The family settled near Bloomington, in what came to be known as Stout's Grove. His mother died soon thereafter, and his father when Isaac was fifteen. Then he made his home with an uncle. There he learned many kinds of hard manual labor. In his manhood he was a farmer, carpenter, brick-mason and house-painter. To him belongs the credit of inventing and patenting the first riding cultivator. The rise of prices consequent upon the Civil War made their manufacture unprofitable. His education came in the log schoolhouse period, but both his mind and heart were finely trained.

He was baptized by Min. James A. Lindsey in 1842 and began at once to speak in the social meetings of the church. A basket meeting had been well announced for a certain Sunday at the Antioch Church, south of Tremont. A great concourse of people assembled, but W. P. Bowles, the star preacher for the occasion, failed to come. The elders assembled and with moral compulsion absolutely impressed Isaac Stout to address the multitude. An elder announced: "Bro. Bowles has not come, so Bro. Isaac Stout will talk to us a while and give the invitation." Mr. Stout shook like a pendant leaf in the wind. At the invitation three persons went forward to become Christians. Mr. Stout sat down. "Take their confessions," said the elder to him. It was announced that Bro. Stout would preach again in the afternoon. He could eat but little dinner, but he preached. Then four more people turned to the Lord. Whereupon, Mr. Stout assuredly gathered that God had called him to preach the gospel. His ministry was mainly in Tazewell County, but evangelistic work reached into McLean, Logan and DeWitt. He was a successful preacher, measured by the best standards. He built with his own hands the chapel of the Concord congregation, from foundation to pulpit. When he came to dedicate it, he spoke not one word about his own labor on the building. In his judgment, far more important interests then demanded the attention of the assembly. He was a fine soul whose modesty was a measure of his greatness.

In 1864 he enlisted in Company A, 108th Illinois Volunteer Infantry, and was at Spanish Ford and the battle of Mobile.

Emanuel Stover.

Ohio, 1822. 1890, Illinois.

Was an active member of the church at Lanark and helpful to the congregations in that part of the State. He was second lieutenant in Company B, Seventy-first Regiment Illinois Volunteers. He served two terms in the House of the Illinois General Assembly. A man of fine character.

J. O. Sutherland

Was born in Marion County, Ind., 1848. He worked at Patoka, Ill., where he began his ministry. He served the church at Sailor Springs and founded the churches at Latham, Riverton, Dawson and Morgansville. He is a plain, sincere man and good preacher, whose thirty years' work in the ministry has been fruitful.

The Sweeneys.

The Sweeney family, the father and four sons all able ministers of the primitive gospel, was one of the great spiritual forces of the Restoration movement. They all served for varying periods in Illinois.

George E. Sweeney.

Kentucky, 1807. 1899, Kentucky.

Was the father. He came to Illinois in 1855. His first work was with the Berean and Scottville Churches, in Macoupin County, then at Barry. Returning to Scottville in 1861, he evangelized for five years in the counties of Macoupin, Sangamon, Morgan and Green. His last pastorate, which closed in the spring of 1868, was at Kansas.

In his funeral discourse at the obsequies of Mr. Sweeney, at Paris, Ky., May 25, 1899, Pres. C. L. Loos said: "Our good Father above gave to our brother unusual vigor of body and mind up to a high degree. It was providentially a munificent inheritance from the sturdy Scotch-Irish stock of his ancestors; his father died one hundred years old. Doubtless, his thirst for knowledge, his keen interest in

things worthy of a human soul, kept alive his intellectual and even his bodily vigor. Some men die in the outer, because they die in the inner, man; they have lost the life of the soul. Internal often begets external decrepitude.

"And his entire rich and strong life, devoted to the greatest cause on earth—the kingdom of God in Jesus Christ. For *seventy-one years* he was a minister of the Word of life. What a record is this in the life of a man! The first year he was a Baptist preacher, a good prelude to the seventy years devoted to the mighty plea for the complete restoration of apostolic Christianity."

Mr. Sweeney's wife was his equal in native endowments of mind, with which she combined a very sweet and gracious disposition.

William G. Sweeney

Was the oldest son. He did comparatively little work in Illinois. His death occurred at Dubuque, Ia., in 1897.

George W. Sweeney

Served for a time in Chicago and elsewhere in Illinois as pastor and evangelist, but most of his life has been passed outside of the State.

Z. T. Sweeney

Is the youngest of the four sons. He and N. S. Haynes began their work in the ministry together—in May, 1868, at Kansas, Ill.—except that Mr. Sweeney had two weeks the start, which he has always held. Shortly thereafter they were invited to conduct a meeting in a near-by schoolhouse in the country. They promised a few. evenings' meetings, as their joint stock of sermons would not warrant anything farther. After the meeting the first evening, they were guests of a childless couple—sincere and devout Christians. The young preachers ever afterward held them in the highest esteem and even admiration. A chapter was read, prayer was offered and the young men were lighted to their sleeping-room on the first floor. At once, the chickens, ducks and geese under the floor set up most unusual and vociferous alarms, as if disturbed by predatory varmints. The outcries soon subsided, and the theologs, having disrobed, climbed upon chairs to get into bed—it was so high. The jump into the immense depths of feathers was like a dive into the crest of an ocean wave. But they were jolly. Then, just as Morpheus waved her magic wand, a mouse scampered across their breasts, hitting Mr. Sweeney first. His cry was distressing, but did not bespeak his courage; for here was the embryo of that Z. T. Sweeney who, in after years, should vanquish any lion of German rationalism who might unconsciously devitalize the glorious gospel of our Lord. He has had wide experiences, is a charming public speaker and is a man of large mould and usefulness.

John S. Sweeney.

Kentucky, 1832.   1908, Kentucky.

Mr. Sweeney came to Illinois in 1854, and began the practice of law at Greenfield. He made his home with Judge Short, a prominent member of the M. E. Church and a leading citizen of the community. One Saturday evening he invited Mr. Sweeney to go with him on the morrow to hear his minister review "Campbellism." That great gospel advocate had made a preaching tour through Illinois in 1853, and many of the orthodox pulpits were busy reviewing his teachings and protecting their flocks against the new "heresies." In his discourse, the M. E. preacher affirmed that Mr. Campbell had said that he "could take the vilest sinner into the water and bring him out a saint." As was the custom, opportunity was given, before the close of the meeting, for any one to ask questions; whereupon, Mr. Sweeney arose and quietly asked where, in his writings, Mr. Campbell had ever made such a statement. The preacher, with a glowering look, replied: "Have you come here to break up my meeting?" Judge Short instantly replied: "No, Bro. Powell; it is a fair question and one that I also would like to have answered." The preacher promised to produce it at another time, and thus the incident closed. Immediately upon the dismission of the congregation, the few Disciples present came to Mr. Sweeney, and, learning from him that he was "of their faith and order," insisted that he answer the discourse which they had just heard. He declined, but thus it was that he was turned from the practice of the law to the preaching of the gospel. He was a faithful student of the Scriptures and a man of fine discrimination, and in him the logical faculty was united with a keen sense of humor. In the first year of his ministry, five hundred people became obedient to the faith under his preaching. Riding along one day, he fell in with a company of people assembled at the usual place for baptizing, on the bank of Apple Creek. The Baptist minister, a Mr. Johnson, was assuring the people that the converts to be then immersed had all "been born again," and had all received the assurance of the forgiveness of their sins at the "mourners' bench," for which he thanked God. Permission being granted, Mr. Sweeney said: "I would like to ask if Baptist converts are all 'born of water' on dry land?" Mr. Johnson replied: "Sir, you are a Campbellite, and desire to disturb our meeting."

A meeting of the ministers was convened in Springfield in the later fifties with the purpose of "disciplining" one of their number. This action Mr. Sweeney earnestly opposed, contending that it was contrary to the congregational independence of the New Testament, and as forming a possible precedent that would result in evil. In such cases, the preacher is responsible to the local church in which he holds membership.

Probably the most eminent service ever rendered the Disciples in Illinois by Mr. Sweeney was in his course toward the Russell defection. Walter Scott Russell was a graduate of Bethany College. Shortly thereafter, he became an extreme and pronounced mystic. Associated with him were some of our leading preachers in the State, who became open advocates of this doctrine. Among these were T. J. Melish;

Frank Apperson, a brilliant young Englishman; F. N. Carman, publisher of the *Christian Sentinel,* the only paper of the Disciples in the State at that time, which indorsed the articles and addresses of Mr. Russell; W. W. Happy, an able and veteran preacher, who was then president of the State Missionary Society, while Samuel Callaway was its treasurer, and Prof. P. Lucas, of Berean, was its secretary. All of these men were in full accord with the views of Mr. Russell. These men thought to reform the Restoration movement on the basis of this inner-light theory. The State Missionary Convention met in Bloomington, September, 1858. The new doctrine was uppermost in the minds of all. It was the general feeling that a real crisis was at hand. On the evening of the second day of the meeting, Mr. Sweeney was to preach. Not one person knew anything of his attitude toward the new teaching. Intense anxiety pervaded the great assembly of the saints. Mr. Sweeney chose for his text, John 16: 13, 14, and unfolded it into a most masterful sermon. It was a pivotal discourse that was to make or unmake myriads, and he rose fully to the occasion. The peculiar teachings of Mr. Russell were clearly shown to be contrary to the Scriptures and enlightened human reason. This was the beginning of its end. The new movement was put upon a course of rapid and ultimate extinction. Mr. Russell died. Professor Lucas went to the law; Messrs. Carman, Callaway and Happy to the Baptists, but later the last named returned to the Disciples. Mr. Melish went to the Baptists and later to the Episcopalians. Berean College went to ruin. And in later years the breach in the Jacksonville Church was wholly healed.

Mr. Sweeney was a participant in about seventy-five public discussions, generally against his inclination.

Frank Talmage.

Pennsylvania, 1874.

Mr. Talmage was educated in the public schools of Philadelphia, his birthplace; in the seminary at Pennington, N. J., and Dickinson College at Carlisle, Pa. He was a minister in the M. E. Church, and after one year's service in Perry County, Pa., was sent by Bishop Kingsley to Missouri in 1866. This was because the ministers of the M. E. Church North were scarce in Missouri at that time, and many of those in the M. E. Church South were unable to take the "ironclad oath," thus leaving Methodist churches in Missouri in bad condition.

In July, 1867, Mr. Talmage left the M. E. Church and became a Christian only. Since then he has continued his ministry among the Disciples. He came to the pastorate of the Marine Church, in Madison County, Ill., in 1872. His useful ministry in that and St. Clair County reached through several years. At times he was associated with John Ellis, the veteran preacher. When conducting a meeting with the Fairview Church, Mr. Talmage baptized the converts in a near-by stream. Some mischievous boys of the neighborhood would come to the place and climb out on a limb of a tree near the pool and make remarks about the baptizings. Brethren were indignant and wished to have the boys arrested, but the preacher dissuaded them. The next day, during the ceremony, one venturesome boy got out on the extreme end of the limb and yelled out, as a candidate was baptized, "Dip him again!" At that moment the overhanging limb broke and the boy fell into the water and disappeared. Serious as was the occasion, the crowd laughed outright as the minister fished that mischievous boy out of the water. This incident ended all that trouble. Among the converts at the Fairview Church were Jonas Tontz and wife. Mr. Tontz was a member of the State Legislature in 1872. Mr. Talmage left Illinois after a few years. He is now preaching at Roswell, N. M.

George W. Tate.

Decatur County, Ind., 1841. 1905, West Salem, Ill.

Grew up on the farm. Received his mental training in the public schools, in Normal School at Kokomo and the

Seminary at Peru. Taught school for several years. Entered ministry in 1873. He was a gospel preacher of the best type. A successful evangelist, pastor, public debater and church-builder. He was interested in the cause of Christ at home and abroad, and always co-operated in every good work.

Dr. G. W. Taylor.

Saratoga County, N. Y., 1815.   1913, Princeton, Ill.

At the age of twelve years, Mr. Taylor left his parental home in Oneida County to make his own way in the world. He then had only twenty-five cents in money and but little education. In 1840 he united with the Congregational Church, but later left it and united with the M. E. Church. About 1851 he visited a brother whose home was near Buffalo. While there, he heard a Christian preacher, whereupon he declared that he had heard "the first gospel sermons." At once he and his wife accepted the common truth. He came to Princeton, Ill., in 1853. His profession was the practice of medicine, but when he was about fifty years of age he was set apart to the work of the ministry, in which he did excellent service. The church at Humboldt, Kan., is a product of his work. Dr. Taylor was always actively identified with all of the co-operative missionary work of the church.

Knox P. Taylor.

Logan County, Ky., 1835.   1812, Bloomington, Ill.

Came to Illinois in 1851, and the years of his virile manhood were lived chiefly in this State. From 1881 to 1904, he devoted his strength to our Bible-school work. He went up and down the State, in its highways and into its byways, with maps, charts, pictures and blackboards. He taught the word of the Lord; he emphasized the value of Sunday-school work, urged better methods and higher efficiency. He did more to help the Disciples in this State to appreciate the value of Bible-school teaching than any other man who has served herein.

Mr. Taylor was an humble man of gentle spirit, kindly impulses and helpful purpose. He was the embodiment of sincerity and simplicity. The professional and perfunctory awakened in him feelings of aversion. He was a great teacher of the Scriptures. By him, people were instructed in Biblical geography, chronology and history, and in great spiritual truths as well.

The men and women of active age in nearly all of our Illinois churches need now to learn what this prophet of God was trying to teach them forty years ago. The value of the Bible-school work is not yet understood nor its importance appreciated in this year of grace.

Mr. Taylor was wholly devoted to his Master's service. He is held in loving and grateful remembrance by thousands of Illinois Disciples with whom he lived and for whom he labored. Great is his reward in heaven.

Harry Robert Trickett.

Nottinghamshire, England, 1840.   1909, Keokuk, Ia.

Came to America in 1852. In his young manhood he returned to England, where he finished his education in King's College, London. He was educated for the law, but soon decided for the ministry. After his return to the United States, he bought a farm in Montebello Township, Hancock County, which was his home to the close of his life. However, he held pastorates in Illinois, Iowa and Missouri. Besides, he did much effective evangelistic work. Mr. Trickett was a great preacher. Judge C. J. Scofield says: "I have heard him preach sermons as able as the best I have ever heard from the pulpit." He took a deep interest in the living questions of the day, sometimes made political speeches, was a brilliant conversationalist and a fine writer. His contributions to religious papers always attracted attention because of their vigorous thought and superior diction. In the closing years of his life it was his custom to write a Christmas sermon for the Nauvoo *Independent.* The closing words of his last sermon were the following: "In all probability, this is the last Christmas sermon I shall write you. Accept as my Christmas gift. It is all I have to give, you know. There will be no Christmas festivities for me. I am old and feeble and lonely, but my heart goes out to you in good wishes. I am very thankful for the warmth and shelter of the hospital, and, while I think and hope that God may give me strength and health again, yet I do not know, nor do I care overmuch. It is well, no matter what happens. Living or dying, I have partaken of the Christmas melodies. I see beyond the shadow of the cross, and have passed into the garden of Joseph of Arithmathea, and am standing among the white lilies of the resurrection. I see that the risen Lord and the Babe of Bethlehem are one, and I cry in the words of the grand old chant, 'O Lamb of God, who taketh away the sin of the world, have mercy on me. Amen and amen.'"

Harvey M. Trimble, of Princeton, Ill.,

Was born near Wilmington, O., Jan. 27, 1842. Mr. Trimble's parents were sturdy members of the Restoration movement. The family came to Princeton in 1843. He attended the public schools and Eureka College. He enlisted as a private in Company K, Ninety-third Regiment Illinois Volunteer Infantry. Was elected sergeant-major, and later was commissioned first lieutenant and adjutant of the regiment. He was in the battles of Champion Hill, campaign and siege of Vicksburg—being under fire almost every day—Missionary Ridge, Allatoona, Savannah, and not a few skirmishes. He was on the march to the sea and campaign of the Carolinas, was present at the surrender of Gen. J. E. Johnston, and then to the grand review at the capital of the nation. Mr. Trimble did not miss a battle in which his regiment was engaged, the casualties of which were 418 out of 718 men who were engaged in action. For fourteen days he was a prisoner of war, coming to his release on his twenty-first birthday. Quite naturally, therefore, since its beginning he has been actively associated with the Grand

Army of the Republic. He was elected its commander-in-chief in 1911.

Returning to Princeton, he studied law and was admitted to the bar. He served as deputy clerk, and master in chancery of the circuit court in Bureau County. He was county judge for more than fifteen years, and circuit judge in the Thirteenth Judicial Circuit six years. The whole length of his service on the bench was twenty-one years and six months. Probably no man who has served the people as a judge in Illinois has had fewer of his decisions reversed by the higher courts.

He has also been a useful officer of the Board of Education in his home city, and of the township high school, which was the first of its kind in the State, and of the Public Library Board.

Mr. Trimble is an elder of the Princeton Church and an interesting gentleman whom it is a pleasure to meet.

Maurice R. Trimble

Was a pioneer preacher of Knox County, Ind. He owned a farm, on which he resided, ten miles north of Vincennes. But much of his work was done in Illinois. Indeed, he was the Nestor of the Restoration movement from Hutsonville to Golconda. His home was at the former place for a time. His courageous and devoted labors laid the foundation for many congregations in that section. In the forties, there were bands of outlaws that overran several counties in southern Illinois. An organization, styling themselves "Regulators," was formed to crush them. These soon became as lawless as the outlaws. Civil anarchy was rampant. Mr. Trimble continued his ministry in the midst of the violent disturbances, publicly denouncing the wrong-doers. On one occasion he was baptizing some converts in the Ohio River, when some of the outlaws made a murderous attack upon him. Mr. Trimble defended his life by resisting the assault to the utmost. When the encounter was over, two of the outlaws were wounded and one of them was not. Gradually the civil disturbance wore itself out and society returned to its normal conditions. Through it all, Mr. Trimble preached the gospel of salvation and peace.

William C. Trimble.

Antioch, O., 1830.   1913, Princeton, Ill.

Mr. Trimble united with the church of Christ in 1842, at the village of Antioch, near his birthplace, under the preaching of Walter Scott. This fact places him among the beginners. He came to Bureau County, Ill., in the fall of 1843, and was associated with the church in Princeton since 1844, which church he served for more than forty years as an elder. He was a faithful preacher and evangelist, and was instrumental in bringing into the church about one thousand people, who were instructed in the gospel. His ministry was wholly devoid of a stipulated financial compensation. For a period, he was noted for his controversies in Christian papers upon some things that he thought to be innovations—a going back to Babylon rather than a restoration of the apostolic church. Among these was the popular conception of "the one-man pastorate in our churches." He, with others, held that it was not warranted by the Scriptures; that one minister should not be expected to do the work of the eldership and of the evangelists. This contention was summarized in the *Christian Standard* by Isaac Errett, its editor, in April, 1885, as follows:

> Let it be understood that in the imperfect condition of most of our churches the employment of one man as a teacher and preacher and a co-operator with the elders in ruling, is justifiable as a necessity, but is not accepted as a finality. It should be the aim and ambition of all churches to reach a more complete organization of forces such as the Scriptures contemplate; namely, a plurality of elders or bishops whose business it shall be to teach, preach and rule, dividing the labor among themselves as may best sustain the interest of the church, and compensated for the time given to their duties, and also according to their necessities. Such an eldership we have seldom had in any of our churches.

Mr. Trimble was hopeful that the Scriptural ideals might

be realized, and was encouraged by the distinct tendency of these later days. "We can never have a most efficient ministry without an efficient officiary."

Allen Harvey Trowbridge.

Salem, Ind., 1826. 1902, Rutland, Ill.

Mr. Trowbridge became a Christian at the age of fifteen. Shortly after his marriage in 1851, he started, in a movers' wagon, across the wild prairies to the new home in Marshall County, Ill. It was a little cottage on the unbroken sea of grass about five miles from Pattensburg, now Belleplain.

In his early ministry he did an extensive missionary work, preaching the gospel, as opportunity offered, in barns, dwellings, groves and schoolhouses. This work laid the foundation for a goodly number of churches. He was associated with the three brothers—Washington, Jefferson and John Houston—formerly so well known in Livingstone County, where they lived, labored, sang and preached for many years. The churches at Toluca, Rutland, Ancona, Minonk, Saunemin, Dana, Flanagan and Washburn are much indebted to him. In his earlier ministry he traveled and served churches within a radius of fifty miles of his home.

Mr. Trowbridge was a good business man, as well as an excellent minister. He gave liberally to missions and all good works. He was one of the early friends of Eureka College, and gave time and means for its support. His four children were educated there.

He was a broad-minded man, companionable in disposition, diligent in business, fervent in spirit, and always seeking first the kingdom of God and his righteousness.

John W. Tyler.

Fayette County, Ky., 1808. 1888, Macon County, Ill.

Mr. Tyler's genealogy is traced to the same line from which came the tenth President of the United States. He united with the Cane Run Baptist Church, near Lexington, in 1834, and soon entered actively the ministry.

In the fall of 1834 he moved to Montgomery County, Ind., and shortly organized there a congregation of believers under the name of the "United Baptist Church of Christ." This name suggests the convictions of Christian truth and the tendencies of Christian feeling that were beginning to manifest themselves in many places about that time. The following year he came to Morgan County, Ill., where he met the great revivalist and reformer, Barton W. Stone. In 1836, Mr. Tyler came to Macon County, where he bought and settled on a farm five miles east of the village of Decatur. By the force of his character, he soon became an influential and leading citizen. He was an intelligent and successful farmer, and accumulated property, but at the same time devoted himself with zeal and energy to the public proclamation of the gospel. His labors were extended into the counties of Shelby, Christian, Sangamon, Logan, DeWitt and Piatt. He was influential in establishing numerous churches and chiefly at his own charges. His ministry continued through a period of fifty-two years. He conducted the funeral of the magnificent pioneer, Joseph Hostetler, at Lovington, in 1870, and in his address said: "I am indebted to Bro. Hostetler for my better understanding of the gospel."

Through a long residence in Macon County, he commanded the confidence and esteem of his fellow-citizens and the love and fellowship of his brethren. He was a farmer, schoolmaster, justice of the peace and minister. He was a genial and cheerful man of optimistic temperament. After his removal to Decatur, he had the misfortune to fall and break one of his limbs at the hip joint. A friend called during his long and painful confinement to inquire about his condition. He replied that he was doing pretty well, but that Dr. McMillen had him nailed up in a lumber-yard just then, but he would be all right when he got out of that! In midsummer of his eightieth year he received a kick upon his head from a horse that brought his beautiful life to a tragic close. He was the father of the brothers, B. B. and J. Z. Tyler.

J. J. Vanhoutin

Is a native of Edgar County, Ill., and has resided there all his life—since 1842. He attended the common country school in winter and worked on his father's farm through summer. In 1861 he entered the military service in Company H, First Missouri Engineers, where he continued for three years and two months. He entered the ministry in 1868. Since then he has served constantly. His work has been done chiefly in Edgar and twenty-seven near-by counties in Illinois and Indiana—mostly in rural congregations and new fields and gospel-destitute places. He has preached in private residences, sheds, halls, groves and schoolhouses. From the schoolhouses the preachers are now debarred by a wrong notion. For years, Mr. Vanhoutin has read from memory the Scriptures to the public assembly. His ministry has been modest, self-sacrificing, useful and fruitful of much good.

H. G. Van Dervoort.

Lafayette, Ind., 1846.

Was brought to McLean County, Ill., in 1849. His early life was spent on the farm. He attended the public schools, developed a hunger for the knowledge of good things and has kept company with many books. In 1864 he took a turn at military service in Company B, 150th Illinois Volunteer Infantry. In 1867 he entered the ministry, and during the next eighteen years preached for most of the Christian congregations—often two or three at a time—in McLean County outside of Bloomington. He served Stanford five years. Besides one short period in Missouri and Kansas each, he has worked for churches in Adams, Green, Hancock and Morgan Counties. Then he has done not a little evangelistic work. During the forty-three years of his continuous ministry, he took only one month for a vacation. In Mr. Van Dervoort the finer elements of Christian manhood are united. The results of his ministerial work are of the best.

Dr. Samuel Van Meter.

Grayson County, Ky., 1824.   1902, Charleston, Ill.

At fifteen, he was apprenticed to a tanner, but bought his time. In 1844 he took up the study of medicine with Dr. T. B. Trower. In 1849 he went to California, practicing his profession on the way. Returning, he settled in Charleston. In 1857, with Dr. H. R. Aller, he established an infirmary there which was very successful. For a period of forty years he was as well known as any man in that part of the State. He was a devout Christian and an efficient elder of the Charleston Church. During the pastorate of F. W. Burnham, Dr. Van Meter frequently voiced the opening prayer at the Sunday morning worship. These were always childlike in faith and simplicity, but beautiful and impressive.

Samuel Vaughn.

Lincoln County, Ky., 1836.

Came with his father's family to Bond County in the fall of 1839. Settled on a farm near Woburn, which is his present home. Received such education as the period and community afforded. Served the Woburn Church as Bible-school superintendent and as an elder, each for thirty-five years. Is still well and active, a teacher in Bible school. He has seldom missed a Sunday from church in forty years. Has served as county commissioner, and in 1900 was a member of the Legislature. He became a Christian at the age of twenty-three and a charter member of the Woburn Church.

John Garland Waggoner.

Moultrie County, Ill., 1844.

Mr. Waggoner's parents both died when he was a little child, so he grew to manhood in the home of Mr. A. H. Edwards, whose wife was his father's sister. Its ideals and influences were most helpful to the boy, and in 1859 he was baptized by Bushrod W. Henry and then decided to give his life to the ministry. He taught schools and supplied pulpits,

JOHN G. WAGGONER.

DANIEL R. HOWE.

DANIEL W. ELLEDGE.

DR. JOHN SCOTT.

thus working his way through college, graduating from Eureka in 1872. Thereafter, he was pastor in Illinois at Harristown, Shelbyville, Eureka for two terms—added making eleven years—Princeton, Canton and Lanark. He served as field secretary of Eureka College for five years, inducing not a few students to come to the school, and turned toward its support about $80,000.

Mr. Waggoner is a superior type of Christian minister. He has never made any claims to "smartness," but he is an unassuming, sincere and faithful preacher of the gospel. His spiritual vision is wide, compassing all the interests of the kingdom of God. He is patient, gentle, sincere and truer than steel to the Christian truth and personal duty. Willingly and cheerfully he goes out of his way to do any one a favor or kindness. Mrs. Susie M. Minges, who has served well as a missionary in Cuba, is his daughter. William H. and Harvey G. Waggoner, both consecrated ministers, are his sons.

When Mr. Waggoner was a young man, he was "working the roads" one day in Moultrie County. At that time, Evangelist S. M. Connor was conducting a series of meetings with the Whitley Creek Church. Becoming quite ill, and hence unable to preach one evening, one of the leading members of the congregation handed Mr. Waggoner fifty cents, saying to him: "Go home and get ready to preach to-night." This was his first financial compensation for preaching.

Lorenzo D. Waldo.

Batavia, N. Y., 1819.   1888, Rockford, Ill.

Educated in the public schools and by the light of his own farm fireside. Grew into the eldership and an earnest ministry. For twenty-five years he preached up and down the Rock River, fifteen of which were given to the Rockford Church. A dozen counties in northern Illinois and southern Wisconsin were blessed by his consecrated life. He was greatly loved by many for his fine character and work.

Thomas S. Wall.

Illinois, 1848.　　　　　　　　　　1884, Illinois.

Mr. Wall was a consecrated preacher who did much hard work, as pastor and evangelist, in Cumberland, Clay, Jasper, Marion and Wayne Counties.

W. W. Weedon.

Columbiana County, O., 1846.

Came to Illinois in 1860. Settled in Wayne County. Attended common and high schools. Farmed and taught school there till 1878, except one year given to military service in the Eighth Regiment Illinois Volunteer Infantry. Entering the Christian ministry in 1878, he has served as pastor the churches at Brownstown, Edinburg and South Fork, near by; Blue Mound, Taylorville, Williamsville, Marion, Assumption, and is now at Mt. Carmel. He was elected to the State Legislature and served in the session of 1890-91. Mr. Weedon has been an active member of, and popular in, a number of fraternal societies. But with him the Lord's work has always held first place. He is a man of fine common sense and brotherly disposition. People like him for what he is. His ministry has always been constructive and far-reaching in its results.

E. C. Weekly.

Kentucky, 1821.　　　　　　　　1897, Chicago, Ill.

Was baptized by Barton W. Stone. In Kentucky, he was a successful builder of chapels. Came to Illinois in 1864, settling in Decatur. He continued his ministerial labors until his failing health forbade any further effort.

Miss Mary S. Welch.

Miss Welch has been one of the most forceful and useful women in DeWitt County. Through her own efforts mainly, she came to be an efficient teacher in the public schools. From 1873 she served as county superintendent of schools

HERBERT L. WILLETT.

CHAS. REIGN SCOVILLE.

WILLIAM F. BLACK.

CLARK BRADEN

for a period of seventeen years at a time when most men did not accord the right of women to this office. Her intelligent faith and faithful work were invaluable to the Clinton Church. She bravely stood by it and fostered it when it was little, poor and despised by the self-righteous. Of late years she has been the superintendent of the Rest-room in Clinton.

Henry Wiley.

Mr. Wiley enlisted, in August, 1861, in Company H, Fifty-ninth Illinois Volunteer Infantry. Promoted to captain in December, 1862. Was in the battles of Pea Ridge, Corinth, Perryville, Stone River, Lookout Mountain, Missionary Ridge, Chickamauga, the Atlanta campaign, Franklin and Nashville.

He is a fine Christian, whose home is at Paris.

Herbert L. Willett.

Michigan, 1864.

Mr. Willett is of the finest mental discipline and tremendous capacity for work. After graduating at Bethany in 1886, he preached seven years. He studied one year at Yale, one at Berlin, and received his doctor's degree from the University of Chicago in 1896. He taught three years in the Bible chairs at Ann Arbor, Mich. After forming the Hyde Park Church, he preached there three years. Then he was with the First Church two years. In 1908 he brought about a union of the last named with the Memorial Baptist Church, known now as the "Memorial Church of Christ," and has since then served as its minister. Besides, he has done much miscellaneous preaching in not a few denominational pulpits in Chicago and elsewhere.

Mr. Willett is one of the most democratic of university men, and of engaging personality. He is always a pleasing and persuasive preacher. It has been said that no honest man can hear him publicly present the proofs of the Scriptures and then say that he does not believe the Bible without a feeling of shame. He is a prolific writer, and for some things that he has thus said he has subjected himself to the criticism of his fellow-Disciples.

A Church Federation Council meeting was held in Chicago in February, 1910. After the session of the day, there was an informal dinner at the Great Northern Hotel, followed by brief speeches by different men. Next to the last to speak was a minister noted for his denominational proclivities. He said that it was puerile to array the Scriptures against denominational Christianity when there were Jewish Christians, Gentile Christians, etc. Then he remarked that the people who had the most to say about unity were the most sectarian of all, and even little. He was once in a Western town where the people were holding a revival, and they advertised as the one true apostolic church of Christ, that there was only one people who had the presumption and littleness to do that, etc. When Mr. Willett rose and began in his most gracious manner, attention was riveted upon him. After a word of introduction, he took up the address just heard by saying: "In regard to our people whom Dr. ―― has done us the honor to mention." Then followed a skillful, polished and thoroughgoing answer. It was a clear, full and unanswerable defense of the Disciples. And there was an eloquent silence that followed it.

At present, Mr. Willett holds an associate professorship of Semitic Languages and Literature in the University of Chicago. In this position he discharges efficiently the duties that are his.

John A. Williams.

Shelby County, Ind., 1818. 1907, Marion County, Ill.

In 1834 his father brought his family to Illinois and settled near the village of Walnut Hill, in Marion County. Here he made a farm on the timber-land, and here John worked, went to school a little and grew to manhood. He became a Christian at the old Mt. Moriah Church and began to preach in his twenty-eighth year. From 1850 his time was mainly given to the ministry of the Word. His evangelistic tours were frequently made on horseback from fifty to one hundred miles. From Shelbyville to Cairo, and from the Wabash to the Mississippi River, he proclaimed the gospel for sixty years. His chief compensation was the assurance of his Master's companionship and his approval of duty unselfishly and faithfully done. Mr. Williams was a superb man physically, being over six feet tall and finely proportioned. His mental powers were far above the average. His knowledge of the Bible was full and clear. His sermons were logical and convincing. His manner was winning. He was known, honored and loved by thousands of people of every kind.

Samuel V. Williams

Came to White County in the fifties and died at Enfield about 1872. He was a very successful country preacher. At one time he went to a co-operation meeting held with the White Oak Church in the edge of Hamilton County. The attendance was large, the interest fine, but the preachers were few. So a young college minister was pressed into service for the occasion. His sermons were good, but did not reach the people. Finally, Mr. Williams arrived, and, of course, did the preaching. His eyes were keen and black, his hair long and black, his voice superior, his general appearance imposing and his knowledge of his subject thorough. The evening was pleasant, the well-seated and well-lighted grove inviting and the large audience expectant. At the close of the discourse a dozen people responded to the gospel invitation, and many others came in the following days.

William T. Williams.

Bath County, Ky., 1810. 1890, Jefferson County, Ill.

He united with the Christian Church and entered its ministry about 1857. For fifteen years before that time he had served as an itinerant Methodist minister. He was a talented, well-educated man, owned and used a large library, had a fine memory—reading much of the Bible without the text—held many public discussions and formed not a few churches in southern Illinois during the last thirty-three years of his life.

John L. Wilson.

Tennessee, 1816.   1881, Illinois.

In 1816, Mr. Wilson's parents came to Illinois and resided in White, Bond and Montgomery Counties, respectively. In 1839 he moved to Mechanicsburg, where he was married in 1843. By the church there he was ordained to the ministry in 1852. He served that congregation one-half time as its pastor for two years. Thereafter, to the close of his life, his energies were devoted to the work of evangelizing.

Physically, Mr. Wilson was a large man, standing more than six feet tall, and was well proportioned. He was a timid man, but his faith in Jesus and his love of the gospel made him a very useful and powerful preacher. On one of his evangelizing tours in central Illinois he came to an assembly of worshipers. The M. E. preacher, according to the custom of his class in that time, was earnestly aiming to show his hearers that the forgiveness of sins, on the human side, is conditioned upon faith only, and is in no way connected in the New Testament with baptism. In his sermon he several times quoted our Lord's commission, as recorded by Mark, as follows: "He that believeth, and so forth, shall be saved." This was too much for Mr. Wilson, so, just before the meeting closed, he publicly announced that he would preach in the schoolhouse at a named date, and that the subject of his sermon would be "And So Forth." Many audiences in central Illinois heard that discourse with pleasure and profit.

In his residence near Harristown he retired to rest March 1, 1881, in his usual apparent excellent health. On the morrow he was not, for God had taken him.

Mathew Wilson.

Tennessee, 1822.   1901, Hot Springs, Ark.

Became a Christian in 1837. Six years thereafter he was consumed with zeal to preach the gospel. But he could not read. His wife, whom he had just married, taught him, and his progress in knowledge was such that he was set apart to the ministry in 1848. A loyalist refugee from Tennessee, he came to Williamson County in 1865 and settled on a farm near Herrin. Then he went preaching wherever people would assemble. He served as evangelist in the six southern counties for six years, and organized more congregations in that section than any other man. He had an impediment in his speech, but none in his Christian zeal.

Charles L. Wood

Was born on his father's farm in Wayne County, Ill., 1868. Attended the schools of the community. He is a man of energy and resolution. For twenty-two years he has given the Christian Churches of Wayne County his best work as a preacher. He served a term in the Spanish-American War. Now he looks after a 320-acre farm, cries an average of 150 public sales a year, and preaches every Lord's Day.

In 1912 he was elected to the House in the forty-eighth General Assembly.

Joseph Wood

Was a Virginian by birth. Traveling on the rivers, he reached the Barney's Prairie settlement in 1815. He was a man of intelligence and influence and earnest religious nature. He served as commissioner of post-roads. His death came rather early in life. He was the first deacon of the Barney's Prairie Church, and a son or grandson of his has been in the officiary of that congregation from 1819 to the present time.

Claiborne Wright.

Indiana, 1819. 1896, Mason, Ill.

Came from Johnson County, Ind., in 1861, and settled on a farm two miles east of Mason. He was the first Christian minister to reside in Effingham County and pioneer preacher of a fine grade.

A poet friend wrote these lines, among others, about him:

> "Claiborne Wright! a name through which we see
> All that a minister of God should be—
> A name itself significant, 'round which
> Our human virtues clustered rank and rich;
> An ample soul perfected on a plan
> That comprehended all the *best* in man,
> And in the largeness of its vision saw
> The beauty of eternal love and law.
>
> "Against all wrong he waged a ceaseless war,
> And kept his soul as stainless as a star;
> Along the awful highways of the world,
> He bore the banner of the Lord unfurled,
> Willing to follow—not afraid to lead
> When duty called him, in the time of need;
> No soldier of the cross—no braver knight
> E'er donned the armor, when the cause was right."

John Yager.

Pennsylvania, 1808.   1894, Illinois.

Mr. Yager became a member of the Christian Denomination in 1829 in Ohio, but in 1834 he transferred his membership to the church of Christ—probably under the ministry of Robert Milligan. He was ordained to the ministry in 1836 and purposed to give himself wholly to its work. His wife objected so earnestly that he gave that up. Coming to Illinois the same year, he bought a large tract of land at Genesse Grove, in Whiteside County, which he held during his lifetime. He became very well versed in the Scriptures and a capable teacher. He was short in stature, but robust and compact in body; a large, well-formed head, a superior mind and a heart aflame with the love of the Master and his pure gospel. He was a born leader of men. His prayers were an inspiration to those who heard them. He was active and aggressive in Christian service for fifty years, and helped in the formation of all the churches of Christ in that part of the State.

Charles Yelton.

Near Lexington, Ky., 1823.   1904, Newton, Ill.

Came to Illinois in 1852 and settled in Jasper County,

which was the place of his residence throughout the larger part of his life. Shortly thereafter he began to preach.

He was a soldier in the Mexican War. In 1861 he became captain of Company H, Thirty-eighth Illinois Infantry. Later, he was chaplain of the 143d Illinois Infantry. In these positions he acquitted himself in a manner becoming a Christian military officer.

His ministry was confined mainly to Jasper and the surrounding counties. There his labors were fruitful in much good. When he prospered in business, he rendered to the Lord of his increase. At an early age the care of his widowed mother and her younger children devolved upon him. His life was full of joyful helpfulness. His last years were passed in Newton, where he delivered his last sermon on the eighty-first anniversary of his birth.

P. F. York.

Indiana, 1849.

Came with his parents to Illinois in 1855, who settled at Wenona. He is a nephew of the Houstons. Was educated at Wenona Seminary and Eureka College. Has now served the ministry of the Christian Church forty-two years—at Paxton, Leroy, Maroa, Girard, Sidell and other places.

CHAPTER VIII.

MISCELLANEA.

DATES.

The dates of many events in pioneer years were fixed in the minds of people by occurrences that could not be easily forgotten. The winter of 1830-31, December to February, was the time of "the deep snow," which covered the ground through central and northern Illinois to the depth of four or five feet. The year 1834 was impressed upon the mind because it was "the sickly season"—many were ill and not a few died. "The sudden freeze" came Dec. 20, 1836. The temperature was warm till noon of that day, when very suddenly the wind veered and at once became so cold that boiling water thrown up into the air came down in icedrops. Ponds and streams were frozen over so quickly that frogs' heads were caught in the ice, and myriads of wild water-fowl were seized in the same manner and perished.

"DISGUISED DEISM" OR "SOCINIANISM."

In 1883, Dr. Jesse H. Smith resided at Chatham, Ill. He was a successful practitioner and an able preacher of the gospel. He was a man of fine character which commanded universal respect. His nephew, J. Addison Smith, was then pastor of the Presbyterian Church (South) at Des Peres, St. Louis Co., Mo. This gentleman in that year addressed the following communication to his cousin, Miss Lillie Smith, at Chatham:

In your last postal card you refer to the conversation we had in the grove. About that conversation, I have this much to say: That I am sorry I mentioned the subject if it is painful to you. I had no wish to hurt your feelings. This you know. I was only stating a fact; viz., that your church was not regarded by the thinking world as an orthodox body. The Synod of Missouri last month sent up another overture to the next General Assembly of our church on this very subject. Our General Assembly has already uttered its voice on this subject, maintaining that the followers of Alexander Campbell are not evangelical, and, consequently, can not be recognized as orthodox ministers in our church courts. The history of the above overture is simply this: A few months ago the Presbytery of La Fayette, in this State, sitting in Sedalia, invited the minister of the Christian Church in that city to sit with the Presbytery as a *visiting brother*. Immediately this sprung the question whether the brother in question was a minister in an orthodox church. Several of the members of the above Presbytery objected to receiving the brother because our highest court, the General Assembly, had declared most emphatically the church in question could not be recognized as a church of Jesus Christ. This question was taken by the above Presbytery to Synod, and we discussed it there, and then sent it up to the next Assembly, that is to meet in Vicksburg, Miss., in May. When the question came up in the Synod of Missouri there was a great deal of feeling on the subject. Many of us were enjoying the hospitality of the members of the Christian Church, and it almost seemed a breach of courtesy for us to openly assail their church. I was the second one to gain the floor of the Synod, and before beginning my speech stated that many of the bre'.iren felt great delicacy in saying anything on the subject in hand, for they were partaking of the hospitality of the members of the church in question. I stated that in my speech there would not be any bitterness or venom, for I had a dear relative, a man of princely gifts, who was a minister in this church. I then showed that the question was not whether this single minister here or there was sound. I believed my uncle was sound and orthodox; but that was not the question before the Synod. It was this: Taking that body as a body, are they orthodox according to the Presbyterian, Methodist, Baptist and Episcopal way of thinking? I then attempted to show that the only way we could get at the question in this form would be to go to the very fountain-head of the system; viz., to Alex. Campbell himself, and, *examining that system there,* to answer whether it was orthodox; I bade the Synod remember that whatever that brother believed was a true exponent of the system. No, for A. Campbell confessed in his debate with Dr. Rice at Lexington, Ky., that *"he had in his church all sorts of men preaching all sorts of doctrines,"* and so what one brother regarded as Campbellism another brother would ignore as such; so, this being true, one would be compelled to go to the fountain-head, Campbell himself, and see what his views were.

And I then stated that the highest authority of this continent, of whom it was said that he did not have a superior in the world, Dabney of Virginia, who was professor of theology for thirty years, once said to me personally that the system of Alex. Campbell was nothing but disguised Deism. I referred the members of Synod to the finest critique of Campbell's system that has ever appeared in America, from the pen of the above Dabney in the *Southern Presbyterian Review* for July, 1880. Then I attempted to show the exact correspondence between Campbell's system and Socinianism. In fact, it has often been said, the truth of which can not be doubted, that Campbell received his system not from himself—it did not originate with him—but from Faustus Socinus, of Poland. Doubtless, you know Alex. Campbell was a licentiate of the Seceder Church, Scotland. He came to America as such, but his father, Thomas Campbell, having been called upon to stand trial before the Presbyterian Church for some little matter, this seems to have irritated young Alex. Campbell, and he then (possibly to spite, as he thought, the Presbyterian Church) began with his father to drift farther and farther away from the church in which he and his father had been licensed. Meeting up with the writings of Socinus, he absorbed them, and here is the starting of the system before us. The points of correspondence between Campbellism and Socinianism are so well defined that they are not questioned. Take only three, to say nothing of others: 1st, original sin; 2nd, atonement; 3rd, the nature and work of the Spirit, and I might add a 4th; viz., the person and work of the Lord Jesus Christ. Now, Lillie, my speech before Synod was so courteous to the feelings of the members of the Christian Church that were present during the discussion—no bitter language was used—so that not one took offense, and when, by appointment of Synod, I had to preach at the Christian Church on Sabbath night, I had a splendid congregation and they treated me with the utmost courtesy.

After repetitions in 110 words, Nephew Smith continues:

Now, Lillie, I am very sorry that this question has been sprung, for you know I do not wish to do or say anything that will give you pain, nor to estrange Uncle Jesse. Now, you may think that I am writing about something of which I am ignorant when I write about your body. But I know whereof I speak. I have known of your body for years. I do not pretend to say anything about your type of religion in the State of Illinois, whether your body there is orthodox or not, but I do pretend to say that I know something about it in Texas and in this State. In Texas your ministers carried on at such a rate that it was regarded by some strict Presbyterians as a desecration of the Sabbath to attend their church, and I was possibly fifteen years of age before I was allowed to hear those of whom it was said that "they ridicule the Holy Spirit." Understand, Lillie, I have met with your people. I have argued with them, and I know what some of them believe and what they do not believe. One of the soundest preachers (regarded sound by your body) of your church in northwestern Missouri had a conversation with me, and from his conversation he denied the personality of the Holy Spirit and makes it [him.—AUTHOR] a mere influence. Remember, he was one of your soundest men in that section of the State. I could say a great deal more on the subject, but I will stop. I am sorry that you requested me to write a letter showing the correspondence between the two systems spoken of. In closing I bid you remember the connection in which I spoke of these two things in that grove. You remember I said I was anxious to have Uncle Jesse when the Presbytery of St. Louis met at my church, but that I was prevented from so doing by the following consideration; viz., that if he were present I would wish him to be invited to sit as a visiting brother, but as soon as this would be mentioned there would be a conflict and clash, as members of Presbytery would oppose such a move on the ground that the body he represented was not orthodox. This, I said, would have hurt uncle's feelings and mine. It was in this way I came to make the remark in question. I am sorry I made it if the mere statement of a truth (so regarded by our Assembly) should cause offense. I dislike these arguments, for they accomplish no good. Sometimes they are forced on us in order to conserve the truth and the gospel of Christ in its purity, as was the case in the Synod. I have no hope of changing your mind on the grand principles involved in these statements. If your system is Scriptural and will do to base your hopes for eternity on, then you keep it. Of course, I must be permitted to acquiesce in the opinion of all orthodox churches of the world—that it is antiscriptural and, consequently, will not do to rest on for eternity. Now, Lillie, remember you requested this letter; take it in the spirit in which it is written.

God bless you richly and you all.

Your affectionate cousin,
J. A. S.

To this loquacious letter Dr. Smith shortly made the following reply:

DEAR SIR: Lillie, on reading your last letter, felt that I should know its contents, and, accordingly, gave it to me to read. Its contents surprised and grieved me no little. And after reading it I feel it my duty to address you, and, if possible, to open your eyes to the heinousness of your sin. First charge—That A. Campbell stole or borrowed his distinctive views of the Christian religion from Socinus. This is as false as perjury and base as slander. It is the repetition of a threadbare slander against the sainted dead. If your salvation from Gehenna depended on the proof of this charge from his writings, your doom would be inevitable. Hear the accused in his own defense. He said nearly sixty years ago: "While I renounce the metaphysical jargon found in creeds on what is called the doctrine of the Trinity, such as eternal generation, etc., I regard Arianism, semi-Arianism and Socinianism as poor, miserable, blind and naked nonsense and absurdity." In the face of this disclaimer, what is your charge but a false fabrication? a slander?

Again, A. Campbell published approvingly fifty-nine years ago: "From my heart I pity the Socinians. I compassionate their temerity, and would not, the Bible being in my hand, rush into the presence of the quick and dead with their sentiments for twice the value of the universe." A. Campbell entertained and taught but one view in reference to the *divine nature* of Jesus Christ and the Holy Spirit; viz., that they are essentially and eternally divine and underived in any sense of generation known to man. We, like the Saviour, receive not honor from men (John 5: 41-44). Those that did so had not the love of God in them. True honor comes from God only, and not from the thinking world, the General Assembly. Here read the enclosed paragraph from A. Campbell. As he said of the Socinians, so say I of you—from my heart I pity you. I compassionate your temerity in ignorantly and willfully slandering the dead in Christ.

Forty years ago, when I knew as little of Socinus and Alex. Campbell as I now do of the man in the moon, I heard your venerable father make the same statement about A. Campbell that you wrote to Lillie. Where he got his information, I never knew, but suppose it was from some retail shop or peddler, as I never knew him to read a line in one of A. Campbell's works in my life. A little second-hand information from your father, seconded by your Virginia idol, seems to constitute your stock in trade. With all your silly pedantry and boasted acquaintance with our people and teaching, I have no idea you ever read any two of A. Campbell's works in your life. If so, which? Will you please answer? You said to Lillie, "The Christian Church is not to be judged by a few sound preachers here and there," and then, without quoting a single sentence from any of our published works to convict us, you seek to condemn us from something you understood *one* of our preachers to say in private and probably excited controversy. Verily, the lame limp and theological policemen usually sit on stools with two legs of unequal length, as in this case.

Your second charge—"That A. Campbell's views of the Christian religion are *nothing* but disguised Deism." I am reluctant to answer this charge because its barefaced falsity demands more severity than I can consistently employ. Do angels of light yet transform themselves into scavengers? To me it sounds like a pansophical egotist. Just such creatures said worse things about the blessed Saviour eighteen hundred years ago. If the statement is not the offspring of ignorance, then the doctrine of total depravity is true in some cases. That old soldier of the Cross, if he knew of this vile aspersion, would justly rebuke me in the day of eternity if I failed to say a word in his exoneration. "Nothing but disguised Deism!" The man who toiled with tongue and pen for half a century in the defense of revealed religion "a Deist"! The man who has done more to eliminate falsehood, destroy priestcraft and reveal the rottenness of human systems and creeds "a Deist"! Angels of God, where are you encamped and how restrained? Thank God for his noble life and imperishable memory! I owe him more this day for a clear and satisfactory conception of the Christian religion than to all the priests and scribes of Christendom. And, now that his sun of life is set and the night of death rests as a mantle upon his ashes, miserable sectarian owls leave their hiding-places to hoot at his memory.

You say, 1st, that you are sorry that you mentioned the subject if it is painful to her, and, 2nd, that you were only stating a *fact*—that her church was not regarded by *the thinking world* as orthodox; and, 3rd, that your General Assembly had decided that we are not evangelical. Reply 1. When a man vends or peddles a slander against a man or religious body, it is a royal apology to tell the wounded, "I am sorry I said it, but it is true and I know it." 2. "Thinking world"! Your pedantic character is accurately photographed by Job 12:2: "No doubt ye are the people, and wisdom will die with you." Again he says (13:4, 5): "But ye are forgers of lies, ye are physicians of no value. O that ye would altogether hold your peace, and it should be your wisdom." 3. "General Association has decided that we are not evangelical." Poor, despised children of God! What next? The pope's bull of excommunication is published—"Ye are not evangelic." The iron bedstead has been made. "Ye are not orthodox," but you through this device and hellish malice can receive the proper stature. Let me say plainly, if our recognition depends upon our falling down and worshiping the image you have set up (your creed), or kissing the big toe of your Holiness, the great Dabney, then we are prepared for lions' dens and fiery furnaces. As to whether we represent a pure Bible Christianity, we court investigation before a proper tribunal, but not before a sectarian court, council and witnesses. If all these should either be dishonest or prejudiced, how could an honest man get justice? From self-styled orthodoxy may the good Lord deliver us; for it was the orthodox priests and rulers that crucified Jesus of Nazareth.

Many years ago a boastful deist of Scotland came to America and challenged the clergy of the United States to measure swords with him. Who met and discomfited this Goliath? The pansophical clergy? No, sir. It was the now sainted dead but vilely aspersed A. Campbell. The bulwark he then threw around the Christian religion will be an honor to himself and a glory to the church to the end of time. His colaborers, ignorantly or spitefully called his followers, have caught his inspiration, and for the last twenty-five years, it is said by those who have investigated the matter, more than fifty per cent. of all the debates in the United States against infidels, atheists and deists have been conducted by them. Under the plea we have made in the last half century, over half a million believing souls have rallied to the Cross of Christ. Here we raise our Ebenezer, and under God will push his victories over sectarianism, deism and atheism till all the Philistian hosts are discomfited and destroyed.

All praise to the saints of God in Sedalia! It is not the first time God's children have heaped coals of fire on the heads of their enemies. The Master taught them, "If your enemy hunger, feed him." Let me be plain with you. Your reference to Mr. Dabney, of Virginia, is both idolatrous and blasphemous, for you say "the highest authority of this continent is Dabney of Virginia." In this bald sentence, even the authority of the Lord Jesus Christ is not excepted. Now, should you not qualify the above statement by the word "human"? I shall not be surprised to learn that you have joined the pious old lady in her reverent exclamation, "Glory to King Beelzebub!"

Finally, one of two things remains for you to do—either furnish the proofs of your allegations, or confess your sin. I will wait and see.

Your uncle,
Dr. J. H. Smith.

A Chicken Story.

The story of the pioneers would be incomplete without mention of their open-hearted hospitality. It was generous to a fault and contributed very much enjoyment to their otherwise circumscribed lives. In those days, chicken was a "company" dish. As soon as the yellow-legged variety was introduced they were at once associated with the Methodist preachers. But these good brethren did not have a monopoly of this toothsome luxury. While the preachers of those days received little cash, and often none, they were royally entertained. The best things to eat were theirs. In every community there was at least one family that gladly welcomed the messengers of the Cross.

In the early day, on a Saturday afternoon, two tired preachers rode up to one of those homes where the latch-key was always out. In a little while the cry of a hen was heard and two small boys, intent on a tragic business, were seen by a passing neighbor. One of the boys held the fowl by the feet and head, with the neck stretched across a log. The other boy stood with uplifted ax. The proceedings moved slowly; so the passing neighbor called out: "Why don't you cut her head off and be done with it? Say, Bub, let go that bill or you'll get your hand cut off sure." The older boy replied: "But we want to chop the neck right up to the head and the old thing won't hold still." "What's the use? Whack away," replied the neighbor. "Lots of use," said the older boy; "there's two preachers in the house, and the neck's all we'll get."

In the seventies, John A. Logan was a candidate for the United States Senate. The Legislature was deadlocked by a tie. Then a Democrat in the House died. But that district was overwhelmingly Democratic; so the Republicans let their nomination go by default. However, a large number of sewing-machine agents got busy in that district. They drove good teams and the wagons were loaded with sewing-machines. On the side they whispered to every solid Republican: "Go to the polls at four o'clock in the afternoon and vote for Mr. Blank; mum is the word." The game won. The Democrats, thinking it unnecessary to vote, stayed at home, and the Republicans elected their candidate. This broke the deadlock, and that vote returned Mr. Logan to the Senate. And that man was one of the boys who years before had stretched the old hen's neck across the log.

The resourcefulness of youth is prophetic.

The Seat of Authority.
The Preachers vs. the Local Church.

Shortly after the close of the pastorate of Alexander Johnson in Springfield, early in 1856, Mr. B. F. Perkey, having preached there a few times, was engaged to serve the congregation as its settled minister. It soon became apparent that his manner of life was bringing reproach on the cause of Christ. Whereupon, the elders of the church waited upon him and advised him that "such was the opposition to his further continuance as pastor that his services could no longer be profitable, and, in their judgment, ought to cease." Already there had been some misunderstanding between Mr. Perkey and a few members of the church,

Then he accused the congregation of violating a compact and doing him great injury. Without any conference with the elders or any knowledge of the church, he mailed a circular to the Christian ministers of the State, calling upon them to meet in Springfield "to consider questions of great importance." Forty-two preachers responded to the call. Mr. Perkey then arraigned the church and one of its members in particular for trial on charges which he had prepared. He demanded that the ministers thus assembled should take upon themselves the task of calling the church to account for its bad faith toward him. The congregation was wholly ignorant of the purpose of this ministerial convention, had not been made a party to its proceedings, and hence had no opportunity of making its defense. But before the convention adjourned it appointed a committee to mete out to the congregation such discipline as, in their judgment, it deserved. In due time the committee made a report, which they styled their "decision." They found that "the grievances of Bro. Perkey are great. The church at Springfield has done him a palpable injury by violating the solemn pact, and should make reparation." This led the congregation to appoint a committee to consider the case. Their report was made to the church and by it adopted Feb. 8, 1857. It *settled* several things. This report bears the unmistakable stamp of that master mind, A. J. Kane. It was as follows:

CHRISTIAN MEETING-HOUSE, Springfield, Feb. 8, 1857.

At a meeting of the congregation in Springfield, Feb. 8, 1857, the following report was read and adopted:

"WHEREAS, Jonathan Atkinson, Theophilus Sweet, E. W. Bakewell and I. N. Carman, the majority of a committee appointed by the late Preachers' Convention held in this city, have presented the elders of this church with a copy of what they style their 'decision,' in which, among other things, they assume to decide as follows:

" 'The grievances of Bro. Perkey are great. The church at Springfield has done him a palpable injury by violating a solemn compact, and justice and love alike bind them to make reparation, as far as possible, for the injury, pecuniary and otherwise, sustained by him and the cause of our Lord Jesus Christ.'

"And, WHEREAS, The investigation of said grievances (as they term it) was altogether partial and *ex parte,* insomuch as they only heard his statement, and such evidence as he saw fit to produce, and did not receive or seek any other, although informed that they could have any information in possession of the elders in relation to matters properly submitted to said committee, nor was the church permitted to select any part of the tribunal;

"Therefore, *Resolved,* That we utterly repudiate and deny the authority arrogated by said committee to try this church or to pass any decision on its action.

"*Resolved,* That a church properly organized is responsible to no tribunal on earth, except to the civil law in cases under its cognizance, and that we regard this action of the committee as an assumption of power, unwarranted by the word of God or the practice of the Christian Church, and a bold attempt to lord it over the heritage of God.

"*Resolved,* That when this church feels itself incompetent to manage its temporal and spiritual affairs, and deems it necessary to have assistance, it not only has the right, but claims the right, to choose a part, at least, of the tribunal to which matters may be properly submitted.

"*Resolved,* That the statement of said committee that 'the church in Springfield has done him a palpable wrong by violating a solemn compact,' is reckless and without foundation.

"*Resolved,* That this church approves the action of the elders in communicating to Elder Perkey 'that such was the opposition to his further continuance as pastor of the congregation, that his services could be no longer profitable and, in their judgment, ought to cease,' and we believe it was done with the best of motives for his good, and for the interest of the cause of Christ.

"*Resolved,* That the church holds itself amenable to no Conference, Synod or Convention, claiming the exclusive right to control its own private and public concerns, but willing and desirous to co-operate with others in promoting the great cause of religion as long as such right is conceded.

"*Resolved,* That while we are disposed to respect the brethren composing the committee, as ministers and proclaimers of the gospel, so long as they confine their operations to the legitimate work to which they are called, we must most decidedly, in the fear of God and in all Christian forbearance, utterly repudiate and set at naught the so-called decision so far as it relates to this church.

"(Signed) A. J. KANE,
"RICHARD LATHAM,
"JOSEPH BENNETT,
"A. C. CONSTANT,
"*Committee.*"

When the "Campbellites" Were Not Evangelical.

The following incident explains itself. It is from the pen of Mr. Henry C. Latham, now a banker of Springfield, written in 1903. In Christian character and reputation he was the equal, if not the superior, of those who disbarred him. He wrote:

In regard to the episode of the Y. M. C. A., it was I who had the experience. About 1864 an attempt was made to organize the Y. M. C. A.; perhaps two hundred young men had assembled in the First Presbyterian Church, and the constitution was presented for adoption. The first item provided that all members of "evangelical" churches should be eligible as members. I raised the question as to what was meant by "evangelical," for it had been hinted that the "Disciples of Christ" were not so considered. They replied that no question should be raised as to my eligibility as a member. I replied I was not asking the question for myself alone, that I had no desire to become a member of any organization where my brothers could not be freely admitted. In the discussion, Bro. J. C. Tully and two men from the Congregational Church came to my aid, and we attempted to amend the constitution by inserting "that any person who believed that Jesus was the Christ, the Son of God, and had accepted him as their Saviour, may become a member," etc. Thereupon, a stranger in the city who happened to be present made a strong speech against the change, and stated that the wording of the constitution as presented had been found necessary to keep out the Unitarians, Universalists and the Campbellites, and before anything was accomplished the meeting adjourned, several stating openly that they did not care to belong to a religious organization where I and my brethren could not be admitted. The attempt at organization at that time failed, but later an organization was effected, and I afterward became president of this same association.

Women as Preachers and Pastoral Helpers.

The entrance of women into the public ministry of the churches of Christ in Illinois was as quiet as the rising sun. They had served with efficiency in so many semi-public relations and places that this final step was easily taken. It seemed to have been Providential. To Mrs. C. C. Babcock, of the Sterling Church, belongs the honor of having been the pioneer in this service. All of her valuable public ministry had the cordial approval of her husband. As far as learned, the other women who have entered the Christian ministry in Illinois are the following: Mary Pickens Buckner, of Augusta; Miss Rachel Crouch, who married Mr. Neil Derrick; Miss Rachel Dangerfield; Miss Daisy Finger; Mrs. Lew D. Hill, wife of Minister Hill; Mrs. Rochester Irwin, wife of Minister Irwin; Mrs. Ida K. Jordon, wife of O. F. Jordon; Miss Bertha Merrill; Mrs. H. E. Monser, wife of Minister Monser; Miss Sadie McCoy, who married Min. J. R. Crank—she was employed by the State Mission Board in 1893 and added 127 people to the churches in 188 days of service; Miss Sadie Olive; Miss Myrtle Park, who married Min. W. H. Storm after a successful pastorate of five years with the Carlock Church; Miss Myrtle Very, Miss Ava S. Walton and Miss Lou Watson.

Among the women missionaries who have gone out from the churches in Illinois there are: Miss Frances Irene Banta, and Miss Nellie Daugherty, who married Dr. James Butchart, to China; Miss Mary Kingsbury, Mrs. Kate Lawrence Brown and Miss Myra Harris McLeoud, to India; Mrs. Marie Jackson McCoy to Japan, and Mrs. Lillian Boyer Hedges to Africa.

In the public ministry of the gospel, women have acquitted themselves well in every way.

Conservatives and Progressives.

In coming out of spiritual Babylon, most of the Disciples of Christ have traveled, for varying periods, through foggy fields of confused thought. The average man, even in enlightened America, does not think clearly and analyze logically. To discriminate between the fundamental and the incidental in New Testament teaching was difficult for many; so fifty years ago two tendencies in Christian thinking were developed and have kept step with the life and growth of the Disciples. The causes and development of these elements are well stated by Prof. B. J. Radford in these words:

There were, as in all parties and organizations, conservatives and progressives in our early churches. When in any movement the progressive element becomes active and aggressive, the conservatives become reactionary. "Extremes beget extremes," and just in proportion as progressives go too fast or too far, the conservatives go too slow, or countermarch. When the progressives, as they often do, both in state and church, show a readiness to adopt new things without much regard as to their constitutionality or orthodoxy, the conservatives begin to suspect and oppose everything they adopt without much regard to its constitutionality or orthodoxy or *desirability*. It was not until after the Civil War that these two tendencies became sufficiently pronounced among us to cause contention and partisanship. But the conservatism of the first decade after the Civil War would be liberal in comparison with its character to-day, and the progressivism of that decade would seem almost reactionary compared with that of to-day. Verily, we see an extreme begetting an extreme. Premising that it would be unfair to our early conservative and progressive leaders to hold them responsible for the extremes into which the movements which they promoted have run, we may say that these two movements in the churches of Christ were led, respectively, by two great and good men—Benjamin Franklin and Isaac Errett. About these gathered captains of hundreds and captains of thousands. The conservatives had an influential and ably edited organ in the *American Christian Review*. This prompted the establishment of the *Christian Standard,* as the organ of the progressive element, which under the sane and brilliant guidance of Isaac Errett became a mighty force in our evangelistic, missionary and educational development.

The great body of the Disciples of Christ in the United States is not aligned with either extreme, but is the middle-of-the-road class. They are open-minded, hospitable toward all truth, and have a supreme regard for the authority of the Bible. The conservatives have differed widely among themselves. Those of this element in Kentucky and Tennessee are of a type and class superior to those in Illinois. Here, for the last twenty-five years, Min. Daniel Sommer, of Indiana, has been the recognized leader. While he has persistently declined to make any reply to direct communications of the writer, his position may be learned from the so-called Sand Creek Address and Declaration, of which he is the accredited author, or, at least, its inspirer. It is as follows:

Meeting assembled at Sand Creek (Church), Shelby Co., Ill., Aug. 17, 1889.
To all those whom it may concern, Greeting:
BRETHREN—For many years, as Disciples of Christ, we have taken the position that in matters of doctrine and practice, where the Bible

speaks, we speak, and where the Bible is silent, we are silent. We have held that nothing should be thought, received or practiced religiously for which we can not produce a "Thus saith the Lord." For a long time the above principles were satisfactorily observed and we were happy and prosperous, with one heart, and we lived in peace and grew in strength through the harmony of our creed for the restoration of primitive apostolic Christianity in spirit and in practice. We discarded all man-made laws, rules, disciplines and confessions of faith as a means of governing the church. We call attention to some painful facts and considerations. There are among us those who teach and practice things not taught nor found in the New Testament. Against these we have repeatedly protested. We complain of and protest against unlawful methods resorted to in order to raise money for religious purposes; the holding of church festivals of various kinds; the selected choir; the man-society and missionary work; the one-man-imported preacher; these being objectionable and unauthorized things now taught and practiced in many congregations to the great grief and mortification of some of the members. To those who teach such things and to those who practice the same we submit that they are not in harmony with the gospel, but in opposition thereto; that it is only safe to teach and practice what the divine record enjoins upon the disciples. We beg you to turn speedily and at once from such things. To you who practice and teach these vicious things we say that we can not tolerate the things of which we complain. This Address and Declaration is not made in the spirit of envy or hate or malice; it is only actuated from a sense of duty, believing that the time has come when a more definite character should be known and recognized between the church and the world. With this end in view, and for the purpose of counteracting the usages and practices, this effort on the part of the congregations below named is made; from a sense of duty we say: That all who are guilty of teaching, allowing or practicing the many innovations and corruptions to which we have referred, after having been admonished and having had time for reflection, if you do not turn from such abominations, we can not and will not longer regard you as brethren.

This document bears thirteen signatures, claiming to represent five country congregations. Kindness impels the withholding of these names. This crass and papistic address is silent on "the organ question," which was the crux of the controversy. To paralyze Christian activities is supreme folly, and to divide churches of Christ by questions of opinion is a heinous sin. It seems never to have occurred to the radical advocates of these opinions that, according to themselves, the Scriptures are silent on most of these things and therefore they themselves should be. A good man and a long-time elder in one of the best churches in the State says: "The conservatives are for the most part good Christian people. They are narrow and need educating. Fifty years ago many of us whom they now call progressives were conservatives. Treat them kindly and in a few years they will be progressives and we will again be conservatives."

All that can be here written of the extreme progressives is this: An association of scholarly and younger men was formed to propagate their peculiar teachings. It was called "The Campbell Institute" and had its headquarters in Chicago, where for a time it published the *Scroll* as the organ of its propaganda. It furnished the ministers who in late years have left the catholic position of the Disciples of Christ for denominationalism. The present position and aims of these progressives are given in the following statement:

1. Constant restatement to ourselves and the Christian world of the conditions which inspired the leaders of the movement to their early efforts, and the historic reasons for the origin, growth and continuance of the Disciples of Christ in the efforts to promote the unity of the church.
2. Present and continued efforts to promote the actual unity of the churches as imposed by our history and justified by the experience of the church during the past century and more.
3. Earnest co-operation with all Christian forces in the efforts to realize this unity. In such a work some body of people will naturally have to take the lead. The Disciples are committed to such efforts by their historic testimony and many notable examples of practical effort in this direction. It is their duty to be leaders and not mere followers in such a crusade. This need involve no compromise in matters of conviction. Nothing would be gained by such a shading of conviction. At the same time, some will be able in all good conscience to go further than others in their overtures for common work and worship, and by efforts of this character the cause of Christian unity will be promoted.
4. That unity will take form most speedily in the actual formation of union churches in localities where Disciples can unite with Baptists, Congregationalists, or others, reducing competition and promoting the interests of the kingdom of God. This type of union will probably become increasingly common as the movement spreads. It will not interfere with such exchanges of courtesies as may promote

good feelings between various religious bodies. But, in the nature of the case, it will give visible demonstration of the practical nature of that unity toward which the church looks with hope. The exchange of ministers by the different religious bodies will be a step in the same direction, where such action involves no surrender of convictions, but only a recognition of the broader fellowship of the churches.

5. The necessary ground and justification for these efforts to realize the ideals of unity in a practical way is the recognition by the Disciples of Christ of the Christian character and brotherhood of all the followers of Jesus of whatever name, and the frank and generous avowal that the convictions and beliefs of all such must be held sacred and significant in any plan of unity. One need not share in all regards the beliefs or customs of his religious neighbors in order to yield to them the right of testimony and practice, under the obligations of conscience and loyalty to Christ. We are not keepers of our brothers' consciences, but we are witnesses of a great and neglected truth, and of the fact that truth is entirely consistent with variety of doctrine and usage, within the broad circle of the Christian faith.

6. What form the united church of the future may take does not concern us. We may have our own beliefs on that question. But we may be assured that the Spirit of God, operating in the lives of believers, will form for Himself a body such as shall be fitted for the largest service in the furtherance of the ideals of the Kingdom of God.

This program elicits little criticism where its advocates hold fast the Deity of Jesus and make the word of God a finality.

SLAVERY.

What was the attitude of the Disciples in Illinois toward slavery? By 1861 they had grown to number possibly twenty thousand in the State. In all discussions upon the question of slavery that culminated in the Dred Scott decision—the deepest and most damning nadir of our national annals— they were active participants. In the thirties, forties and fifties many Disciples came into Illinois from Kentucky, Tennessee and Virginia. Some of those who settled in the border counties were pro-slavery, but the most of these immigrants came because of their aversion to the "peculiar institution." For example, Ben Major, who came from Kentucky and settled in Walnut Grove in the early thirties, freed his slaves and sent his agent with them to New York City in 1834 to pay their passage to Liberia. Of those Disciples who came into Illinois, during the three decades named, from the States east of us, nearly all were antislavery except those from southern Indiana. In the early forties two colonies of Ohio people came to Illinois. Of these, Dr. J. P. Walters, now a resident of Fairfield, says: "The two colonies of Christians who came from Ohio and settled in Wayne County in earlier years were decidedly antislavery in their political convictions, there being abolitionists in each of the companies. These people were important factors in moulding the political sentiment in this county in the years 1840 to 1861. The attitude of the Disciples of Christ during those years throughout this portion of the State was decidedly antislavery, but in border counties pro-slavery sentiment prevailed. In evidence of which it is a fact that this county raised more than its quota of soldiers in every call for volunteers, and that the prevailing religious convictions in quite a number of the military organizations in this part of the State was that of the Disciples of Christ."

Edwards County, sometimes called "Little Britain," because so many English people settled there in the earlier years, was not only opposed to slavery, but outlawed the liquor traffic fifty years ago. The preponderating religious influence in the county during that period has been that of the Disciples.

Hon. W. H. Johnson was a member of the House from White County in the General Assembly of 1882. The family to which he belongs has been noted for its intelligence and patriotism for 150 years. He affirms that most of the Disciples in that part of Illinois in its formative period were opposed to slavery.

The Gale families came from Ohio into Lake County, the Moffett and Hawk families into Carroll County in the early years. These were all antislavery people.

The writer is indebted to Prof. B. J. Radford, the "Sage of Eureka," for the following:

Of the Disciples of Christ who came into Illinois up to 1861, the great majority were immigrants from Kentucky, Tennessee and Virginia.

They were pretty evenly divided between Henry Clay Whigs and Jackson Democrats—the Whigs predominating in the central and the Democrats in the southern portions of the State. The Clay Whigs leaned strongly toward abolitionism and many of them were supporters of the Liberian Colonization Society. The Democrats were mostly pro-slavery, or indifferent to the slavery question.

In the breaking up and recasting of parties in the fifties, the Whigs in the churches of Christ generally became Republicans and the Democrats followed Douglas. When Douglas was repudiated by the pro-slavery Democrats, the majority of his followers among the Disciples remained loyal, but a considerable minority supported Breckenridge—probably one-sixth of the voters in our churches in the State. When the Secession movement began, the patriotic course of Douglas rallied his followers almost unanimously to the defense of the Union. Many of them from our churches entered the military service and a considerable per cent. of them came out Republicans. Not a few of the Breckenridge followers sympathized with the Secessionists, and some of them gave aid and comfort to the enemy. I believe that more than 90 per cent. of our people in the State were loyal, a good showing when we consider their antecedents.

The following are the names of a few representative Disciples of Christ who were active in their antislavery views: Dr. W. P. Naramore, of Stephenson County; Mins. A. H. Trowbridge and H. D. Palmer, of Marshall; Ben Major, of Woodford; William T. Major, of McLean; John Johnson and Min. Geo. W. Minier, of Tazewell; J. W. Simpson and Col. J. W. Judy, of Menard; J. S. Anderson and Min. E. G. Rice, of Morgan; William B. King and William S. Pickerill, of Sangamon; George Redmon, of Edgar; Min. William Schooley, of Clay, and Dr. John Kossouth Ashley, of Wayne. These men were the peers in every way of their contemporaries in these several counties—intelligent, strong, active and forceful citizens—and they were only a few of a great host.

Many Democrats in the North held with Mr. Douglas to the doctrine of "popular sovereignty," but the attack on Fort Sumter, Apr. 12, 1861, by Traitor Beauregard opened their eyes to see the real spirit and aim of the slaveocracy. They would let the black race suffer on, but they could not see our flag shot into the dust. Then quickly indifference gave place to patriotic devotion to the Union, the preservation of whose integrity was then paramount to all things else. From a wide range of personal acquaintance and many sources of information, the conclusion of the writer is that less than two per cent. of the Disciples of Christ in Illinois sympathized enough with the would-be Confederacy to even wish for its success.

It is proper to note here that a number of the great Protestant churches had been split in two by the question of slavery long before its climax was reached in the Civil War. But the Disciples of Christ went through that frightful shock without even a thought of division. Their common faith in the conquering Christ and the catholic gospel subordinated lifelong prejudices and flaming political passions to the interests of the kingdom of God.

Problems of the Rural Churches.

Had President Roosevelt done nothing else than to set the American people to thinking upon questions of country life, his administration would go into history as momentous. The commission that was appointed at his suggestion made its investigation of living conditions in rural localities and submitted its report to Congress, but, for some reason, or no reason, Congress refused to publish it. Parts of it were given to the public by newspapers, and so the leaders in secular education, including particularly scientific agriculture, have taken up the work. And since then the Department of Agriculture has instituted a Rural Organization Service, of which Dr. Thomas N. Carver is the head. There are six million farmers in the United States. Nearly two and a half million of the farms are worked by tenants, which complicates all rural problems.

Christian men are primarily interested in the religious conditions of rural communities. In Illinois, country society has been in a continual flux during the last sixty years. Towns grew as steam railroads were built, and thus many country congregations gave up their lives. These were also further affected by the construction of suburban lines, by the removal of land-owners from the country to towns and cities and renting their lands, by emigration to the farther West, and by the introduction and use of automobiles. The forces of evolution—domestic, social, economic, civic and religious—are active and potent in American life.

Among the ministers of the Christian Church in the State, Min. J. W. Street, of Mackinaw, has given the subject of rural congregations more earnest study than any other. The facts he furnishes should challenge the most serious attention. In his classifications, all churches in places of twelve hundred people or less are counted rural. He bases his conclusions on our year book's data and the Federal census of 1910, and they are as near accurate as they can be made. The total number of Christian Churches in Illinois in 1911 was 745, of which 559 were rural. Of these rural congregations, 173 reported in 1911 a total gain of 5,736; 188 reported an aggregate loss of 5,454, while 198 had neither gained nor lost; thus the net gain for the 559 churches for the year was 282.

For the year closing June 30, 1912, 150 rural churches reported a gain of 4,592 members, 152 of them a loss of 4,407 communicants, and 215 had neither gained nor lost; thus 517 rural churches in that year had a net gain of only 185 members.

These 559 congregations were served by 249 ministers, but many of these preached where they did not reside.

Not until 1910 did the State Board of Missions give particular attention to this wide, important and needy field. The convention of 1913 voted to place a trained expert in this service as soon as the finances would warrant.

Mr. Street says further: In 1910, 168 rural churches gave $1,995 for State Missions; in 1911, 198 gave $2,286 for the same work, and, in 1912, 204 such congregations gave $2,646 for the same cause.

Further, he addressed a list of questions to a number of

ministers in Illinois serving churches in cities of ten thousand or more population, from twenty-three of whom replies were received. First twenty of these twenty-three city ministers were converted in rural churches, as were also fourteen of the Bible-school superintendents and eighteen of the chairmen of the boards of officers; eighteen of these pastors began their ministries in rural communities, but only five of these while so engaged made any specific study of the community with reference to its economic, social, educational and recreational needs. The figures indicate the large contribution that our rural churches have made to our metropolitan ministry.

In looking into the youthhood of Christian ministers, the phrase, "grew up on the farm," occurs with surprising frequency. The great value of rural-church work is illustrated by the lives of two brothers—W. J. and G. T. Carpenter. They were born in Nelson County, Ky., and brought to Illinois by their widowed mother when the younger, George T., was eight years of age. They passed their boyhood's years on a farm in Bureau County. Both secured a college education. They opened a preparatory school Sept. 2, 1861, in the unfinished building at Oskaloosa, Ia. The next year they began the work of the college. The older brother taught there eight years, and then went to California because of his wife's poor health. George T. served as a teacher in the school for ten years, then gave four years to editorial work on the *Evangelist* and returned to the college in 1877 as its president. In 1881 he became chancellor of Drake University and gave efficient service in that position till his death in 1893. Mrs. W. B. Craig is his daughter.

UNCLE JOE AND AUNT ANN WILLSON

(An incident of the earlier days.)

The following incident is from the pleasing pen of Min. T. T. Holton. It well illustrates the simplicity, trustfulness, devotion and fidelity of the earlier days. Mr. Holton was pastor at Vincennes, Ind., at the time. He says:

It was midsummer of 1866, and the sands were hot in the streets of old Vincennes. I was then about six months along in my first pastorate. On many accounts, a vacation would have given me multiplied satisfaction. One Saturday morning there came to my door two old-fashioned persons in a one-horse, old-time buggy. The man in the case beckoned me to approach, and informed me at once that they two were Uncle Joe and Aunt Ann Willson, on their way to Allison Prairie, Ill., for a week's meeting, and desired me to get ready at once and go with them. Said Uncle Joe: "I am old and heavy, and am not able to preach. I want you to go along and do the preaching. I'll manage and maybe exhort a little, and Aunt Ann will put in a word when she feels like, and there is nothing better on hand."

"But, Bro. Willson," I said, "it is now Saturday; there is no one to fill my place to-morrow. And, besides, I would not think it right for me to go away without seeing some of the officers of the church in regard to it." "Bro. Holton, I will wait fifteen minutes; you rush around and see one or two if you think it necessary. And tell them that Uncle Joe wants you, and wants you bad, and wants you right off, for I have an appointment to hold meeting at eleven o'clock this forenoon at a schoolhouse between Vincennes and Allison Prairie." The upshot of it was, I went. "Get right in with us; it will be a little snug, but it's warm and we can stand it." People noticed us as we passed down the street and over the Wabash. "Bro. Willson," said I, "you don't expect that there'll be any meeting a hot day like this, and Saturday at that?" "Indeed, I do. When I was here a year ago I announced it in the hearing of all that I would be thar—Saturday before the first Lord's Day in August—one year from that time. And I'll be there and there'll be a meeting." "Of course, you have written them within a few weeks, reminding them of the appointment." "No, sir; not one word has passed between us in the twelve months. But this is the way I've done for years. They know Uncle Joe'll be there, and I know they'll be there. So be thinking, for you'll have to preach—if I give out." Aunt Ann nodded that that was just the way it would be. Uncle Joe was right. We had a crowd. And all three of us took some part in the meeting. At the close Uncle Joe said to the congregation: "To-night we begin a seven days' meeting on Allison Prairie. And I want you all to be there—this may be Uncle Joe's last trip to Illinois." At night the schoolhouse on Allison Prairie could scarcely hold the people. After preaching, Uncle Joe talked a few minutes while I fanned him with my huge palm-leaf fan. He told the people that he was there for their good, that he simply wanted them to do right, and that less than seven confessions—one for each day—was not to be thought of. He and Aunt Ann met with a hearty greeting. Even the day meetings were well attended. And there was great enthusiasm. It was hot night and day. No one could walk barefooted on the sand till the sun went down. The house was packed with eager listeners every night. And toward the end of the week the yard was full. The people were so close to me I could make no gestures, and I was as wet while preaching as if I had been dipped in the Wabash. Then I took the fan, and Uncle Joe, either sitting or standing, would tell the folks they ought to do right. Aunt Ann did the most of her talking at the day meetings. The necessity for a meeting-house large enough to hold the people was grandly evident, and before the close of the meeting $1,400 was subscribed to that end. On the seventh and last night of the meeting, four young girls were handed through the windows by their parents and friends and managed to get near enough to the preacher for him to take their confessions. Saturday morning found us at Russellville for one more sermon and for baptism. There were several additions at that meeting. And I remember baptizing twenty-two persons at that time. We had other baptisms, I think, during the week, so that at least twenty-seven additions were gained. "My time is up," said Uncle Joe, "and I must go on to Hutsonville, for I told them a year ago I would be there to-night." They gave Uncle Joe and Aunt Ann $28, and they were very glad and thankful. He told me he had preached for years without any pay whatever, except "two bits" that a sister brought in the corner of her apron, and he spent that for ferriage before he got home. He gave large credit to Aunt Ann, who ran the sawmill at home while he was away preaching.

The year following, Uncle Joe was on hand again, making his annual round, and this time he impressed Bro. Alvord into service. And again there were many additions. He notified me that the baptizing would be done just across from Vincennes; so a number of us went out and greeted the veteran, and witnessed the baptisms. And here a singular circumstance happened. There was a gypsy camp near by, and before the meeting concluded an aged gypsy came forward and made the good confession. Upon arising from the water, he put his hand into his pocket, pulled out a silver dollar, and offered it to the preacher. Of course, it was refused. He told me he had been a believer for a long time and had greatly desired to be baptized. He went on his way rejoicing.

I never had the pleasure of meeting Uncle Joe and Aunt Ann again. They have long since gone to their reward. I am hoping to meet them in the city that hath foundations. . . . Joseph Willson took his stand with the Disciples in 1833. He organized over forty churches and received more than two thousand converts. His home was in, or near, Loogootee, Ind., at the time of the above meetings.

CHRISTIAN PAPERS PUBLISHED BY THE DISCIPLES OF CHRIST.

This survey does not include the publications of local churches.

The Christian Messenger.—This was the first periodical published in Illinois in the advocacy of the New Testament order. It was moved by its owner and editor, Barton W. Stone, from Georgetown, Ky., to Jacksonville, Ill., in 1833. It continued with some interruptions till 1847, when it was merged with the *Bible Advocate.* In 1838, Mr. Stone moved to his farm near Jacksonville and the publication of the paper was discontinued for awhile. It was announced in December that it would shortly reappear at Columbia, Mo., but this aim was not reached. At that date it was "hoped that letters may not come to us free from postage." Its publication was begun again in September, 1840, at Jacksonville. It was then a thirty-two-page monthly, with Thomas M. Allen and Jacob Creath, Jr., both of Missouri, as associate editors. In 1843 it was announced that the *Messenger* had not been issued for several months, the ice having blockaded navigation in the Illinois River so that no stock paper could be had. Further, that, by the advice and co-operation of D. P. Henderson, its publication would be resumed soon.

The Berean.—Alexander Graham came from Tuscaloosa, Ala., where he had published *The Disciple,* to Springfield, Ill., in 1838. There he founded *The Berean.* It was a "monthly magazine, neatly gotten up on good paper and contained much sense and valuable information." Evidently it was short-lived.

The Christian was published at Edwardsville in 1847. A. Padon was editor. Price, 75 cents per year. Nothing further has been learned about it.

The Monthly Commentator.—There is still extant a notice of the discontinuance of this publication in 1865 for lack of patronage. Alfred Padon was its editor. No post-office is given. The same notice says that there were three periodicals published by Illinois brethren that year.

The Christian Freeman was published at Jacksonville in 1860. Of it nothing more is known.

The Bible Advocate.—The place of publication was changed from Jacksonville to Carrollton in 1860. E. L. Craig and J. S. Sweeney were its editors. It is highly improbable that two Christian papers were published in Jacksonville the same year; hence, it may be that the *Advocate* was a new name for the *Freeman*.

The Gospel Echo.—A monthly magazine. E. L. Craig, editor. It was published in Quincy in 1859. From 1861 to 1869 it appeared from Carrollton. It is probable that it absorbed the *Bible Advocate* in 1864. In 1865 *The Echo* appeared as a weekly, but its financial support was such that it could not long be continued as such. In 1868, *The Echo* went to Macomb, with J. C. Reynolds as editor. Shortly thereafter, J. H. Garrison became associate editor. In 1869, *The Echo* bought the *Christian Herald*. This was a small monthly owned and edited by J. W. Karr and Dudley Downs. It was started at Wapella in 1865. The next year it was moved to Eureka, where its publication was continued till 1869.

Early in 1872, *The Echo* bought *The Christian*, then published at Kansas City, Mo., and the two papers then consolidated. *The Echo* was moved from Macomb to Quincy in March, 1872. There the paper was issued weekly under the title of *The Gospel Echo and Christian*. One year thereafter the name was shortened to *The Christian*. It was the purpose of the editors of *The Echo* in 1871 to take the paper to Chicago, and arrangements had been fully effected, but the great fire in October burned them all away. The Christian Publishing Company was organized in St. Louis, Mo., in November, 1873, and the Quincy paper went there as part of the company's assets, in January, 1874.

The Evangelist came in its thirteenth year from Oskaloosa, Ia., to Chicago in 1878, where it was published until 1882. B. W. Johnson was its editor. The paper was the property of the "Central Book Concern." An effort was made in 1881 to unite this company with the Christian Publishing Company, of St. Louis, but it went over till 1882, when *The Evangelist* was consolidated with *The Christian* and left the State.

The Christian Sentinel.—A monthly magazine, edited by Dr. W. A. Mallory. He began its publication in Springfield in 1855. John F. Rowe was associate editor. In 1857 it was published in Peoria, with I. N. Carman and O. A. Burgess as editors. Shortly thereafter it disappeared.

The Herald of Truth.—A monthly magazine, the life of which was two years or a little longer. It was first published at De Soto and then at Carbondale. D. H. Banton and John Lindsey were its editors.

The Evangelist at Work was a small paper owned, edited and published by Min. T. S. Wall in Wayne County for a year or two about 1880. Mr. Wall's aim was to reach families with Christian intelligence who were reading no church paper. His effort was wholly unselfish and most commendable.

The Rock was a small weekly paper, owned and edited for several months in the early seventies by Min. T. J. Shelton, who was then pastor of the church at Waverly. The editor was erratic and his paper spicy.

Illinois News—a monthly, four-page paper—was edited and published by the State mission office in the interest of the State work. It was begun in October, 1901, and discontinued January, 1910, inclusive. It was a valuable little paper, but failed because of insufficient financial support. It just about paid its way, but the board of managers were unwilling to employ additional help that seemed necessary for its continuance.

W. H. Boles has published the following papers: 1890-92, *The Idea,* Springfield—temperance; 1894, *Illinois Christian,* Eureka; 1897-99, *The Plow and Hammer,* Alma—religious and educational; 1905-07, *Uncle Sam,* Marissa—temperance and patriotic.

The Christian Century.—The *Christian Oracle* was founded by Min. F. M. Kirkham and Gen. F. M. Drake at Des Moines, Ia., in 1884. Its purpose was to serve particularly the churches of that State. It was moved to Chicago in 1891 and aimed for a larger constituency. For eight years Mr. Kirkham continued as owner and editor. In 1899, J. H. Garrison purchased the paper, and his son, Mr. A. O. Garrison, became managing editor. For a short time, Min. George A. Campbell was editor. In 1900 the stock of the Oracle Publishing Company was bought by a group of men, headed by Min. Charles A. Young, and the name of the paper changed to *The Christian Century.* During the next seven years, Mins. J. J. Haley, F. G. Terrell and H. L. Willett edited the paper. In 1908 the paper was purchased by the New Christian Century Company, a new corporation. Messrs. C. C. Morrison and H. L. Willett became joint editors. At the beginning of 1913, the Disciples Publication Society, a company without capital stock and not for pecuniary profit, was incorporated and purchased the assets of the Century Company. Mr. Morrison is now the sole editor, with Mr. Willett as associate.

BOOKS AND THEIR AUTHORS.

The following is an incomplete list of books that were written by their authors while they resided in Illinois:

E. S. Ames.—The Psychology of Religious Experience; The Divinity of Christ.

N. S. Bastian.—Babylon in Jehovah's Kingdom.

Clark Braden.—Braden-Hughey Debate; Braden-Kelley Debate; Ingersoll Unmasked; Refutation of Accepted Theory of Dates; Refutation of Atheistic Evolution; Problem of Problems; Trials and Crucifixion of Jesus.

J. H. G. Brinkerhoff.—History of Marion County, Illinois.

N. E. Cory.—The Polymathist.

Miss Elmira J. Dickinson.—History of Eureka College.//
H. W. Everest.—The Divine Demonstration; The New Education.//
Errett Gates.—The Early Relation and Separation of Baptists and Disciples; The Disciples of Christ.//
George F. Hall.—Plain Points on Personal Purity; The Model Woman; Some American Evils and Their Remedies; Tabernacle Talks; Pitfalls of the Ballroom; Revivals and How to Have Them; Belgian Hare Standard Manual; The Lord's Exchequer; Temple Addresses.//
N. S. Haynes.—Children's Question Book; Jesus as a Controversialist; History of the Disciples of Christ in Illinois.//
George W. Nance.—Nance Memorial.//
J. C. Myers.—Buds and Flowers.//
D. Walter Potts.—A Fortnight in London Schools.//
B. J. Radford.—Court of Destiny.//
Charles J. Scofield.—A Subtle Adversary; Altar Stairs.//
Robert A. Sickles.—The Mystery of the Immortality of the Soul.//
J. Carroll Stark.—The King and His Kingdom.//
Herbert L. Willett.—Basic Truths of the Christian Faith; The Call of the Christ; Life and Teachings of Jesus; The Moral Leaders of Israel (Part I.); The Moral Leaders of Israel (Part II.); Our Plea for Union and the Present Crisis; Prophets of Israel; The Ruling Quality; Studies in the First Book of Samuel; The Teachings of the Book.//
A. M. Weston.—The Evolution of a Shadow.

The Old Songs.

The songs and the singing were features of the early churches in Illinois. The Disciples desired and sought to have their sacred songs accord with and express the truth as revealed in the word of God. Objectionable matter was eliminated. For example, the invitation hymn beginning,

> "Come, humble sinner, in whose breast
> A thousand thoughts revolve,"

was changed in the fourth stanza from "Perhaps he will accept my plea" to "Surely he will accept my plea;" and in the fifth stanza from "I can but perish if I go" to "I can not perish if I go."

They believed that the attitude of Queen Esther before her tyrant husband, Ahasuerus, was not a fitting likeness of a penitent sinner before the loving Lord who died for him.

They were also careful about the tunes they used. Nothing was sung because it was venerable or stately or had orthodox sanction. The tunes must be such as to enable the heart to understand and be edified. Toward God the singing was worship, and toward men instruction and invitation, encouragement and warning, comfort and inspiration. The singing, being properly regarded as worship, was never turned over to professionals. God's children praised him. There were no choirs, quartets or soloists nor musical instruments, except sometimes a tuning-fork. A musical brother—generally an officer or the preacher—"raised the tune" or "started the hymns." Frequently he marked the time by a patting of his foot on the floor. Generally he "lined out" the words, for hymn-books were few and sold high. But the Disciples did not take kindly to "lining out." It was lacking in simplicity and equality, upon which they insisted.

The first book of their own making which they used was without notes—a pudgy little thing $2\frac{1}{2}$ x $3\frac{7}{8}$ inches, in pearl or five-point type. The book has 1,324 hymns, and the collection equals in its excellence any now in use.

The pioneers sang largely in the minor strains, for there was much opposition, misrepresentation and persecution—even from their fellow-Christians—and their lives were full of hardships and trials. They shared, in a measure, the feelings of the Jews by the rivers of Babylon, where they hung their harps on the willows and sat down and wept. The music of the pioneers had not much of the high notes of triumph, success and victory such as characterize that of our day. It was full of pathos, sweetness, earnestness and strength. Here are a few of the songs they sang through many years:

"How firm a foundation, ye saints of the Lord,
Is laid for your faith in his excellent word."

"Amazing grace! how sweet the sound!
That saved a wretch like me."

"How happy are they who their Saviour obey,
And have laid up their treasures above."

"I would not live alway; I ask not to stay
Where storm after storm rises dark o'er the way."

"O Love divine, how sweet thou art!
When shall I find my wandering heart
All taken up in thee?"

"Blow ye the trumpet, blow
The gladly solemn sound."

"I'm not ashamed to own my Lord
Nor to defend his cause."

"Jesus, I my cross have taken,
All to leave and follow thee."

"Go on, you pilgrims, while below,
In the sure path of peace."

"Am I a soldier of the cross,
A follower of the Lamb?"

"'Tis religion that can give
Sweetest pleasure while we live."

"My Christian friends in bonds of love,
Whose hearts the sweetest union prove."

The last was often sung at the close of their meetings, or when some beloved member was bidden farewell, or the preacher was about to depart to other fields. Then the whole congregation rose, and, going forward, one by one, would shake hands with the one going away, and this was generally attended by a brotherly handshaking throughout the assembly.

The old songs! Mothers sang them as lullabies in their homes and their tired little children were lulled to sleep. Wayworn pilgrims sang them and received new strength and courage. The assemblies of God's children sang them and were aquiver with holy emotion and high purpose. They kept fresh in the Christian conscience the eternal Ought and transformed character into the divine likeness. Age recalls them out of the years long gone and wonders whether the land of endless day is not the place of sublimest songs of eternal youth.

FULLNAME INDEX

----, Ahasuerus 668 Dr 634 Peggy 425 Queen Esther 668
ABBOTT, Minister 76
ABEL, David 136 John M 135
ABERNATHY, Addison 210
ABORN, H 421 Hannah 421
ADAMS, C J 55 Charles J 158 Daniel 330 G F 148 278 297 Geo F 174 464 George F 84 120 284 461 Jas 378 John 119 Mr 394 465 Sarah Flower 513 T H 18
ADAMSON, Adam 349
ADCOCK, Adam 353 Adam K 433
ADES, Cornelius 258 278 Elizabeth 221 John 221 Phebe 221 Sylvanus 256
ADKINS, John 260
ADKINSON, John 175
AGEE, I W 332 Ivan W 56 336
AIDS, Cornelius 193
AINSLER, A C 224
AKERS, Peter 324 339
ALBERT, Caleb 411 Mary J 411
ALBRIGHT, 265 267 Esther 266 Jacob 266
ALBRITON, Beverly 238 George 238
ALCORN, J G 140
ALDEN, G M 110
ALDINGER, F C 157
ALDMON, John 309
ALDRIDGE, William 416
ALKINE, Alvira 327 Catherine 327 Elizabeth 327 James 327 John D 327 John N 327 Silas 325 William 327 Wm N 325
ALLEN, Clara 228 Edward 175 Henry 117 J B 372 459 J Buford 56 365 379 461 J M 42-44 46 48 128 276 297-298

ALLEN (cont)
448 451 461 493 593 J W 94
102-103 106 153 162-163 436
453 459 461 James M 56 John
W 55 461 Mr 248 325 462
Newton 309 Thomas M 663
Thomas S 500
ALLENSWORTH, Catherine 396
ALLER, H R 630
ALLYN, E E 307 Fannie 307 Flora 307 J M 307 R T 307 Richard 519 S E 307 Walter 307
ALSUP, J C 422 J P 323 J T 55 97 261
ALVORD, Bro 662
AMBROSE, John 114
AMES, E S 159-160 666 Lucius 304
AMMERMAN, Sadie 398
ANDERSON, 176 B A 409 B N 130 407 Hanna T 357 J S 657 Lawrence B 290 Mary 251 Mr 208 S H 100 W G 44 283 290 William G 462
ANGEL, Leonard 357
ANSBORN, Catherine 250
ANTHONY, M L 137 360-361
APPERSON, Frank 620
APPLEGATE, G L 349 J H 325
APPLEGATH, Joseph 193
APPLETON, L B 295

ARGO, Alex 134 Benny 134
ARMBRUSTER, Rose J 379
ARMENTROUT, Simon 412
ARMSTRONG, Garrett 451 Geo 259 George 250 Rankin 451 Rosetta 339
ARNE, Mr 394
ARNOLD, Joshua 198 Rebecca 447 Robert 326 Samuel 447 William 418
ARNY, W F M 91
ART, Robert 125 Thomas 125
ARTERBRUN, Sarah 185
ARTERBURN, Dr 267
ASBELL, J M 56
ASHLEY, Alice 463 E M 463 J C 236 429-430 432-433 John Clinton 462 John Kossouth 657 John Kossuth 463 John M 463
ASHMORE, Hiram 79
ASHTON, C M 315
ATEN, A P 60 242 Aaron Prince 463 Emma 243 Mr 464
ATHERTON, Cephas 125 Henry 125 Luke 125
ATKINS, Margaret 185
ATKINSON, A M 152 J 91-92 John 385 Jonathan 37 61 337 339 648 Milo 288
ATTERBERRY, William P 34
ATTOR, Elmer 360
ATWATER, Amzi 346 J M 379

ATWATER (cont)
  Mrs 321
AUGER, John W 138
AUGUSTUS, Fred 188 Henry 188 Larz A 188
AULDRIDGE, John 418
AUSMUS, Oliver 120
AUSTIN, C B 226 Elijah 212 James 430
AVERITT, Elizabeth 302 Ella J 300 Mary 336 Nathan G 302 Nathan J 336 Rebecca 302
AYLES, Elias 464 Parlia Ann 430
AYLESWORTH, B O 127 242 267 351 John 248
BABCOCK, Arthur 440 C C 123 126 367 440 650 Clara C 439-440 Mrs 465
BACON, George E 466
BADENOCH, Joseph 162 Joseph Sr 158
BAILEY, Abram 128 Geo W 140 John 139 168
BAILY, J M 578
BAIN, John 55
BAIRD, Adam 420 Andrew 253 420 Asa M 257 Asa W 256 John 420 Mr 418 Samuel 420
BAKER, Ashley 390 Carrie 402 Col 468 E D 211 378 609 Edward D 88 466 469 Gussie 357 J 381 J T 365 J W 348 James T 213 Joseph 390 L M

BAKER (cont)
  357 Mary Ann 467 Morran 241 Mr 467 P 290 Thos 381 W C 235
BAKEWELL, E W 92 100 286 648
BALCH, Laura 151
BALCOM, Ebon 125
BALDWIN, Levi 122 M H 150-151
BALDWN, Mr 151
BALL, 320 Roy O 292
BALLARD, Charles 454 Joseph 419
BALLENBAUGH, 388
BALLINGER, J W 332 469
BAMBER, R J 261 Robert 166
BANE, Thomas 250
BANGMAN, 601
BANKS, 369
BANSON, John 339
BANTA, Frances Irene 53 651 H T 443
BANTON, D H 665 H D 365
BARBER, 362 Albert U 450 Caroline 362 D C 216 Samuel 222
BARGER, James 72
BARGH, E C 314
BARKER, 298 Jackson 146 Samuel 297
BARNARD, F J 447 Jason 112 Maria 447 Martha 447 S J 447

BARNARD (cont)
  Sympson Y 445
BARNBALL, Henry 226
BARNES, E B 295 Mrs 116
BARNETT, D N 87 H M 55
  Harry 177 J A 177 269 458
  James A 55 John 211
BARNEY, 23 Ann 22 Betsy 22
  Clara 22 George 22 Harry
  366 James 22 Jane 22 Jas F
  192 Richard 22 Sarah 22
  William 22 416
BARNHART, J W 250-251
BARNS, Daniel 257
BARR, Addie 167 Addie V H
  166 J 381
BARRETT, F M 352
BARRICKMAN, Andy 387
  Elizabeth 387 James 387 John
  Sr 387 Mary 387 Sarah S 387
BARROWS, George 321
BARTH, Ephraim 395
BARTHOLOMEW, O A 535
BARTLETT, George 198
BASHAW, W 377
BASSETT, Mr 121 Sarah A 140
BASTIAN, Eunice 65 Mr 65 470
  N S 64 72 148 152 346 385
  392 469 666 Sarah 469
BATCHEL, S J 223
BATEMAN, Lorenzo 450 Mary
  W 450
BAUER, T P 18

BAUFORD, W H 166
BAUGHER, Jesse 390
BAYLES, Sarah C 446
BAYS, D H 18
BEACH, C H 132 Catherine 339
  Samuel 339
BEAN, 369 Geo W 224 James H
  176 Jas B 235
BEAR, Frank 439
BEARD, Andrew 436 J H 97
  James Y 254
BEAUREGARD, Traitor 657
BEBOIT, D R 97
BEBOUT, D R 196
BECKELHYMER, Isaac 56 96-97
  208 330 333-334 383 Mr 331
BECKMAN, J V 302
BECKWORTH, Margaret 259
BEDALL, W B 97
BEDELL, W 388 W B 66
BEEKMAN, H H 333 J V 56 269
  273
BEELER, 298
BEEMAN, M M 208
BEERS, Martha 378 Philo 378
BEGLAR, Adjutant-gen 501
BEHAN, W P 163
BELDING, W A 106 152 157
BELL, 601 Irene 421 J W 221
  James 421 James M 471 Lula
  421 Winifred 421
BELLATTI, Fred 270
BELLCHE, E P 211

BELSHER, E P 385
BELVINS, J R 384
BENEDICK, J D 240
BENFIELD, George 112 Lydia 112 Rebecca 112
BENNET, Calista 362
BENNETT, 362 Clark 122 George 378 H G 262 Harry Gordon 55 Joseph 378 649 Lizzie 271 Lucy 378 Mary 122 Mr 181 W B 387 William 396 Wm 387
BENNIER, Henry 253
BENNINGTON, 320 James 319 Olive 319 Rebecca 319 Robert 319 William 319
BENSON, A T 443 Arch T 442 Archibald T 470 D L 354 John Jr 289 John Sr 289 Jonas 289 William 289
BENTLEY, Gideon 361
BERGMAN, Jacob 286
BERRY, C H 97 C J 270 Charles 471 Charles J 470 Charles L 276 G B 153 G W 435 Geo K 56 J Festus 56 J H 448 T V 267 276 286 493 Thomas 471 Thomas V 470 W M 332 W P 297
BESHERS, B L 323 R L 55 289 291 449
BETTS, W H 204
BEVANS, Nancy 268

BIDDLE, D K 436
BIETZ, Thomas 405
BILLBERRY, 445
BILLINGS, Eliza 384 Jere 142
BINNS, 362 Samuel 79
BIRD, Susanah 319
BIRKS, David 270 John 270 Roland 270
BIVINS, W B 238
BIXBY, Hiram 116
BLACK, A M 370 Elizabeth 319 Evangelist 422 G W 122 Grandpa 219 Henry 220 Isaac 319 J C 434 James 216 219 Joseph 128 Mary A 219 Mrs 373 Salome T 370 W F 47 129 146 149 152 154 166 183 228 309 342 346 353 355 376 392 412 436 471 523 William 128
BLACKERLY, E 300
BLACKSTONE, Mr 571
BLACKWELL, Calvin S 153 Minister 106
BLAINE, James G 468
BLAIR, Stephen 63 229
BLAKE, Catherine 348 Wm S 348
BLAKESLEE, C G 217
BLAKESLEY, C C 126
BLAKSLEE, Charles G 348 Sarah 348
BLANE, Edward 327 George

BLANE (cont)
  327 Madeline 327 Marea 327
  S H 325
BLANK, Mr 647
BLEDSOE, W J 237 Wyatt 198
BLINK, Thomas 232
BLISS, C H 81 86
BLOOMFIELD, Ira J 536 Robert 182
BLOUNT, Jacob B 227
BOBBITT, 336 J J 442 Jonathan 242
BODINE, George 235-236 M L 264
BOGARD, James 231
BOGARDUS, Nancy S 398
BOGGS, Mr 249
BOLES, James 395 Joseph 408 Marion 96 212 235 Mr 473 W H 66 81-82 87 96 230 271 331 392 665 William Henry 472
BOLEYN, Anne 14
BOLIN, C E Jr 359 Charles 362 J O 100 Wm 174
BOLMAN, O C 361
BOLTZ, W V 96
BOND, Melinda 61 Mr 113
BONDURANT, Martha 356 Mary E 475 T A 51 131 Thomas E 101 356 475 Thos E 515
BONHAM, Jay 201
BOOIE, S M 330

BOOK, W H 18
BOONE, H B 127 J T 393 N H 127
BOOTH, Frank S 111
BOOZ, Dr 474 William 32 473 Wm 221
BORDEN, J D 171
BOROP, N A 56
BORTON, Jefferson 333
BOSTICK, Dr 514
BOSTON, Edwin 286
BOTTON, J P 201
BOUGHER, Sarah 390
BOURLAND, Thomas 374
BOVEE, J M 86 123 346 Mr 124
BOVEY, Daniel 349 David 348
BOVIE, Abram 347
BOWEN, F L 56 Frank L 101 368
BOWERS, Charles 270 George 270
BOWLES, A 381 C R 269 David 268 476-477 Elizabeth 268 381 H 304 Hughes 30 176 178 264 272 404 475-476 478 586 Isabel 478 Jesse 115 Jesse P 268 Marial 268 Mr 479-480 Ruth Prather 478 W P 118 176-179 264 266-268 272 285 298 377 380-381 514 615 Walter 477 512 Walter P 30 72 137 174 276 304 375 478 493 549 598 Wattie 480 William F 478

BOWMAN, E M 106-107 165
BOWYER, L E 357
BOYD, 336 Archibald 374 George 250 Henry 345 Mary 336
BOYDSTRUM, Jane 242 John 242
BOYDSTUN, Jacob 245
BOYE, William 430
BOYER, 301 A 189 C C 184-185 Christopher C 481 E E 55 184 289 481 J K 186 John K 185 Mr 571 T A 96 184 204 258 294 320 346 481 Thomas A 55 W F 185-186 W L 186
BOYLES, Hiram 258
BOYNTON, 601
BRACKEN, Arminda 327 George W 327 Louisa 327 Nancy 327 O P 327
BRADBERRY, Curtis 169
BRADBURY, D C 56 Dewitt 248 Nathan 242
BRADEN, Clark 60 63-64 66 75 78-82 85-86 110 200 229 313 481 666 Liddie 132 Mr 83 482 R G 132 W L 132
BRADENBURG, J G T 234
BRADLEY, Emaline 235 J W 239 John 316 Newton 443
BRADNER, Judith 468 Judith H 285
BRADSHAW, 277

BRADY, Charles 129 James 387
BRAMLET, J H 369
BRANCE, Jasper 431
BRANIC, F M 279 329
BRAY, Wm 215
BREAKER, D M 322
BRECKENRIDGE, 657 Senator 468
BREEDEN, H O 55 209 483 J H 101 207 209 482
BREMNER, James 162
BRENENSTUHL, J A 452
BRENNAN, William 299 301
BRENNER, James 151
BREWER, Mary 447
BREWSTER, George 221
BRICKERT, E W 346
BRIDE, Alexander M 203
BRIDGES, C H 356 Geo T 197 George T 199
BRIDGEWATER, Lucy Lyon 219 William 219
BRIGGS, M E 211
BRIGHTWELL, 277
BRINES, Flora V 421 J R 421 Jane 421 Jr 421 Virginia 421
BRINEY, J B 86 377 379
BRINKERHOFF, J H 559 J H G 313 316-317 483 666
BRISTON, Clara 418 Mr 418 N 418
BRISTOW, Alice 418 S P 343 Wm 25

677

BRITT, Jefferson 267
BRITTAIN, A J 366
BROCK, George 429 432 Isaac 429 432 Thompson 245
BROCKER, August 500
BROCKMAN, 324 Samuel 127 T S 533 Thomas 118
BROKAW, Mr 249
BRONAUGH, Amelia M 309 James A 309
BROOKS, H M 184 375 483 J M 78 Theo 392 Theodore 79 294 452 484
BROOM, J H 413
BROWDER, U M 85 484 Uriah Marion 486
BROWER, Mr 123
BROWN, Alpheus 91 119 382 Anna 339 Billy 209 512 Bruce 162 167 C E 379 Clarence 208 David H 421 Ephraim 205 Evangelist 129 George 188 George H 295 George Matthew 484 Huldah 405 J Newton 235 Jessie 46 John 339 353 Joseph 322-323 Julia 339 Kate Lawrence 651 Katherine 185 M T 154 Marion 75 Mattie 137 Matty 484 Mr 113 486 Mrs 109 N S 170 President 40 Putnam 327 R B 123 R L 145 R Leland 97 179 181 196 199 234 315

BROWN (cont)
Reuben 289 Robert 333 404 Samuel 174 Susan 421 Thomas P 286 Tyre 339 W H 85 119 275 285 326 329 332 361 375 392 W M 346 377 William 27 186 282 William M 39 485 Wm 209 Wm H 128 174 378 484 Wm M 139 Zachariah 293 Ziba 241 Ziby 112
BROWNELL, William 298
BROWNING, 361 Adelene 202 Angelina 355 E 221 Frank 355 Geo M 216 Green 218 Nancy 221
BRUBECK, Z M 275
BRUCE, J D 393
BRUNER, F M 48 60 426 454 Francis M 486 H L 48 Henry M 243 Lettie 48 Mr 487 Peter 274
BRUNSON, Cynthia 242
BRUSH, D H 63
BRYAN, Gideon 143 John 394
BRYANT, Daniel 122
BUCHANAN, William 198
BUCK, Hiram 72
BUCKLES, John 487-488 Mary Birks 488 Polly Birks 488 Robert 488
BUCKLEY, Daniel 436 Samuel 270

BUCKNER, C C 161 G W 279 Mary Pickens 651 S G 160 Samuel G 279
BULLOCK, J H 449 J Harry 55 M R 34 446 Thomas 34 592
BUNDY, Dr 442 S H 267 276
BUNN, 485 D P 73-74 Jacob 377
BUNTING, John 429
BURBRIDGE, G W 360 James 124 359-360 362
BURDETT, Malinda 221 Thomas 221
BURGESS, 267 Mr 78 Mrs 105 O A 39 49 57 72-73 76-77 81 103 153 208 298 319 353 448 489 571 584 609 665 T M 55
BURKE, Edmund 42
BURKEY, Daniel 100
BURLESON, James B 305 Nancy A 305
BURNETT, G A 209 Mary A 514
BURNHAM, F W 55 102 262 304 336 379 630 Rhoda 114 Rodney 114 W F 490
BURNS, Charles 190 H T 351 Harry F 157 Sarah 190
BURR, A A 291 330 Albert G 490 Amos A 56
BURROWS, 267 Chas H 76 Dr 77-78
BURT, 265 267 China 266 Flora 224 Joseph 224 Joseph F 449 William 266

BURTON, 418 577 C A 312-313 Minister 376 T H 418
BUSHNELL, Carl 106-107
BUTCHART, Dr 53 James 651 Nellie 53 651
BUTCHER, 429 Jerry 432
BUTLER, J W 59 79 242 424 James W 241 Marie Radcliffe 490 Mr 490 Pardee 118 Thomas D 489
BUTTON, C C 60 M F 60
BUYHER, Isapena 221
BYRUM, Amzi 206
CAFFER, Rachel 150
CAIN, J E 271
CAKE, E B 304
CALBERT, Scott 173
CALDWELL, C H 84 Lydia Ann 328 William 613
CALKINS, Rollo 157 Sarah 248
CALL, Jennie 105
CALLAHAN, Mary 170
CALLAWAY, R W 267 Ralph 325 S B 605 Samuel 620 Samuel T 128
CALLCORD, John 148
CALLENDER, George 41-42
CALLISON, Elizabeth 218 Gillmore 473 Gilmore 218 Josiah 218
CALLOWAY, S T 92 Samuel T 61
CALLUP, C A 163

CALVIN, 15 F N 56 102 115 John 14
CAMERON, Angus 500
CAMMACK, G W 427
CAMP, Geo W 339 J W 56 262 John B 339 Joseph B 339 Mark D 339
CAMPBELL, 190 336 A 96 335 375 462 643 645 A T 165 Alex 642 644 Alexander 22 69-70 118 127 147 187 219 273 280 489 491-492 495 534 554 558 560 571 576 598 609 613 641 Archibald 494 David 343 347 Enos 102 337-338 G Calvin 154 G W 200 Geo A 102 George 72 397 493 597 George A 156 666 J G 73 282 284 288 293-294 298 553 J M 63 J R 357 Jane 494 John 479 John G 176 480 493 Mr 62 71 157 283 348 384 398 425 527 603 618 Mrs 197 R S 121 S F 339 Sally Ann 493 Thomas 179 492 494-495 642 W G 290 W S 200 Walter S 56
CANADA, J L 201
CANADY, Charity 169 Deborah 169
CANDLE, 429
CANFIELD, John 446 Margaret 446
CANNON, W H 96 102 276 295

CANNON (cont) 362 448 467 495 Wm H 55
CANTERBURY, A 200 Carlile 373 John T 373 Livi 373
CANTRALL, Elizabeth 303 Fanny 372 Levi 372 Sarah 372
CANTRELL, C G 56 E A 157
CAPPS, 326
CAREY, H M 331
CARL, Joshua 179 Margaret 179
CARLE, Joshua 495 Margaret 495 W R 100 495
CARLIN, Gov 114-115 Thomas 495
CARLOCK, Abram 289 George 273 Isaac 26 Reuben 27 281-282 289
CARLTON, David 260
CARMAN, F N 620 I N 351 648 665
CARNAHAN, E L 271
CARPENTER, 121 C C 56 123 125 259 G T 60 603 George T 660 J W 55 96 205 383 Jessie 259 W J 55 660
CARR, Fred 446 J H 348-349 James 386 Robert 450
CARRICK, A J 509 D H 275
CARRITHERS, John 259 Minister 262 W P 264 496
CARROLL, H K 95 James 125 Robert 125

CARSON, Lizzie Dodge 60
CARTER, Berry 253 Edward 235-236 George B 434 James 303 James H 240 Nancy Jane 418 Polly 303
CARTMEL, J 373
CARTWRIGHT, R B 363 R D 325 R L 97 182
CARVER, Press 169 Thomas N 658
CASART, Jacob A 450
CASKEY, T W 110
CASSALL, Joseph J 61
CASSELL, H C 96 335 Mrs 104
CASTLE, H C 131 Paul H 449
CATE, Charles A 115
CATHCART, J J 129
CHADSEY, Benjamin 383
CHAFFIN, William 314-315 317
CHALLEN, James 609
CHAMBERLAIN, 362 Elizabeth 302 Griffin 302 Peter 302
CHANCE, David 237 David R 315 318 Wm 25
CHANDLER, Geo 382 George F 55 John 182 496 Riley 406
CHAPIN, J C 163
CHAPLAIN, Baily 266 272
CHAPLIN, Bailey 397 J B 402 R B 267-268 271 Wm 197
CHAPMAN, A L 159 A S 307 C C 106 C M 398 John 310 Ruth 398 W C 260 262

CHASE, Ira J 103 152 167 350-351 353 453 L E 266 294 308 497
CHATRON, Loyola 548
CHEANEY, James W 326
CHENOWETH, Abraham 361 Irving S 55
CHERRY, Albert 308
CHESTNUT, John 232
CHEW, M R 390 Morris R 91-92 Wm 392
CHIDISTER, J W 402
CHILDS, Geo F 106
CHISM, Jesse 293
CHOWNING, Ellen 276 Jas A 427
CHRISTENSON, Mrs 267
CHRISTIAN, Mrs 105 Persis L 103
CHRISTMAN, Martha 387
CHURCH, Samuel 129
CHURCHILL, 376 C 373 Joel 356 John 375 Wileby 375
CLAGGETT, Bernard J 497
CLARK, Champ 279 D M 151 162 Dr 307 E W 338 Frank 259 H D 55 115 276 286 362 Henrietta 104 Jane 306 John 115 Jonas 362 Mary E 109 Mary G 42 R M 34 39 Rachel 172 W A 119 W P 377 William 256 306 Wm 420
CLARY, Sarah E 209

CLAY, Henry 70 657
CLAYPOOL, Andrew 406 David 406
CLEERY, Mary A 305
CLEMENS, J A 55
CLEMENT, Ernest A 163
CLEMENTS, Denman H 299 Evangelist 422 J S 56 96 133 148 159 168 278 284-285 290 294 323 346 441 497
CLEMM, Rebecca 411
CLEMMENTS, Cyrus 252-253
CLEMNER, Wm B 125 444
CLENDENEN, J H 270
CLINE, G W 296 George 297 Uncle Jack 373 W O 156
CLOE, J N 56 J Newton 225
CLOUGH, J S 301
CLOYD, A P 132 W M 132
COATS, J H 385 John H 499
COBB, A P 102 121 146 295 304 379 452 498 Abner P 55 John C 335
COBLE, Wm 232
COCHRAN, John 543
COE, Cephas 259 John 259 Joseph 259 Silas 259
COFFEE, J H 278
COFFEEN, H A 407 H H 60
COFFEY, Robert 427 Wallace 427
COFFMAN, D P 215 Philip 337 609

COGAL, Annie 325
COGSWELL, Henry 157
COKER, Margaret 339
COLCORD, R B 440
COLE, Charles T 137 R L 208
COLEMAN, C B 379 L H 379
COLERIDGE, Samuel Taylor 62
COLESON, Hiram K 55
COLEY, Martha 358
COLLET, Dr 81
COLLIER, Sarah 198 W S 132
COLLINS, Elijah 236 F 200
COLSON, W S 343 Wm 386
COLVER, Nathaniel 471
COMBS, Job 187 Michael 187 506-507
CONDER, Albert 365
CONDIFF, Robert 109
CONKRITE, L R 132
CONNER, A M 56
CONNOR, Americus 148 Anna 112 Daniel 234 498 J W Sr 148 Jacob 112 James 148 184 347 355 392 498 James Sr 405 S M 102 153 295 309 345 498 631 Samuel 148
CONNORAN, James 329 Jas 96
CONNORS, Adelaide 248 P M 288
CONOVER, H 179 James 40 128 John 128 Richard 39 Sarah F 39
CONSTANT, A C 649 G W 381

CONSTANT (cont)
Rezin H 371
COOLEY, L 240 Lathrop 151
COOMBS, Evangelist 422 J V 56 Job 602 Michael 602 Upton 291
COONEIGLE, Jane 494
COOP, Timothy 153
COOPER, 120 M T 207 209
COPELAND, Abner 270 Maria 270 William 270
COPPAGE, Lemuel 118
CORENER, Daniel 171
CORNELIUS, E T 395
CORNELL, Harriett 185
CORRELL, George 235 L J 246-248 Sophia 235
CORRINGTON, Wesley 335
CORTER, Minister 252
CORY, A E 53 55 499 Abram E 279 David 150 N E 129 666 Nathan E 499
COSAT, J J 406 410 413-414 John J 499-500
COSNER, Frank 128
COTHRAN, F C 154
COTMAN, David 149
COTTERELL, Henry A 56
COTTINGHAM, T W 117 120
COTTON, R D 226 267 269
COUCH, Hiram 420 Polly 420 W R 258 420 Walter R 501
COUGHENBERRY, Nathan 225

COULSTON, Margaret 339
COUNTRY, Jake 32
COURSON, Gussie 104
COURTER, Evangelist 422 Maria 420 W R 97 William 415 501 Wm 256
COWAN, F P 327 J J 227 J N 238 John F 228
COWDEN, Mrs 362
COWPERTHWAITE, E E 134
COX, Amos 283 George 443 James 250 Nathan 443 P R 307 Sarah J 443 Walter 145
CRABTREE, Axie 437
CRACKEL, William 144
CRAGUN, E D 56
CRAIG, E L 339 664 Elijah L 112 Emma 587 Joseph 111 Margaret 111 Nancy 111 W B 152 660 Wm Bayard 587
CRAIN, Nina 224
CRAMER, Elizabeth 357
CRAMP, Richard 306
CRANE, J L 72
CRANK, A R 226 J R 55 651 McCoy 333 Sadie 651 Sadie McCoy 221
CRANMER, 15
CRANSTON, Bishop 17
CRAVER, Mary A 194
CRAWFORD, Alice 216 H 216 J H 132 John 132 366 Josiah 205 321 Margaret 216 N B 54

CRAWFORD (cont)
S J 53 57 104 Sarah 115
CRAYCROFT, John 302
CREATH, Jacob 114 118 Jacob Jr 663
CREECH, G N 360
CREIGHTON, E C 411 Evangelist 413 S H 96 411-412 S R 412
CREVISTON, Cloe 327
CRIM, M W 280 W L 202 William L 501
CRITCHFIELD, May 270
CROGAN, Mr 249
CROMKITE, Irving 405
CRON, Grandma 235
CRONCHITE, Roy 406
CRONKHITE, Louisa 411
CROSE, G W 132
CROSS, Benjamin 135 Sadie 229
CROTHERS, E K 286
CROUCH, Rachael 104 Rachel 440 651
CROW, Martha 450 Mary 450 Peter 450 Susan 450 W H 174 358 435
CROWDY, Luther 306
CROWN, Leslie 224-225
CROZIER, Mr 83
CRUM, Abram 174 Elizabeth 306 John T 438 Peter 178-179 Rose Ann 438 Thompson 438 William 306 Wm 438

CRUM-STANLEY, Sarah Jane 438
CRUM-WICK, Margaret Ann 438 Rose Ann 438
CRUMRINE, G T 250 Maria 250 Martha 250 Sarah 250
CULBERTSON, Viola 132
CULLY, Thomas 139 356
CULVER, Mr 123
CUMMINGS, Clark W 56 158 Frank 264
CUNNINGHAM, A B 141 Florence 306 Irvine 414 James 227 John W 227 Mary 306 P L 413 Rachel E 227 W D 99
CUPP, Louis 114
CUPPY, H W 188
CURD, Evaline 185
CURL, John 361 John B 28 113 116 118 533
CURRY, E E 346
CURTIS, James F 384
CURVER, F M 363
CYRUS, 277 C M 248 H A 111 Henry 337
DABNEY, 642 645 C B 55 97 297 382 J B 321 J D 55 97 129 290 359 447 Mr 646 Professor 641 Vaughn 157
DABSON, Elizabeth 209
DAILEY, A D 170
DAILY, Abner 190

DAIRS, F L 97
DAKE, Sarah 374
DAKIN, E Le Roy 163
DALE, Hiram U 55
DALEY, J R 87
DAMON, O H 200
DANDY, John 245
DANGERFIELD, Rachael 334 Rachel 56 651
DANIELS, D O 136 Daniel 299
DARLING, D H 441 Daniel H 502
DARNELL, 267 Sally 266 William 266 Wm 397
DARROW, Elizabeth 203 I 203
DARSIE, James 471 Lloyd 162
DARST, E W 106-107 156 159-161 J P 99 351-352 Jacob 548-549 James P 54 John 34 40 43-44 54 103-104
DARY, Julia 209
DAUGHERTY, Frank 233 Nellie 53 651
DAUGHERTY-BUTCHART, Nellie 210
DAVENPORT, Ben 152 Mr 394 William 34 37 40 88 246 266 272 285 289 298 321 401 448 503 571 582 Wm 91-92 396 588
DAVIDSON, Alexander 424 Anna E 57 Annie E 103 104 C E 116 Caleb 34 148 Clara L

DAVIDSON (cont)
104 Elijah Jr 423 Elijah Sr 423 Elizabeth 423 Margaret Jr 423 Margaret Sr 423 Rose 307 Sarah 307 William M 423
DAVIER, George 450
DAVIES, Minister 75 381 R N 79
DAVIS, A B 396 Alexander B 400 Cordelia 139 David 72 174 Edwards 346 F L 444 F S 56 Frank 292 H A 346 Henry 138-139 560 J A 369 J M 398 J P 267 346 J T 134 James W 383 Joel T 342 John W 500 K B 326 L F 55 205 382-383 M M 18 Milly Ann 319 Minister 73 174 Owen 77 Sarah 139 Steven 210 Thompson 418 Wm H 418
DAVISON, Elijah 424
DAW, Sarah Huey 219
DAWDY, John 242 W H 116
DAWSON, Baily D 92 John 375 565 Lydriam 244 W C 304
DAY, Charles 205 Melissa 256
DAYHOOF, Samuel 198
DEAN, A W 290 C W 158 290 Charles 128 Henry 366
DECK, Jacob 307
DECKER, John 171 Sarah 215
DECKERHOFF, Ida 224
DEE, John V 100
DEEDS, Mary 306

DEFORD, Mrs 260
DEFREESE, Talmage 116
DEIHL, J E 96
DELAY, E 381
DEMAREST, Mary 339
DEMENT, G T 294
DEMILLER, A J 346
DEN, J P 75
DENHAM, A B 416 W W 56 159 204 286
DENNIS, John 118 John C 128 Minnie 104 Oscar 358 R C 78
DENNY, Thomas H 276
DEON, John 609
DEPEW, Clarence L 455
DEPOISTER, Mr 348
DEPOISTERS, L F 330
DEPUTY, James 416
DERRICK, Neil 651 Rachel 651
DETERDING, Sarah Davis 139
DETEST, Mary 435
DETTERDING, Mrs 560
DETWEILER, J S 440
DEVINNEY, Mrs 294
DEVORE, A A 106
DEW, George 60
DEWEESE, B C 323 C C 56 Nimrod 61 W D 55 98 266 293
DIBBLE, P K 279 434
DICE, Frank 407
DICKENS, 298 Methodist Preacher 419

DICKERSON, Joseph 387 P J 66
DICKEY, Laura 151
DICKINSON, E W 42 Elijah Sr 34 448 Elmira J 38 42 57 103 503 667 Miss 105 504
DICKSON, W L 396
DIDLAKE, E H 285
DIEHL, J E 266 346 359 Patricia S 13 Rose 348
DILL, 265
DILLEY, Orin 383
DILLINGHAM, John 200
DILLON, Clista W 132 Davis 132 Geo 407 Isaiah 295 J W 132 Mary A 132 William 295 396
DILLS, T H 267
DILLY, Orin 333
DINGMAN, James 302-303
DINNEL, James H 416
DITZLER, Jacob 75
DIVELY, William 198
DIXON, Alice 446 Jane 446
DOAN, R B 55 266
DOBBINS, Joshua 232
DODD, Dr 138
DODGE, F M 394 John 244 John M 244-245 Jordan 241 244 Margarete 244 Milton 241-242 278 Theodocia 244 Thomas 244
DODSON, Hiram 174 Isaac 333
DONEY, O K 55

DOOLING, Pansy 357
DOOLITTLE, G W 156
DORSEY, 361 Joseph 216
DOTSON, Hiram 176
DOTY, C L 234 Minister 389 Mr 297
DOUGLAS, 657 A S 609 C 203 Eliza 203 Stephen A 468
DOWARD, Z O 348
DOWDY, Alford 242 Cassie 242 Jane 242
DOWLING, L A 248 L H 453 Wm 528
DOWN, Dudley 93
DOWNEN, Otis 435
DOWNS, Dudley 75 174-176 178 183 268 302 368 493 504 507 664 Mr 508 Robert 507
DOYLE, John 100 Mary 601
DRABING, R 270
DRAKE, F M 666 William 364
DRAWN, 219
DRENNEN, Charles 315
DRENNER, 349
DREW, Alfred 213-214 Nancy 213
DRISKELL, Josephine 140
DRON, Wm 214
DRUMMET, Wm 55 250
DRUMMETT, W H 198
DRYDEN, E G 224 John 224 Martha 224 Wm W 224
DUBBER, A E 188

DUDLEY, Marston 200-201
DUFFY, G E 295 J D 357
DUGGAR, Wm 387
DUGGER, W W 322-323
DUNAWAY, Charles 199 John 199
DUNBAR, Melia 394 Susan 147
DUNCAN, James 234 307
DUNGAN, Mr 471
DUNKERSON, Thomas 56 W T 382
DUNKINS, Frank 227 Martha 227
DUNLAP, James 112 Margaret J 112 R E 373 452
DUNN, John 146 Thomas 355
DURHAM, D M 418 421 Elvira 59 Judge 59-60 243
DUTT, Meade E 393
DUVEE, Benj 234 Benjamin 171 173 232
DYER, George 267
EADS, James D 278 John 244
EARL, Henry S 56 286
EARLE, Jane A 591
EARLY, L N 505
EARNEST, Gifford 380
EASTERLING, H B 269
EASTMAN, Fannie 307 Grandma 307 Kate 307 W F 367 440 504
EASTON, J H 355
EATON, C M 254 O M 97 431

EATON (cont)
  Oscar 430
EBERT, William 304
ECK, Edna 53 147
EDDS, Carroll 304
EDMISTON, Jennie 402
EDMONSON, B 242 Cyntha Ann 430
EDSON, C B 156 Charles B 165
EDWARD, II 14
EDWARDS, A H 345 630 Caleb 505 Harvey N 587 John M 276 Mr 266 Robert 324 Stephen 270 Thomas 346 392
EGNEW, Selma 306
EISMINGER, Elizabeth 270 Jacob 270 Mary 270 P 270
ELAM, Evert 116
ELDER, A W 381 Alfred 378 Andrew 128 Charles 128 M R 335 510 Martha 378 Ripley 128
ELDRED, R R 53 56
ELDREDGE, Otis 75
ELDRIDGE, Ottis 182
ELIZABETH, 14
ELKIN, John G 378 Thomas C 378 William F 371 Wm F 378
ELKINS, 376
ELLEDGE, Bro 507 Daniel W 139 187 506 Isaac 182 Mr 508
ELLIFF, Mary 402
ELLIOTT, A J 351 Adeline 332

ELLIOTT (cont)
  Ashley J 510 E E 458 J M 67 Mrs 371
ELLIS, E J 96 Elmer 136 G J 243 Henry 371 Ira 137 John 508 621 Melitus W 371 W M 370
ELLSWORTH, A C 414
ELMORE, C E 228 John 261 William 500
ELSLA, D J 278
ELSTON, Elmura 122
ELSTUN, Mr 171
ELY, Simpson 177
EMERSON, F W 286
EMMERSON, Alan 192-193 F A 330 F W 330
EMMONS, Lucretia 248 Martin 428
ENDER, Levi 329
ENDERS, W D 160 Wm 278
ENDSLEY, Matilda 226
ENGLAND, A T 511 Anna 372 David 373 John 176 264 270 272 276 284 302 373 511 Stephen 23 372-373 Uncle John 512
ENGLE, A J 203 Catherine 203 327 Eliza 203 Elizabeth 327 Ellen 203 Ira 56 Ira A 275 Isaac 203 Joseph 203 L A 135 300 304 327-328 Susan M 203 William 327
ENLOE, Isaac N 116

ENNEFER, S A 55 W L 56
ENSELL, John 295
ENSIGN, Robert Seymour 512
ERASMUS, 15
ERRETT, 219 Isaac 103 152-153 626 652 John 215 W S 48
ESHELMAN, Hattie 357
ETHERIDGE, J S 346
EVANS, C E 96-97 356 412 Chas E 56 David 180 Griffin 138 Horatio 198 J T 141 Jesse W 250 N W 286 T J 140
EVEREST, H W 43 46 104 290 295 379 403 448 459 667 Mr 45
EVERRITT, Isaac 570
EVY, Edward 390
EWELL, Gen 501 Lieut-gen 500
EWERS, J R 161
EWING, A G 34 448 B N 402 C F 267 Charles F 272 E C 338 Ella C 53 Emma Campbell 103 Jane 42 John 307 Mary 272 Minister 332 Shorba A 224
EYCK, Adda Ten 398
EYMAN, James M 300
EYRICK, H L 348
FANBER, D F 451 D T 451
FANNING, James 304
FANNON, F O 313 316 Shorland 56
FARIS, E E 53

FARNER, C L 264
FARR, John 264
FAULDERS, L I 55 L T 349
FEARHEILEY, Anna 421
FENTON, A B 109-110
FERGUSON, William 340
FERRALL, F D 159
FERRELL, B F 228 Peter 500
FERRICE, James 478
FERRIS, Maude Deterding 139 Maude Detterding 105
FERTIG, L G 167
FETTERS, 320 Harley 410
FIDDLAR, Charles 169
FIELD, Mr 239 Wilford 196
FIELDCAMP, Mona 264
FIELDS, Glen 358 Stanton 322
FILLMORE, A D 72 175 185 187 233 392 523 557 Bro 563
FILROE, Minister 85
FILTON, Maria L 421
FINCH, C A 56
FINDALL, Isaac 334
FINDLEY, J F 155
FINGER, Daisy 651 S Daisy 55
FINNELL, R A 380 Rufus 56
FINNIKLE, Hattie 348
FIREBAUGH, B F 132
FISH, John 256
FISHBACK, A J 473 James A 410 Joseph 410
FISHER, A S 35-39 42 Andrew 231 Eli 55 397 452 Elizabeth

FISHER (cont)
    245 H G 295 Jesse 396 John
    245 Pomelia 277 S E 130 133
    200 259 Sarah 38 Stephen E
    55 98 452
FISK, Martha H 336 Nathaniel
    336
FISKE, Minister 329
FITCH, David T 394 Lewis H
    394 Polly M 394
FITZGERALD, Anna 24 186
FLAGG, B F 377 Georgiana 376
FLANNIGAN, Jas W 213 R C
    213
FLECK, Jacob 435
FLEMING, 385 Levi 345
    Minister 389
FLEMMING, Levi 341
FLESHER, Samuel 400
FLICK, John 429 Michael 429
FLICKINGER, C M 355
FLOWER, Alfred 110 190 419
    435 513 Elizabeth S 190
FLYNN, J W 325
FOLEY, G W 236 George 313
FOLLIS, W L 275
FORD, 351 A C 374 E C 63 G W
    383 Rebecca 302 Solomon
    235 W J 49 94 William 352
FORDICE, Jarvis 417
FOREDYCE, Dr 259
FOREMAN, Anderson 61
FORRESTER, George 602 Mr

FORRESTER (cont)
    603
FOSTER, A C 339 A H 324
    Albert 398 Blashel 192 Drew
    427 Harriet 450 John 450
    Mary A 514 Mr 515 Nancy
    114 Robert 74 118 129 209
    220 304 324 329 339 371 375
    450 513-514 555 563 573
    Sarah A 450 Thomas 232 W
    B 514 W S 398 William 193
FOWLER, Francis 211
FOX, Louise 376 Mina 208
FRAKES, Ben 169 James 233
    Lizzie 169 Mrs 476
FRAMPTON, Wm 138
FRANCIS, J M 356
FRANK, A J 188
FRANKLIN, Benjamin 73-74 174
    178 259 268 294 652
    Evangelist 422 J D 293 John
    228 294 John Jr 288 John Sr
    288
FRAZIER, E L 130 148 Harriet
    312 Jacob 312 Simpson 312 T
    L 204
FRAZZEL, Maude 172
FREDERICK, Wm 365
FREEMAN, C W 232 325 Chas
    W 515 Mr 516
FREER, L C P 151
FRENCH, 418 A O 310 A W 418
    C E 128 George 411 George

FRENCH (cont)
  W 411 Irene 411 Irene Jr 411
  Margaret 411 Matilda 411
  Samuel 411
FREYMIRE, W H 53
FRICKERS, Elizabeth 306
FRIEND, John 230 365
FRONT, 396
FROST, A P 497 Adelaide 497
  Elmer 440
FRY, Virgil 165
FUDGE, Elsie 167
FUGATE, S E 433
FULK, Wm 199
FULLER, Alonzo 125 I H 452
FULTON, Elihu 198
FUNK, David I 348-349
FUTCHER, J F 155
GADDIS, Effie L 104
GAFFNEY, Obid 275
GAGE, 238 Darius 246
GAINS, C R 56
GAITHER, Wm 397
GALBRAITH, Jesse 61
GALE, 656 Wm 362
GALLAGHER, A J 74
GALLOWAY, Jas B 232
GALYER, Rebecca 387
GAMBLE, Robert 435
GARD, Seth 22-23 416-417 516
GARDNER, Jas M 170 Leona 519 Lucy 519
GARFIELD, 545 J A 472 James A

GARFIELD (cont)
  248 Mr 249
GARNER, Preacher 567
GARRETT, Mr 171
GARRISON, J H 60 215 244 279
  310 331 334 664 666 Jefferson
  213 O A 666 W E 55 W M
  434
GARST, C W 332 Cassius 297
GARVEY, 376 John 375 Samuel
  372 W F 374
GASH, J S 279 James S 516
GASKIN, Frank 236
GASTON, James 241
GATES, Errett 57 160 531 667
  Flora 309 Guerdon 88 Henry
  M 309 Minister 343
GAUMER, C C 409 C F 412 Clay
  F 413 517
GEE, Old Father 258
GENDERS, Henry 55 175
GERMAN, W C 56
GETZ, Rose 421
GHENT, Carrol 320
GHORMLEY, J F 55 96 226 261
  290 294 449
GIBBS, Louisa 327
GIBERSON, Emma 306 Lelia
  306 Willie 306
GIBSON, Agnes 447 Cyrus 447
  Elmira 447 Hiram 146
  Thomas 122
GIDDENS, John 290

GILBERT, A N 102 337 B R 386
Daniel 229 Minister 331
GILCREST, R A 56
GILCRIST, R A 276 301
GILKEY, Miss 109 Mrs 109
GILL, Mr 267 Thomas 193
GILLASPIE, Logan 415
GILLIAM, William 338
GILLILAND, E A 96 175 210 261 276 295 Ernest A 55 H J 102 J A 203 J H 55 60 210 285-288 295 321 James H 517 John 203
GILLPATRICK, Catherine 336
GILMER, U Y 86
GIMNURA, Henry 136
GISH, Ellis P 56 Gilbert 452 Rufus 450
GIVENS, J P 292 295
GLASFORD, S M 240
GLAZE, E 215
GLEN, John P 26 Nancy 26 Ruth B 26 S 119
GLENN, A A 91 102 Archibald A 518 Mr 519 S P 179 Samuel P 26 178
GLOVER, Annie E 306
GOBLE, Jonathan 360
GODARD, Francis 244
GOFF, Mr 436
GOLDEN, J R 56 102 John R 200 290 521 Minister 291
GOLDSMITH, H O 172 Harry

GOLDSMITH (cont)
172 Tiney 172 William 172
GOLIGHTLY, T J 56 323
GOOD, Stella 387
GOODALL, F M 63 John 63
GOODAN, Garner 378
GOODE, G M 79 83 96 102 295 310 321 372 515 Galen M 519 M M 310 327 334 338 515 519 Mr 80 W S 519
GOODEN, Hardin 360 L 381
GOODIN, Hardin 467
GOODMAN, Minister 389 Mr 521 Thomas 147-148 173 180 184 188 190 343 347 385 507 520 523 Tom 183
GOODNIGHT, T H 278
GOODWIN, Dr 403 Elijah 190 193 355 419-420 425 433 435 437 521-522 George 190 Moses 193 213 419-420 433 436-437 522 559 Mr 436
GOOS, Lewis 325 Louis 291 354 Michael 354
GORDON, D T 172 James B 339 John B 339 W M 347 W T 195-196 William 339
GORIN, Sanford 562
GOSS, Mr 348
GOUGH, William 342
GOULD, Benjamin 214
GRADY, John 450 Mary A 450 R R 450

GRAFF, 231
GRAHAM, Alexander 378 663 Geo 358 H E 398
GRANDY, I B 84
GRANT, Brother 26 John 373 President 463 596 Robert 373 William 25 371
GRAVAT, O B 413
GRAVES, E H 356 J B 335 Thomas 427
GRAY, A C 54 Belle C 235 F S 415 James R 378
GREEN, A W 283 290 Albert 142 Carl 237 Daniel 387 F M 374 Gilbert 354 Gilford 354 James 29 Joseph 375 Martha 354 Phineas 259 W A 55 97 306 334 W G 326 329
GREENMAN, Silas 291
GREER, J W 124
GREGG, Cassie R 132 Eliza J 132 Harmon 75-76 79 134 180 183-184 189 347 522 Harmon Sr 182 Mr 523
GREGORY, John 295
GRESHAM, Jesse 276
GRESSOM, Wm 120
GREY, Jackson 253
GRIDER, Minister 389 Tobias 89 304 341 345 385-386 390 524
GRIDLEY, C 125 Mr 291
GRIFFIN, Clara B 104 Eleazer 128 J L 257 W A 280 William

GRIFFIN (cont) 60 Wm 209
GRIFFITH, Abner 197 G W 96
GRIM, Alfred 259
GRIMES, John M 350 N B 360
GRISSOM, Jesse 435 William 74 84 111 Wm 204-205 207 209
GROGAN, Spencer 270
GRONER, W H 311
GROSS, J P 307
GROVE, Adam 324 Garrison 231
GROVES, Adam J 371 Alzada 219 Cardace 309 H M 310 J 381 Jacob 309 Sarah 253 W G 383 W M 326 524
GRUBB, Lovena C 112
GRUBBS, Thomas 224
GRUBLE, Chester 380
GRUM, Jacob 244
GUEST, Thomas 228
GUILFORD, W M 267
GUNN, H H 413 567 John I 175 524
GUNZENHAUSER, John 241
GUTHERIE, Dora 104
GUTHRIE, Fred 333
HACKER, Mr 348
HACKLEY, G W 370 George W 369 Margaret 369
HADAWAY, L 183 189
HAGERTY, A R 111
HAGIN, F E 53 449 Fred 297

HAGIN (cont)
  Fred E 55 188 254
HAINLINE, 265 Caleb 397 525
HALBIG, Mary E 421
HALE, A M 56 278 309 Anna M 104 454 Anna May 103 Lola V 104 Steven 214
HALE-BABCOCK, Clara Celestia 464
HALEY, Elizabeth 423 Henry E 423 J J 666 Jno G 245 John G 423 William A 132
HALL, 362 Ambrose 176 267 478 B F 240 Claiborn 514 Darius 176 Father 477 Geo F 166 George F 304 448 524 667 J C 269 430 J C T 191-192 525 James 324 John 136 John P 398 Jonathan 525 Joseph 176 195 Mahlon 176 Mr 305 525 Old Mother 477 Thomas A 254 William 193
HALLAM, S K 55 79 278 356
HAMILTON, Geo 349 George 300 Hugh 169 John 339 Lewis 339 Sarah 169 Wm 410
HAMMER, 349 Eliza 348
HAMMOND, Mollie 427
HAMS, Stephen 231
HANCOCK, M J 256 Milan Z 256
HANEY, 347
HANGER, L P 276

HANKS, Dennis 484 Rebecca 303
HANSFORD, Dr 244
HANSON, Uriah 288 William 288
HAPPY, Minister 89 Mr 527 Mrs 104 W W 72 102 128 304 329 339 385 526 560 609 620 W W Jr 338 W W Sr 338 William W Jr 61 William W Sr 61
HARBER, 577 D P 447 David 450 M A 447 Martha 450
HARBERT, Samuel 270
HARBORD, 298
HARDEN, J M 180
HARDIN, J H 50 102 Mr 51 Mrs 120
HARDING, Ralph 168 Ruth 128 W H 97 301
HARDMAN, Henry 394
HARGIS, A O 136
HARGOT, Guy 155
HARKER, J N 56
HARLAN, Asa 209 D J 301 George 209 Levi 384
HARLAND, L D 436
HARLIS, E M 97 287 338
HARLOW, Thomas 332 W E 144
HARMON, Emma 226 W S 299
HARPER, Anna 372 Ellen 197
HARPOLE, J D 360
HARRELL, A J 194 H A 314 H H 387

HARRINGTON, L S 55 Leander 434
HARRIS, Ann 151 D K 360 E F 228 G J 211 J E 55 526 J J 96-97 202 353-354 526 John 209 Z A 431 Zacharia 191
HARRISON, E C 343 Polly 438
HARROLD, Elizabeth 303 Landy 303
HART, E J 55 392 Emily 306 John A 306
HARTFORD, Morgan 205
HARTLEY, E E 182 251 William 187
HARVEY, 312 A G 369 Capt 311 Mary A 369
HARWARD, H G 56
HASSON, Celinda 208 Henry C 208 T N 203
HATCH, Mr 215 William 112
HATCHET, Levi 115
HATCHETT, Levi 279 Levy 424 Livy 114 242
HATFIELD, 336 George 273
HATHAWAY, Emma 604 Mary A 226
HATTEN, A F 319 Mary 319
HAUGHEY, Chas I 251 J M 321 527
HAULMAN, L C 346
HAWES, Esther A 272 J P 267 Peter 269 Sarah 272
HAWK, 656 M B 104 Robert

HAWK (cont)
Moffett Allison 528 William 124
HAWKINS, E L 407 Louisa 312 Mrs 119 Orville 237
HAWKS, Elizabeth 285
HAWLEY, James M 315 R M 80 Samuel 315
HAY, D G 435 Daniel 434 Mary 378 Milton 378 S R 109-110 Samuel R 434
HAYDEN, A S 448 B H 157 Billy 570 M P 200 278 Morgan P 528 W H 56 228 W L 248 William 452 569 Wm 444 609
HAYES, Jennie 306 John 25
HAYNES, Frank 104 J F 308 N S 55 94 102 130 157 174 181 186 204 233 298 304 351-352 439 448 453 459 534 544 617 667
HAYS, Amos 540 Mary 122
HAYWARD, H A 419
HAZELTON, Gervaise 416
HEADINGTON, Joel 61
HEAP, Lysias 63 Ulysses 25
HEAPE, Abraham 354 Cyrus 442 Lysias 352-354 365 528 Minister 235
HEATON, Joseph 405 Wm 211
HECKEL, C A 55 266 299 325 Emma 299
HEDENBERG, Peter 88
HEDENBURG, Peter 609

HEDGES, Geo F 407 Jobe 402 Lillian Boyer 651 Lillie Bowyer 356 Lillie Boyer 53
HEDRICK, David 143 L R 138
HEICKE, Rudolph 405
HELM, T M 381
HENDERSON, D M 309 D P 35 88 118 152 334 338-339 385 448 514 529 560 609 663 D Pat 127 Hickman 170 J P 309 John 309 Maxie Z 309 Mr 82 153 Mrs 109 Nancy 105 S M 337 W C 332 Wm 235
HENDINGTON, Joel 337
HENDRICKS, 362 John 345 John Jr 345 Polly A 345 Synthia 345
HENDRICKSON, John 209 221
HENDRYX, W B 152
HENRY, A W 56 Alonzo 177 B W 90-91 345-346 385 387-388 390 514 Bushrod W 28 72 90-92 147 304 341 391 529 531 539 600 630 J O 29 199 316 342 347 389 530 James O 531 John D 452 Lillian 357 Patrick 20 R B 142 R E 320 Robert E 215 Rolla B 314 531 Thomas 393 VIII 14 W B 29 W S 120
HENSON, Gillum 146
HENTHORN, Henry 432
HERLOCKER, Josiah 280

HERMAN, J 224 Lillie 224 R Lena 224
HERNDON, Benjamin 396 Nancy 396
HERRICK, H N 167
HESS, G M 111 T M 131-134
HESTER, J G 106 Jane 319
HEWETT, Josephus 88
HEWITT, James H 409 Josephus 337 378 609 Mary 358
HIBBS, Hannah D 447 John 445 447
HIBNER, A A 66
HICK, R W 259
HICKERSON, M W 197 Michael 199
HICKMAN, Smith 226
HICKS, 362 J L 357 Minister 86
HIERONYMUS, 265 267 B R 379 397 402 Enoch 396 J P 99 James 272 Jasper 290 President 54 R E 55 269 Robert E 52
HIETT, J W 56 Joseph 402 Josephus 29 William 402
HIGBY, 349 Evalline 378 Lemuel 378
HIGDON, Elmer 201 Ernest 201
HIGGENS, William 450
HIGGINBOTHAM, N F 90
HIGGINS, Barlow 195-196 H J 286 John 420 Ranson 416
HIGGS, J J 159

HIGHT, J F 85-87 238 240
HILL, D B 88 Daniel B 378
 Emely 400 Henry 263 Isaac
 313 J D 172 Jane 336 John 438
 John Sr 313 L D 97 Lew D 56
 212 651 Nehemiah 400
 Roscoe 53 401 S C 85 313
 Thomas 420 W C 311 313
 William 420 William C 312
 532 Wm 433
HILLIARD, Elder 85
HILLIS, L E 61 William D 61
HILMAN, John 408
HIMES, Charles 394 Emiline 394
 Ezra 394 Laura 394 Tyrus
 394
HIMMOND, Maggie 446
HINDLE, Henry 222
HINDS, Andrew 532 578
HINES, E F 407 H 189
HINSHAW, Jehu 293 Martha
 298
HIPSLEY, Caleb 280
HITCH, Allen 278
HITE, J H 392
HITT, R R 578
HITTLE, Geo 400 Mary 400
 Michael 27 265 399-400
 Nancy 400 Strother 266
HOAGLAND, George 97 296 M
 C 332 Martin 128
HOBB, David 384
HOBBS, A I 102 286 346

HOBBS (cont)
 Charlotte 114 David 114 221
 361 385 532 Elizabeth 114
 Nicholas 114 361 Richard
 189
HOBLIT, Merritt 268
HODGE, John 235 John H 92
 John M 91 Nellie F 236
HODGEN, Jacob 361-362 533
HODGES, Hezekiah 365
HODSON, Miles J 297
HOFFMAN, G M 96
HOG, S R 63
HOGE, Perry 259
HOGUE, S E 204
HOLDEN, Hannah 357 W M
 357
HOLLAND, James 245 Mary
 497 William Sr 403 Wm 406
HOLLIER, C C 136 299
HOLLINGSWORTH, J F 131
HOLLINGWORTH, J H 132
HOLLIS, C P 205
HOLLOMAN, T J 56 365
HOLLOWAY, Minister 262
HOLMAN, Mrs 535 Sarah A 534
 Thomas 199
HOLMES, Cailsta 362 Harry 430
 J B 435
HOLT, Almyria 368 S A 364
 William 190 535 Wm 188
HOLTON, Brother 537 James
 226 Mr 294 536 661 Sally E

HOLTON (cont)
    536 T T 102 175-176 267 269 273 276 293 379 402 477 529 550 593 660 Thomas Tilghman 535 William 535
HONDLEY, R L 163
HONEY, J W 231 233 J W Sr 231
HONN, A A 149-150 A C 149 D W 56 96 Daniel K 149 Isaac 149 John D 149 Joseph 149
HONORE, Henry 152
HOOE, L H 181
HOOTON, Ann 221 Wm H 221
HOOVER, 261 Cordelia Davis 139 Guy 155 163 Mrs 560
HOPKINS, Dr 438 Finley 226 J W 207 209 John 198 John W 203 205 Milton 346 Samuel 355 W W 279
HOPPER, W B 196 346 William 426
HOPSON, W H 152 240
HOPWOOD, 261 Josephus 60
HORN, Henry 275
HORNBECK, Alice 126
HORNER, J M 55
HORTON, Margaret 209 W M 203
HOSTELLER, J H 134
HOSTETLER, 538 Christie 343 Clinton 347 Joseph 31 303-304 340 344 355 523 537 552 628 Mr 539 Solomon 340 344

HOSTETTER, Carrie 74
HOTALING, L R 55 Lewis R 260 M 260
HOTCHKISS, Mr 260
HOUGH, J 357 W T 215
HOUGHAM, C D 56 251 284 449
HOUSER, Jefferson 76
HOUSTON, 260 639 E I L 400 J Q A 174 176 249 320 Jefferson 259 261 298 627 Jefferson P 541 John 92 259 261 291 540 627 John Quincy A 541 Minister 262 Mr 541 R F 400 W J 93 Washington 73 259 261 263 298 627 Washington J 541
HOWARD, John 258 John S 541 Martha 245 Mr 207 Panner 258 Stephen 245 William 203 206 William A 542 Wm 209 Wm A 205
HOWE, Catherine 122 D J 56 439 D R 115 123 348 351 364 379 Daniel 349 Daniel R 122 Daniel Radcliffe 540 Henry 124 349 395 438 James 540 James W 122 John 122 W J 153
HOWELL, John 347 John T 344 R E 56 Thomas 237
HOWERTON, Elizabeth 112 James R 112

HOWS, P A 119
HOWSER, Elizabeth 273 Jefferson 267
HOYT, S A 261
HUBARD, H H 106
HUBBARD, Abner 413
HUBBELL, F M 177
HUDSON, Charles J 107 J J 442
HUELIN, Richard 318
HUFF, A L 55 398 A Leroy 313 Bessie 313 Geo J 411 L G 119 Lewie G 55 Oscar 410
HUFFCULT, J L 194
HUFFMAN, Ella Myers 104
HUGGINS, Robert 85
HUGHES, D E 96 205-206 382-383 422 427 D I 328 D T 325 327 Elizabeth 216 327 G W 275 H D 327 J H 114 209-210 James 383 John 76 80 83 211 302 304 M M 275 Margaret 327 Martha 325 Minister 383 Thompson 327 Tomsey 327 William 216
HUGHEY, G W 79 323 George W 76
HULETT, G A 379
HULL, Charles E 542 John D 164 William C 163
HUME, Squire 185
HUMPHREY, Benjamin N 89 Inez 308 S C 276 W A 56 102 304 452
HUNDLEY, James 366
HUNSAKER, Elizabeth 112
HUNT, Amiel 306 J T 192 Mary 192 306 Nancy J 192
HUNTER, A J 188-189 Andrew J 542 James 137 John 189 Mr 543 William 137
HURST, George 168 Nancy O 169 Sarah 197
HURT, Lewis 224 Lewis A 53
HURTLY, William 187
HUSBAND, David 56 230 325 354 364-365 454 Herman 364-365 Mr 231
HUSS, 15
HUSTON, 277 Joseph 291
HYATT, James 346
IDLEMAN, Finis 198 331 344 Finis S 55 James 198
ILES, Elijah 587
IMES, Ellen 418
INFIELD, Mr 156
ING, O C 215
INGERSOLL, 666 G W 170 Robert G 482
INGLE, M M 325
INGLES, Libbie F 60 M 389 Marion 60
INGRAHAM, Daniel 143 Dorman 143 M F 294 Philo 143 William 142-143 Williard F 143 Wm 231
INGRAM, Evangelist 422 J W

INGRAM (cont)
  165 Philo 416 W A 96-97 202
  230 233 W H 201
INMAN, Emma 402
INNES, George 602
INSKIPP, Sarah T 192 W A 192
IRELAND, Eliza 122 Harrison T
  543 John 122 Lou 402 Sarah
  571
IRWIN, John 176 Rochester 252
  259-260 262 452 651
ISAACS, Elijah 121
ISRAEL, Earl 237
IVES, O C 179
JACKMAN, Allen R 415
JACKSON, 657 Catharine 400
  Jesse E 400 W H 387
JACOBS, Fred 186 J T 548 Joel
  213 John 372 Martha A 213
  W W 190
JAMES, Leah 387 Stephen 319
  William B 319
JAMESON, Love H 151 187 550
  597 M 244 Sarah 244
JAMISON, W F 83
JEAKIM, John 410
JEFFERSON, S M 56 286
  Thomas 20
JEFFRIES, E J 310
JEFFS, Samuel 198
JENKINS, J G 179
JENNER, H H 55 250 260 262
  380 452

JENNETTE, Mr 266
JERMANE, W S 211
JEROME, Of Prague 15
JETT, A B 18
JEWELL, W R 81 407
JEWETT, 388 Eunice 65 J E 56
  200 269 276 295 297 402 447
  James E 543
JINNETT, W R 267
JOHANN, Carl 48 Cora 357
JOHNSON, 298 349 362 A L 436-
  437 Alexander 276 424 647
  Arthur 436-437 545 B W 42-
  43 56 162 276 403 448 493 561
  604 665 Barbary 272 Barton
  W 153 Betsy 402 Comfort
  436 Elizabeth 402 G T 349
  Hale 233 544 Huston 237 J B
  56 403 436 561 John 403 436-
  437 561 657 John B 544 John
  T 613 Lucy 436 Luranah 436-
  437 Martha 403 Martin 436
  Melinda 272 Mr 545 619 N H
  276 Polly 436 President 528
  R H 42 56 403 448 561 Robert
  256 420 Silas 225 T J 132 W
  H 434 437 656 W W 177
  William H 545 Wm 397
JOHNSTON, Alexander 209 307
  326 Geo F 349 J E 624 Susan
  A 565
JONES, 336 A P 444 Abner 20-21
  Belle 150 Charles W 614 D

JONES (cont)
   300 E 249 E R 275 Edgar D
   286 Eleanor R 450 F B 269
   305 Gilbert 97 257 277 369
   443 H A 332 H B 150 J 454 J F
   96 J Fred 86 96 249 297 321
   368 441 553 J T 91 James 450
   John 365 John T 35-36 88 102
   320 337 385 448-449 546 609
   614 Joshua 450 M 329 Mace
   150 Martha 420 Mary 226
   577 Minister 401 Mr 99 N A
   307 P W 353 R G 452 S S 96
   113 123 130 133-134 407-409
   546 Sarah V 450 Silas 55 102
   449 Sue E 35 T C 450 W 381
   W F 381
JORDAN, Andrew 200 John 324 Mr 200 O F 55 107 159 444 460
JORDON, E A 547 Ida K 651 J L 339 Mary S 339 Mr 548 O F 395 651
JOSLYN, J H 159
JUDY, 265 Christena 266 Col 326 329 582 Frances 253 Hopkins C 276 J I 321 549 J W 82 100 326 549 605 657 Jacob 266-267 548 John 266 Kate A S 550 Mr 549-550 Richard 253
JUMPS, Samuel 415
JUSTIS, James 179
KABLE, Anna 309

KAHNEY, H J 224
KAISER, Lou Deweese 105
KANE, 485 A J 37 73 92 128-129 176 209 264 278-279 302 304 337 339 346 371 373-378 381 459 512 514 565 648-649 Andrew J 61 550 Caroline Beers 378 Charles P 379 Morrison 550 Mr 551
KARNES, S S 369
KARNS, John 244
KARR, H N 200 J W 664
KAUFMAN, Howard 297
KEARNEY, O A 156 Sarah 435
KEEDY, Charles 348 Jacob 348 Susan 348 Vallee 348
KEELER, Abigail 152 W P 106-107
KEEN, Daniel 23 418 Ira 417 Polly 418 W H 432 Wylie H 428
KELL, James 236
KELLAR, A 91 A H 340 344 346 A L 346 392 551-552 E H 346 552 H G 346 H Y 195 344 346-347 552 Henry Y 90-91 J W 332 James H 90 William 90
KELLER, A L 304 E H 56 H Y 66 258 342 T J 363
KELLEY, 666 E S 85 Louise 554
KELLO, Barton W 437 Isaac 437
KELLOGG, H G 234

KELLUM, John W 171
KELLY, Chatter 389 John S 222 Mr 123 W C 392
KELSEY, J W 426
KENDRICK, George 118
KENNEDY, E R 468 G L 182 Geo S 348 K P 166 Laura 348
KENNER, Alvin 142 190 America 430 B W 436 J M 430
KENT, W H 333
KENYON, G R 159 Mary E 159
KERANS, E F 189 Ross 189
KERN, W H 55
KERNS, W H 361
KERR, W H 414
KERSEY, J M 350-351
KEUSSEFF, Basil S 165
KIGHT, Mary 405
KILBORN, J W 102 346 452 L S 294
KILLAM, Eleanor 387 Ellen 387 Isaac Sr 387 John 242 Lydia 387 Nathan 387 Samuel 387 William 387
KILLION, Jane 325 Paulina 325
KIMBALL, Mr 363
KIMBEL, Lydia E 418
KIMMELL, William 253
KIMMONS, Elizabeth 112 Ira 112 Rebecca 112 Samuel 112 Susanah 112
KINCAID, D L 85 383 Mr 329

KINDIG, B G 451
KINDRED, C G 56 158 165 362 W H 55 97 269
KING, 577 Dr 248 Elizabeth 447 Emma 377 M P 394 R P 430 T 373 William B 657
KINGSBURY, Mary 440 651
KINGSLEY, Bishop 621
KINKADE, William 255
KINNAMAN, Henry 141-142 Samuel 141 Walter 141 Wm 141
KINNER, James 192
KIRK, James 55 103 M K 216
KIRKHAM, F M 162 666
KIRKPATRIC, Wm G 203
KIRKPATRICK, John 24 574 Rosa 231
KISER, Henry 286
KITCHEN, W G 56
KLINE, Ellen 270 Nancy 270 R H 96 Walter 111
KNAPP, C H 159 Nathan M 61 552
KNEE, Jacob 408
KNIGH, Henry 125
KNIGHT, Alonzo 411 Ellen 411 Hosea 411 J W 383 James W 290 James Worcester 553 Jay W 131 M H 288 290 293 Moses H 283 553 Samuel 176 266 269 Sarah 411 Warren 411

KNOWLES, Mariah E 418
KNOX, A R 74 100 247-248 553
   Emma 248 H O 222 James K
   278 Jane 248 John 15 Lottie
   248 Mary 248 Mr 554
   Newton 248 R C 159
KOHL, W F 348 449
KROELL, Grandma 321
KUYKENDALL, H C 170
LACOCK, Bertha 53 N O 293
LAIN, M G 80
LAIR, James M 306 Rosetta A 306
LAKE, John S 373 Maria 394 William 394
LAMAR, 326
LAMASTERS, Emma 172
LAMB, I J 188 Isaac 188
LAMBERT, John 291 Nancy 291
LAMKIN, James H 213 Sally 213 W C 213
LAMONTE, O W 114
LAMOTT, Joseph 254
LAMPHEAR, J W 286
LAMPHERE, Sarah 42
LAMPLUGH, B C 346
LAMPTON, E J 94 96 120 214 216 220-222 447 554
LANAIGER, John 180
LANCASTER, Hannah 266 J P 304 Jerry 337 Joseph 266
LANDES, W 224
LANDIS, Nathaniel 438 Samuel

LANDIS (cont) 438
LANE, Catherine 203 Timps 178
LANGLEY, R P 138
LANGSTON, Jachoniah 372 Nancy 372
LANTERMAN, David 253
LAPPIN, J C 56 204 266 431 John C 555 Robinson 432 S S 56 97 204 267 297 320 431 452 554 W O 55 249 431 William O 555
LARABEE, A 106-107 155-156 160-161 165 167
LARD, Moses E 240
LARIMORE, John 330
LARSON, A F 291 August F 204
LASLIE, Mrs 215
LATHAM, H C 379 Henry C 93 555-556 650 James 555 Richard 378 555 649
LATHERMAN, R 65
LATHROP, Erastus 366 418 J 166
LATIMER, John 242
LATIMORE, Eliza 242 Phoebe 242
LAUGHLIN, A J 162 G H 60 Mr 120
LAVAN, 231
LAVELY, William 92 378
LAW, Alfred P 168
LAWLEY, F M 87

LAWRENCE, Evangelist 331 Grandma 443 Nellie 204 O W 102 114 367
LAWRENCE-BROWN, Kate 286
LAWSON, E L 224
LAYMAN, A C 85
LAYTON, H F 156 J D 345 Mr 109
LEAKE, J F 84
LEATHERMAN, Cyrus 228 293
LEATON, James 68
LEBETTER, Louis 390
LEDBRETTER, W J 342
LEDGERWOOD, H D 56 288 291 Minister 262
LEE, 528 J M 433 James E 213-214 Mary Ann 467 R T 215
LEEK, J F 278
LEEPER, James 339
LEFFINGWELL, S W 454
LEHMAN, L O 55 200 262 440 Louis O 321
LEIGH, A J 116
LEITCHMAN, Abner 182
LEMERT, E M 117
LEMMON, John 290 376 380 556
LEMON, C A 163 John 239 Josephus 239
LENNELL, W W 342
LEONARD, Celestus 194 David 194 Louisa 194 Paschal C 194 S W 233 Silas White 556 Talitha 194

LESCH, L 224 Lattie 224
LESSIG, Ray S 56
LESTER, Amelia 253 J N 56 407 James 381
LEVERING, Joseph 545
LEWIS, C W 72 Daniel 235 Elizabeth 420 H V 253 Minister 128 Nancy 299 420 S R 172 358
LEY, Wm 251
LICHTENBERGER, Charles 430 Dr 152 J P 55 204 299 325 Jane 430
LIDDELL, 83
LIEURANCE, Robert 278
LILE, Wm 365
LILLARD, J T 286
LILLY, 341 E L 345
LINCOLN, Abraham 30 263 467-468 479 484 488 521 587 598 609 Edward Baker 467 Mr 520 Nancy 521 President 42 463 573 Thomas 521
LINDENMEYER, T A 159 T H 253
LINDLY, Cicero J 116 557
LINDSAY, Alfred Sr 176 Catherine 379 David A 277 David Sr 298 J A 89 J C 106 James A 285 320 Jas A 91-92 John 36-37 39 72-73 94 239 267 283 297-298 320-321 446-447 451 M M 104 Mrs 379

LINDSAY (cont)
    William 399
LINDSEY, Alfred 400 476 D A
    275 David 400 Delila 400
    Elizabeth 400 James A 266
    272 396 398-400 557-558 615
    Jane 400 Jas 400 Jas A 582
    John 266 273 351 400-401 558
    665 Mariah 400 Minister 401
    Mr 249 559 S B 342 Wm 400
LINES, I R 165 Jane I 192
LINN, L M 96 328-329 331 334
    365 386 389
LIPPENCOTT, Gen 518
LITTLETON, H C 85-86 127 204
    383 606 Henry C 559
LIVINGS, A G 140 Catherine
    140
LLOYD, Eliza 270 W R 286
LOAR, John 105 Minister 262
LOBINGIER, Henry Schell 153
LOCKE, James 291 Ursley 291
LODGE, John M 245
LOGAN, America T 378 Daniel
    96 427-428 Daniel Jr 431
    Evangelist 376 G W 342 J B
    73 John A 466 528 647 Mary
    378 Stephen T 378
LOLLAR, F M 143 232 559 G M
    143 G W 234
LOMAX, S 363 Taylor 242
LONDON, David 260
LONG, 577 Anna 348 Anthony

LONG (cont)
    410 C N 294 Elias A 167
    Fannie 348 Florence V 348
    Mr 123 R A 458 Samuel 211
    Sarah 211 Susan 348 Uriah
    278 W N 138
LOOKABILL, H R 226
LOOMIS, A A 390
LOOS, C L 448 616 Charles
    Louis 41 285
LORANCE, Wm 207
LORD, M N 151 240 Mr 152
LORMAN, Emma Veatch 60
LORTON, Mr 119
LOTT, J B 200 O H 200
LOUCKS, W G 18
LOUIS, Mary 222
LOVELY, W 394
LOVINGS, Frank 344 John 344
LOVINS, A A 386
LOWE, Elmer 114 Joseph 111
    114 266-267 273 294 Samuel
    129 175 200 266-267 273 279
    294 297 356 William 114
LOWELL, Mr 308
LOWERY, Henry 331
LOYD, J W 392
LUCAS, 327 A G 120 209 D R 79
    82 120 326 359 J R 148 346
    John 224 Minister 329 367
    Mr 83 P 620
LUCCOCK, J B 73 John 178 294
    John B 72

LUCY, George W 424
LUDLOW, J D 132
LUMB, Martha 436
LUMBECK, John 268
LUMM, Fenton 437 559 Fentore 428 Jonas 428 560
LUSE, Joseph 142
LUTHER, 14-15 Martin 13 Willard T 433
LUTTRIL, Jackson 446
LYMAN, J D 300
LYNN, J E 102 379-380
LYON, Clyde 383 395 Clyde L 55 D J 263 O L 287
LYTLE, D A 97 J 134
LYTTLE, Miss 115
MABLE, H C 116
MACCLINTOCK, W D 160
MACE, Isaac W 150
MACKNET, Rhoda 306
MACY, Johnathan 449
MADDEN, D W 56 286
MADISON, John 221 Rebecca 221 W D 56 William 158
MAGARITY, Rhoda J 450 Sarah C 450 William S 450
MAGEE, Ivan W 267
MAHAN, Elizabeth A 305 Sarah 305 Thomas 305-306
MAHON, P G 308
MAIN, Andrew 359
MAJOR, Ben 34-36 448 503 563 592 655 657 Elizabeth 285 Jo

MAJOR (cont)
563 John 285 Judith H 285 L S 151-152 156 Minister 401 W T 88 William T 62 285 657 William Trabue 564 Wm T 91-92 571
MALLORY, Dr 371 Susan A 565 W A 92 300 328 374-377 665 William A 565 William C 61
MALOAN, W A 102
MALONE, Alfred C 168 Eliza 112 Isaac 398 Mr 364 Nancy A 112 W A 278
MALTMAN, H L 296 383
MANFORD, Minister 79
MANIRE, B F 110
MANLEY, A P 418
MANN, Horace 33 45 Malinda 192
MANNING, R S 249
MANSFIELD, 336
MAPES, G W 123 217 279 Geo W 122 George Watson 566 Samuel 130 133-134 Wm 413
MARION, Francis 232
MARKHAM, James 331 Maria 331 Nancy 331
MARKLE, 601 A B 260 Minister 262
MARLAN, Jonah 435 Naomi 435
MARLATT, Peter 405
MARLOW, C W 55 141 144 297

MARLOW (cont)
354 T J 385
MARR, Jessie 159
MARROW, Byron 427
MARSH, Clark 55 Clark H 425 Wesley 248
MARSHALL, Israel 242 Israel M 245
MARSTON, C C 79
MARTIN, 261 567 A 316-317 Betsy 319 Elizabeth 249 Evangelist 422 Geo W 566 Isaac 176 J E 241 J H 413-414 J L 413 J M 60 278 James 319-320 John 133 Levina 26 M J 346 Margaret 280 Mary 319 Minister 412 Mr 123 568 P 249 Parley 407 Presley 185 R M 132 413-414 Rolla 133 Rolla M 134 201 409 411 499 566 Walter 133
MARVIN, Universalist 327
MASHER, F M 159
MASLAN, James A 428
MASON, 267 388 David 473 Henry 438 J C 110 332 James 438 Jane 227 John 227 Thomas 214
MASSIE, Betsey 218
MASTERS, J E 310
MATHERS, J F 409
MATHES, J 355 J C 148 355 J M 193 John C 354-355 Ruth J

MATHES (cont)
355 W R 360 William 346
MATHEWS, H B 451 Richard 155
MATHIS, Caleb 259 G W 259
MATLOCK, T J 114
MATTHEWS, Luther 439
MATTHEWS-GREIDLY, Carrie 439
MATTS, Alonzo 325
MAUPIN, B F 138 W T 44 56 94 139
MAVITY, H S 269 J H 413 Thos W 55
MAXWELL, Alethee 319 Father 285 Israel 242 R C 276 Samuel E 259 William 242 319
MAYFIELD, J B 190 351 James M 216
MAYNARD, C H 360
MCALISTER, Robert 150
MCBEAN, John L 55 Mr 157
MCBETH, 601
MCBRAIN, John E 236
MCBRIAN, J C 235
MCCALL, R R 239-240
MCCANCE, David 394-395
MCCARTHY, James 312 Jane 312
MCCARTNEY, Ewing 210 J F 66 323 M N 67
MCCARY, William 198

MCCASH, Albert 173 Andrew 173 I N 173 301 I S 171 173 Isaac 386 Levi 173
MCCAULY, Mr 109
MCCLANE, E T 418
MCCLARY, Elizabeth M 418 John G 418 Mr 418
MCCLEARY, J B 259
MCCLEAVE, J W 254
MCCLENNAHAN, Elijah 395
MCCLINTOCK, W H 360
MCCLURE, Elizabeth 218 J 377 J S 216 James 215 218 403 M J 86 Mary 403 Mr 220
MCCLURE-SMITH, Hattie 218
MCCOLLEY, G W 263 W G 295 392
MCCOLLOUGH, J H 115
MCCOLLUM, 561 A 89 Alex 139 Alexander 560
MCCONNELL, James 226 Turlie 405 W T 56 325 356
MCCORCLE, Eliza 403 Isabel 403 Richard B 403
MCCORD, 445
MCCORKLE, J B 128 209 260-261 450 John Byram 561 Minister 451 Richard B 561
MCCORMICK, J H 345
MCCOY, 124 Marie Jackson 413 651 R D 53 55 Sadie 651 Sarah C 96 454
MCCULLOUGH, J H 102-103

MCCULLOUGH (cont) 286
MCCUNE, J L 56 John L 319
MCCUNNE, John L 452
MCCURDY, Mr 364 Mrs 260
MCDANIEL, Asa 160 William 285
MCDANIELS, Jas L 145
MCDERMONT, J M 226
MCDOWELL, Lou 402
MCELROY, G W 56 George 305 S W 333
MCELWAIN, Margaret 122
MCFADDEN, Thrissa 327 William 327
MCFARLAND, M 455
MCGARVEY, J W 59
MCGEE, John 411 Martha 411 Rebecca 411 Samuel 24 186 217 411 William 411
MCGINNIS, Mr 563 W H 349 562
MCGLAUGHLIN, Allen 410 O P 410 Viola 410
MCGREGOR, W K 155
MCGUFFEY, 554
MCGUFFIN, J W 307 John 375 John C 374 John Henry 563
MCGUIRE, Jas 129
MCINTIRE, Minister 336
MCINTYRE, Benjamin 335
MCKAY, J M 159
MCKENSIE, Mrs Dr 294

MCKIBBEN, Harriett 192
MCKINGHT, J P 96
MCKINLEY, President 543
MCKINNEY, Mr 134
MCKINNIE, Maggie 136
MCKINSEY, James 191
MCKNIGHT, J P 55 351
MCLAIN, J R 87
MCLEOUD, Myra Harris 232 651
MCLORD, Evargartine 447 Lucenda 446
MCMAHAN, J C 222
MCMANIS, G G 122 Geo G 121 123 George 595
MCMANUS, Geroge G 563
MCMILLAN, James 78 257 Joseph 222
MCMILLEN, 388 Dr 628 James 253 420 Lydia 420 Paul 237
MCMORRIS, L 90 Lindsay 388
MCMULLIN, John 344
MCNABB, Ann 378 Ebenezer 304
MCNEELEY, James 428
MCNEELY, Bridget E 430 William 430
MCNEMAR, Osceola 229 291
MCNIECE, 257
MCNIGHT, Nancy J 309
MCNITT, Mr 123
MCNUTT, J M 346 Sarah 169 William 84

MCPHERSON, J H 56 James 533 James D 91 John 308 L C 53 Lowell C 55 Mr 120 R P 56 Taylor 519
MCQUARY, Allen 216
MCREE, James 375
MCREYNOLDS, Paul 55
MCSALY, Alma 226
MCVEY, Mr 520 Richard 519
MEACHAM, Albert 143 Hannah 112
MEADE, Gen 501
MEADOWS, Bro J 244 Elijah 242 Fred 112 Henry 244 James 325 Lemuel 242 Melinda 244 Mother 245 Nancy 244 Polly 244 W 245 William 242
MEANS, Mr 25 T K 24
MECOY, John 84 John F 240
MEDBURY, C S 56 154 289 301 375 447
MEEK, Daniel 448 Jane 242 Julia 242 Sarah 242
MEEKS, John 196 199
MELANCTHON, 15
MELISH, Mr 620 T J 619
MELOAN, W A 362 W E 330
MELTON, J R 424
MENGES, Melvin 53 55 297
MERRIFIELD, Fred 163
MERRILL, Bertha 651
MERRIMAN, F A 381
MERRY, H O 276

MERSHON, C M 165
MESNARD, W S 196
METCALF, C H 307 J D 307 568
METZLER, M 134
MEYERS, Daniel 312 L B 208
MILES, J J 174 Nelson A 610
MILLER, 327 Adam 569 Amos 191 Charles H 276 D D 78 169 174 257 262 271 277 325 421 431 D R 82 David 124 569 David D 568 E 348 E J 387 E W 116 Ean 255 Elinor R 400 G A 289 295 349 449 G W 340 Geo A 55 I F 319 Isaac 266 390 J C 357 J D 392 J Fred 392 J J W 211 360 J W 86 111 J Wood 18 Jacob 198-199 James 387 James J W 570 Jeremiah 268 John 56 140 205 242 262 267 351 354 568 Katie 224 Lodusky 306 Mary Ann 319 Mr 83 267 422 570 Roy A 268 Sarah 266 272 Sarah A 268 273 W O 279 Walker 266 Wilford 398 William 265-266
MILLICAN, A A 314
MILLIGAN, Morgan 138 Robert 638
MILLINGER, J H 151
MILLION, Paul E 344
MILLISON, J B 299 301
MILLS, Charles 198 Glen 201

MILLS (cont) Sarah 436
MILNER, Jesse 428
MILTEER, T Wilson 250
MILTON, 572
MINER, Walter 440
MINGES, Susie M 631
MINIER, Bro 274 572 G W 91 266 268 271-273 276 291 297-298 376 396-397 493 598 Geo W 657 George W 37 267 537 540 570 Minister 401 Mr 92 571 Sarah 122 571 T L 360 402
MINTON, 147
MITCHELL, 577 Cyprus R 55 Eliza J 450 Ira 304 397 J Pleasant 450 James 73 174 266 269 291 296 298 397 450 493 Joe J 192 John O 450 Mary 402 Nancy 450 Nancy O 450 P L 368 R J 402 Rodney J 402 Sarah 450 Sophia 402 Susan 450 William 450
MIZE, L S 308
MOBLEY, Mordecai 378 549 573
MOFFETT, 656 Abraham 124 F L 56 Frank L 125 Garner 124-125 Robert 125 348-349 Thomas 124 W R 155
MOFFITT, F L 96
MOLER, Isaac W 150 Jessie 150

MOLER (cont)
　Martha 150
MONAHAN, Enos 209
MONEHAN, John W 316
MONNAHAN, J W 317
MONSER, H E 97 388 440 651
　Harold E 182 295 J W 56 133
　259 267 355
MONTGOMERY, Caroline 103
　Charles 327 Cleva 327
　Hannah 447 Susan 327 Tyra
　103
MOOBERRY, Seville M 398
MOODY, Oliver 53
MOOMAW, Otho 56 Otto C 286
MOONEY, M J 224
MOORE, A B 221 Eli 420 F L 242
　573 Frank L 176 Isaac 307 J
　H 446-447 James 141 Juliett
　446 L B 446 Mary L 446
　Milan 175 Robert 286 292-
　293 Robin 237 S C 354 S G
　111 Sarah 221 Sister 307
MOOTHART, 301
MOREHOUSE, Jacob 387
MOREY, John F 197 Moses D
　197
MORGAN, A J 116 David 232 F
　M 317 427 449 J D 315 386 J
　M 135 346 386 John A 422
　Joseph D 316 L W 267 Moses
　136 Nellie 173
MORLAN, John 428 431

MORPHEW, Ezra 194 Phebe 194
MORRALL, George 193
MORREL, G W 233
MORRELL, G W 366 574 Geo W
　415 421 George 257
MORRIS, J M 243 454 Vera 297
　W G 106
MORRISON, C C 165 379-380
　666 Mary 24 186-187 Mary L
　379 Prussia 109
MORROW, Father 264 William
　176 178 304 Wm 174
MORSE, David 608
MORTON, Joseph 61 S D 197
MOSBARGER, Hannah 355
　Jacob 354-355 Peter 355 W H
　355
MOSELY, John 129 Thomas 129
MOSES, Helen E 149
MOSS, J J 100 240 440 Jasper 349
　R H 358
MOTT, James 324
MOULDS, George 264
MOULDSEA, 261
MOULTON, Levi 403
MOXLEY, John 438
MOYER, James E 420
MOZLEY, Norman Sr 238
MUCKLEY, Wm 209
MULKEY, 385 C F 231 575 D C
　25 Isaac 229 353-354 365 392
　442 576 J M 89 312 J N 212
　353-354 John 24 John M 25

MULKEY (cont)
202 574-575 John N 188 John Newton 575 John Sr 25 Jonathan H 25 574 Minister 235 Newton 442 Philip 24 513 575 William F 574
MULLIGAN, L M 347
MULLIKIN, E M 148
MULLIN, Abram 250 David 250
MULLINS, G G 109 George G 161 Harvey 256-257 Mr 162
MUNN, L L 402
MUNNELL, Samuel 406 Thomas 66 219 459
MUNROE, William 355
MUNSON, B 203
MURDOCK, Frank 437
MURPHY, Bedford 278 Chas P 251 Elizabeth 244 Frances 423 Henry 241 Irene 244 Isaac 242 424 J E 241 John E 92 241-242 244 394 423 426 Joseph 424 Joseph E 426 Mr 115 Nancy 245 P H 91 242 P J 242 Patrick 114 278 Patrick H 58 241 424 576 President 59 Seth C 244-245 William 245
MUSGROVE, Joel 169
MUSICK, Fielding 275 Henry 274 Robert 266 272
MYERS, A M 34 E B 34 Elias B 40 J C 405-406 410 414 667

MYERS (cont)
Jonas 221 L B 96 126 Margaret 221 Uphema 221
NANCE, A G 326 A J 385 Clement D 438 Clement Sr 576-577 591 David 438 Geo W 298 440 George W 667 Hyram 394 J D 440 Mary 577 Mary A 450 Mr 577 Robert 450 Ruth 438
NAPOLEON, 151
NARAMORE, M O 159 Milton O 106-107 W P 395 577 657
NAY, Bruce 189 D W 189 Ezra 189 Roley 55 189 S W 189
NAYLOR, Alexander 129
NEAL, Archie 377
NEGRO, Bro Richard 424 Sister Polly 424
NELSON, W E 74 461 551 William 579 William E 578
NETHERCUTT, M W 97
NETZ, 349
NEVILLE, Belle 132 J H 39 John H 38 Professor 37 40
NEVINS, J H 333 Mr 259
NEW, John B 493 John C 188 597
NEWCOMB, H O 43 Joseph Sr 296
NEWELL, Mr 263
NEWKIRK, James 402
NEWMAN, David 405 William 150

NEWNAN, C B 96 382
NEWPORT, R U 71
NEWTON, R H 55 267 295 Robert H 395
NICHOLS, Albert 266 276 Burden 237 Fred S 55 368 J D 369 L T 85 Maggie 159 Roland A 162
NICHOLSON, B T 407 Robert 359
NICKS, Quinton 193
NIFING, Jack 306
NILES, Mary 192 Thomas 192
NOBLE, 301
NORRIS, Romelia 252-253 Wm 449
NORTH, Catherine 403 Ruful 403
NORTHCUT, A D 89
NORTHCUTT, A D 135-136 138-139 299 303-304 334 375 391 Andrew D 580 Jeremiah 580 Mr 137 300 581
NORTON, E M 97 406 408 414 Eldon 405 J H 165 John 405 Minister 376
NUTTY, Samuel 398
O'BANNON, Matilda 332 Matilda Dorsey 311
O'CONNOR, T J 18
O'HAIR, W S 184
O'KANE, John 187 193 329 351 550 597

O'KELLEY, James 20
O'NEAL, Elizabeth 447
OATMAN, Adolphus G 450 Clement 447 Eliza 447 Hardin 447 James R 450 Jesse 447 John 31 395 447 577 Joseph 447 Letitia A 450 Mr 448 Nancy 447
OBOLD, Henry 421
ODELL, J B 435 Joseph 430 Samuel 198 T G 111
ODLE, Charlotte 213 John 213
OGDEN, Deborah 170
OGLE, J 363 J T 55 261 Josephus 329
OGLESBY, 601 Judith 303 Richard J 29 303 531
OLIVE, Miss 388 Sadie 651 William 310
OLIVER, John 405
OLLOMON, Peter 235
OMER, Ivan 111 R A 114 306
ORAHOOD, Orren 405 Roby 291
ORANGE, Daniel 190 Elizabeth 190 Elizabeth S 190 John B 190
ORENDORFF, Malinda 281 Thomas 281
ORGAN, C L 56 252 Ermess 430 James T 430 Sitzina 213
ORR, E A 106 Robert 177 W E 159

ORVIS, Minister 77
OSBORN, Elijah 331 Eliza 331 H W 88 91 Harrison 129 371 Harrison W 29 92 James 331 Mary 331 Minister 376 William 331
OSBORNE, Charles L 136 H W 340 Harrison 327 Harrison W 337 581 L C 412 Uncle Harrison 582
OSBURN, C E 369
OTT, E A 165 248
OVERBAUGH, F C 344
OVERMAN, William 299
OVIATT, O Q 55
OWEN, Elizabeth 319 Geoge 276 George 174 George Carroll 582 J W 298 John 297 327 Nathan 319 Robert 69 W D 83 153 W T 212
OWENS, George 129 178-179 Greenburg 140 John T 266 Martha 140 Mr 141 R J 169
OXER, Rosa Lee 139
PACE, Harvey T 234 236 Martha E 234
PACKARD, Mary 447
PADEN, Alford 304
PADON, A 663 Alfred 664
PAGE, A N 130 301 396 582 Andrew 321 J J 391 Jackson 343 John 90 Mary A Grove 582 O J 168 322 Oliver J 583

PAINTER, H H 88 Mr 176 Nancy 355
PALMER, C R 159 D H 134 David 221 H D 89 91 102 319 396 571 657 Henry D 88 92 288-289 319 401 489 582-583 John M 514 Minister 401 583 Mr 584 Patsey 319 Potter 153 Susan 221
PARK, Jonathan 296-298 Myrtle 651
PARKE, Lucy W 450 Mary 450 Myrtle B 55 289
PARKER, B E 585 Flora 369 I A J 239 364 369 584 J E 97 266 329 364 585 J F M 121 364 James R 172 John F M 585 L G 585 Lesly 364 Lucie M 227 Mr 585 Nancy 228 Patsey 450 W A 585
PARKERSON, Minister 595
PARKINSON, Milton 17
PARKS, Robert 353
PARMENTER, Nancy J 418
PARRICK, John 115
PARROTT, D J 333 W A 333
PARSLEY, Jas C 235
PARSONS, J L 96 153
PARVIN, I L 269 Ira L 55
PASFIELD, George 587 H P 378
PATRICK, 445
PATTEN, Margaret 219
PATTERSON, C H 120 G W 304

PATTERSON (cont)
   Geo A 341 George 401 Kit 134 Levi 345 Minister 117 William 216 Wm 392
PATTON, Daniel 253 J S 385 Minister 127
PAUL, Charles 339
PAYNE, Anna 381 Calvin 270 W C 159
PEARL, Evangelist 422 G W 96 126 184 348-349 440
PEARRE, Caroline Neville 57 102 Mrs 105
PEARSON, E B 53 Earnest 261 J W 358 360
PECCLA, Abner 327 Elizabeth 327 Jane 327
PEELER, Abner 88 176 266 272 476 525 585 Albert 298 Dell 408 Joseph N 327 Minister 401 Mr 586
PEIFER, W H 398
PELLATT, W H 72
PEMBERTON, Charlotte 213 Jesse 213 Joshua 213 Mary C 213 Millie 213 W C 213
PENDER, J T 85
PENDLETON, W K 76
PENNER, Carrie 224
PEPPER, Mr 147 Samuel 147
PERDUE, Edward 245 Jane 245
PERKEY, B F 647 Elder 649 Mr 648

PERKINS, Abijah 226 J W 134 185 188 500
PERRY, James W 263 Lewis C 118 Mr 308 Wm 445
PETERS, Geo L 55 H H 53 55 189 431 457 Polly 270 Pop 134
PETERSON, J C 204
PETTIT, Alford 215 Jonathan 157 Wm 215
PEUGH, C B 438
PHILIPS, F M 314 R M 313
PHILLIPS, F M 444 Joseph 432 L P 346 390 W B 287
PHINNEY, Mr 240
PIATT, Byron 449 Harry 177 John H 177
PICKENS, 238
PICKENS-BUCKNER, Mary 215
PICKERELL, C B 446 J H 300 L B 55 452
PICKERILL, L B 102 586 William S 657
PICKRELL, 376 512 Emma 375 587 J H 378 J Henry 587 Jesse 586 W S 587 William S 586 Wm S 375
PIERCE, C R 324-325 Elijah C 325 G W 325 J E 123 Manda A 325 Nancy 325
PIERSON, Wm 135
PILKINGTON, Wm 413
PILLSBURY, Judge 83

PINE, Minister 411
PINKERTON, B J 448 T W 304
PINNELL, A J 186 Edward 186 W O 587
PIPER, J R 311 John 369-370 Jonathan 362 Laura 309 369
PIPPIN, Leroy 211
PIQUE, R H 86
PIRKEY, A E 200 Oval 59
PIRTLE, Andrew 288 Thomas 288
PIXLEY, 143 Abigail 23 Job 23
PLAIN, Willis 333
PLATT, G E 346
PLEAK, F M 386
PLOWMAN, Lottie 309 Susan 309
PLUMB, Col 248-249
PLUMMER, Hiram S 234 Martha E 234
POE, Felin 141
POGUE, Hiram 387 Rachel 387
POHRER, 349
POLK, Eliza 319 Isaac 319
POLLARD, W D 294
POND, George 112
PONTIUS, M L 262 351
POOL, James 22 416-417 419 516 588
POOLE, C W 225
POOR, W 381
POPE, B F 63 Pleasant 63
PORTER, Alice 463 H G 356 J M

PORTER (cont)
297 J W 56 260 269 297 Lura Thompson 103 Mrs 104 Robert D 194 Wm D 194
POTTER, M 447 Mr 123 Samuel 301
POTTS, A A 394 Agnes 394 D Walter 394 667 J H 394 J W 333
POUNDS, W G 181
POWEL, 347
POWELL, Bro 618 Ervilla 327 Franklin 327 Henry H 349 Hiram 373 J N 327 Jemima 327 John 263 302 John A 324 Joseph 232 M W 292 Stephen 327
POWERS, Frank 257
POYNTER, D J 56 589 Minister 262 W A 321 589 W C 56 451 William 227 290 448-449 William C 588
POYNTON, Arthur 435 William 435
PRATER, 388
PRATHER, Bazil 198 Edward 211 Elijah 198 Elisha 198 L E 444 Phoche 172
PRATT, Alonzo 450 B C 56 Jim 439 Mrs 303
PRATZ, Lois E A 53
PRICE, C E 60 C J 163 C M 18 J H 393 John 118 Jonathan 242

PRICE (cont)
    Mr 120 William 324 351 Wm 55
PRICHARD, Henry 387 Isabel 387
PRIEST, L R 166-167 R F 166
PRIMM, William 324
PRITCHARD, H O 54 Henry R 597
PRITCHETT, J W 302 T A 302
PROCTOR, Alexander 448 S S 132
PROMPELLY, Amanda 277
PROPHATER, J E 291 Mr 249
PROPST, E A 325 Elizabeth 327 Lucinda 327 Mary A 325
PROTOFF, Daniel 165
PROVINE, Anna 309
PROVOLT, Jerry 341
PRUETT, Henry 382
PRUITT, 336 S C 269
PRYANT, Sarah 420
PUCKET, Goodwin 436
PUCKETT, Edward 429 G W 353-354 P J 430 Thomas 430
PURCELL, 190 Bishop 70
PURDY, Geo L 279
PURLEE, C D 290 Ellis 186 Mr 332
PURSELL, W T 166
PURSLEY, Charlotte 358
PURSLEY-BROWN, Ethel 358
PURSLEY-REYNOLDS, Jennie
PURSLEY-REYNOLDS (cont) 358
PURVIS, J T 433
PUTERBAUGH, H J 401 Solomon 401
PUTNAM, Eban 420 Samuel 420
PYATT, Minister 89
PYLE, Minister 353 Mr 353
QUIGG, John F 402
QUIMBY, 362
QUINLAN, J 330 J G 55
QUISENBERRY, 265
RADCLIFF, J M 85 239 Juliet 122 Rachel 122
RADCLIFFE, J M 84
RADFORD, B J 45 55 129 286 302 403 448 453 651 656 667 B J Sr 34 Chas T 55 Professor 37 41 47 Reuben 378
RAGAN, George A 161
RAGGIO, M D 152 165
RAGLAND, Nancy 423 Richard 423
RAGSDALE, Alva 56 287
RAILSBACK, Ann P 402 James E 402 Louisa 396 402 Thomas F 395-396
RAINES, John A 127
RAINEY, T W 328
RAINS, J A 129
RAINWATER, Clarence 362
RALPH, John 608
RANDALL, Marshall 299

RANEY, T W 325
RANSBURG, Alice 398 Cora 398 Grace 398
RATTS, R 189
RAY, Mattie 172 Robert 172
READ, Eli 143 Lafayette 418 Mary 421 William 142-143 Wm 231
REDDING, Isaac 128
REDGRAVE, C C 18
REDINBAUGH, Katherine 194 Michael 194
REDMAN, Charles 422
REDMON, 231 Dr 408 Geo W 188 George 657
REECE, J H 294
REED, 601 Daniel 144 Ely 418 Ernest 449 George 257 J A 589 Thomas 257 Wm G F 154
REEDER, I J 427
REESE, J 151
REEVES, Esther 447
REICHEL, H C 55 264 351 449
REID, Silas 24 W W 433
RENNER, William 124
REYNARD, C O 393
REYNOLDS, 388 Alex 424 Alexander 88 118 Charles 244 E B 241 E W 156 H J 55 244 J B 244-245 J C 93 216 220 242 279 332 424 576 664 Jane 214 John C 58 76 589 Joseph 198 Phebe 244 Rachel

REYNOLDS (cont) 244 Samuel 297 W J 111
RHODES, Aaron 288 E B 112 Ebenezer 27-28 281-282 Elijah 222 Jane M 112 Jeremiah 281 John H S 281 O M 288 Samuel 281 Silas 530 Solomon 112 W J 283 Walter 268
RIBEA, Wm 327
RICE, A H 93 129 Allen H 276 C R 325 Dr 641 E G 128 328 335 338-340 657 Elbert G 589 Erastus 112 Euphrazina 112 Hugh B 452 Lizzie 309 Mr 590 N L 70 Nathan 390 Tolvin 435 William 336
RICH, Rose 433
RICHARDS, A 381 Charles 452 Jesse 296 O A 55 Sylvester 432 Townsend 428 432 William 214
RICHARDSON, A 377 A A 577 Aaron A 445 451 C F 333 Cleopatra G 306 Frank 577 Georgia 306 H T 306 Harry B 306 J L 129 James M 451 M T 306 Susan 424 W F 55 402
RICHERSON, Alley 370 Jerry 370
RICHEY, Edward 278
RICHHART, William 389
RICHMOND, Josiah 250

RICKEY, Clara 250
RIDGELEY, William 419
RIDGELY, Irene 104
RIGDON, 601 Charles 205 John 88-89 118 205 278 Sidney 597 Wm 209
RIGG, Eliza J 418
RIGGS, 336 J M 590 Scott 590 Stephen 179 Willis 242
RIJNHART, Susie C 379
RILEY, C C 206 Calvin 267 Wash 199
RITCHEY, Francis 221 John 221 Mary 221 Zerilda 221
ROACH, A C 223 455
ROADY, J C 306
ROBBINS, J W 96 236
ROBERSON, Isabel 242 Minister 262 Thomas 242
ROBERTS, A P 86 Alvina 325 David 360 F G 97 J A 102 J R 86 John 449 Maggie 185 R B 79 132 148 174 T T 185 W A 234 W E 382 W L 374
ROBERTSON, Barney 432 Carrie 410 H C 387 M B 26 Margaret 387 Mary 410 N H 290 297 Norman H 229 R H 410
ROBESON, F K 131 James 179 285 288-291 293-294 296-298 320 397 445-448 451 493 582 590 Jane A 591 Jimmie 284

ROBESON (cont)
Minister 401 Mr 591 Uncle Jimmy 577 592
ROBINSON, A S 382 Isaac 335 James 174 Joel 335 John 15 John M 435 L M 176 207 266-267 269 272 Levi Mac 593 Mary 435 William 339
ROBISON, Minister 118
RODE, Wm 197
RODECKER, William 198
RODGERS, Martha 224
ROE, John 250
ROGERS, Edwin 55 John 142 176 John I 493 S F 437 W D 411
ROLAND, L N 309
ROLL, Harris 421
ROLLISON, J P 261
ROMINE, J B 204
RONLEY, Charles 342
ROOSEVELT, President 658
ROPP, Alice 53
RORHER, Simon 304
ROSBORO, J F 254 312-313
ROSE, J C 299 J S 181 190 433 Mr 191
ROSENBURGER, S D 142
ROSS, 603 Albert F 300 Andrew 121-123 571 594-595 Bert 298 C W 97 Charles W 55 210 332 596 Chas W 126 Emory 53 G W 348-349 383 Geo W

ROSS (cont)
    55 210 George W 278 300 596
    J R 221 James 118 James D
    300 James M 300 James R
    278 Jimmie 320 John 121-122
    311 349 594-595 Joseph 121
    594-595 Mr 123 221 Nancy E
    300 W S 66 William 594
ROTCHFORD, M W 352
ROTH, Elsie 297
ROTHENBERGER, W F 161
ROUGHAN, Charles 500
ROUNDS, W S 180
ROUSE, Edward 343
ROUTH, R H 111
ROUTT, John L 596
ROWE, Charles 174 251 302 335
    356 452 Charles O 371 593
    Eugene 224 G H 56 310 John
    F 407 665 Mr 594
ROWELL, J H 42
ROWLAND, James 250
ROWLISON, C C 55 200 289
ROYAL, J B 203 209 220 280 329
    383 Joseph B 596
ROYER, Oscar 438
RUBLE, 362 J 355
RUBY, Mary 374
RUCKER, Elizabeth 303 John
    303
RUDD, John 261
RUDDLE, Stephen A 115
RUDE, G L 190 Gershom 523

RUDE (cont)
    Gershom L 597
RULON, Abner 396
RUSSEL, W S 338
RUSSELL, 527 H J 166 Mr 620
    Sarah 420 W J 56 W S 62
    Walter Scott 61 619
RUST, W H 56
RUSTIN, W S 264
RUTH, Jeremiah 436
RYAN, Elizabeth 268 George G
    268 Melville 268 Wielan 276
    William 176 272-273 298 571
    William B 268 598 Wm 178
    264 396 Wm P 177
SABIN, A L 290 Dr 290 293 Mr
    259
SAILOR, J C 224
SALEE, J S 402
SAMMS, Alfred 277
SAMSON, Bernhardin 13 Mary
    325
SAMUELS, David 354 Ruth 354
SANBORN, C R 81
SANDERS, James 135 137 302-
    303 Joseph 362
SANDERSON, H M Sr 366
SANGSTER, Emma 176
SARGENT, Elijah 400
SARVIS, Guy 160
SAUNDERS, C F 165 Jonathan R
    378 Minister 150 Platt 151
SAVAGE, Henry S Sr 129 Sarah

721

SAVAGE (cont)
  Frances 129
SAYLES, Dennis 418 George T 373 H F 348
SCHEITLAN, John B 243
SCHICK, P W 288 298 Peter 174
SCHOCKLEY, Deacon 350
SCHOOLEY, Minister 432 O D 140 Philadelphia 140 William 140-141 657
SCHOOLY, Mr 532 Wm 197
SCHOONOVER, S M 157
SCHROEDER, George W 253
SCHULZE, Hyram 215
SCOAN, John 159
SCOFIELD, C J 216 623 Charles J 599 667 Elizabeth 216 Mr 600
SCOGENS, P O 179
SCONCE, 385 J W 90 John 386 John W 343 600
SCOTT, 83 Andrew 25-26 97 295 357 371 410 601 Benjamin Jr 211 Benjamin Sr 211 C L 387 Catherine 403 Charles L 601 Dr 602 Dred 655 F A 56 Hervey 382 I N 602 Ira 547 James 176 476 James R 26 John 136 205 601 Judge 599 Levi T 601 Lucy 372 Martha 371 Martin 285 Mary 601 Mr 548 603 Narcissa 192 Peter 403 Samuel 288 T D 136 T J

SCOTT (cont)
  333 Walter 602 626 William 192
SCOVILLE, C R 164 346 Evangelist 422
SCRIVENS, C A 56 C H 291 Charles 264
SEALOCK, B H 55 295 326 350 375
SEARCY, Samuel 168
SEARLE, J L 271
SEARLES, Irving A 153
SEARS, E W 170 585 Robert 413
SEATON, J A 267 269 297 James A 112
SECRIST, John 205
SEELY, Mrs 109
SEFTON, Geo M 147 John 198 William 198
SEILER, David K 421 Rosaline 421
SELBY, C E 267
SELLS, Jacob 122
SERENA, J A 55 295 Joseph 321
SEVERS, A L 237
SEWARD, J I 386
SEWELL, Minister 129
SEYMORE, Edith E M 409
SEYSTER, D F 55 348-349 David Franklin 603
SHADDLE, Jesse B 143
SHADLE, Mr 367
SHAFER, D P 18 Henry 128

SHAKESPEARE, 572
SHAMBAUGH, Wm 360
SHANE, Frank 196
SHANKLIN, D H 134
SHARP, C M 155 Charles M 58 Cragy 121 Cragy J 603 Craigie Sr 449 E O 97 446 Edward O 157 Henry 80 T C 80
SHARPE, E O 331
SHARPLES, David 451-452 Martin 382 Minister 262
SHARPLESS, David 209
SHASTID, John G 362
SHAUL, C F 333
SHAW, 396 Aaron 355 Adam 348 Anna 355 H P 335 Herbert P 55 James 70 76 Knowles 153 162 243 440 448 Lillian Chalman 158 Mr 71 T J 360 W F 55 Will F 167 225
SHEARER, W S 167
SHEELY, 349
SHEERER, G E 330
SHEIK, Peter 269
SHELBY, N A 193
SHELLENBERGER, J H 348
SHELLHORN, Cassie 421
SHELT, Minister 239
SHELTON, S T 424 Samuel 424 T J 333 665 W B 197
SHEPARD, B F 382 Emmons 246
SHEPHERD, John 438 S 90

SHEPPARD, M C 170
SHERMAN, L Y 610
SHERWOOD, C W 125 349 367-368 438-439 Charles 348 604 Charles W 603 Chas W 439 Minister 367
SHICK, F M 256 Marion 366
SHIELDS, D H 279 448-449 David H 55 G F 129 Guy 209 William 72
SHINN, C M 275
SHIRK, Mr 123
SHIRLEY, Arnold 56 Elizabeth 268 Henry 268 James W 268 William R 268
SHOAFF, Eliza 23
SHOCKEY, Edward 300 Thomas 300 W P 133 413 W S 404 W W 300 Wm 174
SHOCKLEY, 351 W P 279
SHOEMAKER, Amos 125 Joel 325 Miss 435
SHOENERT, Christ 418
SHOOK, Samuel 315 317
SHOPTAUGH, J A 189 J N 189
SHORE, John T 169
SHORES, James 267
SHORT, C F 174 C P 374 C W 178 Charles 269 Judge 618 Mr 519 Richard 179
SHORTRIDGE, Elias 329
SHOUP, William 378
SHOWMAN, John 259

723

SHREEVES, Joshua 215
SHRUSEBERRY, John 430
SHUEY, T J 97
SHURE, Angline 327
SHURTLEFF, D W 127 S M 295
SHURTS, John W 56
SICK, Mr 394
SICKLES, Robert A 374 667
SIMER, W J 313-314 317 604
SIMMONDS, Elizabeth 272
SIMMONS, Elizabeth 213 G B 212 George 432 Wm 213
SIMMS, Minister 115 William 575 William H 188 William T 188 Wm 190
SIMONSON, Lorena 352
SIMPSON, Emma 604 J W 550 657 James 61 James W 328 604 John A 276 Jordan 300 Kate A S 550 W E 270
SIMS, Austin 340 George 515 J J 307 Minister 332
SINCLAIR, C C 55 Ellmore 55 John A 55
SINGER, Wm 138
SITHERWOOD, G D 286 George D 99
SKATES, Jonathan 117
SKEEN, Mary 374
SKELTON, John 428 Leroy 55 174 266-268 273 286 302 320
SKIDMORE, Albert 172 Maggie 172

SLADE, Geo P 140 Minister 140 W P 436
SLAGLE, Ellin 306
SLATER, Mr 397
SLICK, Isaac 259 Joseph G 176
SLOAN, Elizabeth 418 John J 418 Julia 182
SLYTER, D C 398
SMALL, James 18
SMART, J H 60 102 279 290 313-314 334 Jerome H 605
SMITH, 568 A J 247 A S 203 Adda 407 Alice 213 Andrew J 247 B H 294 B K 493 Benj H 152 C T 116 Charles 197-199 Dr 643 E M 305 Elias 21 Elijah 237 Eliza 387 Eliza Wadsworth 350 Ephraim 244 F 85 F E 55 F P 55 Frank 80 Franklin 306 G W 86 Geo P 256 Green W 84-85 Hannah 227 244 Harris 408 Henry B 451 Isaac 339 J Addison 640 J F 55 200 J H 646 J H O 106 162-163 J N 126 439 J S 289 J T 56 119-120 389 Jesse 642-643 Jesse H 306 640 John 387 414 John M 131 John T 361 Jonathan 253 Lillie 640 642-644 M J 203 Margaret T 306 Mary 447 Minister 79 Miss 109 Mr 164 Mrs 197 218 Nephew 642 O

SMITH (cont)
L 55 237 295 Polly 391 Sallie Ann 213 Samuel B 405 Singer De Loss 209 Sue S 42 Susan 306 T E 245 Thomas 203 Unity 203 Uriah 203 W G 55 W M 389 Wesley 198 William 218 Wm G 329
SMITHER, A C 208
SMITHERS, Henry 269 382
SMITHFEETERS, Sarah 214
SMITHSON, C M 97 197-198 250-251 605 H H 198 605 Ramsey 80
SMOOT, C E 56 328 Chas 325
SMYSER, 341 Rebecca 345 S M 345
SNIFF, W W 55 200 227
SNIVELY, Geo L 56 362 George 205 George L 606
SNOOKS, C M 414
SNOW, James 312 318 M M 275
SNYDER, Caroline 277 John W 284
SOCINUS, 643-644 Faustus 642
SOLOMON, Aslver 305 Dempsey 309 Joel 205 Lucy 309 W W 433
SOMMER, Daniel 390 652
SOREY, M Lee 56
SOUTHERLAND, J O 136
SOUTHERN, Abram 340
SOUTHGATE, G R 290 298

SPARKS, A J 138
SPARLIN, Wright 168
SPARLING, David 232 Henry 87
SPAULDING, Louise 309
SPEARS, Dr 147
SPECK, J R 56 96
SPEECE, 396
SPEER, Dr 601 J K 76 328 Minister 329
SPENCE, Lizzie 260 Minister 262
SPENCER, H V 75 I R 262 Mr 259 Thomas 255
SPERLING, Mr 438
SPICER, A R 56 389 W E 55 440
SPIEGEL, O P 167
SPIELMAN, Mary E 348
SPILLAR, Eliza 443
SPILLER, Elijah 24 William 442
SPITLER, C T 348 Frank 150 S T 289
SPOONER, 301 Edwin A 430 John 241 Virginia 430
SPRECHER, Letha 348
SPRIGGS, E A 57
SPRINGER, W G 179 Wm G 174
STACHELL, Ida 224
STAGNER, J J 298 J M 296 J S 175 288 292 John S 290 John S Jr 290 Speed 290 293
STAMBAUGH, F M 97 J H 356
STANBUS, L 224

STANDISH, J 193
STANLEY, E J 266 439 Ellis J 607 F B 439 Minister 117 Mr 120 Pleasant 438 T B 267 348-349 439 Thomas B 607 Thomas J 438 Wm 438
STAR, Adam 355
STARBUCK, F L 295 297 L F 264
STARK, B F 193 E C 130 363 607 Elizabeth 218-219 George 218 J C 449 J Carroll 116 221 278 453 608 667 James 214 218-219 221 338 609 John 218 221-222 Mr 364 Robert 218-219 S I 189 Sarah 169
STARKE, 238
STARKEY, E E 159
STARR, Charles 237 Sarah A 101
STAUFFER, C Lee 57 349 C R 56 C Roy 349
STEBBINS, Edward 279
STEEL, Andrew 116
STEELE, Amanda 377 Betsey 218 Etta 377 James 149 John D 218 M E 194 Mr 367
STEERS, 362
STEPHENS, C M 451 Margaret A 194
STEPHENSON, Mary Ann 447 Miss 115
STEVENS, Benedict 246 E B 152-153 Nathan 344 Rebecca 340

STEVENSON, G W 312 Marion 57 161 204 208 455 R E 269
STEWARD, John 420
STEWART, A P 79 117 120 Edwin 162 J F 119 James F 57 610 John T 587 Maud 249 Mr 611 O W 56 96 294 531 Oliver W 223 610 W B 416
STILE, Mr 435
STINE, Peter 429 Stephen 429
STIPP, George Y 567 T L 84-85 226 404 406 413 567 611
STITT, Margaret 450 P Buckner 450
STIVERS, B T 256 Horace 299 J T 56 Marshall 256
STOCKDALE, Parker 162
STOFFER, L D 119
STOKES, D 381 Matthew 81
STONE, B W 24 88 329 335 337 514 609 Barton W 21 23 25 30 118 210 309 338 383 485 497 577 581 591 611 628 632 663 Elizabeth 115 Jesse E 116 Marsena 536 Mr 339 612-614 Paul N 309 T S 67
STOOPS, Hughey 207
STORM, 385 Greenup 387 Homer 387 Jackson 341 387 John 390 John Jr 387 Minister 389 Myrtle 651 W H 651 W R 387
STORMS, Jack 345

STORY, J E 194 334
STOTLAR, Eliza 443 Samuel 443
STOUT, Elijah 57 174 266 397 I 396 Isaac 266 268 273 297 397-398 614-615 J E 97 172 John E 57 Marion 119 Stephen 397
STOVER, Emanuel 124 616
STRAND, Fred 438
STRATTON, 320
STRAWN, J W 335
STRAXER, Jacob 201
STREATOR, Dr 251 J M 148
STREET, J W 409 659 John W 56 Wm 333
STREETER, W N 374
STREIBICH, Harry 351 Harry M 56
STRICKLAND, Pastor 155 Warren G 303
STRODES, 336
STROM, John Sr 387
STRONG, Cyrus 130 Eva 309 Sallie 267 W H 362 William 385 Wm 361 Wm H 533
STROSNIDER, Maud 249 Mr 249
STROUD, Mr 571 Sarah 272
STROUP, Laurie 192
STUCKEY, James 410
STUMBAUGH, Fanny M 398
SULLIVAN, Evangelist 454
SUMMERBELL, Minister 75

SUMMERS, Abram 178
SUMNER, Betsy 271 Frank 269 Margaret 268 Norman 268
SUMPTER, William 278
SUTHERLAND, H J 234 J O 275 377 616 J R 256 Jacob 232 Jos R 56 P W 255
SUTTON, 250 F W 56-57 262 G R 311
SWAFORD, J W 107
SWAIN, Darius 306
SWAN, 362 H 433 M 286
SWANER, J M 407
SWANK, Jane 327 Mary Ann 327
SWEARINGEN, Isaac 450
SWEARINGER, Van B 134
SWEENEY, G E 93 Geo E 190 Geo W 56 153 George E 616 George W 617 J S 73 118 120 152 276 327 330 332 381 385 664 John S 72 78 93 210-211 618 Mr 619-620 William G 617 Z T 57 153 184 186 190 392 617-618
SWEET, Henry 395 Jane 411 Mr 26 329 Theophilus 25 88 91 328 371 384 648
SWIFT, Toller 458
SWINDLE, D D 84
SWINFORD, S F 229
SWISHER, Edward 408 Jacob 413

SWORD, F A 125 Mr 100
SYBRANT, John 127-128
SYKES, Hermann 327 Sarah 327
SYLVESTER, W T 180
SYMONDS, J H 122
TABOR, D V 117 Elisha 378
TACKET, Enfield 391
TAFT, A J 304 John 129
TALBOT, J C 109-110
TALMAGE, Frank 80 620 Mr 621
TANDY, H F 174 356 H P 217 334
TANHAUSER, Solomon 67
TANNER, Joseph 222
TARMEN, Elizabeth 291 Thomas 291
TATE, Benj W 234 Benjamin W 231 233 Geo W 231 George W 621 James A 610 R W 263
TATTERSHELL, Flora 410 Jessie 410
TAULBEE, J M 331
TAYLOR, A D 233 A W 161 448 Aunt Sallie 382 B S 194 G W 123 622 Geo W 319 J M 395 J T 449 J W 371 378 J Z 96 353 379 537 James 371 John 118-119 306 John Wycliffe 382 K P 297 Knox P 286 441 454 622 Malinda 327 Margaret J 319 Mr 259 623 Nancy 336 Preston 295 T A 481 Thomas

TAYLOR (cont)
O 336 W A 120 W B 107 159 164 166
TEAGARDEN, Quince 407
TEBO, George F 119 Nancy 119
TEBUS, Wm 275
TEETER, Margaret D 227 Robert 227
TENNESON, J M 96
TENNEY, J B 267
TERRELL, F G 666 Frank G 163
TERRY, A H 388
TETER, W H 211
TETZEL, John 13
THACKABERRY, F C 123 F M 56
THAYER, Dr 302 J W 301
THEIMS, William 235
THEROLIS, William 398
THOMALSON, Charles 125
THOMAS, A S 138 Anna 348 B F 186 Barnett 182 G W 57 Henry 122 J N 56 289 John 150 L R 57 M M 301 Mary E 348 Mildred F 348 R E 56 S M 56 Susan 348
THOMPSON, A J 60 102 242 C B 260 Catherine 272 D A 231 David G 272 E S 145 Evangelist 422 Frank 110 435 G W 356 H P 260 J J 230 J W 138 John 209 Julia Y 447 L G 267 L J 307 Leonard G 307

THOMPSON (cont)
    Lura V 104 M W 447 Mary Ann 111 Minister 79 Mr 259 Nancy 418 Thomas 418 William 351
THORNBERRY, Mary B 106 Mr 349
THORNTON, Gen 392 Lillie 224
THRAPP, Mr 338 R F 56 102 200 267 337
THRASH, John 167
THROGMORTON, W P 82 86
THUER, Galveston 275
THURMAN, Sister 307
TICHNOR, 336
TIFFIN, T O 334
TILFORD, William 350
TILGHMAN, Sally Price 535
TILLOTSON, Mary 411
TIMMONS, Clarence L 279 Otto 237
TINKER, Jacob 197
TINKLER, John 314
TINSLEY, Thad 167
TIPSWORD, Griffin 199
TITUS, Daniel 422 Mary E 112 Susanah 112
TODD, Jane 450 John 565
TOLAND, George 149-150 J C 150
TOLER, B C 203
TOMLINSON, I G 234
TONTZ, Jonas 621
TOOF, J T 58 60 115 T J 153
TORRENCE, Joseph 138
TOTHEROH, Elizabeth 228
TOWNE, C S 404
TOWNLEY, Clarence 278
TOWNS, Noah 428
TRAILOR, Jesse L 328 Obedience 328
TRAINS, J D 140
TRAMBO, Mr 109
TRAVER, Levi 112 Phoebe 112
TRAVIS, Daniel 447 Mr 254 Rhoda 447
TREAT, W B F 76 253 259 366 548
TRICKETT, H R 96 205 278 Harry Robert 623
TRIMBLE, Harvey M 624 M R 254 256-258 Mathew 123 Maurice R 71 169 256 329 419-420 497 522 625 William C 626 Wm C 123
TRIPP, Benjamin 438 David 124
TROUT, D S 224 F A 224
TROUTNER, Joseph 359
TROWBRIDGE, 320 A H 100 250 261 449 657 Allen Harvey 627 Mr 249
TROWER, T B 630
TRUE, Ellen F 39 Herod W 500
TRUEX, Minister 212
TRUNKEY, J H 165
TRUNNEL, Caroline 450 Ellis

TRUNNEL (cont)
    350 Harriet 450 Nancy J 450
TRYER, John 438
TRYON, Nancy 355
TUCKER, A R 145 E N 248
    Harry E 56 Nathan 450
    Sarah 450 Sarah A 450
    Solomon 450 Thomas 450
    Wilson 450
TULLEY, J C 174
TULLY, J C 250 650
TURLEY, B 373 C 381 Elmer 270
    H D 373-374 Mary F 373 S S
    313 Samuel 277
TURNBAUGH, W E 362
TURNER, Alexander 256 Emily
    Booth 101 Ephraim D 256
    Helen E 149 Homer 136 John
    B 178 Margaret 194 Sister
    114 W F 351
TURNEY, D B 86 George W 430
    W F 392
TURPIN, Charlotte 303
TYLER, B B 44 57 299 332 493
    577 629 J W 139 299 304 343 J
    Z 299 629 John 299 John W
    135 137 298 302-303 341 539
    627 Mr 628
TYNER, D C 215
TYNG, A B Sr 352
UNDERWOOD, 24 B F 73 79-80
    82 Charles C 54 George 198
    H J 156 Minister 202 Mr 83 T

UNDERWOOD (cont)
    J 372
UPDIKE, Evangelist 422 J V 18
UPDYKE, James D 253
UPTON, David 213
URBANK, James 383
UTT, E A 306
VANARSDALE, G B 351
VANBUSKIRK, D R 99 286 493
    R D 96
VANCAMP, Mr 519
VANCE, Clara B 449 J L 449
    Jehiel 408
VANDAMENT, Henry 256
VANDERCOOK, H A 156
VANDERLIP, Elizabeth 112
    Phoebe A 112 Rosena 112
VANDERVOORT, C R 351 Dr
    248 Elijah 319 H G 174 211
    283 290 297 629 H S 361
    Sarah 319
VANDUSEN, H A 314 318
VANETTA, Frances E 403
VANHOOSER, Wm 139
VANHOUTEN, John J 187
VANHOUTIN, J J 184 629
VANMATRE, Lewis 366
VANMETER, Dr 147 Samuel
    630
VANPELT, Samuel 361 William
    361
VANSENDEN, Samantha 421
VANWORKMAN, Mr 197-198

VAUGHN, Alice 214 Col 530
    Samuel 630
VAWTER, Elijah 91 J M 147 Mr
    92 S D 56 264 449
VEACH, H L 97
VENDERVEER, E T 211
VENNUM, F B 131
VENTRES, K C 261
VENTRESS, K C 56 97
VERMILION, P D 207 304
VERMILLION, P D 120 560
VERNON, F H 409 James 18
VERTREECE, John 242
VERY, Myrtle 651
VIETE, Maggie 162
VILLIARS, Charles 412
VINCENT, Ann 26 Daniel 26
VIOLETT, E E 433
VISSERING, John 250
VIVION, J B 243
VOCE, W W 208
VOGEL, Peter 56 110 328 365
VOLKER, F C 190
WADDELL, C H 322
WADE, David 221 Edward 221
    Nancy 221 Sarah 276
WADSWORTH, M G 369 Mary
    368 Mary E 370
WAGGLE, Daniel 74
WAGGONER, E 90 Elijah 389 H
    G 56 Harvey G 631 J G 56
    101-102 104 123 204 248 263
    345 392 448 John Garland

WAGGONER (cont)
    630 Susie M 631 W H 56 99
    William H 631
WAGNER, Albert 398 Clay 348
    D G 348 D H 348 Mary E 348
WAIT, C L 156
WAKEFIELD, Paul 379
WALDEN, Charles F 171
WALDO, L D 348-349 439
    Lorenzo D 631
WALK, David 75 110 174 181
    496
WALKER, 27 265 Anderson 430
    433 D K 181 Daniel 114 Ira J
    132 Lucy 114 Malinda 281
    Noah 133 Sallie 283 W D 191
WALL, T S 665 Thomas 232
    Thomas S 632
WALLACE, Alden R 110
    Andrew 478 Cicero 166-167
    Isabel 478 L S 424 Rachel 390
    Robert 241 S L 426 Smith 241
    Thomas 426
WALLER, Maj 143
WALLICK, Joe S 609
WALLING, Wm 182
WALSER, John 415
WALTER, Amos 422 Joseph 381
WALTERS, J P 656 W 404
WALTMIRE, Jerome 396-397
WALTON, Ava S 221 651
    Elizabeth 219 Elizabeth
    Stark 220 Georgenia 31

WALTON (cont)
  Georgenia Daw 218 J O 97 220 382 Simeon B 219-220
WAMMACK, Joel 144
WARD, E 330 Elijah 187 Eliza 129 Jacob 61 129 Jesse 431-432 Minister 331 Sarah Frances 129 Tipton 180 W B 444 W D 159
WARE, John 250 Samuel 250
WARFIELD, B F 276
WARNER, G W 269 297 454 Sarah 348
WARREN, L C 133 Minister 329 P P 385 390 R P 322
WARRENER, R O 88
WARRINER, Belle 152 486 Dr 152 298 R O 486 W O 285
WASSON, Joseph 420
WATERS, J W 346 Jemima 268 Samuel 268
WATKINS, Amos 298 320 445 B U 493 Elmia 445 Martha 445 W D 128 Warren 445
WATRONS, Horace 236
WATSON, Chas H 176 James 189 L F 228 Lou 333 651 Mehitabel 176 Mr 249 259 Nancy 176 Russell 284 W H 250 W T 343
WAUGHOP, Clara B 320
WEAGLEY, Samuel G 61
WEAKLEY, Ellen 227 Thomas B

WEAKLEY (cont)
  227
WEATHERFORD, Mr 275
WEAVER, C M 86 C S 53 275 Clifford S 56 T F 96 276 346 T M 120
WEBB, 120 298 Cynthia 176
WEEDON, W W 102 138 422 434 632
WEEKLEY, C E 304
WEEKLY, E C 301 632
WEEKS, Benjamin 390
WEESE, Clara 209
WEIMER, G M 57
WELCH, J M 184 John H 199 Mary S 632
WELLS, Mcelvain 353
WELSH, Mary 175
WELTY, John 349
WESLEY, John 15
WEST, S 377
WESTON, A M 45 667
WETZEL, D N 56
WETZELL, Catherine 176 D N 189 David 176-177
WHARTON, W B 181
WHEATLEY, Isaac 353 R A 353 Robert J 353
WHEELER, 601
WHERRY, John 121 364
WHIPP, Amanda 327 Jackson 326 L A 326 Melissa 327
WHITAKER, Edward 428 Isaac

WHITAKER (cont)
428 J W 366
WHITE, 151 A J 162 Aaron B 326 Bertha 413 Capt 556 David 231 Emily 132 Etta C 377 H 179 I N 86 J K P 214 Jane 328 Mrs 109 Oliver 135 Orman 333 Pauline 351 William G 328 Wm 355
WHITESIDE, Minister 73
WHITESIDES, B F 373 George W 270 M D 373
WHITFIELD, Willis 530
WHITMAN, Elvira 59 Josiah 245 423 Julia 423 Sarah 423 Squire 423 William 423-424
WHITMER, Peter 99-100 286 441
WHITNAH, C L 204 H A 204
WHITTAKER, C G 224
WHITTON, Margaret 312
WICKERSHAM, Antha 430 Sampson 430
WIDNEY, Charles 348-349
WIFFIN, Thomas 353
WIGGINTON, M J 309
WIGGLE, Almira 222 David 222
WILBUR, W 311
WILCOX, 261 Alanson 608 Bert 136
WILCOXEN, J C 208 James 204
WILEY, Henry 633 James 147 L 270 Leroy 147 188 M 270 N S 186 Stephen 147

WILHITE, Evangelist 422
WILHOIT, Angeline 185 J G 186 Pendleton 185 Sarah 185
WILKENS, R M 357
WILKES, J W 331 L B 379
WILLARD, Aliff C 300 Perry 367
WILLETT, H L 102 160 163 666 Herbert L 57 460 633 667 Mr 634
WILLFORD, Wm H 442
WILLIAMS, Abner 353 Alex 198 Alfred 172 B 377 B T 179 Catherine 402 Charles 56 224 Charles O 375 D W 309 Daniel 353 E T 379 Emma 172 Frederick 63 353 G W 357 George 124 H 190 H H 407 Hezekiah 188 I G 420 431-432 J C 216 J D 97 120 275 383 James A 306 Jane 172 Jesse C 216 John 85 156 421 441 John A 116-117 140 213 236 253 312 314-317 354 427 634 John D 146 K A 363 Louisa 443 Martha 303 Mary A 216 Mary E 309 Mr 242 N P 402 Nancy 242 R E 286 Richard 124 Robert 264 Roger 15 Samuel 213 309 Samuel V 635 Vashti 421 William 172 353 443 William T 314 635 Wm H 171

WILLIS, Amanda J 447 Amos 193 Edward 192 G B 247 Nancy 192 W W 192
WILLOUGHBY, W D 57
WILLSON, Aunt Ann 660-662 J F 329 John 328 Uncle Joe 660-662
WILSON, 349 A A 295 339 Alonzo A 287 Anna M 210 Arthur 286 Arthur A 56 Daniel 280 Edward 395 Elizabeth 250 J R 451 Jane 250 Jesse 26 Joe 168 John 137 174 178 301-302 306 346 375-376 415 John L 139 636 Jonathan 250 Lucinda E 306 Mathew 442 444 636 Matthew 203 239 Mrs 109 Robert 159 S R 138 Samuel 371 443 Virginia 216 William 291 Wm 406
WINDERS, Tamar 420 Warren 420
WINDSOR, W 377
WINEMAN, Nancy F 370
WINGARD, Allen 226
WINTER, Phila 248
WINTERS, Harriett 192 J F 427
WISE, 349 E E 116 G W 276
WISHER, C C 57 296
WISWELL, A B 339 Elizabeth 339 Emma 339
WITCHEN, Robert 259

WITMER, Abram 348-349
WITTS, Carlile 373
WITWER, E B 107
WOLF, 349 Fred 276 Jacob 258 Joe 168 Josiah 258 Leslie 53 Mr 123 Sarah 276
WOLFE, G L 237 Gen 494 Leslie 257 Leslie E 57 Minister 238
WOLFORD, M C R 278 S 377
WONDERLICK, Philip 203
WOOD, Adelphia 372 C L 431 Charles L 428 433 637 D H 417 G M 297 John 90 Joseph 23 417 516 637 L F 334 Minister 170 O H 23 Samuel 428 433 Susan 435 Thomas 143 W W 159
WOODRUFF, Mr 394
WOODS, Ann C 192 Belle 307 Dixon 231 Eliza 192 Hiram 102 408 John T 192 Mary 231 Patrick 231
WOODWARD, Horace A 420 Sophia 420
WOODWORTH, 378
WOOLLEY, John G 611
WOOSLEY, Elijah 450 Joshua 447 Mary 447 450 Senith A 450 William T 450
WOOTEN, Minister 238
WORK, J W 159
WORSHAM, Cynthia 358
WRAY, B L 259 446 Burton L 56

WRAY (cont)
  Mr 260
WREE, George 302
WRIGHT, 147 Andrew 76-77 267 Catherine 194 Catherine M 194 Charlotte 194 Claiborne 194 637 Col 482 David P 421 Edward 331 Ellen Jane 194 G W 179 J B 258 347-349 J F 87 J H 77 94 162 267 295 347 James 185 Jefferson 194 John 433 M 270 Martha 391 N J 57 259 Nathan 188-189 347 507 O P 305 392 Reuben 391 State Evangelist 348 Susan 194 William 67 Wm T 194
WYATT, 362
WYCLIFFE, 15
WYCOFF, J W 300 Peter W 300
WYLDER, J R 333
YAGER, John 438-439 638 Josiah 403
YATES, Gov 565 Minister 79 120 Richard 371 W F 134
YEAGER, John 125
YEARGIN, John 533
YEARNSHAW, J M 124 John G

YEARNSHAW (cont)
  122 Mr 394
YELTON, Charles 638
YEUELL, Claris 18
YEUNS, Eliza 325 Lewis 325
YOAR, Jesse 392
YORK, P F 57 412 639
YOST, George 229
YOUNG, 572 C A 165 Charles A 666 Dr 279 288 298 Elder 214 G P 122 H 221 Mr 175 Oscar 407 P G 352 571 R A 211
YOUNGBLOOD, Frank 405 Joseph 405
YOUNGER, A S 342
YOWELL, Elizabeth S 325 James 325 William C 325
ZEHR, R F 224
ZELLER, Carrie F 103 105
ZENDT, S H 56 204 262 287 289 440
ZIMMERLY, Jacob 182
ZIMMERMAN, Dr 177 John 174 W B 189
ZINCK, Gilbert 57
ZINK, Gilbert 186
ZOLLARS, E V 159 379
ZOUND, Ellis 392
ZWINGLI, 13 15

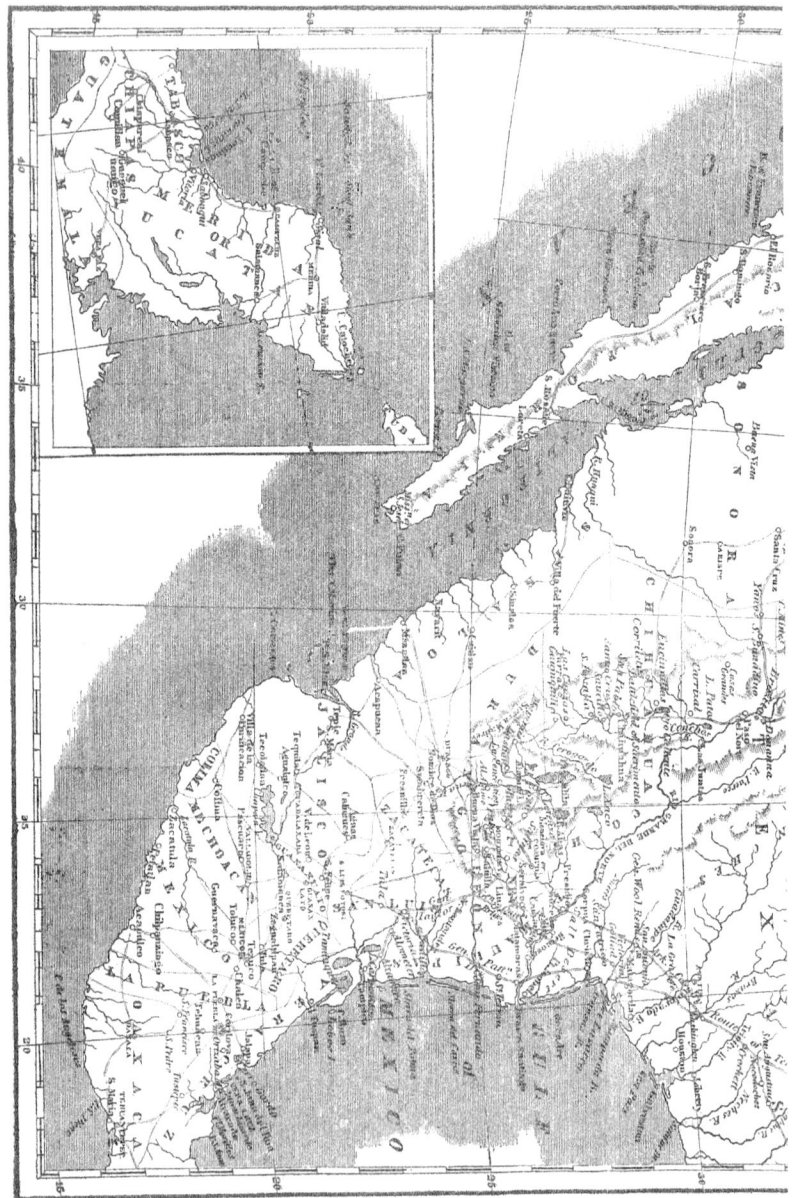

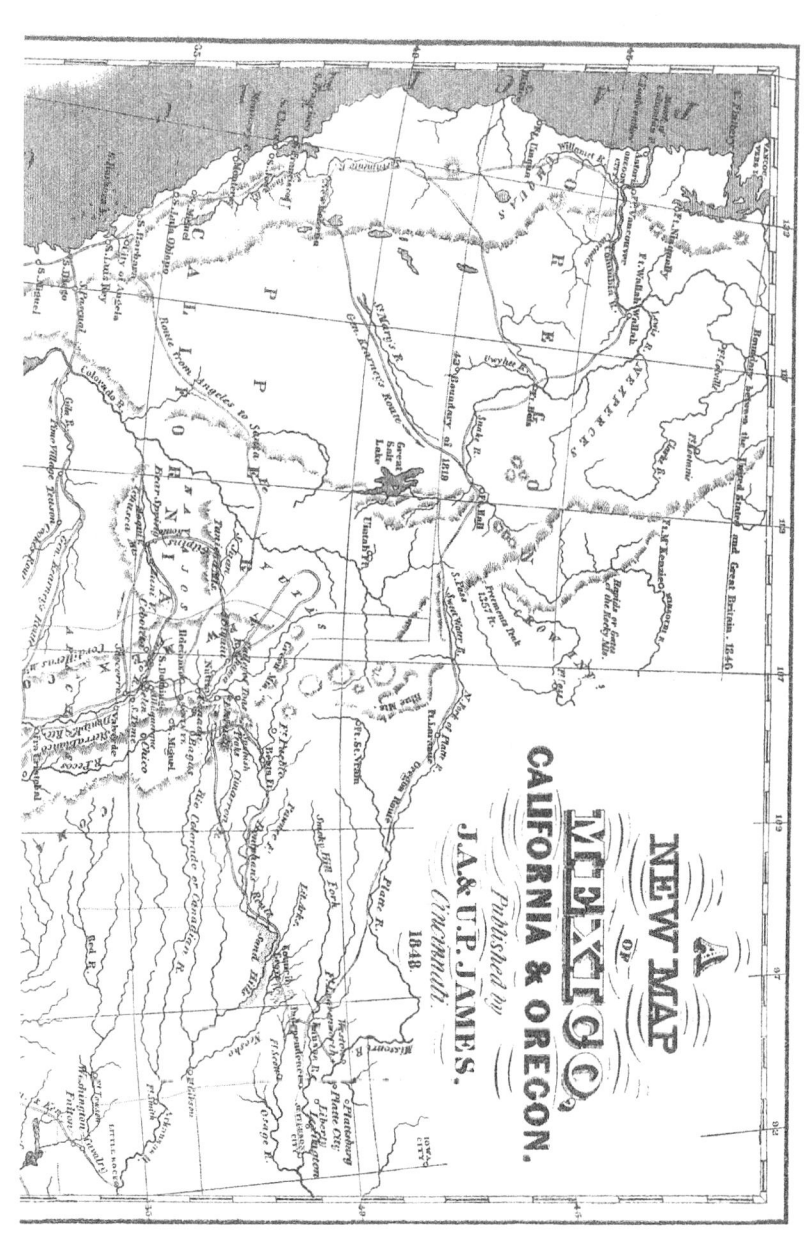

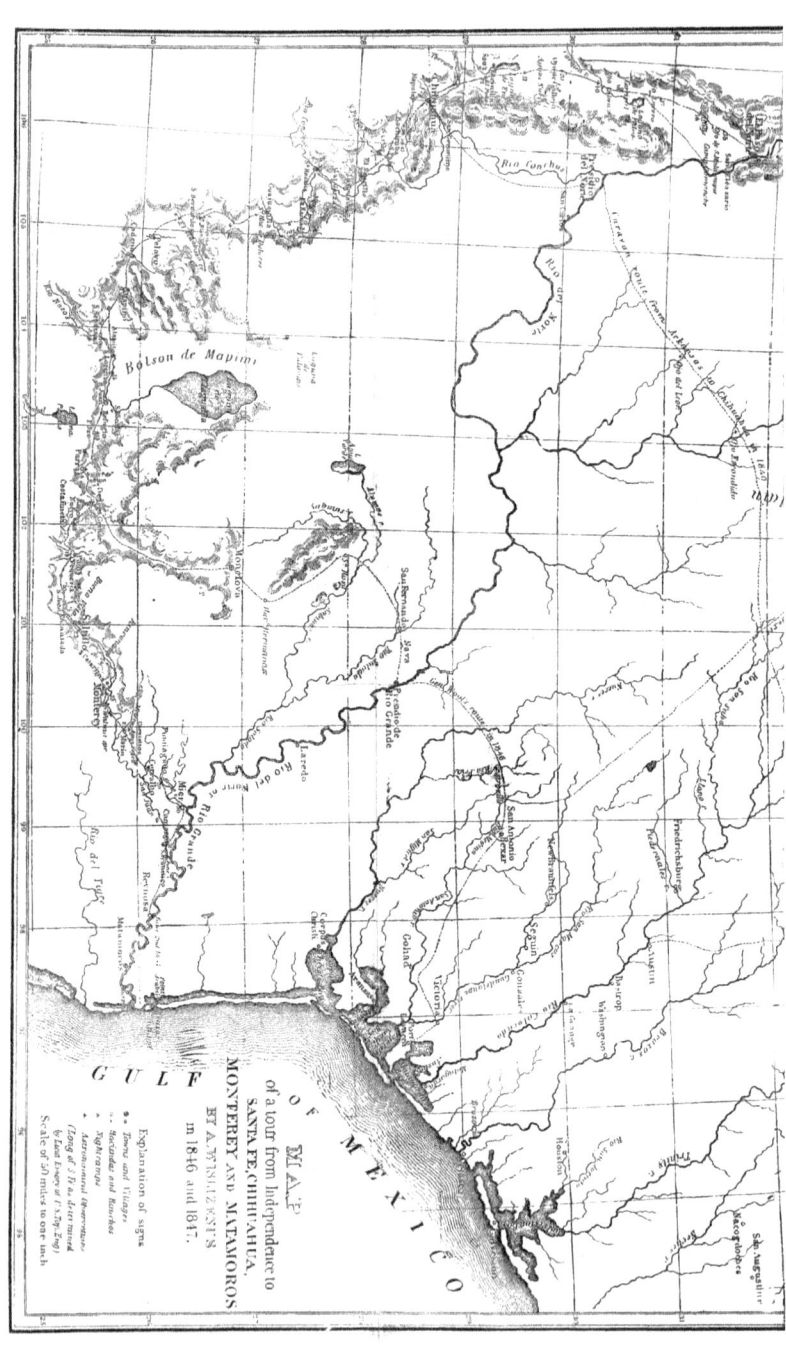

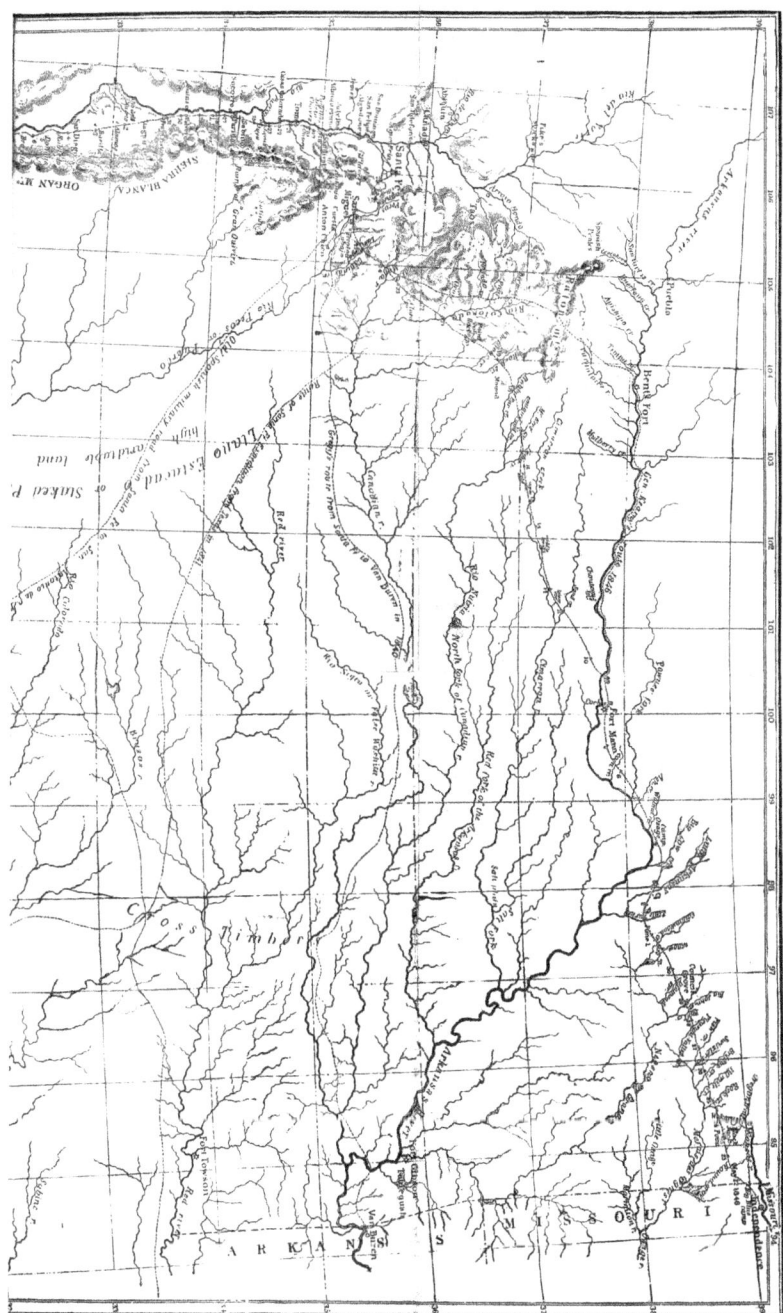

www.ingramcontent.com/pod-product-compliance
Lightning Source LLC
Chambersburg PA
CBHW071212290426
44108CB00013B/1164